III. Business Judgment

Test Focus:

—Analyzing business situations and drawing subsequent conclusions about them

Plan of Attack:

1. Underline the main points as you read.

2. *Define the decision-making factors* that fit into the 5 categories for evaluation on the data evaluation questions:
   a. Major objective in making the decision (the desired result)
   b. Major factor in making the decision (a basic consideration)
   c. Minor factor in making the decision (a secondary consideration)
   d. Major assumption in making the decision (a supposition)
   e. Unimportant issue in making the decision (an issue that is insignificant or not relevant)

IV. Mathematics

Test Focus:

—Understanding the basic principles of arithmetic, algebra, and geometry
—Dealing with numbers—in verbal problems and straight calculations
—Interpreting tables and graphs

Plan of Attack:

1. Save time-consuming problems for later. (*When you skip a problem, be sure you skip that number on the answer sheet.*)

2. Read each question carefully and make sure you:
   a. Look at the answers before starting work on the problem. (Estimation can save a lot of time.)
   b. Express your answer in the requested units
   c. Really answer the question

3. *Quick Tips*—For further formulas see page 224.
   a. *Arithmetic*
      - Any item multiplied by zero is zero.
      - Any item divided by zero is not defined.
      - In calculations with mixed numbers, change the mixed numbers to fractions.
      - The order of terms in a *ratio* is important. (Be sure to express each term in the same units.)
      - In dealing with *decimals*:
        —Adding zero to the right of the decimal does not change the value.
        —To multiply by 10, move the decimal one place to the right.
        —To divide by 10, move the decimal one place to the left.
      - When computing *percentages*, you will find it is usually easier to change the percentages to decimals or fractions.
      - Don't confuse decimals and percentages. If units are percentages, an entry of .2 means .2% or .002.
      - Laws of *exponents*:

$$b^n \times b^m = b^{n+m}$$
$$a^n \times b^n = (a \cdot b)^n$$

b. *Algebra*

- Only *like* algebraic terms may be combined.
- *Always check your answer in the original equation.*
- In *algebraic expressions,* break problems down to their simplest form and try to eliminate any equivalent answer choices. In simplifying, remember to:

  —Multiply and divide before adding and subtracting

  —Simplify exponents and fractions

  —Combine like terms

  (If an expression has more than 1 set of parentheses, get rid of the inner parentheses first and work outward through the rest of the parentheses.)

c. *Geometry*

Angles

straight angle = 180°
perpendicular (right) angle = 90°
acute angle = less than 90°
obtuse angle = greater than 90°

d. *Charts and Graphs*

- Look at the entire table or graph.
- Determine the units being used, and express your answer in the correct units.
- Try to calculate the answer by estimating, or rounding off, numbers.
- Use your pencil or paper edge to measure line and bar graphs.
- *Circle Graphs*—Use the *ratio* of percentages to find the answer. Don't spend time finding the actual amounts before finding the ratio of the amounts.

V. Data Sufficiency

Test Focus:

—Ability to reason, using a basic knowledge of arithmetic, algebra, and geometry

Plan of Attack:

1. *Don't waste time calculating the exact answer.* You need determine only if sufficient data are available for the solution.

2. *Don't make extra assumptions* on inference questions.

3. On inference questions pertaining to circle graphs, be careful to compare only like percentages.

How to Succeed on the GMAT

The Basics

Budget your time. Calculate the time you may spend on each question so that you aren't caught short at the end. Be sure not to linger on a question you can't answer.

Don't random guess. Random guessing is a poor policy; wrong answers do count against you. If you are able to eliminate some choices, however, "calculated" guessing can help your score.

Read directions carefully. Sections change, so don't start out with a false assumption.

Consider all choices. You must pick the best choice, not just a good choice.

Mark your answer grid clearly. Use the proper soft-lead pencil (No. 2) or a mechanical pencil, and blacken the choice completely. Be sure erasures are done cleanly with a good eraser.

The Finer Points

(For further help, see Chapters 4 and 5)

I. Reading Recall

Test Focus:

—Remembering main points and significant details

—Drawing inferences

Plan of Attack:

1. Concentrate on discovering and underlining the *central theme* of the passage—the key to answering all questions. The central theme is usually found in the:
   a. *Title* (if there is one)
   b. *Topic sentence.* Topic sentences are usually at the:
      - Beginning of a paragraph
      - End of a paragraph
   c. *First few paragraphs* in longer selections

2. Determine the *structure* of the passage. Note facts, words, and phrases that signal a shift in emphasis or thought or that indicate the relationship of one idea to another.
   a. Words announcing the summary sentence:

accordingly	hence	lastly
as a result	in conclusion	therefore
finally	in short	thus

b. Words announcing items of equal elements:

above all	another	furthermore
again	as well as	likewise
also	besides	moreover
and	first	

c. Words announcing an illustration:

for example	in such cases	namely
for instance	in the same manner	specifically
in other words	just as	the following

d. Words indicating a change of direction:

although	in spite of	notwithstanding
despite	instead	regardless

e. Words designating contrast of equals:

but	nevertheless	still
however	otherwise	yet

f. Words calling attention to important ideas:

don't overlook	notice that	of significance is

g. All-inclusive and negative words:

under all circumstances	never
always	only
every	no
entirely	not
at all times	none

3. Concentrate on *significant details.* Try underlining main points as you read.

4. An *inference* is not stated. Look for clues such as:
   a. Frequency—How often the same idea is stated
   b. Fairness—Whether arguments are balanced
   c. Wording—Whether emotional or "loaded" words are used

5. *Review all underlined sections before your time is finished.*

II. Verbal Aptitude

Test Focus:

—Grasping the meanings of words
—Determining word and idea relationships

ANTONYMS (opposites)
Plan of Attack:

Make sure the answer is opposite in meaning, and that both words correspond in:

1. *Tense* (present to present, past to past, etc.)
2. *Part of Speech* (noun to noun, adverb to adverb, etc.)

WORD-PAIR RELATIONSHIPS (similarities between 2 sets of words)
Plan of Attack:

Determine the *rationale* existing between the word-pair. This can involve many possible relationships. Some of the more common ones are mentioned in detail on pages 106, 107.

SENTENCE COMPLETION
Plan of Attack:

1. Learn to recognize the implication of the sentence. This will help you to locate the *key words* in the sentence that can supply hints to the missing words.
2. Your answer must not only be *logical,* but must be *grammatically correct.*

Barron's How to Prepare for the Graduate Management Admission Test (GMAT)

Formerly Admission Test for Graduate Study in Business–ATGSB

by

EUGENE D. JAFFE, M.B.A., Ph.D.

Associate Professor of Marketing, Director of Continuing Management Education
Graduate School of Business, St. John's University

and

STEPHEN HILBERT, Ph.D.

Associate Professor of Mathematics
Ithaca College

Barron's
Educational Series, Inc.
Woodbury, New York

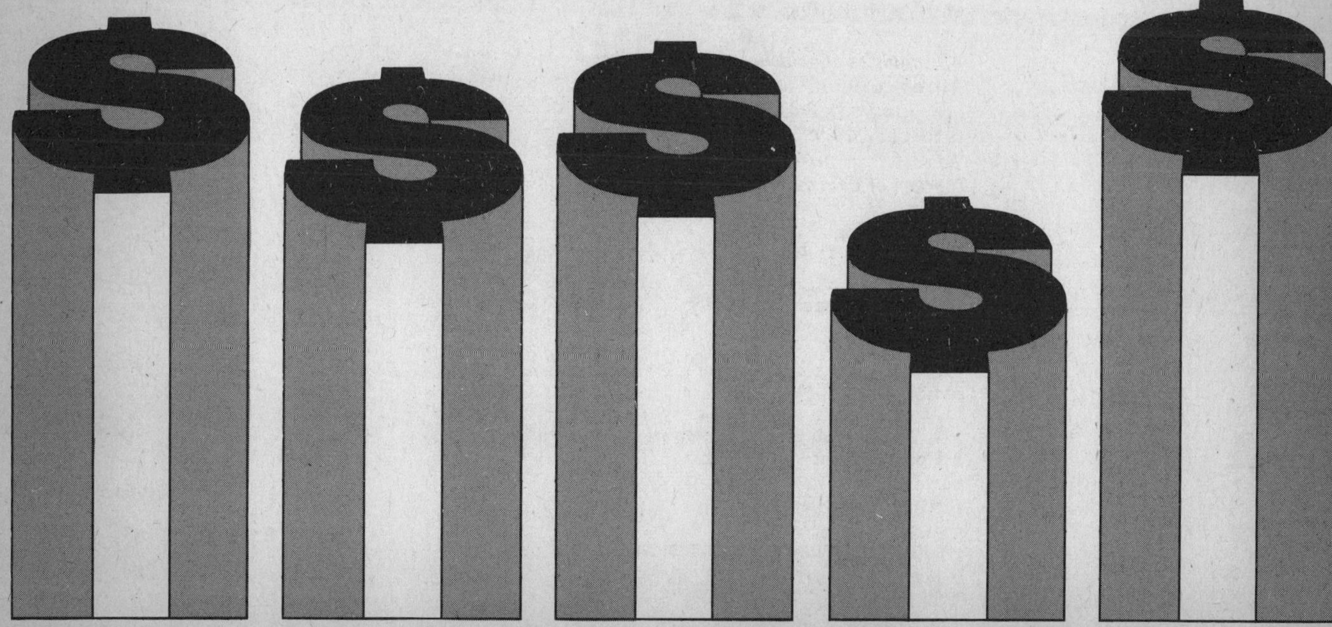

All inquiries should be addressed to:
Barron's Educational Series, Inc.
113 Crossways Park Drive
Woodbury, New York 11797

Library of Congress Catalog Card No. 75-11771

Paper Edition
International Standard Book No. 0-8120-0508-2

Library of Congress Cataloging in Publication Data

Jaffe, Eugene D.
Barron's how to prepare for the graduate management admission test (GMAT)

1. Business education–Examinations, questions, etc.
I. Hilbert, Stephen, joint author. II. Title.
HF1118.J33 371.2'64 75-11771
ISBN 0-8120-0508-2

PRINTED IN THE UNITED STATES OF AMERICA

For Liora, Iris and Nurit

Table of Contents

Preface

Barron's How to Prepare for the Graduate Management Admission Test (GMAT) is designed to assist students planning to take the official Graduate Management Admission Test administered by the Educational Testing Service of Princeton, New Jersey. Since the results of the GMAT are used by many graduate schools of business as a means for measuring the qualifications of their applicants, it is important that the prospective student do as well as he possibly can on this exam. His admission to business school may well depend on it.

A study guide, although not able to guarantee a perfect score, can provide a good deal of assistance in test preparation by enabling the student to become familiar with the material he will encounter on the exam and supplying him with ample opportunity for practice and review. With this in mind, we have developed a study guide that goes further than the simple simulation of the official GMAT in its effort to offer a sound basis of test preparation. Besides containing six practice tests with questions (and answers) similar to those the student will encounter on the actual exam, it offers invaluable advice on *how* to prepare for the exam, ranging from a general discussion of the purpose and format of the GMAT to a step-by-step program of subject analysis and review designed to help the student discover his weak points and take measures to correct them.

Review sections for each subject area appearing on the exam have been especially developed to meet the specific needs of students who may feel a deficiency in any of these areas. Each review provides both an explanation of the material and exercises for practice work. The six practice exams included in the guide have self-scoring tables to help the student evaluate his results and check his progress. All answers to the test questions are fully explained to ensure complete understanding. A glossary of business terms, a general vocabulary list, and a list of business schools requiring the GMAT add to the value of this guide as a means of preparation for this important test.

The authors would also like to extend their appreciation to Mrs. Susan Hilbert and Ms. Dawn Murcer for their excellent job in typing the manuscript, to Professor Shirley Hockett for several helpful discussions, and to Professor Justin Longenecker for his generous advice.

How to Use This Guide

The step-by-step study program appearing below outlines the recommended study plan you should follow when preparing for the GMAT. By making use of this procedure, you will be able to take full advantage of the material presented in this guide.

1. Familiarize yourself with the purpose and general format of the GMAT (Chapter I).

2. Study the analysis of each type of question on the exam (Chapter II).

3. Take the GMAT Diagnostic Test and use the Self-scoring Table at the end of the test to evaluate your results.

4. Study the review sections (Chapter IV), spending more time on areas where you scored poorly on the Diagnostic Test.

5. Take the five sample GMAT tests and evaluate your results after completing each one.

6. Review again any areas you discover you are still weak in after you have evaluated your test results.

7. Use the General Vocabulary List and Glossary of Business Terms to help increase your knowledge of word meanings and supplement your review.

Acknowledgments

The authors gratefully acknowledge the kindness of all organizations concerned with granting us permission to reprint passages, charts, and graphs. The copyright holders and publishers of quoted passages are listed on this and the following pages.

Sources and permissions for charts and graphs appear on the appropriate pages throughout the book through the courtesy of the following organizations: the New York Times Company; U.S. Department of Labor; Dow Jones & Company, Inc; Office of Management and the Budget; U.S. Department of Health, Education, and Walfare; United Nations Economics Bulletin for Europe; Social Security Bulletin; Statistical Abstract of the U.S.; U.S. Department of Commerce, Bureau of Economic Analysis; Federal Reserve Bank of New York; European Economic Community; U.S. Department of Commerce, Bureau of the Census; New York State Department of Labor; Federal Power Commission; U.S. Treasury Department; U.S. Bureau of Labor Statistics; Institute of Life Insurance; and the Statistical Abstract of Latin America.

Page 11, Sample Passage: Maynard and Davis, *Sales Management,* © 1957, The Ronald Press Company, New York.

Page 23, Passage 1: *Trade Policy Toward Low-Income Countries,* copyright 1967 by the Committee for Economic Development.

Page 54, Passage 2: from *Basic Problems in Marketing Management* by Edwin C. Greif. © 1967 by Wadsworth Publishing Company, Inc., Belmont, California 94002. Reprinted by permission of the publisher.

Page 257, Passage 1: *Improving Executive Development in the Federal Government,* copyright 1964 by the Committee for Economic Development.

Page 258, Passage 2: from *Legal Aspects of Marketing* by Marshall C. Howard. Copyright 1964 by McGraw-Hill Book Company. Used with permission of McGraw-Hill Book Company.

Page 259, Passage 3: Harold B. Scott, "Government Policies and Attitude Toward U.S.–East European and Mainland China Trade," in Arvind V. Phatak, (ed), *Building Business Bridges To Eastern Europe And Mainland China,* Temple University, Bureau of Economic and Business Research, 1972.

Page 288, Passage 2: reprinted with permission from Cruickshank and Davis, *Cases in Management* (Homewood, Ill.: Richard D. Irwin, Inc., 1954 c.).

Page 320, Passage 2: N. Sethi, *The Setting of Administrative Management in India,* St. John's University, Business Research Institute, 1969.

Page 321, Passage 3: G. R. Crone's, *Background to Geography,* 1964, published in the United States by Dufour Editions, Inc., Chester Springs, PA.

Page 346, Passage 1: Maynard and Davis, *Sales Management,* © 1957, The Ronald Press Company, New York.

Page 348, Passage 2: reprinted by permission of The World Publishing Company from *Basic Marketing* by Robert S. Raymond. Copyright © 1967 by Robert S. Raymond.

Page 379, Passage 1: *The Hebrew Impact on Western Civilization,* edited by Dagobert Runes. The Philosophical Library.

Page 380, Passage 2: *Budgeting for National Objectives,* copyright 1966 by the Committee for Economic Development.

Page 381, Passage 3: from *The American Guide,* edited by Henry G. Alsberg, Copyright © 1949, by permission of Hastings House, Publishers.

Page 408, Passage 1: reprinted with permission from Cruickshank and Davis, *Cases in Management* (Homewood, Ill.: Richard D. Irwin, Inc., 1954 c.).

Page 471, Passage 2: reprinted with permission from Cruickshank and Davis, *Cases in Management* (Homewood, Ill.: Richard D. Irwin, Inc., 1954 c.).

Page 474, Passage 1: from W. D. Howells, "The Man of Letters as a Man of Business," in *Literature and Life.* Copyright 1911 by Harper & Brothers. Reprinted with permission of William White Howells.

Page 475, Passage 2: reprinted with permission of Macmillan Publishing Co., Inc., from *Interpretations* by Walter Lippmann. Copyright 1932 by Walter Lippmann, renewed 1960 by Allan Nevins.

Page 502, Passage 2: from *Our Dynamic World: A Survey in Modern Geography* by A. Joseph Wraight. © 1966 by the author. Reproduced by permission of the publisher Chilton Book Company, Radnor, Pennsylvania.

Page 532, Passage 2: reprinted with permission from Cruickshank and Davis, *Cases in Management* (Homewood, Ill.: Richard D. Irwin, Inc., 1954 c.).

Page 80, Example 2: "Skye, Lonely Scottish Isle," *Newark Sunday News,* June 9, 1968, C 16, Sec. 2.

Page 82, Example 4: David Gunter, "Kibbutz Life Growing Easier," *Newark News,* May 6, 1968, p. 5.

Page 86, Example 2: Reprinted with permission from "Understanding Foreign Policy," by Saul K. Padover, *Public Affairs Pamphlet #280.* Copyright, Public Affairs Committee, Inc.

Page 89, Exercise A: from *New Students and New Places* by the Carnegie Commission on Higher Education. Copyright 1971 The Carnegie Foundation for the Advancement of Teaching. Used with permission of McGraw-Hill Book Company.

Portions of the "Reading Comprehension Review": Eugene J. Farley, *Barron's How to Prepare for the High School Equivalency Examination Reading Interpretation Test,* © 1970 Barron's Educational Series, Inc., Woodbury, N.Y.

Portions of the "Verbal Aptitude Review": Samuel C. Brownstein and Mitchel Weiner, *Barron's How to Prepare for the Graduate Record Examination,* © 1973 Barron's Educational Series, Inc., Woodbury, N.Y.

ONE
AN INTRODUCTION TO THE GMAT

The most productive approach to undertaking the actual study and review necessary for any examination is first to determine the answers to some basic questions: What? Where? When? and How? In this case, what is the intent of the Graduate Management Admission Test (GMAT)? What does it measure? Where and when is the exam given? And most important, how can the candidate specifically prepare himself to demonstrate aptitude and ability to study business at the graduate level?

The following discussion centers on the purpose behind the Graduate Management Admission Test and presents a study program to follow in preparing for this exam, including a special section to acquaint you with the general format and procedure used on the GMAT.

The Purpose of the GMAT

The purpose of the GMAT is to measure the candidate's ability to *think systematically* and to employ the *reading and analytical skills* that he has acquired throughout his years of schooling. The types of questions that are used to test this ability are discussed in the next chapter. It should be noted that the test does not aim to measure the student's knowledge of *specific business or academic subjects.* No specific business experience is necessary, nor will any specific academic subject area be covered. The candidate is assumed to have knowledge of basic algebra, geometry, and arithmetic.

In effect, the GMAT provides college admission officials with an *objective* measure of academic abilities to supplement subjective criteria used in the selection process, such as interviews, grades, and references. In other words, the test is used as a means for measuring ability other than college grades. Suppose you are an average student in a college with high grading standards. Your overall grade average may be lower than that of a student from a college with lower grading standards. The GMAT allows you and the other student to be tested under similar conditions using the same grading standard. In this way, a more accurate picture of all-around ability can be established.

Where to Apply

Information about the exact dates of the exam, fees, testing locations, and a test registration form can be found in the GMAT Bulletin of Information for Candidates published by ETS. You can obtain a copy by writing:

Graduate Management Admission Test
Educational Testing Service
Box 966
Princeton, New Jersey 08540

The Graduate Management Admission Test (GMAT) is generally given in November, January, March, and July. Since the majority of business schools send out their acceptances in the spring, it is wise to take this exam as early as possible to ensure that the schools you are applying to receive your scores in time.

The Test Format

In recent years the GMAT (formerly the ATGSB) has contained five types of questions—Reading Recall, Verbal Aptitude, Mathematics, Data Sufficiency, and Business Judgment. The following chart outlines the frequency with which these questions have appeared on the exam in the past few years, the number of questions included in each section, and the total time allotted for their completion. Most exams tend to repeat either the Reading Recall or Mathematics sections, but the repetition of other types of questions is not unfeasible. It is obviously impossible to predict the format of future exams, but this outline can give you an idea of the general format you can expect.

Outline of Recent GMATs

FORM 1

SECTION	TYPE OF QUESTION	NUMBER OF QUESTIONS	READING TIME (MINUTES)	ANSWERING TIME (MINUTES)
I	Reading Recall	30	15	20
II	Mathematics	55	–	75
III	Verbal Aptitude	40	–	20
IV	Data Sufficiency	15	–	15
V	Reading Recall	30	15	20
VI	Mathematics	35	–	40

TOTAL TEST TIME = 3 Hours, 40 Minutes

FORM 2

SECTION	TYPE OF QUESTION	NUMBER OF QUESTIONS	READING TIME (MINUTES)	ANSWERING TIME (MINUTES)
I	Business Judgment	20	–	35
II	Mathematics	55	–	75
III	Verbal Aptitude	40	–	20
IV	Data Sufficiency	15	–	15
V	Reading Recall	30	15	20
VI	Mathematics	35	–	40

TOTAL TIME = 3 Hours, 40 Minutes

FORM 3

SECTION	TYPE OF QUESTION	NUMBER OF QUESTIONS	READING TIME (MINUTES)	ANSWERING TIME (MINUTES)
I	Reading Recall	30	15	20
II	Mathematics	55	–	75
III	Verbal Aptitude	40	–	20
IV	Data Sufficiency	15	–	15
V	Reading Recall	30	15	20
VI	Data Sufficiency	25	–	25

TOTAL TIME = 3 Hours, 25 Minutes

FORM 4

SECTION	TYPE OF QUESTION	NUMBER OF QUESTIONS	READING TIME (MINUTES)	ANSWERING TIME (MINUTES)
I	Reading Recall	30	15	20
II	Mathematics	55	–	75
III	Verbal Aptitude	40	–	20
IV	Data Sufficiency	15	–	15
V	Reading Recall	30	15	20
VI	Reading Recall	20	15	10

TOTAL TIME = 3 Hours, 25 Minutes

Each section of the GMAT must be completed within a specified time limit. If you should finish the section before the allotted time has elapsed, you must spend the remaining time working on that section *only*. You may *not* work on other sections of the test at all. It is a good idea to have a watch with you during the exam so that you can keep track of how much time you have and budget it accordingly.

Specific directions telling you exactly how to answer the questions appear at the beginning of each section of the exam. Keep in mind that although the directions for answering the sample questions in this guide are designed to simulate as closely as possible those on the actual test, the format of the test you take may vary. Therefore, it is important that you read the directions on the actual test very carefully before attempting to answer the questions. You also should be certain of the exact time limit you are allowed.

How to Prepare for the GMAT

You should now be aware of the purpose of the GMAT and have a general idea of the format of the test. With this basic information, you are in the position to begin your study and review. The rest of this guide represents a study plan which will enable you to prepare for the GMAT. If used properly, it will help you diagnose your weak areas and take steps to remedy them.

Begin your preparation by becoming as familiar as possible with the various types of questions that appear on the exam. The analysis of typical GMAT questions in the next chapter is designed for this purpose. When you feel you understand this material completely, take the Diagnostic Test that follows and evaluate your results on the self-scoring table provided at the end of the test. (An explanation of how to use these tables appears below.) A low score in any area indicates that you should spend more time reviewing that particular material. Study the review section for that area until you feel you have mastered it and then take one of the sample GMATs at the back of the book. Continue this pattern of study until you are completely satisfied with your performance. For best results, try to simulate exam conditions as closely as possible when taking sample tests.

The Self-scoring Tables

Results of the GMAT are evaluated by three scores: verbal and quantitative, both rated on a scale of 0 to 60, and a total score rated on a scale of 200 to 800. There are no passing or failing scores, but generally few students score below 10 or above 46 on the verbal and quantitative sections, and below 250 or above 700 on the total. Normally two-thirds of those taking the test score between 22 and 38 on the verbal and quantitative sections and between 400 and 600 on the total. A score of 500 is indicative of the 50th percentile; half taking the test score above 500, the other half below.

The self-scoring tables for each sample test in this guide can be used as a means of evaluating your weaknesses in particular subject areas and should give you a rough estimate of how you will do when you take the actual test.

After completing a sample test, first determine the number of *correct* answers you had for each section. Next, subtract *one-fourth* the number of *wrong* answers for each part from the number of correct answers. This is done to compensate for guessing. For example, suppose that in section 1 of a certain test you answered 24 out of 30 questions correctly. This means that you had 6 incorrect responses (30 minus 24). Subtract $\frac{1}{4}$ of 6 ($1\frac{1}{2}$) from 24 to obtain a final score of $22\frac{1}{2}$. Record this score in the appropriate score box in the Self-scoring Table as shown below.

Self-scoring Table

PART	SCORE	RANK
1	$22\frac{1}{2}$	GOOD
2		
3		
4		
5		
6		

Then, compare this score with those contained in the Self-scoring Scale. Insert the rank, either POOR, FAIR, GOOD, or EXCELLENT, in the appropriate box in the Self-scoring Table.

Self-scoring Scale

PART	POOR	FAIR	GOOD	EXCELLENT
1	0–15	16–21	22–25	26–30
2	0–29	30–40	41–47	48–55
3	0–20	21–28	29–34	35–40
4	0–7	8–10	11–12	13–15
5	0–10	11–14	15–16	17–20
6	0–18	19–25	26–30	31–35

A rank of FAIR or POOR in any area indicates that you need to spend more time reviewing that material.

TWO
AN ANALYSIS OF TYPICAL GMAT QUESTIONS

A logical first step in preparing for the GMAT is to become as familiar as possible with the types of questions that usually appear on this exam. The following analysis of typical GMAT questions explains the purpose behind each type and the best method for answering it. Samples of the questions with a discussion of their answers are also presented. More detailed discussions and reviews for each type of question are presented elsewhere in this book.

Reading Recall

The purpose of these questions is to test your ability to understand and remember *main points* and *significant details* contained in material you have read and to determine how well you can draw inferences from this material. Generally, each Reading Recall section contains three passages of several paragraphs each. You are allowed 15 minutes to read all three passages. After this time has elapsed you are given another 20 minutes to answer questions based on these passages. You may not refer to the passages while answering the questions, but instead must rely on your memory to supply the desired information.

The best way to approach the Reading Recall question is to concentrate as much as possible on the *significant details* in the passages. A good method for fixing these ideas in your memory is to underline main points as you read. Try to budget your time so that you can cover all the material during the allotted 15 minutes. If you finish all three passages before time is called, you will be able to use the material you have underlined as a means of quick review.

The following passage will give you an idea of the format of the Reading Recall section. As you read, underline what you believe to be the main ideas presented. Limit your reading time to 7 minutes. Spend another 7 minutes answering the questions that follow, remembering not to refer back to the passage for assistance. When you have finished, compare your responses with the analysis of answers provided at the end.

Sample Passage

Part A: TIME—7 minutes

Some economists believe that the United States can be utilized as a "land bridge" for the shipment of containerized cargo between Europe and the Far East. Under the land-bridge concept, containerized freight traveling between Europe and the Far East would be shipped by ocean carrier to the United States East Coast, unloaded and placed on special railway flatcars, and shipped via railroad to a West Coast port. At this port, the containers would then be loaded on ships bound to a Far East port of entry. This procedure would be reversed for material traveling in the opposite direction. Thus, a land transportation system would be substituted for marine transportation during part of the movement of goods between Europe and the Far East.

If a land-bridge system of shipment were deemed feasible and competitive with alternative methods, it would open a completely new market for both United States steamship lines and railroads. At present, foreign lines carry all Far East–Europe freight. American carriers get none of this trade, and the all-water route excludes the railroads.

The system established by a land-bridge could also serve to handle goods now being shipped between the United States West Coast and Europe, or goods shipped between the Far East and the United States Gulf and East Coasts. Currently, there are 20 foreign lines carrying West Coast freight to Europe via the Panama Canal, but not one United States line. Thus, in addition to the land-bridge getting this new business for the railroads, it also gives the United States East Coast ships an opportunity to compete for this trade.

While this method of shipment will probably not add to the labor requirements at East and West Coast piers, it does have the potential of absorbing some of the jobs that the containerization of current cargo has eliminated or could eliminate. Thus, the possibility of creating new jobs for longshoremen is not an expected benefit of such a system, but it will most certainly create other labor requirements. The land-bridge concept has the potential of offering new job openings for United States railway workers and seamen. In addition, there would be expansion of labor requirements for people in the shipbuilding and container manufacturing business.

By making United States rail transportation an export service, the land-bridge system would have a favorable effect on our balance of payments. Such a system also has the potential of relieving the United States government of part of the burden it now bears in the form of subsidies to the shipping industry. The federal government subsidizes the construction and operation of scheduled vessels. Some 52 percent of the income from their operation comes from the government in that these ships are used for all our military and other government-related export shipments. The land-bridge requirement for scheduled sailings could effect a shift from the use of these subsidized lines for shipment of government goods to commercial cargo of the land bridge. This would then open some of the lucrative government business to the unscheduled, unsubsidized lines.

QUESTIONS TO

Sample Passage

Part B: TIME—7 minutes

DIRECTIONS: Answer the following questions pertaining to information contained in the passage you have just read. You may not turn back to this passage for assistance.

A B C D E
|| || || || ||

1. According to the passage, if a land-bridge system were feasible, it would
   (A) create employment in the bridge-building industry
   (B) decrease the amount of air freight
   (C) create a new market for steamship lines and railroads
   (D) make American railroads more efficient
   (E) increase foreign trade

2. The author implies that which of the following would be provided employment by the development of a land-bridge?

    I. Longshoremen
    II. U.S. railway workers
    III. U.S. seamen

    (A) I only
    (B) III only
    (C) I and II only
    (D) II and III only
    (E) I, II, and III

A B C D E

3. According to the passage, the major alternative to a U.S. land-bridge is the

    (A) Panama Canal
    (B) Suez Canal
    (C) air-freight system
    (D) all land route
    (E) military transport system

A B C D E

4. The passage states that a land-bridge would improve United States

    (A) foreign trade
    (B) balance of payments
    (C) railroad industry
    (D) international relations
    (E) gold reserves

A B C D E

5. A land-bridge would *not*

    (A) aid U.S. steamship lines
    (B) handle goods shipped between Europe and the Far East
    (C) create new jobs for longshoremen
    (D) supply new business for U.S. railroads
    (E) create business for unscheduled shipping lines

A B C D E

Answers and Analysis

The sample passage with main points underlined appears below:

Some economists believe that the United States can be utilized as a "land bridge" for the shipment of containerized cargo between Europe and the Far East. Under the land-bridge concept, containerized freight traveling between Europe and the Far East would be shipped by ocean carrier to the United States East Coast, unloaded and placed on special railway flatcars, and shipped via railroad to a West Coast port. At this port, the containers would then be loaded on ships bound to a Far East port of entry. This procedure would be reversed for material traveling in the opposite direction. Thus, a land transportation system would be substituted for marine transportation during part of the movement of goods between Europe and the Far East.

If a land-bridge system of shipment were deemed feasible and competitive with alternative methods, it would open a completely new market for both United States steamship lines and railroads. At present, foreign lines carry all Far East-Europe freight. American carriers get none of this trade and the all-water route excludes the railroads.

The system established by a land-bridge could also serve to handle goods now being shipped between the United States West Coast and Europe, or goods shipped between the Far East and the United States Gulf and East Coasts. Currently, there are 20 foreign lines carrying West Coast freight to Europe via the Panama Canal, but not one United States line. Thus, in addition to the land-bridge getting this new business for the railroads, it also gives the United States East Coast ships an opportunity to compete for this trade.

While this method of shipment will probably not add to the labor requirements at East and West Coast piers, it does have the potential of absorbing some of the jobs that the containerization of current cargo has eliminated or could eliminate. Thus, the possibility of creating new jobs for longshoremen is not an expected benefit of such a system, but it will most certainly create other labor requirements. The land-bridge concept has the potential of offering new job openings for United States railway workers and seamen. In addition, there would be expansion of labor requirements for people in the shipbuilding and container manufacturing business.

By making United States rail transportation an export service, the land-bridge system would have a favorable effect on our balance of payments. Such a system also has the potential of relieving the United States government of part of the burden it now bears in the form of subsidies to the shipping industry. The federal government subsidizes the construction and operation of scheduled vessels. Some 52 percent of the income from their operation comes from the government in that these ships are used for all our military and other government-related export shipments. The land-bridge requirement for scheduled sailings could effect a shift from the use of these subsidized lines for shipment of government goods to commercial cargo of the land bridge. This would then open some of the lucrative government business to the unscheduled, unsubsidized lines.

Answers to Part B:

1. **(C)** 2. **(D)** 3. **(A)** 4. **(B)** 5. **(C)**

Analysis:

1. **(C)** See paragraph 2.
2. **(D)** See paragraph 4.
3. **(A)** Paragraph 3 discusses use of the Panama Canal as a route for freight lines.
4. **(B)** See paragraph 5.
5. **(C)** See paragraph 4. It specifically states that longshoremen wouldn't benefit.

Verbal Aptitude

This section of the GMAT is designed to test your ability to grasp the meanings of words and to determine the relationships that exist between words and ideas in a given situation. Verbal aptitude thus reflects your capacity for communication and understanding, and is a basic measure of your vocabulary range.

The Verbal Aptitude section of the exam usually consists of three types of questions: antonyms, analogies, and sentence completions. The following discussion will give you an idea of how to approach each of these types when you encounter them on the exam.

Antonyms

An antonym is a word that is opposite in meaning to another word. For example, an antonym for *good* would be *bad.* On the exam you are given a key word printed in capital letters accompanied by five lettered choices. You must select the lettered word that comes closest to being *opposite* in meaning to the capitalized word. Your choice should be a word that corresponds in tense or part of speech to the key word. Try the following sample question.

BUILD: (A) destroy (B) deceive (C) furnish (D) demur (E) depart

A B C D E
|| || || || ||

ANSWER: (*A*) destroy

ANALYSIS: Build is a verb in the present tense meaning to construct. (B) deceive means to trick, (C) furnish means to equip, (D) demur means to hesitate, and (E) depart means to leave. Clearly, (A) destroy, meaning to demolish, is the word that is opposite in meaning to the key word, build.

Word-Pair Relationships

In the context of the GMAT a word-pair relationship, or analogy, can be defined as a similarity existing between two given sets of words. An example of this would be the statement BOY : GIRL :: man : woman (read boy is to girl as man is to woman). The similarity between the two word-pairs should be apparent.

You are asked to select from five lettered word-pairs the combination which has a similar relationship to the key word-pair (stem) which appears in capital letters. When making your selection, you should first establish the type of relationship (rationale) existing between the key words. (In the example BOY : GIRL this can be stated as A is the male counterpart of B.) After the rationale of the key word has been determined, a corresponding word-pair can be logically located among the choices.

Try the sample question below.

RITUAL : WORSHIP :: (A) meal : recipe (B) paragon : person (C) protocol : diplomacy (D) geography : geology (E) medicine : magic

A B C D E
|| || || || ||

ANSWER: (*C*) protocol : diplomacy

ANALYSIS: The rationale of the stem can be stated as A is the ceremony associated with B. Since protocol is the ceremony associated with diplomacy, the most similar word-pair is (C).

Sentence Completions

These questions require you to complete a sentence by selecting from five alternatives the word or set of words which when inserted into blanks in the given sentence best complete the meaning of that sentence. Look for key words in the sentence that will supply hints to the missing words. Make sure to choose only those words which are *logical* in the context of the sentence and also *grammatically* correct.

Try the sample questions below, choosing the set of words that best completes the meaning of the sentence.

SAMPLE 1:

A B C D E
|| || || || ||

In economics, inflation is sometimes defined as too much ________ chasing after too few ________.

(A) money . . . goods
(B) production . . . dollars
(C) output . . . supplies
(D) productivity . . . workers
(E) advertising . . . consumers

ANSWER: (*A*) money . . . goods

ANALYSIS: In this sentence the desired information is a definition of inflation (the key word). Choices (B) through (E) may all be eliminated because they don't supply this information. Choice (A) clearly completes the meaning of the sentence.

SAMPLE 2:

A B C D E
|| || || || ||

A strike is taken as a last resort, only when other ________ fail.

(A) excuses
(B) companies
(C) adjustments
(D) measures
(E) admonitions

ANSWER: (*D*) measures

ANALYSIS: Strike is the key word here. In the context of the sentence, the answer will be a word describing a strike. Of the five alternatives, measures is the only logical choice.

Business Judgment

The objective of the Business Judgment section is to test your ability to analyze business situations and draw subsequent conclusions about them. On this section you are asked to read a passage discussing various aspects of a business situation leading to the need for a decision. After you complete the passage, you are given two sets of questions to answer.

The first set, data evaluation, contains a number of factors relating to the passage which you must evaluate as being a *major objective*, a *major factor*, a *minor factor*, a *major assumption*, or an *unimportant issue* in the decision-making process. The second set, data application, contains general questions each requiring selection of the answer that comes closest to describing an objective or objectives in the passage. You are permitted to refer to the passage while answering the questions.

As in the Reading Recall passages, it is helpful to underline main points as you read. However, when reading the Business Judgment passages, you should concentrate on defining decision-making factors that fit into the categories for evaluation in the data evaluation questions.

Read the sample passage below, underlining what you feel to be

1. Major Objectives
2. Major Factors
3. Minor Factors
4. Major Assumptions
5. Unimportant Issues

After you have finished, answer the questions that follow. Allow yourself 12 minutes to complete the entire exercise. You may consult the passage for assistance.

Sample Passage

TIME—12 minutes

Early in 1953, the soft drink world began to watch an interesting experiment, the introduction of soft drinks in cans. Grocery outlets up to that time had enjoyed about one-half of all sales, but it was felt that if the new package was successful, local bottling plants might give way to great central plants, possibly operated by companies with established names in the grocery fields, with shipments being made in carload lots. Local bottlers faced a great decision. If the change were to prove permanent, they should perhaps hasten to add can-filling machines lest they lose their market. Coca Cola, Canada Dry, White Rock, and many other bottlers experimented with the new plan. An eastern chain put out privately branded cans.

A basic limitation was a cost factor of about three cents per can, whereas bottle cost was but a fraction of a cent, since a bottle averaged about twenty-four round trips. It was, however, known that at that time about one-third of all beer sales were made in cans and furthermore, that other beverages had paved the way for consumer acceptance of a canned product. Beer prices normally were from three to four times those of soft drinks.

Many leaders in the industry felt that it might well be that consumer advertising emphasizing the convenience of using a nonreturnable package might offset both habit and the extra cost to the consumer. One of the principal bottling companies undertook a rather large-scale market research project to find useful guides to future action.

Sample Data Evaluation Questions

DIRECTIONS: Evaluate each of the following factors used in decision-making which relate to the passage you have just read by selecting

(A) for a *Major Objective*—the result desired by the executive;

(B) for a *Major Factor*—a primary consideration, spelled out in the passage, that influences the decision;

(C) for a *Minor Factor*—a less important consideration in the decision;

(D) for a *Major Assumption*—a conclusion reached by the executive not necessarily supported by the factors present;

(E) for an *Unimportant Issue*—a consideration not directly related to the problem.

1. Introduction of soft drinks in cans

2. A large-scale market research project

3. Cost of soft drinks in cans

4. Grocery outlets accounted for one-half of sales

5. The beer market was smaller than that of soft drinks

Sample Data Application Question

DIRECTIONS: Answer the following question using information contained in the passage.

6. Which of the following reasons are given for one of the bottling companies to launch a market research project?

I. Desire to corner the soft-drink market

II. Determine whether consumers would be willing to pay a higher price for canned soft-drinks

III. Test consumer reaction to canned soft-drinks

(A) I only
(B) III only
(C) I and II only
(D) II and III only
(E) I, II, and III

Answers and Analysis

The sample passage with suggested underlining appears below.

Early in 1953, the soft drink world began to watch an interesting experiment, the introduction of soft drinks in cans. Grocery outlets up to that time had enjoyed about one-half of all sales, but it was felt that if the new package was successful, local bottling plants might give way to great central plants, possibly operated by companies with established names in the grocery fields, with shipments being made in carload lots. Local bottlers faced a great decision. If the change were to prove permanent, they should perhaps hasten to add can-filling machines lest they lose their market. Coca Cola, Canada

Dry, White Rock, and many other bottlers experimented with the new plan. An eastern chain put out privately branded cans.

A basic limitation was a cost factor of about three cents per can, whereas bottle cost was but a fraction of a cent, since a bottle averaged about twenty-four round trips. It was, however, known that at that time about one-third of all beer sales were made in cases, and furthermore, that other beverages had paved the way for consumer acceptance of a canned product. Beer prices normally were from three to four times those of soft drinks.

Many leaders in the industry felt that it might well be that consumer advertising emphasizing the convenience of using a nonreturnable package might offset both habit and the extra cost to the consumer. One of the principal bottling companies undertook a rather large-scale market research project to find useful guides to future action.

Answers to Data Evaluation Questions:

1. **(A)** 2. **(B)** 3. **(B)** 4. **(C)** 5. **(E)**

Analysis:

1. **(A)** The introduction of soft drinks in cans is certainly the *Major Objective* here and the major decision to be made; the major outcome would be consumer acceptance of canned soft drinks.

2. **(B)** The market research project will gather information allowing management to make a decision; without such information, presumably, no decision could be reached. Therefore, the project is a *Major Factor*.

3. **(B)** The cost of canned soft drinks is a *Major Factor* in making the decision because it is crucial to consumer acceptance. If the soft drinks are priced too high, consumers may not be willing to purchase them.

4. **(C)** Grocery stores are related to the issue of whether consumers would accept the new product and thus a *Minor Factor*. If consumers accept the project, grocery stores would have to stock the item.

5. **(E)** It does not state in the passage that the "beer market was smaller than that of soft drinks." Therefore, the only possible answer to this question is (E), *Unimportant Issue*.

Answer to Data Application Question

ANSWER: (*D*) II and III only.

ANALYSIS: The correct answer is (D) because the passage states that some of the major uncertainties as to whether to offer canned soft drinks is their high cost and the purchasing habits of consumers, i.e., whether they would prefer canned soft drinks and be willing to pay a premium (high) price for them. Alternative (A), I only, is factually incorrect since no mention is made that the bottler in question desires to "corner the market," but rather to obtain some answers to the central problem—that of consumer reaction to canned soft drinks.

Mathematics

The Mathematics section of the GMAT is designed to test your ability to work with numbers. There are a variety of questions in this section dealing with the basic principles of arithmetic, algebra and geometry. These questions may take the form of word problems or require straight calculation. In addition, many questions involving the interpretation of tables and graphs are usually included.

The typical Mathematics section consists of 55 questions that must be answered within a time limit of 75 minutes. Often a shorter section of perhaps 35 questions with a 40 minute time limit will also appear on an exam. Although the majority of questions are not that difficult, it is not always possible to answer all of them within the allotted time. For this reason, you should be aware of certain procedures that will help you make the most of the time you have.

Strategy for GMAT Mathematics Questions

In order to maximize your score on this section, you must answer all the questions you can. *Don't waste time* on a question you can't figure out in a minute or two. You will score better if you answer 2 or 3 easy questions in the time it takes to answer one difficult one. Since the last questions may be easier than the first questions, try to *budget your time* so that you will have a chance to try each question.

Don't waste time on *unnecessary calculations*. If you can answer the question by *estimating* or doing a rough calculation, the time you save can be used to answer other questions. Keep this in mind especially when considering problems that involve tables and graphs. In many cases you can make estimates which will simplify your calculations and still be accurate enough to answer the question. Using estimates is a skill that can turn a good score into an excellent one.

For line and bar graphs, use your pencil as a ruler. It is more accurate than simply "eyeballing" columns which are not adjacent.

You should understand that random guessing will not help your score on these sections, since a percentage of your wrong answers is subtracted from your correct answers. If you can eliminate all but two of the answers for a particular question, it will probably help your score to guess an answer for that question.

Solve the sample questions below, allowing yourself 12 minutes to complete all of them. As you work, try to make use of the above strategy. Any figure that appears with a problem is drawn as accurately as possible to provide information that may help in answering the question. All numbers used are real numbers.

Sample Mathematics Questions

TIME—12 minutes

1. A B C D E
|| || || || ||

1. A train travels from Albany to Syracuse a distance of 120 miles at the average rate of 50 miles per hour. The train then travels back to Albany from Syracuse. The total

traveling time of the train is 5 hours and 24 minutes. What was the average rate of speed of the train on the return trip to Albany?

(A) 60 mph
(B) 48 mph
(C) 40 mph
(D) 50 mph
(E) 35 mph

2. A parking lot charges a flat rate of X dollars for any amount of time up to two hours, and $\frac{1}{6}X$ for each hour or fraction of an hour after the first two hours. How much does it cost to park for 5 hours and 15 minutes?

2. A B C D E

(A) $3X$
(B) $2X$
(C) $1\frac{2}{3}X$
(D) $1\frac{1}{2}X$
(E) $1\frac{1}{6}X$

Use the following table for questions 3–5.

Number of Students by major in State University		
	1950	1970
Division of Business	990	2,504
Division of Sciences	350	790
Division of Humanities	1,210	4,056
Division of Engineering	820	1,600
Division of Agriculture	630	1,050
TOTAL	4,000	10,000

3. From 1950 to 1970, the percentage of university students enrolled in Engineering

3. A B C D E

(A) stayed roughly the same
(B) increased by more than 4%
(C) increased by more than 1% but less than 4%
(D) decreased by more than 4%
(E) decreased by more than 1% but less than 4%

4. The number of students enrolled in Business from 1950 to 1970

4. A B C D E

(A) almost tripled
(B) increased by a factor of about 2.5
(C) roughly doubled
(D) stayed about the same
(E) decreased by 40%

5. By 1970 how many of the divisions had an enrollment greater than 200% of the enrollment of that division in 1950?

5. A B C D E

(A) 0
(B) 1
(C) 2
(D) 3
(E) 4

Use the graph below for questions 6 and 7.

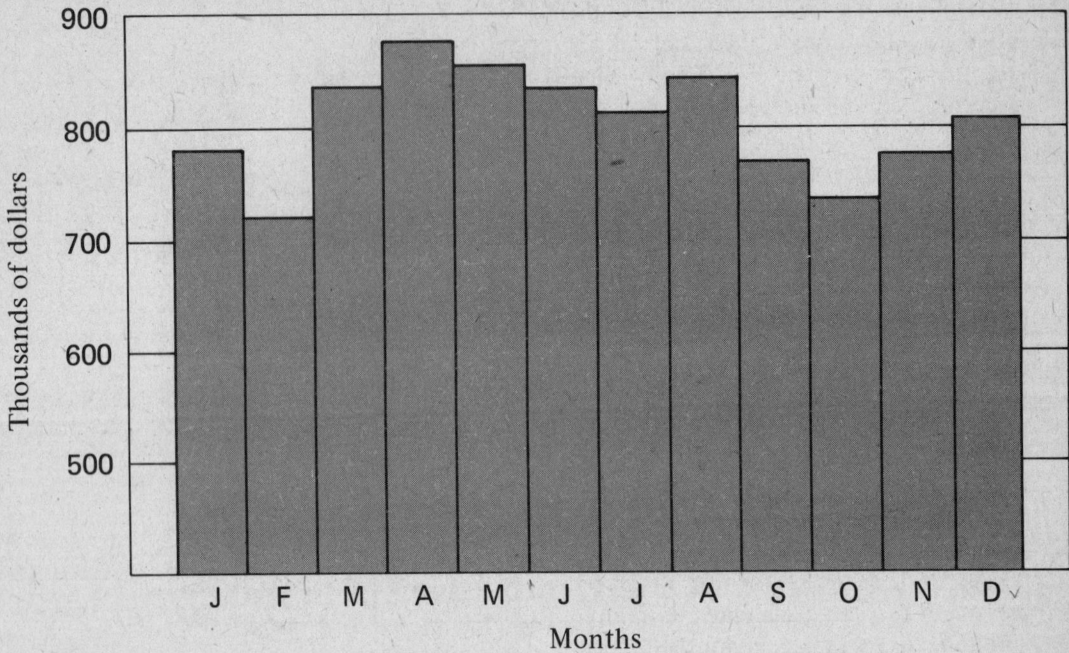

The graph gives monthly sales of the XYZ corporation in thousands of dollars for each month in 1970.

6. A B C D E

6. In what month were sales the least?

(A) January
(B) February
(C) October
(D) December
(E) March

7. A B C D E

7. Which of the following statements are true?

I. Of Spring, Summer, and Fall, Spring was the season which had the highest total sales.

II. Sales in April were greater than the combined sales of January and February.

III. The greatest change in sales occurred between August and September.

(A) I only
(B) I and II
(C) II only
(D) II and III
(E) I and III

Answers and Analysis

ANSWERS:

1. **(C)**
2. **(C)**
3. **(D)**
4. **(B)**
5. **(D)**
6. **(B)**
7. **(A)**

ANALYSIS:

1. **(C)** The train took 120/50 = $2\frac{2}{5}$ hours to travel from Albany to Syracuse. Since the total traveling time of the train was $5\frac{2}{5}$ hours, it must have taken the train 3 hours for the trip from Syracuse to Albany. Since the distance traveled is 120 miles, the average rate of speed on the return trip to Albany was (1/3)(120) mph = 40 mph.

2. **(C)** It costs X for the first 2 hours. If you park 5 hours and 15 minutes there are 3 hours and 15 minutes left after the first 2 hours. Since this time is charged at the rate of $X/6$ for each hour or fraction thereof, it costs $4(X/6)$ for the last 3 hours and 15 minutes. Thus the total is $X + \frac{4}{6}X = 1\frac{2}{3}X$.

3. **(D)** Since 820/4,000 = .205, the percentage of university students enrolled in Engineering in 1950 was 20.5%; since 1,600/10,000 = .16, the percentage in 1970 was 16%. Thus the percentage of university students enrolled in Engineering decreased by 4.5%.

4. **(B)** In 1950 there were 990 Business students and in 1970 there were 2,504. Since (2.5)(1,000) = 2,500, the correct answer is thus (B) increased by a factor of about 2.5. Note that this is an easy way to save yourself time. Instead of dividing 990 into 2,504 to find the exact rate of increase, simply use numbers close to the original numbers to get an estimate. In many cases this gives enough information to answer the question and saves valuable time.

5. **(D)** If a division in 1970 has more than 200% of the number of students it had in 1950 that means that the number of students more than doubled between 1950 and 1970. Therefore simply double each entry in the 1950 column and if this is less than the corresponding entry in the 1970 column, that division has more than 200% of the number of students it had in 1950. Since (2)(990) = 1980 which is less than 2,504, the number of Business students more than doubled. Since (2)(1,210) = 2,420 which is less than 4,056, Humanities more than doubled, and because (2)(350) = 700 which is less than 790, Sciences more than doubled. Engineering did not double in size because (2)(820) = 1640 which is larger than 1,600. Also since (2)(630) = 1,260, which is larger than 1,050, the number of Agricultural students in 1970 was less than 200% of the number of Agricultural students in 1950. Therefore three of the divisions (Business, Humanities, and Sciences) more than doubled between 1950 and 1970.

6. **(B)** Use your pencil as a rulér to compare February to October; the other answers are obviously wrong.

7. **(A)** June and March were about the same; May was a little larger than August and April was much greater than July; so Spring sales were higher than Summer sales. It is easy to see Spring sales were higher than Fall sales. Therefore, statement I is true. (Use your pencil as a substitute for a ruler to compare columns which are not next to each other.) Since April sales were about $900,000 and sales in February and January were each larger than $700,000, the combined sales in January and February were larger than $1,400,000. Therefore, statement II is false. Between August and September the change was roughly $50,000 but between February and March the change was more than $100,000. Thus statement III is false.

Data Sufficiency

This section of the GMAT is designed to test your reasoning ability. Like the Mathematics section, it requires a basic knowledge of the principles of arithmetic, algebra, and geometry. Each Data Sufficiency question consists of a mathematical problem and two statements containing information relating to it. You must decide whether the problem can be solved by using information from (A) the first statement alone but not the second alone, (B) the second statement alone but not the first alone, (C) both statements together but not each separately (D) either of the statements alone, or (E) neither of the statements together. Generally, you are allowed one minute to answer each question. Thus, if a section contains 15 questions, it will be 15 minutes in length. As in the Mathematics section, time is of the utmost importance. Approaching Data Sufficiency problems properly will help you use this time wisely.

Always keep in mind the fact that you are never asked to supply an answer for the problem; you need only determine if there is sufficient data available to find the answer. Therefore, *don't waste time figuring out the exact answer.* Once you know whether or not it is possible to find the answer with the given information you are through. If you spend too much time doing unnecessary work on one question you may not be able to finish the entire section.

Because of the nature of these questions, it may be possible in certain instances to improve your score by making an educated guess. If, for example, you know that the first statement alone is sufficient but are not sure about the second one alone, you are already limited to just two choices—(A) the first statement alone but not the second statement alone is sufficient, or (D) either of the statements alone is sufficient. The same holds true if you are sure that the second statement alone is sufficient but are uncertain of the first statement. Since you get one point for each correct answer and only lose $\frac{1}{4}$ of a point for an incorrect answer, you won't run the risk of substantially lowering your score by guessing.

Read the following directions carefully and then try the sample Data Sufficiency questions below. Allow yourself 6 minutes total time. All numbers used are real numbers. A figure given for a problem is intended to provide information consistent with that in the question, but not necessarily consistent with the additional information contained in the statements.

Sample Data Sufficiency Questions

TIME—6 minutes

DIRECTIONS: Each of the following problems has a question and two statements which are labeled (1) and (2). Use the data given in (1) and (2) together with other available information (such as the number of hours in a day, the definition of *clockwise*, mathematical facts, etc.) to decide whether the statements are *sufficient* to answer the question. Then choose

(A) if you can get the answer from (1) alone but not from (2) alone;

(B) if you can get the answer from (2) alone but not from (1) alone;

(C) if you can get the answer from (1) and (2) together, although neither statement by itself suffices;

(D) if statement (1) alone suffices *and* statement (2) alone suffices;

(E) if you cannot get the answer from statements (1) and (2) together, but need even more data.

1. A B C D E

1. A rectangular field is 40 yards long. Find the area of the field.

(1) A fence around the entire boundary of the field is 140 yards long.
(2) The field is more than 20 yards wide.

2. Is X a number greater than zero? 2.A B C D E

(1) $X^2 - 1 = 0$
(2) $X^3 + 8 = 0$

3. An industrial plant produces bottles. In 1961 the number of bottles produced by the plant was twice the number produced in 1960. How many bottles were produced altogether in the years 1960, 1961 and 1962? 3.A B C D E

(1) In 1962 the number of bottles produced was 3 times the number produced in 1960.
(2) In 1963 the number of bottles produced was one half the total produced in the years 1960, 1961, and 1962.

4. A man 6 feet tall is standing near a light on the top of a pole. What is the length of the shadow cast by the man? 4.A B C D E

(1) The pole is 18 feet high.
(2) The man is 12 feet from the pole.

5. Find the length of RS if z is 90° and $PS = 6$. 5.A B C D E

(1) $PR = 6$
(2) $x = 45°$

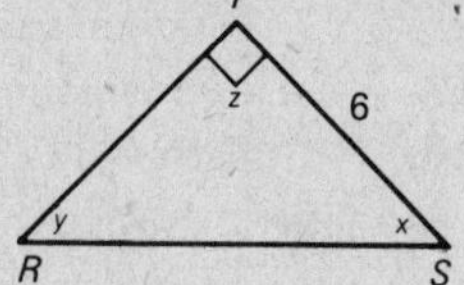

6. Working at a constant rate and by himself, it takes worker U 3 hours to fill up a ditch with sand. How long would it take for worker V to fill up the same ditch working by himself?

(1) Working together but at the same time U and V can fill in the ditch in 1 hour $52\frac{1}{2}$ minutes.
(2) In any length of time worker V fills in only 60% as much as worker U does in the same time.

Answers and Analysis

ANSWERS:

1. (A)	4. (C)
2. (B)	5. (D)
3. (E)	6. (D)

ANALYSIS:

1. (A) The area of a rectangle is the length multiplied by the width. Since you know the length is 40 yards, you must find out the width in order to solve the problem. Since statement (2) simply says the width is greater than 20 yards you can not find out the exact width using (2). So (2) alone is not sufficient. Statement (1) says the length of a fence around the entire boundary of the field is 140 yards. The length of this fence is the perimeter of the rectangle, the sum of twice the length and twice the width. If we replace the length by 40 in $P = 2L + 2W$ we have $140 = 2(40) + 2W$ and solving for W yields $2W = 60$, or $W = 30$ yards. Hence the area is $(40)(30) = 1200$ square yards. Thus (1) alone is sufficient but (2) alone is not.

2. **(B)** Statement (1) means $X^2 = 1$, but there are two possible solutions to this equation, $X = 1$, $X = -1$. Thus using (1) alone you can not deduce whether X is positive or negative. Statement (2) means $X^3 = -8$ but there is only one possible (real) solution to this, $X = -2$. Thus X is not greater than zero which answers the question. And (2) alone is sufficient.

3. **(E)** T, the total produced in the three years, is the sum of $P_0 + P_1 + P_2$, where P_0 is the number produced in 1960, P_1 the number produced in 1961, and P_2 the number produced in 1962. You are given that $P_1 = 2P_0$. Thus $T = P_0 + P_1 + P_2 = P_0 + 2P_0 + P_2 = 3P_0 + P_2$. So we must find out P_0 and P_2 to answer the question. Statement (1) says $P_2 = 3P_0$; thus by using (1) if we can find the value of P_0 we can find T. But (1) gives us no further information about P_0. Statement (2) says T equals the number produced in 1963, but it does not say what this number is. Since there are no relations given between production in 1963 and production in the individual years 1960, 1961, or 1962 you can not use (2) to find out what P_0 is. Thus (1) and (2) together are not sufficient.

4. **(C)** Sometimes it may help to draw a picture. By proportions or by similar triangles the height of the pole, h, is to 6 feet as the length of the shadow, s, + the distance to the pole, x, is to s. So $h/6 = (s + x)/s$. Thus $hs = 6s + 6x$ by cross-multiplication. Solving for s gives $hs - 6s = 6x$, or $s(h - 6) = 6x$, or, finally we have $s = 6x/(h - 6)$. Statement (1) says $h = 18$; thus $s = 6x/12 = x/2$, but using (1) alone we can not deduce the value x. Thus (1) alone is not sufficient. Statement (2) says x equals 12; thus, using (1) and (2) together we deduce $s = 6$, but using (2) alone all we can deduce is that $s = 72/(h - 6)$, which cannot be solved for s unless we know h. Thus using (1) and (2) together we can deduce the answer but (1) alone is not sufficient nor is (2) alone.

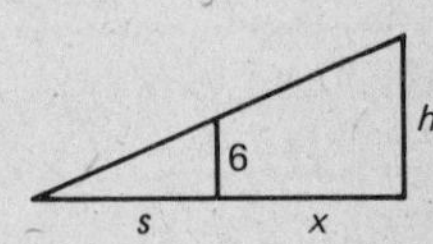

5. **(D)** Since z is a right angle, $(RS)^2 = (PS)^2 + (PR)^2$, so $(RS)^2 = (6)^2 + (PR)^2$, and RS will be the positive square root of $36 + (PR)^2$. Thus if you can find the length of PR the problem is solved. Statement (1) says $PR = 6$, thus $(RS)^2 = 36 + 36$, so $RS = 6\sqrt{2}$. Thus (1) alone is sufficient. Statement (2) says $x = 45°$ but since the sum of the angles in a triangle is 180° and z is 90° then $y = 45°$. So x and y are equal angles and that means the sides opposite x and opposite y must be equal or $PS = PR$. Thus $PR = 6$ and $RS = 6\sqrt{2}$ so (2) alone is also sufficient.

6. **(D)** (1) says U and V together can fill in the ditch in $1\frac{7}{8}$ hours. Since U can fill in the ditch in 3 hours, in 1 hour he can fill in one-third of the ditch. Hence, in $1\frac{7}{8}$ hours U would fill in $(1/3)(15/8) = \frac{5}{8}$ of the ditch. So V fills in $\frac{3}{8}$ of the ditch in $1\frac{7}{8}$ hours. Thus V would take $(8/3)(15/8) = 5$ hours to fill in the ditch working by himself. Therefore statement (1) alone is sufficient. According to statement (2) since U fills the ditch in 3 hours, V will fill $\frac{3}{5}$ of the ditch in 3 hours. Thus V will take 5 hours to fill in the ditch working by himself.

Answer Sheet – Diagnostic Test

Section I — Reading Recall

1.A B C D E
2.A B C D E
3.A B C D E
4.A B C D E
5.A B C D E
6.A B C D E
7.A B C D E
8.A B C D E
9.A B C D E
10.A B C D E
11.A B C D E
12.A B C D E
13.A B C D E
14.A B C D E
15.A B C D E
16.A B C D E
17.A B C D E
18.A B C D E
19.A B C D E
20.A B C D E
21.A B C D E
22.A B C D E
23.A B C D E
24.A B C D E
25.A B C D E
26.A B C D E
27.A B C D E
28.A B C D E
29.A B C D E
30.A B C D E

Section II — Mathematics

31.A B C D E
32.A B C D E
33.A B C D E
34.A B C D E
35.A B C D E
36.A B C D E
37.A B C D E
38.A B C D E
39.A B C D E
40.A B C D E
41.A B C D E
42.A B C D E
43.A B C D E
44.A B C D E
45.A B C D E
46.A B C D E
47.A B C D E
48.A B C D E
49.A B C D E
50.A B C D E
51.A B C D E
52.A B C D E
53.A B C D E
54.A B C D E
55.A B C D E
56.A B C D E
57.A B C D E
58.A B C D E
59.A B C D E
60.A B C D E
61.A B C D E
62.A B C D E
63.A B C D E
64.A B C D E
65.A B C D E
66.A B C D E
67.A B C D E
68.A B C D E
69.A B C D E
70.A B C D E
71.A B C D E
72.A B C D E
73.A B C D E
74.A B C D E
75.A B C D E
76.A B C D E
77.A B C D E
78.A B C D E
79.A B C D E
80.A B C D E
81.A B C D E
82.A B C D E
83.A B C D E
84.A B C D E
85.A B C D E

Section III — Verbal Aptitude

86.A B C D E
87.A B C D E
88.A B C D E
89.A B C D E
90.A B C D E
91.A B C D E
92.A B C D E
93.A B C D E
94.A B C D E
95.A B C D E
96.A B C D E
97.A B C D E
98.A B C D E
99.A B C D E
100.A B C D E
101.A B C D E
102.A B C D E
103.A B C D E
104.A B C D E
105.A B C D E
106.A B C D E
107.A B C D E
108.A B C D E
109.A B C D E
110.A B C D E
111.A B C D E
112.A B C D E
113.A B C D E
114.A B C D E
115.A B C D E
116.A B C D E
117.A B C D E
118.A B C D E
119.A B C D E
120.A B C D E
121.A B C D E
122.A B C D E
123.A B C D E
124.A B C D E
125.A B C D E

Section IV — Data Sufficiency

126. A B C D E
127. A B C D E
128. A B C D E
129. A B C D E
130. A B C D E
131. A B C D E
132. A B C D E
133. A B C D E
134. A B C D E
135. A B C D E
136. A B C D E
137. A B C D E
138. A B C D E
139. A B C D E
140. A B C D E

Section V — Business Judgment

141. A B C D E
142. A B C D E
143. A B C D E
144. A B C D E
145. A B C D E
146. A B C D E
147. A B C D E
148. A B C D E
149. A B C D E
150. A B C D E
151. A B C D E
152. A B C D E
153. A B C D E
154. A B C D E
155. A B C D E
156. A B C D E
157. A B C D E
158. A B C D E
159. A B C D E
160. A B C D E

Section VI — Mathematics

161. A B C D E
162. A B C D E
163. A B C D E
164. A B C D E
165. A B C D E
166. A B C D E
167. A B C D E
168. A B C D E
169. A B C D E
170. A B C D E
171. A B C D E
172. A B C D E
173. A B C D E
174. A B C D E
175. A B C D E
176. A B C D E
177. A B C D E
178. A B C D E
179. A B C D E
180. A B C D E
181. A B C D E
182. A B C D E
183. A B C D E
184. A B C D E
185. A B C D E
186. A B C D E
187. A B C D E
188. A B C D E
189. A B C D E
190. A B C D E
191. A B C D E
192. A B C D E
193. A B C D E
194. A B C D E
195. A B C D E

THREE GMAT DIAGNOSTIC TEST

Now that you have become familiar with the various types of questions appearing on the GMAT and have had a chance to sample each type, you probably have an idea of what to expect from an actual exam. The next step, then, is to take a sample test to see how you do.

The diagnostic test that follows has been designed to resemble the format of recent GMATs. When taking it, try to simulate actual test conditions as closely as possible. For example, you may want to time yourself as you work on each section so that you don't go over the allotted time limit for that section. After you have completed the test, check your answers and use the self-scoring chart to evaluate the results. Use these results to determine which review sections you should spend the most time studying before you attempt the 5 sample GMATs at the end of the book. To assist you in your review, all answers to mathematics questions are keyed so that you can easily refer to the section in the Mathematics Review that discusses the material covered in a particular question.

Diagnostic Test

Section I Reading Recall

TOTAL TIME: 35 minutes

Part A: TIME—15 minutes

DIRECTIONS: This part contains three reading passages. You are to read each one carefully. You will have fifteen minutes to study the three passages and twenty minutes to answer questions based on them. When answering the questions, you will *not* be allowed to refer back to the passages.

Passage 1:

The economic condition of the low-income regions of the world is one of the great problems of our time. Their progress is important to the high-income countries, not only for humanitarian and political reasons but also because rapid economic growth in the low-income countries could make a substantial contribution to the expansion and prosperity of the world economy as a whole.

The governments of most high-income countries have in recent years undertaken important aid programs, both bilaterally and multilaterally, and have thus demonstrated their interest in the development of low-income countries. They have also worked within the General Agreement on Tariffs and Trade (GATT) for greater freedom of trade and, recognizing the special problems of low-income countries, have made special trading arrangements to meet their needs. But a faster expansion of trade with high-income countries is necessary if the low-income countries are to enjoy a satisfactory rate of growth.

This statement is therefore concerned with the policies of high-income countries toward their trade with low-income countries. Our recommendations are based on the conviction that a better distribution of world resources and a more rational utilization of labor are in the general interest. A liberal policy on the part of high-income countries with respect to their trade with low-income countries will not only be helpful to the low-income countries but, when transitional adjustments have taken place, beneficial to the high-income countries as well.

It is necessary to recognize however, that in furthering the development of low-income countries, the high-income countries can play only a supporting role. If development is to be successful, the main effort must necessarily be made by the people of the low-income countries. The high-income countries are, moreover, likely to provide aid and facilitate trade more readily and extensively where the low-income countries are seen to be making sound and determined efforts to help themselves, and thus to be making effective use of their aid and trade opportunities.

It is, then, necessary that the low-income countries take full account of the lessons that have been learned from the experience of recent years, if they wish to achieve successful development and benefit from support from high-income countries. Among the most important of these lessons are the following:

Severe damage has been done by inflation. A sound financial framework evokes higher domestic savings and investment as well as more aid and investment from abroad. Budgetary and monetary discipline and a more efficient financial and fiscal system help greatly to mobilize funds for investment and thereby decisively influence the rate of growth. Foreign aid should also be efficiently applied to this end.

The energies of the people of low-income countries are more likely to be harnessed to the task of economic development where the policies of their governments aim to offer economic opportunity for all and to reduce excessive social inequalities.

Development plans have tended to concentrate on industrial investment. The growth of industry depends, however, on concomitant development in agriculture. A steady rise in productivity on the farms, where in almost all low-income countries a majority of the labor force works, is an essential condition of rapid over-all growth. Satisfactory development of agriculture is also necessary to provide an adequate market for an expanding industrial sector and to feed the growing urban population without burdening the balance of payments with heavy food imports. Diminishing surpluses in the high-income countries underline the need for a faster growth of agricultural productivity in low-income countries. Success in this should, moreover, lead to greater trade in agricultural products among the low-income countries themselves as well as to increased exports of some agricultural products to the high-income countries.

There can be no doubt about the urgency of the world food problem. Adequate nourishment and a balanced diet are not only necessary for working adults but are crucial for the mental and physical development of growing children. Yet, in a number of low-income countries where the diet is already insufficient the production of food has fallen behind the increase in population. A continuation of this trend must lead to endemic famine. The situation demands strenuous efforts in the low-income countries to improve the production, preservation, and distribution of food so that these countries are better able to feed themselves.

Passage 2:

The concept of "standard of living" is a wide and multifaceted one. In the absence of comprehensive measurement, it is commonly expressed empirically in terms of consumption or in terms of income.

One of the most comprehensive expressions of standard of living is total consumption over an extended period, where consumption is defined not only as family purchases but also as (1) consumption of goods and services produced by the family; (2) consumption of public services provided without payment; and (3) consumption of goods and services received as compensation for labor, over and above wages and salary. It may be assumed that total consumption is less subject to incidental fluctuations than income. Moreover, it reflects not only current income but also past income and savings, windfalls, and expectations regarding future income.

Current monetary income constitutes the main indicator for the standard of living; however, standard of living is not determined solely by current income, but also by past income, accumulated assets and expectations for future income. Moreover, the standard of living of a family is influenced by the value of the public services from which it benefits and the rate of taxes which it has to pay.

Between 1964 and 1970 the standard of living of the urban population rose. During this period, average real income increased by approximately 5% per annum. During the economic recession (1966–67), the income of all strata was adversely affected, particularly that of lower income groups. Since the end of the recession, a trend of decreasing inequality in income distribution has occurred, most noticeably among the lower income brackets. In 1970, the degree of income inequality was similar to that of the year 1964, despite the fact that during the latter period two external factors—an increase in welfare payments and the aging of the population—acted towards increasing the degree of inequality.

In the period under review, the standard of living of families originating from Asia and Africa improved relative to that of all families. This improvement found expression in higher income levels, better housing, a higher ownership rate of consumer durables and an increase in the proportion of families in higher income brackets. However, even after the improvement in their relative position during the past decade, their average income is still only 70% of the overall average for all families.

One of the important factors behind the income differential between families of African and Asian origins and the rest of the population is the level of education. In recent years the gap between these two groups has narrowed among the younger generation, but it is still substantial. Unless the education gap is significantly reduced between these two groups, other means employed in an attempt to produce more income equality will be thwarted. More resources must be immediately put to the task of improving educational opportunities for families of African and Asian origin, without of course, reducing the educational facilities and opportunities open to the rest of the population.

Passage 3:

Much has been written about the need for increasing our knowledge of marketing in other countries and how different marketing systems operate in delivering goods and services to consumers. American businessmen have long been interested in foreign markets for the purpose of stimulating trade. Analysis of the mechanisms of a given country's internal trade and the structural and environmental factors of its marketing system are necessary to the success of an American firm's marketing efforts abroad.

Knowledge of a country's marketing system is of equal importance to the potential investor. Information pertaining to channels of distribution, promotional facilities, and the marketing experience of management should have weight in the investment decision equal to factors such as financing, the possibility of expropriation, and plant location. Moreover, American businessmen are certainly not limited to investment in manufacturing industry abroad; there may be profitable opportunities for the introduction of American marketing institutions and techniques in other countries. The extent to which American dollars should be channeled into the introduction of American marketing innovations depends upon the answers to the following questions: (1) to what extent is it possible to "transplant" American marketing operations or institutions to foreign countries, and (2) would such transplantations, if successful, contribute to the economic development of the recipient country?

In light of the above, research is needed to determine the factors responsible for the acceptance and growth of marketing innovations so that an understanding of the adoption process can aid American businessmen contemplating the introduction of similar marketing techniques in other developing countries.

Take the case of an American marketing innovation: self-service. Whether self-service shops can be successful outside the United States depends upon sufficient population density, consumer income and the availability of suitable store locations and manpower. But even when these environmental forces are positive, cultural constraints may still serve as a barrier to the development of self-service. For example, a packaged foods industry cannot develop unless culturally developed habits of buying only "fresh" foods and produce can be overcome. Moreover, consumers must be sufficiently literate to select products from store shelves without the help of sales clerks.

The traditional pattern of shopping (in many countries) at different locations for each category of goods—e.g. dairy products, vegetables, meat, etc.—is a custom that has been learned and reinforced over many years. It does not break down easily. Daily shopping trips may be more of a social endeavor, providing the housewife contact with her friends at the local market or grocery, although hand-to-mouth buying may also result from low incomes and lack of refrigeration and storage facilities.

In Israel, the first supermarket was successful in changing the shopping patterns of many housewives who traditionally shopped at different stores for meat, dairy products, vegetables and fruit, and baked goods. Housewives preferred the self-service shop because it reduced total shopping time and offered quality food at lower prices. Working women switched to the self-service shop because it is open during their lunch hour, unlike the small shops that close at midday for several hours. Besides introducing a wider assortment of products at lower prices, standardized packaging, pricing, and quality was afforded the Israeli consumer. Although prepackaged meats and produce were not accepted by many consumers at first, there are indications that buying habits have changed. For example, packaged meat now accounts for about 25 percent of total sales of Israel's two major self-service food chains. In addition, the rate of increase of packaged meat sales at one chain (Consumer Union) is now greater than that of other commodities.

If there is still time remaining, review the passages until all 15 minutes have elapsed.
Do not look at Part B until that time.

Part B: TIME—20 minutes

QUESTIONS TO

Passage 1:

DIRECTIONS: Answer the following questions pertaining to information contained in the three passages you have just read. You may not turn back to these passages for assistance.

1. The economic conditions of low-income countries are important to high-income countries because of

I. Humanitarian reasons
II. Political reasons
III. Cultural reasons

(A) I only
(B) III only
(C) I and II only
(D) II and III only
(E) I, II, and III

2. According to the passage, governments of most high-income countries have

(A) not worked for freer trade with low-income countries
(B) undertaken important aid programs for low-income countries
(C) injected massive doses of capital into low-income countries
(D) provided training programs for low-income country entrepreneurs
(E) helped improve the educational systems of low-income countries

3. The major subject of the passage is concerned with

(A) trade relations of high-income countries towards low-income countries
(B) foreign trade problems of low-income countries
(C) fiscal and monetary problems of low-income countries
(D) trade arrangements under the GATT organization
(E) general economic problems of low-income countries

4. If low-income countries expect aid from high-income countries, they must

(A) spend the aid wisely
(B) put their own house in order first
(C) learn from the experience of developed countries
(D) curb inflation
(E) all the above

5. Which of the following policies is mentioned for its influence upon the rate of economic growth?

(A) an efficient financial and fiscal system
(B) a trade surplus
(C) a democratic government
(D) little reliance upon foreign aid
(E) a budgetary surplus

6. Industrial growth depends upon a parallel growth of the

(A) labor force
(B) agricultural system
(C) balance of payments
(D) urban population
(E) monetary system

7. The passage states that participation of high-income countries is limited to

(A) ten percent of their GNP
(B) a supporting role
(C) regulations stipulated by GATT
(D) what low-income countries can absorb
(E) monetary aid only

8. In order to better use foreign aid, low-income countries should

(A) not take more than they can use
(B) budget the capital wisely
(C) reduce excessive social inequalities
(D) concentrate on commercial development
(E) establish agricultural communes

9. Which of the following statements represents a major problem in the agricultural systems of low-income countries?

I. The increase in food production is less than population growth.
II. Food distribution is inefficient.
III. Food prices are too high.

(A) I only
(B) III only
(C) I and II only
(D) II and III only
(E) I, II, and III

10. If low-income countries could develop economically at a faster rate, the result would be

(A) less inflation
(B) lower deficits in their balance of trade
(C) liberal trade policies
(D) better distribution of world resources
(E) more equitable fiscal policies

QUESTIONS TO

Passage 2:

11. The author expresses "standard of living" in terms of

(A) total goods and services produced
(B) consumption of goods and services
(C) real income
(D) per-capita income
(E) discretionary income

12. Which income period best expresses "standard of living"?

(A) past income
(B) current income
(C) future income
(D) all of the above
(E) none of the above

13. Consumption is defined as

(A) total family purchases
(B) total family purchases plus goods and services produced by the family
(C) public services provided by the state
(D) income minus expenditures on necessities
(E) goods and services actually consumed

14. Between 1964 and 1970, average real income

(A) remained stable
(B) increased by about 5 percent
(C) decreased slightly
(D) decreased during the recession
(E) decreased by 5 percent

15. According to the passage, income inequality (during 1970)

(A) declined among all strata
(B) declined most significantly among lower income groups
(C) widened between the rich and the poor strata
(D) did not change appreciably
(E) declined among older groups in the population

16. The author believes that inequality of income might be narrowed if

(A) the tax structure is reformed
(B) the educational gap between different population groups is reduced
(C) more jobs could be found for people of Asian-African origin
(D) real incomes increased
(E) a system of price controls were implemented

17. The standard of living of Asian-African immigrants improved as measured by all of the following factors *except*

(A) higher income levels
(B) better housing
(C) increased ownership of consumer durables
(D) a shift in population centers
(E) an increased proportion of these families in higher income brackets

18. It may be inferred that the author of the passage is a(n)

(A) engineer
(B) food specialist
(C) economist
(D) bank president
(E) efficiency expert

19. Even though the income level of families of Asian-African origin increased relatively, their average income is still

(A) only about equal to that of other groups
(B) about 70 percent of the overall national average
(C) close to the national average, but slightly below
(D) about 50 percent of the national average
(E) about 25 percent of the national average

20. Between 1964 and 1970, the standard of living of the urban population

(A) declined
(B) increased
(C) stagnated
(D) remained about constant
(E) doubled

QUESTIONS TO

Passage 3:

21. According to the author, knowledge of foreign marketing systems is essential because it

(A) cements relations between countries
(B) helps us to know about other people
(C) stimulates foreign trade
(D) improves channels of distribution
(E) teaches us something about our own marketing system

22. The passage implies that marketing can contribute to

(A) improving goods and services
(B) economic development
(C) more efficient promotion and advertising
(D) full employment
(E) growth of economic institutions

23. The introduction of American marketing techniques abroad depends upon the

(A) educational level in the host country
(B) amount of investment capital available
(C) efficient channels of distribution
(D) extent to which the technique(s) can be "transplanted"
(E) none of the above

24. A most important constraint to the introduction of self-service shops seems to be

(A) cultural barriers
(B) income
(C) education
(D) capital formation
(E) population dispersion

25. In Israel, daily shopping trips to the food market occur because of

(A) a lack of supermarkets
(B) social reasons as much as economic ones
(C) low per-capita incomes
(D) poor transportation facilities
(E) fluctuating food supplies

26. Working women prefer self-service shops owing to

(A) lower food prices
(B) better quality food products
(C) more convenient shopping hours
(D) wider choice of commodities
(E) pre-packaged meats and vegetables

27. Concerning the transfer of American marketing techniques abroad, the author concludes that

(A) most countries can accept these techniques
(B) they are not operable in most countries
(C) more research is needed into this subject
(D) the transfer depends upon capital availability
(E) only developed countries can use American marketing techniques

28. The author states that adoption of self-service is a function of

I. Household income
II. Cultural and structural constraints
III. Population density

(A) I only
(B) III only
(C) I and II only
(D) II and III only
(E) I, II and III

29. The article from which this passage was extracted probably appeared in a(n)

(A) academic journal
(B) accounting journal
(C) management textbook
(D) popular magazine
(E) newspaper editorial

30. Based on the Israeli experience, we can conclude that the adoption of self-service by developing countries

(A) is hopeless
(B) shows some promise
(C) no conclusion can be made
(D) the authors are extremely optimistic
(E) none of the above

If there is still time remaining, you may review the questions in this section only.
You may not look at Part A or turn to any other section of the test.

Section II Mathematics

TIME: 75 minutes

DIRECTIONS: Solve each of the following problems; then indicate the correct answer on the answer sheet. [On the actual test you will be permitted to use any space available on the examination paper for scratch work.]

NOTE: A figure that appears with a problem is drawn as accurately as possible so as to provide information that may help in answering the question. Numbers in this test are real numbers.

31. If 32 students in a class are female and there are 18 male students in the class, what percentage of the class is female?

(A) 32%
(B) 36%
(C) 56.25%
(D) 64%
(E) 72%

32. If $x + y = 2$ and $y = 5$ what is $x - y$?

(A) −8
(B) −5
(C) −3
(D) 2
(E) 8

Use the following graph for questions 33–35.

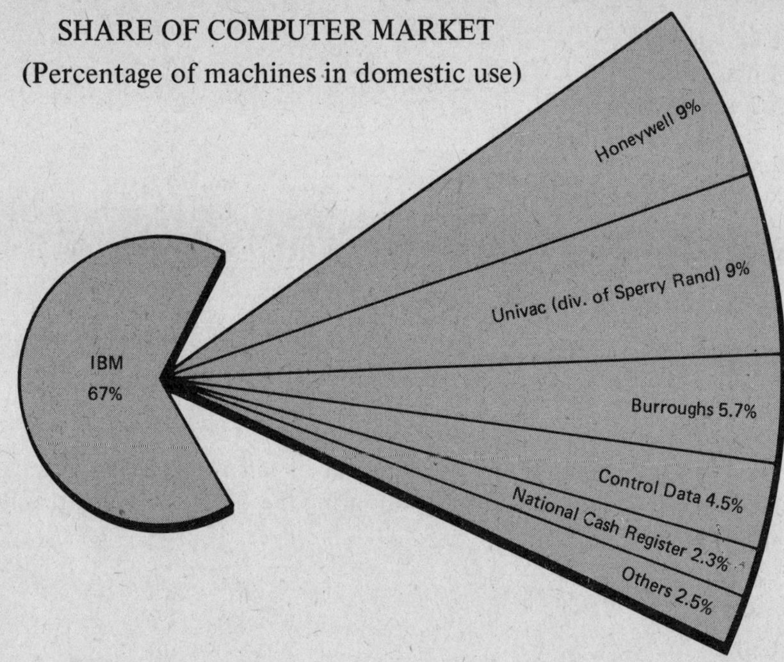

33. IBM's share of the computer market is roughly x times the total of all other companies; x equals

(A) $\frac{1}{10}$
(B) $\frac{1}{2}$
(C) $1\frac{1}{2}$
(D) 2
(E) 3

34. If Control Data and National Cash Register merged, the merged firm's new rank in share of the market would be

(A) 2
(B) 3
(C) 4
(D) 5
(E) 6

35. Consider the following statements

I. Univac's share of the market is greater than those of Burroughs and Control Data combined.
II. Honeywell and Univac together have less than a third of IBM's share of the market.
III. IBM's share of the market is 30 times larger than that of National Cash Register.

Which of the above statements are true?

(A) II only
(B) III only
(C) I and II
(D) I and III
(E) I, II and III

36. If a job takes 12 men 4 hours to complete, how long should it take 15 men to complete the job?

(A) 2 hrs. 40 min.
(B) 3 hrs.
(C) 3 hrs. 12 min.
(D) 3 hrs. 24 min.
(E) 3 hrs. 30 min.

37. Apples cost 10¢ each. If the price of apples rises by 12%, how much will a dozen apples cost?

(A) 12¢
(B) $1.20
(C) $1.32
(D) $1.34
(E) $1.36

38. How long must a driver take to drive the final 70 miles of a trip if he wants to average 50 miles an hour for the entire trip and during the first part of the trip he drove 50 miles in $1\frac{1}{2}$ hours?

(A) 54 min
(B) 1 hr
(C) 66 min
(D) 70 min
(E) 75 min

Use the following table for questions 39–41.

MAJOR WAGE NEGOTIATIONS IN 1973

Month	Employer	Unions	Workers Covered
January	Popular Price Dresses	Ladies Garment Workers	59,950
February	N.J. Apparel Contractors	Ladies Garment Workers	27,050
March	Con Edison	Utility Workers	16,800
April	Goodyear	Rubber Workers	23,000
May	General Electric Co.	Electrical Workers (I.U.E.)	90,000
	Int. Paper Kraft Division	United Paperworkers, Electrical Brotherhood	11,500
	Nat. Skirt and Sportswear Assn. N.Y. Coat and Suit Assn.	Ladies Garment Workers	51,500
June	Westinghouse Electric	Electrical Workers (I.U.E.)	36,300
	Calif. Processors	Teamsters	56,550
	Nat. Master Freight	Teamsters	450,000
	Railroads	United Transportation Union	135,000
July	U.S. Postal Service	Postal Workers	600,000
September	Major Automobile Makers	Auto Workers	670,250
October	Mack Truck	Auto Workers	13,900
December	Budd	Auto Workers	19,200

Source: U.S. Dept. of Labor.

39. For how many months in 1973 are there major wage negotiations which involve fewer than 150,000 workers?

(A) 4
(B) 5
(C) 6
(D) 7
(E) 8

40. How many workers will have wage negotiations handled by the Ladies Garment Workers Union in 1973?

(A) 51,500
(B) 87,000
(C) 102,000
(D) 130,000
(E) 138,500

41. Of those workers whose wages will be negotiated in 1973, which union represents the largest number?

(A) Ladies Garment Workers
(B) Meat Cutters
(C) Teamsters
(D) Postal Workers
(E) Auto Workers

42. If a rectangle has length L and the width is one half of the length, then the area of the rectangle is

(A) L
(B) L^2
(C) $\frac{1}{2}L^2$
(D) $\frac{1}{4}L^2$
(E) $2L$

43. Eggs cost 50¢ a dozen for the first 100 dozen a store buys from a wholesaler and 47¢ a dozen for all those bought in addition to the first 100 dozen. How much does it cost to buy 150 dozen eggs from the wholesaler?

(A) $70.50
(B) $72.00
(C) $73.50
(D) $123.50
(E) $150.00

44. If the product of two numbers is 5 and one of the numbers is $\frac{3}{2}$, then the sum of the two numbers is

(A) $4\frac{1}{3}$
(B) $4\frac{2}{3}$
(C) $4\frac{5}{6}$
(D) $5\frac{1}{6}$
(E) $6\frac{1}{2}$

45. Which of the following sets of numbers can be used as the lengths of the sides of a triangle?

I. [5,7,12]
II. [2,4,10]
III. [5,7,9]

(A) I only
(B) III only
(C) I and II only
(D) I and III only
(E) II and III only

46. What is the next number in the sequence 2,5,8 . . . ?

(A) 7
(B) 9
(C) 10
(D) 11
(E) 12

47. A dealer owns a group of station wagons and motorcycles. If the number of tires (excluding spare tires) on the vehicles is 30 more than twice the number of vehicles, then the number of station wagons the dealer owns is

(A) 10
(B) 15
(C) 20
(D) 30
(E) insufficient information given

Use this graph for questions 48–51.

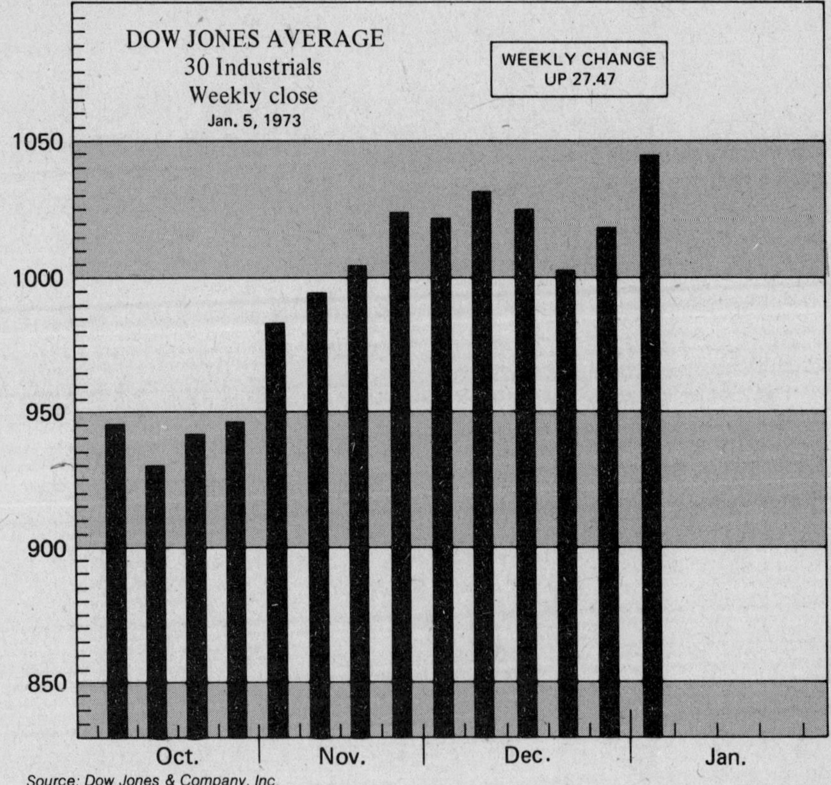

Source: Dow Jones & Company, Inc.

48. In which week during the last three months of 1972 was the average close at the highest value?

(A) first week in Nov.
(B) fourth week in Nov.
(C) second week in Dec.
(D) third week in Dec.
(E) fifth week in Dec.

49. Between which two successive weeks (of those shown) did the average drop the most?

(A) first and second weeks in Oct.
(B) fourth week in Oct. and first week in Nov.
(C) third and fourth weeks in Nov.
(D) first and second weeks in Dec.
(E) third and fourth weeks in Dec.

50. What was the lowest value of the average during the time shown?

(A) 910
(B) 922
(C) 931
(D) 939
(E) 970

51. During how many weeks (of those shown) was the average close between 960 and 1000?

(A) 2
(B) 3
(C) 4
(D) 5
(E) 6

52. If the two sides of a right triangle adjacent to the right angle are 5 and 12,then the third side of the triangle is

(A) 7
(B) 9
(C) 11
(D) 13
(E) 15

53. Rich sold his skis for $160.00 and his ski boots for $96.00. He made a profit of 20% on his boots and took a 10% loss on his skis. He ended up with a

(A) loss of $1.78
(B) loss of $1.50
(C) gain of $3.20
(D) gain of $7.53
(E) gain of $17.06

54. It costs 10¢ each to print the first 500 copies of a newspaper. It costs $(10 - x/50)$¢ each for every copy after the first 500. What is x if it cost $75.00 to print 1,000 copies of the newspaper?

(A) 2.5
(B) 100
(C) 25
(D) 250
(E) 300

55. The amount of coal necessary to heat a home cost $53.00 in 1972 and will increase at the rate of 15% a year. The amount of oil necessary to heat the same home cost $45.00 in 1972 but will increase at the rate of 20% a year. In 1974 which of the following methods would heat the home for the cheapest price?

(A) Use of only coal
(B) Use of only oil
(C) Use of coal or oil since they cost the same amount
(D) Use of oil for 8 months and coal for 4 months
(E) Use of coal for 8 months and oil for 4 months

56. If the side of a square increases by 30%, then its area increases by

(A) 9%
(B) 30%
(C) 60%
(D) 69%
(E) 130%

57. Train Y leaves New York at 1 A.M. and travels east at an average speed of x mph. If train Z leaves New York at 2 A.M. and travels east, at what average rate of speed will train Z have to travel in order to catch train Y by 5:30 A.M.?

(A) $\frac{5}{6}x$
(B) $\frac{9}{8}x$
(C) $\frac{6}{5}x$
(D) $\frac{9}{7}x$
(E) $\frac{3}{2}x$

Use this graph for question 58.

ANTIPOLLUTION FUNDING DURING THE 70s
(Cost in billions of dollars for 1971–1980)

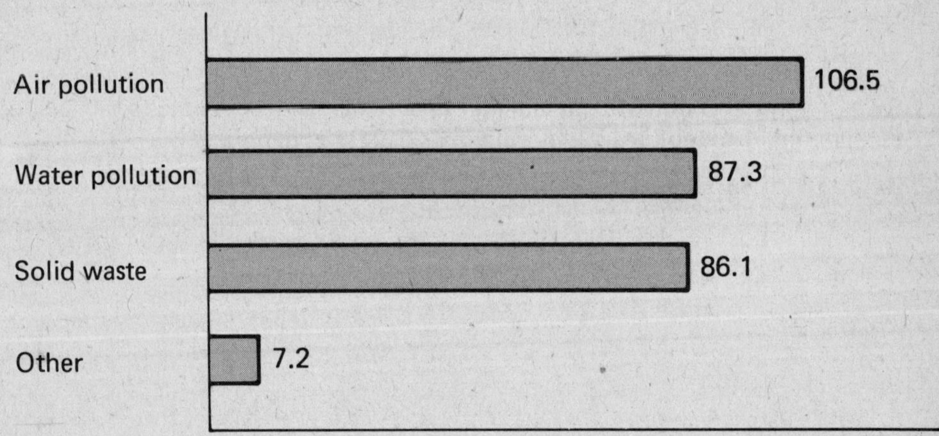

58. The ratio of air pollution funding to water pollution funding is about

(A) 2 to 1
(B) 3 to 2
(C) 6 to 5
(D) 5 to 6
(E) 2 to 3

59. If 30 boxes of pencils cost a total of $5.10, then 4 boxes of pencils should cost

(A) 52¢
(B) 68¢
(C) 78¢
(D) 85¢
(E) 93¢

60. A worker is paid r dollars for each hour he works up to 8 hours a day. For any time worked over 8 hours he is paid at the rate of $(1.5)r$ dollars an hour. The total amount of dollars the worker will earn if he works 11 hours in a day is

(A) $(4.5)r$
(B) $(5.5)r$
(C) $(9.25)r$
(D) $(11)r$
(E) $(12.5)r$

61. If the product of 3 consecutive integers is 120, then the sum of the integers is

(A) 9
(B) 12
(C) 14
(D) 15
(E) 17

Use the table below for questions 62 and 63.

Grants from the *XYZ* Foundation	1971	1972
Colleges	5.2	4.9
Medical research	3.1	3.5
Other	1.7	1.8
Total	10.0	10.2

62. Medical research grants between 1971 and 1972,

(A) decreased by 4%
(B) stayed about the same
(C) increased by about 10%
(D) increased by about 13%
(E) increased by about 21%

63. What percent of the total grants of the *XYZ* Foundation for both years was received by colleges?

(A) 49.8
(B) 50
(C) 50.2
(D) 50.5
(E) 51

64. Mechanics are paid twice the hourly wage of salesmen. Custodial workers are paid one-third the hourly wage of mechanics. What fraction of the hourly wage of custodial workers are salesmen paid?

(A) $\frac{1}{3}$
(B) $\frac{1}{2}$
(C) $\frac{2}{3}$
(D) $\frac{4}{3}$
(E) $\frac{3}{2}$

65. If x and y are negative, then which of the following statements are always true?

I. $x + y$ is positive
II. xy is positive
III. $x - y$ is positive

(A) I only
(B) II only
(C) III only
(D) I and III only
(E) II and III only

66. An unloaded truck travels 10 miles on a gallon of gas. When the same truck is loaded it travels only 85% as far on a gallon of gas. How many gallons of gas will the loaded truck use to travel 50 miles?

(A) 5
(B) 5.67
(C) 5.88
(D) 6.02
(E) 6.3

67. If $8a = 6b$ and $3a = 0$ then

(A) a and b are equal
(B) $a = 6$
(C) $\frac{b}{a} = \frac{4}{3}$
(D) $a = 6$ and $b = 8$
(E) $\frac{a}{b} = \frac{3}{4}$

68. A horse can travel at the rate of 5 miles per hour for the first two hours of a trip. After the first two hours the horse's speed drops to 3 miles per hour. How many hours will it take the horse to travel 20 miles?

(A) 4
(B) 5
(C) $5\frac{1}{3}$
(D) $5\frac{1}{2}$
(E) $5\frac{2}{3}$

Use the following table for questions 69–72

THE BUDGET DOLLAR

1972 Fiscal year, estimated — Where it comes from		1973 Fiscal year, estimated — Where it comes from
41¢	Individual Income Taxes	38¢
8¢	Excise Taxes	7¢
16¢	Corporation Income Taxes	14¢
5¢	Borrowing	10¢
25¢	Social Insurance Taxes and Contributions	26¢
5¢	Other	5¢

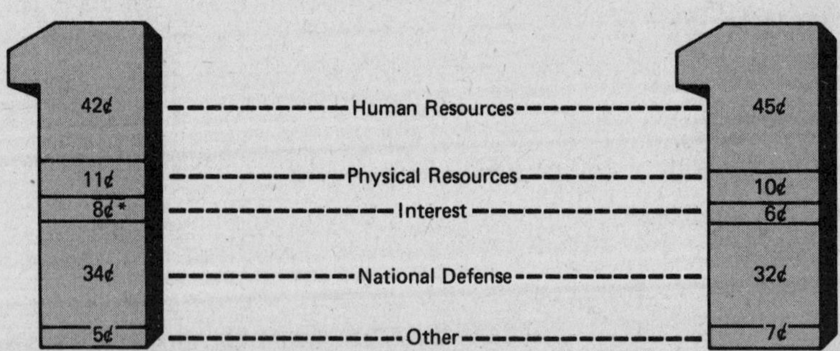

*Excludes interest paid to trust funds

Source: Office of Management and the Budget

69. In each year the category which provided the most income was

(A) borrowing
(B) individual income taxes
(C) human resources
(D) social insurance taxes
(E) national defense

70. The percentage of the budget allocated to human resources between 1972 and 1973 is expected to

(A) decline by 3%
(B) decline by 2%
(C) stay the same
(D) rise by 2%
(E) rise by 3%

71. In 1973 which one of the following categories was estimated to require the largest amount of the budget?

(A) human resources
(B) national defense
(C) physical resources
(D) interest and national defense
(E) physical resources and national defense

72. Which of the following statements can be inferred from the graph?

I. The amount of money collected from excise taxes declined from 1972 to 1973.
II. The government will borrow twice as much money in 1973 as it did in 1972.
III. Of the total amount of income in 1972 and 1973, 15% came from Corporation Income Taxes.

(A) None
(B) III only
(C) I and II only
(D) II and III only
(E) I, II, and III

73. If the ratio of the radii of two circles is 3 to 2, then the ratio of the areas of the two circles is

(A) 2 to 3
(B) 3 to 4
(C) 4 to 9
(D) 9 to 4
(E) 3 to 2

74. −5 times (− 4) is

(A) −20
(B) 54
(C) 20
(D) −54
(E) −5

75. If $\frac{1}{x} < \frac{1}{y}$ then

(A) $x > y$
(B) x and y are negative
(C) x and y are positive
(D) $x < y$
(E) none of the preceding statements follows

76. A manufacturer of boxes wants to make a profit of x dollars. When he sells 5,000 boxes it costs 5¢ a box to make the first 1,000 boxes and then it costs y¢ a box to make the remaining 4,000 boxes. What price in dollars should he charge for the 5,000 boxes?

(A) $5{,}000 + 1{,}000y$
(B) $5{,}000 + 1{,}000y + 100x$
(C) $50 + 10y + x$
(D) $5{,}000 + 4{,}000y + x$
(E) $50 + 40y + x$

Use the following graph for questions 77–80.

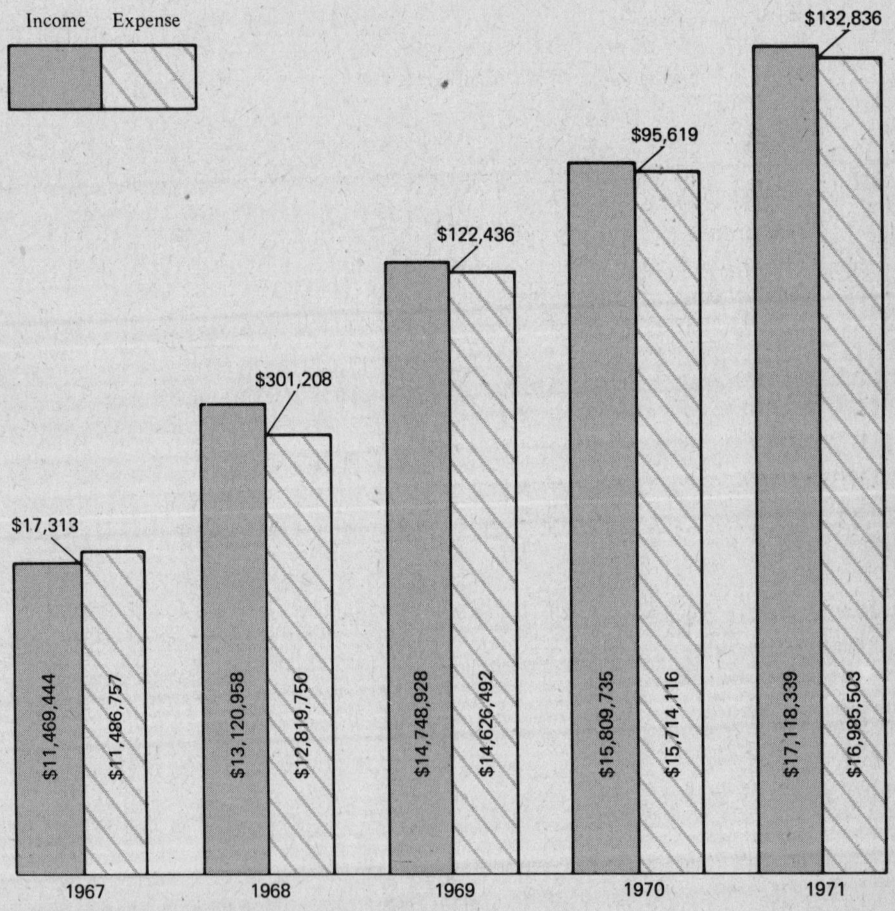

© 1973 by the New York Times Company. Reprinted by permission.

77. In what year was the profit (income minus expenses) the greatest?

(A) 1967
(B) 1968
(C) 1969
(D) 1970
(E) 1971

78. In how many of the years was the profit larger than in the preceding year?

(A) 0
(B) 1
(C) 2
(D) 3
(E) 4

79. Between which two successive years was the rise (in dollars) in income the greatest?

(A) 1967 and 1968
(B) 1968 and 1969
(C) 1969 and 1970
(D) 1970 and 1971
(E) insufficient information to determine

80. Which of the following statements can be inferred from the graph?

I. The company made a profit in all the years shown on the graph. F
II. The company's profit increased in every year between 1969 and 1971. F
III. The company's expenses increased in each year shown on the graph. T

(A) I only
(B) II only
(C) III only
(D) I and III only
(E) I, II, and III

81. If $x - 2$ is less than y then

(A) x and y are positive
(B) y is less than $x + 2$
(C) y is greater than x
(D) $y + 2$ is greater than x
(E) none of the preceding

82. Wheat costs \$2.00 a bushel and corn costs \$3.00 a bushel. If the price of wheat rises 10% a month and the price of corn is unchanged, how many months will it take before a bushel of corn costs less than a bushel of wheat?

(A) 2
(B) 3
(C) 4
(D) 5
(E) 6

83. If $\frac{1}{2}+\frac{1}{4}=\frac{x}{15}$, then x is

(A) 10
(B) 11.25
(C) 12
(D) 13.75
(E) 14

84. If $x+y+z+w=15$, then at least k of the numbers x, y, z, w must be positive where k is

(A) 0
(B) 1
(C) 2
(D) 3
(E) 4

85. If the length of a rectangle is increased by 11%, then the area of the rectangle is increased by

(A) 11%
(B) 21%
(C) 110%
(D) 111%
(E) 121%

If there is still time remaining, you may review the questions in this section only. You may not turn to any other section of the test.

Section III Verbal Aptitude

TIME: 20 minutes

Antonyms

DIRECTIONS: For each question below, select the lettered word or phrase that comes closest to being *opposite* in meaning to the word appearing in capital letters. Be sure to consider all meanings carefully.

86. ABANDONMENT: (A) desertion (B) renunciation (C) maintenance (D) profligation (E) abjuration

87. ADROIT: (A) prim (B) unskillful (C) correct (D) strong (E) apt

88. PRESCRIBE: (A) soothe (B) impose (C) enjoin (D) prohibit (E) describe

89. SPECIOUS: (A) genuinely logical (B) sometimes funny (C) constricted (D) inadmissible (E) avoidable

90. HAUGHTY: (A) intelligent (B) mature (C) chilly (D) meek (E) arrogant

91. INSOLENT: (A) solvent (B) outrageous (C) polite (D) lazy (E) indigent

92. ASSIDUOUS: (A) courteous (B) inactive (C) careless (D) stylish (E) sensual

93. DISCRETE: (A) wet (B) joined (C) large (D) soft (E) near

94. INTREPID: (A) vulgar (B) intrusive (C) chronic (D) cowardly (E) jealous

95. NOXIOUS: (A) wholesome (B) disheveled (C) deleterious (D) perfumed (E) potent

96. OFFICIOUS: (A) modest (B) unofficial (C) obtrusive (D) subordinate (E) negligent

97. PRECURSORY: (A) glassy (B) subsequent (C) fortunate (D) unpretentious (E) satisfactory

98. FACETIOUS: (A) serious (B) facile (C) pleasant (D) obstinate (E) jocose

99. VERSATILE: (A) unsteady (B) immovable (C) vacillating (D) smooth (E) torpid

Word-Pair Relationships

DIRECTIONS: For each question below, determine the relationship between the pair of capitalized words and then select the lettered pair of words which have a similar relationship to the first pair.

100. ARTIST : PAINT :: (A) doctor : patient (B) mechanic : car (C) physics : formula (D) chemist : discovery (E) sculptor : clay

101. TIMIDITY : COWARDICE :: (A) honor : weakness (B) virtue : dishonesty (C) economy : parsimony (D) shirker : valor (E) protected : silent

102. NEUROSIS : PSYCHOSIS :: (A) sickness : doctor (B) cold : influenza (C) nervousness : reaction (D) remedy : treatment (E) flood : rain

103. SPHERE : HEMISPHERE :: (A) circle : quadrant (B) polygon : hexagon (C) angle : square (D) triangle : rectangle (E) linear : curvilinear

104. VESTMENT : ECCLESIASTICAL :: (A) mountain : clouds (B) uniform : military (C) scientific : alchemy (D) forecast : reality (E) light : spiritual

105. INAUGURATION : PRESIDENT :: (A) promotion : executive (B) nomination : officer (C) elected : politician (D) ordination : priest (E) lottery : winner

106. RULE : NATION :: (A) command : army (B) prevent : irregularity (C) anarchy : chaos (D) tension : motivation (E) solve : problem

107. HARMONY : MUSIC :: (A) agreement : mathematics (B) electrons : physics (C) eclipse : astronomy (D) abjure : sociology (E) politics : history

108. VOLT : ELECTRICITY :: (A) inch : distance (B) metric : kilometer (C) letter : alphabet (D) oxygen : water (E) ocean : wave

109. SCORE : MUSICIAN :: (A) prayer : religion (B) blueprint : engineer (C) scalpel : surgeon (D) orders : soldier (E) hours : clock

110. TAX : EXEMPTION :: (A) crime : transgression (B) obligation : debt (C) fine : payment (D) disease : immunity (E) trial : forfeit

111. COGENT : REASON :: (A) inspiring : emotion (B) potent : fear (C) lovely : philosophy (D) truthful : law (E) graceful : duty

112. FIRE : EXTINGUISH :: (A) brake : hold (B) urgency : exigency (C) war : army (D) pass : intercept (E) fight : referee

Sentence Completions

DIRECTIONS: For each sentence below, select the lettered word or set of words which, when inserted in the sentence blanks, best complete the meaning of that sentence.

113. Economic development is likely to be ________ if stock market conditions are not ________.

(A) speeded . . . constrained
(B) hampered . . . favorable
(C) forthcoming . . . propitious
(D) justified . . . deleterious
(E) maintained . . . honored

114. Leibnitz considered his law of historical continuity to be ______.

(A) dogmatic
(B) descriptive
(C) axiomatic
(D) absurd
(E) evoked

115. In a surprising number of cases, the ______ from automobile to farm-implement manufacturing was relatively easy.

(A) transition
(B) conformity
(C) success
(D) strategy
(E) business

116. The immediate ______ of ______ change in any period are births, deaths, and the net number of migrants.

(A) producers . . . economic
(B) result . . . social
(C) consequence . . . rapid
(D) determinants . . . population
(E) effect . . . social

117. The measurement of ______ has long been a central problem in applied economics.

(A) energy
(B) productivity
(C) sales
(D) land
(E) currency

118. The more frequently persons ______ with one another, the more alike their ______ tend to become.

(A) interact . . . activities
(B) eat . . . speech
(C) travel . . . income
(D) disagree . . . schisms
(E) study . . . economics

119. The theories of the two anthropologists look ______ opposed.

(A) reliably
(B) possibly
(C) academically
(D) diametrically
(E) accedingly

120. Brazil is the largest and most ______ Latin country in the world.

(A) aggressive
(B) populous
(C) prodigious
(D) alluring
(E) flourishing

121. ________ plays an important part in the development of Australia by bringing new life and skills into the country.

(A) Capital
(B) Investment
(C) Immigration
(D) Trade
(E) Emigration

122. Economic development in Kenya is taking place through accelerated growth of the ________ sector.

(A) internal
(B) trade
(C) developing
(D) industrial
(E) institutional

123. The economist Mills pointed out that the true province of economic law was ________ and not ________.

(A) production . . . distribution
(B) interest . . . capital
(C) prices . . . products
(D) stability . . . inflation
(E) theoretical . . . practical

124. Keynes argued that the economy hung on the amount of ________ which business carried out.

(A) activity
(B) service
(C) profits
(D) development
(E) investment

125. While the United States exceeds the Soviet Union in Gross National Product, the Soviets believe that this ________ will in time ________.

(A) gap . . . increase
(B) lead . . . diminish
(C) measure . . . evaporate
(D) condition . . . improve
(E) position . . . exacerbate

If there is still time remaining, you may review the questions in this section only.
You may not turn to any other section of the test.

Section IV Data Sufficiency

TIME: 15 minutes

DIRECTIONS: Each of the following problems has a question and two statements which are labeled (1) and (2). Use the data given in (1) and (2) together with other available information (such as the number of hours in a day, the definition of *clockwise*, mathematical facts, etc.) to decide whether the statements are *sufficient* to answer the question. Then fill in space

(A) if you can get the answer from (1) alone but not from (2) alone;

(B) if you can get the answer from (2) alone but not from (1) alone;

(C) if you can get the answer from (1) and (2) together, although neither statement by itself suffices;

(D) if statement (1) alone suffices *and* statement (2) alone suffices;

(E) if you cannot get the answer from statements (1) and (2) together, but need even more data.

All numbers used in this section are real numbers. A figure given for a problem is intended to provide information consistent with that in the question, but not necessarily with the additional information contained in the statements.

126. A rectangular field is 40 yards long. Find the area of the field.

(1) A fence around the outside of the field is 140 yards long.
(2) The distance from one corner of the field to the opposite corner is 50 yards.

127. Is x greater than 0?

(1) $x^3 + 1 = 0$
(2) $x^2 - \frac{1}{2} = 0$

128. There are 450 boxes to load on a truck. *A* and *B* working independently but at the same time take 30 minutes to load the truck. How long should it take *B* working by himself to load the truck?

(1) *A* loads twice as many boxes as *B*.
(2) *A* would take 45 minutes by himself.

129.

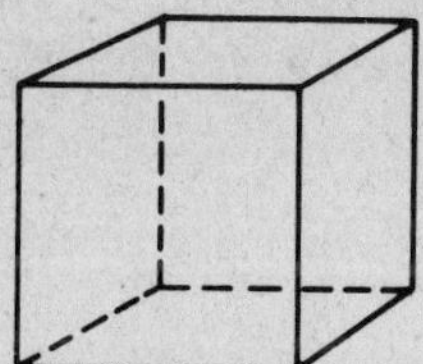

Is the figure above a cube?

(1) The lengths of all edges are equal.
(2) The angle between any two edges that meet is a right angle.

130. A car drives around a circular track once. A second car drives from point *A* to point *B* in a straight line. Which car travels further?

(1) The car driving around the circular track takes a longer time to complete its trip than the car traveling in a straight line.
(2) The straight line from *A* to *B* is $1\frac{1}{2}$ times as long as the diameter of the circular track.

131. Find $x + y$

(1) $x - y = 6$
(2) $2x + 3y = 7$

132. Find the length of AC if AB has length 3 and x is 45.

(1) $z = 45$
(2) $y = 90$

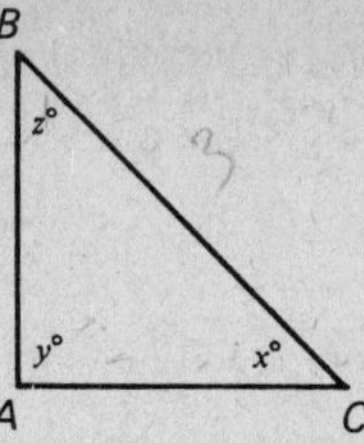

133. How much did it cost Mr. Jones to insure his car for the year 1971?

(1) He spent $300.00 for car insurance in 1970.
(2) The total amount he spent for car insurance in 1969, 1970, and 1971 was $905.00

134. It costs 50 cents in tolls, 2 dollars in gas, and at least 1 dollar for parking to drive (round trip) from Utopia to Green Acres each day. The train offers a weekly ticket. Which is the cheaper way to travel per week?

(1) The weekly train ticket costs 15 dollars.
(2) Parking costs a total of 6 dollars.

135. Is $ABCD$ a rectangle?

(1) AD and BC bisect each other at E.
(2) Angle ACD is 90°.

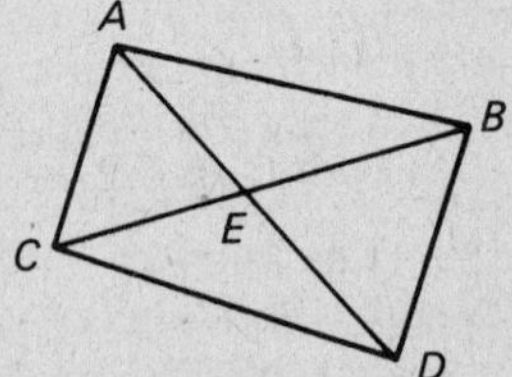

136. A worker is hired for five days. He is paid $5.00 more for each day of work than he was paid for the preceding day of work. What was the total amount he was paid for the five days of work?

(1) He had made 50% of the total by the end of the third day.
(2) He was paid twice as much for the last day as he was for the first day.

137. Is y larger than x?

(1) $x + y = 2$
(2) $\frac{x}{y} = 2$

138. Does a circle with diameter d have greater area than a square of side s?

(1) $d < (\sqrt{2})s$
(2) $d < s$

139. 5 apples cost 80 cents. How much will it cost to buy 10 apples and 3 oranges?

(1) Oranges cost 6 for 50 cents.
(2) 10 apples and 6 oranges cost $2.10.

140. A pair of skis originally sold for $160.00. After a discount of x%, the skis were discounted y%. Do the skis cost less than $130.00 after the discounts?

(1) $x = 20$ (2) $y = 15$

If there is still time remaining, you may review the questions in this section only. You may not turn to any other section of the test.

Section V Business Judgment

TIME: 35 minutes

DIRECTIONS: Read the following two passages. After you have completed each of them you will be asked to answer two sets of questions. The first of these, data evaluation, involves determining the importance of specific factors included in the passage. The second, data application, consists of general questions relating to the passage. When answering questions, you may consult the passage.

Passage 1:

The problems of marketing citrus, like any other product, vary from area to area within Western Europe. There are however, two major problems which face citrus growers. One, which is a regional problem, concerns the restrictive and protective practices of the Common Market. The other, which is an overall problem, is the generally static level of citrus consumption.

In the early 1960's when the Common Market set out its agricultural policies, it included citrus under the general heading of "fruit and vegetables." Citrus was, therefore, treated in the same way as commodities grown within the EEC area; the purpose of the policies was and is to protect home-grown produce, although, in fact, the only Citrus growing area in the group is Italy which produces oranges only in sufficient quantities to meet between 4% and 6% of the total EEC consumption of this fruit. Whereas duties on most other fruit and vegetables entering the Common Market area from outside have been replaced by "variable prices," citrus entering the area is burdened with a duty which has gradually increased in size. Conversely, the home grown Italian oranges are now marketed among members of the EEC free of duty.

The quality standards adopted by the EEC are the International (Geneva) standards, originally intended to be applied at the point of shipping. The EEC is however, applying them at point of docking, thereby penalizing those countries whose crops have to travel long distances.

Most exporting citrus countries—including the USA, Brazil, Israel, Italy and South Africa—have been accustomed to using the chemical "diphenyl" as an external preservative. The World Health Organization has confirmed that the quantities applied (100–110 p.p.m.) offer no danger to the consumer.

The EEC however, will not accept more than 70 p.p.m. of diphenyl. This makes it difficult for exporters whose goods have to travel long distances, to maintain high standards at the point of arrival.

Under EEC regulations, all fruit treated with diphenyl must have marking to this effect on the container and the shops marketing the goods must be advised of the use of the chemical. Yet harmful chemicals are used on fruit and vegetables grown within the EEC, without any requirement that their use be declared.

In considering his country's coming program for the export of citrus fruit to EEC countries, Mr. Limon had to assess the effect that the above constraints would have on the development of a strong marketing strategy. With this in mind, he set out to prepare his report for his government's export authority.

Data Evaluation Questions

DIRECTIONS: Evaluate each of the following factors used in decision-making which relate to the passage you have just read by selecting

(A) for a *Major Objective*—the result desired by the executive;

(B) for a *Major Factor*—a primary consideration, spelled out in the passage, that influences the decision;

(C) for a *Minor Factor*—a less important consideration in the decision;

(D) for a *Major Assumption*—a conclusion reached by the executive not necessarily supported by the factors present;

(E) for an *Unimportant Issue*—a consideration not directly related to the problem.

141. Static level of citrus consumption.

142. EEC citrus quality standards.

143. Development of a citrus export strategy.

144. Harmful chemicals are used on fruit grown in EEC countries.

145. Italy is a member of the Common Market.

Data Application Questions

DIRECTIONS: Answer each of the following questions using information contained in the passage.

146. It can be inferred from the passage that diphenyl

I. can be used in large quantities
II. is used by citrus exporters
III. preserves the quality of citrus

(A) I only
(B) III only

(C) I and II only
(D) II and III only
(E) I, II and III

147. Trade barriers or restrictions to the export of citrus to EEC countries include

I. discriminatory quality standards
II. tariffs
III. stable citrus consumption

(A) I only
(B) III only
(C) I and II only
(D) II and III only
(E) I, II and III

148. Citrus producing countries that are members of the EEC include

I. South Africa
II. Israel
III. Italy

(A) I only
(B) III only
(C) I and II only
(D) II and III only
(E) I, II and III

149. The EEC quality standards are

I. the International (Geneva) standards
II. discriminatory
III. complicated

(A) I only
(B) III only
(C) I and II only
(D) II and III only
(E) I, II and III

150. It may be inferred from the passage that some goods sold among EEC member countries

I. are exempt from duty
II. travel long distances
III. have strong demand

(A) I only
(B) III only
(C) I and II only
(D) II and III only
(E) I, II and III

Passage 2:

The Parks Company, located in New York City, has engaged exclusively in the manufacture of baking powder since it was founded seventy-five years ago. Current sales are approximately $800,000 annually. The sales volume, measured in commodity units instead of dollars, shows a decline of about 11 percent over the past decade. The company has a small office force and employs approximately 50 people in the production process, which is divided into (1) the mixing department, (2) the assembly department, and (3) the final inspection and packing department.

In 1935, distribution was foreign as well as national. Today the sale of the product is confined to New England and the Middle Atlantic states. Mr. Andrew H. Pendler, the president, attributes this significant decrease in both market area and sales volume to high tariff rates, sterner competition, and trade dislocations caused by World War II.

Mr. Gordon Janis, the sales manager, after studying the market closely, arrived at a different set of reasons why sales have been dropping. In the first place, according to Janis, sales to commercial consumers have diminished to practically nothing. Many modern bakeries buy the necessary chemicals and manufacture their own baking powder. Secondly, the population has become urbanized. Formerly, when a larger portion of the citizenry was suburban, many housewives did their own baking. Today people in cities are close to bakeries and other outlets where they can buy the finished product, and improved transportation has enabled fresh bakery products to be readily available at retail outlets. The third reason which Mr. Janis considers significant is the growing popularity of ready-mixes. The natural tendency of practically all human beings is to get as much as they can for a minimum of effort. Since ready-mixes do save housewives a good deal of labor, this type of product has been well received.

Mr. Janis believes that the company "cannot cope with the first two factors," and therefore his suggestion for increasing sales is to branch out and manufacture ready-mix baking products which will compare favorably with nationally known brands. Management was particularly receptive to Janis' idea because production of ready-mixes would require only minor changes in personnel and the cost of additional machinery would be relatively small.

Without further investigation, the manufacture of Parks' ready-mixes was started. After several months, ready-mix sales still amounted to less than 10 per cent of gross sales, and 85 per cent of ready-mix sales were in New York City. The entire position of the company was in jeopardy. Both Mr. Pendler and Mr. Janis were worried about the business, but neither seemed to know what to do.

Data Evaluation Questions

DIRECTIONS: Evaluate each of the following factors used in decision-making which relate to the passage you have just read by selecting

(A) for a *Major Objective*—the result desired by the executive;

(B) for a *Major Factor*—a primary consideration, spelled out in the passage, that influences the decision;

(C) for a *Minor Factor*—a less important consideration in the decision;

(D) for a *Major Assumption*—a conclusion reached by the executive not necessarily supported by the factors present;

(E) for an *Unimportant Issue*—a consideration not directly related to the problem.

151. Declining sales volume

152. The company is located in New York

153. Production of a ready-mix baking product

154. Urbanization of the population

155. Increased world trade

Data Application Questions

DIRECTIONS: Answer each of the following questions using information contained in the passage.

156. According to company management, sales volume declined owing to

I. High tariff rates
II. Increased competition
III. World War II

(A) I only
(B) III only
(C) I and II only
(D) II and III only
(E) I, II and III

157. Parks sales volume had declined by about

(A) 1 percent
(B) 5 percent
(C) 10 percent
(D) 15 percent
(E) 25 percent

158. Baking powder sales declined because

I. Bakeries made their own powder
II. Housewives switched to ready-mixes
III. Manufacturing costs increased

(A) I only
(B) III only
(C) I and II only
(D) II and III only
(E) I, II and III

159. The Parks Company management can be characterized as

I. Good decision makers
II. Good market researchers
III. Poor businessmen

(A) I only
(B) III only
(C) I and II only
(D) II and III only
(E) I, II and III

160. According to the passage, the decision to make ready-mixes was based on the following consideration(s)

I. Management was worried about the business
II. Ready-mixes were growing in popularity
III. Production of ready-mixes was possible without incurring major additional capital and labor costs

(A) I only
(B) III only
(C) I and II only
(D) II and III only
(E) I, II and III

If there is still time remaining, you may review the questions in this section only. You may not turn to any other section of the test.

Section VI Mathematics

TIME: 40 minutes

DIRECTIONS: Solve each of the following problems; then indicate the correct answer on the answer sheet. [On the actual test you will be permitted to use any space available on the examination paper for scratch work.]

NOTE: A figure that appears with a problem is drawn as accurately as possible so as to provide information that may help in answering the question. Numbers in this test are real numbers.

161. If a car travels at a constant rate of 50 mph, how long will it take to travel $222\frac{1}{2}$ miles?

(A) 3 hrs. 44 min.
(B) 4 hrs.
(C) 4 hrs. 22 min.
(D) 4 hrs. 27 min.
(E) 4 hrs. 44 min.

162. What is the length of *AB?*
Angle *ACB* is 90°; $AC = 5$; $CB = 6$.

(A) 7 (B) 7.5 (C) 7.67 (D) $\sqrt{61}$ (E) 8

A
C
B

163. If $x < 2$ and $y > 2$ then $x < y$

(A) always
(B) only if $y > 0$
(C) only if $x > 0$
(D) never
(E) sometimes

Use the following graph for questions 164–167.

U.S. POPULATION GROWTH RATE

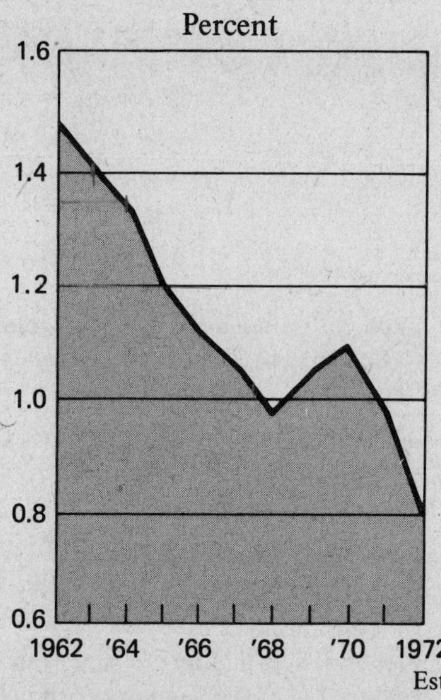

164. If the population at the beginning of 1964 was 175,654,003, then by approximately how many people did the population grow in 1964?

(A) 1,109,950
(B) 2,005,220
(C) 2,107,850
(D) 2,110,000
(E) 2,283,500

165. According to the graph the population of the U.S. was greatest in which of the following years?

(A) 1962
(B) 1966
(C) 1968
(D) 1970
(E) 1972

166. Which of the following statements can be deduced from the information on the graph?

I. The population of the U.S. was constantly growing in the years 1962–1972.
II. The rate at which the population was growing decreased from 1967 to 1970.
III. The population was growing faster in 1970 than in any of the years since 1964.

(A) I only
(B) II only
(C) III only
(D) I and II only
(E) I and III only

167. The population of the U.S. grew at the slowest rate during

(A) 1965
(B) 1967
(C) 1968
(D) 1970
(E) 1971

168. To increase the cross sectional area of a circular pipe by 44%, the diameter of the pipe should be increased by

(A) 4%
(B) 12%
(C) 16%
(D) 20%
(E) 44%

169. A car has 10 gallons of gas in its tank. The car gets $15 - x/10$ miles to the gallon when it travels at the rate of x mph. How many miles will the car travel at 45 mph before it runs out of gas?

(A) 105
(B) 110
(C) 115
(D) 120
(E) 150

170. If 3 men working independently and at the same rate turn out 210 boxes an hour, how many employees working at the same rate are necessary to produce 490 boxes an hour?

(A) 5
(B) 6
(C) 7
(D) 8
(E) 9

171. If one conveyer belt moves 4 tons of coal in 36 minutes and another conveyer moves 5 tons of coal in 40 minutes, how long should it take both conveyers working independently to move 3 tons of coal?

(A) $11\frac{2}{5}$ min
(B) $12\frac{12}{17}$ min
(C) $13\frac{4}{13}$ min
(D) 24 min
(E) 27 min

172. A company's profit rate is 5% on its first $1,000 of sales each day and $4\frac{1}{4}$% on all sales in excess of $1,000 for that day. How many dollars profit will the company make in a day when its sales are $5,235?

(A) $205.40
(B) $222.48
(C) $229.99
(D) $272.49
(E) $285.37

Use the following graph for questions 173–176.

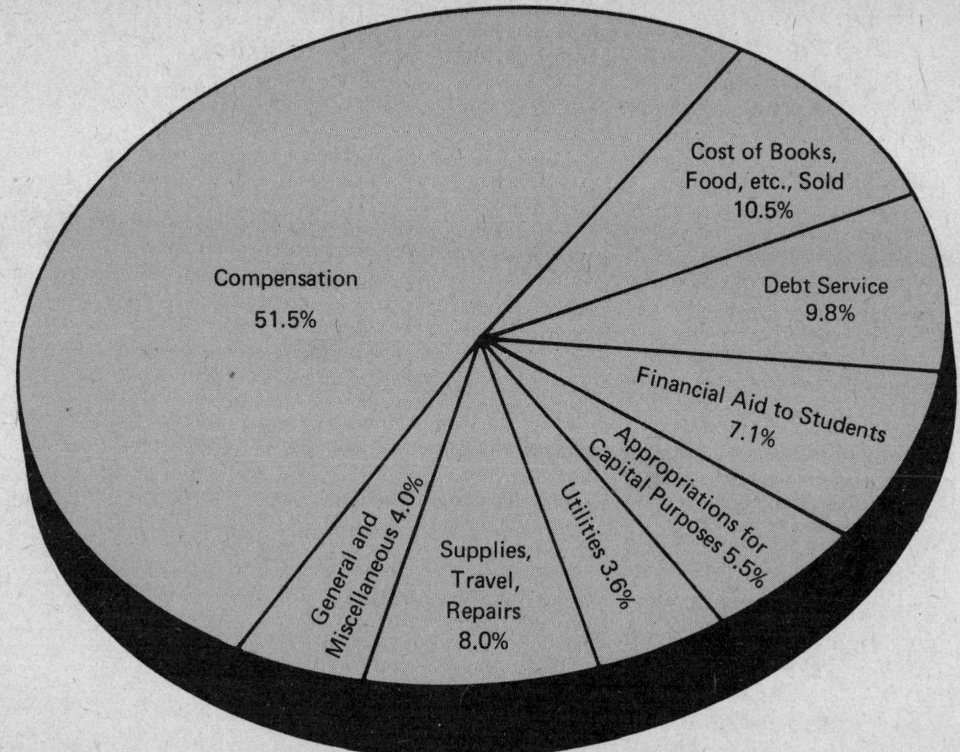

Total expenses of the college were $16,985,503 for the year.

173. How much was spent on financial aid to students and utilities?

(A) $817,500.10
(B) $1,717,550.03
(C) $1,687,503.00
(D) $1,732,604.00
(E) $1,817,448.82

174. In how many categories was more than $1,000,000 spent?

(A) 1
(B) 2
(C) 3
(D) 4
(E) 5

175. If the college spent roughly x times as much for compensation as it did on the books, food, etc. that it sold, then x is

(A) 1/5
(B) 1/2
(C) 3
(D) 5
(E) 7

176. Of all the categories shown, the one that cost the college the least was

(A) compensation
(B) miscellaneous
(C) utilities
(D) debt services
(E) appropriations for capital

177. If $x + y = 3$ then $2x + 2y$ is equal to

(A) 3
(B) 6
(C) 8
(D) 10
(E) none of these

178. If $x > 3$ then $1/x$ is

(A) $>1/3$
(B) $<1/3$
(C) <0
(D) negative
(E) >3

179. If a bank charges interest at a rate of 5% on the first 1,000 dollars of a loan and 4% on the balance of the loan over the first thousand dollars, then what percent of 5,000 will it charge on a loan of $5,000?

(A) 4.1
(B) 4.2
(C) 4.25
(D) 4.33
(E) 5

Use the following graph for questions 180–182.

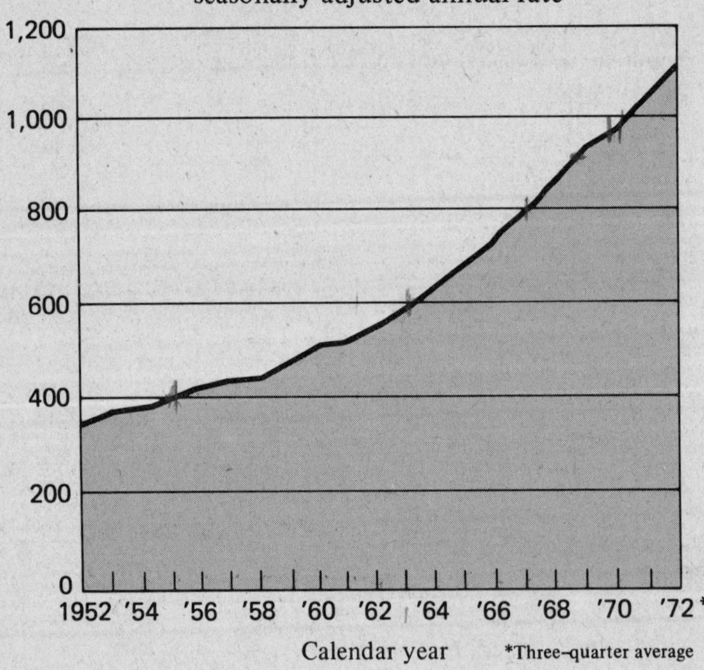

180. Between 1955 and 1970 the U.S. Gross National Product (GNP) increased by a factor of roughly

(A) 1.7
(B) 2
(C) 2.3
(D) 2.5
(E) 3

181. The Gross National Product was greater than 800 billion in how many of the years shown?

(A) 2
(B) 4
(C) 6
(D) 8
(E) 9

182. Which of the following statements are true?

I. The GNP has gone up every year between 1954 and 1970.
II. The GNP has quadrupled between 1952 and 1972.
III. The GNP was above 600 billion dollars in more of the years shown than it was below 600 billion.

(A) I only
(B) II only
(C) I and II only
(D) I and III only
(E) II and III only

Use the following table for questions 183–185.

DISTRIBUTION OF EMPLOYEES BY JOB		
RANK OF EMPLOYEE	NO. OF EMPLOYEES	AVERAGE YEARLY WAGE PER EMPLOYEE
Partner	15	$38,000
Manager	50	20,000
Supervisor	105	16,000
Foreman	300	13,000
Line Employee	2,500	9,000

183. How much in wages does the company pay per year?

(A) $25,000,000
(B) $28,375,000
(C) $29,650,000
(D) $30,050,000
(E) $31,530,000

184. The average wage per employee is about

(A) $8,000
(B) $9,000
(C) $9,500
(D) $10,000
(E) $10,500

185. Which of the following statements can be deduced from the data?

I. The ratio of managers to foremen is 1 to 6.
II. Only 15 people are paid more than $22,000 a year.
III. 2,500 of the employees are paid less than $9,000 a year.

(A) I only
(B) I and II only
(C) I and III only
(D) II and III only
(E) I, II and III

186. A toy was originally priced at $13.00 and then was discounted 10%. After a month the toy was sold at another 10% discount. How much was the toy sold for?

(A) $10.05
(B) $10.40
(C) $10.53
(D) $10.62
(E) $10.73

187. How much interest will $5,500 earn in a year at a rate of 6%?

(A) $30
(B) $33
(C) $300
(D) $330
(E) $333

188. If the price of a stock doubles every six months and it is currently selling at $1.00 a share, how long will it take before the stock is selling for more than $63 a share?

(A) 3 years
(B) 3.5 years
(C) 4 years
(D) 4.5 years
(E) 8 years

189. The next number in the sequence 1,3,9,27, . . . is

(A) 36
(B) 45
(C) 54
(D) 63
(E) 81

Use the following table for questions 190–192.

HOURS OF WORK NEEDED TO PURCHASE CERTAIN PRODUCTS
(By Average Employee)

	1971	1972
One dozen eggs	10 min.	8 min.
Pair of shoes	3 hrs.	2 hrs. 45 min.
Suit	15 hrs.	15.5 hrs.
20 lbs. of potatoes	45 min.	42 min.
Automobile	600 hrs.	620 hrs.
Haircut	30 min.	30 min.
Bottle of milk	5 min.	4 min.
5 lbs. of meat	1 hr.	1 hr.

190. How much longer did the employee have to work in 1971 to purchase 10 lbs. of potatoes and 5 dozen eggs than he did in 1972?

(A) 5 min.
(B) 10 min.
(C) 15 min.
(D) 20 min.
(E) 25 min.

191. Which of the following items cost the least in 1971?

(A) haircut
(B) one dozen eggs
(C) bottle of milk
(D) one pound of meat
(E) 4 lbs. of potatoes

192. Which of the following conclusions can be inferred from the table?

I. The employees were paid more in 1972 than they were in 1971.
II. The price of a haircut was the same in 1972 as it was in 1971.
III. In each year only two of the items shown on the table required more than 10 hours of work.

(A) I only
(B) II only
(C) III only
(D) II and III
(E) I, II and III

193. If $\frac{x}{y} = 2$, then $\frac{y^2}{x^2}$ is equal to

(A) ¼
(B) ½
(C) 1
(D) 2
(E) 4

194. An employer pays two workers *X* and *Y* a total of $550 a week. *X* is paid 120% of the amount that *Y* is paid. How much is *Y* paid each week?

(A) $200
(B) $235
(C) $250
(D) $260
(E) $300

195. A worker can work overtime a maximum of 2 days a week. If he makes x dollars a day when he works no overtime and he makes $x + y$ when he works overtime, what is the maximum amount he can make in a 5 day week?

(A) $5x$
(B) $3x + 3y$
(C) $3x + 2y$
(D) $5x + 2y$
(E) $5x + 5y$

If there is still time remaining, you may review the questions in this section only. You may not turn to any other section of the test.

Answers

Section I Reading Recall

1. **(C)**	9. **(C)**	17. **(D)**	25. **(B)**
2. **(B)**	10. **(D)**	18. **(C)**	26. **(C)**
3. **(A)**	11. **(B)**	19. **(B)**	27. **(C)**
4. **(E)**	12. **(D)**	20. **(B)**	28. **(E)**
5. **(A)**	13. **(E)**	21. **(C)**	29. **(A)**
6. **(B)**	14. **(B)**	22. **(B)**	30. **(B)**
7. **(B)**	15. **(B)**	23. **(D)**	
8. **(C)**	16. **(B)**	24. **(A)**	

Section II Mathematics

(Numbers in parentheses indicate the section in the Mathematics Review where material concerning the question is discussed.)

31. **(D)** (I–4)	50. **(C)** (IV–3)	69. **(B)** (IV–2)
32. **(A)** (II–2)	51. **(A)** (IV–3)	70. **(E)** (IV–2)
33. **(D)** (IV–2)	52. **(D)** (III–4)	71. **(A)** (IV–2)
34. **(C)** (IV–2)	53. **(A)** (I–4)	72. **(A)** (IV–2)
35. **(A)** (IV–2)	54. **(D)** (II–3)	73. **(D)** (III–7, II–5)
36. **(C)** (II–3)	55. **(B)** (I–4)	74. **(C)** (I–6)
37. **(D)** (I–4)	56. **(D)** (III–7)	75. **(E)** (II–7)
38. **(A)** (II–3)	57. **(D)** (II–3)	76. **(E)** (I–4, II–3)
39. **(E)** (IV–1)	58. **(C)** (IV–3, II–5)	77. **(B)** (IV–4)
40. **(E)** (IV–1)	59. **(B)** (II–5)	78. **(C)** (IV–4)
41. **(E)** (IV–1)	60. **(E)** (II–3)	79. **(A)** (IV–4)
42. **(C)** (III–7)	61. **(D)** (I–1)	80. **(C)** (IV–4)
43. **(C)** (II–3, II–2)	62. **(D)** (IV–1)	81. **(D)** (II–7)
44. **(C)** (II–2)	63. **(B)** (IV–2)	82. **(D)** (I–8)
45. **(B)** (III–4)	64. **(E)** (II–3)	83. **(B)** (I–2)
46. **(D)** (II–6)	65. **(B)** (II–7)	84. **(B)** (I–6)
47. **(B)** (II–2, II–3)	66. **(C)** (I–2)	85. **(A)** (III–7, I–4)
48. **(C)** (IV–3)	67. **(A)** (I–2, II–2)	
49. **(E)** (IV–4)	68. **(C)** (II–3)	

Section III Verbal Aptitude

86. **(C)**	88. **(D)**	90. **(D)**	92. **(C)**
87. **(B)**	89. **(A)**	91. **(C)**	93. **(B)**

94. **(D)**
95. **(A)**
96. **(A)**
97. **(B)**
98. **(A)**
99. **(B)**
100. **(E)**
101. **(C)**
102. **(B)**
103. **(A)**
104. **(B)**
105. **(D)**
106. **(A)**
107. **(A)**
108. **(A)**
109. **(B)**
110. **(D)**
111. **(A)**
112. **(D)**
113. **(B)**
114. **(C)**
115. **(A)**
116. **(D)**
117. **(B)**
118. **(A)**
119. **(D)**
120. **(B)**
121. **(C)**
122. **(D)**
123. **(A)**
124. **(E)**
125. **(B)**

Section IV Data Sufficiency

126. **(D)**
127. **(A)**
128. **(D)**
129. **(C)**
130. **(B)**
131. **(C)**
132. **(D)**
133. **(E)**
134. **(A)**
135. **(C)**
136. **(D)**
137. **(C)**
138. **(D)**
139. **(D)**
140. **(A)**

Section V Business Judgment

141. **(B)**
142. **(B)**
143. **(A)**
144. **(E)**
145. **(C)**
146. **(D)**
147. **(C)**
148. **(B)**
149. **(C)**
150. **(A)**
151. **(B)**
152. **(E)**
153. **(A)**
154. **(B)**
155. **(E)**
156. **(C)**
157. **(C)**
158. **(C)**
159. **(B)**
160. **(D)**

Section VI Mathematics

(Numbers in parentheses indicate the section in the Mathematics Review where material concerning the question is discussed.)

161. **(D)** (II–3)
162. **(D)** (III–4)
163. **(A)** (II–7)
164. **(E)** (IV–3)
165. **(E)** (IV–3)
166. **(A)** (IV–3)
167. **(E)** (IV–3)
168. **(D)** (III–7, I–4)
169. **(A)** (II–3)
170. **(C)** (II–3)
171. **(B)** (II–3)
172. **(C)** (I–4)
173. **(E)** (IV–2)
174. **(E)** (IV–2)
175. **(D)** (IV–2)
176. **(C)** (IV–2)
177. **(B)** (II–2)
178. **(B)** (II–7)
179. **(B)** (I–4)
180. **(D)** (IV–3)
181. **(C)** (IV–3)
182. **(A)** (IV–3)
183. **(C)** (IV–1)
184. **(D)** (IV–1, I–7)
185. **(A)** (IV–1)
186. **(C)** (I–4)
187. **(D)** (I–4)
188. **(A)** (II–6)
189. **(E)** (II–6)
190. **(E)** (IV–1)
191. **(C)** (IV–1)
192. **(C)** (IV–1)
193. **(A)** (II–2)
194. **(C)** (II–2)
195. **(D)** (II–1)

Analysis

Section I Reading Recall

1. **(C)** See paragraph 1: "Their progress is important to the high-income countries, not only for humanitarian and political reasons. . . ."

2. **(B)** Paragraph 2: "governments of most high-income countries have in recent years undertaken important aid programs. . . ."

3. **(A)** See paragraphs 3 and 4 especially.

4. **(E)** All are mentioned. See paragraphs 4, 6, 7 and 8.

5. **(A)** Paragraph 6: "a more efficient financial and fiscal system help greatly to mobilize funds for investment" and following.

6. **(B)** See paragraph 8; the section which states that industrial growth depends upon agricultural productivity.

7. **(B)** See paragraphs 2 and especially 4: "high-income countries can play only a supporting role."

8. **(C)** See paragraph 7: "governments aim . . . to reduce excessive social inequalities."

9. **(C)** Only the first two are mentioned. I is mentioned in paragraph 9, II is implied in paragraphs 8 and 9.

10. **(D)** See paragraph 3: If low income countries could speed their economic growth, then "a better distribution of world resources" would occur.

11. **(B)** In paragraph 2, this definition is given: "it is commonly expressed empirically in terms of consumption or in terms of income."

12. **(D)** See the last sentence of paragraph 2.

13. **(E)** See paragraph 2, item 3.

14. **(B)** This is given in paragraph 4.

15. **(B)** In paragraph 4 it is stated that the degree of income inequality in 1970 was the same as that in 1964, when "a trend of decreasing inequality . . . among the lower income brackets" had occurred.

16. **(B)** See paragraph 6: "Unless the education gap is significantly reduced . . . more income equality will be thwarted."

17. **(D)** See paragraph 5: The standard of living improvement was expressed in "high income levels, better housing, a higher ownership rate of consumer durables and an increase in the proportion of families in higher income brackets."

18. **(C)** The entire passage deals with standards of living and income levels of population groups, an important subject of economics.

19. **(B)** See paragraph 5: "their average income is still only 70% of the overall average for all families."

20. **(B)** See the first sentence of paragraph 4: "Between 1964 and 1970 the standard of living of the urban population rose."

21. **(C)** See paragraph 1: "American businessmen have long been interested in foreign markets for the purpose of stimulating trade."

22. **(B)** See the statement that such "transplantations" could aid economic development as given in paragraph 2.

23. **(D)** Paragraphs 2 and 3 deal with this issue.

24. **(A)** See paragraph 4 ff, e.g., the resistance to packaged foods, new shopping behavior, etc.

25. **(B)** See paragraph 5: "Daily shopping trips may be more of a social endeavor."

26. **(C)** See paragraph 6: "it reduced total shopping time . . . working women switched . . . because it is open during their lunch hour."

27. **(C)** See paragraph 3: "research is needed to determine the factors responsible for the acceptance and growth of marketing innovations."

28. **(E)** All three. The first two are specifically stated in paragraph 4, the last is inferred from the passage.

29. **(A)** is most appropriate. Alternatives (B), (D) and (E) can be immediately excluded, (C) is excluded because "Management" is not the *major* topic discussed.

30. **(B)** The Israeli experience shows that there is hope that similar countries might successfully adopt self-service.

Section II Mathematics

31. **(D)** There are 50 students in the class. Since $\frac{32}{50} = .64$, females make up 64% of the class.

32. **(A)** Since y is 5 and $x + y = 2$, $x + 5 = 2$. Add -5 to each side of the equation to obtain $x = -3$. Therefore, $x - y = -3 - (5) = -8$.

33. **(D)** IBM's share of the market is 67% and the total share of the other companies is 33%. Since 2(33)% = 66%, the answer is roughly 2.

34. **(C)** If the two firms merge, their share would would be (4.5 + 2.3)%. The merged firm would have a 6.8% market share which would make it fourth behind IBM, Honeywell, and Univac.

35. **(A)** Statement I is false since Univac has 9% of the market which is less than 5.7% + 4.5% or 10.2%. Statement II is true since together Univac and Honeywell have a share amounting to 18% of the market which is less than one third of the 67% which IBM controls. Statement III is false since 30(2.3)% = 69% which is larger than 67%.

36. **(C)** Since 15 is $\frac{5}{4}$ of 12, it takes 15 men only $\frac{4}{5}$ as long as 12 men to do the job. $\frac{4}{5}$ of 4 = $3\frac{1}{5}$ hours, or 3 hrs. 12 min.

37. **(D)** The new price of apples is (1.12)10¢ = 11.2¢ each. Therefore, 12(11.2)¢ = 134.4¢ = $1.34.

38. **(A)** The total length of the trip will be 120 miles. Hence to average 50 mph for the trip, he must take 2.4 hrs. total traveling time. Since he has already traveled for 1.5 hrs., he must complete the trip in 2.4–1.5 or .9 hrs. or 54 min.

39. **(E)** Jan., Feb., March, April, Aug., Oct., Nov., and Dec.

40. **(E)** The wage negotiations will involve 87,000 in Jan. and Feb., and 51,500 in May. So the total is 138,500.

41. **(E)** The Auto Workers have one agreement involving 670,250. This agreement by itself makes their coverage the largest.

42. **(C)** Area = length times width = $(L)(\frac{1}{2}L) = \frac{1}{2}L^2$.

43. **(C)** The first 100 dozen cost (100)(50¢) = $50.00 Since the total purchase is 150 dozen, the last 50 dozen cost 47¢ each. So the total cost is $50.00 + 50(47¢) = $50.00 + $23.50 = $73. 50.

44. **(C)** Let x be the unknown number. Then $\left(\frac{3}{2}\right)x = 5$; so $x = (5)\left(\frac{2}{3}\right) = \frac{10}{3}$. The sum of the two numbers is $x + \frac{3}{2} = \frac{10}{3} + \frac{3}{2} = \frac{29}{6} = 4\frac{5}{6}$.

45. **(B)** The length of any side of a triangle must be less than the sum of the lengths of the other two sides. Since 5 + 7 = 12 and 10 is greater than 2 + 4, I and II cannot be the sides of a triangle. 5 + 7 is greater than 9, 5 + 9 is greater than 7, and 7 + 9 is greater than 5. Therefore, there is a triangle whose sides have lengths of 5, 7, and 9.

46. **(D)** $2+3=5$ and $5+3=8$, so the next number is $8+3$ or 11.

47. **(B)** Each station wagon has 4 tires and each motorcycle has 2 tires. Let x be the number of station wagons and let y be the number of motorcycles. Then $4x + 2y$ is the total number of tires which must equal $2(x+y)+30$. Thus, $4x + 2y = 2x + 2y + 30$ yielding $4x = 2x+30$ with $2x=30$ or $x=15$.

48. **(C)** Use your pencil to compare the height of the columns.

49. **(E)** (B), (C), (D), are wrong since the average rose. The drop was roughly 35 pts. between the first and second weeks in October compared to about 25 pts. between the third and fourth weeks in December.

50. **(C)** The week with lowest value was the second week in October. (Each notch between 900 and 950 indicates 5 pts.)

51. **(A)** The average closed between 960 and 1,000 only at the end of the first and second weeks of November.

52. **(D)** The square of the hypotenuse, the side opposite the right angle, equals $(5)^2 + (12)^2$ or $25 + 144$ or 169. So the length of the side opposite the right angle is $\sqrt{169}$ or 13.

53. **(A)** Price = (cost)(rate). Let x be the original cost of the skis. Then $\$160 = x(.9)$, so $x = \$177.78$. Let y be the original cost of the boots then $\$96 = y(1.2)$, so $y = \$80$. So he made $\$96 - \$80 = \$16$ on the boots and lost $\$177.78 - \$160 = \$17.78$ on the skis. Therefore, he lost \$1.78.

54. **(D)** The cost in cents of printing 1000 copies equals $500(10) + (1000 - 500)\left(10 - \frac{x}{50}\right) = 5000 + 500\left(10 - \frac{x}{50}\right)$. Therefore, $7500 = 5000 + 5000 - 10x$, $10x = 2500$, and $x = 250$.

55. **(B)** The increase in cost between 1972 and 1973 is the product (cost in 1972) · (rate of increase). The cost in 1973 will be the cost in 1972 (1 + rate of increase). Also, the cost in 1974 will equal (cost in 1973) (1 + rate of increase) or (cost in 1972) $(1 + \text{rate of increase})^2$. So the cost of coal for 1974 = $\$(53)(1.15)^2 = \$(53)(1.32225) = \$70.09$, and the cost of oil for 1974 = $\$(45)(1.2)^2 = \$(45)(1.44) = \$64.80$. Since oil is cheaper than coal, (D) and (E) are incorrect because replacing oil by coal for any amount of time raises the cost.

56. **(D)** Let s be the side of the original square. Since the side of the increased square is $1.3s$, the area of the increased square is $1.69(s^2)$. Therefore, the área has increased by $1.69(s^2) - s^2$ or by $.69(s^2)$ or 69%.

57. **(D)** By 5:30 A.M. train Y will have traveled $(4\frac{1}{2})x$ miles. So train Z must travel $(4\frac{1}{2})x$ miles in $3\frac{1}{2}$ hours. The average rate of speed necessary is $\frac{4\frac{1}{2}x}{3\frac{1}{2}}$ which equals $\frac{\frac{9}{2}x}{\frac{7}{2}}$ or $\frac{9}{7}x$.

58. **(C)** $(6)(18) = 108$ and $(5)(18) = 90$. To make quick estimates, check the amount funded for water pollution if air pollution received 100. For example, if the ratio were 3 to 2, water pollution would get only 66.7 billion dollars.

59. **(B)** Let x be the cost in cents of 4 boxes of pencils. $\frac{4}{30} = \frac{x}{5.10}$, which means $x = \$\left(\frac{4}{30}\right)(5.10) = \$.68 = 68¢$.

60. **(E)** The amount the worker is paid for working T hours if T is larger than 8 is $8r + (T - 8)(1.5)r$. When $T = 11$, the worker will be paid $8r + 3(1.5)r = (12.5)r$.

61. **(D)** The product of three consecutive integers is of the form $x(x + 1)(x + 2)$. A good approximation to this is $(x + 1)^3$. Since $5^3 = 125$, a good guess is 4, 5, 6. This is correct because $(4)(5)(6) = 120$. The sum of these three numbers is 15.

62. **(D)** Medical research grants increased by .4 between 1971 and 1972. The fractional increase is $\frac{.4}{3.1}$. Since $\frac{.4}{3.2} = \frac{1}{8} = 12.5\%$, 13% is the best estimate.

63. **(B)** Total amount was 20.2 and the total amount the colleges received was 10.1. The colleges received $\frac{10.1}{20.2}$ or $\frac{1}{2}$ or 50%.

64. **(E)** Let M be the mechanic's hourly wage, C the custodial worker's hourly wage, and S the salesman's hourly wage. Then $M = 2S$, and $C = \frac{1}{3}M$ or $M = 3C$, hence $3C = 2S$, $S = \frac{3}{2}C$.

65. **(B)** Statement I is false since $(-1) + (-2) = -3$, and III is false since $(-1) - (-2) = 1$. But II is true since $(-x)(-y) = xy$, for all x and y.

66. **(C)** The loaded truck gets (.85)10 miles or 8.5 miles per gallon. The loaded truck will require $\frac{50}{8.5}$ or 5.88 gallons to travel 50 miles.

67. **(A)** Since $3a = 0$, a must equal 0, which implies that $b = 0$. Note that $\frac{b}{a}$ and $\frac{a}{b}$ are not defined.

68. **(C)** The horse will travel 10 miles in the first two hours. The horse will take $\frac{10}{3}$ or $3\frac{1}{3}$ hours to travel the final 10 miles. So the total time is $5\frac{1}{3}$ hours.

69. **(B)** Income is part of "Where it comes from."

70. **(E)** In 1972 human resources received 42% of each budget dollar and in 1973 it received 45% of each budget dollar. So this budget allocation was estimated to rise by 3%.

71. **(A)** Note that the question refers to 1973.

72. **(A)** Statement I is false since the graph indicates only that the percentage of the total collected was less. (If the total in 1973 was much larger, the amount collected from excise taxes could have increased.) II is false since, again, the graph gives only percentages not amounts. III is false for the same reason.

73. **(D)** Let r_1 be the radius of the first circle and r_2 the radius of the second circle. Then $\frac{r_1}{r_2} = \frac{3}{2}$, so $r_1 = \left(\frac{3}{2}\right)r_2$, and $\pi(r_1)^2 = \pi\frac{9}{4}(r_2)^2$. Since the area of a circle is π (radius)^2, then the ratio of the areas is 9 to 4.

74. **(C)** $(-5)(-4) = (5)(4)$.

75. **(E)** Let $x = -3$ and $y = 2$, then $\frac{1}{-3} < \frac{1}{2}$, so (A), (B), and (C) are false. Let $x = 3$ and $y = 2$; then $\frac{1}{3} > \frac{1}{2}$ so (D) is false. (E) is the only correct answer.

76. **(E)** The selling price of the boxes should equal x plus the cost. The cost in cents of making 5,000 boxes is (1,000)5¢ + (4,000)y which equals $50 + 40y$ in dollars. So the selling price should be $50 + 40y + x$.

77. **(B)** The profit is indicated by the arrow.

78. **(C)** 1968 and 1971.

79. **(A)** The rise in income was greater than $1,600,000 only between 1967 and 1968, and between 1968 and 1969. The gain was greater in the former.

80. **(C)** Statement I is false since there was a loss in 1967. II is false since the profits decreased from 1968 to 1969.

81. **(D)** If $x - 2 < y$, then $x < y + 2$.

82. **(D)** The price of wheat in dollars will be $2(1.10)^n$ a bushel after n months, and this will be greater than 3 when $(1.10)^n$ is greater than 1.5. $(1.1)^2 = 1.21$, $(1.1)^3 = 1.331$, $(1.1)^4 = 1.4641$, $(1.1)^5 = 1.61051$; therefore, after 5 months the price of wheat will be higher.

83. **(B)** If $\frac{1}{2} + \frac{1}{4} = \frac{x}{15}$, then since $\frac{1}{2} + \frac{1}{4} = \frac{3}{4}$, we have that $\frac{3}{4} = \frac{x}{15}$. So $x = \frac{45}{4} = 11\frac{1}{4} = 11.25$.

84. **(B)** If three of the numbers were negative, then as long as the fourth is greater than the absolute value of the sum of the other three, the sum of all four will be positive. For example, $(-50) + (-35) + (-55) + 155 = 15$.

85. **(A)** Area $= LW$. The increased length is $1.11L$ and W is unchanged; so the increased area is $(1.11L)W = (1.11)(LW) = (1.11)A$. Therefore, the increase in area is $1.11A - A = .11A$; and the area is increased by 11%.

Section III Verbal Aptitude

86. **(C)** ABANDONMENT: desertion, dereliction. *Antonym:* maintenance

87. **(B)** ADROIT: skillful, clever. *Antonym:* unskillful

88. **(D)** PRESCRIBE: appoint, ordain. *Antonym:* prohibit

89. **(A)** SPECIOUS: plausible, showy. *Antonym:* genuinely logical

90. **(D)** HAUGHTY: arrogant, disdainful. *Antonym:* meek

91. **(C)** INSOLENT: rude, impertinent. *Antonym:* polite

92. **(C)** ASSIDUOUS: diligent, careful. *Antonym:* careless

93. **(B)** DISCRETE: separate. *Antonym:* joined

94. **(D)** INTREPID: brave, fearless. *Antonym:* cowardly

95. **(A)** NOXIOUS: hurtful, deadly. *Antonym:* wholesome

96. **(A)** OFFICIOUS: busy, meddling. *Antonym:* modest

97. **(B)** PRECURSORY: preceding, prefatory. *Antonym:* subsequent

98. **(A)** FACETIOUS: pleasant, jocular. *Antonym:* serious

99. **(B)** VERSATILE: unsteady, wavering. *Antonym:* immovable

100. **(E)** An artist creates by using paint. A sculptor uses clay.

101. **(C)** Cowardice is an extreme and negative degree of timidity. Parsimony is a negative degree of economy.

102. **(B)** Neurosis is a milder form of mental disease than psychosis. A cold is a milder form of physical disease than influenza.

103. **(A)** A hemisphere is half (or part of) a sphere. A quadrant is one-third (or part of) a circle.

104. **(B)** Vestment is clothing worn in ecclesiastical circles. A uniform is clothing worn in military circles.

105. **(D)** A president is inaugurated. A priest is ordained.

106. **(A)** The leader rules a nation. The leader commands an army.

107. **(A)** Harmony is the pleasing combination of tones in a musical chord. Agreement is the pleasing combination of numbers in a mathematical equation.

108. **(A)** A volt is a measure (actually of electromagnetic force) of electricity. An inch is a measure of distance.

109. **(B)** A musician uses a score to play a composition. An engineer uses a blueprint to build a structure.

110. **(D)** Exemption prevents one from paying taxes. Immunization prevents one from contracting a disease.

111. **(A)** Something that is cogent appeals to reason. Something that is inspiring appeals to emotion.

112. **(D)** One can stop a pass by intercepting the ball. One can stop a fire by extinguishing it.

113. **(B)** Another possibility is (A), but "conditions are not constrained" has an unclear meaning.

114. **(C)** Axiomatic, or an established principle is implied since Liebnitz' "historical continuity" is a law.

115. **(A)** From automobile to farm-implement implies a transition.

116. **(D)** The most meaningful in this sentence; births, deaths, and the net number of migrants are the determinants of population change.

117. **(B)** is the only logical answer.

118. **(A)** As people in given societies or groups *interact* with one another, their *activities* or behavior tends to be alike.

119. **(D)** *Diametrically*, or directly opposed.

120. **(B)** Another possibility is (C) prodigious, or *enormous*, but that is already mentioned: "Brazil is the *largest* country."

121. **(C)** Immigration can bring new *life* and skills into the country; none of the other possibilities can.

122. **(D)** is the only clear answer, the others are ambiguous.

123. **(A)** Mills believed that production was the key to economic growth, while distribution was redundant. None of the other alternatives have any meaning in the context of the sentence.

124. **(E)** Business investment is one of the important determinants of economic activity and growth. Alternative (A) could be considered, but it is too broad and lacks specificity.

125. **(B)** The Soviets do not believe that this gap will increase as in (A), but rather that it will diminish.

Section IV Data Sufficiency

126. **(D)** Area = (length)(width) = 40(width). So to find the area we must know the width. The perimeter of a rectangle is twice (length + width). (1) tells us the perimeter equals 140 yds. Since the length is 40 yds, the width is 30 yds, so (1) is sufficient. If we connect 2 opposite corners of the field, then it is divided into 2 right triangles where the side opposite the right angle has length 50 and one of the other sides has length 40. Since $(40)^2 + (\text{width})^2 = (50)^2$ the width is 30, and (2) is sufficient by itself.

127. **(A)** Statement (1) is $x^3 + 1 = 0$, which means $x^3 = 1$, the only solution to this equation is -1. So x is not greater than 0. Therefore, (1) alone is sufficient. Statement (2) says $x^2 - \frac{1}{2} = 0$ or $x^2 = \frac{1}{2}$. There are two possible solutions to this equation, one positive and the other negative. So (2) by itself is not sufficient.

128. **(D)** Statement (1) is sufficient since it implies that A loaded 300 boxes in 30 minutes and B loaded 150 boxes. So B should take 90 minutes to load the 450 boxes by himself. (2) is also sufficient since it implies A loads 10 boxes per minute; hence A loads 300 boxes in 30 minutes, and by the above argument we can deduce that B will take 90 minutes.

129. **(C)** A cube is a solid with 6 faces, all of which are congruent squares. Statement (1) is not sufficient since a solid with 2 of the faces as diamonds (rhombus) is not a cube but does satisfy (1). . Statement (2) is not sufficient since a solid with 2 or 4 of the faces congruent rectangles is not a cube . But (1) and (2) together mean that each face is a congruent square.

130. **(B)** The first car will travel a distance equal to the circumference of the circle, which is π times the diameter. Since π is greater than $1\frac{1}{2}$, (2) is sufficient. (1) is not sufficient since one car might have traveled at a faster rate than the other.

131. **(C)** Statement (1) tells us only that $x = 6 + y$, so it is not sufficient. In the same way (2) alone will give only one of the unknowns in terms of the other. However, if we use both (1) and (2), we obtain a system of two equations which can be solved for x and y.

132. **(D)** Since we know that the sum of the angles in a triangle is 180° and that $x = 45$, (1) implies (2) and (2) implies (1). Either one is sufficient, since if $z = 45$, then $x = z$ and the sides opposite the equal angles are equal. Hence $AC = AB = 3$.

133. **(E)** Using (1) and (2) together it is possible to determine only the total paid in 1969 and 1971. No relation is given between the amounts paid in 1969 and 1971; thus there is not enough information to determine the cost in 1971.

134. **(A)** It costs \$10 in gas, \$2.50 in the tolls, and at least \$5 in parking to drive each week. So driving costs at least \$17.50 a week. (1) is sufficient. Without information on the price of the train ticket we can not compare the two methods, so (2) is not sufficient.

135. **(C)** Statement (1) is not sufficient since the diagonals of *any* parallelogram bisect each other. Statement (2) is not sufficient since the other angles of the figure do not have to be right angles. However, (1) and (2) together are sufficient. Statement (1) implies the figure is a parallelogram. In a parallelogram, opposite angles are equal and the sum of all four angles must be 360°. Thus, if one of the angles in a parallelogram is 90°, all of the angles are right angles and the parallelogram is a rectangle.

136. **(D)** Let x be the amount he was paid on the first day; then he was paid $x + 5$, $x + 10$, $x + 15$, and $x + 20$ for the remaining days of work. The total amount he was paid is $5x + 50$. Thus if we can find x, we can find the total amount he was paid. Statement (1) is sufficient since after 3 days his total pay was $x + x + 5 + x + 10$ or $3x + 15$; this is equal to $\frac{1}{2}(5x + 50)$. So $3x + 15 = 2.5(x) + 25$ which implies $x = 20$. Statement (2) is sufficient since he was paid $x + 20$ on the last day and so $x + 20 = 2x$ which implies $x = 20$.

Remember that to answer the question it is not necessary to actually *solve* the equations given in statements 1 and 2. You only have to know that they will give you an equation which can be solved for x. Don't bother to actually solve the problem since you only have a limited amount of time to work all the questions in this section.

137. **(C)** Statement (1) alone is not sufficient since $x = 3$, $y = -1$, and $x = -1$, $y = 3$ satisfy $x + y = 2$. Statement (2) alone is not sufficient since $x = 2$, $y = 1$ and $x = -2$, $y = -1$ satisfy (2). However, since (2) says $x = 2y$, using (1) $x + y = 2y + y = 2$ we see that $y = \frac{2}{3}$ and $x = \frac{4}{3}$. So (1) and (2) together are sufficient.

138. **(D)** Area of the circle is $\pi r^2 = \pi\left(\frac{d}{2}\right)^2 = \frac{\pi}{4}d^2$ and the area of the square is s^2. Statement (2) is sufficient. $d < s$ implies $d^2 < s^2$ and $\frac{\pi}{4}$ is less than 1. So $\frac{\pi}{4}d^2 < d^2 < s^2$. (Note that since d and s are both positive $d < s$ does imply $d^2 < s^2$.) Since $\sqrt{2}$ is greater than 1, statement (1) implies (2) so (1) alone is sufficient.

139. **(D)** 10 apples will cost \$1.60. Hence if we can discover the cost of three oranges we can solve the problem. Statement (1) is sufficient since (1) implies 3 oranges will cost 25¢. Statement (2) is also sufficient since we know 10 apples cost \$1.60, thus (2) implies (1) which we know to be sufficient.

140. **(A)** Since 80% of \$160 = \$128, we know that after the first discount the skis cost less than \$130. Any further discount will only lower the price. So (1) alone is sufficient. Statement (2) alone is not sufficient since if x were 10%, (2) would tell us the price was less than \$130; but if x were 1%, (2) would imply that the price was greater than \$130.

Section V Business Judgment

141. **(B)** The static level of demand for citrus is a major factor in the development of a marketing strategy. Given this level, the question is whether marketing strategy, such as advertising, can increase the demand for the products.

142. **(B)** The EEC's citrus quality standards are a major factor influencing export strategy since they are intended to make it difficult for non-EEC producers to sell to Common Market countries.

143. **(A)** The development of a marketing strategy for the export of citrus to the Common Market is the decision maker's major objective.

144. **(E)** That harmful chemicals are used on fruit grown in the Common Market does not influence the marketing strategy of the decision maker.

145. **(C)** That Italy is a member of the EEC is a minor factor; that Italy grows citrus *is* a major factor, however.

146. **(D)** Diphenyl is a preservative agent used to protect citrus shipped long distances. See paragraphs 4 and 5.

147. **(C)** Tariffs (import taxes) and discriminatory quality standards (see the discussion on diphenyl) were used by EEC countries to restrain the exports of non-EEC countries.

148. **(B)** Italy. See paragraph 2.

149. **(C)** See paragraph 3.

150. **(A)** The passage states, in paragraph 2, that oranges were sold to other EEC countries duty free. It may be inferred that other products are so treated.

151. **(B)** Declining sales volume was a symptom rather than a cause of the company's problem; therefore, it is a major factor requiring a decision as to how the decline can be corrected.

152. **(E)** Company location had no direct bearing on the issues discussed in the passage.

153. **(A)** The production of ready-mixes is the major objective of management. Whether the decision was a correct one can be discerned by the reader; nevertheless, this is the direction in which management decided to go.

154. **(B)** The urbanization of the population leading to the consumption of commercially-baked food products was a major factor in management's consideration to manufacture a home-baking product.

155. **(E)** The increase in world trade had no direct bearing on the company's problem. As management saw it, an increase in *tariff rates* abroad caused a decline in their overseas sales.

156. **(C)** See paragraph 2: high tariff rates, sterner competition, and trade distortions (caused in part by tariffs and other trade barriers).

157. **(C)** It was 11 percent. See paragraph 1.

158. **(C)** Manufacturing costs were not a factor. See paragraph 3.

159. **(B)** To have let sales decline for so long without taking any action and then finally reacting in a superficial way—making decisions without adequate research and consideration—is poor managerial action.

160. **(D)** Management was certainly worried about the business, but this apprehension did not directly lead to *specific* action as factors I and II did.

Section VI Mathematics

161. **(D)** The time needed to travel 222.5 miles when traveling at a constant rate of 50 mph is $\frac{222.5}{50}$ or 4.45 hrs. Since .45 hrs. = (.45)(60) min. = 27 min., the correct answer is 4 hrs. 27 min.

162. **(D)** Because angle ACB is a right angle, $(AC)^2 + (CB)^2 = (AB)^2$. Thus $(AB)^2 = 25 + 36 = 61$. Therefore, $AB = \sqrt{61}$.

163. **(A)** Since any number less than 2 is less than any number greater than 2, x is always less than y.

164. **(E)** Estimate the growth rate by 1.3% since the rate was between 1.2% and 1.4% in 1964. A quick estimate for the growth is (.013)(175,000,000), which is 2,275,000. Since this estimate is less than the actual increase (because 175,000,000 is less than the population at the beginning of 1964) the only possible answer is (E). All the other answers are less than 2,275,000.

165. **(E)** Since the population was growing in all the years shown, the population would be the largest in the last year shown, 1972.

166. **(A)** Statement I is true since the growth rate was always greater than 0%. Statement II is false because the growth rate for 1970 is greater than the growth rate for 1968. Statement III is false since the rate was higher in 1964 than in 1970.

167. **(E)** You can use your pencil to see that the growth rate was lower in 1971 than in 1968. All the other possible years had growth rates greater than 1%.

168. **(D)** Area $= \pi r^2$ and $2r = d$; thus, Area $= \pi\left(\frac{d}{2}\right)^2 = \frac{\pi}{4}d^2$. So to increase the area by 44%, d^2 must be increased by 44%. Hence, if d_1 is the increased diameter, $(d_1)^2 = (1.44)\ d^2$ which means $d_1 = 1.2d$ (since $\sqrt{1.44} = 1.2$). Therefore, the diameter must be increased by 20%.

169. **(A)** When the car travels at 45 mph, it will get $15 - \frac{45}{10}$ or 10.5 miles per gallon. The car has 10 gallons of gas so it will travel (10)(10.5) or 105 miles before it runs out of gas.

170. **(C)** If 3 men produce 210 boxes, then each man produces 70 boxes. Therefore $\frac{490}{70}$ or 7 men will produce 490 boxes.

171. **(B)** Conveyer 1 moves 4 tons in 36 minutes or $\frac{4}{36} = \frac{1}{9}$ tons per minute. Conveyer 2 moves 5 tons in 40 minutes or $\frac{5}{40} = \frac{1}{8}$ tons per minute. Working together the conveyers will move $\left(\frac{1}{8} + \frac{1}{9}\right)$ or $\frac{17}{72}$ tons per minute. Thus if x is the amount of time it takes to move 3 tons of coal, then $\left(\frac{17}{72}\right)x = 3$. Therefore, $x = (3)\left(\frac{72}{17}\right) = \frac{216}{17} = 12\frac{12}{17}$ minutes.

172. **(C)** The company makes 5% on the first \$1,000, so it makes (.05)(\$1,000) or \$50 on the first \$1,000 of sales. On the remaining \$4,235 of sales, the company makes 4¼%; so it makes (.0425)(\$4,235) or \$179.99. Therefore, the total profit is \$229.99.

173. **(E)** Financial aid to students and utilities together received 10.7% of the expenses. The total expenses were \$16,985,503. Therefore, (.107)(\$16,985,503), which equals \$1,817,448.82, was spent on financial aid to students and utilities.

174. **(E)** If we can find out what percentage of 16,958,503, one million is, then we can simply compare that percent with those given in the graph. This is certainly quicker than multiplying out the exact amount spent on each category. Since 1,000,000/17,000,000 = .0592 and 1,000,000/16,900,000 = .0588 then 1,000,000/16,958,503 is between 5.88% and 5.92%. Notice this is much faster than actually dividing 16,958,503 into 1,000,000. Now it is easy to see that compensation, cost of books, debt service, financial aid, and supplies were the only categories with expenditures greater than 1,000,000.

175. **(D)** 51.5 is roughly 5 times 10.5.

176. **(C)** The only category which received less than 4% of the budget was utilities.

177. **(B)** $2x + 2y = 2(x + y) = (2)(3)$, since $x + y = 3$. Therefore, 6 is the correct answer.

178. **(B)** If $x > 3$, then both numbers are positive. Therefore, $\frac{1}{x} < \frac{1}{3}$.

179. **(B)** The total interest on the loan will be (.05)(\$1,000) + (.04)(\$4,000) = \$50 + \$160 = \$210. The percentage will be 210/5,000 = .042 or 4.2%.

180. **(D)** In 1955 the GNP was about 400 billion; in 1970 it was about 1,000 billion and (2.5)(400) = 1,000.

181. **(C)** The GNP was greater than 800 billion only for the years 1967 to 1972 (inclusive), which is a total of 6 years.

182. **(A)** Statement I is true. Statement II is false because the GNP was greater than 300 billion in 1952, but less than 1,200 billion in 1972. Statement III is false since the GNP did not reach 600 billion until 1963 and hence was less than 600 billion for 11 of the 21 years shown.

183. **(C)** The total wages paid to the employees of each rank is the number of employees at that rank times the average wage for that rank. So the total wages in thousands of dollars is (15)(38) + (50)(20) + (105)(16) + (300)(13) + (2500)(9) or 570 + 1000 + 1680 + 3900 + 22500 which equals 29,650 × 1000 or $29,650,000.

184. **(D)** Average wage per employee is the total wages divided by the number of employees, which is 2,970. So the average wage is 29,650,000/2,970. Since 29,700,000 is only 50,000 more than 29,650,000 and 29,700,000/2,970 = 10,000, then 10,000 is an estimate a little larger than the actual average wage. Therefore, (E) is wrong. The product (9,500)(2,970) is 28,215,000, which is 1,435,000 less than 29,650,000. So 10,000 is a better estimate than 9,500. (A) and (B) are obviously wrong.

185. **(A)** Statement I is true since there are 50 managers and 300 foremen and $\frac{50}{300} = \frac{1}{6}$. Statements II and III are false since the table only gives average wages for the different ranks and does not give individual salaries.

186. **(C)** The toy was priced at ($13)(.90) after the first discount and was finally sold at another 10% discount. Therefore, it was sold for ($13)(.90)(.90) = ($13)(.81) = $10.53.

187. **(D)** (.06)($5,500) = $330.00.

188. **(A)** The stock will be selling at $2.00 after 6 months, $4.00 after a year, etc. Therefore, after k 6-month periods, the stock will be selling at $(\$2.00)^k$. Since $2^5 = 32$ and $2^6 = 64$, the stock will be selling at less than $63 after $2\frac{1}{2}$ years but at more than $63 after 3 years.

189. **(E)** (3)(1) = 3, (3)(3) = 9, (3)(9) = 27; so (3)(27) = 81. Another method yields $3^0 = 1$, $3^1 = 3$, $3^2 = 9$, $3^3 = 27$, $3^4 = 81$.

190. **(E)** Each dozen eggs required 2 minutes more of work and every 20 lbs. of potatoes required 3 minutes more of work. Therefore, the total amount of extra work required was (5)(2) + (5)(3) or 25 minutes.

191. **(C)** A bottle of milk was the only item that required less than 10 minutes of work in 1971.

192. **(C)** Statements I and II are false because no information is given about the prices of the objects on the list or the employees' wages in 1971 or 1972. Statement III is true; in both years only an automobile and a suit required more than 10 hours of work.

193. **(A)** Since $\frac{x}{y}$ is not zero, $\frac{y}{x} = 1/\frac{x}{y} = \frac{1}{2}$. But $\frac{y^2}{x^2} = \left(\frac{y}{x}\right)^2 = \left(\frac{1}{2}\right)^2 = \frac{1}{4}$.

194. **(C)** Let x be the amount X is paid and y be the amount Y is paid. Since $x = (1.2)y$, $x + y = (2.2)y$. But we know $x + y = \$550$; so $(2.2)y = \$550$. Dividing each side, we have $y = \$250$.

195. **(D)** There are only 2 days he can work overtime, so there are at most 2 days he can make $x + y$ per day. On the other 3 days the most he can make is x per day. So his maximum salary for the 5 days is $2(x + y) + 3x = 5x + 2y$.

Evaluating Your Score

Tabulate your score for each section of the Diagnostic Test according to the directions on page 3 and record the results in the Self-scoring Table below. Then find your rank for each score on the Self-scoring Scale and record it in the appropriate box.

Self-scoring Table

PART	SCORE	RANK
1		
2		
3		
4		
5		
6		

Self-scoring Scale

PART	POOR	FAIR	GOOD	EXCELLENT
1	0–15	16–21	22–25	26–30
2	0–29	30–40	41–47	48–55
3	0–20	21–28	29–34	35–40
4	0– 7	8–10	11–12	13–15
5	0–10	11–14	15–16	17–20
6	0–18	19–25	26–30	31–35

The following Review sections cover material for each type of question on the GMAT. Spend more time studying those sections for which you had a rank of FAIR or POOR on the Diagnostic Test.

FOUR

REVIEW AND PRACTICE FOR THE GMAT

By taking the Diagnostic Test and evaluating your results, you now have an indication of what your strong and weak points are. Your next step is to begin a more intensive review of test material, concentrating particularly on those areas in which you rated FAIR or POOR, but also covering material you did well on so that you will be certain you fully understand all of the topics.

Study the following sections carefully and do the practice exercises that are provided. The *Reading Comprehension Review* will also assist you in preparing for both Reading Recall and Business Judgment questions. For further business review, use the *Glossary of Business Terms* in the following chapter. Mathematics and Data Sufficiency are covered in the *Mathematics Review* which is keyed to answers for sample tests for easy reference. The *Logic Review* contains a discussion of principles of logic that can be applied to many areas of the exam. In the same manner the *General Vocabulary List* not only supplements the *Verbal Aptitude Review* but also presents words appearing throughout the GMAT.

READING COMPREHENSION REVIEW

A large proportion of the GMAT is designed to test your ability to comprehend material contained in reading passages. The Reading Recall sections of the exam are concerned with determining how well you remember the main points and significant details in the material you have read and also your capacity for drawing inferences from this material. The objective of the Business Judgment areas is to test your ability to analyze business situations and draw subsequent conclusions about them. In each case, success depends on the extent of your reading comprehension skills. The following discussion is designed to help you formulate an approach to reading passages that will enable you to better understand the material you will be asked to read on the GMAT. Practice exercises at the end of this review will give you an opportunity to try out this approach.

Basic Reading Skills

A primary skill necessary for good reading comprehension is the understanding of the meanings of individual words. Knowledge of a wide and diversified vocabulary enables you to detect subtle differences in sentence meaning that may hold the key to the meaning of an entire paragraph or passage. For this reason, it is important that you familiarize yourself with as many words as possible. The *General Vocabulary List* in Chapter five is a good place to begin.

A second reading skill to be developed is the ability to discover the central theme of a passage. By making yourself aware of what the entire passage is about, you are in a position to relate what you read to this central theme, logically picking out the main points and significant details as you go along. Although the manner in which the central theme is stated may vary from passage to passage, it can usually be found in the title (if one is presented), in the "topic sentence" of a paragraph in shorter passages, or in longer passages, by reading several paragraphs.

A third essential skill is the capacity to organize mentally how the passage is put together and determine how each part is related to the whole. This is the skill you will have to use to the greatest degree on the GMAT where you must pick out significant and insignificant factors, remember main details, and relate information you have read to the central theme.

In general, a mastery of these three basic skills will provide you with a solid basis for better reading comprehension wherein you will be able to read carefully to draw a conclusion from the material, decide the meanings of words and ideas presented and how they in turn affect the meaning of the passage, and recognize opinions and views that are expressed.

Applying Basic Reading Skills

The only way to become adept at the three basic reading skills outlined above is to practice using the techniques involved as much as possible. Studying the meanings of new words you encounter, not only in the vocabulary lists in this Guide but also in all your reading material, will soon help you establish a working knowledge of many words. In the same manner, making an effort to locate topic sentences, general themes, and specific details in material you read will enable you to improve your skills in these areas. The following drills will help. After you have read through them and answered the questions satisfactorily, you can try the longer practice exercises at the end.

Finding the Topic Sentence

The term "topic sentence" is used to describe the sentence that gives the key to an entire paragraph. Usually the topic sentence is found in the beginning of a paragraph. However, there is no absolute rule. A writer may build his paragraph to a conclusion, putting the key sentence at the end. Here is an example in which the topic sentence is located at the beginning:

EXAMPLE 1:

The world faces a serious problem of overpopulation. Right now many people starve from lack of adequate food. Efforts are being made to increase the rate of food production, but the number of people to be fed increases at a faster rate.

The idea is stated directly in the opening sentence. You know that the passage will be about "a serious problem of overpopulation." Like a heading or caption, the topic sentence sets the stage or gets your mind ready for what follows in that paragraph.

Before you try to locate the topic sentence in a paragraph you must remember that this technique depends upon reading and judgment. Read the whole passage first. Then try to decide which sentence comes closest to expressing the main point of the paragraph. Do not worry about the position of the topic sentence in the paragraph; look for the most important statement. Find the idea to which all the other sentences relate.

Try this passage yourself to identify the topic sentence:

EXAMPLE 2:

During the later years of the American Revolution, the Articles of Confederation government was formed. This government suffered severely from a lack of power. Each state distrusted the others and gave little authority to the central or federal government. The Articles of Confederation produced a government which could not raise money from taxes, prevent Indian raids, or force the British out of the United States.

What is the topic sentence? Certainly the paragraph is about the Articles of Confederation. However, is the key idea in the first sentence or in the second sentence? In this instance, the *second* sentence does a better job of giving you the key to this paragraph—the lack of power that describes the Articles of Confederation. The sentences that complete the paragraph relate more to the idea of "lack of power" than to the time when the government was formed. Don't assume that the topic sentence is always the first sentence of a paragraph. Try this:

EXAMPLE 3:

There is a strong relation between limited education and low income. Statistics show that unemployment rates are highest among those adults who attended school the fewest years. Most jobs in a modern industrial society require technical or advanced training. The best pay goes with jobs that demand thinking and decisions based on knowledge. A few people manage to overcome their limited education by personality or a "lucky break." However, studies of lifetime earnings show that the average high school graduate earns more than the average high school dropout, who in turn earns more than the average adult who has not finished eighth grade.

Here, the first sentence contains the main idea of the whole paragraph. One more example should be helpful:

EXAMPLE 4:

They had fewer men available as soldiers. Less than one third of the railroads and only a small proportion of the nation's industrial production was theirs. For most of the war their coastline was blockaded by Northern ships. It is a tribute to Southern leadership and the courage of the people that they were not defeated for four years.

In this case you will note that the passage builds up to its main point. The topic sentence is the last one. Practice picking out the topic sentences in other material you read until it becomes an easy skill.

Finding the General Theme

A more advanced skill is the ability to read several paragraphs and relate them to one general theme or main idea. The procedure involves careful reading of the entire passage and deciding which idea is the central or main one. You can tell you have the right idea when it is most frequent, most important, or every sentence relates to it. As you read the next passage note the *underlined* parts.

EXAMPLE 1:

True democracy means direct rule by the people. A good example can be found in a modern town meeting in many small New England towns. All citizens aged twenty-one or over may vote. They not only vote for officials, but they also get together to vote on local laws (or ordinances). The small size of the town and the limited number of voters make this possible.

In the cities, voters cast ballots for officials who get together to make the laws. Because the voters do not make the laws directly, this system is called indirect democracy or representative government. There is no problem of distance to travel, but it is difficult to run a meeting with hundreds of thousands of citizens.

Representation of voters and a direct voice in making laws are more of a problem in state or national governments. The numbers of citizens and the distances to travel make representative government the most practical way to make laws.

Think about the passage in general and the underlined parts in particular. Several examples discuss voting for officials and making laws. In the first paragraph both of these are done by the voters. The second paragraph describes representative government in which voters elect officials who make laws. The last paragraph emphasizes the problem of size and numbers and says that representative government is more practical. In the following question, put all these ideas together.

A B C D E

The main theme of this passage is that

(A) the United States is not democratic
(B) citizens cannot vote for lawmakers
(C) representative government does not make laws
(D) every citizen makes laws directly
(E) increasing populations lead to less direct democracy

The answer is choice (E). Choices (B), (C), and (D) can be eliminated because they are not true of the passage. Choice (A) may have made you hesitate a little. The passage makes comments about *less direct* democracy, but it never says that representative government is *not democratic*.

The next 3 passages offer further practice in finding the main theme. Answer the question following each example and check the analysis to make sure you understand.

EXAMPLE 2:

Skye, 13 miles off the northwest coast of Scotland, is the largest and most famous of the Hebrides. Yet fame has neither marred its natural beauty nor brought affectation to its inhabitants. The scene and the people are almost as they were generations ago.

The first sight that impresses the visitor to Skye is its stark beauty. This is not beauty of the usual sort, for the island is not a lush green "paradise." It is, on the other hand, almost devoid of shrubbery. Mountains, moorlands, sky, and sea combine to create an overpowering landscape. Endless stretches of rocky hills dominate the horizon. Miles of treeless plains meet the eye. Yet this scene has a beauty all its own.

And then cutting into the stark landscape are the fantastic airborne peaks of the Cuillins, rising into the clear skies above. The Cuillins are the most beloved mountains in Scotland and are frequently climbed. Their rugged, naked grandeur, frost-sculptured ridges and acute peaks even attracted Sir Edmund Hilary.

The main idea of this passage is

A B C D E
|| || || || ||

(A) the sky over Skye
(B) the lack of trees on Skye
(C) the natural beauty of Skye
(D) the lack of affectation on Skye
(E) the Cuillins in the skies of Skye

All of the answers have some truth to them. The problem is to find the *best* answer. Four of the choices are mentioned in the passage only by a small comment. But choice (C) is throughout every part of the passage. The clue to the correct answer was the frequency or how often the same theme was covered.

EXAMPLE 3:

Trade exists for many reasons. No doubt it started from a desire to have something different. Men also realized that different men could make different products. Trade encouraged specialization, which led to improvement in quality.

Trade started from person to person, but grew to involve different towns and different lands. Some found work in transporting the goods or selling them. Merchants grew rich as the demand for products increased. Craftsmen were able to sell more products at home and abroad. People in general had a greater variety of things to choose.

The knowledge of new products led to an interest in the lands which produced them. More daring persons went to see other lands. Others stayed at home, but asked many questions of the travellers. As people learned about the products and the conditions in other countries, they compared them with their own. This often led to a desire for better conditions or a hope for a better life. Trade was mainly an economic force, but it also had other effects.

The general theme of the passage deals with how

A B C D E
|| || || || ||

(A) trade makes everyone rich
(B) trade divides the world
(C) products are made
(D) trade changes people's lives
(E) people find new jobs

This is not easy as you may feel that all the choices are good. Most of them were mentioned in some part of the passage. However, you must select the *best* choice. If you had trouble, let us analyze the passage.

Paragraph one emphasizes a "desire for something different" and "improvement." The second paragraph refers to "found work," "merchants grew rich," "craftsmen sell more," and "greater variety of things to choose." The third paragraph covers "interest in the lands," "compared them with their own," "desire for better conditions" and "better life." All these are evidence of the same general theme of how trade brings changes in the lives of people. Choice (D) is the best answer.

Choice (A) is tempting because of the comment on merchants getting rich. However, this idea is not found all through the passage. Choice (B) may catch the careless thinker. Trade does not divide the world, even though the passage talks about dividing jobs. Choice (C) is weak. Some comment is made about making products, but not in all parts of the passage. Choice (E) is weak for the same reason as choice (C).

EXAMPLE 4:

The enormous problems of turning swamps and desert into fields and orchards, together with the ideal of share-and-share-alike, gave birth to the kibbutz.

In those days, the kibbutz member had to plow the fields with a rifle slung over his shoulder.

Today security is still a factor in the kibbutz. Shelters are furrowed into the ground along every walk among the shade trees, near the children's house, where all the young children of the kibbutz live, and near the communal dining room.

But the swamps have been conquered, and the desert is gradually becoming green. And while kibbutz members once faced deprivation and a monotonous diet, today they reap the harvest of hard work and success.

One such kibbutz is Dorot, at the gateway to the Negev desert and typical of the average size Israeli communal settlement.

Life on the kibbutz has become more complex through growth and prosperity. While once the land barely yielded enough for a living, Dorot, like many other kibbutzim, now exports some of its crops. It also has become industrialized, another trend among these settlements. Dorot has a factory which exports faucets to a dozen countries, including the United States.

A B C D E
|| || || || ||

The main theme of this article is

(A) faucets are a sign of growth and prosperity in the kibbutz
(B) with the solving of agricultural problems the kibbutz has become a more complex society
(C) since security is a problem for the kibbutz, it has become industrialized
(D) Dorot is the prosperous gateway to the Negev desert
(E) kibbutzim are good places to live because they are located in swamps and deserts

Choice (A) receives brief mention at the end of the passage. It is an idea in the passage, but certainly not the general idea of the passage. Choice (D) is the same kind of answer as choice (A)—it is too specific a fact. Choice (E) is unrelated to the passage. We now have choices (B) and (C) as possible answers. Choice (C) seems reasonable until you analyze it. Did the need for security *cause* the industrialization? Or are there better examples of how life has become more complex now that agricultural problems have been solved? The evidence leans more to choice (B).

In summary, in order to find the general theme:

1. Read at your normal speed
2. Locate the topic sentence in each paragraph
3. Note ideas that are frequent or emphasized
4. Find the idea to which most of the passage is related

Finding Logical Relationships

In order to fully understand the meaning of a passage, you must first look for the general theme and then relate the ideas and opinions found in the passage to this general theme. In this way, you can determine not only what is important but also how the ideas interrelate to form the whole. From this understanding, you will be better able to answer questions that refer to the passage.

As you read the following passages, look for general theme and supporting facts, words or phrases that signal emphasis or shift in thought, and the relation of one idea to another.

EXAMPLE 1:

The candidate who wants to be elected pays close attention to statements and actions that will make the voters see him favorably. In ancient Rome candidates wore pure white togas (the Latin word *candidatus* means "clothed in white") to indicate that they were pure, clean, and above any "dirty work." However, it is interesting to note that such a toga was not worn after election.

In more modern history, candidates allied themselves with political parties. Once a voter knows and favors the views of a certain political party, he may vote for anyone with that party's label. Nevertheless, divisions of opinion develop so that today there is a wide range of candidate views in any major party.

1. From the first paragraph the best of these conclusions is that after an election

   (A) all candidates are dishonest
   (B) candidates do not have to use the toga as a symbol
   (C) candidates do not change their ideas
   (D) officials are always honest
   (E) policies always change

A B C D E
|| || || || ||

You noted the ideas about a candidate in Rome. You saw the word "however" signal a shift in ideas or thinking. Now the third step rests with your judgment. You cannot jump to a conclusion; you must see which conclusion is reasonable or fair. Choices (A), (D), and (E) should make you wary. They say "all" or "always" which means without exception. The last sentence is not that strong or positive. Choices (B) and (C) must be considered. There is nothing in the paragraph that supports the fact that candidates do not change their ideas. This forces you into choice (B) as the only statement logically related to what the paragraph said.

2. A fair statement is that most candidates from the same political party today are likely to

A B C D E

(A) have the same views
(B) be different in every view
(C) agree on almost all points
(D) agree on some points and disagree on others
(E) agree only by accident

Here again, the burden rests on your judgment after following ideas and word clues. The paragraph makes the point that there is a wide range of views. That eliminates choice (A). Choice (B) is not logical because the candidates would not likely be in the same party if they disagree on every view. The remaining choices are different degrees of agreement. Choice (E) is weak because candidates are too interested to arrive at agreement only by accident. The wide range mentioned seems to oppose choice (C) and favor choice (D) as a little more likely. You may say that choice (C) sounds pretty good. Again we stress that *you are picking the very best choice,* not just a good choice. This is what we mean by reflecting carefully on all possibilities and selecting the best available choice.

EXAMPLE 2:

In 1812 Napoleon had to withdraw his forces from Russia. The armies invaded successfully and reached the city of Moscow. There was no question of French army disloyalty or unwillingness to fight. As winter came, the Russian army moved out of the way, leaving a wasted land and burned buildings. Other conquered European nations seized upon Napoleon's problems in Russia as their chance to rearm and to break loose from French control.

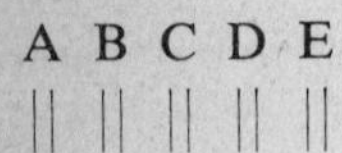

According to the passage, the main reason for Napoleon's withdrawal from Russia was the

(A) disloyalty of the French troops
(B) Russian winter
(C) burned buildings
(D) planned revolts in other countries
(E) Russian army

In this passage, only choice (A) is totally incorrect. Choice (E) is very weak because the Russian army was not able to stop the invasion. The choices narrow to which is the best of (B), (C), and (D). It seems that all three answers are supported by the passage. There needs to be some thought and judgment by you. Which of these could be overcome easily and which could be the strongest reason for Napoleon leaving Russia? The burned buildings could be overcome by the troops making other shelters. The Russian winter was severe and the army did not want to face it. However, marching out of Russia in the winter was also a great problem. Napoleon probably would have stayed in Moscow except for a more serious problem—the loss of control he had established over most of Europe, thus, answer (D) is best.

EXAMPLE 3:

By 1915 events of World War I were already involving the United States and threatening its neutrality. The sinking of the British liner *Lusitania* in that year by a German submarine caused great resentment among Americans. Over a hundred United States citizens were killed in the incident. President Wilson had frequently deplored the use of submarines by Germany against the United States. Since the U.S. was neutral, it was not liable to acts of war by another nation.

However, Wilson resolved to represent the strong feeling in the country (notably in the Midwest) and in the Democratic Party that U.S. neutrality should be maintained. He felt that the United States should have "peace with honor," if possible.

There were also people, mostly in the East, that wanted to wage a preventive war against Germany. Such men as Theodore Roosevelt bitterly attacked Wilson as one who talked a great deal but did nothing.

By 1917 Germany again used unrestricted submarine warfare and Wilson broke off relations with Germany. In February British agents uncovered the Zimmerman Telegram. This was an attempt by the German ambassador to Mexico to involve that nation in a war against the United States. And in March several American merchant ships were sunk by German submarines. His patience at an end, Wilson at last took the position of a growing majority of Americans and asked Congress to declare war on Germany. Thus, United States entered World War I.

1. This passage tries to explain that

(A) Wilson wanted the U.S. to go to war against Germany
(B) Wilson tried to avoid war with Germany
(C) Germany wanted the U.S. to enter the war
(D) Other nations were pressuring U.S. to enter the war
(E) Mexico was our main enemy

1. A B C D E

2. We can conclude from the passage that most citizens of United States in 1917 were

(A) totally opposed to war with Germany
(B) in favor of war before Wilson was
(C) willing to accept war after Wilson persuaded them
(D) neutral
(E) trying to avoid war

2. A B C D E

3. The last event in the series of happenings that led to a declaration of war against Germany was the

(A) Zimmerman Telegram
(B) attacks on U.S. merchant ships
(C) Wilson's war message to Congress
(D) change of public opinion
(E) sinking of the *Lusitania*

3. A B C D E

In question 1, the key is to note Wilson's actions discussed in paragraph two. Near the end of the passage there is a phrase about "his patience at end." These describe a man who was trying to avoid a conflict as in answer choice (B).

Question 2 rests on two ideas. There was a change in the feeling of the American people about war. The other idea is whether Wilson changed to lead them or he responded after he felt that they had changed. The phrase "took the position of a growing majority of Americans" tells us that Wilson followed the change in opinion as in answer choice (B).

In question 3, you need to check the sequence of events. A declaration of war followed the president's request.

Making Inferences

An inference is not stated. It is assumed by the reader from something said by the writer. An inference is the likely or probable conclusion rather than the direct logical one. It usually involves an opinion or viewpoint that the writer wants the reader to follow or assume. In another kind of inference the reader figures out the author's opinion even though it is not stated. The clues are generally found in which facts are presented and in the choice of words and phrases. Opinion is revealed by its one-sided nature in which no opposing facts are given. It is shown further by "loaded" words that reveal feelings.

It is well worth noting that opinionated writing is often more interesting than straight factual accounts. Some writers are very colorful, forceful, or amusing in presenting their views. You should understand that there is nothing wrong with reading opinion. You should read varied opinions, but know that they are opinions. Then make up your own mind.

Not every writer will insert his opinion obviously. However, you can get clues from how often the same idea is said (frequency), whether arguments are balanced on both sides (fairness), and the choice of wording (emotional or loaded words). Look for the clues in this next passage.

EXAMPLE 1:

Slowly but surely the great passenger trains of the United States have been fading from the rails. Short-run commuter trains still rattle in and out of the cities. Between major cities you can still find a train, but the schedules are becoming less frequent. The Twentieth Century Limited, The Broadway Limited, and other luxury trains that sang along the rails at 60 to 80 miles an hour are no longer running. Passengers on other long runs complain of poor service, old equipment, and costs in time and money. The long distance traveller today accepts the noise of jets, the congestion at airports, and the traffic between airport and city. A more elegant and graceful way is becoming only a memory.

1. A B C D E

1. With respect to the reduction of long run passenger trains, this writer expresses

(A) regret
(B) pleasure
(C) grief
(D) elation
(E) anger

Before you choose the answer, you must assume what the writer's feeling is. He does not actually state his feeling, but clues are available so that you may infer what it is. Choices (B) and (D) are impossible, because he gives no word that shows he is pleased by the change. Choice (C) is too strong as is choice (E). Choice (A) is the most reasonable inference to make. He is sorry to see the change. He is expressing regret.

2. A B C D E

2. The author seems to feel that air travel is

(A) costly
(B) slow
(C) streamlined
(D) crude
(E) uncomfortable

Here we must be careful because he says very little about air travel. However, his one sentence about it presents three negative or annoying points. The choice now becomes fairly clear.

EXAMPLE 2:

When the United States started at the end of the eighteenth century, it was a small and weak country, made up mostly of poor farmers. Foreign policy, reflecting this domestic condition, stressed "no entangling alliances." The State Department then had a staff of less than half a dozen persons, whose total salary was $6,600 (of which $3,500 went to the Secretary of State), and a diplomatic service budget (July, 1790) of $40,000. Militarily, too, the country was insignificant. The first United States army, soon after the American Revolution, was made up of one captain (John Doughty) and 80 men. Clearly, the United States did not consider itself a real power and was not taken seriously by the rest of the world.

It was not until immense changes took place INSIDE the United States that the country began to play an important role in foreign affairs. By the beginning of the twentieth century, the United States had ceased to be a predominantly agricultural nation and had become an industrial one. Its population had grown more than 30 times its original number. George Washington was president of 3,000,000 Americans; Theodore Roosevelt, of 100,000,000.

1. A small country today cannot expect to play an important part in world affairs unless it 1. A B C D E

(A) has wealth
(B) has powerful allies
(C) is strong internally
(D) is none of the above
(E) is all of the above

(NOTE: This is a slightly different style of question. You must look at each of the answer choices in (A)–(C). As you consider the passage and what it suggests for a small country today, you add your own knowledge. Each of the answer choices in (A)–(C) makes good sense. Therefore, answer choice (E) is the best answer because it includes all of the good ones in (A)–(C). Again, this is not designed to trick you. The purpose of such a question is to be sure that you have read all the choices before you have made a selection of the best one.)

2. The writer seems to think that the main factor in making the United States a world power was 2. A B C D E

(A) industrialization
(B) passing of time
(C) growth of population
(D) the presidency of Theodore Roosevelt
(E) avoiding entangling alliances

The passage does not answer the question directly. You must infer or assume what is meant by the author. However, there is a clue in the author's comment that changes inside a country make a big difference in its foreign policy. The big internal changes noted are population and industrial power. By drawing on your knowledge and by interpreting the passage, you will be led to choice (A) for this question.

In Example 3 you will find three short statements by three different writers. The questions will require that you make inferences about each writer and then make comparisons of one against the other two.

EXAMPLE 3:

Writer I

No nation should tolerate the slacker who will not defend his country in time of war. The so-called conscientious objector is a coward who accepts the benefits of his country but will not accept the responsibility. By shirking his fair share, he forces another person to assume an unfair burden.

Writer II

A democratic nation should have room for freedom of conscience. Religious training and belief may make a man conscientiously opposed to participation in war. The conscientious objector should be permitted to give labor service or some form of non-combat military duty. His beliefs should be respected.

Writer III

The rights of the conscientious objector should be decided by each individual. No government should dictate to any person or require him to endanger his life if the person, in conscience, objects. There need be no religious basis. It is enough for a free individual to think as he pleases and to reject laws or rules to which he conscientiously objects.

1.A B C D E || || || || ||

1. A balanced opinion on this subject is presented by
   (A) Writer I
   (B) Writer II
   (C) Writer III
   (D) all of the writers
   (E) none of the writers

2.A B C D E || || || || ||

2. We can conclude that the writer most likely to support a person who refuses any military service is
   (A) Writer I
   (B) Writer II
   (C) Writer III
   (D) all of the writers
   (E) none of the writers

3.A B C D E || || || || ||

3. An authoritarian person is most likely to agree with
   (A) Writer I
   (B) Writer II
   (C) Writer III
   (D) all of the writers
   (E) none of the writers

Look for clues in the language or choice of words that are loaded with feeling such as "slacker," "so-called," and "shirking" by Writer I and "dictate," "endanger," and "as he pleases" by Writer III. Compare them with the language used by Writer II. The second help is to connect what these writers say with views you have heard or read. We are not asking you to take any of these opinions. You are using your skill in reading what the writers think and adding it to your own knowledge. Then you make logical or related inferences.

Now that you have spent time reviewing the three basic skills you should master for better reading comprehension ability, try the practice exercises that follow. Answers to these exercises appear after Exercise C. You should also try to spend time using this reading approach as you read other material not related to the GMAT.

Practice Exercises

The following three reading passages are similar to those found on the GMAT. You should read each one and then, without consulting the passage for assistance, answer the questions that follow. On the actual exam you are asked to read all three passages before answering the questions. Passages are separated here for practice purposes.

EXERCISE A

TOTAL TIME: 12 minutes

Part A: TIME—5 minutes

DIRECTIONS: This part contains a reading passage. You will have 5 minutes to study the passage and 7 minutes to answer questions based on it. When answering the questions you will *not* be allowed to refer back to the passage.

For the most part, American institutions of higher education managed to expand their resources and facilities to absorb the rapidly increasing numbers of students seeking to enroll in the 1960s. Students who could not qualify for the most selective four-year institutions were admitted to less selective four-year institutions or to two-year colleges. Only toward the end of the decade were there signs of serious stresses and strains resulting from financial stringency in both public and private institutions.

The outlook for smooth absorption of the increased numbers of students who will be seeking higher education in the 1970s is at present very uncertain. Campus unrest, which is leading some state legislatures to "punish" public institutions of higher education by withholding funds and which is causing some alumni and other private donors to hold back on gifts to colleges and universities, may abate somewhat if we withdraw from the Indochina war, but most sophisticated observers do not expect unrest to disappear on campuses. Cutbacks in federal government support of higher education may prove to be temporary if a decline in military expenditures facilitates increased appropriations for education and other social services. But a more persistent problem is likely to be the fiscal stringency faced by state and local governments (with the latter representing a significant source of financing of two-year colleges).

Appropriations for higher education must compete at state and local levels with rapidly rising expenditures for welfare, elementary and secondary education, and other public services. State and local governments face serious difficulties in meeting these mounting costs because they tend to rely heavily on sales taxes and, in the case of local governments, property taxes—taxes yielding revenues that tend to rise less rapidly than personal income. In contrast, the tax revenues of the federal government, which rely in large part on personal and corporate income taxes, tend to rise more rapidly than personal income.

In fact, from the perspective of the fall of 1971, it appears likely that higher education will *not* be in a position to absorb the increased numbers of students seeking admission in the 1970s without greatly increased federal government support, along the lines recommended by the Carnegie Commission. In the absence of such increased federal government support, students and their parents in both public and private institutions will have to meet an increased proportion of the rising costs of education through greatly increased tuition and fees. That requirement will be to the detriment of enrollment of many students from low-income families and even of a good many students from middle-income families, and public institutions may continue to be forced to turn away qualified applicants on an increased scale.

Assuming, however, that adequate funds are forthcoming from public sources, that growth is not inhibited by changes in the demand for college graduates or by structural changes in higher education, and that the age distribution of students does not change very much, enrollment trends in the 1970s and the following two decades will be determined by (1) changes in the rate of growth of the college-age population and (2) a continuation of the long-run upward trend in enrollment rates, which in turn primarily reflects the influence of three interrelated and overlapping factors: (a) the upward trend in high school graduation rates, (b) the rise in real per-capita income, and (c) changes in the occupational structure which result in an increased demand for persons holding academic degrees.

How will enrollment be distributed among types of institutions in future years? If changes in the 1970s reflect the shifts that occurred from 1963 to 1970, the most rapid growth of enrollment to 1980 is likely to occur in the two-year institutions. Their enrollment will increase 70 percent and may be expected to increase these institutions' share of total enrollment from 28 to 31 percent. Most of this growth will occur in the public two-year colleges, which are likely to account for 96 percent of all enrollment in two-year institutions in 1980, as compared with 94 percent in 1970.

The comprehensive colleges are also estimated to experience rapid growth. Although their enrollment is likely to increase 58 percent in the 10-year period, their share of the total is projected to rise only from 31 to 32 percent. This estimate would be only slightly altered if, as seems likely, some of the public liberal arts colleges were to broaden their programs so that they would be entitled to classification as comprehensive colleges by 1980.

Interestingly, the projections suggest that the most slowly growing group of institutions will be the doctoral-granting institutions, although they will experience a substantial 37 percent increase in enrollment. But their share of the total is likely to fall from 30 to about 27 percent. Moreover, the more prestigious the institution, the less rapid the rate of enrollment growth is likely to be. This reflects the fact that the less prestigious doctoral-granting institutions tend to be younger, and thus in an earlier and more rapid stage of development.

If there is still time remaining, review the passage until all 5 minutes have elapsed.
Do not look at Part B until that time.

Part B: TIME—7 minutes

DIRECTIONS: Answer the following questions pertaining to information in the passage you have just read. You may not turn back to that passage for assistance.

1. According to the passage, American institutions of higher education

1. A B C D E

(A) failed to absorb all applicants in the 1960s
(B) were financially strained
(C) expanded their resources and facilities
(D) worsened academically
(E) increased in number

2. According to the author, the outlook for absorption of increased numbers of students is

2. A B C D E

(A) favorable
(B) doubtful
(C) uncertain
(D) optimistic
(E) plausible

3. It is stated in the passage that enrollment trends in the 1970s will be influenced by

3. A B C D E

(A) costs of education
(B) changes in the rate of growth of educational institutions
(C) changes in the educational system
(D) changes in the rate of growth of college-age population
(E) none of the above

4. Another factor mentioned by the author that can influence enrollment trends is

4. A B C D E

(A) changes in the demand for college graduates
(B) attitudes of high school students
(C) the general economic climate
(D) growth of the service industry
(E) the future of extra-curricular college activities

5. It can be inferred that the author believes that increased federal support

5. A B C D E

(A) should be welcomed only as a last resort
(B) is essential to support increased enrollment
(C) should be used only in public institutions
(D) could lead to higher income taxes
(E) would result in higher tuition costs

6. The author states that campus unrest has caused

6. A B C D E

(A) a decline in enrollment
(B) disruption of classes
(C) a decline in gift-giving to colleges
(D) student support for the Indochina war
(E) increased costs for police protection

7.A B C D E

7. The author believes that campus unrest is

(A) a passing phenomenon
(B) of little effect on enrollment
(C) unlikely to disappear quickly
(D) of little consequence
(E) the work of a minority

8.A B C D E

8. It is the author's opinion that higher education will

(A) not be able to absorb increased enrollments without more federal support
(B) face a decrease in demand for a college degree
(C) rely on higher personal and corporate income taxes
(D) experience quite substantial enrollment increases
(E) be affected by a changing labor market for Ph.D's

9.A B C D E

9. According to the passage, enrollment in two-year institutions will

(A) increase by 70 percent
(B) increase by 20 percent
(C) remain somewhat stable
(D) decline slightly
(E) decline rapidly

10.A B C D E

10. The most slowly growing group of institutions will be

(A) comprehensive colleges
(B) four-year colleges
(C) doctoral-granting institutions
(D) two-year colleges
(E) private colleges

EXERCISE B

TOTAL TIME: 12 minutes

Part A: TIME—5 minutes

DIRECTIONS: This part contains a reading passage. You will have 5 minutes to study the passage and 7 minutes to answer questions based on it. When answering the questions you will *not* be allowed to refer back to the passage.

On August 15, 1971, the President announced a far-reaching New Economic Policy designed to check the rise in prices and wages, strengthen the Nation's external economic position and stimulate economic activity at home. To curb the rate of inflation, prices, wages, and rents were subjected to a 90-day freeze, which was followed by a comprehensive but more flexible system of controls. To improve the Nation's balance of payments, the President suspended the convertibility of the dollar into gold and other reserve assets and imposed a temporary 10-percent surcharge on imports. And to strengthen the domestic economy, the President proposed, in addition to these measures, a fiscal package whose stimulus came from a set of tax cuts, which were passed by the Congress in December in somewhat altered form.

Results of the new program were visible in varying degrees by the end of the year. They were most apparent in the slowdown of price and wage increases during the freeze. On the international front the major industrial countries agreed to a realignment of currencies more favorable to the U.S. competitive position and to prompt discussions concerning trade barriers and long-term monetary reform. The strong upsurge in the purchases of automobiles from mid-August through November was partly a result of the proposed removal of the Federal excise tax, but much of it was apparently an attempt by consumers to buy automobiles before prices were increased in the post-freeze period. Perhaps the most significant effect of the combined package was the impact on public confidence. From mid-August to the end of the year, there was slow but steady improvement in confidence that the rate of inflation was subsiding and the pace of the economic recovery was gathering strength.

The decision to embark on the New Economic Policy (NEP) came from an increasing awareness in the Administration that the ambitious goals it had set in the beginning of the year were not being met. Progress in the fight against inflation was proceeding too slowly, and its future success was uncertain. At the same time, the recovery was also progressing, but not fast enough to cut the rate of unemployment. More crucial than either of these for the timing of the decisions was the serious weakening of the dollar in international markets. As the summer wore on, there were no signs of a resolution of the financial crisis that in May caused the Swiss franc and the Austrian schilling to be revalued and the German mark and the Netherlands guilder to be set free to float in value. In the second quarter, the U.S. balance of payments on the official reserve transactions basis had recorded a deficit of $23 billion at a seasonally adjusted annual rate, and in July and August pressure against the dollar reached enormous proportions. Funds totalling $3.7 billion moved into foreign official reserve accounts in the week ended August 15. The time had come to deal decisively with the international financial problem that had persisted for at least a dozen years despite the efforts of four successive Administrations.

If there is still time remaining, review the passage until all 5 minutes have elapsed.
Do not look at Part B until that time.

Part B: TIME—7 minutes

DIRECTIONS: Answer the following questions pertaining to information in the passage you have just read. You may not turn back to that passage for assistance.

1. A provision of the President's New Economic Policy was

(A) wage and price controls
(B) increased income taxes
(C) a surcharge on exports
(D) reduced tariffs
(E) devaluation of the dollar

1.A B C D E

2.A B C D E

2. Imports were subjected to a

(A) 90-day freeze
(B) system of price controls
(C) quota system
(D) 10-percent surcharge
(E) most-favored nation basis

3.A B C D E

3. The decision to embark on the NEP came about because of

(A) public pressure
(B) devaluation of the dollar
(C) an act of Congress
(D) slowdown of inflation
(E) failure to meet the Administration's economic goals

4.A B C D E

4. What currencies were set free to float in value?

(A) dollar
(B) Swiss franc
(C) German mark
(D) British pound
(E) Italian lira

5.A B C D E

5. The international financial problem had persisted for

(A) 12 years
(B) 4 years
(C) 12 months
(D) 2 years
(E) since World War II

6.A B C D E

6. Increased automobile purchases in the United States were the result of

(A) rising incomes
(B) a surge in car imports
(C) removal of the Federal excise tax
(D) significant body restyling
(E) unknown factors

7.A B C D E

7. The President suspended the convertibility of the dollar into gold to improve the country's

(A) monetary system
(B) balance of payments
(C) dollar reserves
(D) foreign exchange holdings
(E) scarce resources

8.A B C D E

8. As a result of the President's NEP, the passage states that the public's confidence

(A) waned
(B) showed little change
(C) showed no change
(D) showed slow but steady improvement
(E) greatly increased

9. During the period under discussion in the passage, unemployment

(A) declined
(B) increased
(C) stayed about the same
(D) was not mentioned in the passage
(E) was mentioned without comment

9. A B C D E

10. Which of the following men was President during the time period under discussion?

(A) Kennedy
(B) Roosevelt
(C) Nixon
(D) Johnson
(E) Truman

10. A B C D E

EXERCISE C

TOTAL TIME: 12 minutes

Part A: TIME—5 minutes

DIRECTIONS: This part contains a reading passage. You will have 5 minutes to study the passage and 7 minutes to answer questions based on it. When answering the questions you will *not* be allowed to refer back to the passage.

The sudden and summary demise of the SST program supplied final evidence of a process that started in the mid-sixties; our generation stands, at present, at one of the sharp turning points of human culture characterized by fairly general rejection of an old value system.

We grew up in a world that regarded material progress through technological improvement as the main glory of our times. We learned to admire our productive machinery as a generator of greater self-fulfillment by freeing us from the toil of past generations. We interpreted the conquest of distance through rapid transportation as a way of creating freer and better understanding among the inhabitants of our planet. As our younger generation has taken stock of our hopes and actual accomplishments, however, it has found that a world built on technology is a hollow one. Our expectations were too utopian and, therefore, our actual achievements have lost the creditability of our ideals.

A new orientation is emerging. It does not build its hopes on the more efficient creation of goods and services as the ultimate answer to miseries. Instead, it regards technology as a source of our ills rather than the solution to them. The factories, once visited by streams of admiring townfolk, now stand in the public eye as the source of pollution. Supersonic planes are no longer the embodiment of the ultimate conquest of distance. The important element of their existence is now the nuisance of their noise. Automation is no longer valued as the source of leisure time; it draws criticism as the creator of structural unemployment.

Middle-aged men are ill advised to argue their ideological-social beliefs with the younger generation. As value systems replace each other, being "right" or "wrong" loses most of its meaning. Demography itself assures the ultimate domination by the younger generation; the young will outlive us.

There is, however, room for rational analysis in the economic impact of this change in cultures. The SST case has proven it; the preferences of the alienated are now a strong enough factor to determine the contractions and expansions of the public purse.

There can be little doubt that their attitudes as citizens, as consumers and even as investors will have a crucial impact upon the economic structure.

Mankind has experienced recurrent trouble in dealing with the intricacies of advanced civilizations. Saint Augustine's Christian purism was a rejection of Roman sophistication. Calvin's puritanistic views represented deep distrust of Renaissance worldliness. Jean Jacques Rousseau's XVIII century turn to natural life expressed the reservations of a sensitive man to complexities beyond his understanding. High moments of civilization have a general tendency to produce counter-cultures and alienated reactions: a yearning for a world with fewer complexities and closer to the intimate scale of man's own life.

Life at present abounds with similar symptoms. Leading schools report a growing interest among graduating collegians for careers in farming. Clothing styles among the young, a good indicator of cultural change, reflect a taste for the simple, non-commercial product. The traditionalist tweedy line is being replaced by items from the Army and Navy surplus store. Girls turn to home sewing and create their own styles inspired by folkloric elements. Over-urbanized vacation spots are losing out to wandering and camping. "Roughing it" is now in style. The rediscovery of nature mixes well with the embracement of conservationist causes. The latter, formerly a conservative movement among the landed gentry against the intrusion of new elements, is now a mass issue.

If there is still time remaining, review the passage until all 5 minutes have elapsed. Do not look at Part B until that time.

Part B: TIME—7 minutes

DIRECTIONS: Answer the following questions pertaining to information in the passage you have just read. You may not turn back to that passage for assistance.

1. A B C D E

1. An appropriate title for the passage could be

(A) *Youth in Rebellion*
(B) *Demographics of Youth*
(C) *Dethroning Technology*
(D) *Demise of the SST*
(E) *Old and New Ideologies*

2. A B C D E

2. The demise of the SST is indicative of

(A) an upsurge of patriotism
(B) rejection of technology if it is a source of ills
(C) a misunderstanding of progress
(D) costly failures
(E) rebellious youth

3. A B C D E

3. Progress, according to the passage, used to mean

(A) establishment of science-based industry
(B) an increase in material goods
(C) better transportation
(D) greater self-fulfillment
(E) more wealth

4. The author states that automation is viewed by young people as a(n)

(A) potential source of leisure time
(B) labor saving device
(C) aid to economic growth
(D) creator of structural unemployment
(E) complement to technology

4. A B C D E

5. Some colleges report that graduates have taken a growing interest in

(A) politics
(B) sewing
(C) transportation
(D) farming
(E) auto mechanics

5. A B C D E

6. The desire by youth for a simpler life closer to nature is expressed by the term

(A) conservationism
(B) counter-culture
(C) renaissance
(D) purism
(E) conservatism

6. A B C D E

7. Which historical person desired a return to the "natural life"?

(A) Rousseau
(B) Calvin
(C) Saint Simon
(D) Saint Augustine
(E) Luther

7. A B C D E

8. The author believes that the older generation should

(A) not argue their ideological beliefs with the young generation
(B) take on the beliefs of the young generation
(C) take a "business as usual" attitude
(D) try to persuade young people to be more conservative
(E) take no action at all

8. A B C D E

9. According to the passage, young people will have an impact on the economy because of all the following except

(A) they will comprise a large number of the population
(B) they will influence investment
(C) their incomes will rise
(D) they have more voting power
(E) they are more militant

9. A B C D E

10. In general, the passage points out that attitudes and values of the youth generation are

(A) basically the same as their parents
(B) influenced by what they learn in college
(C) basically different from that of their parents
(D) volatile, in that they change every year or two
(E) favorably disposed to conspicuous consumption

10. A B C D E

Answers and Analysis

EXERCISE A

1. **(C)** See paragraph 1, line 1: ". . . American institutions of higher education managed to expand their resources and facilities. . . ."

2. **(C)** Paragraph 2, see line 1: "The outlook for smooth absorption of the increased numbers of students in the 1970s is at present very uncertain."

3. **(D)** See paragraph 5, item 1: "changes in the rate of growth of the college age population."

4. **(A)** See paragraph 5, item c: "changes in the occupational structure which result in an increased demand for persons holding academic degrees."

5. **(B)** See paragraph 5, line 1, and also paragraph 4, line 1: ". . . it appears likely that higher education will *not* be in a position to absorb the increased numbers of students seeking admission in the 1970s without greatly increased federal government support. . . ."

6. **(C)** See paragraph 2, line 2: "Campus unrest . . . is leading some state legislatures [to withhold] funds . . . and . . . is causing some alumni to hold back on gifts. . . ."

7. **(C)** See paragraph 2: ". . . most sophisticated observers do not expect unrest to disappear. . . ."

8. **(A)** See the explanation to question 5 above.

9. **(A)** This figure is given in paragraph 6.

10. **(C)** See paragraph 8, line 1: ". . . the most slowly growing group of institutions will be the doctoral-granting. . . ."

EXERCISE B

1. **(A)** This is inferred in paragraph 1, line 1, and specifically mentioned in line 2.

2. **(D)** Also mentioned in paragraph 1: ". . . the President . . . imposed a temporary 10-percent surcharge on imports."

3. **(E)** See paragraph 3, line 1: "The decision to embark on the NEP came from. . . ." and following.

4. **(C)** See paragraph 3: ". . . the German mark and the Netherlands guilder to be set free to float in value."

5. **(A)** See the last line of the passage: ". . . the international financial problem that had persisted for at least a dozen years. . . ."

6. **(C)** Paragraph 2: "The strong upsurge in the purchases of automobiles . . . was partly a result of the proposed removal of the Federal excise tax. . . ."

7. **(B)** Paragraph 1: "To improve the Nation's balance of payments, the President suspended the convertibility of the dollar into gold. . . ."

8. **(D)** See paragraph 2: ". . . the most significant effect of the combined package [i.e. the NEP] was the impact on public confidence."

9. **(C)** Paragraph 3: "Progress in the fight against inflation was proceeding too slowly, and its future success was uncertain."

10. **(C)** Obviously President Nixon, since the NEP was announced in August, 1971. See paragraph 1, line 1.

EXERCISE C

1. **(C)** The passage deals with the supposed rejection of technology and material progress by youth.

2. **(B)** See for example, paragraph 3: ". . . it regards technology as a source of our ills. . . ."

3. **(B)** See paragraph 2: "We grew up in a world that regarded material progress through technological improvement. . . ."

4. **(D)** See paragraph 3: "Automation . . . draws criticism as the creator of structural unemployment."

5. **(D)** See paragraph 7, line 2.

6. **(B)** This is expressed in paragraph 6, last line.

7. **(A)** See paragraph 6.

8. **(A)** See paragraph 4: "Middle-aged men are ill-advised to argue . . . with the younger generation."

9. **(E)** These reasons are found in paragraphs 4 and 5.

10. **(C)** The youth have apparently rejected the value systems of their parents, as exemplified by the issues raised in the passage.

VERBAL APTITUDE REVIEW

The Verbal Aptitude section of the GMAT usually contains three parts — antonyms, word-pair relationships, and sentence completions — each designed to test your ability to grasp the meanings of words and to determine the relationships that exist between words and ideas in a given situation. Success with this section depends largely on your grasp of a wide range of vocabulary and your understanding of how to answer each type of question. A discussion of these questions with practice exercises for further review follows. You will also benefit by using the *General Vocabulary List* starting on page 233 to familiarize yourself with as many new words as possible.

Antonyms

You will recall that an antonym is a word that is *opposite* in meaning to another word as, for example, *fat* is an antonym for *thin.* On the exam you are given a key word printed in capital letters followed by five lettered choices. You must select the lettered word that comes closest to being *opposite* in meaning to the capitalized word.

There are two main points to remember in approaching questions of this type. First, when choosing the antonym for a key word, be sure that both words correspond in tense (present to present, past to past, etc.) or part of speech (noun to noun, adverb to adverb, etc.). Otherwise, your choice won't be a true opposite. Second, a large command of vocabulary is essential for success with antonym questions. You must know the meanings of all five choices and the key word in order to determine which choice is correct. Keeping these points in mind, try the following practice exercises. Answers are given after Exercise D.

Practice Exercises

Antonyms

EXERCISE A

DIRECTIONS: For each question below, select the lettered word or phrase that comes closest to being *opposite* in meaning to the word appearing in capital letters. Be sure to consider all meanings carefully.

1.A B C D E

1. ABOMINATE: (A) love (B) loathe (C) abhor (D) despise (E) attach

2.A B C D E

2. RAVENOUS: (A) famished (B) nibbling (C) sated (D) starving (E) unsatisfied

3.A B C D E

3. PITHY: (A) central (B) federal (C) homogeneous (D) tautological (E) gregarious

4.A B C D E

4. ADAMANT: (A) yielding (B) primitive (C) elementary (D) primeval (E) inflexible

5. EPHEMERAL: (A) evergreen (B) deciduous (C) biennial (D) everlasting (E) tactile
5. A B C D E

6. SYNTHETIC: (A) cosmetics (B) artificial (C) plastic (D) viscous (E) natural
6. A B C D E

7. VIVACIOUS: (A) animated (B) dramatic (C) versatile (D) phlegmatic (E) vigilant
7. A B C D E

8. AUDACITY: (A) quivering (B) cowardice (C) conciseness (D) patricide (E) bravado
8. A B C D E

9. IRASCIBLE: (A) pictorial (B) piscatorial (C) bellicose (D) cranky (E) good-natured
9. A B C D E

10. BUCOLIC: (A) citified (B) rustic (C) intoxicated (D) sick (E) healthy
10. A B C D E

11. INFINITESIMAL: (A) everlasting (B) colossal (C) picayune (D) microscopic (E) telescopic
11. A B C D E

12. GELID: (A) lurid (B) torpid (C) torrid (D) piebald (E) vapid
12. A B C D E

13. CIRCUITOUS: (A) diameter (B) direct (C) roundabout (D) labyrinth (E) radius
13. A B C D E

14. PROVINCIAL: (A) urbane (B) governmental (C) local (D) rural (E) native
14. A B C D E

15. CLANDESTINE: (A) open (B) daylight (C) miasma (D) pugnacious (E) banal
15. A B C D E

16. ABHOR: (A) detest (B) absolve (C) accuse (D) bedizen (E) adore
16. A B C D E

17. FLAMBOYANT: (A) decorated (B) apparition (C) plain (D) female (E) terse
17. A B C D E

18. REDUNDANT: (A) tautological (B) repeated (C) curt (D) voluble (E) opulent
18. A B C D E

19. IMPOVERISHED: (A) impecunious (B) affluent (C) rococo (D) iniquitous (E) pendent
19. A B C D E

20. OBSEQUIOUS: (A) fawning (B) servile (C) supercilious (D) improper (E) first
20. A B C D E

21.A B C D E || || || || || **21.** DISCRETE: (A) wise (B) foolish (C) unkempt (D) separate (E) continuous

22.A B C D E || || || || || **22.** FATUOUS: (A) inane (B) thin (C) witty (D) planned (E) stout

23.A B C D E || || || || || **23.** AMENABLE: (A) responsive (B) intractable (C) indifferent (D) agreeable (E) correct

24.A B C D E || || || || || **24.** FALLACIOUS: (A) erroneous (B) faulty (C) accurate (D) afraid (E) plucky

25.A B C D E || || || || || **25.** ALTRUISM: (A) honesty (B) tolerance (C) bigotry (D) thievery (E) selfishness

EXERCISE B

DIRECTIONS: For each question below, select the lettered word or phrase that comes closest to being *opposite* in meaning to the word appearing in capital letters. Be sure to consider all meanings carefully.

1.A B C D E || || || || || **1.** INDIFFERENT: (A) curious (B) varied (C) uniform (D) alike (E) uninquisitive

2.A B C D E || || || || || **2.** COHESIVE: (A) attached (B) detached (C) associated (D) affiliated (E) sticky

3.A B C D E || || || || || **3.** INSIPID: (A) tasty (B) silly (C) angry (D) active (E) emaciated

4.A B C D E || || || || || **4.** DISCORD: (A) noise (B) amity (C) irritation (D) scrap (E) use

5.A B C D E || || || || || **5.** PRIORITY: (A) anxiety (B) irregular (C) subsequence (D) pious (E) impious

6.A B C D E || || || || || **6.** CRABBED: (A) fished (B) saccharine (C) sour (D) apple (E) orange

7.A B C D E || || || || || **7.** CORROBORATION: (A) proof (B) arrest (C) invalidation (D) alibi (E) alias

8.A B C D E || || || || || **8.** DECORUM: (A) ribaldry (B) balladry (C) high collar (D) solo (E) freedom

9. VIVACIOUS: (A) surgery (B) awake (C) girlish (D) inactive (E) boyish — 9. A B C D E

10. INGENUOUS: (A) clever (B) stupid (C) naive (D) young (E) sophisticated — 10. A B C D E

11. ALLEVIATE: (A) allow (B) aggravate (C) instigate (D) belittle (E) refuse — 11. A B C D E

12. OBSOLETE: (A) automobile (B) fancy (C) free (D) renovated (E) old — 12. A B C D E

13. BLASÉ: (A) indifferent (B) awed (C) afraid (D) cultured (E) worldly — 13. A B C D E

14. SANGUINE: (A) bloody (B) gloomy (C) happy (D) thin (E) red-faced — 14. A B C D E

15. LANGUID: (A) pusillanimous (B) indifferent (C) sad (D) vigorous (E) motley — 15. A B C D E

16. RESPITE: (A) recess (B) intermission (C) exertion (D) friendly (E) angry — 16. A B C D E

17. OBLOQUY: (A) shame (B) fame (C) name (D) colloquy (E) inquiry — 17. A B C D E

18. PLACATE: (A) nettle (B) label (C) soothe (D) reply (E) retaliate — 18. A B C D E

19. COMPLACENT: (A) satisfied (B) agreeable (C) nasty (D) querulous (E) asking — 19. A B C D E

20. ASSENT: (A) save (B) inquire (C) resent (D) introduce (E) disavow — 20. A B C D E

21. HUSBANDRY: (A) munificence (B) wife (C) frugality (D) matrimony (E) widower — 21. A B C D E

22. NOISOME: (A) quiet (B) salubrious (C) eager (D) foul (E) deodorant — 22. A B C D E

23. PERMANENT: (A) indifferent (B) tardy (C) mutable (D) improper (E) disheveled — 23. A B C D E

24. COVETOUS: (A) unfinished (B) uncovered (C) undesirous (D) birdlike (E) plying — 24. A B C D E

25. CORPOREAL: (A) sergeant (B) private (C) commissioned officer (D) spiritual (E) boatswain — 25. A B C D E

EXERCISE C

DIRECTIONS: For each question below, select the lettered word or phrase that comes closest to being *opposite* in meaning to the word appearing in capital letters. Be sure to consider all meanings carefully.

1.A B C D E

1. ZEALOT: (A) heretic (B) hypocrite (C) person who is careless (D) person who is rich (E) person who is indifferent

2.A B C D E

2. ABSTEMIOUS: (A) fastidious (B) punctilious (C) pusillanimous (D) dissipated (E) prodigal

3.A B C D E

3. SATIETY: (A) starvation (B) dissatisfaction (C) unfeigned (D) lowest class (E) grandeur

4.A B C D E

4. DECIDUOUS: (A) undecided (B) hesitant (C) evergreen (D) annual (E) perennial

5.A B C D E

5. INNOCUOUS: (A) large (B) toxic (C) spotless (D) impeccable (E) sober

6.A B C D E

6. GERMANE: (A) Teutonic (B) healthful (C) irrelevant (D) massive (E) puny

7.A B C D E

7. EGREGIOUS: (A) notorious (B) splendid (C) abortive (D) maturing (E) birdlike

8.A B C D E

8. NEPOTISM: (A) midnight (B) partiality (C) impartiality (D) dawn (E) noon

9.A B C D E

9. AUTONOMOUS: (A) magnanimous (B) ambiguous (C) exiguous (D) dependent (E) operated by hand

6.A B C D E

10. EXCULPATE: (A) pardon (B) destroy (C) create (D) convict (E) admonish

11.A B C D E

11. EARTHY: (A) pithy (B) salty (C) watery (D) refined (E) moldy

12.A B C D E

12. CONTENTIOUS: (A) pacific (B) bellicose (C) satisfied (D) dissatisfied (E) hungry

13.A B C D E

13. GAINSAY: (A) deny (B) lose money (C) audit (D) applaud (E) affirm

14. AMELIORATE: (A) harden (B) coarsen (C) aggravate (D) improve (E) scrape — 14. A B C D E

15. IGNOMINIOUS: (A) disgraceful (B) erudite (C) scholarly (D) incognito (E) laudatory — 15. A B C D E

16. EVANESCENT: (A) permanent (B) incandescent (C) ephemeral (D) putrid (E) perfunctory — 16. A B C D E

17. CORPULENT: (A) sallow (B) partnership (C) emaciated (D) entrepreneur (E) red-blooded — 17. A B C D E

18. JOCUND: (A) round (B) flat (C) jocular (D) jugular (E) melancholy — 18. A B C D E

19. HIBERNAL: (A) Irish (B) estival (C) English (D) festival (E) wintry — 19. A B C D E

20. EBULLIENT: (A) intoxicated (B) placid (C) effervescent (D) gregarious (E) jovial — 20. A B C D E

21. ASSUAGE: (A) meat (B) abate (C) individual (D) irritate (E) demonstrate — 21. A B C D E

22. INDIGENOUS: (A) alien (B) digestible (C) comestible (D) pleased (E) irate — 22. A B C D E

23. DEARTH: (A) birth (B) scantiness (C) abundance (D) bright (E) morning — 23. A B C D E

24. DELETERIOUS: (A) sane (B) intoxicated (C) sober (D) wholesome (E) adding — 24. A B C D E

25. FELL: (A) downed (B) risen (C) propitious (D) cruel (E) officer — 25. A B C D E

EXERCISE D

DIRECTIONS: For each question below, select the lettered word or phrase that comes closest to being *opposite* in meaning to the word appearing in capital letters. Be sure to consider all meanings carefully.

1. EXEMPLARY: (A) deplorable (B) imitative (C) good (D) conduct (E) addition — 1. A B C D E

2. CHOLERIC: (A) red (B) serene (C) severe (D) stern (E) irritable — 2. A B C D E

3.A B C D E || || || || ||
3. BAROQUE: (A) commoner (B) boat (C) rococo (D) simple (E) stupid

4.A B C D E || || || || ||
4. DILETTANTE: (A) amateur (B) professional (C) late (D) early (E) advancing

5.A B C D E || || || || ||
5. AMORPHOUS: (A) diaphanous (B) translucent (C) organized (D) opaque (E) chaotic

6.A B C D E || || || || ||
6. CAPRICIOUS: (A) whimsical (B) consistent (C) goatlike (D) honest (E) hypocritical

7.A B C D E || || || || ||
7. SALUBRIOUS: (A) healthy (B) plagued (C) rustic (D) fashioned (E) miasmic

8.A B C D E || || || || ||
8. DISPARITY: (A) equality (B) aspersion (C) allusion (D) equanimity (E) suture

9.A B C D E || || || || ||
9. APOTHEGM: (A) perpendicular (B) pithy statement (C) prolix statement (D) terse statement (E) letter

10.A B C D E || || || || ||
10. CHARY: (A) lavish (B) malevolent (C) insinuating (D) sparing (E) irritable

11.A B C D E || || || || ||
11. CANDOR: (A) hypocrisy (B) ingenuousness (C) sweetmeat (D) pleasure (E) velocity

12.A B C D E || || || || ||
12. EQUIVOCATE: (A) lie (B) whisper (C) balance (D) tell truth (E) be unequal

13.A B C D E || || || || ||
13. ESTRANGED: (A) reconciled (B) separated (C) foreign (D) traded (E) embarrassed

14.A B C D E || || || || ||
14. PRETENTIOUS: (A) real (B) excusing (C) modest (D) unpardonable (E) typical

15.A B C D E || || || || ||
15. SUB ROSA: (A) under the rose (B) clandestinely (C) fashionable (D) open (E) simple

16.A B C D E || || || || ||
16. SUBSERVIENT: (A) obsequious (B) omnipresent (C) oligarchy (D) haughty (E) miserly

17.A B C D E || || || || ||
17. UNTENABLE: (A) rented (B) maintainable (C) occupied (D) permanent (E) picayune

18. HERBIVOROUS: (A) ravenous (B) omnivorous (C) carnivorous (D) voracious (E) veracious — 18. A B C D E

19. OPULENCE: (A) glamor (B) sobriety (C) badinage (D) penury (E) petulance — 19. A B C D E

20. THRENODY: (A) elegy (B) eulogy (C) ballade (D) paean (E) epic — 20. A B C D E

21. VAUNTED: (A) lauded (B) belittled (C) crept (D) worried (E) wicked — 21. A B C D E

22. CEDE: (A) yield (B) harvest (C) annex (D) examine (E) mimic — 22. A B C D E

23. OBFUSCATE: (A) clarify (B) magnify (C) intensify (D) belittle (E) becloud — 23 A B C D E

24. CONCAVE: (A) hollow (B) solid (C) convex (D) complex (E) broken — 24. A B C D E

25. PRECIPITATE: (A) wary (B) steep (C) audacious (D) masterly (E) conquered — 25. A B C D E

Answer Key

Antonyms

EXERCISE A

1. A	11. B	21. E
2. C	12. C	22. C
3. D	13. B	23. B
4. A	14. A	24. C
5. D	15. A	25. E
6. E	16. E	
7. D	17. C	
8. B	18. C	
9. E	19. B	
10. A	20. C	

EXERCISE B

1. A	11. B	21. A
2. B	12. D	22. B
3. A	13. B	23. C
4. B	14. B	24. C
5. C	15. D	25. D
6. B	16. C	
7. C	17. B	
8. A	18. A	
9. D	19. D	
10. E	20. E	

EXERCISE C

1. E	11. D	21. D
2. D	12. A	22. A
3. A	13. E	23. C
4. C	14. C	24. D
5. B	15. E	25. C
6. C	16. A	
7. B	17. C	
8. C	18. E	
9. D	19. B	
10. D	20. B	

EXERCISE D

1. A	11. A	21. B
2. B	12. D	22. C
3. D	13. A	23. A
4. B	14. C	24. C
5. C	15. D	25. A
6. B	16. D	
7. E	17. B	
8. A	18. C	
9. C	19. D	
10. A	20. D	

Word-Pair Relationships

The purpose of this type of question, also known as an analogy, is to test your ability to determine relationships existing between pairs of words. This may involve finding a relationship between a tangible situation and a more abstract grouping or it may center around synonyms, antonyms, cause and effect, or other areas.

On the GMAT you are given a pair of words printed in capital letters and five other lettered pairs. You must select the pair of words from among the five lettered choices that best matches the relationship of the first pair. For example:

TREE : FOREST :: (A) daisy : meadow (B) grass : lawn (C) wheat : field (D) flower : garden (E) frog : pond

The first step in finding the answer to a word-pair relationship problem is to determine the relationship (rationale) existing between the initial word-pair. In this instance it is that a forest would not exist without trees. Looking at the choices you can see that B is the correct answer because a lawn would not exist without grass—TREE is to FOREST as *grass* is to *lawn.* The other choices are not satisfactory because a meadow can exist without daisies, a field can exist without wheat, gardens don't necessarily have to have flowers (e.g., vegetable garden), and ponds don't need frogs to exist.

Consider the following example:

POSSESS : LOSE :: (A) hesitate : advance (B) cease : recur (C) undertake : perform (D) continue : desist (E) produce : supply

The initial words are opposite in meaning. Therefore, you can immediately eliminate choices C and E as they represent synonyms. Choice A is poor because hesitate and advance aren't clear opposites. Choice B is better, but the concept of repetition in recur is not found in lose. Choice D is the best answer—POSSESS is to LOSE as *continue* is to *desist.*

As has been noted, there are many possible relationships that can exist between words. The following list presents some of the more common ones you may encounter.

1. Worker and article created

carpenter : house
writer : book
composer : symphony

2. Worker and tool used

carpenter : saw
writer : typewriter
surgeon : scalpel

3. Tool and object worked on

pencil : paper
saw : wood

4. The act the tool does to the object it works on

saw : wood (cuts)
knife : bread (cuts)
brake : car (stops)

5. Time sequence

early : late
dawn : twilight
sunrise : sunset

6. Cause and effect

germ : disease
carelessness : accident
explosion : debris

7. Degree of intensity

tepid : hot
joy : ecstasy
admiration : love

8. Class – species

furniture : chair
insect : grasshopper
mammal : whale
dog : poodle

9. Type – characteristic

cow : herbivorous
tiger : carnivorous

10. Grammatical relationships

I : mine (first person nominative case : first person possessive case)
wolf : vulpine (noun : adjective)
have : had (present tense : past tense)
alumnus : alumni (masculine singular noun : masculine plural noun)

11. Synonyms

lie : prevaricate
kind : benevolent

12. Antonyms

never : always
love : hate
fancy : plain
real : fictional

13. Homonyms

hour : our
their : there
wear : where

14. Rhyming

had : bad
some : come
fall : tall

15. Person and thing he seeks

alchemist : gold
prospector : gold

16. Person and thing he learns to avoid

child : fire
pilot : reef

17. Part to the whole

soldier : regiment
star : constellation

18. Sex

duck : drake
bull : cow

The following exercises will give you more practice in solving word-pair relationships. Use the *General Vocabulary List* to find the meanings of any words you don't know. Answers to all exercises are located after Exercise D.

Practice Exercises

Word-Pair Relationships

EXERCISE A

DIRECTIONS: For each question below, determine the relationship between the pair of capitalized words and then select the lettered pair of words which have a similar relationship to the first pair.

1.A B C D E

1. QUIXOTIC : FEASIBLE :: (A) sudden : workable (B) theoretical : practical (C) fashionable : efficient (D) precise : practicable (E) sad : adept

2.A B C D E

2. DEBATE : FORENSIC :: (A) drama : histrionic (B) opera : spoken (C) concerto : harmonizing (D) argument : domestic (E) novel : original

3.A B C D E

3. ANTHOLOGY : POEMS :: (A) antipasto : hors d'oeuvres (B) volume : book (C) encyclopedia : words (D) thesaurus : synonyms (E) medley : arrangement

4.A B C D E

4. ANHYDROUS : SATURATED :: (A) dry : wet (B) sweet : wet (C) cloying : full (D) stolid : liquid (E) physics : chemistry

5. WINE : GRAPES :: (A) champagne : raisins (B) liquor : intoxicating (C) vineyard : winery (D) whiskey : hops (E) vodka : potatoes — 5. A B C D E

6. NOTABLE : NOTORIOUS :: (A) philanthropic : benevolent (B) philandering : pleasant (C) heinous : atrocious (D) nefarious : secret (E) philanthropic : miserly — 6. A B C D E

7. ENTREPRENEUR : LABORER :: (A) profits : wages (B) arbitrator : capitalist (C) mediator : conflict (D) moonlighting : worker (E) capitalism : communism — 7. A B C D E

8. MORPHINE : SEDATES :: (A) drug : addicts (B) liquor : intoxicates (C) medicine : soothes (D) oil : smears (E) bandage : heals — 8. A B C D E

9. *HAMLET* : SOLILOQUY :: (A) *Macbeth* : tragedy (B) trust : monopoly (C) *Rigoletto* : quartet (D) *Othello* : jealousy (E) play : act — 9. A B C D E

10. CONTINENT : IMMORAL :: (A) land : evil (B) dissolute : lascivious (C) wanton : restrained (D) shore : reef (E) conscience : sin — 10. A B C D E

11. MENDICANT : IMPECUNIOUS :: (A) critic : quizzical (B) complainer : petulant (C) hat : askew (D) liar : poor (E) philanthropist : prodigal — 11. A B C D E

12. APOSTATE : RELIGION :: (A) loyal : faith (B) traitor : country (C) renegade : Indian (D) vital : church (E) disloyal : colonies — 12. A B C D E

13. DERMATOLOGIST : SKIN :: (A) paleontologist : statues (B) genealogist : genes (C) cardiologist : heart (D) astrologist : future (E) psychologist : insanity — 13. A B C D E

14. SEE : EYES :: (A) grapple : iron (B) grass : hands (C) lisp : speech (D) limp : limbs (E) sneeze : nostrils — 14. A B C D E

15. CYNOSURE : BRILLIANT :: (A) student : attentive (B) map : legible (C) rock : large (D) word : common (E) magnet : attractive — 15. A B C D E

16. NUMERATOR : DENOMINATOR :: (A) fraction : decimal (B) divisor : quotient (C) ratio : proportion (D) dividend : divisor (E) top : bottom — 16. A B C D E

17. NOISOME : GARBAGE :: (A) liquid : perfume (B) heavy : metal (C) loud : music (D) warmth : snow (E) fragrant : incense — 17. A B C D E

18.A B C D E **18.** SAD : DOLOROUS :: (A) rich : wealthy (B) smart : smattering (C) grief : healthy (D) giver : free (E) gratitude : frugal

19.A B C D E **19.** SCHOOL : TUITION :: (A) game : loss (B) lawyer : client (C) hospital : insurance (D) church : tithe (E) library : fine

20.A B C D E **20.** DISSERTATION : IDEAS :: (A) propaganda : facts (B) novel : theme (C) poem : emotions (D) play : acting (E) essay : novel

21.A B C D E **21.** NAIVE : INGENUOUS :: (A) ordinary : ingenious (B) old : wise (C) simple : kind (D) eager : reserved (E) sophisticated : urbane

22.A B C D E **22.** TERMAGANT : SHREW :: (A) anteater : mouse (B) virago : scold (C) supporter : nag (D) single : married (E) male : female

23.A B C D E **23.** CLOUD : STORM :: (A) container : contained (B) portent : disaster (C) cumulus : gale (D) thunder : lightning (E) rain : wind

24.A B C D E **24.** CONDUIT : WATER :: (A) pump : oil (B) behavior : liquid (C) artery : blood (D) wire : sound (E) electricity : television

25.A B C D E **25.** BREAD : OVEN :: (A) ceramics : kiln (B) silo : corn (C) pottery : wheel (D) iron : furnace (E) cake : stove

EXERCISE B

DIRECTIONS: For each question below, determine the relationship between the pair of capitalized words and then select the lettered pair of words which have a similar relationship to the first pair.

1.A B C D E **1.** LATITUDE : EQUATOR :: (A) direction : declension (B) weight : length (C) warp : woof (D) longitude : International Date Line (E) north pole : Arctic Circle

2.A B C D E **2.** ANTIMACASSAR : SOFA :: (A) rug : floor (B) table : chair (C) door : window (D) picture : frame (E) pillow : bed

3.A B C D E **3.** PERIMETER : ADDITION :: (A) arithmetic : geometric (B) exponential : quadratic (C) linear : logarithmic (D) triangle : sphere (E) area : multiplication

4. ACTUARY : INSURANCE :: (A) librarian : school (B) historian : dates (C) veterinarian : animal husbandry (D) agronomist : agreement (E) vegetarian : meat

4. A B C D E

5. ISOLATIONIST : ALOOF :: (A) altruist : selfish (B) pessimist : mournful (C) scholar : proud (D) bigot : tolerant (E) segregationist : gregarious

5. A B C D E

6. WATER : CONDUIT :: (A) electricity : magnet (B) elevator : shaft (C) shell : rifle (D) noise : cannon (E) soda : bottle

6. A B C D E

7. PLAINTIFF : DEFENDANT :: (A) court : law (B) injured : accused (C) judge : jury (D) district attorney : lawyer (E) nobleman : serf

7. A B C D E

8. EXPLOSIVE : VOLCANO :: (A) cold : mountain (B) arid : desert (C) humid : valley (D) misty : morning (E) fertile : plain

8. A B C D E

9. BIZARRE : EXOTIC :: (A) stage : dancer (B) commonplace : routine (C) wild : tame (D) ordinary : exceptional (E) lively : livid

9. A B C D E

10. DOCTOR : DISEASE :: (A) psychiatrist : maladjustment (B) teacher : pupils (C) scholar : knowledge (D) judge : crime (E) lawyer : law

10. A B C D E

11. SHOWER : DELUGE :: (A) irritation : rage (B) April : May (C) passion : affection (D) surprise party : exceptional (E) flow : surge

11. A B C D E

12. DRAMA : PLAYWRIGHT :: (A) act : actor (B) words : author (C) poetics : poet (D) review : critic (E) opera : musician

12. A B C D E

13. ALWAYS : NEVER :: (A) often : rarely (B) frequently : occasionally (C) constantly : frequently (D) intermittently : casually (E) occasionally : constantly

13. A B C D E

14. PRESIDENT : POPE :: (A) elected : chosen (B) ballot : smoke (C) proclamation : bull (D) temporal : secular (E) leader : religion

14. A B C D E

15. PERMANENT : EVANESCENT :: (A) durable : fleeting (B) lasting : glittering (C) eternal : everlasting (D) hairdo : bleach (E) wave : scene

15. A B C D E

16. ORNITHOLOGIST : BIRDS :: (A) aquarium : fish (B) anthropologist : insects (C) archeologist : artifacts (D) architect : buildings (E) botanist : animals

16. A B C D E

17.A B C D E || || || || ||

17. VERBS : ACTION :: (A) nouns : amplification (B) pronouns : demonstration (C) adjectives : modification (D) adverbs : connection (E) prepositions : definition

18.A B C D E || || || || ||

18. OAFISH : ASTUTE :: (A) net : gun (B) ocean : mountain (C) wise : smart (D) lake : thorough (E) simpleton : sage

19.A B C D E || || || || ||

19. SUGGEST : DEMAND :: (A) deny : request (B) affection : consolation (C) hint : blunder (D) give : receive (E) take : grab

20.A B C D E || || || || ||

20. VINDICABLE : REPREHENSIBLE :: (A) mild : serious (B) bitter : sad (C) mild : sad (D) solid : porous (E) vivid : dull

21.A B C D E || || || || ||

21. MULTIPLICATION : DIVISION :: (A) increase : decrease (B) zero : infinity (C) calculate : estimate (D) digit : series (E) integers : numbers

22.A B C D E || || || || ||

22. ABAB CDCD EFEF GG : ABBA ABBA CDE CDE :: (A) Italian : Petrarchan (B) Milton : Wordsworth (C) Shakespeare : Wordsworth (D) ballad : sonnet (E) Miltonic : Petrarchan

23.A B C D E || || || || ||

23. TRIANGLE : QUADRILATERAL :: (A) plane : solid (B) pentagon : hexagon (C) rectangle : octagon (D) cone : cube (E) regular : irregular

24.A B C D E || || || || ||

24. FINE : IMPRISONMENT :: (A) sentence : judgment (B) bail : bond (C) jury : judge (D) magistrate : judge (E) misdemeanor : felony

25.A B C D E || || || || ||

25. EINSTEIN : RELATIVITY :: (A) Aristotle : calculus (B) Newton : gravity (C) Pasteur : biology (D) Edison : mechanics (E) Galileo : chemistry

EXERCISE C

DIRECTIONS: For each question below, determine the relationship between the pair of capitalized words and then select the lettered pair of words which have a similar relationship to the first pair.

1.A B C D E || || || || ||

1. LIQUEFY : PETRIFY :: (A) water : stone (B) soften : frighten (C) cash in : strengthen (D) solvent : rich (E) insolvent : bankrupt

2.A B C D E || || || || ||

2. BELT : TROUSERS :: (A) braces : garters (B) trunk : tree (C) pillar : society (D) cables : trolley (E) cables : bridge

3. GASOLINE : PETROL :: (A) motor : car (B) engine : trunk (C) light : heavy (D) elevator : lift (E) refined : crude

3. A B C D E

4. RHYTHM : RHYME :: (A) poet : versifier (B) accent : sound (C) prose : poetry (D) versification : scansion (E) blank verse : free verse

4. A B C D E

5. SCHOLAR : ENTREPRENEUR :: (A) books : superstition (B) learning : studying (C) university : laboratory (D) knowledge : profits (E) knowledge : research

5. A B C D E

6. NECTAR : AMBROSIA :: (A) frankincense : myrrh (B) vegetable : fruit (C) taste : smell (D) goddess : god (E) drink : food

6. A B C D E

7. MUSLIN : BROCADE :: (A) ornate : decorated (B) simple : torn (C) gaudy : rich (D) plain : figured (E) multicolored : variegated

7. A B C D E

8. DERIVATION : LEXICOGRAPHER :: (A) evolution : biologist (B) origin : typographer (C) politics : anarchist (D) laws : court (E) foundation : roofer

8. A B C D E

9. EPAULET : SHOULDER :: (A) medal : chest (B) knapsack : back (C) sash : window (D) sword : scabbard (E) decoration : uniform

9. A B C D E

10. SHEEP : WOOL :: (A) fodder : animal (B) otter : fur (C) flax : cotton (D) animal : vegetable (E) stupid : good

10. A B C D E

11. NAIL : PUNCTURE :: (A) sword : scabbard (B) scalpel : incision (C) easel : picture (D) needle : sew (E) tire : flat

11. A B C D E

12. MISDEMEANOR : FELONY :: (A) imprisonment : bail (B) joy : ecstasy (C) gale : breeze (D) judge : magistrate (E) coward : criminal

12. A B C D E

13. SECRET SERVICE : F.B.I. :: (A) soldier : army (B) local : national (C) treasury : justice (D) policemen : detectives (E) open : undercover

13. A B C D E

14. FATUOUS : INANE :: (A) clever : inchoate (B) querulous : picayune (C) fatal : mordant (D) portentous : significant (E) cloying : viscous

14. A B C D E

15. LUNGS : BLOOD :: (A) heart : circulation (B) arteries : veins (C) carburetor : car (D) glands : secretions (E) carburetor : gasoline

15. A B C D E

16. A B C D E

16. SCALES : JUSTICE :: (A) weights : measures (B) markets : courts (C) torch : liberty (D) laurel : peace (E) balance : right

17. A B C D E

17. DIAPHANOUS : CACOPHONOUS :: (A) twofold : multiple (B) sheer : transparent (C) sheer : opaque (D) harmonious : discordant (E) transparent : noisy

18. A B C D E

18. BLEEDING : TOURNIQUET :: (A) drowning : resuscitation (B) sunstroke : fatigue (C) traffic : red light (D) coughing : elixir (E) disease : microbe

19. A B C D E

19. DETRITUS : GLACIERS :: (A) ice : icebergs (B) thaw : cold (C) silt : rivers (D) sediment : bottom (E) dregs : society

20. A B C D E

20. EXCULPATE : INCRIMINATE :: (A) exonerate : involve (B) free : fine (C) blame : criticize (D) blame : pardon (E) excuse : free

21. A B C D E

21. TRUMPET : BRASS :: (A) drums : hide (B) bugle : bronze (C) cello : string (D) orchestra : band (E) horn : metal

22. A B C D E

22. SANDPAPER : ABRASIVE :: (A) polish : floors (B) pumice : emulsion (C) gasoline : refined (D) oil : lubricant (E) gratuity : irritant

23. A B C D E

23. ALBEIT : ALTHOUGH :: (A) preposition : conjunction (B) conjunction : conjunction (C) conjunction : preposition (D) adjective : conjunction (E) conjunction : adverb

24. A B C D E

24. HABITS : INSTINCTS :: (A) work : play (B) training : heredity (C) acquired : cultivated (D) natural : unusual (E) birds : animals

25. A B C D E

25. AMBULATORY : BEDRIDDEN :: (A) wheelchair : bed (B) healthy : sick (C) strong : weak (D) broken arm : broken limb (E) free : confined

EXERCISE D

DIRECTIONS: For each question below, determine the relationship between the pair of capitalized words and then select the lettered pair of words which have a similar relationship to the first pair.

1. A B C D E

1. PARIAH : FAVORITE :: (A) nephew : son (B) hypnotism : comatose (C) sycophant : obsequious (D) ostracism : nepotism (E) chosen : accepted

2. GOLF : HOLES :: (A) badminton : feather (B) football : kick (C) baseball : innings (D) tennis : net (E) swimming : pool

2. A B C D E

3. INFANCY : SENILITY :: (A) conclusion : climax (B) incipient : critical (C) dawn : dusk (D) day : night (E) January : October

3. A B C D E

4. TIRADE : ABUSIVE :: (A) monologue : lengthy (B) aphorism : boring (C) prologue : precedent (D) encomium : laudatory (E) critique : insolent

4. A B C D E

5. GOOSE : GANDER :: (A) lion : lioness (B) shark : sharkskin (C) duck : drake (D) male : female (E) master : slave

5. A B C D E

6. BUSHEL : POTATOES :: (A) container : fruit (B) ounce : coal (C) wood : cord (D) point : diamond (E) bricks : mortar

6. A B C D E

7. PADDLE : CANOE :: (A) engine : train (B) auto : motor (C) oar : row (D) walk : run (E) steer : rudder

7. A B C D E

8. THERMOMETER : TEMPERATURE :: (A) minute : time (B) gauge : pressure (C) calendar : year (D) stopwatch : speed (E) barometer : air current

8. A B C D E

9. SYNTHESIS : CONSTRUCTION :: (A) artificial : building (B) dissection : analysis (C) excuse : denial (D) inductive : logical (E) artificial : true

9. A B C D E

10. PLEBISCITE : UKASE :: (A) vote : musical instrument (B) lack : abundance (C) public : ruler (D) written : oral (E) cancel : construct

10. A B C D E

11. IAMBIC : DACTYLIC :: (A) poem : essay (B) accent : sound (C) two : three (D) rhythm : hand (E) anapest : trochee

11. A B C D E

12. PARTNERSHIP : CORPORATION :: (A) two : many (B) local : national (C) agreement : conspiracy (D) conspiracy : plot (E) unlimited : limited

12. A B C D E

13. INKBLOT : EYE CHART :: (A) blurs : letters (B) blotter : spectacles (C) physician : specialist (D) psychiatrist : optometrist (E) oculist : ophthalmologist

13. A B C D E

14.A B C D E

14. TULIP : ZINNIA :: (A) Dutch : Swiss (B) garden : meadow (C) bulb : seed (D) annual : perennial (E) flower : grass

15.A B C D E

15. LIGAMENTS : BONES :: (A) fat : muscles (B) invertebrates : vertebrates (C) tear : fracture (D) invertebrates : mammals (E) heart : arm

16.A B C D E

16. LIKE : AS :: (A) conjunction : conjunction (B) conjunction : preposition (C) me : I (D) me : me (E) comparison : contrast

17.A B C D E

17. DEBATER : LARYNGITIS :: (A) actor : applause (B) doctor : diagnosis (C) writer : paper (D) pedestrian : lameness (E) swimmer : wet

18.A B C D E

18. DAFFODILS : TREES :: (A) spring : summer (B) fish : frogs (C) lake : meadow (D) snakes : grass (E) garden : orchard

19.A B C D E

19. KNIGHT : SHIELD :: (A) fencer : saber (B) soldier : carbine (C) welder : goggles (D) mechanic : wrench (E) lord : escutcheon

20.A B C D E

20. FURLONG : MILE :: (A) second : hour (B) degree : thermometer (C) foot : yard (D) ounce : pound (E) pint : gallon

21.A B C D E

21. SECURITY COUNCIL : ASSEMBLY :: (A) veto : no veto (B) Senate : House of Representatives (C) United Nations : League of Nations (D) strong : weak (E) unpopular : popular

22.A B C D E

22. CONVICTION : INTELLECT :: (A) speech : propaganda (B) belief : religion (C) facts : statistics (D) court : home (E) persuasion : emotion

23.A B C D E

23. BEREAVED : CONDOLENCES :: (A) guilty : accusation (B) faulty : eraser (C) robbed : insurance (D) victorious : wealth (E) destitute : charity

24.A B C D E

24. MERCURY : VENUS :: (A) furthest : nearest (B) asteroid : planet (C) Roman : Greek (D) speed : love (E) martial : marital

25.A B C D E

25. BRUSH : PAINT :: (A) hammer : nail (B) polish : floor (C) trowel : cement (D) match : fire (E) rake : lawn

Answer Key

Word-Pair Relationships

EXERCISE A

1. **B**	11. **B**	21. **E**
2. **A**	12. **B**	22. **B**
3. **D**	13. **C**	23. **B**
4. **A**	14. **B**	24. **C**
5. **E**	15. **E**	25. **A**
6. **E**	16. **D**	
7. **A**	17. **E**	
8. **B**	18. **A**	
9. **C**	19. **D**	
10. **C**	20. **C**	

EXERCISE B

1. **D**	11. **A**	21. **B**
2. **A**	12. **D**	22. **C**
3. **E**	13. **A**	23. **B**
4. **C**	14. **C**	24. **E**
5. **B**	15. **A**	25. **B**
6. **B**	16. **C**	
7. **B**	17. **C**	
8. **B**	18. **E**	
9. **B**	19. **E**	
10. **A**	20. **A**	

EXERCISE C

1. **A**	11. **B**	21. **C**
2. **E**	12. **B**	22. **D**
3. **D**	13. **C**	23. **B**
4. **B**	14. **D**	24. **B**
5. **D**	15. **E**	25. **E**
6. **E**	16. **C**	
7. **B**	17. **E**	
8. **A**	18. **C**	
9. **A**	19. **C**	
10. **B**	20. **A**	

EXERCISE D

1. **D**	11. **C**	21. **A**
2. **C**	12. **E**	22. **E**
3. **C**	13. **D**	23. **E**
4. **D**	14. **C**	24. **D**
5. **C**	15. **C**	25. **C**
6. **D**	16. **C**	
7. **A**	17. **D**	
8. **B**	18. **E**	
9. **B**	19. **C**	
10. **C**	20. **E**	

Sentence Completions

This type of question is designed to test your skills in vocabulary *usage* and your ability to recognize consistency among the elements in a sentence. You are given a sentence in which one or two words have been omitted. You must select from five lettered choices the word or words that when inserted in the sentence blanks best completes the meaning of the sentence.

In effect, these questions are a form of reading comprehension. If you are able to recognize the implication of a sentence, you will be able to choose the words that relate to this implication. At times your knowledge of a particular fact may help you choose the correct answer, but for the most part you must depend upon your ability to understand and use language. For this reason you should make sure you understand the *usage* of all vocabulary words you learn.

When answering sentence completion questions, look for key words to assist you in determining the idea being expressed in each sentence. Consider the following examples.

Because the enemy had a reputation for engaging in sneak attacks, we were ____ on the alert.

(A) inevitably
(B) frequently
(C) constantly
(D) evidently
(E) occasionally

A B C D E
|| || || || ||

The key words here are *sneak attacks* and *alert*. The missing word refers to the degree of alertness necessary for protection against sneak attacks. Since one must always be on the alert when faced with the possibility of sneak attacks, choice C, constantly, is the best answer. Choices B and E can be eliminated because neither indicates steady alertness. Choices A and D are possible answers, but C is the best choice.

____ has introduced the tremendous problem of the ____ of the hundreds of workers replaced by machines.

(A) Specialization . . . relocation
(B) Automation . . . retraining
(C) Unemployment . . . education
(D) Disease . . . recovery
(E) Machinery . . . training

A B C D E
|| || || || ||

In this sentence the key words are *problem* and *replaced by machines.* Choice B, automation . . . retraining and Choice E, machinery . . . training, both pertain to machines. Choice B, however, is better because *automation* implies replacing by machines and *retraining* states the problem resulting from this replacement. The other choices don't fit into the context of the sentence.

The following exercises will help you become more adept at sentence completions. Answers to the exercises appear after Exercise D.

Practice Exercises

Sentence Completions

EXERCISE A

DIRECTIONS: For each sentence below, select the lettered word or set of words which, when inserted in the sentence blanks, best complete the meaning of that sentence.

1.A B C D E
|| || || || ||

1. The literary artist, concerned solely with the creation of a book or story as close to perfection as his powers will permit, is generally a quiet individual, contemplative, ____.

(A) effuse
(B) somnolent
(C) retiring
(D) poetic
(E) gregarious

2.A B C D E
|| || || || ||

2. He was so ____ at tying fishermen's flies that he was asked to demonstrate his technique at sports fairs and exhibitions.

(A) applicable
(B) adroit
(C) fancy
(D) gauche
(E) impressed

3.A B C D E
|| || || || ||

3. No punishment is too severe for such an ____ crime; it is almost impossible to understand its enormity.

(A) avaricious
(B) apposite
(C) exemplary
(D) arbitrary
(E) egregious

4.A B C D E
|| || || || ||

4. He was so convinced that people were driven by ____ motives that he could not believe that anyone could be unselfish.

(A) selfless
(B) personal
(C) altruistic
(D) ulterior
(E) intrinsic

5. When the infant displayed signs of illness, the anxious parents called in a ____.

(A) podiatrist
(B) pediatrician
(C) practitioner
(D) pedagogue
(E) plagiarist

5. A B C D E

6. I can recommend him for this position because I have always found him ____ and reliable.

(A) voracious
(B) veracious
(C) vindictive
(D) valorous
(E) mendacious

6. A B C D E

7. No hero of ancient or modern times can surpass the Indian with his lofty contempt of death and the ____ with which he sustained the cruelest affliction.

(A) assent
(B) fortitude
(C) guile
(D) concern
(E) reverence

7. A B C D E

8. Sitting so close to the ____ section of the orchestra, I found that the incessant beating of the drums gave me a headache.

(A) string
(B) brass
(C) wind
(D) percussion
(E) front

8. A B C D E

9. I could not wish for a more ____ occasion on which to announce my plans for enlarging our establishment.

(A) ominous
(B) propitious
(C) magnificent
(D) pronounced
(E) portentous

9. A B C D E

10. We ask for ____ from others, yet we are never merciful ourselves.

(A) clemency
(B) culpability
(C) sincerity
(D) selectivity
(E) consideration

10. A B C D E

11. To prevent a repetition of this dreadful occurrence, we must discover the ____ element in the food that was served.

(A) unknown
(B) toxic
(C) benign
(D) tawdry
(E) heinous

11. A B C D E

12. The concept of ____ grouping of people with similar interests and abilities was very popular among educators.

(A) segregated
(B) integrated
(C) heterogeneous
(D) homogeneous
(E) congruent

12. A B C D E

13. A B C D E

13. His theories were so ____ that few could see what he was trying to establish.

(A) logical
(B) erudite
(C) scholarly
(D) theoretical
(E) nebulous

14. A B C D E

14. When I first began to study words in families, I was unaware that *protagonist* was the opposite of *antagonist*, that ____ was the opposite of *zenith*.

(A) *apex*
(B) *rood*
(C) *solstice*
(D) *nadir*
(E) *hegira*

15. A B C D E

15. Your ____ attitude will alienate any supporters you may have won to your cause.

(A) fascinating
(B) humanitarian
(C) logical
(D) truculent
(E) tortuous

16. A B C D E

16. We do not mean to be disrespectful when we refuse to follow the advice of our ____ leader.

(A) venerable
(B) respectful
(C) famous
(D) gracious
(E) dynamic

17. A B C D E

17. I fail to understand why there is such a ____ atmosphere; we have lost a battle, not a war.

(A) funereal
(B) blatant
(C) giddy
(D) sanguine
(E) haughty

18. A B C D E

18. When he recited the passage by ____, he revealed that he was reproducing ____ without understanding their meaning.

(A) sounds—meaning
(B) sounds—pronunciation
(C) effects—cause
(D) rote—sounds
(E) ideas—message

19. A B C D E

19. Something that is ____ is not ____.

(A) trite—boring
(B) violent—vivid
(C) common—a cliché
(D) elastic—resilient
(E) hackneyed—original

20. A B C D E

20. When he realized that he had been induced to sign the contract by ____, he threatened to institute legal proceedings to ____ the agreement.

(A) force—nullify
(B) innuendo—negate
(C) chicanery—cancel
(D) flattery—liquidate
(E) hypnotism—validate

21. An individual who is ____ is incapable of ____.

(A) fettered – flight
(B) modest – shame
(C) penurious – thought
(D) militant – fear
(E) ambitious – failure

21. A B C D E

22. His ____ was so marked that I teasingly suggested that he had seen a ____.

(A) clumsiness – vision
(B) pallor – spectre
(C) demeanor – physician
(D) separation – lawyer
(E) visage – ghost

22. A B C D E

23. A ____ statement is an ____ comparison.

(A) sarcastic – unfair
(B) blatant – overt
(C) sanguine – inherent
(D) metaphorical – implied
(E) bellicose – ardent

23. A B C D E

24. The hostess attempted to ____ a romantic atmosphere that would bring the two young people together in ____.

(A) simulate – conflict
(B) expand – fealty
(C) introduce – cacophony
(D) contrive – matrimony
(E) present – collusion

24. A B C D E

25. Old legends of extinct religions come down to us as ____ and ____.

(A) romance – chivalry
(B) myths – fables
(C) dreams – visions
(D) predictions – prophecies
(E) miracles – epiphanies

25. A B C D E

EXERCISE B

DIRECTIONS: For each sentence below, select the lettered word or set of words which, when inserted in the sentence blanks, best complete the meaning of that sentence.

1. As I recall my plane trip around the world last July and August, I think my greatest difficulty was the adjustment to the different ____ served with the food in the various cities we visited.

(A) ingredients
(B) condiments
(C) qualities
(D) grades
(E) varieties

1. A B C D E

2. After several ____ attempts to send the missile into space, the spacecraft was finally launched successfully.

(A) abortive
(B) difficult
(C) experimental
(D) preliminary
(E) excellent

2. A B C D E

3. A B C D E

3. He worked _____ at his task for weeks before he felt satisfied that the results would justify his long effort.

(A) occasionally
(B) regularly
(C) patiently
(D) assiduously
(E) intermittently

4. A B C D E

4. His book was marred by the many _____ remarks, which made us forget his main theme.

(A) inappropriate
(B) humorous
(C) digressive
(D) opinionated
(E) slanted

5. A B C D E

5. Overindulgence _____ character as well as physical stamina.

(A) strengthens
(B) stimulates
(C) debilitates
(D) maintains
(E) provides

6. A B C D E

6. He was not _____ and preferred to be alone most of the time.

(A) antisocial
(B) gracious
(C) gregarious
(D) cordial
(E) handsome

7. A B C D E

7. The reasoning in this editorial is so _____ that we cannot see how anyone can be deceived by it.

(A) coherent
(B) special
(C) cogent
(D) specious
(E) chauvinistic

8. A B C D E

8. Since you have failed three of the last four tests, you cannot afford to be _____ about passing for the term.

(A) courteous
(B) relevant
(C) sanguine
(D) passive
(E) indolent

9. A B C D E

9. You are afraid to attack him directly; you, therefore, are resorting to _____.

(A) guile
(B) effrontery
(C) criticism
(D) innuendo
(E) condemnation

10. A B C D E

10. His _____ remarks are often embarrassing because of their frankness.

(A) sarcastic
(B) sadistic
(C) frank
(D) urbane
(E) ingenuous

11. The pioneers' greatest asset was not their material wealth but their ____.

(A) fortitude
(B) simplicity
(C) largesse
(D) companions
(E) possessions

11. A B C D E

12. Your ____ tactics may compel me to cancel the contract because the job must be finished on time.

(A) dilatory
(B) offensive
(C) obstructive
(D) infamous
(E) confiscatory

12. A B C D E

13. Some students are ____ and want to take only the courses for which they see immediate value.

(A) theoretical
(B) stupid
(C) pragmatic
(D) foolish
(E) opinionated

13. A B C D E

14. Because I find that hot summer weather ____ me and leaves me very tired, I try to leave the city every August and go to Maine.

(A) irritates
(B) bores
(C) enervates
(D) boils
(E) disturbs

14. A B C D E

15. Americans do not feel that ____ obedience and implicit submission to the will of another is necessary in order to maintain good government.

(A) titular
(B) blind
(C) partial
(D) verbal
(E) stark

15. A B C D E

16. Because his occupation required that he work at night and sleep during the day, he had an exceptionally ____ complexion.

(A) ghastly
(B) ruddy
(C) livid
(D) plain
(E) pallid

16. A B C D E

17. It is almost impossible at times to capture the ____ of words when we translate them into a foreign language.

(A) implications
(B) meanings
(C) denotations
(D) connotations
(E) essence

17. A B C D E

18. A B C D E

18. As ____ head of the organization, he attended social functions and civic meetings but had no ____ in the formulation of company policy.

(A) titular—voice
(B) complete—vote
(C) titular—pride
(D) real—competition
(E) actual—superior

19. A B C D E

19. Unlike the Shakespearean plays, the "closet dramas" of the nineteenth century were meant to be ____ rather than ____.

(A) seen—acted
(B) read—acted
(C) quiet—loud
(D) sophisticated—urbane
(E) produced—acted

20. A B C D E

20. The collapse of the financial empire set up by the small group was more than a ____; it affected millions of small ____.

(A) threat—men
(B) vision—speculators
(C) debacle—investors
(D) disaster—homeowners
(E) calamity—prospectors

21. A B C D E

21. Employers who retire people who are willing and able to continue working should realize that ____ age is not an effective ____ in determining whether an individual is capable of working.

(A) physical—barrier
(B) chronological—factor
(C) intellectual—criterion
(D) chronological—criterion
(E) declining—standard

22. A B C D E

22. Her true feelings ____ themselves in her sarcastic asides; only then was her ____ revealed.

(A) concealed—sweetness
(B) manifested—bitterness
(C) hid—sarcasm
(D) developed—anxiety
(E) grieved—charm

23. A B C D E

23. To ____ is to try to ____ an individual.

(A) gainsay—corrupt
(B) evacuate—dismiss
(C) exhume—bury
(D) proselytize—convert
(E) inhibit—frighten

24. A B C D E

24. When I listened to his cogent arguments, all my ____ were ____ and I was forced to agree with his point of view.

(A) senses—stimulated
(B) doubts—confirmed
(C) friends—present
(D) questions—asked
(E) doubts—dispelled

25. She was ____ because her plans had gone ____.

(A) pleased – awry
(B) imminent – efficiently
(C) foiled – well
(D) importunate – splendidly
(E) distraught – awry

25. A B C D E

EXERCISE C

DIRECTIONS: For each sentence below, select the lettered word or set of words which, when inserted in the sentence blanks, best complete the meaning of that sentence.

1. The ties that bind us together in common activity are so ____ that they can disappear at any moment.

(A) tentative
(B) tenuous
(C) restrictive
(D) consistent
(E) tenacious

1. A B C D E

2. I did not anticipate reading such an ____ discussion of the international situation in the morning newspaper; normally, such a treatment could be found only in scholarly magazines.

(A) erudite
(B) arrogant
(C) ingenious
(D) overt
(E) analytical

2. A B C D E

3. We need more men of culture and enlightenment; we have too many ____ among us.

(A) boors
(B) students
(C) philistines
(D) pragmatists
(E) philosophers

3. A B C D E

4. The Trojan War proved to the Greeks that cunning and ____ were often more effective than military might.

(A) treachery
(B) artifice
(C) strength
(D) wisdom
(E) beauty

4. A B C D E

5. His remarks were filled with ____, which sounded lofty but presented nothing new to the audience.

(A) aphorisms
(B) platitudes
(C) bombast
(D) adages
(E) symbols

5. A B C D E

6. Achilles had his ____, Hitler had his Elite Corps.

(A) myrmidons
(B) antagonists
(C) arachnids
(D) myriads
(E) anchorites

6. A B C D E

7. A B C D E

7. In order to photograph _____ animals, elaborate flashlight equipment is necessary.

(A) predatory
(B) wild
(C) nocturnal
(D) live
(E) rare

8. A B C D E

8. He was deluded by the _____ who claimed he could cure all diseases with his miracle machine.

(A) salesman
(B) inventor
(C) charlatan
(D) doctor
(E) practitioner

9. A B C D E

9. The attorney protested that the testimony being offered was not _____ to the case and asked that it be stricken from the record as irrelevant.

(A) favorable
(B) coherent
(C) harmful
(D) beneficial
(E) germane

10. A B C D E

10. Automation threatens mankind with an increased number of _____ hours.

(A) meager
(B) useless
(C) active
(D) complex
(E) idle

11. A B C D E

11. I was so bored with the verbose and redundant style of that writer that I welcomed the change to the _____ style of this author.

(A) prolix
(B) consistent
(C) terse
(D) logistical
(E) tacit

12. A B C D E

12. Such doltish behavior was not expected from so _____ an individual.

(A) exasperating
(B) astute
(C) cowardly
(D) enigmatic
(E) democratic

13. A B C D E

13. Disturbed by the _____ nature of the plays being presented, the Puritans closed the theaters in 1642.

(A) mediocre
(B) fantastic
(C) moribund
(D) salacious
(E) witty

14. A B C D E

14. John left his position with the company because he felt that advancement was based on _____ rather than on ability.

(A) chance
(B) seniority
(C) nepotism
(D) superciliousness
(E) maturation

15. He became quite overbearing and domineering once he had become accustomed to the ____ shown to soldiers by the natives; he enjoyed his new sense of power. 15. A B C D E

(A) ability
(B) domesticity
(C) deference
(D) culpability
(E) insolence

16. Epicureans live for the ____ of their senses. 16. A B C D E

(A) mortification
(B) removal
(C) gratification
(D) gravity
(E) lassitude

17. I grew more and more aware of Iago's ____ purpose as I watched him plant the seeds of suspicion in Othello's mind. 17. A B C D E

(A) noble
(B) meritorious
(C) fell
(D) insincere
(E) hypocritical

18. Her reaction to his proposal was ____; she rejected it ____. 18. A B C D E

(A) inevitable – vehemently
(B) subtle – violently
(C) clever – obtusely
(D) sympathetic – angrily
(E) garrulous – tersely

19. ____ is the mark of the ____. 19. A B C D E

(A) Timorousness – hero
(B) Thrift – impoverished
(C) Avarice – philanthropist
(D) Trepidation – coward
(E) Vanity – obsequious

20. If you carry this ____ attitude to the conference, you will ____ any supporters you may have at this moment. 20. A B C D E

(A) belligerent – delight
(B) truculent – alienate
(C) conciliatory – defer
(D) supercilious – attract
(E) ubiquitous – alienate

21. It hurt my pride to be forced to ____ a person who always insulted me; nevertheless, I tried to ____ him. 21. A B C D E

(A) rebuke – condign
(B) respect – avenge
(C) propitiate – conciliate
(D) repudiate – evaluate
(E) intimidate – redeem

22. Because ____ is such an unsightly disease, its victims have frequently been shunned. 22. A B C D E

(A) leprosy
(B) cancer
(C) halitosis
(D) poverty
(E) tuberculosis

23.A B C D E
|| || || || ||

23. I am not attracted by the ____ life of the ____, always wandering through the countryside, begging for charity.

(A) proud – almsgiver
(B) noble – philanthropic
(C) urban – hobo
(D) natural – philosopher
(E) peripatetic – vagabond

24.A B C D E
|| || || || ||

24. The sugar dissolved in the water ____; finally all that remained was an almost ____ residue on the bottom of the glass.

(A) quickly – lumpy
(B) immediately – fragrant
(C) gradually – imperceptible
(D) subsequently – glassy
(E) spectacularly – opaque

25.A B C D E
|| || || || ||

25. It is foolish to vent your spleen on an ____ object; still, you make ____ enemies that way.

(A) inanimate – fewer
(B) immobile – bitter
(C) interesting – curious
(D) insipid – fewer
(E) humane – more

EXERCISE D

DIRECTIONS: For each sentence below, select the lettered word or set of words which, when inserted in the sentence blanks, best complete the meaning of that sentence.

1.A B C D E
|| || || || ||

1. Architects travel to Greece and ____ to study the Parthenon and the Pantheon.

(A) Cyprus
(B) Turkey
(C) France
(D) Spain
(E) Italy

2.A B C D E
|| || || || ||

2. The discoveries of science often are a mixed blessing; on the one hand they give us valuable pesticides that enable the farmer to grow more abundant crops and on the other hand they ____ the benefits by destroying the balance of nature.

(A) compromise
(B) misplace
(C) mollify
(D) damage
(E) counteract

3.A B C D E
|| || || || ||

3. If we ____ these experienced people to positions of unimportance because of their political persuasions, we shall lose the services of valuably trained personnel.

(A) define
(B) propel
(C) relegate
(D) constrict
(E) detract

4. His ____ directions misled us; we did not know which of the two roads to take.

(A) foolish
(B) complicated
(C) extenuating
(D) ambiguous
(E) arbitrary

4. A B C D E

5. I am afraid that you will have to alter your ____ views in the light of the tragic news that has just arrived.

(A) roseate
(B) tragic
(C) contrary
(D) narrow
(E) dour

5. A B C D E

6. You were frightened by a concept that you ____ in your own mind.

(A) accepted
(B) idealized
(C) sought
(D) externalized
(E) created

6. A B C D E

7. Although there are ____ outbursts of gunfire, we can report that the major rebellion has been suppressed.

(A) bitter
(B) heinous
(C) meager
(D) nocturnal
(E) sporadic

7. A B C D E

8. He was guided by ____ rather than by ethical considerations.

(A) expediency
(B) precepts
(C) morality
(D) consequence
(E) sophistry

8. A B C D E

9. We now know that what constitutes practically all matter is empty space; relatively enormous ____ in which revolve with lightning velocity infinitesimal particles so small that they have never been seen or photographed.

(A) seas
(B) particles
(C) areas
(D) skies
(E) voids

9. A B C D E

10. To be ____ is to be without ____.

(A) credulous—gullibility
(B) considerate—incredibility
(C) belligerent—pugnacity
(D) maudlin—tenacity
(E) gullible—skepticism

10. A B C D E

11. His listeners enjoyed his ____ wit but his victims often ____ at its satire.

(A) lugubrious—suffered
(B) taut—smiled
(C) bitter—smarted
(D) lugubrious—smiled
(E) trenchant—winced

11. A B C D E

12. A B C D E || || || || ||

12. An occasional ____ remark spoiled the ____ that made the paper memorable.

(A) trite – clichés
(B) colloquial – verisimilitude
(C) hackneyed – originality
(D) urbane – sophistication
(E) jocund – gaiety

13. A B C D E || || || || ||

13. Unlike the carefully weighed and ____ compositions of Dante, Goethe's writings have always the sense of ____ and enthusiasm.

(A) inspired – vigor
(B) spontaneous – immediacy
(C) contrived – languor
(D) planned – immediacy
(E) developed – construction

14. A B C D E || || || || ||

14. In Homer's work, Achilles is the ____ of Greek warriors; Odysseus ____ the shrewd man.

(A) epitome – abhors
(B) antithesis – exemplifies
(C) paragon – exemplifies
(D) prototype – eschews
(E) adversary – abhors

15. A B C D E || || || || ||

15. ____ enables us to know the past and to use it in preparing for the future.

(A) Beauty
(B) Truth
(C) Language
(D) Antiquity
(E) Thought

16. A B C D E || || || || ||

16. Victims of glaucoma find that their ____ vision is impaired and that they can no longer see objects not directly in front of them.

(A) peripatetic
(B) peripheral
(C) periphrastic
(D) ocular
(E) perspicacious

17. A B C D E || || || || ||

17. The child's earliest words deal with concrete objects and actions; it is much later that he is able to grapple with ____.

(A) decisions
(B) abstractions
(C) maxims
(D) opponents
(E) mathematics

18. A B C D E || || || || ||

18. It is regrettable that the author saved many of his most brilliant lines for the ____; by that time, most of the audience had left.

(A) ingenue
(B) epilogue
(C) climax
(D) curtain
(E) book

19. It would be difficult for one so ____ to be led to believe that all men are equal and that we must disregard race, color, and creed.

19. A B C D E

(A) emotional
(B) broadminded
(C) tolerant
(D) intolerant
(E) democratic

20. The ____ of our civilization from an agricultural society to today's complex industrial world was accompanied by upheaval and, all too often, war.

20. A B C D E

(A) adjustment
(B) migration
(C) phasing
(D) metamorphosis
(E) route

21. To be ____ is to be ____.

21. A B C D E

(A) petulant – agreeable
(B) turbid – swollen
(C) torpid – sluggish
(D) turgid – clear
(E) evergreen – deciduous

22. Man is essentially a ____ animal and tends to ____ others.

22. A B C D E

(A) selfish – resent
(B) vicarious – work with
(C) maudlin – belittle
(D) perverse – adopt
(E) gregarious – associate with

23. Singers have a definite advantage over musicians who play an instrument; they can appeal to us through ____ as well as ____.

23. A B C D E

(A) personality – charm
(B) emotions – sounds
(C) thoughts – ideas
(D) ideas – music
(E) sight – personality

24. Because the inspector gave the plant a ____ examination, he ____ many defects.

24. A B C D E

(A) semiannual – uncovered
(B) significant – neglected
(C) perfunctory – overlooked
(D) pertinent – unveiled
(E) routine – discovered

25. The playwright was known not for his original ideas but for his ____ of ideas that had been propounded by others.

25. A B C D E

(A) invention
(B) reiteration
(C) consideration
(D) enlightenment
(E) rejection

Answer Key

Sentence Completions

EXERCISE A

1. **C**	11. **B**	21. **A**
2. **B**	12. **D**	22. **B**
3. **E**	13. **E**	23. **D**
4. **D**	14. **D**	24. **D**
5. **B**	15. **D**	25. **B**
6. **B**	16. **A**	
7. **B**	17. **A**	
8. **D**	18. **D**	
9. **B**	19. **E**	
10. **A**	20. **C**	

EXERCISE B

1. **B**	11. **A**	21. **D**
2. **A**	12. **A**	22. **B**
3. **D**	13. **C**	23. **D**
4. **C**	14. **C**	24. **E**
5. **C**	15. **B**	25. **E**
6. **C**	16. **E**	
7. **D**	17. **D**	
8. **C**	18. **A**	
9. **D**	19. **B**	
10. **E**	20. **C**	

EXERCISE C

1. **B**	11. **C**	21. **C**
2. **A**	12. **B**	22. **A**
3. **C**	13. **D**	23. **E**
4. **B**	14. **C**	24. **C**
5. **B**	15. **C**	25. **A**
6. **A**	16. **C**	
7. **C**	17. **C**	
8. **C**	18. **A**	
9. **D**	19. **D**	
10. **D**	20. **B**	

EXERCISE D

1. **E**	11. **E**	21. **C**
2. **E**	12. **C**	22. **C**
3. **C**	13. **D**	23. **D**
4. **D**	14. **C**	24. **C**
5. **A**	15. **C**	25. **B**
6. **E**	16. **B**	
7. **E**	17. **B**	
8. **A**	18. **B**	
9. **E**	19. **D**	
10. **E**	20. **D**	

MATHEMATICS REVIEW

The Mathematics and Data Sufficiency areas of the GMAT require a working knowledge of mathematical principles, including an understanding of the fundamentals of algebra, geometry, and arithmetic, and the ability to interpret graphs. The following review covers these areas thoroughly and if used properly, will prove helpful in preparing for the mathematical parts of the GMAT.

Read through the review carefully. You will notice that each topic is keyed for easy reference. Use the key number next to each answer given in the Sample Tests to refer to those sections in the review that cover material you may have missed and therefore will need to spend more time on.

I. Arithmetic

I–1. Whole Numbers

1–1
The numbers 0,1,2,3, . . . are called whole numbers or *integers*. So 75 is an integer but $4\frac{1}{3}$ is not an integer.

1–2
If the integer k divides m evenly, then we say *m is divisible by k* or *k is a factor of m*. For example, 12 is divisible by 4, but 12 is not divisible by 5. 1,2,3,4,6,12 are all factors of 12.

If k is a factor of m, then there is another integer n such that $m = k \times n$; in this case, m is called a *multiple of k*.

Since $12 = 4 \times 3$, 12 is a multiple of 4 and also 12 is a multiple of 3. 5,10,15, and 20 are all multiples of 5 but 15 and 5 are not multiples of 10.

Any integer is a multiple of each of its factors.

1–3
Any whole number is divisible by itself and by 1. If p is a whole number greater than 1, which has *only* p and 1 as factors, then p is called a *prime number*. 2,3,5,7,11,13,17,19 and 23 are all primes. 14 is not a prime since it is divisible by 2 and by 7.

A whole number which is divisible by 2 is called an *even* number; if a whole number is not even, then it is an *odd* number. 2,4,6,8,10 are even numbers, and 1,3,5,7 and 9 are odd numbers.

A collection of numbers is *consecutive* if each number is the successor of the number which precedes it. For example, 7,8,9 and 10 are consecutive, but 7,8,10,13 are not. 4,6,8,10 are consecutive even numbers. 7,11,13,17 are consecutive primes. 7,13,19,23 are not consecutive primes since 11 is a prime between 7 and 13.

1–4

Any whole number can be written as a product of factors which are prime numbers.

To write a number as a *product of prime factors:*

(A) Divide the number by 2 if possible; continue to divide by 2 until the factor you get is not divisible by 2.
(B) Divide the result from (A) by 3 if possible; continue to divide by 3 until the factor you get is not divisible by 3.
(C) Divide the result from (B) by 5 if possible; continue to divide by 5 until the factor you get is not divisible by 5.
(D) Continue the procedure with 7,11, and so on, until all the factors are primes.

EXAMPLE 1: Express 24 as a product of prime factors.

(A) $24 = 2 \times 12$, $12 = 2 \times 6$, $6 = 2 \times 3$ so $24 = 2 \times 2 \times 2 \times 3$. Since each factor (2 and 3) is prime, $24 = 2 \times 2 \times 2 \times 3$.

EXAMPLE 2: Express 252 as a product of primes.

(A) $252 = 2 \times 126$, $126 = 2 \times 63$ and 63 is not divisible by 2, so $252 = 2 \times 2 \times 63$.
(B) $63 = 3 \times 21$, $21 = 3 \times 7$ and 7 is not divisible by 3. Since 7 is a prime, then $252 = 2 \times 2 \times 3 \times 3 \times 7$ and all the factors are primes.

1–5

A number m is a *common multiple* of two other numbers k and j if it is a multiple of each of them. For example, 12 is a common multiple of 4 and 6, since $3 \times 4 = 12$ and $2 \times 6 = 12$. 15 is not a common multiple of 3 and 6, because 15 is not a multiple of 6.

A number k is a *common factor* of two other numbers m and n if k is a factor of m and k is a factor of n.

The *least common multiple* (L.C.M.) of two numbers is the smallest number which is a common multiple of both numbers. To find the least common multiple of two numbers k and j:

(A) Write k as a product of primes and j as a product of primes.
(B) If there are any common factors *delete* them in *one* of the products.
(C) Multiply the remaining factors; the result is the least common multiple.

EXAMPLE 1: Find the L.C.M. of 12 and 11.

(A) $12 = 2 \times 2 \times 3$, $11 = 11 \times 1$.
(B) There are no common factors.
(C) The L.C.M. is $12 \times 11 = 132$.

EXAMPLE 2: Find the L.C.M. of 27 and 63.

(A) $27 = 3 \times 3 \times 3$, $63 = 3 \times 3 \times 7$.
(B) $3 \times 3 = 9$ is a common factor so delete it once.
(C) The L.C.M. is $3 \times 3 \times 3 \times 7 = 189$.

You can find the L.C.M. of a collection of numbers in the same way except that if in step (B) the common factors are factors of more than two of the numbers, then delete the common factor in *all but one* of the products.

EXAMPLE 3: Find the L.C.M. of 27, 63 and 72.

(A) $27 = 3 \times 3 \times 3$, $63 = 3 \times 3 \times 7$, $72 = 2 \times 2 \times 2 \times 3 \times 3$.
(B) Delete 3×3 from two of the products.
(C) The L.C.M. is $3 \times 7 \times 2 \times 2 \times 2 \times 3 \times 3 = 21 \times 72 = 1{,}512$.

I–2. Fractions

2–1

A FRACTION is a number which represents a ratio or division of two whole numbers (integers). A fraction is written in the form $\frac{a}{b}$. The number on the top, a, is called the numerator; the number on the bottom, b, is called the denominator. The denominator tells how many equal parts there are (for example, parts of a pie); the numerator tells how many of these equal parts are taken. For example, $\frac{5}{8}$ is a fraction whose numerator is 5 and whose denominator is 8; it represents taking 5 of 8 equal parts, or dividing 8 into 5.

A fraction can not have 0 as a denominator since division by 0 is not defined.
A fraction with 1 as the denominator is the same as the whole number which is its numerator. For example, $\frac{12}{1}$ is 12, $\frac{0}{1}$ is 0.

If the numerator and denominator of a fraction are identical, the fraction represents 1. For example, $\frac{3}{3} = \frac{9}{9} = \frac{13}{13} = 1$. Any whole number, k, is represented by a fraction with a numerator equal to k times the denominator. For example, $\frac{18}{6} = 3$, and $\frac{30}{5} = 6$.

2–2

Mixed Numbers. A mixed number consists of a whole number and a fraction. For example, $7\frac{1}{4}$ is a mixed number; it means $7 + \frac{1}{4}$ and $\frac{1}{4}$ is called the fractional part of the mixed number $7\frac{1}{4}$. Any mixed number can be changed into a fraction:

(A) Multiply the whole number by the denominator of the fraction.
(B) Add the numerator of the fraction to the result of step A.
(C) Use the result of step B as the numerator and use the denominator of the fractional part of the mixed number as the denominator. This fraction is equal to the mixed number.

EXAMPLE 1: Write $7\frac{1}{4}$ as a fraction.

(A) $4 \cdot 7 = 28$
(B) $28 + 1 = 29$
(C) so $7\frac{1}{4} = \frac{29}{4}$.

A fraction whose numerator is larger than its denominator can be changed into a mixed number.

(A) Divide the denominator into the numerator; the result is the whole number of the mixed number.
(B) Put the remainder from step A over the denominator; this is the fractional part of the mixed number.

EXAMPLE 2: Change $\frac{35}{8}$ into a mixed number.

(A) Divide 8 into 35; the result is 4 with a remainder of 3.
(B) $\frac{3}{8}$ is the fractional part of the mixed number.
(C) So $\frac{35}{8} = 4\frac{3}{8}$.

We can regard any whole number as a mixed number with 0 as the fractional part. For example, $\frac{18}{6} = 3$.

In calculations with mixed numbers, change the mixed numbers into fractions.

2–3

Multiplying Fractions. To multiply two fractions, multiply their numerators and divide this result by the product of their denominators.

In word problems, *of* usually indicates multiplication.

EXAMPLE: John saves $\frac{1}{3}$ of $240. How much does he save?

$$\frac{1}{3} \cdot \frac{240}{1} = \frac{240}{3} = \$80, \text{ the amount John saves.}$$

2–4

Dividing Fractions. One fraction is a *reciprocal* of another if their product is 1. So $\frac{1}{2}$ and 2 are reciprocals. To find the reciprocal of a fraction, simply interchange the numerator and denominator (turn the fraction upside down). This is called *inverting* the fractions. So when you invert $\frac{15}{17}$ you get $\frac{17}{15}$. When a fraction is inverted the inverted fraction and the original fraction are reciprocals. Thus $\frac{15}{17} \cdot \frac{17}{15} = \frac{255}{255} = \frac{1}{1} = 1$.

To divide one fraction (the dividend) by another fraction (the divisor), invert the divisor and multiply.

EXAMPLE 1: $\frac{5}{6} \div \frac{3}{4} = \frac{5}{6} \cdot \frac{4}{3} = \frac{20}{18}$

EXAMPLE 2: A worker makes a basket every $\frac{2}{3}$ hour. If the worker works for $7\frac{1}{2}$ hours, how many baskets will he make? We want to divide $\frac{2}{3}$ into $7\frac{1}{2}$, $7\frac{1}{2} = \frac{15}{2}$, so we want to divide $\frac{15}{2}$ by $\frac{2}{3}$. Thus

$$\frac{15}{2} \div \frac{2}{3} = \frac{15}{2} \cdot \frac{3}{2} = \frac{45}{4} = 10\frac{1}{4} \text{ baskets.}$$

2–5

Dividing and Multiplying by the Same Number. Since multiplication or division by 1 does not change the value of a number, you can multiply or divide any fraction by 1 and the fraction will remain the same. Remember that $\frac{a}{a} = 1$ for any non-zero number a. Therefore, if you multiply or divide any fraction by $\frac{a}{a}$, the result is the same as if you multiplied the numerator and denominator by a or divided the numerator or denominator by a.

If you multiply the numerator and denominator of a fraction by the same non-zero number the fraction remains the same.

If you divide the numerator and denominator of any fraction by the same non-zero number, the fraction remains the same.

Consider the fraction $\frac{3}{4}$. If we multiply 3 by 10 and 4 by 10, then $\frac{30}{40}$ must equal $\frac{3}{4}$.

When we multiply fractions, if any of the numerators and denominators have a common factor (see page 135 for factors) we can divide each of them by the common factor and the fraction remains the same. This process is called *cancelling* and can be a great time-saver.

EXAMPLE: Multiply $\frac{4}{9} \cdot \frac{75}{8}$. Since 4 is a common factor of 4 and 8, divide 4 and 8 by 4 getting $\frac{4}{9} \cdot \frac{75}{8} = \frac{1}{9} \cdot \frac{75}{2}$. Since 3 is a common factor of 9 and 75 divide 9 and 75 by 3 to get $\frac{1}{9} \cdot \frac{75}{2} = \frac{1}{3} \cdot \frac{25}{2}$. So $\frac{4}{9} \cdot \frac{75}{8} = \frac{1}{3} \cdot \frac{25}{2} = \frac{25}{6}$.

2–6

Equivalent Fractions. Two fractions are equivalent or equal if they represent the same ratio or number. In the last section, you saw that if you multiply or divide the numerator and denominator of a fraction by the same non-zero number the result is equivalent to the original fraction. For example, $\frac{7}{8} = \frac{70}{80}$ since $70 = 10 \times 7$ and $80 = 10 \times 8$.

In the test there will only be five choices, so your answer to a problem may not be the same as any of the given choices. You may have to express a fraction as an equivalent fraction.

To find a fraction with a known denominator equal to a given fraction:

(A) divide the denominator of the given fraction into the known denominator;
(B) multiply the result of (A) by the numerator of the given fraction; this is the numerator of the required equivalent fraction.

EXAMPLE: Find a fraction with denominator 30 which is equal to $\frac{2}{5}$:

(A) 5 into 30 is 6;
(B) $6 \cdot 2 = 12$ so $\frac{12}{30} = \frac{2}{5}$.

2–7

Reducing a Fraction to Lowest Terms. A fraction has been reduced to lowest terms when the numerator and denominator have no common factors.

For example, $\frac{3}{4}$ is reduced to lowest terms, but $\frac{3}{6}$ is not because 3 is a common factor of 3 and 6.

> To reduce a fraction to lowest terms, cancel all the common factors of the numerator and denominator. (Cancelling common factors will not change the value of the fraction.)

For example, $\frac{100}{150}=\frac{10\cdot 10}{10\cdot 15}=\frac{10}{15}=\frac{5\cdot 2}{5\cdot 3}=\frac{2}{3}$. Since 2 and 3 have no common factors, $\frac{2}{3}$ is $\frac{100}{150}$ reduced to lowest terms. A fraction is equivalent to the fraction reduced to lowest terms.

If you write the numerator and denominator as products of primes, it is easy to cancel all the common factors.

$$\frac{63}{81}=\frac{3\cdot 3\cdot 7}{3\cdot 3\cdot 3\cdot 3}=\frac{7}{9}$$

2–8

Adding Fractions. If the fractions have the same denominator, then the denominator is called a *common denominator*. Add the numerators, and use this sum as the new numerator with the common denominator as the denominator of the sum.

EXAMPLE 1: $\frac{5}{12}+\frac{3}{12}=\frac{5+3}{12}=\frac{8}{12}=\frac{2}{3}$

EXAMPLE 2: Jim uses 7 eggs to make breakfast and 8 eggs for supper. How many dozen eggs has he used? 7 eggs are $\frac{7}{12}$ of a dozen and 8 eggs are $\frac{8}{12}$ of a dozen. He used $\frac{7}{12}+\frac{8}{12}=\frac{7+8}{12}=\frac{15}{12}=\frac{5}{4}=1\frac{1}{4}$ dozen eggs.

If the fractions don't have the same denominator, you must first find a common denominator. Multiply all the denominators together; the result is a common denominator.

EXAMPLE: To add $\frac{1}{2}+\frac{2}{3}+\frac{7}{4}$, $2\cdot 3\cdot 4=24$ is a common denominator.

There are many common denominators; the smallest one is called the *least common denominator*. For the previous example, 12 is the least common denominator.

Once you have found a common denominator, express each fraction as an equivalent fraction with the common denominator, and add as you did for the case when the fractions had the same denominator.

EXAMPLE: $\frac{1}{2}+\frac{2}{3}+\frac{7}{4}=?$

(A) 24 is a common denominator.

(B) $\frac{1}{2}=\frac{12}{24}, \frac{2}{3}=\frac{16}{24}, \frac{7}{4}=\frac{42}{24}.$

(C) $\frac{1}{2}+\frac{2}{3}+\frac{7}{4}=\frac{12}{24}+\frac{16}{24}+\frac{42}{24}=\frac{12+16+42}{24}=\frac{70}{24}=\frac{35}{12}.$

2-9

Subtracting Fractions. When the fractions have the same denominator, subtract the numerators and place the result over the denominator.

EXAMPLE: $\frac{3}{5}-\frac{2}{5}=\frac{3-2}{5}=\frac{1}{5}$

When the fractions have different denominators

(A) Find a common denominator.
(B) Express the fractions as equivalent fractions with the same denominator.
(C) Subtract.

EXAMPLE: $\frac{3}{5}-\frac{2}{7}=?$

(A) A common denominator is $5 \cdot 7 = 35$.

(B) $\frac{3}{5}=\frac{21}{35}, \frac{2}{7}=\frac{10}{35}.$

(C) $\frac{3}{5}-\frac{2}{7}=\frac{21}{35}-\frac{10}{35}=\frac{21-10}{35}=\frac{11}{35}.$

2-10

Complex Fractions. A fraction whose numerator and denominator are themselves fractions is called a *complex fraction.* For example $\frac{2/3}{4/5}$ is a complex fraction. A complex fraction can always be simplified by dividing the fraction.

EXAMPLE 1: $\frac{2}{3} \div \frac{4}{5} = \frac{\cancel{2}^{1}}{3} \cdot \frac{5}{\cancel{4}_{2}} = \frac{1}{3} \cdot \frac{5}{2} = \frac{5}{6}$

EXAMPLE 2: It takes $2\frac{1}{2}$ hours to get from Buffalo to Cleveland traveling at a constant rate of speed. What part of the distance is traveled in $\frac{3}{4}$ of an hour?

$\frac{3/4}{2\ 1/2}=\frac{3/4}{5/2}=\frac{3}{4}\cdot\frac{2}{5}=\frac{3}{2}\cdot\frac{1}{5}=\frac{3}{10}$ of the distance.

I–3. Decimals

3–1

A collection of digits (the digits are 0,1,2, . . . ,9) after a period (called the decimal point) is called a *decimal fraction.* For example, .503, .5602, .32, and .4 are all decimal fractions.

Every decimal fraction represents a fraction. To find the fraction a decimal fraction represents:

(A) Take the fraction whose denominator is 10 and whose numerator is the first digit to the right of the decimal point.
(B) Take the fraction whose denominator is 100 and whose numerator is the second digit to the right of the decimal point.
(C) Take the fraction whose denominator is 1,000 and whose numerator is the third digit to the right of the decimal point.
(D) Continue the procedure until you have used each digit to the right of the decimal place. The denominator in each step is 10 times the denominator in the previous step.
(E) The *sum* of the fractions you have obtained in (A), (B), (C), and (D) is the fraction that the decimal fraction represents.

EXAMPLE 1: Find the fraction .503 represents.

(A) $\frac{5}{10}$

(B) $\frac{0}{100}$

(C) $\frac{3}{1000}$

(D) All the digits have already been used.

(E) So $.503 = \frac{5}{10} + \frac{0}{100} + \frac{3}{1000} = \frac{500}{1000} + \frac{0}{1000} + \frac{3}{1000} = \frac{503}{1000}$.

EXAMPLE 2: What fraction does .78934 represent?

(A) $\frac{7}{10}$

(B) $\frac{8}{100}$

(C) $\frac{9}{1000}$

(D) $\frac{3}{10,000}, \frac{4}{100,000}$

(E) So $.78934 = \frac{7}{10} + \frac{8}{100} + \frac{9}{1000} + \frac{3}{10,000} + \frac{4}{100,000} = \frac{78,934}{100,000}$.

Notice that the denominator of the last fraction you obtain in step (D) is a common denominator for all the previous denominators. Since each denominator is 10 times the previous one, the denominator of the final fraction of part (D) will be the product of r copies of 10 multiplied together (called 10^r) where r is the number of digits which appear in the decimal fraction. Therefore, a decimal fraction represents a fraction whose denominator is 10^r where r is the number of digits in the decimal fraction and whose numerator is the number represented by the digits of the decimal fraction.

EXAMPLE 3: What fraction does .5702 represent?

There are 4 digits in .5702. Therefore, the denominator is $10 \times 10 \times 10 \times 10 =$ 10,000, and the numerator is 5,702. Therefore, $.5702 = \frac{5{,}702}{10{,}000}$.

You can add any number of zeros to the right of a decimal fraction without changing its value.

EXAMPLE: $.3 = \frac{3}{10} = \frac{30}{100} = .30 = .30000 = \frac{30{,}000}{100{,}000} = .300000000 \ldots$

3–2

We call the first position to the right of the decimal point the tenths place, since the digit in that position tells you how many tenths you should take. (It is the numerator of a fraction whose denominator is 10.) In the same way, we call the second position to the right the hundredths place, the third position to the right the thousandths, and so on. This is similar to the way whole numbers are expressed, since 568 means $5 \times 100 + 6 \times 10 + 8 \times 1$. The various digits represent different numbers depending on their position: the first place to the left of the decimal point represents units, the second place to the left represents tens, and so on.

The following diagram may be helpful:

T	H	T	U		T	H	T
H	U	E	N		E	U	H
O	N	N	I	•	N	N	O
U	D	S	T		T	D	U
S	R		S		H	R	S
A	E				S	E	A
N	D					D	N
D	S					T	D
S						H	T
						S	H
							S

Thus, 5,342.061 means 5 thousands + 3 hundreds + 4 tens + 2 + 0 tenths + 6 hundredths + 1 thousandth.

3–3

A DECIMAL is a whole number plus a decimal fraction; the decimal point separates the whole number from the decimal fraction. For example, 4,307.206 is a decimal which represents 4,307 added to the decimal fraction .206. A decimal fraction is a decimal with zero as the whole number.

3–4

A fraction whose denominator is a multiple of 10 is equivalent to a decimal. The denominator tells you the last place that is filled to the right of the decimal point. Place the decimal point in the numerator so that the last place to the right of the decimal point corresponds to the denominator. If the numerator does not have enough digits, add the appropriate number of zeros *before* the numerator.

EXAMPLE 1: Find the decimal equivalent of $\frac{5{,}732}{100}$.

Since the denominator is 100, you need two places to the right of the decimal point so $\frac{5{,}732}{100} = 57.32$.

EXAMPLE 2: What is the decimal equivalent of $\frac{57}{10{,}000}$?

The denominator is 10,000, so you need 4 decimal places. Since 57 only has two places, we add two zeros in front of 57; thus, $\frac{57}{10{,}000} = .0057$.

Do not make the error of adding the zeros to the right instead of to the left of 57; .5700 means $\frac{5{,}700}{10{,}000}$ not $\frac{57}{10{,}000}$.

3–5

Adding Decimals. Decimals are much easier to add than fractions. To add a collection of decimals:

(A) Write the decimals in a column with the decimal points vertically aligned.
(B) Add enough zeros to the right of the decimal point so that every number has an entry in each column to the right of the decimal point.
(C) Add the numbers in the same way as whole numbers.
(D) Place a decimal point in the sum so that it is directly beneath the decimal points in the decimals added.

EXAMPLE 1: How much is 5 + 3.43 + 16.021 + 3.1?

$$\text{(A)}\quad \begin{array}{r} 5 \\ 3.43 \\ 16.021 \\ +\ 3.1 \\ \hline \end{array} \qquad\qquad \text{(B)}\quad \begin{array}{r} 5.000 \\ 3.430 \\ 16.021 \\ +\ 3.100 \\ \hline \end{array}$$

$$\text{(C)}\quad \begin{array}{r} 5.000 \\ 3.430 \\ 16.021 \\ +\ 3.100 \\ \hline \end{array}$$

$$\text{(D)}\quad 27.551$$

The answer is **27.551**.

EXAMPLE 2: If John has \$.50, \$3.25, and \$6.05, how much does he have altogether?

$$\begin{array}{r} \$\ .50 \\ 3.25 \\ +\ 6.05 \\ \hline \$9.80 \end{array}$$

So John has \$9.80.

3–6

Subtracting Decimals. To subtract one decimal from another:

(A) Put the decimals in a column so that the decimal points are vertically aligned.
(B) Add zeros so that every decimal has an entry in each column to the right of the decimal point.
(C) Subtract the numbers as you would whole numbers.
(D) Place the decimal point in the result so that it is directly beneath the decimal points of the numbers you subtracted.

EXAMPLE 1: Solve 5.053 − 2.09.

(A) $\begin{array}{r} 5.053 \\ -\ 2.09 \\ \hline \end{array}$

(B) $\begin{array}{r} 5.053 \\ -\ 2.090 \\ \hline \end{array}$

(C) $\begin{array}{r} 5.053 \\ -\ 2.090 \\ \hline \end{array}$

(D) 2.963

The answer is **2.963.**

EXAMPLE 2: If Joe has \$12 and he loses \$8.40, how much money does he have left?

Since \$12.00 − \$8.40 = \$3.60, he has \$3.60 left.

3–7

Multiplying Decimals. Decimals are multiplied like whole numbers. *The decimal point of the product is placed so that the number of decimal places in the product is equal to the total of the number of decimal places in all of the numbers multiplied.*

EXAMPLE 1: What is (5.02)(.6)?

(502)(6) = 3012. There were 2 decimal places in 5.02 and 1 decimal place in .6, so the product must have 2 + 1 = 3 decimal places. Therefore, (5.02)(.6) = 3.012.

EXAMPLE 2: If eggs cost \$.06 each, how much should a dozen eggs cost?

Since (12)(.06) = .72, a dozen eggs should cost \$.72.

> **Computing Tip.** To multiply a decimal by 10, just move the decimal point to the right one place; to multiply by 100, move the decimal point two places to the right and so on.

EXAMPLE: $9{,}983.456 \times 100 = 998{,}345.6$

3–8

Dividing Decimals. To divide one decimal (the dividend) by another decimal (the divisor):

(A) Move the decimal point in the divisor to the right until there is no decimal fraction in the divisor (this is the same as multiplying the divisor by a multiple of 10).
(B) Move the decimal point in the dividend the same number of places to the right as you moved the decimal point in step (A).
(C) Divide the result of (B) by the result of (A) as if they were whole numbers.
(D) The number of decimal places in the result (quotient) should be equal to the number of decimal places in the result of step (B).

EXAMPLE 1: Divide .05 into 25.155.

(A) Move the decimal point two places to the right in .05; the result is 5.
(B) Move the decimal point two places to the right in 25.155; the result is 2515.5.
(C) Divide 5 into 25155; the result is 5031.
(D) Since there was one decimal place in the result of (B); the answer is 503.1.

The work for this example might look like this:

$$\begin{array}{r} 503.1 \\ .05\overline{)25.155} \end{array}$$

You can always check division by multiplying.

$(503.1)(.05) = 25.155$ so we were correct.

If you write division as a fraction, example 1 would be expressed as $\frac{25.155}{.05}$.

You can multiply both the numerator and denominator by 100 without changing the value of the fraction, so

$$\frac{25.155}{.05} = \frac{25.155 \times 100}{.05 \times 100} = \frac{2515.5}{5.}.$$

So step (A) and (B) always change the division of a decimal by a decimal into the division by a whole number.

To divide a decimal by a whole number, divide them as if they were whole numbers. Then place the decimal point in the quotient so that the quotient has as many decimal places as the decimal (the dividend).

EXAMPLE 2: $\frac{55.033}{1.1} = \frac{550.33}{11.} = 50.01.$

EXAMPLE 3: If oranges cost 6¢ each, how many oranges can you buy for $2.52?

$$6¢ = \$.06,$$

so the number of oranges is

$$\frac{2.52}{.06} = \frac{252}{6} = 42.$$

Computing Tip. To divide a decimal by 10, move the decimal point *to the left* one place; to divide by 100, move the decimal point two places to the left, and so on.

EXAMPLE: Divide 5,637.6471 by 1,000.

The answer is 5.6376471, since to divide by 1,000 you move the decimal point 3 places to the left.

3–9

Converting a Fraction into a Decimal. To convert a fraction into a decimal, divide the denominator into the numerator. For example, $\frac{3}{4} = \frac{3.00}{4} = .75$. Some fractions give an infinite decimal when you divide the denominator into the numerator, for example, $\frac{1}{3} = .333\ldots$ where the three dots mean you keep on getting 3 with each step of division. .333 . . . is an *infinite decimal.*

If a fraction has an infinite decimal, use the fraction in any computation.

EXAMPLE 1: What is $\frac{2}{9}$ of $3,690.90?

Since the decimal for $\frac{2}{9}$ is .2222 . . . use the fraction $\frac{2}{9}$.
$\frac{2}{9} \times \$3{,}690.90 = 2 \times \$410.10 = \$820.20.$

You should know the following decimal equivalents of fractions:

$\frac{1}{100} = .01$	$\frac{1}{6} = .1666\ldots$
$\frac{1}{50} = .02$	$\frac{1}{5} = .2$
$\frac{1}{40} = .025$	$\frac{1}{4} = .25$
$\frac{1}{25} = .04$	$\frac{1}{3} = .333\ldots$
$\frac{1}{20} = .05$	$\frac{3}{8} = .375$
$\frac{1}{16} = .0625$	$\frac{2}{5} = .4$
$\frac{1}{15} = .0666\ldots$	$\frac{1}{2} = .5$
$\frac{1}{12} = .0833\ldots$	$\frac{5}{8} = .625$
$\frac{1}{10} = .1$	$\frac{2}{3} = .666\ldots$
$\frac{1}{9} = .111\ldots$	$\frac{3}{4} = .75$
$\frac{1}{8} = .125$	$\frac{7}{8} = .875$
$\frac{3}{2} = 1.5$	

Any decimal with . . . is an infinite decimal.

I–4. Percentage

4–1

PERCENTAGE is another method of expressing fractions or parts of an object. Percentages are expressed in terms of hundredths, so 100% means 100 hundredths or 1. 50% would be 50 hundredths or $\frac{1}{2}$.

A decimal is converted to a percentage by multiplying the decimal by 100. Since multiplying a decimal by 100 is accomplished by moving the decimal point two places to the right, *you convert a decimal into a percentage by moving the decimal point two places to the right*. For example, .134 = 13.4%.

If you wish to convert a percentage into a decimal, you divide the percentage by 100. There is a shortcut for this also. To divide by 100 you move the decimal point two places to the left.

Therefore, *to convert a percentage into a decimal, move the decimal point two places to the left*. For example, 24% = .24.

A fraction is converted into a percentage by changing the fraction to a decimal and then changing the decimal to a percentage. A percentage is changed into a fraction by first converting the percentage into a decimal and then changing the decimal to a fraction. You should know the following fractional equivalents of percentages:

$1\% = \frac{1}{100}$	$25\% = \frac{1}{4}$	$80\% = \frac{4}{5}$
$2\% = \frac{1}{50}$	$33\frac{1}{3}\% = \frac{1}{3}$	$83\frac{1}{3}\% = \frac{5}{6}$
$4\% = \frac{1}{25}$	$37\frac{1}{2}\% = \frac{3}{8}$	$87\frac{1}{2}\% = \frac{7}{8}$
$5\% = \frac{1}{20}$	$40\% = \frac{2}{5}$	$100\% = 1$
$8\frac{1}{3}\% = \frac{1}{12}$	$50\% = \frac{1}{2}$	$120\% = \frac{6}{5}$
$10\% = \frac{1}{10}$	$60\% = \frac{3}{5}$	$125\% = \frac{5}{4}$
$12\frac{1}{2}\% = \frac{1}{8}$	$62\frac{1}{2}\% = \frac{5}{8}$	$133\frac{1}{3}\% = \frac{4}{3}$
$16\frac{2}{3}\% = \frac{1}{6}$	$66\frac{2}{3}\% = \frac{2}{3}$	$150\% = \frac{3}{2}$
$20\% = \frac{1}{5}$	$75\% = \frac{3}{4}$	

Note, for example, that $133\frac{1}{3}\% = 1.33\frac{1}{3} = 1\frac{1}{3} = \frac{4}{3}$.

When you compute with percentages, it is usually easier to change the percentages to decimals or fractions.

EXAMPLE 1: A company has 6,435 bars of soap. If the company sells 20% of its bars of soap, how many bars of soap did it sell?

Change 20% into .2. Thus, the company sold (.2)(6,435) = 1287.0 = 1,287 bars of soap. An alternative method would be to convert 20% to $\frac{1}{5}$. Then, $\frac{1}{5} \times 6{,}435 =$ 1,287.

EXAMPLE 2: In a class of 60 students, 18 students received a grade of B. What percentage of the class received a grade of B?

$\frac{18}{60}$ of the class received a grade of B. $\frac{18}{60} = \frac{3}{10} = .3$ and $.3 = 30\%$, so 30% of the class received a grade of B.

EXAMPLE 3: If the population of Dryden was 10,000 in 1960 and the population of Dryden increased by 15% between 1960 and 1970, what was the population of Dryden in 1970?

The population increased by 15% between 1960 and 1970, so the increase was (.15)(10,000) which is 1,500. The population in 1970 was 10,000 + 1,500 = 11,500.

A quicker method: the population increased 15%, so the population in 1970 is 115% of the population in 1960. Therefore, the population in 1970 is 115% of 10,000 which is (1.15)(10,000) = 11,500.

4–2

Interest and Discount. Two of the most common uses of percentages are in interest and discount problems.

The rate of interest is usually given as a percentage. The basic formula for interest problems is:

$$\boxed{\text{INTEREST} = \text{AMOUNT} \times \text{TIME} \times \text{RATE}}$$

You can assume the rate of interest is the annual rate of interest unless the problem states otherwise; so you should express the time in years.

EXAMPLE 1: How much interest will $10,000 earn in 9 months at an annual rate of 6%?

9 months is $\frac{3}{4}$ of a year and $6\% = \frac{3}{50}$, so using the formula, the interest is \$10,000 $\times \frac{3}{4} \times \frac{3}{50} = \$50 \times 9 = \$450$.

EXAMPLE 2: What annual rate of interest was paid if $5,000 earned $300 in interest in 2 years?

Since the interest was earned in 2 years, $150 is the interest earned in one year. $\frac{150}{5,000} = .03 = 3\%$, so the annual rate of interest was 3%.

This type of interest is called *simple interest.*

There is another method of computing interest called *compound interest.* In computing compound interest, the interest is periodically added to the amount (or principal) which is earning interest.

EXAMPLE 3: What will $1,000 be worth after three years if it earns interest at the rate of 5% compounded annually?

Compounded annually means that the interest earned during one year is added to the amount (or principal) at the end of each year. The interest on $1,000 at

5% for one year is $(1,000)(.05) = $50. So you must compute the interest on $1,050(not $1,000) for the second year. The interest is $(1,050)(.05) = $52.50. Therefore, during the third year interest will be computed for $1,102.50. During the third year the interest is $(1,102.50)(.05) = $55.125 = $55.13. Therefore, after 3 years the original $1,000 will be worth $1,157.63.

If you calculated simple interest on $1,000 at 5% for three years, the answer would be $(1,000)(.05)(3) = $150. Therefore, using simple interest, $1,000 is worth $1,150 after 3 years. Notice that this is not the same as the money was worth using compound interest.

You can assume that interest means simple interest unless a problem states otherwise.

The basic formula for discount problems is:

DISCOUNT = COST × RATE OF DISCOUNT

EXAMPLE 1: What is the discount if a car which cost $3,000 is discounted 7%?

The discount is $3,000 × .07 = $210.00 since 7% = .07.

If we know the cost of an item and its discounted price, we can find the rate of discount by using the formula

$$\text{rate of discount} = \frac{\text{cost} - \text{price}}{\text{cost}}.$$

EXAMPLE 2. What was the rate of discount if a boat which cost $5,000 was sold for $4,800?

Using this formula, we find that the rate of discount equals

$$\frac{5{,}000 - 4{,}800}{5{,}000} = \frac{200}{5{,}000} = \frac{1}{25} = .04 = 4\%.$$

After an item has been discounted once, it may be discounted again. This procedure is called *successive* discounting.

EXAMPLE 3: A bicycle originally cost $100 and was discounted 10%. After three months it was sold after being discounted 15%. How much was the bicycle sold for?

After the 10% discount the bicycle was selling for $100(.90) = $90. An item which costs $90 and is discounted 15% will sell for $90(.85) = $76.50, so the bicycle was sold for $76.50.

Notice that if you added the two discounts of 10% and 15% and treated the successive discounts as a single discount of 25%, your answer would be that the bicycle sold for $75, which is incorrect. Successive discounts are *not* identical to a single discount of the sum of the discounts. The previous example shows that successive discounts of 10% and 15% are not identical to a single discount of 25%.

I–5. Rounding off Numbers

5–1

Many times an approximate answer can be found more quickly and may be more useful than the exact answer. For example, if a company had sales of $998,875.63 during a year, it is easier to remember that the sales were about $1 million.

Rounding off a number to a decimal place means finding the multiple of the representative of that decimal place which is closest to the original number. Thus, rounding off a number to the nearest hundred means finding the multiple of 100 which is closest to the original number. Rounding off to the nearest tenth means finding the multiple of $\frac{1}{10}$ which is closest to the original number. After a number has been rounded off to a particular decimal place, all the digits to the right of that particular decimal place will be zero.

EXAMPLE 1: Round off 9,403,420.71 to the nearest hundred.

You must find the multiple of one hundred which is closest to 9,403,420.71.

The answer is 9,403,400.

To round off a number to the *r*th decimal place:

(A) Look at the digit in the place to the right of the *r*th place;
(B) *If the digit is 0,1,2,3, or 4, change all the digits in places to the right of the rth place to 0* to round off the number.
(C) *If the digit is 5,6,7,8, or 9, add 1 to the digit in the rth place and change all the digits in places to the right of the rth place to 0* to round off the number.

For example, the multiple of 100 which is closest to 5,342.1 is 5,300. Most problems dealing with money are rounded off if the answer contains a fractional part of a cent. This is common business practice.

EXAMPLE 2: If 16 donuts cost $1.00, how much should three donuts cost?

Three donuts should cost $\frac{3}{16}$ of $1.00. Since $\frac{3}{16} \times 1. = .1875$, the cost would be $.1875. In practice, you would round it up to $.19 or 19¢.

Rounding off numbers can help you get quick, approximate answers. Since many questions require only rough answers, you can save time on the test by rounding off numbers.

EXAMPLE 3: If 5,301 of the 499,863 workers employed at the XYZ factory don't show up for work on Monday, about what percentage of the workers don't show up?

(A) 1 (B) 2 (C) 3 (D) 4 (E) 5

You can quickly see that the answer is (A) by rounding off both numbers to the nearest thousand before you divide, because $\frac{5{,}000}{500{,}000} = \frac{1}{100} = .01 = 1\%$. The exact answer is $\frac{5{,}301}{499{,}863} = .010604$, but it would take much longer to get an exact answer.

EXAMPLE 4: Round off 43.79 to the nearest tenth.

The place to the right of tenths is hundredths, so look in the hundredths place. Since 9 is bigger than 5, add 1 to the tenths place. Therefore, 43.79 is 43.8 rounded off to the nearest tenth.

If the digit in the rth place is 9 and you need to add 1 to the digit to round off the number to the rth decimal place, put a zero in the rth place and add 1 to the digit in the position to the left of the rth place. For example, 298 rounded off to the nearest 10 is 300; 99,752 to the nearest thousand is 100,000.

I–6. Signed Numbers

6–1

A number preceded by either a plus or a minus sign is called a SIGNED NUMBER. For example, +5, −6, −4.2, and +¾ are all signed numbers. If no sign is given with a number, a plus sign is assumed; thus, 5 is interpreted as +5.

Signed numbers can often be used to distinguish different concepts. For example, a profit of $10 can be denoted by +$10 and a loss of $10 by −$10. A temperature of 20 degrees below zero can be denoted −20°.

6–2

Signed numbers are also called DIRECTED NUMBERS. You can think of numbers arranged on a line, called a number line, in the following manner:

Take a line which extends indefinitely in both directions, pick a point on the line and call it 0, pick another point on the line to the right of 0 and call it 1. The point to the right of 1 which is exactly as far from 1 as 1 is from 0 is called 2, the point to the right of 2 just as far from 2 as 1 is from 0 is called 3, and so on. The point halfway between 0 and 1 is called ½, the point halfway between ½ and 1 is called ¾. In this way, you can identify any whole number or any fraction with a point on the line.

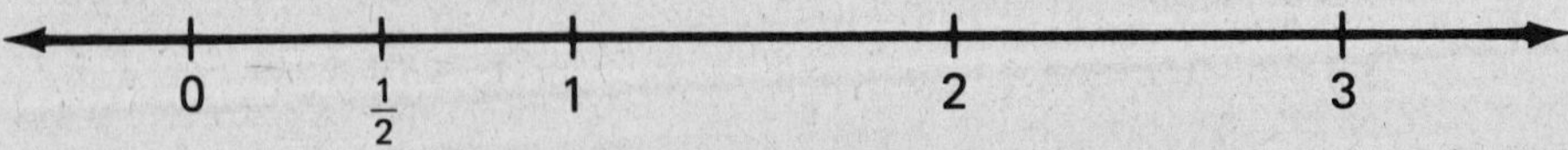

All the numbers which correspond to points to the right of 0 are called *positive numbers*. The sign of a positive number is +.

If you go to the left of zero the same distance as you did from 0 to 1, the point is called −1; in the same way as before, you can find $-2, -3, -\frac{1}{2}, -\frac{3}{2}$ and so on.

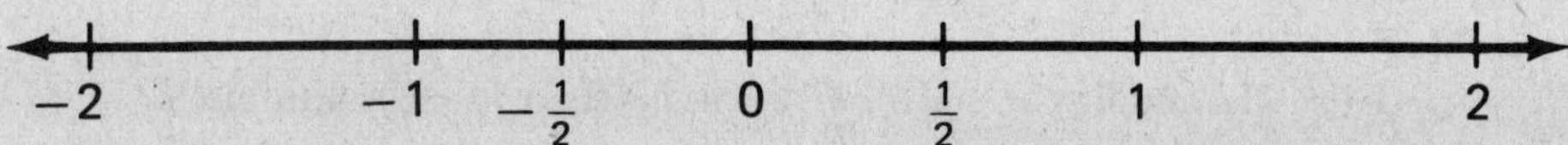

All the numbers which correspond to points to the left of zero are called *negative numbers*. Negative numbers are signed numbers whose sign is −. For example, −3, −5.15, −.003 are all negative numbers.

> *0 is neither positive nor negative; any nonzero number is positive or negative but not both.* So $-0 = 0$.

6-3

Absolute Value. The absolute value of a signed number is the distance of the number from 0. The absolute value of any nonzero number is *positive*. For example, the absolute value of 2 is 2; the absolute value of −2 is 2. The absolute value of a number a is denoted by $|a|$, so $|-2| = 2$. The absolute value of any number can be found by dropping its sign, $|-12| = 12$, $|4| = 4$. *Thus* $|-a| = |a|$ *for any number a.* The only number whose absolute value is zero is zero.

6-4

Adding Signed Numbers:

Case I. Adding numbers with the *same sign:*

(A) The sign of the sum is the same as the sign of the numbers being added.
(B) Add the absolute values.
(C) Put the sign from step (A) in front of the number you obtained in step (B).

EXAMPLE 1: What is $-2 + (-3.1) + (-.02)$?

(A) The sign of the sum will be −.
(B) $|-2| = 2$, $|-3.1| = 3.1$, $|-.02| = .02$, and $2 + 3.1 + .02 = 5.12$.
(C) The answer is −5.12.

Case II. Adding *two* numbers with *different signs:*

(A) The sign of the sum is the sign of the number which is largest in absolute value.
(B) Subtract the absolute value of the number with the smaller absolute value from the absolute value of the number with the larger absolute value.
(C) The answer is the number you obtained in step (B) preceded by the sign from part (A).

EXAMPLE 2: How much is −5.1 + 3?

(A) The absolute value of −5.1 is 5.1 and the absolute value of 3 is 3, so the sign of the sum will be −.
(B) 5.1 is larger than 3, and 5.1 − 3 = 2.1.
(C) The sum is −2.1.

Case III. Adding *more than two* numbers with *different signs:*

(A) Add all the positive numbers; the result is positive (this is Case I).
(B) Add all the negative numbers; the result is negative (this is Case I).
(C) Add the result of step (A) to the result of step (B), by using Case II.

EXAMPLE 3: Find the value of 5 + 52 + (−3) + 7 + (−5.1).

(A) 5 + 52 + 7 = 64.
(B) −3 + (−5.1) = −8.1.
(C) 64 + (−8.1) = 55.9, so the answer is 55.9.

EXAMPLE 4: If a store made a profit of $23.50 on Monday, lost $2.05 on Tuesday, lost $5.03 on Wednesday, made a profit of $30.10 on Thursday, and made a profit of $41.25 on Friday, what was its total profit (or loss) for the week? Use + for profit and − for loss.

The total is 23.50 + (−2.05) + (−5.03) + 30.10 + 41.25 which is 94.85 + (−7.08) = 87.77. So the store made a profit of $87.77.

6–5

Subtracting Signed Numbers. When subtracting signed numbers:

(A) Change the sign of the number you are subtracting (the subtrahend).
(B) Add the result of step (A) to the number being subtracted from (the minuend) using the rules of the preceding section.

EXAMPLE 1: Subtract 4.1 from 6.5.

(A) 4.1 becomes −4.1.
(B) 6.5 + (−4.1) = 2.4.

EXAMPLE 2: What is 7.8 − (−10.1)?

(A) −10.1 becomes 10.1.
(B) 7.8 + 10.1 = 17.9.

So we subtract a negative number by adding a positive number with the same absolute value, and we subtract a positive number by adding a negative number of the same absolute value.

6–6

Multiplying Signed Numbers. Case I. Multiplying two numbers:

(A) Multiply the absolute values of the numbers.
(B) If both numbers have the same sign, the result of step (A) is the answer, i.e. the product is positive. If the numbers have different signs, then the answer is the result of step (A) with a minus sign.

EXAMPLE 1: $(-5)(-12) = ?$

(A) $5 \times 12 = 60$
(B) Both signs are the same, so the answer is 60.

EXAMPLE 2: $(4)(-3) = ?$

(A) $4 \times 3 = 12$
(B) The signs are different, so the answer is -12. You can remember the sign of the product in the following way:

$$(-)(-) = + \quad (+)(+) = + \quad (-)(+) = - \quad (+)(-) = -$$

Case II. Multiplying more than two numbers:

(A) Multiply the first two factors using Case I.
(B) Multiply the result of (A) by the third factor.
(C) Multiply the result of (B) by the fourth factor.
(D) Continue until you have used each factor.

EXAMPLE 3: $(-5)(4)(2)(-\frac{1}{2})(\frac{3}{4}) = ?$

(A) $(-5)(4) = -20$
(B) $(-20)(2) = -40$
(C) $(-40)(-\frac{1}{2}) = 20$
(D) $(20)(\frac{3}{4}) = 15$, so the answer is 15.

The sign of the product is + if there are no negative factors or an even number of negative factors. The sign of the product is − if there are an odd number of negative factors.

6–7

Dividing Signed Numbers: Divide the absolute values of the numbers; the sign of the quotient is determined by the same rules as you used to determine the sign of a product. Thus,

$$+ \div + = +, - \div - = +, + \div - = -, - \div + = -.$$

EXAMPLE 1: Divide 53.2 by −4.

53.2 divided by 4 is 13.3. Since one of the numbers is positive and the other negative, the answer is −13.2.

EXAMPLE 2: $\frac{-5}{-2} = \frac{5}{2}$

I-7. Averages and Medians

7-1

Mean. The *average* or *arithmetic mean* of a collection of N numbers is the result of dividing the sum of all the numbers in the collection by N.

EXAMPLE 1: The scores of 9 students on a test were 72, 78, 81, 64, 85, 92, 95, 60, and 55. What was the average score of the students?

Since there are 9 students, the average is the total of all the scores divided by 9. So the average is $\frac{1}{9}$ of $(72 + 78 + 81 + 64 + 85 + 92 + 95 + 60 + 55)$, which is $\frac{1}{9}$ of (682) or $75\frac{7}{9}$.

EXAMPLE 2: The temperature at noon in Coldtown, U.S.A. was 5° on Monday, 10° on Tuesday, 2° below zero on Wednesday, 5° below zero on Thursday, 0° on Friday, 4° on Saturday, and 1° below zero on Sunday. What was the average temperature at noon for the week?

Use negative numbers for the temperatures below zero. The average temperature is the average of 5, 10, −2, −5, 0, 4 and −1, which is $\frac{5 + 10 + (-2) + (-5) + 0 + 4 + (-1)}{7} = \frac{11}{7} = 1\frac{4}{7}$. Therefore, the average temperature at noon for the week is $1\frac{4}{7}$.

EXAMPLE 3: If the average annual income of 10 workers is $15,665 and two of the workers each made $20,000 for the year, what is the average annual income of the remaining 8 workers?

The total income of all 10 workers is 10 times the average income which is $156,650. The two workers made a total of $40,000, so the total income of the remaining 8 workers was $156,650 − $40,000 = $116,650. Therefore, the average annual income of the 8 remaining workers is $\frac{\$116{,}650}{8} = \$14{,}581.25$.

7-2

The Median. The number which is in the middle if the numbers in a collection of numbers are arranged in order is called the *median*. In example 1 above, the median score was 78, and in example 2, the median temperature for the week was 0. Notice that the medians were different from the averages. In example 3, we don't have enough data to find the median although we know the average.

In general, the median and the average of a collection of numbers are different.

If the number of objects in the collection is even, the median is the average of the two numbers in the middle of the array. For example, the median of 64, 66, 72, 75, 76, and 77 is the average of 72 and 75 which is 73.5.

I-8. Powers, Exponents, and Roots

8-1

If b is any number and n is a whole number greater than 0, b^n means the product of n factors each of which is equal to b. Thus,

$$b^n = b \times b \times b \times \cdots \times b \text{ where there are } n \text{ copies of } b.$$

If $n = 1$, there is only one copy of b so $b^1 = b$. Here are some examples,

$$2^5 = 2 \times 2 \times 2 \times 2 \times 2 = 32,\ (-4)^3 = (-4) \times (-4) \times (-4) = -64,\ \frac{3^2}{4} = \frac{3 \times 3}{4} = \frac{9}{4},$$

$$1^n = 1 \text{ for any } n,\ 0^n = 0 \text{ for any } n.$$

b^n is read as "b raised to the nth power." b^2 is read "b squared." b^2 is always greater than 0 (positive) if b is not zero, since the product of two negative numbers is positive. b^3 is read "b cubed," b^3 can be negative or positive.

You should know the following squares and cubes:

$1^2 = 1$	$8^2 = 64$
$2^2 = 4$	$9^2 = 81$
$3^2 = 9$	$10^2 = 100$
$4^2 = 16$	$11^2 = 121$
$5^2 = 25$	$12^2 = 144$
$6^2 = 36$	$13^2 = 169$
$7^2 = 49$	$14^2 = 196$
	$15^2 = 255$
$1^3 = 1$	$3^3 = 27$
$2^3 = 8$	$4^3 = 64$
	$5^3 = 125$

If you raise a fraction, $\frac{p}{q}$, to a power, then $\left(\frac{p}{q}\right)^n = \frac{p^n}{q^n}$. For example,

$$\left(\frac{5}{4}\right)^3 = \frac{5^3}{4^3} = \frac{125}{64}.$$

EXAMPLE 1: If the value of an investment triples each year, what percent of its value today will the investment be worth in 4 years?

The value increases by a factor of 3 each year. Since the time is 4 years, there will be four factors of 3. So the investment will be worth $3 \times 3 \times 3 \times 3 = 3^4$ as much as it is today. $3^4 = 81$, so the investment will be worth 8,100% of its value today in four years.

8-2

Exponents. In the expression b^n, b is called the base and n is called the *exponent*. In the expression 2^5, 2 is the base and 5 is the exponent. The exponent tells how many factors there are.

> The *two basic formulas for problems involving exponents* are:
>
> (A) $b^n \times b^m = b^{n+m}$
>
> (B) $a^n \times b^n = (a \cdot b)^n$
>
> (A) and (B) are called *laws of exponents.*

EXAMPLE 1: What is 6^3?

Since $6 = 3 \times 2$, $6^3 = 3^3 \times 2^3 = 27 \times 8 = 216$.

or

$6^3 = 6 \times 6 \times 6 = 216$.

EXAMPLE 2: Find the value of $2^3 \times 2^2$.

Using (A), $2^3 \times 2^2 = 2^{2+3} = 2^5$ which is 32. You can check this, since $2^3 = 8$ and $2^2 = 4$; $2^3 \times 2^2 = 8 \times 4 = 32$.

8-3

Negative Exponents. $b^0 = 1$ *for any nonzero number b.* By one of the laws of exponents (A) above, $b^n \times b^0$ should be $b^{n+0} = b^n$. If we still want (A) to be true, then b^0 must be 1. (NOTE: 0^0 is not defined.)

Using the law of exponents once more, you can define b^{-n} where n is a positive number. If (A) holds, $b^{-n} \times b^n = b^{-n+n} = b^0 = 1$, so $b^{-n} = \frac{1}{b^n}$. *Multiplying by* b^{-n} *is the same as dividing by* b^n.

EXAMPLE 1:

$$2^{-3} = \frac{1}{2^3} = \frac{1}{8};\ 2^0 = 1$$

EXAMPLE 2:

$$\left(\frac{1}{2}\right)^{-1} = \frac{1}{1/2} = 2$$

EXAMPLE 3: Find the value of $\frac{6^4}{3^3}$.

$$\frac{6^4}{3^3} = \frac{(3 \cdot 2)^4}{3^3} = \frac{3^4 \cdot 2^4}{3^3} = 3^4 \times 2^4 \times 3^{-3} = 3^4 \times 3^{-3} \times 2^4 = 3^1 \times 2^4 = 48.$$

8–4

Roots. If you raise a number d to the nth power and the result is b, then d is called the nth root of b, which is usually written $\sqrt[n]{b} = d$. Since $2^5 = 32$, then $\sqrt[5]{32} = 2$. The second root is called the square root and is written $\sqrt{\ }$; the third root is called the cube root. If you read the columns of the table on page 159 from right to left, you have a table of square roots and cube roots. For example, $\sqrt{225} = 15$; $\sqrt{81} = 9$; $\sqrt[3]{64} = 4$.

There are two possibilities for the square root of a positive number; the positive one is called the square root. Thus we say $\sqrt{9} = 3$ although $(-3) \times (-3) = 9$.

Since the square of any nonzero number is positive *the square root of a negative number is not defined as a real number.* Thus $\sqrt{-2}$ is not a real number. There are cube roots of negative numbers. $\sqrt[3]{-8} = -2$, because $(-2) \times (-2) \times (-2) = -8$.

You can also write roots as exponents; for example,

$$\sqrt[n]{b} = b^{1/n};\ \text{so}\ \sqrt{b} = b^{1/2},\ \sqrt[3]{b} = b^{1/3}.$$

Since you can write roots as exponents, formula (B) above is especially useful.

$a^{1/n} \times b^{1/n} = (a \cdot b)^{1/n}$ or $\sqrt[n]{a \times b} = \sqrt[n]{a} \times \sqrt[n]{b}$. This formula is the basic formula for simplifying square roots, cube roots and so on. *On the test you must state your answer in a form which matches one of the choices given.*

EXAMPLE 1: $\sqrt{54} = ?$

Since $54 = 9 \times 6$, $\sqrt{54} = \sqrt{9 \times 6} = \sqrt{9} \times \sqrt{6}$. Since $\sqrt{9} = 3$, $\sqrt{54} = 3\sqrt{6}$.

You can not simplify by adding square roots unless you are taking square roots of the same number. For example,

$$\sqrt{3} + 2\sqrt{3} - 4\sqrt{3} = -\sqrt{3},\ \text{but}\ \sqrt{3} + \sqrt{2}\ \text{is not equal to}\ \sqrt{5}.$$

EXAMPLE 2: Simplify $6\sqrt{12} + 2\sqrt{75} - 3\sqrt{98}$.

Since $12 = 4 \times 3$, $\sqrt{12} = \sqrt{4 \times 3} = \sqrt{4} \times \sqrt{3} = 2\sqrt{3}$;
$75 = 25 \times 3$, so $\sqrt{75} = \sqrt{25} \times \sqrt{3} = 5\sqrt{3}$;
and $98 = 49 \times 2$, so $\sqrt{98} = \sqrt{49} \times \sqrt{2} = 7\sqrt{2}$.
Therefore, $6\sqrt{12} + 2\sqrt{75} - 3\sqrt{98} = 6 \times 2\sqrt{3} + 2 \times 5\sqrt{3} - 3 \times 7\sqrt{2} = 12\sqrt{3} + 10\sqrt{3} - 21\sqrt{2} = 22\sqrt{3} - 21\sqrt{2}$.

EXAMPLE 3: Simplify $27^{1/3} \times 8^{1/3}$.

$27^{1/3} = \sqrt[3]{27} = 3$ and $8^{1/3} = 2$, so $27^{1/3} \times 8^{1/3} = 3 \times 2 = 6$. Notice that 6 is $\sqrt[3]{216}$ and $27^{1/3} \times 8^{1/3} = (27 \times 8)^{1/3} = 216^{1/3}$.

II. Algebra

II–1. Algebraic Expressions

1–1

Often it is necessary to deal with quantities which have a numerical value which is unknown. For example, we may know that Tom's salary is twice as much as Joe's salary. If we let the value of Tom's salary be called T and the value of Joe's salary be J, then T and J are numbers which are unknown. However, we do know that the value of T must be twice the value of J, or $T = 2J$.

T and $2J$ are examples of algebraic expressions. An algebraic expression may involve letters in addition to numbers and symbols; however, *in an algebraic expression a letter always stands for a number.* Therefore, you can multiply, divide, add, subtract and perform other mathematical operations on a letter. Thus, x^2 would mean x times x. Some examples of algebraic expressions are: $2x + y$, $y^3 + 9y$, $z^3 - 5ab$, $c + d + 4$, $5x + 2y(6x - 4y + z)$. When letters or numbers are written together without any sign or symbol between them, multiplication is assumed. Thus $6xy$ means 6 times x times y. $6xy$ is called a term; terms are separated by + or − signs. The expression $5z + 2 + 4x^2$ has three terms, $5z$, 2, and $4x^2$. Terms are often called monomials (mono = one). If an expression has more than one term, it is called a *polynomial,* (poly = many). The letters in an algebraic expression are called *variables* or *unknowns*. When a variable is multiplied by a number, the number is called the *coefficient* of the variable. So in the expression $5x^2 + 2yz$, the coefficient of x^2 is 5, and the coefficient of yz is 2.

1–2

Simplifying Algebraic Expressions. *Since there are only five choices of an answer given for the test questions, you must be able to recognize algebraic expressions which are equal.* It will also save time when you are working problems if you can change a complicated expression into a simpler one.

Case I. Simplifying expressions which don't contain parentheses:

(A) Perform any multiplications or divisions before performing additions or subtractions. Thus, the expression $6x + y \div x$ means add $6x$ to the quotient of y divided by x. Another way of writing the expression would be $6x + \frac{y}{x}$. This is not the same as $\frac{6x + y}{x}$.

(B) The order in which you multiply numbers and letters in a term does not matter. So $6xy$ is the same as $6yx$.

(C) The order in which you add terms does not matter; for instance, $6x + 2y - x = 6x - x + 2y$.

(D) If there are roots or powers in any terms, you may be able to simplify the term by using the laws of exponents. For example, $5xy \cdot 3x^2y = 15x^3y^2$.

(E) Combine like terms. *Like terms* (or similar terms) are terms which have exactly the same letters raised to the same powers. So x, $-2x$, $\frac{1}{3}x$ are like terms. For example, $6x - 2x + x + y$ is equal to $5x + y$. In combining like terms, you simply add or subtract the coefficients of the like terms, and the result is the coefficient of that term in the simplified expression. In our example above, the coefficients of x were $+6$, -2, and $+1$; since $6-2+1=5$ the coefficient of x in the simplified expression is 5.

(F) Algebraic expressions which involve divisions or factors can be simplified by using the techniques for handling fractions and the laws of exponents. Remember dividing by b^n is the same as multiplying by b^{-n}.

EXAMPLE 1: $3x^2 - 4\sqrt{x} + \sqrt{4x} + xy + 7x^2 = ?$

(D) $\sqrt{4x} = \sqrt{4}\sqrt{x} = 2\sqrt{x}$.
(E) $3x^2 + 7x^2 = 10x^2$, $-4\sqrt{x} + 2\sqrt{x} = -2\sqrt{x}$.

The original expression equals $3x^2 + 7x^2 - 4\sqrt{x} + 2\sqrt{x} + xy$. Therefore, the simplified expression is $10x^2 - 2\sqrt{x} + xy$.

EXAMPLE 2: Simplify $\dfrac{21x^4y^2}{3x^6y}$.

(F) $\dfrac{21}{3}x^4y^2x^{-6}y^{-1}$.
(B) $7x^4x^{-6}y^2y^{-1}$.
(D) $7x^{-2}y$, so the simplified term is $\dfrac{7y}{x^2}$.

EXAMPLE 3: Write $\dfrac{2x}{y} - \dfrac{4}{x}$ as a single fraction.

(F) A common denominator is xy so $\dfrac{2x}{y} = \dfrac{2x \cdot x}{y \cdot x} = \dfrac{2x^2}{xy}$, and $\dfrac{4}{x} = \dfrac{4y}{xy}$.

Therefore, $\dfrac{2x}{y} - \dfrac{4}{x} = \dfrac{2x^2}{xy} - \dfrac{4y}{xy} = \dfrac{2x^2 - 4y}{xy}$

Case II. Simplifying expressions which have parentheses:

The first rule is to perform the operations inside parentheses first. So $(6x+y) \div x$ means divide the sum of $6x$ and y by x. Notice that $(6x+y) \div x$ is different from $6x + y \div x$.

The main rule for getting rid of parentheses is the distributive law, which is expressed as $a(b+c) = ab + ac$. In other words, if any monomial is followed by an expression contained in a parenthesis, then *each* term of the expression is multiplied by the monomial. Once we have gotten rid of the parentheses, we proceed as we did in Case I.

EXAMPLE 4: $2x(6x-4y+2) = (2x)(6x) + (2x)(-4y) + (2x)(2) = 12x^2 - 8xy - 4x$.

If an expression has more than one set of parentheses, get rid of the *inner parentheses first* and then *work out* through the rest of the parentheses.

EXAMPLE 5: $2x-(x+6(x-3y)+4y)=?$

To remove the inner parentheses we multiply $6(x-3y)$ getting $6x-18y$. Now we have $2x-(x+6x-18y+4y)$ which equals $2x-(7x-14y)$. Distribute the minus sign (multiply by -1), getting $2x-7x-(-14y)=-5x+14y$. Sometimes brackets are used instead of parentheses.

EXAMPLE 6: Simplify $-3x\left[\frac{1}{2}(3x-2y)-2(x(3+y)+4y)\right]$

$$=-3x\left[\frac{1}{2}(3x-2y)-2(3x+xy+4y)\right]$$

$$=-3x\left[\frac{3}{2}x-y-6x-2xy-8y\right]$$

$$=-3x\left[-\frac{9}{2}x-2xy-9y\right]$$

$$=\frac{27}{2}x^2+6x^2y+27xy.$$

1–3

Adding and Subtracting Algebraic Expressions. Since algebraic expressions are numbers, they can be added and subtracted.

The only algebraic terms which can be combined are like terms.

EXAMPLE 1: $(3x+4y-xy^2)+(3x+2x(x-y))=?$

The expression $=(3x+4y-xy^2)+(3x+2x^2-2xy)$, removing the inner parentheses;
$=6x+4y+2x^2-xy^2-2xy$, combining like terms.

EXAMPLE 2: $(2a+3a^2-4)-2(4a^2-2(a+4))=?$

It equals $(2a+3a^2-4)-2(4a^2-2a-8)$, removing inner parentheses;
$=2a+3a^2-4-8a^2+4a+16$, removing outer parentheses;
$=-5a^2+6a+12$, combining like terms.

1–4

Multiplying Algebraic Expressions. When you multiply two expressions, you multiply *each term of the first by each term of the second.*

EXAMPLE 1: $(b-4)(b+a)=b(b+a)-4(b+a)=?$

$$=b^2+ab-4b-4a.$$

EXAMPLE 2: $(2h-4)(h+2h^2+h^3)=?$

$$=2h(h+2h^2+h^3)-4(h+2h^2+h^3)$$
$$=2h^2+4h^3+2h^4-4h-8h^2-4h^3$$
$$=-4h-6h^2+2h^4, \text{ which is the product.}$$

If you need to multiply more than two expressions, multiply the first two expressions, then multiply the result by the third expression, and so on until you have used each factor. Since algebraic expressions can be multiplied, they can be squared, cubed, or raised to other powers.

EXAMPLE 3: $(x-2y)^3=(x-2y)(x-2y)(x-2y).$

$$\text{Since } (x-2y)(x-2y)=x^2-2yx-2yx+4y^2$$
$$=x^2-4xy+4y^2,$$

$$(x-y)^3=(x^2-4xy+4y^2)(x-2y)$$
$$=x(x^2-4xy+4y^2)-2y(x^2-4xy+4y^2)$$
$$=x^3-4x^2y+4xy^2-2x^2y+8xy^2-8y^3$$
$$=x^3-6x^2y+12xy^2-8y^3.$$

The order in which you multiply algebraic expressions does not matter. Thus $(2a+b)(x^2+2x)=(x^2+2x)(2a+b)$.

1–5

Factoring Algebraic Expressions. If an algebraic expression is the product of other algebraic expressions, then the expressions are called factors of the original expression. For instance, we claim that $(2h-4)$ and $(h+2h^2+h^3)$ are factors of $-4h-6h^2+2h^4$. We can always check to see if we have the correct factors by multiplying; so by example 2 above we see that our claim is correct. We need to be able to factor algebraic expressions in order to solve quadratic equations. It also can be helpful in dividing algebraic expressions.

First remove any monomial factor which appears in every term of the expression.

Some examples:

$$3x+3y=3(x+y)\text{: 3 is a monomial factor.}$$
$$15a^2b+10ab=5ab(3a+2)\text{: } 5ab \text{ is a monomial factor.}$$
$$\frac{1}{2}hy-3h^3+4hy=h\left(\frac{1}{2}y-3h^2+4y\right),$$
$$=h\left(\frac{9}{2}y-3h^2\right)\text{: } h \text{ is a monomial factor.}$$

You may also need to factor expressions which contain squares or higher powers into factors which only contain linear terms. (Linear terms are terms in which variables are raised only to the first power.) The first rule to remember is that since $(a+b)(a-b)=a^2+ba-ba-b^2=a^2-b^2$, the difference of two squares can always be factored.

EXAMPLE 1: Factor $(9m^2-16)$.

$9m^2=(3m)^2$ and $16=4^2$, so the factors are $(3m-4)(3m+4)$.

Since $(3m-4)(3m+4)=9m^2-16$, these factors are correct.

EXAMPLE 2: Factor $x^4y^4 - 4x^2$.

$x^4y^4 = (x^2y^2)^2$ and $4x^2 = (2x)^2$, so the factors are $x^2y^2 + 2x$ and $x^2y^2 - 2x$.

You also may need to factor expressions which contain squared terms and linear terms, such as $x^2 + 4x + 3$. The factors will be of the form $(x + a)$ and $(x + b)$. Since $(x + a)(x + b) = x^2 + (a + b)x + ab$, you must look for a pair of numbers a and b such that $a \cdot b$ is the numerical term in the expression and $a + b$ is the coefficient of the linear term (the term with exponent 1).

EXAMPLE 3: Factor $x^2 + 4x + 3$.

You want numbers whose product is 3 and whose sum is 4. Look at the possible factors of three and check whether they add up to 4. Since $3 = 3 \times 1$ and $3 + 1$ is 4, the factors are $(x+3)$ and $(x+1)$. Remember to check by multiplying.

EXAMPLE 4: Factor $y^2 + y - 6$.

Since -6 is negative, the two numbers a and b must be of opposite sign. Possible pairs of factors for -6 are -6 and $+1$, 6 and -1, 3 and -2, and -3 and 2. Since $-2 + 3 = 1$, the factors are $(y + 3)$ and $(y - 2)$. So $(y + 3)(y - 2) = y^2 + y - 6$.

EXAMPLE 5: Factor $a^3 + 4a^2 + 4a$.

Factor out a, so $a^3 + 4a^2 + 4a = a(a^2 + 4a + 4)$. Consider $a^2 + 4a + 4$; since $2 + 2 = 4$ and $2 \times 2 = 4$, the factors are $(a + 2)$ and $(a + 2)$. Therefore, $a^3 + 4a^2 + 4a = a(a + 2)^2$.

If the term with the highest exponent has a coefficient unequal to 1, divide the entire expression by that coefficient. For example, to factor $3a^3 + 12a^2 + 12a$, factor out a 3 from each term, and the result is $a^3 + 4a^2 + 4a$ which is $a(a+2)^2$. Thus, $3a^3 + 12a^2 + 12a = 3a(a + 2)^2$.

There are some expressions which can not be factored, for example, $x^2 + 4x + 6$. In general, if you can't factor something by using the methods given above, don't waste a lot of time on the question. Sometimes you may be able to check the answers given to find out what the correct factors are. The factoring you have to do on the test should not be any more difficult than the examples in this section.

1–6

Division of Algebraic Expressions. The main things to remember in division are:

(1) When you divide a sum, you can get the same result by dividing each term and adding quotients. For example, $\frac{9x + 4xy + y^2}{x} = \frac{9x}{x} + \frac{4xy}{x} + \frac{y^2}{x} = 9 + 4y + \frac{y^2}{x}$.

(2) You can cancel common factors, so the results on factoring will be helpful. For example, $\frac{x^2-2x}{x-2}=\frac{x(x-2)}{x-2}=x$.

You can also divide one algebraic expression by another using long division.

EXAMPLE 1: $(15x^2+2x-4)\div 3x-1$.

$$\begin{array}{r|l} & 5x+2 \\ 3x-1 & 15x^2+2x-4 \\ & \underline{15x^2-5x} \\ & 7x-4 \\ & \underline{6x-2} \\ & x-2 \end{array}$$

So the answer is $5x+2$ with a remainder of $x-2$.

You can check by multiplying,

$(5x+2)(3x-1)=15x^2+6x-5x-2$

$=15x^2+x-2$; now add the remainder $x-2$

and the result is $15x^2+x-2+x-2=15x^2+2x-4$.

Division problems where you need to use (1) and (2) are more likely than problems involving long division.

II-2. Equations

2-1

AN EQUATION is a statement that says two algebraic expressions are equal. $x+2=3$, $4+2=6$, $3x^2+2x-6=0$, $x^2+y^2=z^2$, $\frac{y}{x}=2+z$, and $A=LW$ are all examples of equations. We will refer to the algebraic expressions on each side of the equals sign as the left side and the right side of the equation. Thus, in the equation $2x+4=6y+x$, $2x+4$ is the left side and $6y+x$ is the right side.

2-2

If we assign specific numbers to each variable or unknown in an algebraic expression, then the algebraic expression will be equal to a number. This is called *evaluating* the expression. For example, if you evaluate $2x+4y^2+3$ for $x=-1$ and $y=2$, the expression is equal to $2(-1)+4\cdot 2^2+3=-2+4\cdot 4+3=17$.

If we evaluate each side of an equation and the number obtained is the same for each side of the equation, then the specific values assigned to the unknowns are called a *solution of the equation.* Another way of saying this is that the choices for the unknowns satisfy the equation.

EXAMPLE 1: Consider the equation $2x + 3 = 9$.

If $x = 3$, then the left side of the equation becomes $2 \cdot 3 + 3 = 6 + 3 = 9$, so both sides equal 9, and $x = 3$ is a solution of $2x + 3 = 9$. If $x = 4$, then the left side is $2 \cdot 4 + 3 = 11$. Since 11 is not equal to 9, $x = 4$ is *not* a solution of $2x + 3 = 9$.

EXAMPLE 2: Consider the equation $x^2 + y^2 = 5x$.

If $x = 1$ and $y = 2$, then the left side is $1^2 + 2^2$ which equals $1 + 4 = 5$. The right side is $5 \cdot 1 = 5$, since both sides are equal to 5, $x = 1$ and $y = 2$ is a solution.

If $x = 5$ and $y = 0$, then the left side is $5^2 + 0^2 = 25$ and the right side is $5 \cdot 5 = 25$, so $x = 5$ and $y = 0$ is also a solution.

If $x = 1$ and $y = 1$, then the left side is $1^2 + 1^2 = 2$ and the right side is $5 \cdot 1 = 5$. Therefore, since $2 \neq 5$, $x = 1$ and $y = 1$ is not a solution.

There are some equations which *do not have any solutions which are real numbers.* Since the square of any real number is positive or zero, the equation $x^2 = -4$ does not have any solutions which are real numbers.

2–3
Equivalence. One equation is *equivalent* to another equation, if they have exactly the same solutions. The basic idea in solving equations is to transform a given equation into an equivalent equation whose solutions are obvious.

The two main tools for solving equations are:

(A) If you add or subtract the same algebraic expression to or from *each side* of an equation, the resulting equation is equivalent to the original equation.
(B) If you multiply or divide both sides of an equation by the same *nonzero* algebraic expression, the resulting equation is equivalent to the original equation.

The most common type of equation is the linear equation with only one unknown. $6z = 4z - 3$, $3 + a = 2a - 4$, $3b + 2b = b - 4b$, are all examples of linear equations with only one unknown.

Using (A) and (B), you can solve a linear equation in one unknown in the following way:

(1) Group all the terms which involve the unknown on one side of the equation and all the terms which are purely numerical on the other side of the equation. This is called *isolating the unknown.*
(2) Combine the terms on each side.
(3) Divide each side by the coefficient of the unknown.

EXAMPLE 1: Solve $6x + 2 = 3$ for x.

(1) Using (A) subtract 2 from each side of the equation. Then $6x + 2 - 2 = 3 - 2$ or $6x = 3 - 2$.
(2) $6x = 1$.
(3) Divide each side by 6. Therefore, $x = \frac{1}{6}$.

You should always check your answer in the original equation.

$$\text{Since } 6\left(\frac{1}{6}\right) + 2 = 1 + 2 = 3,\ x = \frac{1}{6} \text{ is a solution.}$$

EXAMPLE 2: Solve $3x + 15 = 3 - 4x$ for x.

(1) Add $4x$ to each side and subtract 15 from each side; $3x + 15 - 15 + 4x = 3 - 15 - 4x + 4x$.
(2) $7x = -12$.
(3) Divide each side by 7, so $x = \frac{-12}{7}$ is the solution.

CHECK:

$$3\left(\frac{-12}{7}\right) + 15 = \frac{-36}{7} + 15 = \frac{69}{7} \text{ and } 3 - 4\left(\frac{-12}{7}\right) = 3 + \frac{48}{7} = \frac{69}{7}.$$

If you do the same thing to each side of an equation, the result is still an equation but it may not be equivalent to the original equation. Be especially careful if you square each side of an equation. For example, $x = -4$ is an equation; square both sides and you get $x^2 = 16$ which has both $x = 4$ and $x = -4$ as solutions. *Always check your answer in the original equation.*

If the equation you want to solve involves square roots, get rid of the square roots by squaring each side of the equation. Remember to check your answer since squaring each side does not always give an equivalent equation.

EXAMPLE 3: Solve $\sqrt{4x + 3} = 5$.

Square both sides: $(\sqrt{4x + 3})^2 = 4x + 3$ and $5^2 = 25$, so the new equation is $4x + 3 = 25$. Subtract 3 from each side to get $4x = 22$ and now divide each side by 4. The solution is $x = \frac{22}{4} = 5.5$. Since $4(5.5) + 3 = 25$ and $\sqrt{25} = 5$, $x = 5.5$ is a solution to the equation $4x + 3 = 5$.

If an equation involves fractions, multiply through by a common denominator and then solve. Check your answer to make sure you did not multiply or divide by zero.

EXAMPLE 4: Solve $\frac{3}{a} = 9$ for a.

Multiply each side by a: the result is $3 = 9a$. Divide each side by 9, and you obtain $\frac{3}{9} = a$ or $a = \frac{1}{3}$. Since $\frac{3}{1/3} = 3 \cdot 3 = 9$, $a = \frac{1}{3}$ is a solution.

2–4

You may be asked to solve two equations in two unknowns. Use one equation to solve for one unknown in terms of the other; now change the second equation into an equation in only one unknown which can be solved by the methods of the preceding section.

EXAMPLE 1: Solve for x and y: $\begin{cases} \frac{x}{y} = 3 \\ 2x + 4y = 20. \end{cases}$

The first equation gives $x = 3y$. Using $x = 3y$, the second equation is $2(3y) + 4y = 6y + 4y$ or $10y = 20$, so $y = \frac{20}{10} = 2$. Since $x = 3y$, $x = 6$.

CHECK:

$$\frac{6}{2} = 3, \text{ and } 2 \cdot 6 + 4 \cdot 2 = 20, \text{ so } x = 6 \text{ and } y = 2 \text{ is a solution.}$$

EXAMPLE 2: If $2x + y = 5$ and $x + y = 4$, find x and y.

Since $x + y = 4$, $y = 4 - x$, so $2x + y = 2x + 4 - x = x + 4 = 5$ and $x = 1$. If $x = 1$, then $y = 4 - 1 = 3$. So $x = 1$ and $y = 3$ is the solution.

CHECK:

$$2 \cdot 1 + 3 = 5 \text{ and } 1 + 3 = 4.$$

Sometimes we can solve two equations by adding them or by subtracting one from the other. If we subtract $x + y = 4$ from $2x + y = 5$ in example 2, we have $x = 1$. However, it is generally quicker to use the previous method.

2–5

Solving Quadratic Equations. If the terms of an equation contain squares of the unknown as well as linear terms, the equation is called *quadratic*. Some examples of quadratic equations are $x^2 + 4x = 3$, $2z^2 - 1 = 3z^2 - 2z$, and $a + 6 = a^2 + 6$.

To solve a quadratic equation:

(A) Group all the terms on one side of the equation so that the other side is *zero*.
(B) Combine the terms on the nonzero side.
(C) Factor the expression into linear expressions.
(D) Set the linear factors equal to zero and solve.

The method depends on the fact that if a product of expressions is zero then at least one of the expressions must be zero.

EXAMPLE 1: Solve $x^2 + 4x = -3$.

(A) $x^2 + 4x + 3 = 0$
(C) $x^2 + 4 + 3 = (x + 3)(x + 1) = 0$
(D) So $x + 3 = 0$ or $x + 1 = 0$. Therefore, the solutions are $x = -3$ and $x = -1$.

CHECK:

$(-3)^2 + 4(-3) = 9 - 12 = -3$
$(-1)^2 + 4(-1) = 1 - 4 = -3$, so $x = -3$ and $x = -1$ are solutions.

A quadratic equation will usually have 2 different solutions, but it is possible for a quadratic to have only one solution or even no solution.

EXAMPLE 2: If $2z^2 - 1 = 3z^2 - 2z$, what is z?

(A) $0 = 3z^2 - 2z^2 - 2z + 1$
(B) $z^2 - 2z + 1 = 0$
(C) $z^2 - 2z + 1 = (z - 1)^2 = 0$
(D) $z - 1 = 0$ or $z = 1$

CHECK:

$2 \cdot 1^2 - 1 = 2 - 1 = 1$ and $3 \cdot 1^2 - 2 \cdot 1 = 3 - 2 = 1$, so $z = 1$ is a solution.

Equations which may not look like quadratics may be changed into quadratics.

EXAMPLE 3: Find a if $a - 3 = \frac{10}{a}$.

Multiply each side of the equation by a to obtain $a^2 - 3a = 10$, which is quadratic.

(A) $a^2 - 3a - 10 = 0$
(C) $a^2 - 3a - 10 = (a - 5)(a + 2)$
(D) So $a - 5 = 0$ or $a + 2 = 0$.

Therefore, $a = 5$ and $a = -2$ are the solutions.

CHECK:

$5 - 3 = 2 = \frac{10}{5}$ so $a = 5$ is a solution.

$-2 - 3 = -5 = \frac{10}{-2}$ so $a = -2$ is a solution.

You can also solve quadratic equations by using the *quadratic formula.* The quadratic formula states that the solutions of the quadratic equation $ax^2 + bx + c = 0$ are $x = \frac{1}{2a}[-b + \sqrt{b^2 - 4ac}]$ and $x = \frac{1}{2a}[-b - \sqrt{b^2 - 4ac}]$.

1

This is usually written $x = \frac{1}{2a}[-b \pm \sqrt{b^2 - 4ac}]$. Use of the quadratic formula would replace steps (C) and (D).

EXAMPLE 4: Find x if $x^2 + 5x = 12 - x^2$.

(A) $x^2 + 5x + x^2 - 12 = 0$
(B) $2x^2 + 5x - 12 = 0$

So $a = 2$, $b = 5$ and $c = -12$. Therefore, using the quadratic formula, the solutions are $x = \frac{1}{4}[-5 \pm \sqrt{25 - 4 \cdot 2 \cdot (-12)}] = \frac{1}{4}[-5 \pm \sqrt{121}]$. So we have $x = \frac{1}{4}[-5 \pm 11]$. The solutions are $x = \frac{3}{2}$ and $x = -4$.

CHECK:

$$\left(\frac{3}{2}\right)^2 + 5 \cdot \frac{3}{2} = \frac{9}{4} + \frac{15}{2} = \frac{39}{4} = 12 - \frac{9}{4} = 12 - \left(\frac{3}{2}\right)^2$$
$$(-4)^2 + 5(-4) = 16 - 20 = -4 = 12 - 16 = 12 - (-4)^2$$

NOTE: If $b^2 - 4ac$ is negative, then the quadratic equation $ax^2 + bx + c = 0$ has no real solutions because negative numbers do not have real square roots.

The quadratic formula will always give you the solutions to a quadratic equation. If you can factor the equation, factoring will usually give you the solution in less time. Remember, you want to answer as many questions as you can in the time given. So factor if you can. If you don't see the factor immediately, then use the formula.

II-3. Word Problems

3-1

The general method for solving word problems is to translate them into algebraic problems. The quantities you are seeking are the unknowns, which are usually represented by letters. The information you are given in the problem is then turned into equations. Words such as "is," "was," "are," and "were" mean equals, and words like "of" and "as much as" mean multiplication.

EXAMPLE 1: A coat was sold for \$75. The coat was sold for 150% of the cost of the coat. How much did the coat cost?

You want to find the cost of the coat. Let \$$C$ be the cost of the coat. You know that the coat was sold for \$75 and that \$75 was 150% of the cost. So \$75 = 150% of \$$C$ or $75 = 1.5C$. Solving for C you get $C = \frac{75}{1.5} = 50$, so the coat cost \$50.

CHECK:

$$(1.5)\ \$50 = \$75.$$

EXAMPLE 2: Tom's salary is 125% of Joe's salary. Mary's salary is 80% of Joe's salary. Their combined salary is \$61,000. What is Mary's salary?

Let M = Mary's salary, J = Joe's salary and T = Tom's salary. The first sentence says $T = 125\%$ of J or $T = \frac{5}{4}J$, and $M = 80\%$ of J or $M = \frac{4}{5}J$. The second sentence says that $T + M + J = \$61{,}000$. Using the information from the first sentence, $T + M + J = \frac{5}{4}J + \frac{4}{5}J + J = \frac{25}{20}J + \frac{16}{20}J + J = \frac{61}{20}J$. So $\frac{61}{20}J = 61{,}000$; solving for J you have $J = \frac{20}{61} \times 61{,}000 = 20{,}000$. Therefore, $T = \frac{5}{4} \times \$20{,}000 = \$25{,}000$ and $M = \frac{4}{5} \times \$20{,}000 = \$16{,}000$.

CHECK:

$$\$25{,}000 + \$16{,}000 + \$20{,}000 = \$61{,}000.$$

So Mary's salary is \$16,000.

EXAMPLE 3: Steve weighs 25 pounds more than Jim. Their combined weight of Jim and Steve is 325 pounds. How much does Jim weigh?

Let S = Steve's weight in pounds and J = Jim's weight in pounds. The first sentence says $S = J + 25$, and the second sentence becomes $S + J = 325$. Since $S = J + 25$, $S + J = 325$ becomes $(J + 25) + J = 2J + 25 = 325$. So $2J = 300$ and $J = 150$. Therefore, Jim weighs 150 pounds.

CHECK:

If Jim weighs 150 pounds, then Steve weighs 175 pounds and $150 + 175 = 325$.

EXAMPLE 4: A carpenter is designing a closet. The floor will be in the shape of a rectangle whose length is 2 feet more than its width. How long should the closet be if the carpenter wants the area of the floor to be 15 square feet?

The area of a rectangle is length times width, usually written $A = LW$, where A is the area, L is the length, and W is the width. We know $A = 15$ and $L = 2 + W$. Therefore, $LW = (2 + W)\ W = W^2 + 2W$; this must equal 15. So we need to solve $W^2 + 2W = 15$ or $W^2 + 2W - 15 = 0$. Since $W^2 + W - 15$ factors into $(W + 5)(W - 3)$, the only possible solutions are $W = -5$ and $W = 3$. Since W represents a width, -5 cannot be the answer; therefore the width is 3 feet. The length is the width plus two feet, so the length is 5 feet. Since $5 \times 3 = 15$, the answer checks.

3–2

Distance Problems. A common type of word problem is a distance or velocity problem. The basic formula is

$$\boxed{\text{DISTANCE TRAVELED} = \text{RATE} \times \text{TIME.}}$$

The formula is abbreviated $d = rt$.

EXAMPLE 1: A train travels at an average speed of 50 miles per hour for $2\frac{1}{2}$ hours and then travels at a speed of 70 miles per hour for $1\frac{1}{2}$ hours. How far did the train travel in the entire 4 hours?

The train traveled for $2\frac{1}{2}$ hours at an average speed of 50 miles per hour, so it traveled $50 \times \frac{5}{2} = 125$ miles in the first $2\frac{1}{2}$ hours. Traveling at a speed of 70 miles per hour for $1\frac{1}{2}$ hours, the distance traveled will be equal to $r \times t$ where $r = 70$ m.p.h. and $t = 1\frac{1}{2}$, so the distance is $70 \times \frac{3}{2} = 105$ miles. Therefore, the total distance traveled is $125 + 105 = 230$ miles.

EXAMPLE 2: The distance from Cleveland to Buffalo is 200 miles. A train takes $3\frac{1}{2}$ hours to go from Buffalo to Cleveland and $4\frac{1}{2}$ hours to go back from Cleveland to Buffalo. What was the average speed of the train for the round trip from Buffalo to Cleveland and back?

The train took $3\frac{1}{2} + 4\frac{1}{2} = 8$ hours for the trip. The distance of a round trip is $2(200) = 400$ miles. Since $d = rt$ then 400 miles $= r \times 8$ hours. Solve for r and you have $r = \frac{400 \text{ miles}}{8 \text{ hours}} = 50$ miles per hour. Therefore the average speed is 50 miles per hour.

The speed in the formula is the average speed. If you know that there are different speeds for different lengths of time, then you must use the formula more than once, as we did in example 1.

3–3

Work Problems. In this type of problem you can always assume all workers in the same category work at the same rate. The main idea is: If it takes k

workers 1 hour to do a job then *each worker does* $\frac{1}{k}$ *of the job in an hour* or he works at the rate of $\frac{1}{k}$ of the job per hour. If it takes m workers h hours to finish a job then each worker does $\frac{1}{m}$ of the job in h hours so he does $\frac{1}{h}$ of $\frac{1}{m}$ in an hour. Therefore, each worker *works at the rate of* $\frac{1}{mh}$ *of the job per hour.*

EXAMPLE 1: If 5 men take an hour to dig a ditch, how long should it take 12 men to dig a ditch of the same type?

Since 5 workers took an hour, each worker does $\frac{1}{5}$ of the job in an hour. So 12 workers will work at the rate of $\frac{12}{5}$ of the job per hour. Thus if T is the time it takes for 12 workers to do the job, $\frac{12}{5} \times T = 1$ hour and $T = \frac{5}{12} \times 1$ hour, so

$$T = \frac{5}{12} \text{ hours or 25 minutes.}$$

EXAMPLE 2: Worker A takes 8 hours to do a job. Worker B takes 10 hours to do the same job. How long should it take worker A and worker B working together, but independently, to do the same job?

Worker A works at a rate of $\frac{1}{8}$ of the job per hour, since he takes 8 hours to finish the job. Worker B finished the job in 10 hours, so he works at a rate of $\frac{1}{10}$ of the job per hour. Therefore, if they work together they should complete $\frac{1}{8} + \frac{1}{10} = \frac{18}{80} = \frac{9}{40}$, so they work at a rate of $\frac{9}{40}$ of the job per hour together. So if T is the time it takes them to finish the job, $\frac{9}{40}$ of the job per hour $\times$ T hours must equal 1 job. Therefore,

$$\frac{9}{40} \times T = 1 \text{ and } T = \frac{40}{9} = 4\frac{4}{9} \text{ hours.}$$

EXAMPLE 1: There are two taps, tap 1 and tap 2, in a keg. If both taps are opened, the keg is drained in 20 minutes. If tap 1 is closed and tap 2 is open, the keg will be drained in 30 minutes. If tap 2 is closed and tap 1 is open, how long will it take to drain the keg?

Tap 1 and tap 2 together take 20 minutes to drain the keg, so together they drain the keg at a rate of $\frac{1}{20}$ of the keg per minute. Tap 2 takes 30 minutes to drain the keg by itself, so it drains the keg at the rate of $\frac{1}{30}$ of the keg per minute. Let r be the rate at which tap 1 will drain the keg by itself. Then $\left(r + \frac{1}{30}\right)$ of the keg per minute is the rate at which both taps together will drain the keg, so $r + \frac{1}{30} = \frac{1}{20}$. Therefore, $r = \frac{1}{20} - \frac{1}{30} = \frac{1}{60}$, and tap 1 drains the keg at the rate of $\frac{1}{60}$ of the keg per minute, so it will take 60 minutes or 1 hour for tap 1 to drain the keg if tap 2 is closed.

II–4. Counting Problems

4–1

An example of the first type of counting problem is: 50 students signed up for both English and Math. 90 students signed up for either English or Math. If 25 students are taking English but not taking Math, how many students are taking Math but not taking English?

In these problems, "either . . . or . . ." means you can take both, so the people taking both are counted among the people taking either Math or English.

You must avoid counting the same people twice in these problems. The formula is:

the number taking English or Math = the number taking English + the number taking Math − the number taking both.

You have to subtract the number taking both subjects since they are counted once with those taking English and counted again with those taking Math.

A person taking English is either taking Math or not taking Math, so there are 50 + 25 = 75 people taking English, 50 taking English and Math and 25 taking English but not taking Math. Since 75 are taking English, 90 = 75 + number taking Math − 50; so there are 90 − 25 = 65 people taking Math. 50 of the people taking Math are taking English so 65 − 50 or 15 are taking Math but not English.

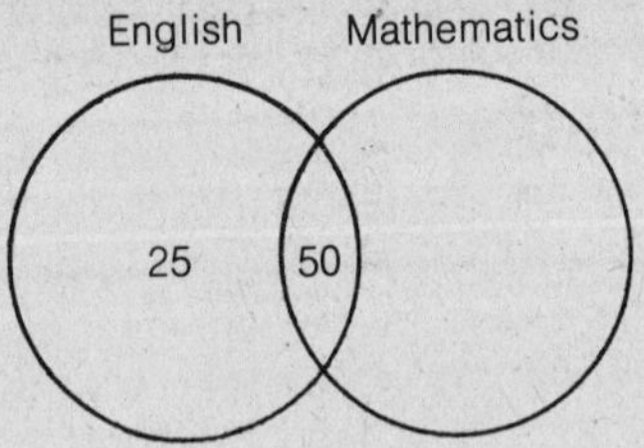

The figure shows what is given. Since 90 students signed up for English or Mathematics. 15 must be taking Mathematics but not English.

EXAMPLE 1: In a survey, 60% of those surveyed owned a car and 80% of those surveyed owned a T.V. If 55% owned both a car and a T.V., what percent of those surveyed owned a car or a T.V. or both?

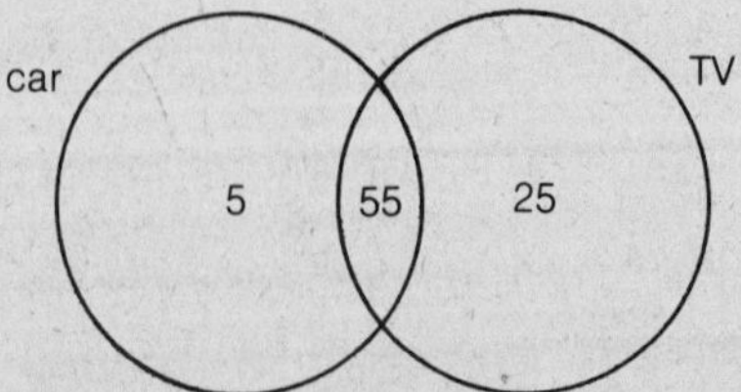

The basic formula is:

people who own a car or a T.V. = people who own a car
+ people who own a T.V. − people who own both a car and a T.V.

So the people who own a car or a T.V. = 60% + 80% − 55% = 85%. Therefore, 85% of the people surveyed own either a car or a T.V.

If we just add 60% and 80% the result is 140% which is impossible. This is because the 55% who own both are counted twice.

4–2

If an event can happen in m different ways, and each of the m ways is followed by a second event which can occur in k different ways, then the first event can be followed by the second event in $m \cdot k$ different ways. This is called the *fundamental principle of counting.*

EXAMPLE 1: If there are 3 different roads from Syracuse to Binghamton and 4 different roads from Binghamton to Scranton, how many different routes are there from Syracuse to Scranton which go through Binghamton?

There are 3 different ways to go from Syracuse to Binghamton. Once you are in Binghamton, there are 4 different ways to get to Scranton. So using the fundamental principle of counting, there are $3 \times 4 = 12$ different ways to get from Syracuse to Scranton going through Binghamton.

EXAMPLE 2: A club has 20 members. They are electing a president and a vice president. How many different outcomes of the election are possible? (Assume the president and vice president must be different members of the club.)

There are 20 members, so there are 20 choices for president. Once a president is chosen, there are 19 members left who can be vice president. So there are $20 \cdot 19 = 380$ different possible outcomes of the election.

II–5. Ratio and Proportion

5–1

Ratio. A ratio is a comparison of two numbers by division. The ratio of a to b is written as $a{:}b = \frac{a}{b} = a \div b$. We can handle ratios as fractions, since a ratio is a fraction. In the ratio $a{:}b$, a and b are called the *terms* of the ratio. *Since* a:b *is a fraction,* b *can never be zero.* The fraction $\frac{a}{b}$ is usually different from the fraction $\frac{b}{a}$ $\left(\text{for example } \frac{3}{2} \text{ is not the same as } \frac{2}{3}\right)$ so *the order of the terms in a ratio is important.*

EXAMPLE 1: If an orange costs 20¢ and an apple costs 12¢, what is the ratio of the cost of an orange to the cost of an apple?

The ratio is $\frac{20¢}{12¢} = \frac{5}{3}$ or 5:3. Notice that the ratio of the cost of an apple to the cost of an orange is $\frac{12¢}{20¢} = \frac{3}{5}$ or 3:5. So the order of the terms is important.

A ratio is a number, so if you want to find the ratio of two quantities they must be expressed in the same units.

EXAMPLE 2: What is the ratio of 8 inches to 6 feet?

Change 6 feet into inches. Since there are 12 inches in a foot, 6 feet = 6×12 inches = 72 inches. So the ratio is $\frac{8 \text{ inches}}{72 \text{ inches}} = \frac{1}{9}$ or 1:9. If you regard ratios as fractions, the units must cancel out. In example 2, if you did not change units the ratio would be $\frac{8 \text{ inches}}{6 \text{ feet}} = \frac{4}{3}$ inches/feet, which is not a number.

If two numbers measure different quantities, their quotient is usually called a rate. For example, $\frac{50 \text{ miles}}{2 \text{ hours}}$ which equals 25 miles per hour is a rate of speed.

5–2

Proportion. A proportion is a statement that two ratios are equal. For example, $\frac{3}{12} = \frac{1}{4}$ is a proportion; it could also be expressed as 3:12 = 1:4 or 3:12 :: 1:4.

In the proportion $a:b = c:d$, the terms on the outside, (a and d), are called the *extremes*, and the terms on the inside, (b and c), are called the *means*. Since $a:b$ and $c:d$ are ratios, b and d are both different from zero, so $bd \neq 0$. Multiply each side of $\frac{a}{b} = \frac{c}{d}$ by bd; you get $(bd)\left(\frac{a}{b}\right) = ad$ and $(bd)\left(\frac{c}{d}\right) = bc$. Since $bd \neq 0$, the proportion $\frac{a}{b} = \frac{c}{d}$ is equivalent to the equation $ad = bc$. This is usually expressed in the following way.

In a proportion the product of the extremes is equal to the product of the means.

EXAMPLE 1: Find x if $\frac{4}{5} = \frac{10}{x}$.

In the proportion $\frac{4}{5} = \frac{10}{x}$, 4 and x are the extremes and 5 and 10 are the means, so $4x = 5 \cdot 10 = 50$.

Solve for x and we get $x = \frac{50}{4} = 12.5$.

Finding the products ad and bc is also called *cross-multiplying the proportion:* $\frac{a}{b} \times \frac{c}{d}$. So cross-multiplying a proportion gives two equal numbers. The proportion $\frac{a}{b} = \frac{c}{d}$ is read "a is to b as c is to d."

EXAMPLE 2: Two numbers are in the ratio 5:4 and their difference is 10. What is the larger number?

Let m and n be the two numbers. Then $\frac{m}{n} = \frac{5}{4}$ and $m - n = 10$. Cross-multiply the proportion and you get $5n = 4m$ or $n = \frac{4}{5}m$. So $m - n = m - \frac{4}{5}m = \frac{1}{5}m = 10$ and $m = 50$, which means $n = \frac{4}{5} \cdot 50 = 40$. Therefore, the larger number is 50.

CHECK:

$$\frac{50}{40} = \frac{5}{4} \text{ and } 50 - 40 = 10.$$

Two variables, a and b, are *directly proportional* if they satisfy a relationship of the form $a = kb$, where k is a number. The distance a car travels in two hours and its average speed for the two hours are directly proportional, since $d = 2s$ where d is the distance and s is the average speed expressed in miles per hour. Here $k = 2$. Sometimes the word *directly* is omitted, so a and b are proportional means $a = kb$.

EXAMPLE 3: If m is proportional to n and $m = 5$ when $n = 4$, what is the value of m when $n = 18$?

There are two different ways to work the problem.

I. Since m and n are directly proportional, $m = kn$; and $m = 5$ when $n = 4$, so $5 = k \cdot 4$ which means $k = \frac{5}{4}$. Therefore, $m = \frac{5}{4}n$. So when $n = 18$, $m = \frac{5}{4} \cdot 18 = \frac{90}{4} = 22.5$.

II. Since m and n are directly proportional, $m = kn$. If n' is some value of n, then the value of m corresponding to n' we will call m', and $m' = kn'$. So $\frac{m}{n} = k$ and $\frac{m'}{n'} = k$; therefore, $\frac{m}{n} = \frac{m'}{n'}$ is a proportion. Since $m = 5$ when $n = 4$, $\frac{m}{n} = \frac{5}{4} = \frac{m'}{18}$. Cross-multiply and we have $4m' = 90$ or $m' = \frac{90}{4} = 22.5$.

If two quantities are proportional, you can always set up a proportion in this manner.

EXAMPLE 4: If a machine makes 3 yards of cloth in 2 minutes, how many yards of cloth will the machine make in 50 minutes?

The amount of cloth is proportional to the time the machine operates. Let y be the number of yards of cloth the machine makes in 50 minutes; then $\frac{2 \text{ minutes}}{50 \text{ minutes}} = \frac{3 \text{ yards}}{y \text{ yards}}$, so $\frac{2}{50} = \frac{3}{y}$. Cross multiply, and you have $2y = 150$, so $y = 75$. Therefore, the machine makes 75 yards of cloth in 50 minutes.

Since a ratio is a number, the units must cancel; so put the numbers which measure the same quantity in the same ratio.

Any two units of measurement of the same quantity are directly proportional.

EXAMPLE 5: How many ounces are there in $4\frac{3}{4}$ pounds?

Let x be the number of ounces in $4\frac{3}{4}$ pounds. Since there are 16 ounces in a pound, $\frac{x \text{ ounces}}{16 \text{ ounces}} = \frac{4\,^3\!/_4 \text{ pounds}}{1 \text{ pound}}$. Cross-multiply to get $x = 16 \cdot 4\frac{3}{4} = 16 \cdot \frac{19}{4} = 76$; so $4\frac{3}{4}$ pounds $= 76$ ounces.

You can always change units by using a proportion. You should know the following measurements:

LENGTH:	1 foot = 12 inches
	1 yard = 3 feet
AREA:	1 square foot = 144 square inches
	1 square yard = 9 square feet
TIME:	1 minute = 60 seconds
	1 hour = 60 minutes
	1 day = 24 hours
	1 week = 7 days
	1 year = 52 weeks
VOLUME:	1 quart = 2 pints
	1 gallon = 4 quarts
WEIGHT:	1 ounce = 16 drams
	1 pound = 16 ounces
	1 ton = 2000 pounds

EXAMPLE 6: On a map, it is $2\frac{1}{2}$ inches from Harrisburg to Gary. The actual distance from Harrisburg to Gary is 750 miles. What is the actual distance from town A to town B if they are 4 inches apart on the map?

Let d miles be the distance from A to B; then $\frac{2\,^1\!/_2 \text{ inches}}{4 \text{ inches}} = \frac{750 \text{ miles}}{d \text{ miles}}$. Cross-multiply and we have $\left(2\frac{1}{2}\right)d = 4 \times 750 = 3{,}000$, so $d = \frac{2}{5} \times 3{,}000 = 1{,}200$. Therefore, the distance from A to B is 1,200 miles. Problems like this one are often called scale problems.

Two variables, a and b, are *indirectly proportional* if they satisfy a relationship of the form $k = ab$, where k is a number. So the average speed of a car and the time it takes the car to travel 300 miles are indirectly proportional, since $st = 300$ where s is the speed and t is the time.

EXAMPLE 7: m is indirectly proportional to n and $m = 5$ when $n = 4$. What is the value of m when $n = 18$?

Since m and n are indirectly proportional, $m \cdot n = k$, and $k = 5 \cdot 4 = 20$ because $m = 5$ when $n = 4$. Therefore, $18m = k = 20$, so $m = \frac{20}{18} = \frac{10}{9}$ when $n = 18$.

Other examples of indirect proportion are work problems (see page 174).

If two quantities are directly proportional, then when one increases, the other increases. If two quantities are indirectly proportional when one quantity increases, the other decreases.

5–3

It is also possible to compare three or more numbers by a ratio. The numbers A, B, and C are in the ratio 2:4:3 means $A{:}B = 2{:}4$, $A{:}C = 2{:}3$, and $B{:}C = 4{:}3$. The order of the terms is important. $A{:}B{:}C$ is read A is to B is to C.

EXAMPLE 1: What is the ratio of Tom's salary to Martha's salary to Anne's salary if Tom makes \$15,000, Martha makes \$12,000 and Anne makes \$10,000?

The ratio is 15,000:12,000:10,000 which is the same as 15:12:10. You can cancel a factor which appears in *every* term.

EXAMPLE 2: The angles of a triangle are in the ratio 5:4:3; how many degrees are there is the largest angle?

The sum of the angles in a triangle is 180°. If the angles are $a°$, $b°$, and $c°$, then $a + b + c = 180$, and $a{:}b{:}c{:} = 5{:}4{:}3$. You could find b in terms of a since $\frac{a}{b} = \frac{5}{4}$ and c in terms of a since $\frac{a}{c} = \frac{5}{3}$ and then solve the equation for a.

A quicker method for this type of problem is:

(1) Add all the numbers, so $5 + 4 + 3 = 12$.
(2) Use each number as the numerator of a fraction whose denominator is the result of step (1), getting $\frac{5}{12}, \frac{4}{12}, \frac{3}{12}$.
(3) Each quantity is the corresponding fraction (from step (2)), of the total.

Thus

$a = \frac{5}{12}$ of 180 or 75, $b = \frac{4}{12}$ of 180 or 60, and $c = \frac{3}{12}$ of 180 or 45.
So the largest angle is 75°.

CHECK:

$$75{:}60{:}45 = 5{:}4{:}3 \text{ and } 75 + 60 + 45 = 180.$$

II–6. Sequence and Progressions

6–1

A SEQUENCE is an ordered collection of numbers. For example, 2,4,6,8,10, . . . is a sequence. 2,4,6,8,10 are called the *terms* of the sequence. We identify the terms by their position in the sequence; so 2 is the first term, 8 is the 4th term and so on. The dots mean the sequence continues; you should be able to figure out the succeeding terms. In the example, the sequence is the sequence of even integers, and the next term after 10 would be 12.

EXAMPLE 1: What is the eighth term of the sequence 1,4,9,16,25, . . . ?

Since $1^2 = 1$, $2^2 = 4$, $3^2 = 9$, the sequence is the sequence of squares of integers, so the eighth term is $8^2 = 64$.

6–2

An *arithmetical progression* is a sequence of numbers with the property that the *difference* of any two consecutive numbers is always the same. The numbers 2,6,10,14,18,22, . . . constitute an arithmetical progression, since each term is 4 more than the term before it. 4 is called the common difference of the progression.

If d is the common difference and a is the first term of the progression, then the nth term will be $a + (n - 1)d$. So a progression with common difference 4 and initial term 5 will have $5 + 6(4) = 29$ as its 7th term. You can check your answer. The sequence would be 5,9,13,17,21,25,29, . . . so 29 is the seventh term.

A sequence of numbers is called a *geometric progression* if the *ratio* of consecutive terms is always the same. So 3,6,12,14,48, . . . is a geometric progression since $\frac{6}{3} = 2 = \frac{12}{6} = \frac{24}{12} = \frac{48}{24}, \ldots$. *The nth term of a geometric series is* ar^{n-1} where a is the first term and r is the common ratio. If a geometric progression started with 2 and the common ratio was 3, then the fifth term should be $2 \cdot 3^4 = 2 \cdot 81 = 162$. The sequence would be 2,6,18,54,162, . . . so 162 is indeed the fifth term of the progression.

We can quickly add up the first n terms of a geometric progression which starts with a and has common ratio r. *The formula for the sum of the first n terms* is $\frac{ar^n - a}{r - 1}$ when $r \neq 1$. (If $r = 1$ all the terms are the same so the sum is na.)

EXAMPLE 1: Find the sum of the first 7 terms of the sequence 5,10,20,40, ...

Since $\frac{10}{5} = \frac{20}{10} = \frac{40}{20} = 2$, the sequence is a geometric sequence with common ratio 2. The first term is 5, so the sum of the first 7 terms is

$$\frac{5 \cdot 2^7 - 5}{2 - 1} = 5(2^7 - 1) = 5(128 - 1) = 5 \cdot 127 = 635.$$

CHECK:

The first seven terms are 5,10,20,40,80,160,320, and $5 + 10 + 20 + 40 + 80 + 160 + 320 = 635$.

II-7. Inequalities

7-1

A number is positive if it is greater than 0, so 1, $\frac{1}{1000}$, and 53.4 are all positive numbers. Positive numbers are signed numbers whose sign is +. If you think of numbers as points on a number line (see section 6, page 155), positive numbers correspond to points to the right of 0.

A number is negative if it is less than 0. $-\frac{4}{5}$, -50, and $-.0001$ are all negative numbers. Negative numbers are signed numbers whose sign is −. Negative numbers correspond to points to the left of 0 on a number line.

0 is the only number which is neither positive nor negative.

$a > b$ means the number a is greater than the number b, that is $a = b + x$ where x is a positive number. If we look at a number line, $a > b$ means a is to the right of b. $a > b$ can also be read as b is less than a, which is also written $b < a$. For example, $-5 > -7.5$ because $-5 = -7.5 + 2.5$ and 2.5 is positive.

The notation $a \leqslant b$ means a is less than or equal to b, or b is greater than or equal to a. For example, $5 \geqslant 4$; also $4 \geqslant 4$. $a \neq b$ is not equal to b.

If you need to know whether one fraction is greater than another fraction, put the fractions over a common denominator and compare the numerators.

EXAMPLE 1: Which is larger, $\frac{13}{16}$ or $\frac{31}{40}$?

A common denominator is 80.

$\frac{13}{16} = \frac{65}{80}$, and $\frac{31}{40} = \frac{62}{80}$;

since $65 > 62$,

$\frac{65}{80} > \frac{62}{80}$,

so $\frac{13}{16} > \frac{31}{40}$.

7-2

Inequalities have certain properties which are similar to equations. We can talk about the left side and the right side of an inequality, and we can use algebraic expressions for the sides of an inequality. For example, $6x < 5x + 4$. A value for an unknown *satisfies an inequality,* if when you evaluate each side of the inequality the numbers satisfy the inequality. So if $x = 2$, then $6x = 12$ and $5x + 4 = 14$ and since $12 < 14$, $x = 2$ satisfies $6x < 5x + 4$. Two inequalities are equivalent if the same collection of numbers satisfy both inequalities.

The following basic principles are used in work with inequalities:

(A) Adding the same expression to *each* side of an inequality gives an equivalent inequality (written $a < b \Leftrightarrow a + c < b + c$ where $\Leftrightarrow$ means equivalent).

(B) Subtracting the same expression from *each* side of an inequality gives an equivalent inequality ($a < b \Leftrightarrow a - c < b - c$).

(C) Multiplying or dividing *each* side of an inequality by the same *positive* expression gives an equivalent inequality ($a < b \Leftrightarrow ca < cb$ for $c > 0$).

(D) Multiplying or dividing each side of an inequality by the same *negative* expression *reverses* the inequality ($a < b \Leftrightarrow ca > cb$ for $c < 0$).

(E) If both sides of an inequality have the same sign, inverting both sides of the inequality *reverses* the inequality.

$$0 < a < b \Leftrightarrow 0 < \frac{1}{b} < \frac{1}{a}$$

$$a < b < 0 \Leftrightarrow \frac{1}{b} < \frac{1}{a} < 0$$

(F) If two inequalities are of the same type (both greater or both less), adding the respective sides gives the same type of inequality.

$$(a < b \text{ and } c < d, \text{ then } a + c < d + d)$$

Note that the inequalities are *not* equivalent.

(G) If $a < b$ and $b < c$ then $a < c$.

EXAMPLE 1: Find the values of x for which $5x - 4 < 7x + 2$.

Using property (B) subtract $5x + 2$ from each side, so $(5x - 4 < 7x + 2) \Leftrightarrow -6 < 2x$. Now use property (C) and divide each side by 2, so $-6 < 2x \Leftrightarrow -3 < x$.

So any x greater than -3 satisfies the inequality. It is a good idea to make a spot check. -1 is > -3; let $x = -1$ then $5x - 4 = -9$ and $7x + 2 = -5$. Since $-9 < -5$, the answer is correct for at least the particular value $x = -1$.

EXAMPLE 2: Find the values of a which satisfy $a^2 + 1 > 2a + 4$.

Subtract $2a$ from each side, so
$(a^2 + 1 > 2a + 4) \Leftrightarrow a^2 - 2a + 1 > 4$.
$a^2 - 2a + 1 = (a - 1)^2$ so
$a^2 - 2a + 1 > 4 \Leftrightarrow (a - 1)^2 > 2^2$.

We need to be careful when we take the square roots of inequalities. If $q^2 > 4$ and if $q > 0$, then $q > 2$; but if $q < 0$, then $q < -2$. We must look at two cases in example 2. First, if $(a - 1) \geq 0$ then

$(a - 1)^2 > 2^2 \Leftrightarrow a - 1 > 2$ or $a > 3$.
If $(a - 1) < 0$ then $(a - 1)^2 > 2^2 \Leftrightarrow a - 1 < -2 \Leftrightarrow a < -1$.
So the inequality is satisfied if $a > 3$ or if $a < -1$.

CHECK:

$$(-2)^2 + 1 = 5 > 2(-2) + 4 = 0, \text{ and } 5^2 + 1 = 26 > 14 = 2 \cdot 5 + 4.$$

Some inequalities are not satisfied by *any* real number. For example, since $x^2 \geq 0$ for all x, there is no real number x such that $x^2 < -9$.

You may be given an inequality and asked whether other inequalities follow from the original inequality. You should be able to answer such questions by using properties (A) through (G).

If there is any property of inequalities you can't remember, try out some specific numbers. If $x < y$, then what is the relation between $-x$ and $-y$? Since $4 < 5$ but $-5 < -4$, the relation is probably $-x > -y$, which is true by (C).

Probably the most common mistake is forgetting to reverse the inequalities if you multiply or divide by a negative number.

III. Geometry

III–1. Angles

1–1

If two straight lines meet at a point they form an *angle*. The point is called the *vertex* of the angle and the lines are called the *sides* or *rays* of the angle. The sign for angle is ∠ and an angle can be denoted in the following ways:

(A) $\angle ABC$ where B is the vertex, A is a point on one side, and C a point on the other side.

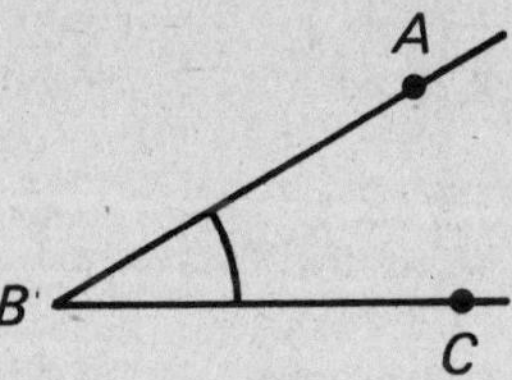

(B) $\angle B$ where B is the vertex.

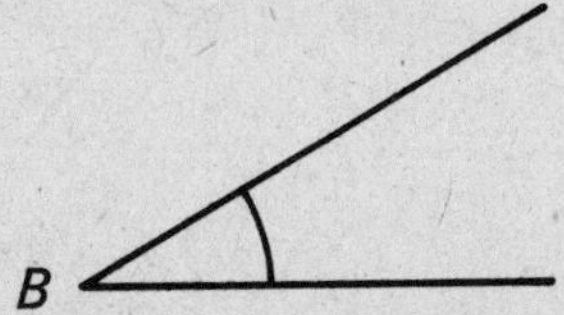

(C) $\angle 1$ or $\angle x$ where x or 1 is written inside the angle.

Angles are usually measured in degrees. We say that an angle equals x degrees, when its measure is x degrees. Degrees are denoted by °. An angle of 50 degrees is 50°. $60' = 1°$, $60'' = 1'$ where $'$ is read minutes and $''$ is read seconds.

1–2

Two angles are *adjacent* if they have the same vertex and a common side and one angle is not inside the other.

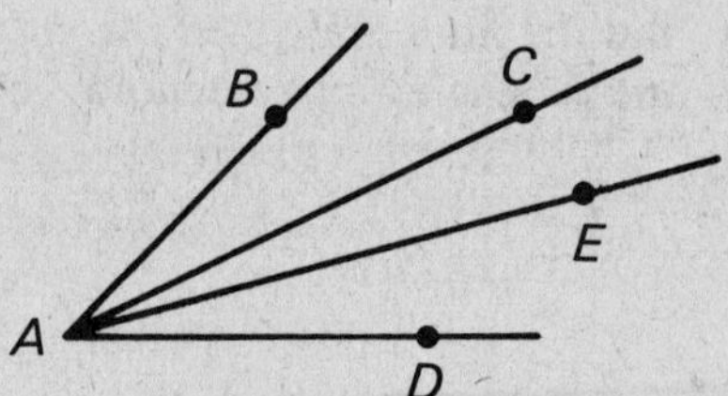

$\angle BAC$ and $\angle CAD$ are adjacent, but $\angle CAD$ and $\angle EAD$ are not adjacent.

If two lines intersect at a point, they form 4 angles. The angles opposite each other are called *vertical* angles. $\angle 1$ and $\angle 3$ are vertical angles. $\angle 2$ and $\angle 4$ are vertical angles.

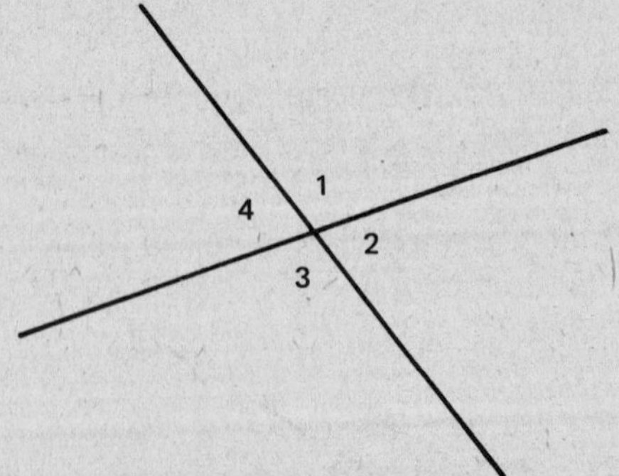

Vertical angles are equal,

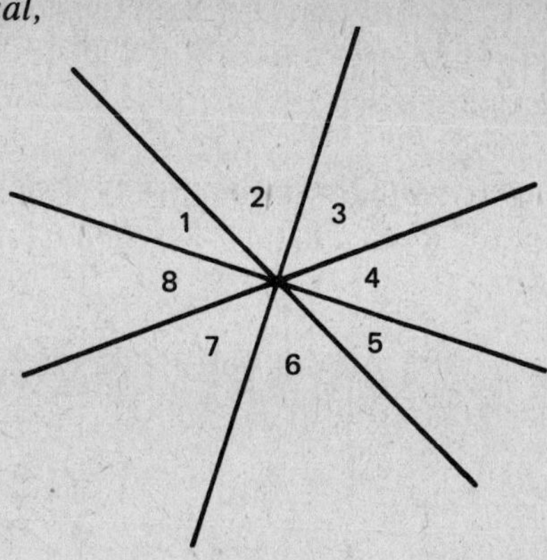

so $\angle 1 = \angle 5$, $\angle 2 = \angle 6$, $\angle 3 = \angle 7$, $\angle 4 = \angle 8$.

1–3

A straight angle is an angle whose sides lie on a straight line. *A straight angle equals 180°.*

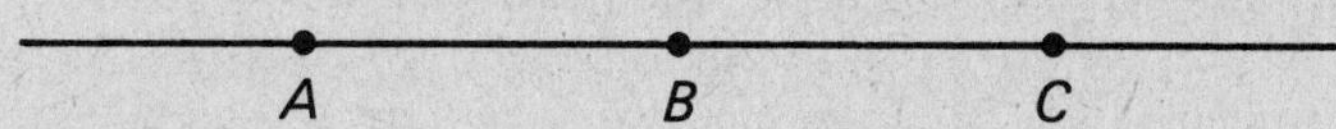

$\angle ABC$ is a straight angle.

If the sum of two adjacent angles is a straight angle, then the angles are *supplementary* and each angle is the supplement of the other.

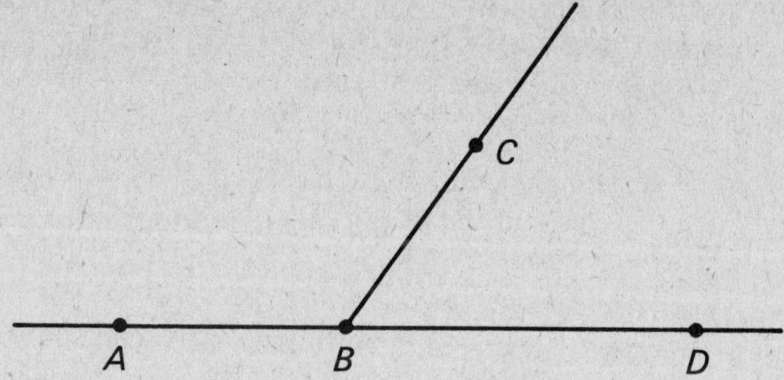

$\angle ABC$ and $\angle CBD$ are supplementary.

If an angle of $x°$ and an angle of $y°$ are supplements, then $x + y = 180$.

If two supplementary angles are equal, they are both *right angles.* A right angle is half of a straight angle. A right angle = 90°.

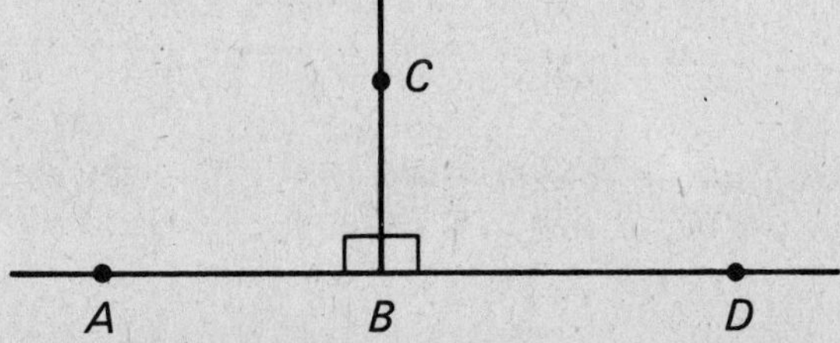

$\angle ABC = \angle CBD$ and they are both right angles. A right angle is denoted by ∟. When 2 lines intersect and all four of the angles are equal, then each of the angles is a right angle.

If the sum of two adjacent angles is a right angle, then the angles are *complementary* and each angle is the complement of the other.

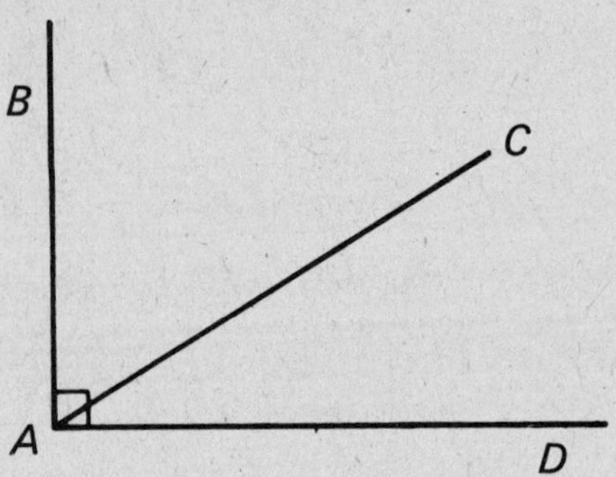

$\angle BAC$ and $\angle CAD$ are complementary.

If an angle of $x°$ and an angle of $y°$ are complementary, then $x + y = 90$.

EXAMPLE 1: If the supplement of angle x is three times as much as the complement of angle x, how many degrees is angle x?

Let d be the number of degrees in angle x; then the supplement of x is $(180 - d)°$, and the complement of x is $(90 - d)°$. Since the supplement is 3 times the complement, $180 - d = 3(90 - d) = 270 - 3d$ which gives $2d = 90$, so $d = 45$.

Therefore, angle x is 45°.

If an angle is divided into two equal lines by a straight line, then the angle has been *bisected* and the line is called the *bisector* of the angle.

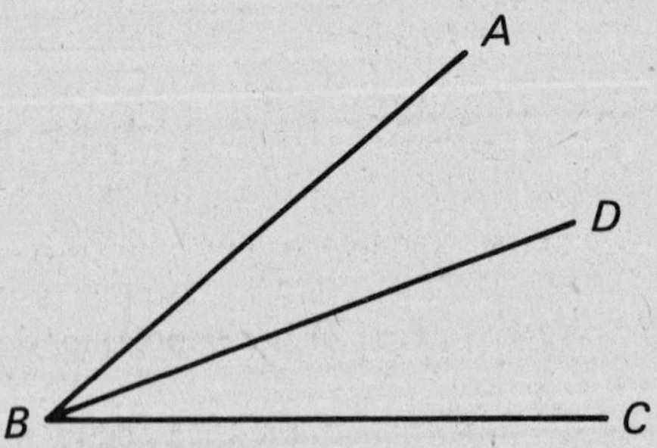

BD bisects $\angle ABC$; so $\angle ABD = \angle DBC$.

An *acute angle* is an angle less than a right angle. An *obtuse* angle is an angle greater than a right angle, but less than a straight angle.

$\angle 1$ is an acute angle, and $\angle 2$ is an obtuse angle.

III–2. Lines

2–1

A line is understood to be a straight line. A line is assumed to extend indefinitely in both directions. *There is one and only one line between two distinct points.* There are two ways to denote a line:

(1) (A) by a single letter: l is a line;

l

(2) (B) by two points on the line: A B AB is a line.

A *line segment* is the part of a line between two points called *endpoints.* A line segment is denoted by its endpoints.

A B

AB is a line segment. If a point P on a line segment is equidistant from the endpoints, then P is called the *midpoint* of the line segment.

A P B

P is the midpoint of AB if the length of $AP =$ the length of PB. Two line segments are equal if their lengths are equal; so $AP = PB$ means the line segment AP has the same length as the line segment PB.

When a line segment is extended indefinitely in one direction, it is called a *ray*. A ray has one endpoint.

AB is a ray which has *A* as its endpoint.

2-2

P is a *point of intersection* of two lines if *P* is a point which is on both of the lines. *Two different lines can not have more than one point of intersection,* because there is only one line between two points.

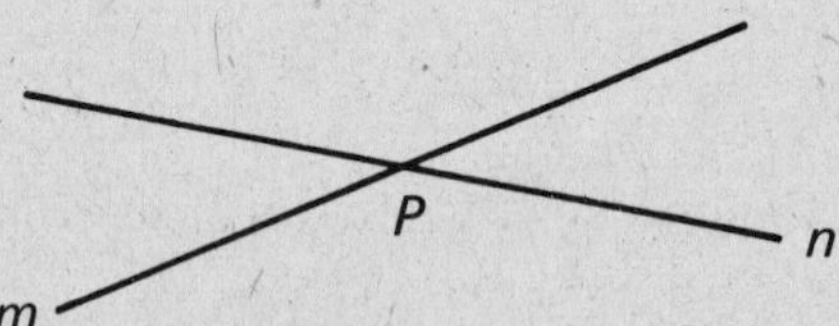

P is the point of intersection of *m* and *n*. We also say *m and n intersect at P*.

Two lines in the same plane are parallel if they do not intersect no matter how far they are extended.

m and *n* are parallel, but *k* and *l* are not parallel since if *k* and *l* are extended they will intersect. Parallel lines are denoted by the symbol ‖; so $m \parallel n$ means *m* is parallel to *n*.

If two lines are parallel to a third line, then they are parallel to each other.

If a third line intersects two given lines, it is called a *transversal.* A transversal and the two given lines form eight angles. The four inside angles are called *interior* angles. The four outside angles are called *exterior* angles. If two angles are on opposite sides of the transversal they are called *alternate* angles.

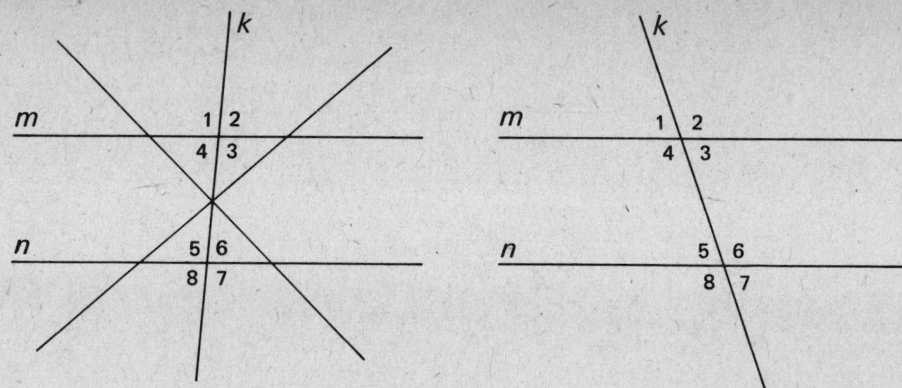

k is a transversal of the lines *m* and *n*. Angles 1, 2, 7, and 8 are the exterior angles, and angles 3, 4, 5, and 6 are the interior angles. $\angle 4$ and $\angle 6$ are an example of a pair of alternate angles. $\angle 1$ and $\angle 5$, $\angle 2$ and $\angle 6$, $\angle 3$ and $\angle 7$, and $\angle 4$ and $\angle 8$ are pairs of *corresponding* angles.

If two parallel lines are intersected by a transversal then:

(1) Alternate interior angles are equal.
(2) Corresponding angles are equal.
(3) Interior angles on the same side of the transversal are supplementary.

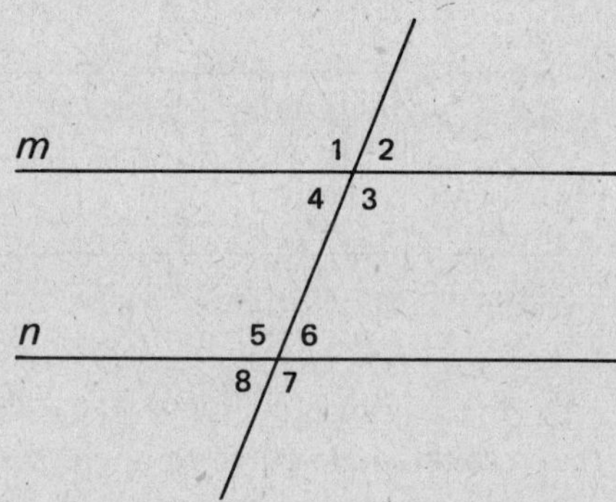

If we use the fact that vertical angles are equal, we can replace "interior" by "exterior" in (1) and (3).

m is parallel to *n* implies:

(1) $\angle 4 = \angle 6$ and $\angle 3 = \angle 5$
(2) $\angle 1 = \angle 5$, $\angle 2 = \angle 6$, $\angle 3 = \angle 7$ and $\angle 4 = \angle 8$
(3) $\angle 3 + \angle 6 = 180°$ and $\angle 4 + \angle 5 = 180°$

The reverse is also true. Let *m* and *n* be two lines which have *k* as a transversal.

(1) If a pair of alternate interior angles are equal, then *m* and *n* are parallel.
(2) If a pair of corresponding angles are equal, then *m* and *n* are parallel.
(3) If a pair of interior angles on the same side of the transversal are supplementary, then *m* is parallel to *n*.

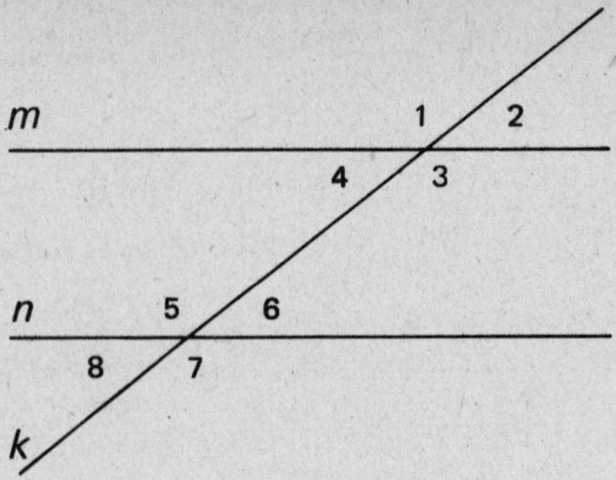

If $\angle 3 = \angle 5$, then $m \parallel n$. If $\angle 4 = \angle 6$ then $m \parallel n$. If $\angle 2 = \angle 6$ then $m \parallel n$. If $\angle 3 + \angle 6 = 180°$, then $m \parallel n$.

EXAMPLE 1: If m and n are two parallel lines and angle 1 is 60°, how many degrees is angle 2?

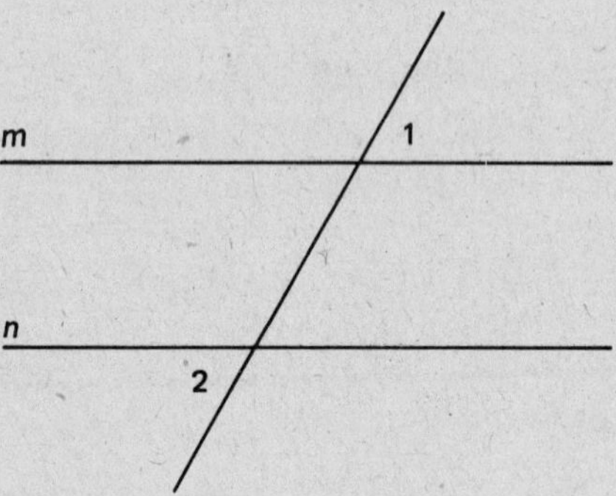

Let $\angle 3$ be the vertical angle equal to angle 2.

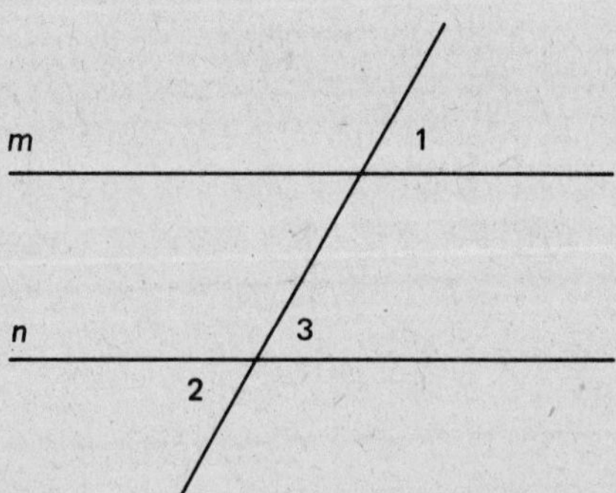

$\angle 3 = \angle 2$. Since m and n are parallel, corresponding angles are equal. Since $\angle 1$ and $\angle 3$ are corresponding angles, $\angle 1 = \angle 3$. Therefore, $\angle 1 = \angle 2$, and $\angle 2$ equals 60° since $\angle 1 = 60°$.

2–3

When two lines intersect and all four of the angles formed are equal, the lines are said to be *perpendicular*. If two lines are perpendicular, they are the sides of right angles whose vertex is the point of intersection.

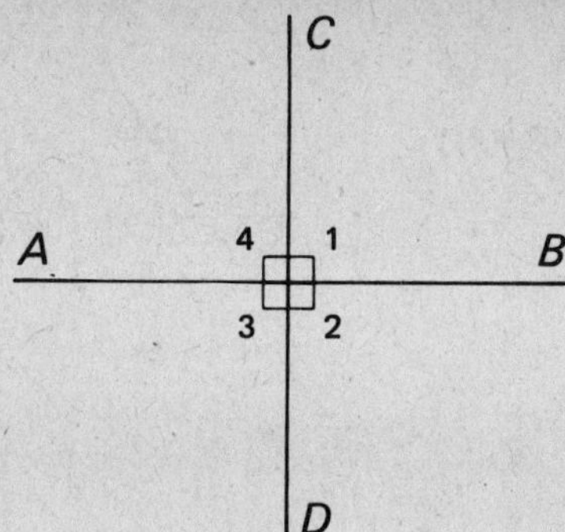

AB is perpendicular to CD, and angles 1, 2, 3, and 4 are all right angles. $\perp$ is the symbol for perpendicular; so $AB \perp CD$.

If two lines in a plane are perpendicular to the same line, then the two lines are parallel.

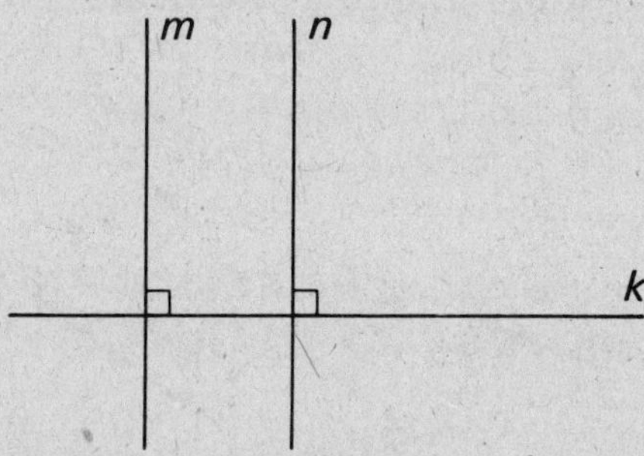

$m \perp k$ and $n \perp k$ implies that $m \parallel n$.

If *any one* of the angles formed when two lines intersect is a right angle, then the lines are perpendicular.

III–3. Polygons

A POLYGON is a closed figure in a plane which is composed of line segments which meet only at their endpoints. The line segments are called *sides* of the polygon, and a point where two sides meet is called a *vertex* (plural *vertices*) of the polygon.

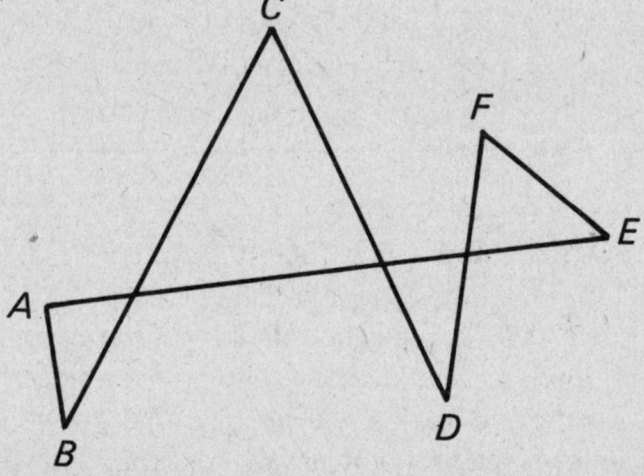

$ABCDEF$ is not a polygon since the line segments intersect at points which are not endpoints.

Some examples of polygons are:

A polygon is usually denoted by the vertices given in order.

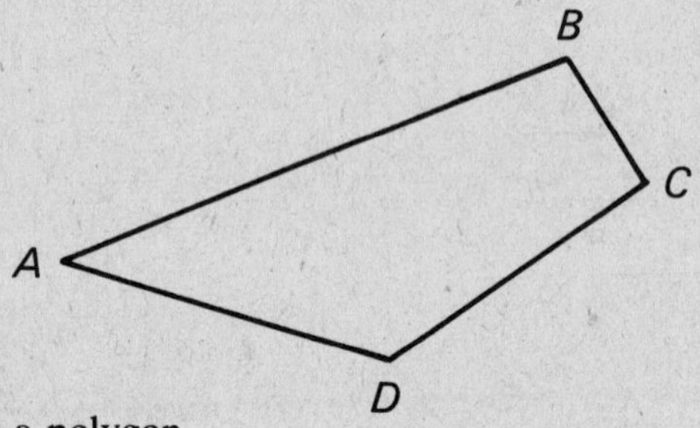

ABCD is a polygon.

A *diagonal* of a polygon is a line segment whose endpoints are nonadjacent vertices. The *altitude* from a vertex *P* to a side is the line segment with endpoint *P* which is perpendicular to the side.

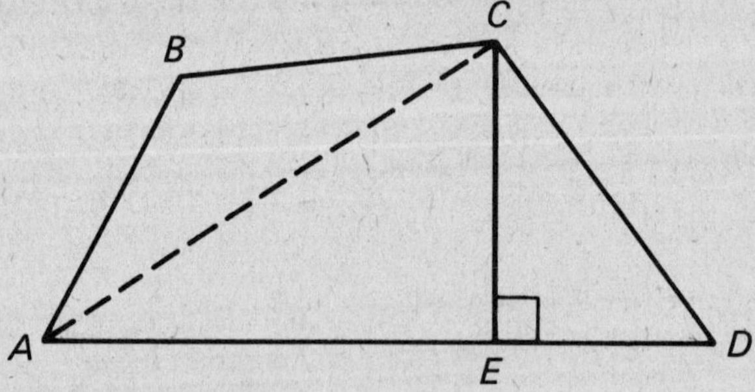

AC is a diagonal, and *CE* is the altitude from *C* to *AD*.

Polygons are classified by the number of angles or sides they have. A polygon with three angles is called a *triangle;* a four-sided polygon is a *quadrilateral;* a polygon with five angles is a *pentagon;* a polygon with six angles is a *hexagon;* an eight-sided polygon is an *octagon.* The number of angles is always equal to the number of sides in a polygon, so a six-sided polygon is a hexagon. The term *n*-gon refers to a polygon with *n* sides.

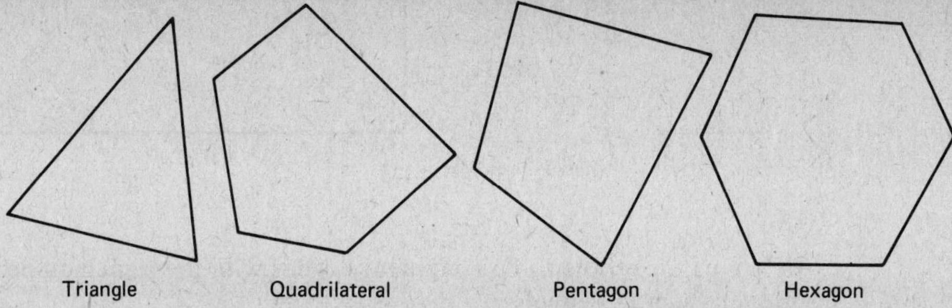

If the sides of a polygon are all equal in length and if all the angles of a polygon are equal, the polygon is called a *regular* polygon.

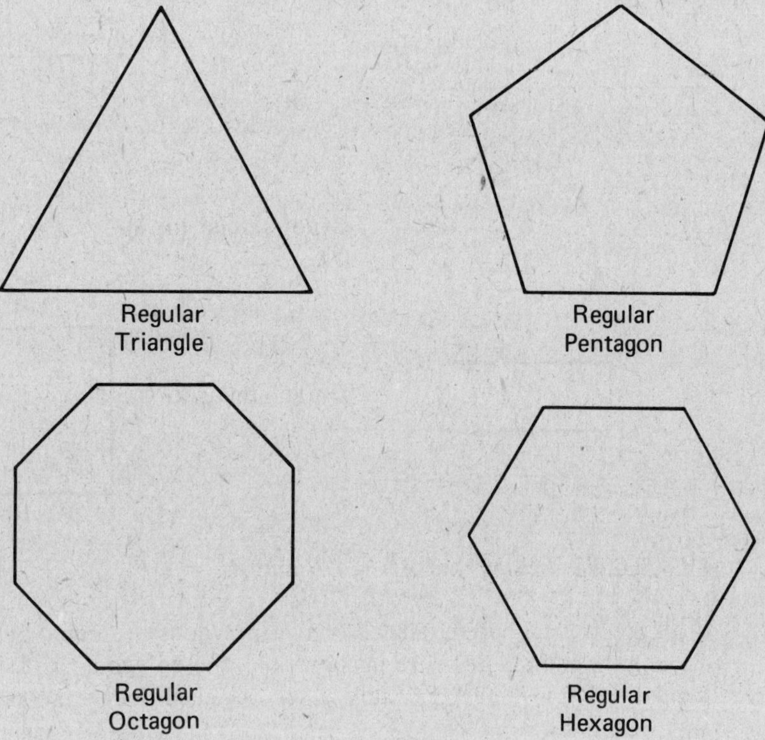

If the corresponding sides and the corresponding angles of two polygons are equal, the polygons are *congruent*. Congruent polygons have the same size and the same shape.

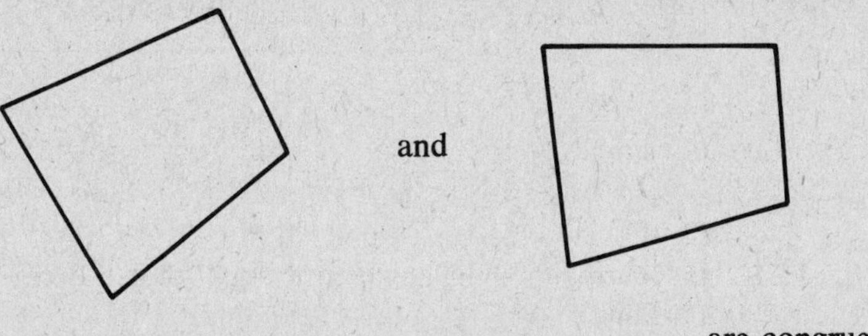

are congruent but

and

are not congruent.

In figures for problems on congruence, sides with the same number of strokes through them are equal.

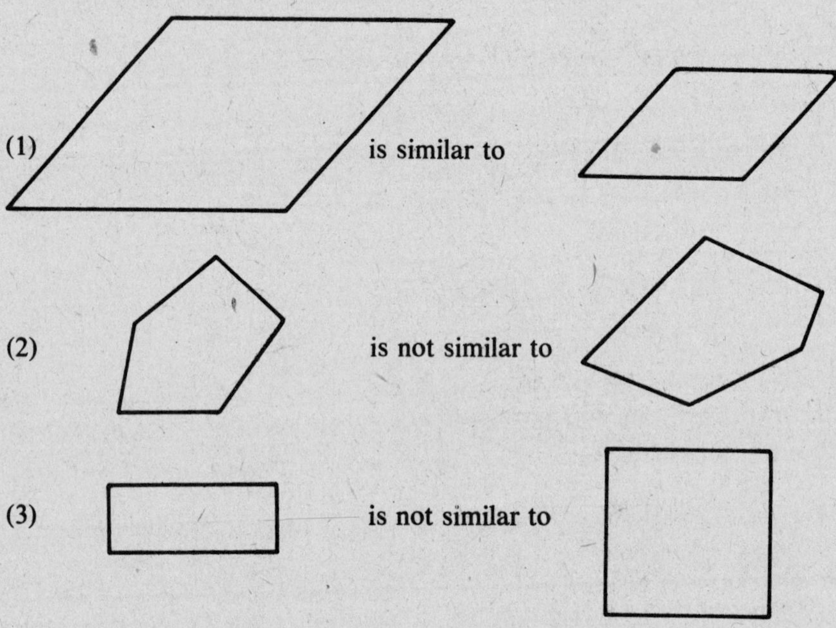

This figure indicates that $AB = DE$ and $AC = DF$.

If all the corresponding angles of two polygons are equal and the lengths of the corresponding sides are proportional, the polygons are said to be *similar*. Similar polygons have the same shape but need not be the same size.

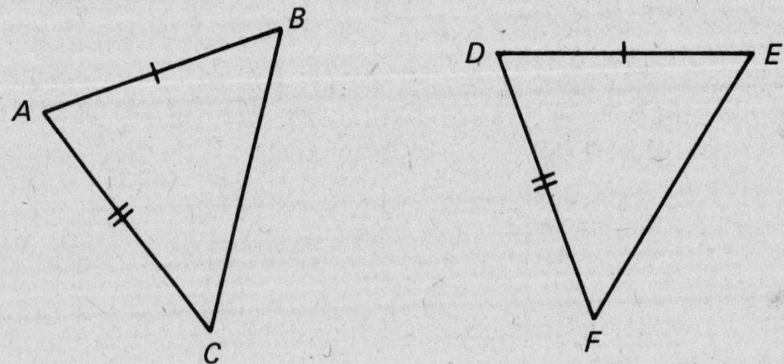

In (3) the corresponding angles are equal, but the corresponding sides are not proportional.

The sum of all the angles of an n-gon is $(n-2)180°$. So the sum of the angles in a hexagon is $(6-2)180° = 720°$.

III–4. Triangles

4–1

A TRIANGLE is a 3-sided polygon. If two sides of a triangle are equal, it is called isosceles. If all three sides are equal, it is an *equilateral* triangle. If all of the sides have different lengths, the triangle is *scalene*. When one of the angles in a triangle is a right angle, the triangle is a *right triangle*. If one of the angles is obtuse we have an *obtuse triangle*. If all the angles are acute, the triangle is an *acute triangle*.

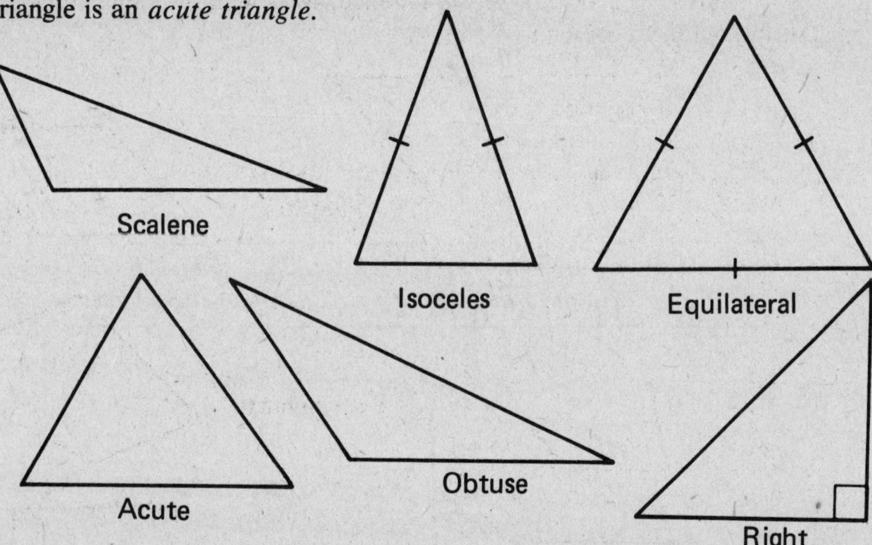

The symbol for a triangle is △; so △ABC means a triangle whose vertices are A, B, and C.

The sum of the angles in a triangle is 180°.

The sum of the lengths of any two sides of a triangle must be longer than the remaining side.

If two angles in a triangle are equal, then the lengths of the sides opposite the equal angles are equal. If two sides of a triangle are equal, then the angles opposite the two equal sides are equal. In an equilateral triangle all the angles are equal and each angle = 60°. If each of the angles in a triangle is 60°, then the triangle is equilateral.

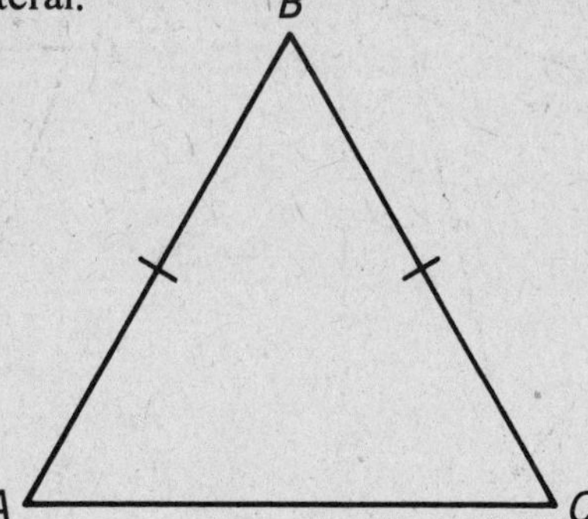

If $AB = BC$, then $\angle BAC = \angle BCA$.

If one angle in a triangle is larger than another angle, the side opposite the larger angle is longer than the side opposite the smaller angle. If one side is longer than another side, then the angle opposite the longer side is larger than the angle opposite the shorter side.

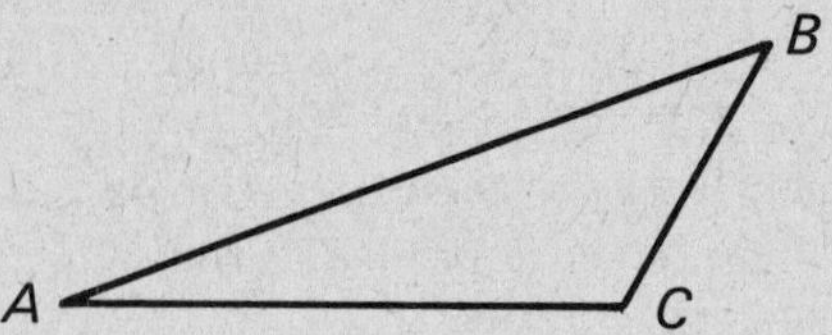

$AB > AC$ implies $\angle BCA > \angle ABC$.

In a right triangle, the side opposite the right angle is called the *hypotenuse*, and the remaining two sides are called *legs*.

> *The Pythagorean Theorem* states that *the square of the length of the hypotenuse is equal to the sum of the squares of the lengths of the legs.*

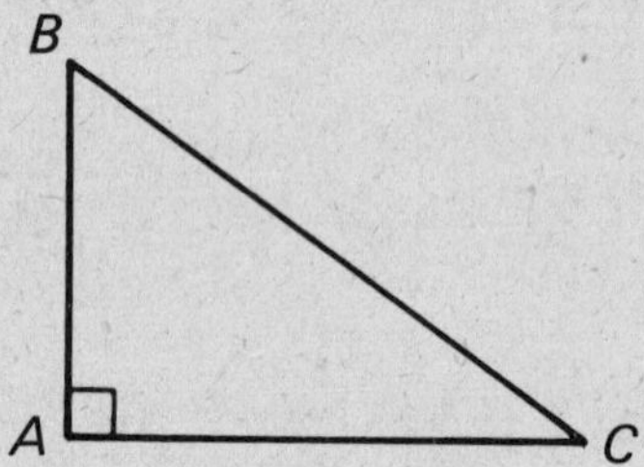

$(BC)^2 = (AB)^2 + (AC)^2$

If $AB = 4$ and $AC = 3$ then $(BC)^2 = 4^2 + 3^2 = 25$ so $BC = 5$. If $BC = 13$ and $AC = 5$, then $13^2 = 169 = (AB)^2 + 5^2$. So $(AB)^2 = 169 - 25 = 144$ and $AB = 12$.

If the lengths of the three sides of a triangle are a, b, and c and $a^2 = b^2 + c^2$, then the triangle is a right triangle where a is the length of the hypotenuse.

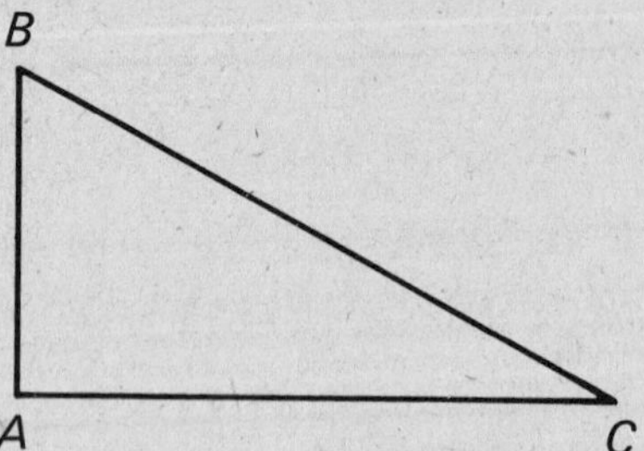

If $AB = 8$, $AC = 15$, and $BC = 17$, then since $17^2 = 8^2 + 15^2$, $\angle BAC$ is a right angle.

4–2

CONGRUENCE. Two triangles are congruent, if two pairs of corresponding sides and the corresponding *included* angles are equal. This is called *Side-Angle-Side* and is denoted by S.A.S.

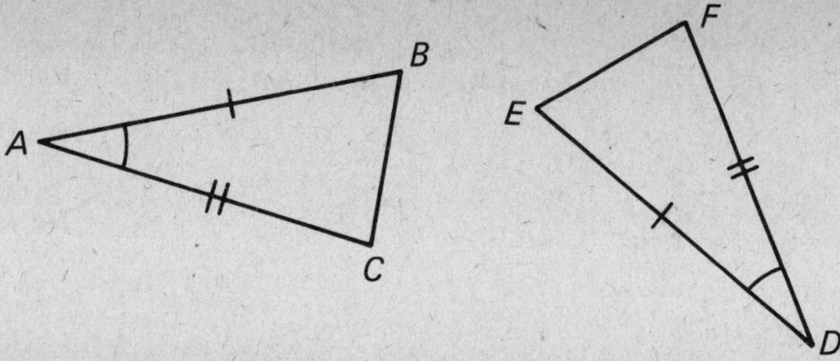

$AB = DE$, $AC = DF$ and $\angle BAC = \angle EDF$ imply that $\triangle ABC \cong \triangle DEF$. $\cong$ means congruent.

Two triangles are congruent if two pairs of corresponding angles and the corresponding *included* side are equal. This is called *Angle-Side-Angle* or A.S.A.

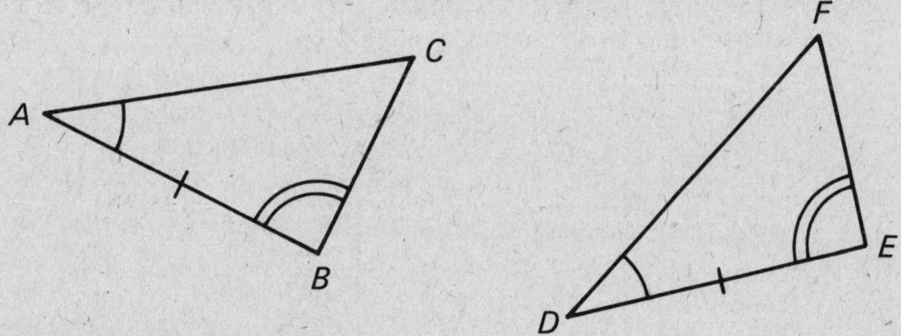

If $AB = DE$, $\angle BAC = \angle EDF$, and $\angle CBA = \angle FED$ then $\triangle ABC \cong \triangle DEF$.

If all three pairs of corresponding sides of two triangles are equal, then the triangles are congruent. This is called *Side-Side-Side* or S.S.S.

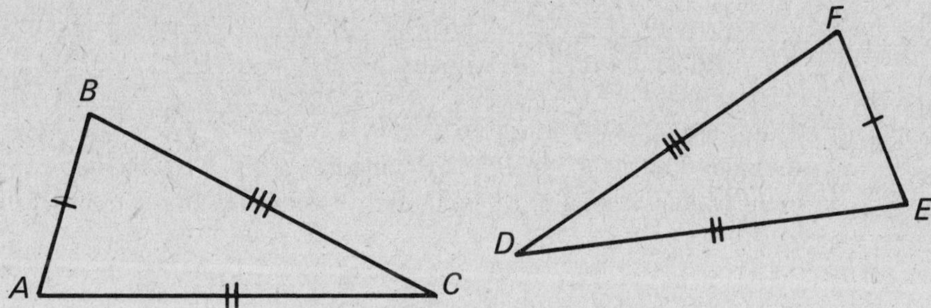

$AB = EF$, $AC = ED$, and $BC = FD$ imply that $\triangle ABC \cong \triangle EFD$.

Because of the Pythagorean Theorem, if any two corresponding sides of two right triangles are equal, the third sides are equal and the triangles are congruent.

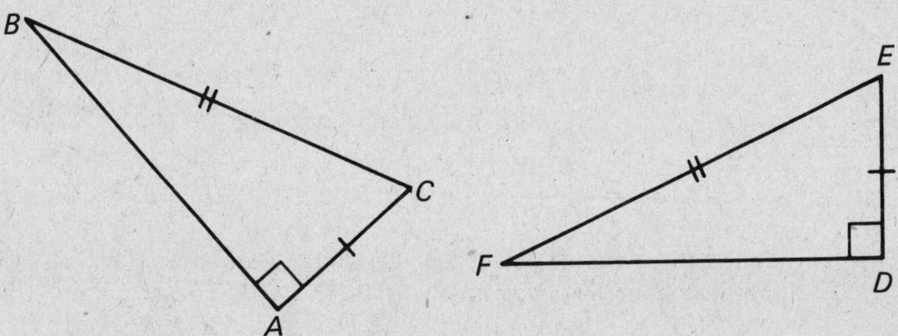

$AC = DE$ and $BC = EF$ imply $\triangle ABC \cong \triangle DFE$.

In general, if two corresponding sides of two triangles are equal, we cannot infer that the triangles are congruent.

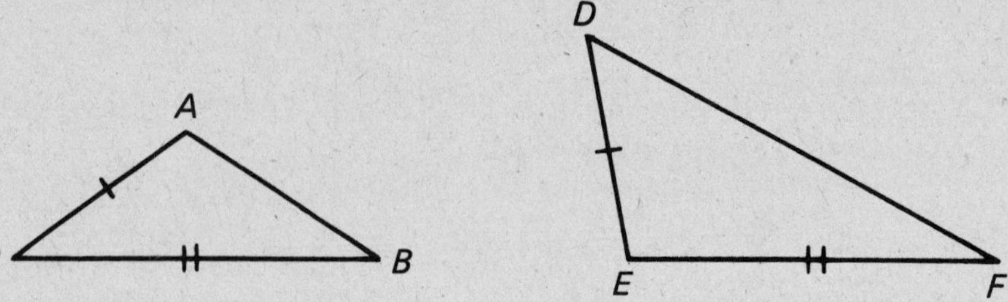

$AC = DE$ and $CB = EF$, but the triangles are not congruent.

If two sides of a triangle are equal, then the altitude to the third side divides the triangle into two congruent triangles.

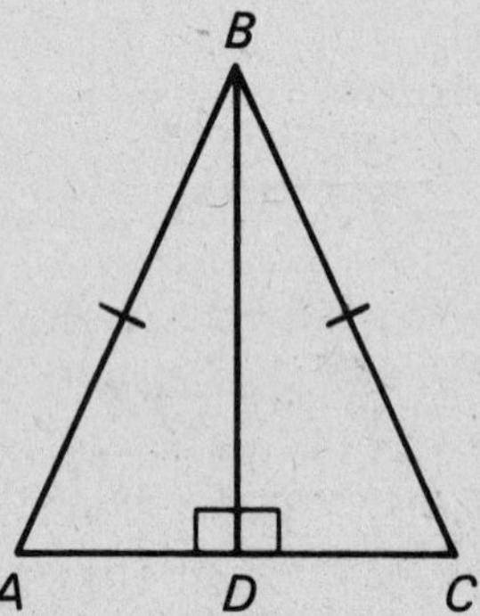

$AB = BC$ and $BD \perp AC$ implies $\triangle ADB \cong \triangle CDB$.

Therefore, $\angle ABD = \angle CBD$, so BD bisects $\angle ABC$. Since $AD = DC$, D is the midpoint of AC so BD is the median from B to AC. A *median* is the segment from a vertex to the midpoint of the side opposite the vertex.

EXAMPLE 1: $EF = ?$

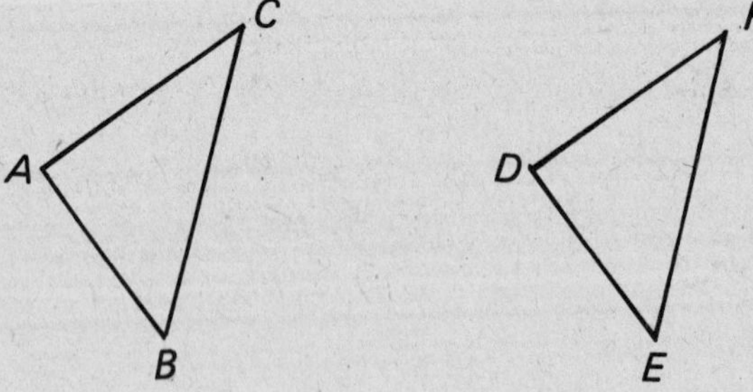

$AB = 4$, $AC = 4.5$ and $BC = 6$, $\angle BAC = \angle EDF$, $DE = 4$ and $DF = 4.5$

Since two pairs of corresponding sides (AB and DE, AC and DF) and the corresponding included angles ($\angle BAC$, $\angle EDF$) are equal, the triangles ABC and DEF are congruent by S.A.S. Therefore, $EF = BC = 6$.

4–3

Similarity. *Two triangles are similar if all three pairs of corresponding angles are equal.* Since the sum of the angles in a triangle is 180°, it follows that if two corresponding angles are equal, the third angles must be equal.

If you draw a line which passes through a triangle and is parallel to one of the sides of the triangle, the triangle formed is similar to the original triangle.

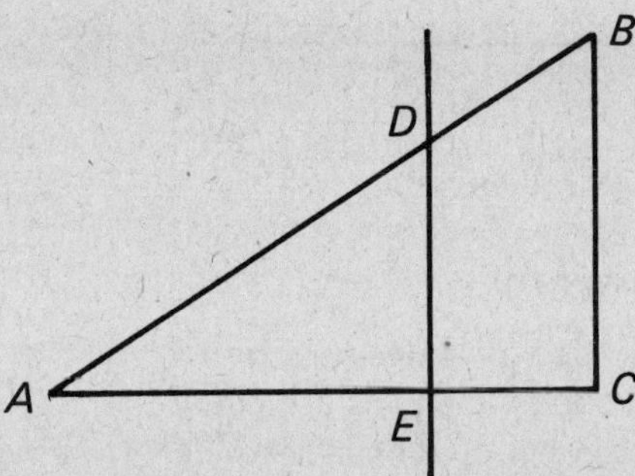

If $DE \parallel BC$ then $\triangle ADE \sim \triangle ABC$ ~ means similar.

EXAMPLE 1: A man 6 feet tall casts a shadow 4 feet long; at the same time a flagpole casts a shadow which is 50 feet long. How tall is the flagpole?

The man with his shadow and the flagpole with its shadow can be regarded as the pairs of corresponding sides of two similar triangles.

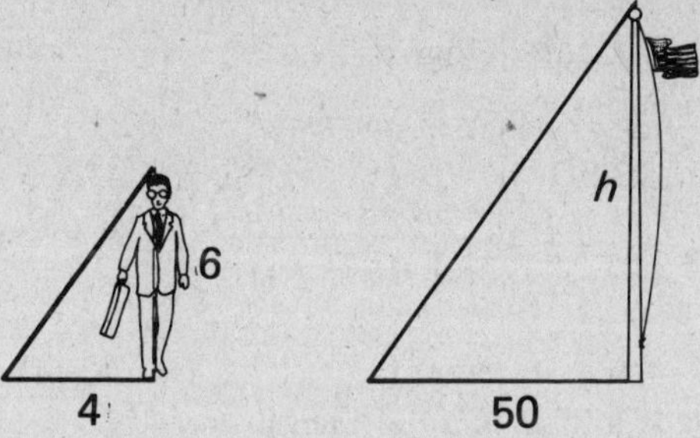

Let h be the height of the flagpole. Since corresponding sides of similar triangles are proportional, $\frac{4}{50} = \frac{6}{h}$. Cross-multiply getting $4h = 6 \cdot 50 = 300$; so $h = 75$. Therefore, the flagpole is 75 feet high.

III–5. Quadrilaterals

A QUADRILATERAL is a polygon with four sides. The sum of the angles in a quadrilateral is 360°. If the opposite sides of a quadrilateral are parallel, the figure is a *parallelogram*.

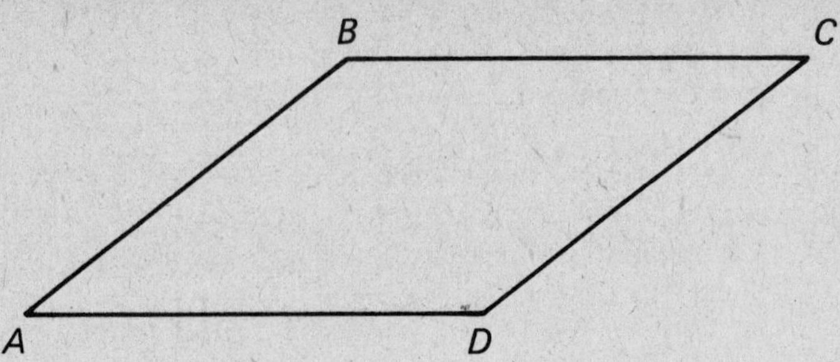

ABCD is a parallelogram.

In a parallelogram:

(1) The opposite sides are equal.
(2) The opposite angles are equal.
(3) A diagonal divides the parallelogram into two congruent triangles.
(4) The diagonals bisect each other. (A line *bisects* a line segment if it intersects the segment at the midpoint of the segment.)

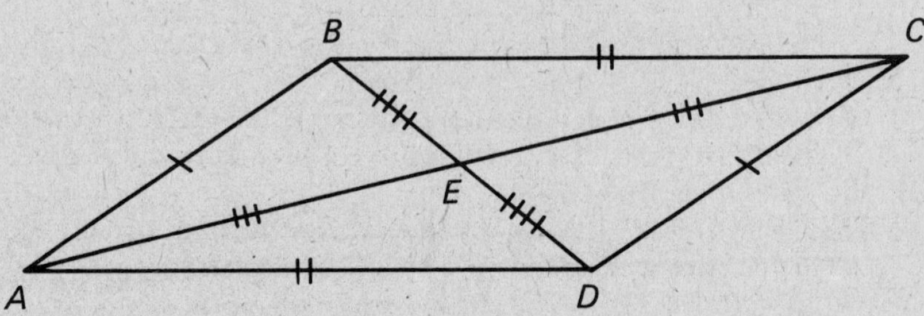

ABCD is a parallelogram.

(1) $AB = DC$, $BC = AD$.
(2) $\angle BCD = \angle BAD$, $\angle ABC = \angle ADC$.
(3) $\triangle ABC \cong \triangle ADC$, $\triangle ABD \cong \triangle CDB$.
(4) $AE = EC$ and $BE = ED$.

If *any* of the statements (1), (2), (3) and (4) are true for a quadrilateral, then the quadrilateral is a parallelogram.

If all of the sides of a parallelogram are equal, the figure is called a *rhombus*.

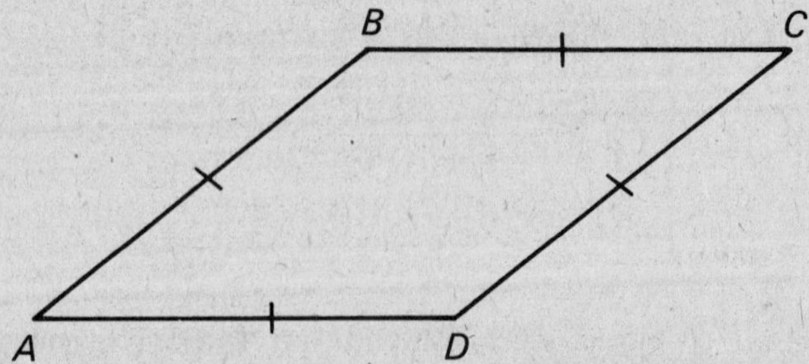

ABCD is a rhombus.

The diagonals of a rhombus are perpendicular.

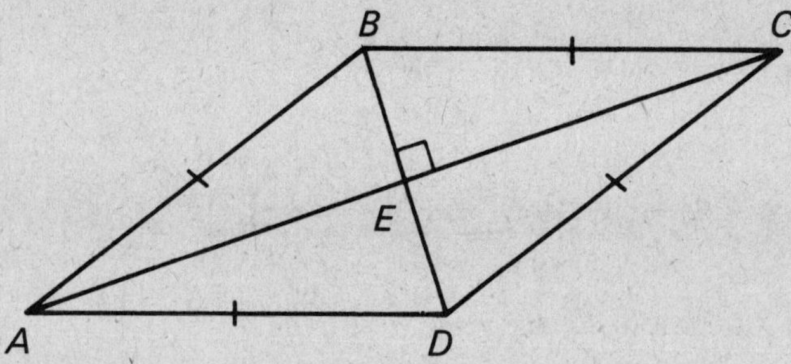

$BD \perp AC$; $\angle BEC = \angle CED = \angle AED = \angle AEB = 90°$.

If all the angles of a parallelogram are right angles, the figure is a *rectangle*.

$ABCD$ is a rectangle.

Since the sum of the angles in a quadrilateral is 360°, if *all* the angles of a quadrilateral are equal then the figure is a rectangle. The diagonals of a rectangle are equal. The length of a diagonal can be found by using the Pythagorean Theorem.

If $ABCD$ is a rectangle, $AC = BD$ and $(AC)^2 = (AD)^2 + (DC)^2$.

If all the sides of a rectangle are equal, the figure is a *square*.

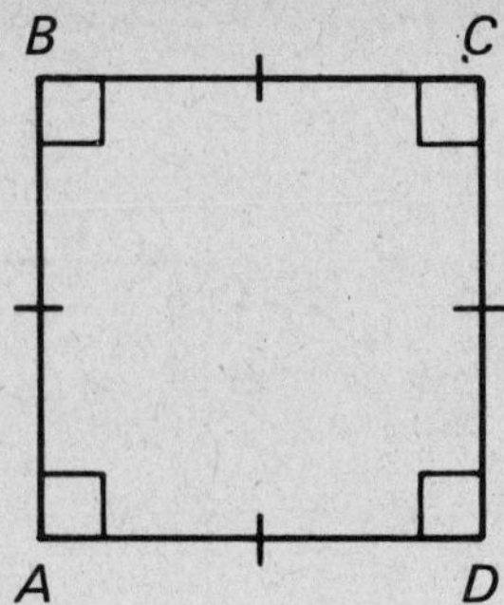

ABCD is a square.

If all the angles of a rhombus are equal, the figure is a square. The length of the diagonal of a square is $\sqrt{2}\, s$ where s is the length of a side.

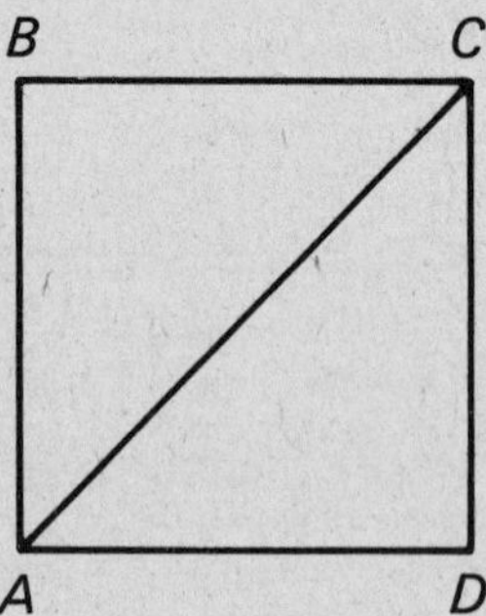

In square $ABCD$, $AC = (\sqrt{2})AD$.

A quadrilateral with two parallel sides and two sides which are not parallel is called a *trapezoid.* The parallel sides are called *bases,* and the non-parallel sides are called *legs.*

If $BC \parallel AD$ then $ABCD$ is a trapezoid; BC and AD are the bases.

III–6. Circles

A CIRCLE is a figure in a plane consisting of all the points which are the same distance from a fixed point called the *center* of the circle. A line segment from any point on the circle to the center of the circle is called a *radius* (plural: radii) of the circle. All radii of the same circle have the same length.

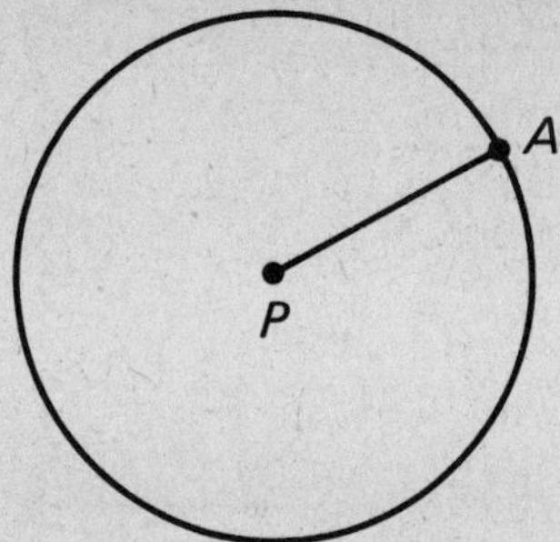

This circle has center P and radius AP.

A circle is **denoted** by a single letter, usually its center. Two circles with the same center are *concentric*.

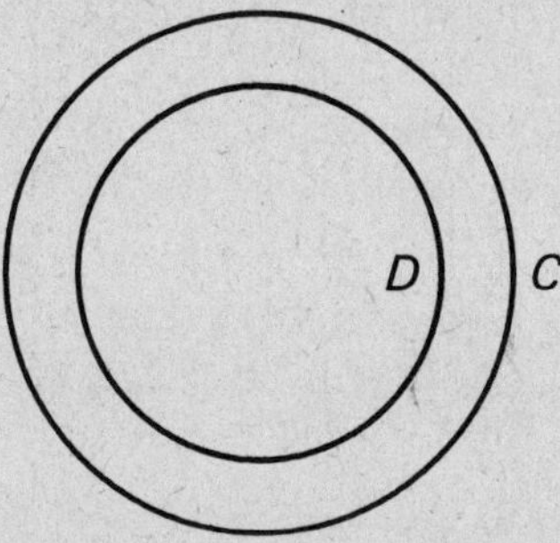

C and D are concentric circles.

A line segment whose endpoints are on a circle is called a *chord*. A chord which passes through the center of the circle is a *diameter*. *The length of a diameter is twice the length of a radius.* A diameter divides a circle into two congruent halves which are called *semicircles*.

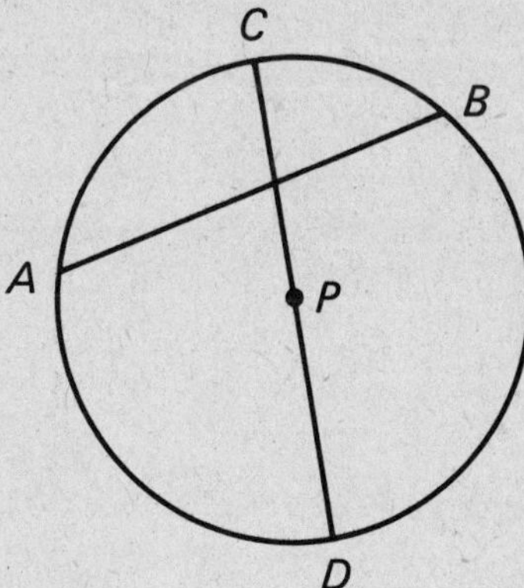

P is the center of the circle.
AB is a chord and CD is a diameter.

A diameter which is perpendicular to a chord bisects the chord.

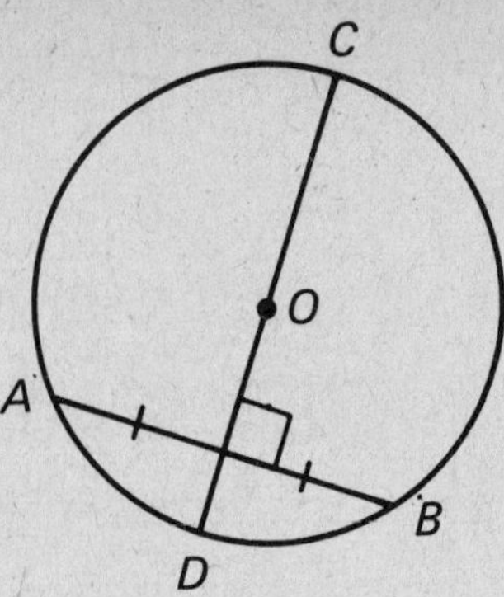

O is the center of this circle and $AB \perp CD$; then $AE = EB$.

If a line intersects a circle at one and only one point, the line is said to be a *tangent* to the circle. The point common to a circle and a tangent to the circle is called the *point of tangency*. The radius from the center to the point of tangency is perpendicular to the tangent.

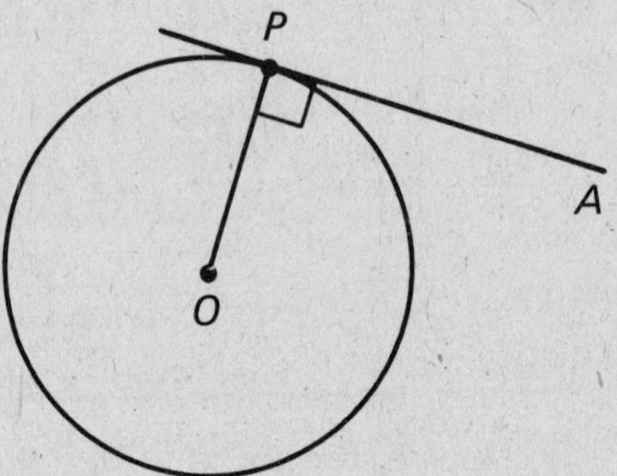

AP is tangent to the circle with center O. P is the point of tangency and $OP \perp PA$.

A polygon is *inscribed* in a circle if all of its vertices are points on the circle.

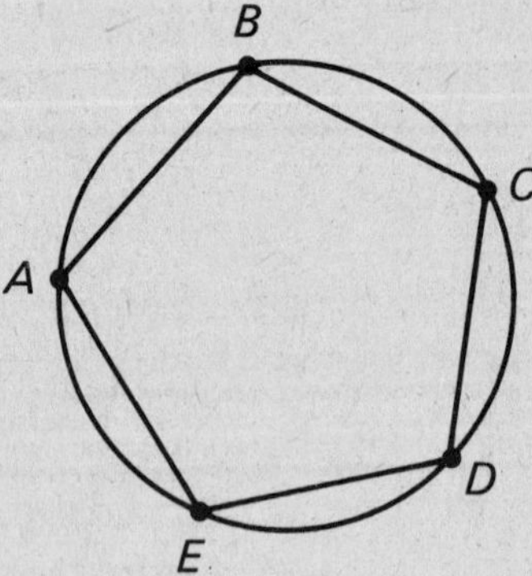

$ABCDE$ is an inscribed pentagon.

An angle whose vertex is a point on a circle and whose sides are chords of the circle is called an *inscribed angle*. An angle whose vertex is the center of a circle and whose sides are radii of the circle is called a *central angle*.

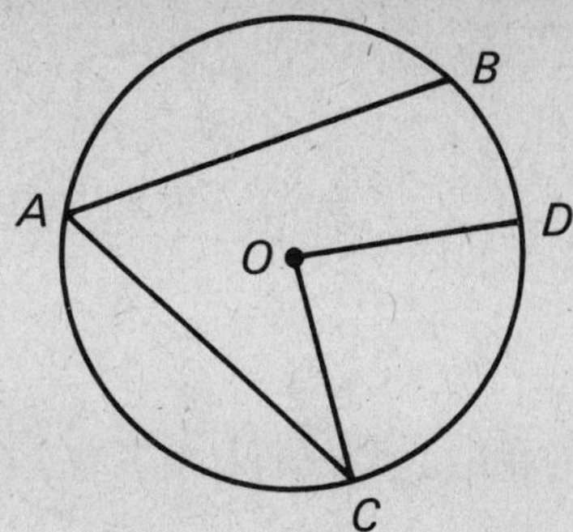

$\angle BAC$ is an inscribed angle.
$\angle DOC$ is a central angle.

An *arc* is a part of a circle.

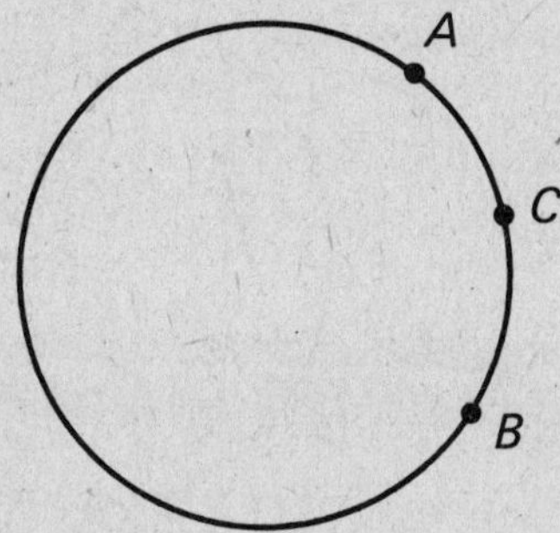

ACB is an arc. Arc ACB is written $\widehat{ACB}$.

If two letters are used to denote an arc, they represent the smaller of the two possible arcs. So $\widehat{AB} = \widehat{ACB}$.

An arc can be measured in degrees. The entire circle is 360°; thus an arc of 120° would be $\frac{1}{3}$ of a circle.

A central angle is equal in measure to the arc it intercepts.

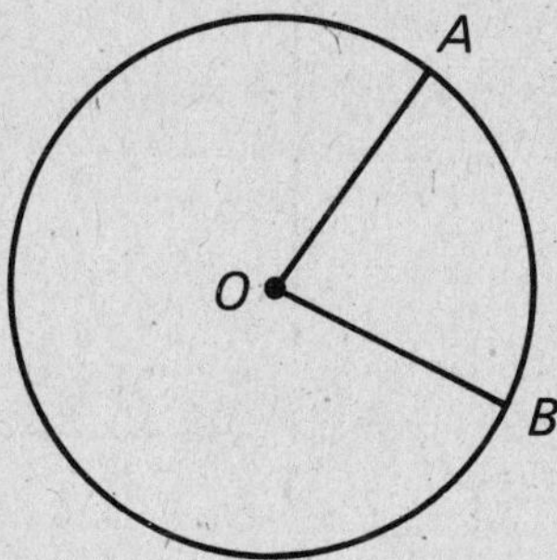

$\angle AOB = \widehat{AB}$

An inscribed angle is equal in measure to $\frac{1}{2}$ the arc it intercepts.

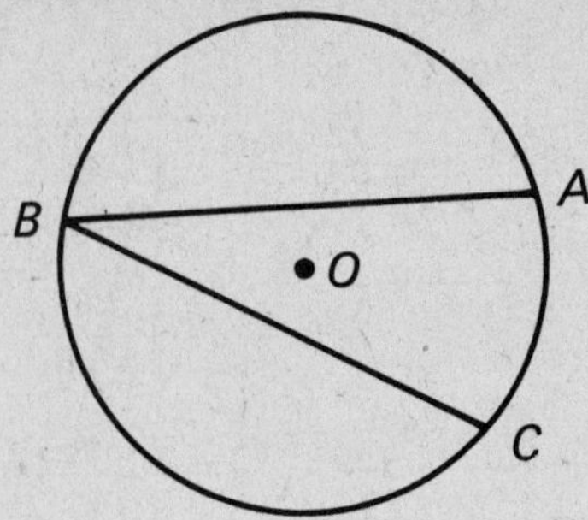

$\angle ABC = \frac{1}{2}\widehat{AC}$.

An angle inscribed in a semicircle is a *right angle.*

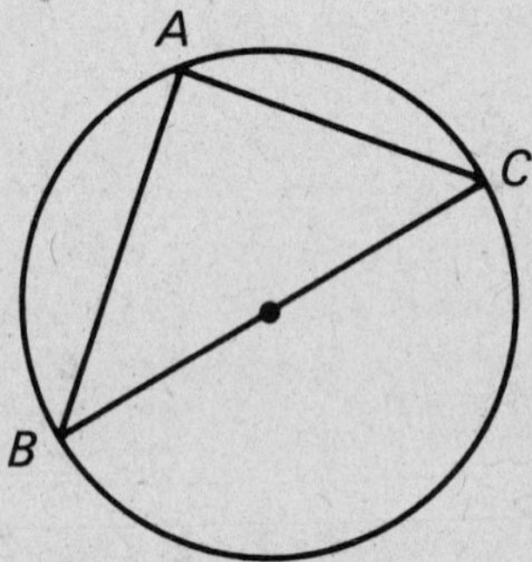

If BC is a diameter, then $\angle BAC$ is inscribed in a semicircle; so $\angle BAC = 90°$.

III–7. Area and Perimeter

7–1

The area A of a square equals s^2, where s is the length of a side of the square. Thus, $A = s^2$.

If $AD = 5$ inches, the area of square $ABCD$ is 25 square inches.

The area of a rectangle equals length times width; if L is the length of one side and W is the length of a perpendicular side, then the area $A = LW$.

If $AB = 5$ feet and $AD = 8$ feet, then the area of rectangle $ABCD$ is 40 square feet.

The area of a parallelogram is base × height; $A = bh$, where b is the length of a side and h is the length of an altitude to the base.

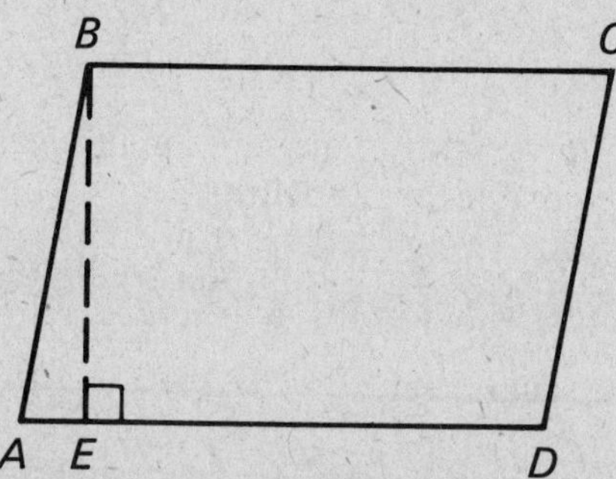

If $AD = 6$ yards and $BE = 4$ yards, then the area of the parallelogram $ABCD$ is $6 \cdot 4$ or 24 square yards.

The area of a trapezoid is the (average of the bases) × height. $A = [(b_1 + b_2)/2]^h$ where b_1 and b_2 are the lengths of the parallel sides and h is the length of an altitude to one of the bases.

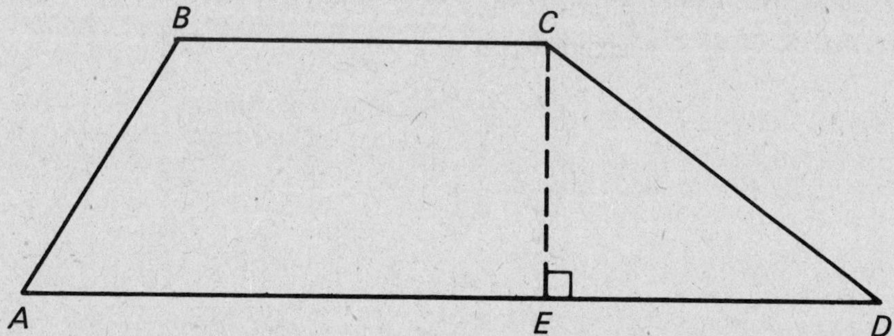

If $BC = 3$ miles, $AD = 7$ miles, and $CE = 2$ miles, then the area of trapezoid $ABCD$ is $[(3 + 7)/2] \cdot 2 = 10$ square miles.

The area of a triangle is $\frac{1}{2}$ (base × height); $A = \frac{1}{2}bh$, where b is the length of a side and h is the length of the altitude to the base.

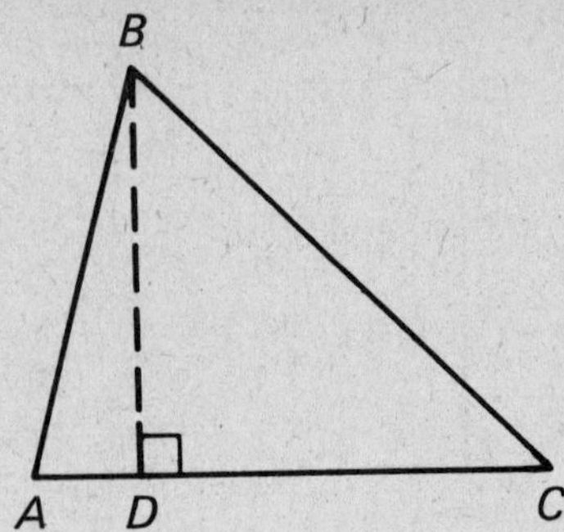

If $AC = 5$ miles and $BD = 4$ miles, then the area of the triangle is $\frac{1}{2} \times 5 \times 4 = 10$ square miles.

Since the legs of a right triangle are perpendicular to each other, the area of a right triangle is one-half the product of the lengths of the legs.

EXAMPLE 1: If the lengths of the sides of a triangle are 5 feet, 12 feet, and 13 feet, what is the area of the triangle?

Since $5^2 + 12^2 = 25 + 144 = 169 = 13^2$, the triangle is a right triangle and the legs are the sides with lengths 5 feet and 12 feet. Therefore, the area is $\frac{1}{2} \times 5 \times 12 = 30$ square feet.

If we want to find the area of a polygon which is not of a type already mentioned, we break the polygon up into smaller figures such as triangles or rectangles, find the area of each piece, and add these to get the area of the given polygon.

The area of a circle is πr^2 where r is the length of a radius. Since $d = 2r$ where d is the length of a diameter, $A = \pi\left(\frac{d}{2}\right)^2 = \pi\frac{d^2}{4}$. π is a number which is approximately $\frac{22}{7}$ or 3.14; however, there is *no fraction which is exactly equal to* π. π is called an *irrational number*.

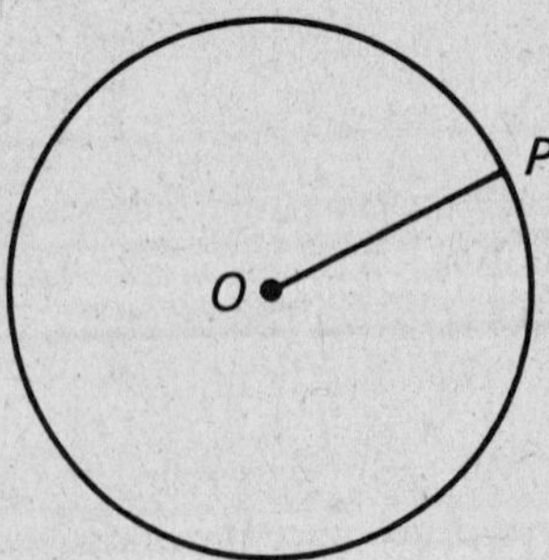

If $OP = 2$ inches, then the area of the circle with center O is $\pi 2^2$ or 4π square inches. The portion of the plane bounded by a circle and a central angle is called a *sector* of the circle.

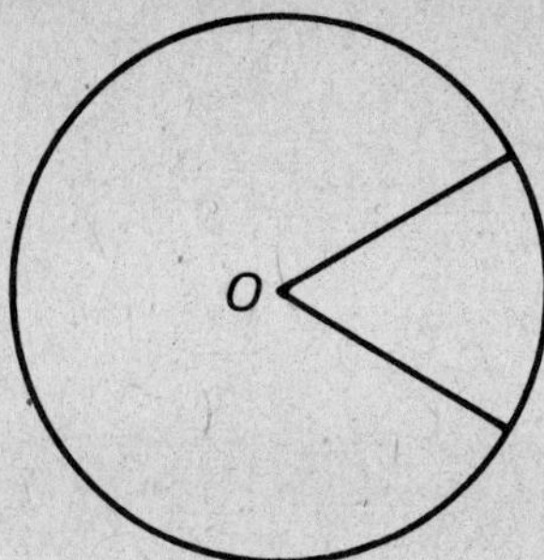

The shaded region is a sector of the circle with center O. The area of a sector with central angle $n°$ in a circle of radius r is $\frac{n}{360}\pi r^2$.

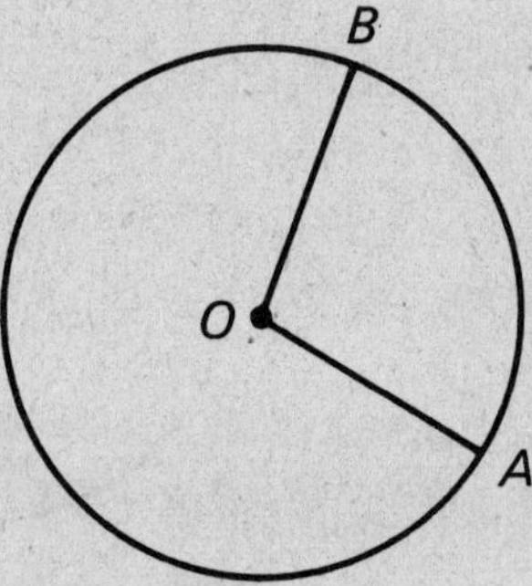

If $OB = 4$ inches and $\angle BOA = 100°$, then the area of the sector is $\frac{100}{360}\pi \cdot 4^2 = \frac{5}{18} \cdot 16\pi = \frac{40}{9}\pi$ square inches.

7–2

The *perimeter* of a polygon is the sum of the lengths of the sides.

EXAMPLE 1: What is the perimeter of a regular pentagon whose sides are 6 inches long?

A pentagon has 5 sides. Since the pentagon is regular, all sides have the same length which is 6 inches. Therefore, the perimeter of the pentagon is 5×6 which equals 30 inches or 2.5 feet.

The *perimeter of a rectangle is* $2(L + W)$ where L is the length and W is the width.
The *perimeter of a square is* $4s$ where s is the length of a side of the square.

The *perimeter of a circle* is called the *circumference* of the circle. The *circumference of a circle is* πd *or* $2\pi r$, where d is the length of a diameter and r is the length of a radius.

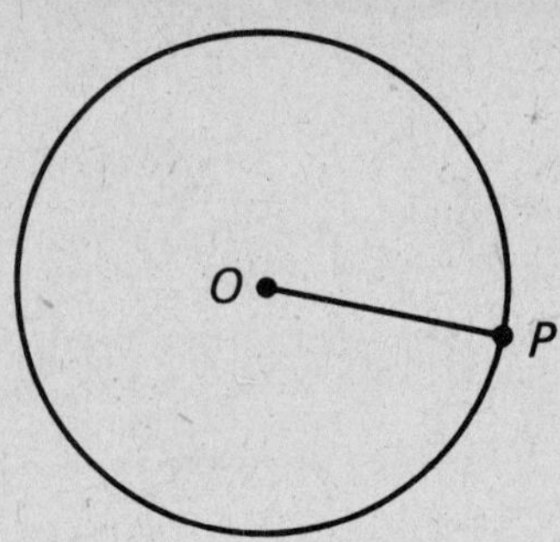

If O is the center of a circle and $OP = 5$ feet, then the circumference of the circle is $2 \times 5\pi$ or 10π feet.

The length of an arc of a circle is $(n/360)\ \pi d$ where the central angle of the arc is $n°$.

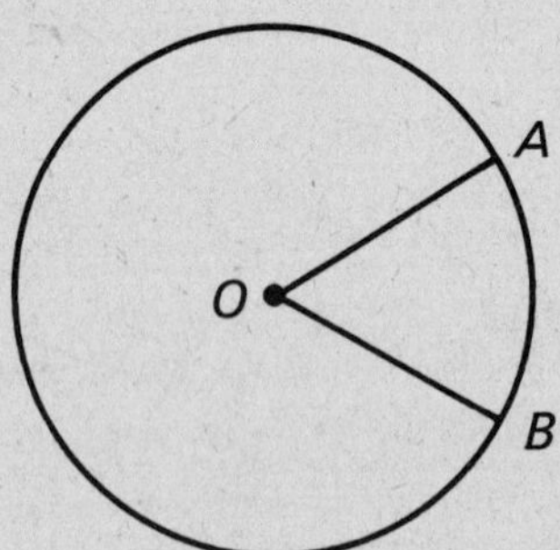

If O is the center of a circle where $OA = 5$ yards and $\angle AOB = 60°$, then the length of arc AB is $\frac{60}{360}\pi \times 10 = \frac{10}{6}\pi = \frac{5}{3}\pi$ yards.

EXAMPLE 2: How far will a wheel of radius 2 feet travel in 500 revolutions? (Assume the wheel does not slip.)

The diameter of the wheel is 4 feet; so the circumference is 4π feet. Therefore, the wheel will travel $500 \times 4\pi$ or $2{,}000\pi$ feet in 500 revolutions.

III–8. Volume and Surface Area

8–1

The volume of a rectangular prism or box is length times width times height.

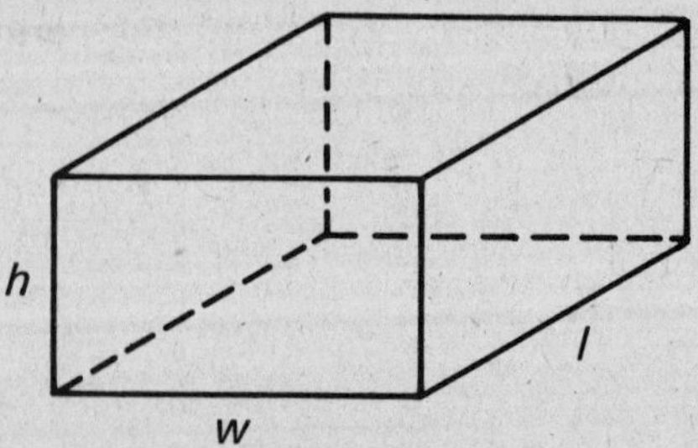

$$V = lwh$$

EXAMPLE 1: What is the volume of a box which is 5 feet long, 4 feet wide, and 6 feet high?

The volume is $5 \times 4 \times 6$ or 120 cubic feet.

If each of the faces of a rectangular prism is a congruent square, then the solid is a *cube*. The volume of a cube is the length of a side (or edge) cubed.

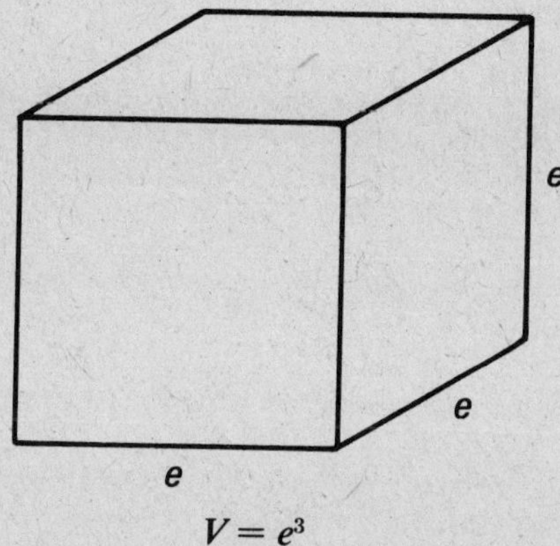

$$V = e^3$$

If the side of a cube is 4 feet long, then the volume of the cube is 4^3 or 64 cubic feet.

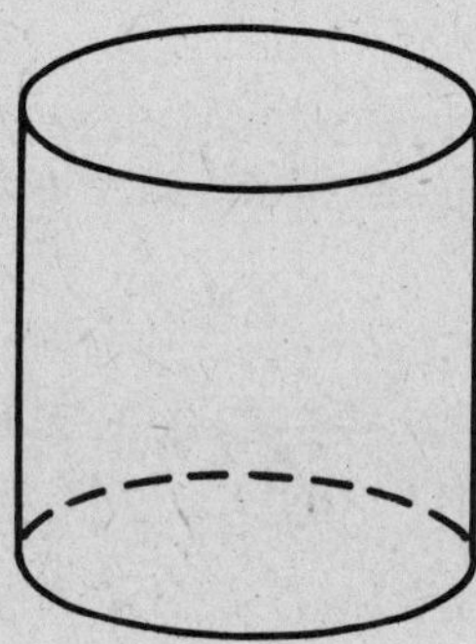

This solid is a circular cylinder. The top and the bottom are congruent circles. Most tin cans are circular cylinders. The volume of a circular cylinder is the product of the area of the circular base and the height.

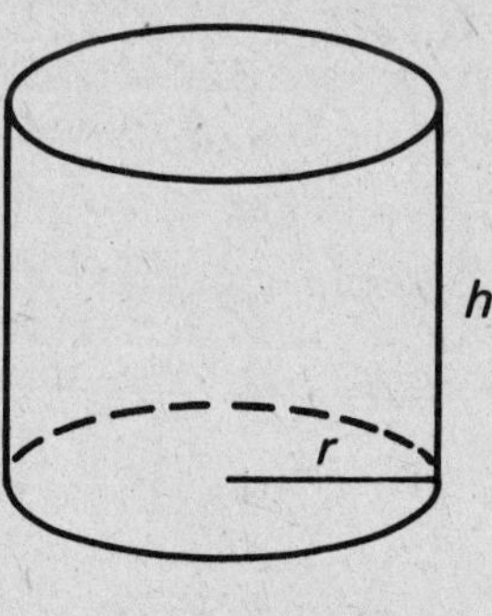

$$V = \pi r^2 h$$

EXAMPLE 2: A circular pipe has a diameter of 10 feet. A gallon of oil has a volume of 2 cubic feet. How many gallons of oil can fit into 50 feet of the pipe?

Think of the 50 feet of pipe as a circular cylinder on its side with a height of 50 feet and a radius of 5 feet. Its volume is $\pi \cdot 5^2 \cdot 50$ or $1{,}250\pi$ cubic feet. Since a gallon of oil has a volume of 2 cubic feet, 50 feet of pipe will hold $1{,}250\pi/2$ or 625π gallons of oil.

A *sphere* is the set of points in space equidistant from a fixed point called the center. The length of a segment from any point on the sphere to the center is called the radius of the sphere. *The volume of a sphere of radius r is* $\frac{4}{3}\pi r^3$.

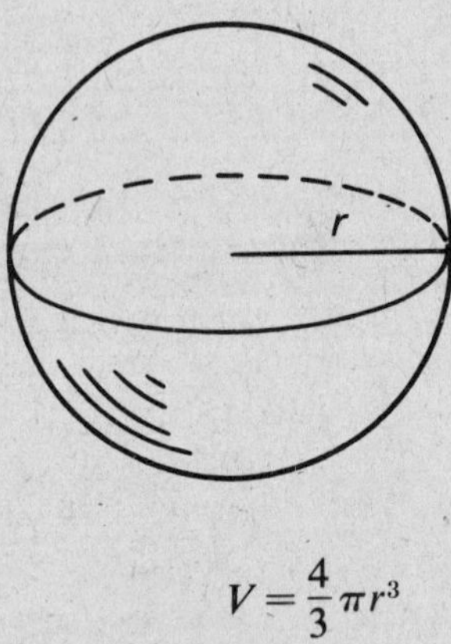

$$V = \frac{4}{3}\pi r^3$$

The volume of a sphere with radius 3 feet is $\frac{4}{3}\pi 3^3 = 36\pi$ cubic feet.

8–2

The surface area of a rectangle prism is $2LW + 2LH + 2WH$ where L is the length, W is the width, and H is the height.

EXAMPLE 1: If a roll of wallpaper covers 30 square feet, how many rolls are needed to cover the walls of a rectangular room 10 feet long by 8 feet wide by 9 feet high?

We have to cover the surface area of the walls which equals $2(10 \times 9 + 8 \times 9)$ or $2(90 + 72)$ or 324 square feet. (Note that the product represents the area of the floor or the ceiling.) Since a roll covers 30 square feet, we need $\frac{324}{30} = 10\frac{4}{5}$ rolls.

The surface area of a cube is $6e^2$ where e is the length of an edge.

The area of the circular part of a cylinder is called the lateral area. The lateral area of a circular area is $2\pi rh$. If we unroll the circular part, we get a rectangle whose dimensions are the circumference of the circle and the height of the cylinder. The total surface area is $2\pi rh + 2\pi r^2$.

EXAMPLE 2: How much tin is needed to make a tin can in the shape of a circular cylinder whose radius is 3 inches and whose height is 5 inches?

The area of both the bottom and top is $\pi \cdot 3^2$ or 9π square inches. The lateral area is $2\pi \cdot 3 \cdot 5$ or 30π square inches. Therefore, we need $9\pi + 9\pi + 30\pi$ or 48π square inches of tin.

III–9. Coordinate Geometry

In coordinate geometry, every point in the plane is associated with an ordered pair of numbers called *coordinates*. Two perpendicular lines are drawn; the horizontal line is called the x-axis and the vertical line is called the y-axis. The point where the two axes intersect is called the *origin*. Both of the axes are number lines with the origin corresponding to zero (see I–6.) Positive numbers on the x-axis are to the right of the origin, negative numbers to the left. Positive numbers on the y-axis are above the origin, negative numbers below the origin. The coordinates of a point P are (x,y) if P is located by moving x units along the x-axis from the origin and then moving y units up or down. *The distance along the x-axis is always given first.*

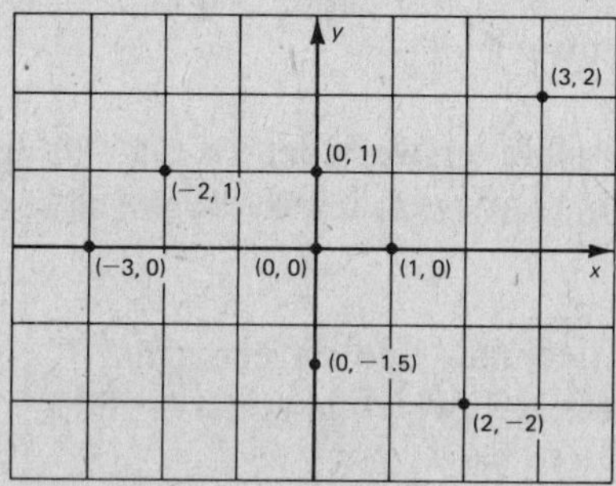

The numbers in parentheses are the coordinates of the point. Thus "$P = (3,2)$" means that the coordinates of P are (3,2). *The distance between the point with coordinates (x,y) and the point with coordinates (a,b) is* $\sqrt{(x-a)^2+(y-b)^2}$. You should be able to answer most questions by using the distance formula.

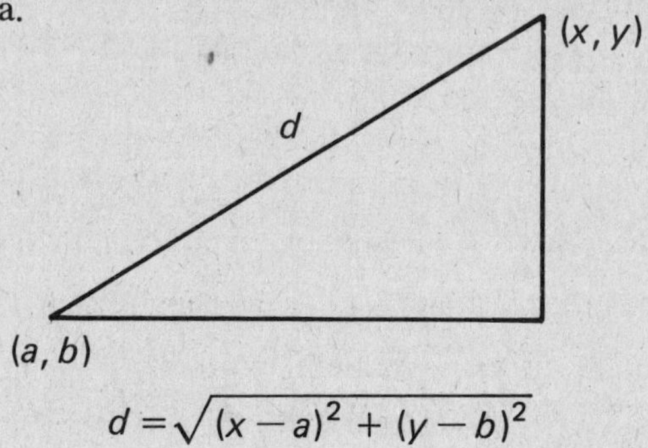

$$d = \sqrt{(x-a)^2 + (y-b)^2}$$

EXAMPLE 1: Is $ABCD$ a parallelogram? $A = (3,2)$, $B = (1,-2)$, $C = (-2,1)$, $D = (1,5)$.

The length of AB is $\sqrt{(3-1)^2+((2-(-2))^2} = \sqrt{2^2+4^2} = \sqrt{20}$. The length of CD is $\sqrt{(-2-1)^2+(1-5)^2} = \sqrt{3^2+4^2} = \sqrt{25}$. Therefore, $AB \neq CD$, so $ABCD$

cannot be a parallelogram, since in a parallelogram the lengths of opposite sides are equal.

Geometry problems occur frequently in the data sufficiency questions. *If you are not provided with a diagram, draw one for yourself.* Think of any conditions which will help you answer the question; perhaps you can see how to answer a different question which will lead to an answer to the original question. It may help to draw in some diagonals, altitudes, or other auxiliary lines in your diagram.

IV. Tables and Graphs

IV–1. Tables

General Hints. You *must* know how to interpret tables and graphs to score well on the Mathematics part of the test. In some recent tests, about half of the questions in the sections on mathematics have dealt with charts and graphs.

(A) Make sure to look at the *entire* table or graph.

(B) Figure out what *units* the table or graph is using. Make sure to express your answer in the correct units.

(C) Look at the possible answers before calculating. Since many questions only call for an approximate answer, it may be possible to round off (see I–5) saving time and effort.

(D) Don't confuse decimals and percentages. If the units are percentages, then an entry of .2 means .2% which is equal to .002.

(E) In inference questions, only the information given can be used.

(F) See if the answer makes sense.

EXAMPLE: (Refer to the table on page 217.)

1.A B C D E

1. What percent of the babies born in the U.S. in 1947 died before the age of 1 year?

(A) 3.22
(B) 4.7
(C) 26.7
(D) 32.2
(E) 47

To find a percentage, use the information given in the rate columns. The rate is given *per thousand*. In 1947 the rate was 32.2 per thousand which is $\frac{32.2}{1000}=.0322$ or 3.22%. So the correct answer is (A). If you assumed incorrectly that the rate was per hundred, you would get the incorrect answer (D); if you looked in the wrong column you might get (B) or (E) as your answer.

2.A B C D E

2. Which state had the most infant deaths in 1940?

(A) California
(B) New Mexico
(C) New York
(D) Pennsylvania
(E) Texas

Infant Deaths (Under 1 Year of Age) and Rates Per 1,000 Live Births, by States: 1940 to 1950

STATE	NUMBER OF INFANT DEATHS					RATE PER 1,000 LIVE BIRTHS				
	1940	1947	1948	1949	1950	1940	1947	1948	1949	1950
United States	110,984	119,173	113,169	111,531	103,825	47.0	32.2	32.0	31.3	29.2
Alabama	3,870	3,301	3,228	3,345	3,044	61.5	37.5	37.8	39.6	36.8
Arizona	983	973	1,083	1,034	953	85.5	50.8	56.4	51.0	45.8
Arkansas	1,810	1,445	1,363	1,539	1,209	47.0	29.5	28.4	33.7	26.5
California	4,403	7,233	6,885	6,574	6,115	39.2	29.4	28.6	26.8	25.0
Colorado	1,270	1,234	1,267	1,153	1,167	60.4	37.5	38.4	35.1	34.4
Connecticut	868	1,150	1,026	943	886	34.0	25.2	24.3	23.1	21.8
Delaware	217	239	214	224	235	47.7	31.0	29.5	30.4	30.7
District of Columbia	554	691	531	576	603	49.3	31.9	25.5	29.1	30.4
Florida	1,818	2,285	2,103	2,088	2,078	53.8	38.2	35.3	33.8	32.1
Georgia	3,744	3,251	3,169	3,101	3,064	57.8	34.2	34.2	33.3	33.5
Idaho	506	478	481	431	434	42.9	29.4	29.8	27.0	27.1
Illinois	4,398	5,672	5,123	5,195	4,868	35.3	28.9	27.7	27.4	25.6
Indiana	2,595	2,949	2,760	2,746	2,520	42.1	30.6	29.8	29.1	27.0
Iowa	1,636	1,817	1,610	1,591	1,555	36.5	28.5	26.6	25.7	24.8
Kansas	1,106	1,251	1,151	1,136	1,130	38.3	28.1	26.9	25.9	25.7
Kentucky	3,387	2,971	3,073	3,139	2,616	53.1	37.1	39.8	41.2	34.9
Louisiana	3,268	2,773	2,779	2,810	2,639	64.3	37.2	37.9	37.2	34.6
Maine	810	853	706	713	650	53.2	35.7	32.0	32.5	30.9
Maryland	1,590	1,794	1,537	1,636	1,465	49.1	31.6	28.8	30.5	27.0
Massachusetts	2,458	3,027	2,613	2,347	2,240	37.5	28.1	26.8	24.5	23.3
Michigan	4,032	5,080	4,639	4,545	4,230	40.7	31.5	30.0	28.9	26.3
Minnesota	1,758	2,165	1,959	1,893	1,889	33.2	28.6	26.9	25.6	25.1
Mississippi	2,869	2,448	2,474	2,631	2,385	54.4	36.8	37.9	39.6	36.7
Missouri	2,885	2,929	2,585	2,563	2,510	46.9	32.5	30.3	30.0	29.2
Montana	537	484	461	457	441	46.5	32.1	30.7	29.7	28.2
Nebraska	792	894	835	761	796	36.0	27.8	26.8	24.1	25.0
Nevada	109	134	147	118	139	51.7	33.2	39.8	32.1	37.9
New Hampshire	341	399	361	333	282	40.9	30.1	29.1	27.9	24.5
New Jersey	2,121	2,965	2,585	2,534	2,467	35.5	27.9	26.5	26.0	25.2
New Mexico	1,488	1,379	1,438	1,408	1,211	100.6	67.9	70.1	65.1	54.8
New York	7,297	9,123	8,258	7,878	7,429	37.2	28.2	27.3	26.1	24.7
North Carolina	4,631	3,938	3,858	4,113	3,674	57.6	34.9	35.3	38.1	34.5
North Dakota	593	523	487	517	453	45.1	30.6	29.4	30.7	26.6
Ohio	4,744	5,817	5,693	5,315	4,990	41.4	29.5	30.5	28.1	26.8
Oklahoma	2,238	1,733	1,731	1,531	1,514	49.9	32.3	34.4	30.8	30.2
Oregon	585	895	897	869	812	33.2	24.7	25.5	24.6	22.5
Pennsylvania	7,404	7,741	6,442	6,567	6,126	44.7	31.1	28.4	29.2	27.6
Rhode Island	410	522	444	395	450	37.9	28.2	26.3	24.0	27.8
South Carolina	3,042	2,352	2,331	2,283	2,220	68.2	39.5	40.4	39.0	38.6
South Dakota	466	511	525	448	473	38.7	30.9	32.0	26.0	26.6
Tennessee	2,954	3,144	3,098	3,331	2,961	53.5	36.3	37.7	40.2	36.4
Texas	8,675	8,161	9,131	8,628	7,630	68.3	41.1	46.2	42.7	37.4
Utah	539	545	568	535	503	40.4	25.1	27.4	25.3	23.7
Vermont	309	303	271	301	221	44.5	31.2	28.9	32.4	24.5
Virginia	3,335	3,142	3,163	3,162	2,836	58.5	36.6	38.5	38.1	34.6
Washington	992	1,643	1,537	1,530	1,522	35.2	28.1	27.5	27.1	27.3
West Virginia	2,269	2,091	2,108	2,082	1,822	53.7	38.0	40.2	39.6	36.1
Wisconsin	2,046	2,476	2,148	2,202	2,121	37.3	29.5	26.3	26.5	25.7
Wyoming	232	249	293	280	247	44.7	34.0	39.5	37.4	32.5

Source: Department of Health, Education, and Welfare, Public Health Service, National Office of Vital Statistics; annual report, *Vital Statistics of the United States.*

Source: Statistical Abstract of the U.S. 1957

Look in the numbers column under 1940. Only Texas had more than 8,000 in 1940, so the correct answer is (E). New Mexico had a *higher rate*, but the question asked for the *highest amount. Make sure you answer the question which is asked.*

3.A B C D E

3. Which of the following statements can be inferred from the table?

I. In 1950 less than $1/20$ of the babies born in the U.S. died before the age of 1 year.
II. The number of infant deaths in the U.S. decreased from 1945 to 1950.
III. More than 5% of the infant deaths in the U.S. in 1950 occurred in California.
IV. The number of infant deaths in North America in 1950 was less than 150,000.

(A) I only
(B) II only
(C) I and III only
(D) I, III, IV only
(E) I, II, III, IV

Analysis:

Statement I can be inferred since $1/20$ of 1,000 = 50 which exceeds the rate per thousand of 29.2 in 1950.

Statement II can't be inferred since the table has no information about 1945. Infant deaths decreased between 1940 and 1950, but that doesn't mean they decreased between 1945 and 1950.

Statement III can be inferred from the table. The total number of infant deaths in 1950 was 103,825, and 6,115 occurred in California. A calculation of 6,115/103,825 could be made, but it is much quicker to find 5% of 103,825 which is 5,191. Since 6,115 is greater than 5,191, more than 5% of the infant deaths in the U.S. occurred in California.

Statement IV can't be inferred, because the table only gives information about the U.S. and there are other countries in North America.

So the correct answer is (C).

IV–2. Circle Graphs

CIRCLE GRAPHS are used to show how various sectors share in the whole. Circle graphs are sometimes called pie charts. Circle graphs usually give the percentage that each sector receives.

EXAMPLE: (Refer to the graph on page 219.)

1.A B C D E

1. The amount spent on materials in 1960 was 120% of the amount spent on

(A) research in 1960
(B) compensation in 1960
(C) advertising in 1970
(D) materials in 1970
(E) legal affairs in 1960

When using circle graphs to find ratios of various sectors, don't find the amounts each sector received and then the ratio of the amounts. Find the *ratio of the percentages,*

Expenditures of General Industries
By major categories

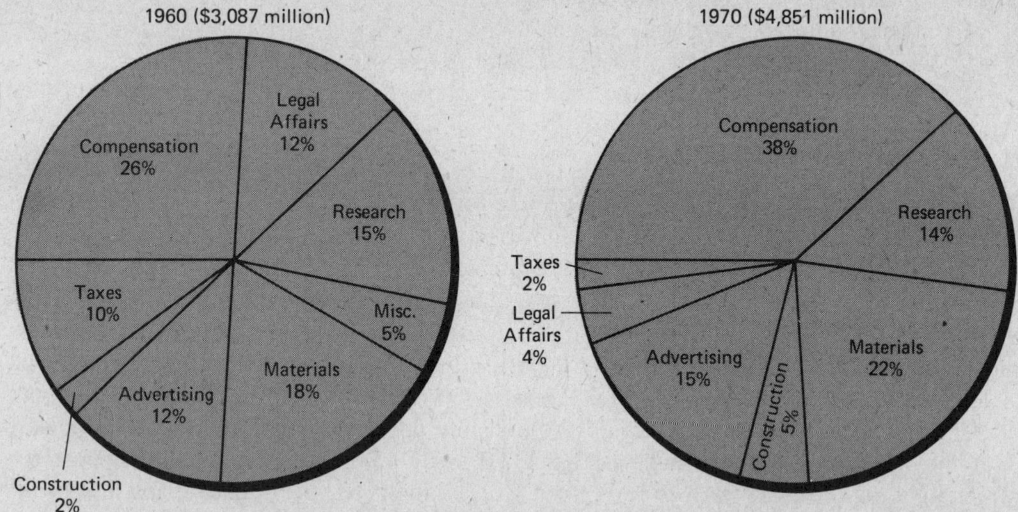

which is much quicker. In 1960, 18% of the expenditures were for materials. We want x where 120% of $x = 18\%$; so $x = 15\%$. Any category which received 15% of 1960 expenditures gives the correct answer, but only one of the five choices is correct. Here, the answer is (A) since research received 15% of the expenditure in 1960. Check the 1960 answers first since you need look only at the percentages, which can be done quickly. Notice that (C) is incorrect, since 15% of the expenditures for 1970 is different from 15% of the expenditures for 1960.

2. The fraction of the total expenditures for 1960 and 1970 spent on compensation was about 2.A B C D E

(A) $\frac{1}{5}$
(B) $\frac{1}{4}$
(C) $\frac{1}{3}$
(D) $\frac{3}{7}$
(E) $\frac{1}{2}$

In 1960, 26% of $3,087 million was spent on compensation and in 1970 compensation received 38% of $4,851 million. The total expenditures for 1960 and 1970 are $(3,087 + 4,851) million. So the exact answer is [(.26)(3,087) + (.38)(4,851)]/(3,087 + 4,851). Actually calculating the answer, you will waste a lot of time. Look at the answers and think for a second.

We are taking a weighted average of 26% and 38%. To find a weighted average, we multiply each value by a weight and divide by the total of all the weights. Here 26% is given a weight of 3,087 and 38% a weight of 4,851. The following general rule is often useful in average problems: The average or weighted average of a collection of values can *never* be:

(1) less than the smallest value in the collection, or
(2) greater than the largest value in the collection.

Therefore, the answer to the question must be greater than or equal to 26% and less than or equal to 38%.

Since $\frac{1}{5} = 20\%$ and $\frac{1}{4} = 25\%$, which are both less than 26%, neither (A) nor (B) can be the correct answer. Since $\frac{3}{7} = 42\frac{6}{7}\%$ and $\frac{1}{2} = 50\%$, which are both greater than 38%, neither (D) nor (E) can be correct. Therefore, by elimination (C) is the correct answer.

3.A B C D E

3. The amount spent in 1960 for materials, advertising, and taxes was about the same as

   (A) $\frac{5}{4}$ of the amount spent for compensation in 1960
   (B) the amount spent for compensation in 1970
   (C) the amount spent on materials in 1970
   (D) $\frac{5}{3}$ of the amount spent on advertising in 1970
   (E) the amount spent on research and construction in 1970

First calculate the combined percentage for materials, advertising, and taxes in 1960. Since 18% + 12% + 10% = 40%, these three categories accounted for 40% of the expenditures in 1960. You can check the one answer which involves 1960 now. Since $\frac{5}{4}$ of 26% = 32.5%, (A) is incorrect. To check the answers which involve 1970, you must know the amount spent on the three categories above in 1960. 40% of 3,087 is 1234.8; so the amount spent on the three categories in 1960 was $1,234.8 million. You could calculate the amount spent in each of the possible answers, but there is a quicker way. Find the *approximate* percentage that 1,234.8 is of 4,087, and check this against the percentages of the answers. Since $\frac{12}{48} = \frac{1}{4}$, the amount for the 3 categories in 1960 is about 25% of the 1970 expenditures. Compensation received 38% of 1970 expenditures, so (B) is incorrect. Materials received 22% and research and construction together received 20%; since advertising received 15%, $\frac{5}{3}$ of the amount for advertising yields 25%. So (D) is probably correct. You can check by calculating 22% of 4,851 which is 1,067.22, while 25% of 4,851 = 1,212.75. Therefore, (D) is correct.

In inference questions involving circle graphs, *do not compare different percentages.* Note in question 3 that the percentage of expenditures in 1960 for the three categories (40%) is *not equal* to 40% of the expenditures in 1970.

IV–3. Line Graphs

LINE GRAPHS are used to show how a quantity changes continuously. Very often the quantity is measured as time changes. If the line goes up, the quantity is increasing; if the line goes down, the quantity is decreasing; if the line is horizontal, the quantity is not changing. To measure the height of a point on the graph, use your pencil or a piece of paper (for example, the admission card to the exam) as a straight edge.

EXAMPLE: (Refer to the graph on page 221.)

1.A B C D E

1. The ratio of productivity in 1967 to productivity in 1940 was about

   (A) 1:4
   (B) 1:3
   (C) 3:1
   (D) 4:1
   (E) 9:1

In 1967 productivity had an index number of 400, and the index numbers are based on 1940 = 100. So the ratio is 400:100 = 4:1. Therefore, the answer is (D). [If you used (incorrectly) output or employment (instead of productivity) you would get the wrong answer (E) or (C); if you confused the order of the ratio you would have incorrectly answered (A).]

TRENDS IN INDUSTRIAL INVESTMENT, LABOUR PRODUCTIVITY, EMPLOYMENT AND OUTPUT, 1940 TO 1967

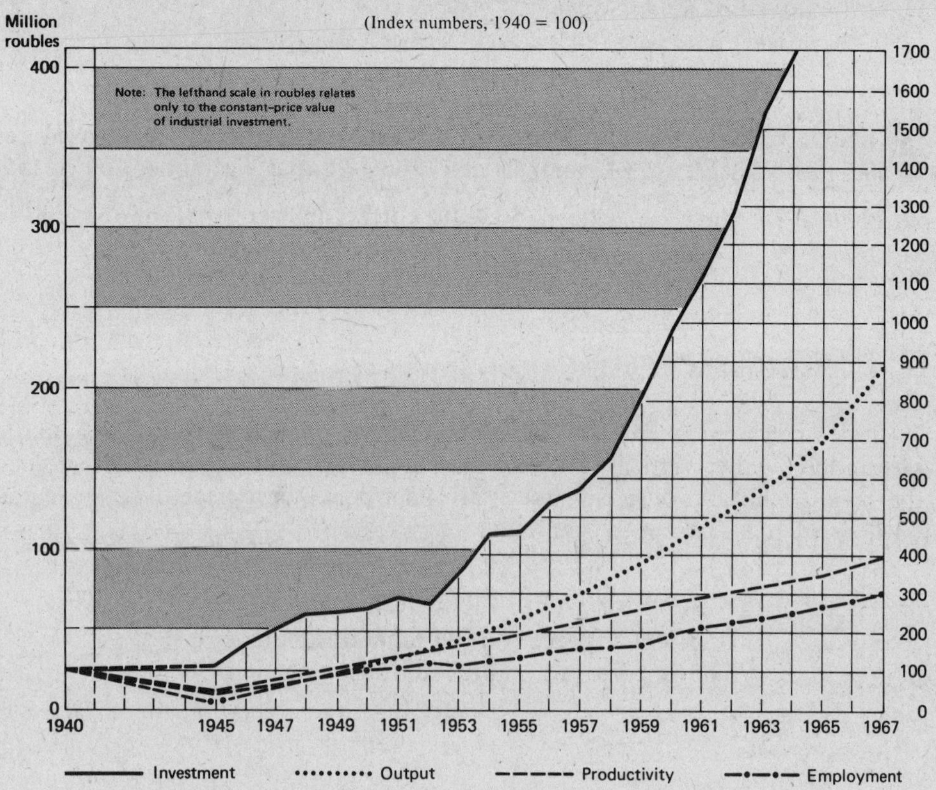

Source: United Nations Economics Bulletin for Europe

2. If 1 rouble = \$3, then the constant-price value of industrial investment in 1959 was about

2.A B C D E

(A) \$1.9 million
(B) \$200 million
(C) \$420,000,000
(D) \$570,000,000
(E) \$570,000 million

In 1959, the value was about 190 million roubles. (It was a little below 200 million.) The answers are all in dollars, so multiply 190 by 3 to get \$570 million or \$570,000,000 (D). If you are not careful about units, you may answer (B) or (E), which are incorrect.

3. Employment was at its minimum during the years shown in

3.A B C D E

(A) 1940
(B) 1943
(C) 1945
(D) 1953
(E) 1967

The minimum of a quantity displayed on a line graph is the lowest place on the line. Thus in 1945, (C), the minimum value of employment was reached.

4.A B C D E

4. Between 1954 and 1965, output
   (A) decreased by about 10%
   (B) stayed about the same
   (C) increased by about 200%
   (D) increased by about 350%
   (E) increased by about 500%

The line for output goes up between 1954 and 1965, so output increased between 1954 and 1965. Therefore, (A) and (B) are wrong. Output was about 200 in 1954 and about 700 in 1965. Since $\frac{700}{200} = 3.5 = 350\%$, the correct answer is (D).

IV-4. Bar Graphs

Quantities can be compared by the height or length of a bar in a bar graph. A bar graph can have either vertical or horizontal bars. You can compare different quantities or the same quantity at different times. Use your pencil or a piece of paper to compare bars which are not adjacent to each other.

DISABILITY BENEFICIARIES REPORTED AS REHABILITATED:
Number, as percent of all rehabilitated clients
of State vocational rehabilitation agencies,
Years 1955–1971

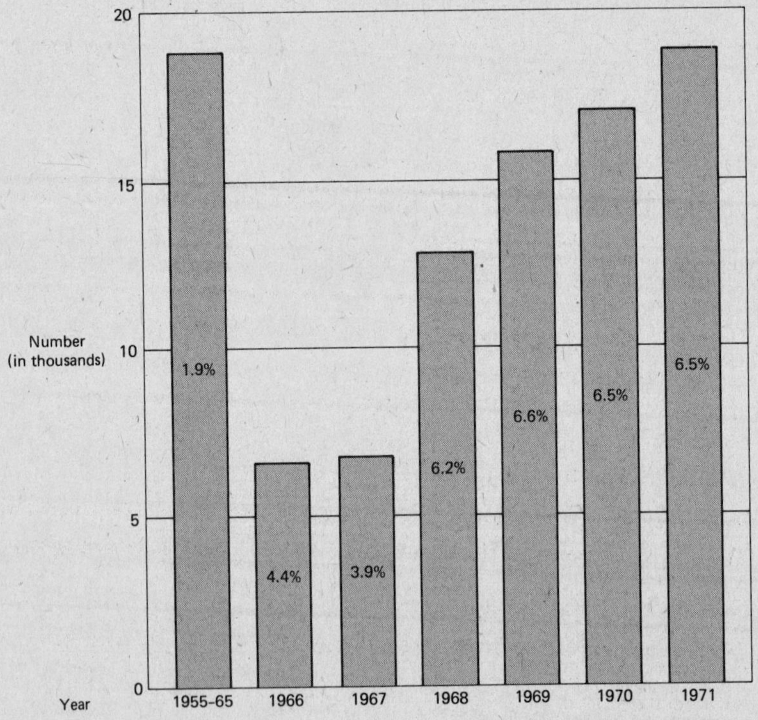

Source: Social Security Bulletin

EXAMPLE: (Refer to the graph on page 222.)

1. Between 1967 and 1971, the largest number of disability beneficiaries were reported as rehabilitated in the year

(A) 1967
(B) 1968
(C) 1969
(D) 1970
(E) 1971

1.A B C D E

The answer is (E) since the highest bar is the bar for 1971. The percentage of disability beneficiaries out of all rehabilitated beneficiaries was higher in 1969, but the *number* was lower.

2. Between 1955 and 1965, about how many clients were rehabilitated by State vocational rehabilitation agencies?

(A) 90,000
(B) 400,000
(C) 1,000,000
(D) 1,900,000
(E) 10,000,000

2.A B C D E

1.9% of those rehabilitated were disability beneficiaries, and there were about 19,000 disability beneficiaries rehabilitated. So if T is the total number rehabilitated, then 1.9% of $T = 19{,}000$ or $.019T = 19{,}000$. Thus, $T = 19{,}000/.019 = 1{,}000{,}000$ and the answer is (C).

IV–5. Cumulative Graphs

You can compare several categories by a graph of the cumulative type. These are usually bar or line graphs where the height of the bar or line is divided up proportionately among different quantities.

FEDERAL PRISONERS RECEIVED FROM THE COURTS, BY MAJOR OFFENSE GROUPS: Years 1944–1952

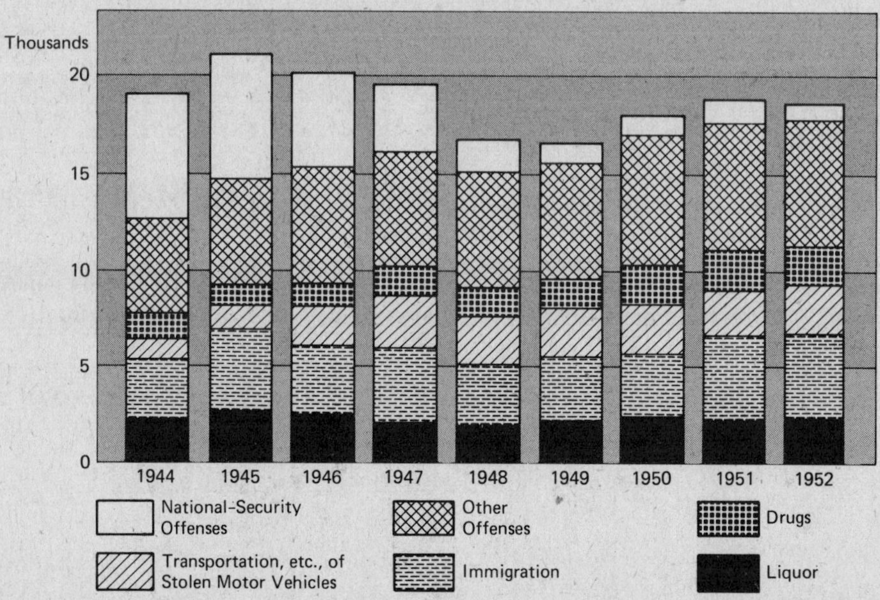

Source: Statistical Abstract of the U.S. 1953

1.A B C D E

1. In 1946, roughly what percent of the federal prisoners received from the courts were national-security offenders?

(A) 15
(B) 20
(C) 25
(D) 30
(E) 35

The total number of prisoners in 1946 was about 20,000, and national security offenders accounted for the part of the graph from just above 15,000 to just above 20,000. Therefore, there were about 20,000 − 15,000 = 5,000 prisoners convicted of national-security offenses. Since 5,000/20,000 = $\frac{1}{4}$ = 25%, the correct answer is (C).

2.A B C D E

2. Of the combined total for the four years 1947 through 1950, the largest number of offenders were in the category

(A) national-security offenses
(B) other offenses
(C) drugs
(D) immigration
(E) liquor

The correct answer is (B). Since other offenses had the most offenders in each year, that category must have the largest total number of offenders. [If you answered this question for the years 1944–1946, then (A) would be correct.]

3.A B C D E

3. Which of the following statements can be inferred from the graph?

I. The number of federal prisoners received from the courts decreased each year from 1946 to 1948.
II. More than 40% of the prisoners between 1944 and 1952 came from the other offenses category.
III. 2% of the federal prisoners received in 1952 were convicted on heroin charges.

(A) I only
(B) III only
(C) I and II only
(D) I and III only
(E) I, II, and III

Statement I is true, since the height of the bar for each year was lower than the height of the bar for the previous year in 1946, 1947, and 1948.

Statement II is not true. For most of the years, other offenses accounted for about 25–30%, and it never was more than 40% in any year. Therefore, it could not account for more than 40% of the total.

Statement III can not be inferred. There is a category of drug offenders, but there is no information about specific drugs.

So, the correct answer is (A).

REVIEW OF FORMULAS

(Numbers next to the formulas refer to the section of the Math Review where the formula is discussed.)

Interest = Amount × Time × Rate	I–4
Discount = Cost × Rate of Discount	I–4
Price = Cost × (100% − Rate of Discount)	I–4
$x = \frac{1}{2a}[-b \pm \sqrt{b^2 - 4ac}]$ (quadratic formula)	II–2
Distance = Speed × Time	II–3
$a^2 + b^2 = c^2$ when a and b are the legs and c is the hypotenuse of a right triangle	III–4
Diameter of a circle = 2 × Radius	III–6
Area of a square = s^2	III–7
Area of a rectangle = LW	III–7
Area of a triangle = $\frac{1}{2}bh$	III–7
Area of a circle = πr^2	III–7
Area of a parallelogram = bh	III–7
Area of a trapezoid = $\frac{1}{2}(b_1 + b_2)h$	III–7
Circumference of a circle = πd	III–7
Perimeter of a square = $4s$	III–7
Perimeter of a rectangle = $2(L + W)$	III–7
Volume of a box = lwh	III–8
Volume of a cube = e^3	III–8
Volume of a cylinder = $\pi r^2 h$	III–8
Volume of a sphere = $\frac{4}{3}\pi r^3$	III–8
Surface area of a box = $2LW + 2LH + 2WH$	III–8
Surface area of a cube = $6e^2$	III–8
Surface area of a cylinder = $2\pi rh + 2\pi r^2$	III–8
Distance between points (x,y) and (a,b) is $\sqrt{(x-a)^2 + (y-b)^2}$	III–9

Hints for Answering Mathematics Questions

1. Make sure you answer the question you are asked to answer.
2. Look at the answers before you start to work out a problem; you can save a lot of time.
3. Don't waste time on superfluous computations.
4. *Estimate* whenever you can to save time.
5. Budget your time so you can try all the questions. (Bring a watch.)
6. You probably won't be able to answer all the questions; don't waste time worrying about it.
7. Do all the problems you know how to work *before* you start to think about those that you can't answer in a minute or two.
8. If you skip a question, make sure you skip that number on the answer sheet.
9. Don't make extra assumptions on inference questions (see the Logic Review section).
10. Work efficiently; don't waste time worrying during the test.
11. Make sure you express your answer in the units asked for.
12. On data sufficiency questions, don't do any more work than is necessary. (Don't solve the problem; you only have to know that the problem can be solved.)

BASIC LOGIC REVIEW

A knowledge of the principles of elementary logic presented in this section can be helpful in many areas of the GMAT. Aside from the obvious benefits of having a sound reasoning ability to apply in solving Data Sufficiency and Mathematics problems, a capacity for logical thinking can also be extremely useful in the Verbal Aptitude area of the exam, where you are required to find logical relationships between words, and in the Reading Recall and Business Judgment sections where sound thinking is certain to increase your understanding of the passages you read. With this in mind, study the following material carefully.

Implications

Many types of questions on the exam ask you to determine if a statement can be inferred or deduced from certain given information. To say that a statement q can be inferred from a statement p means that whenever statement p is true, statement q must be true. This concept may also be expressed as *p implies q, q follows from p,* or *q can be deduced from p.* It is written $p \Rightarrow q$. Statement q is called the *conclusion* and statement p is called the *hypothesis* of the implication.

For an implication $p \Rightarrow q$ to be false, it is only necessary to find one case where the conclusion q is false and the hypothesis p is true.

EXAMPLE 1: Let p represent the statement *Tom owns a motorcycle.* Let q represent the statement *Tom owns a motor vehicle.* Can q be inferred from p?

Yes. All motorcycles are motor vehicles. Therefore, if Tom has a motorcycle he has a motor vehicle. (p is true, and q is true). Whenever p is true, so $p \Rightarrow q$.

Even though $p \Rightarrow q$ is true, $q \Rightarrow p$ is not necessarily true.

EXAMPLE 2: Let p and q represent the same statements used in **example** 1.

Does p follow from q?

No. Not all motor vehicles are motorcycles. Therefore, Tom could own a motor vehicle (q) without owning a motorcycle (p). Statement q is true but statement p is false. Since both statements must be true for the deduction to be true, $q \Rightarrow p$ is false.

EXAMPLE 3:

HOURS OF WORK NEEDED TO PURCHASE
(By Average Employee)

	1971	1972
One dozen eggs	10 min.	8 min.
Pair of shoes	3 hrs.	2 hrs. 45 min.
Suit	15 hrs.	15.5 hrs.
2 lbs. of potatoes	45 min.	42 min.
Automobile	600 hrs.	620 hrs.
Haircut	30 min.	30 min.
Bottle of milk	5 min.	4 min.
5 lbs. of meat	1 hr.	1 hr.

Which of the following conclusions can be inferred from the table?

I. The employees were paid more in 1972 than they were in 1971.
II. The price of a haircut was the same in 1972 as it was in 1971.
III. In each year only two of the items shown on the table required more than 10 hours of work.

(A) I only
(B) II only
(C) III only
(D) II and III
(E) I, II, and III

This is an example of a type of inference problem found on the ATGSB. The correct answer is C, statement III only. Statement I can not be inferred from the table since the table gives no information about the prices of the items in dollars. Statement II can not be inferred from the table since there is no information about the monetary wages of the average employee. Statement III can be inferred since only a suit and an automobile took more than ten hours of work in each year according to the table.

Do not make the mistake of assuming information which is not given. If you assumed that the price of eggs rose or stayed the same between 1971 and 1972 then you could infer statement I.

Connectives

If you connect two or more statements, you form a compound statement. The truth value of the statements which make up the compound statement and the connectives used in forming the compound statement will both affect the truth value of the compound statement.

Conjunction

The *conjunction* of two statements, p and q, may be expressed as *p and q,* or as *both p and q.* It is written $p \wedge q$. The conjunction $p \wedge q$ is true *only* when both of the statements p and q are true. If either one of the statements is false,then $p \wedge q$ is false. For example, let p represent the statement *Tom owns a boat.* Let q represent the statement *Tom owns a car.* The conjunction $p \wedge q$ is expressed verbally as *Tom owns a boat and Tom owns a car,* or as *Tom owns a boat and a car.* It is true *only* when Tom owns both a car and a boat. The statement would be false, for example, if Tom owned a car but did not own a boat.

The conjunction of more than two statements is true if each of the statements is true. If *any* of the statements are false, the conjunction is false. Verbal equivalents would be *p and q and r, each p, q, and r,* or *all of p, q, and r.* Consider the statement *Tom, Mary, and John each own a car.* This is the conjunction of the statements *Tom owns a car, Mary owns a car,* and *John owns a car.* The statement is true only if each of the three people own a car. The statement would be false if someone did not own a car. For example, the statement is false if Tom and Mary each own a car but John does not own a car.

EXAMPLE: Refer to the table given in Example 3 of the section on Implications. Let $p \wedge q$ represent the statement *An average employee had to work more than 2 hours and 50 minutes in each of the years 1971 and 1972 to purchase a pair of shoes.* Can $p \wedge q$ be inferred from the table?

No. This statement is the conjunction of two statements p and q where p is the statement *The average employee had to work more than 2 hours and 50 minutes in 1971 to purchase a pair of shoes,* and q is the statement *The average employee had to work more than 2 hours and 50 minutes in 1972 to purchase a pair of shoes.* Statement p is true but q is false so the statement *p and q* is false. Therefore, $p \wedge q$ can not be inferred from the table.

Disjunction

The disjunction of two statements, p and q, is expressed verbally as *either p or q,* or as *p or q.* The disjunction of p and q is written symbolically as $p \vee q$. Statement $p \vee q$ is false *only* when both p and q are false. It is true if at least one of the statements p and q is true. This can be shown in the following manner. Let p represent the statement *Tom owns a boat.* Let q represent the statement *Tom owns a car.* Disjunction $p \vee q$ is expressed verbally as *Tom owns a boat or a car.* Disjunction $p \vee q$ is true if Tom owns a boat, or if Tom owns a car, or if Tom owns both a boat and a car. It is false only if Tom owns neither a boat nor a car.

The disjunction of more than two statements is true if *any* of the statements is true. The disjunction is false *only* when *every* one of the statements is false. Verbal equivalents of $p \vee q \vee r$ would be *p or q or r,* or *at least one of p, q, and r is true.* Let $p \vee q \vee r$ represent the statement: *Tom or Mary or John owns a car,* the disjunction of the three statements, *Tom owns a car* (p), *Mary owns a car* (q), and *John owns a car* (r). The disjunction is false only if *none* of the three people (Tom, Mary, John) owns a car. The statement would be true if *any* one of the people (Tom, Mary, John) owns a car.

EXAMPLE: Refer to the table given in Example 3 of the section on Implications. Let $p \vee q \vee r$ represent the statement *In at least one of the years 1970, 1971, and 1972, the average employee had to work more than 2 hours and 50 minutes to purchase a pair of shoes.* Can $p \vee q \vee r$ be inferred from the table?

Yes. This statement is the disjunction of p, q, and r where p is the statement *An average employee had to work more than 2 hours and 50 minutes in 1970 to purchase a pair of shoes,* q the statement *An average employee had to work more than 2 hours and 50 minutes in 1971 to purchase a pair of shoes,* and r the statement *An average employee had to work more than 2 hours and 50 minutes in 1972 to purchase a pair of shoes.* Since q is true, the disjunction is true, even though r is false and there is no information about p on the table.

Compare the sections on Conjunctions and Disjunctions so that you clearly see the differences that exist between the two.

Carrying this idea a step further, it is possible to show that $\sim p \wedge \sim q$ is *not* a negation of $p \wedge q$. The truth set of $\sim p \wedge \sim q$ is the area common to the truth set of $\sim p$ and the truth set of $\sim q$.

The Venn Diagram for $\sim p$ is

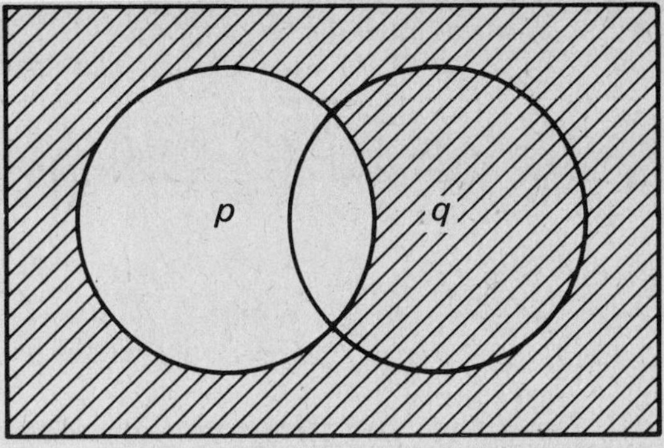

The Venn Diagram for $\sim q$ is

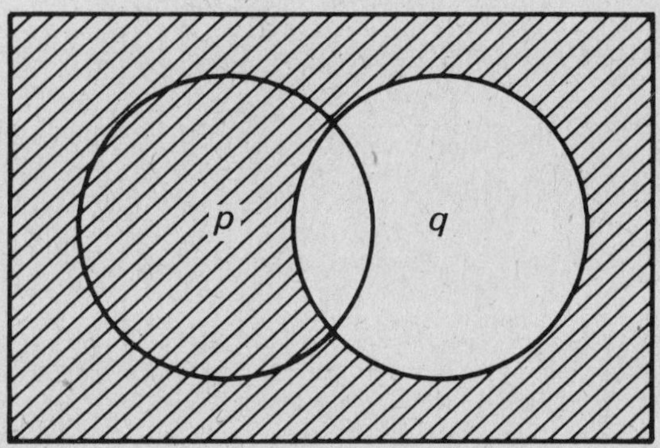

Therefore, taking the truth sets common to each statement and combining them, you can arrive at the Venn Diagram for $\sim p \wedge \sim q$, which is

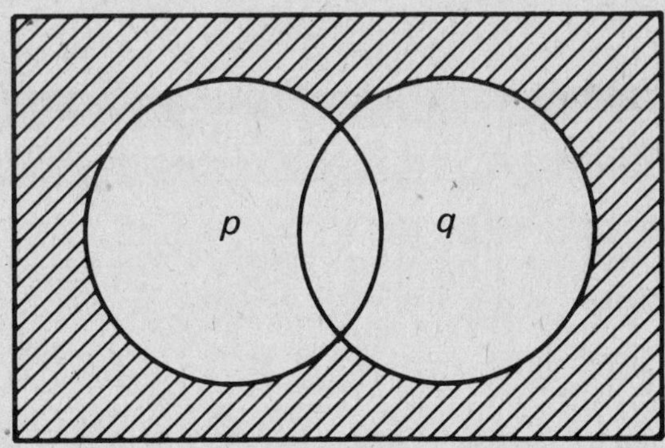

By comparing this diagram with the diagram for $p \wedge q$, you can see that the two are not interchanged. Thus, $\sim p \wedge \sim q$ is not the negation of $p \vee q$, and the two statements are not equivalent. This is an important fact to remember when solving counting problems.

As an illustration of this point, consider the following. Let p represent the statement *A car has a radio.* Let q represent the statement *A car has a heater.* Then, $p \wedge q$ represents the statement *A car has a radio and a heater.* In the same manner, $\sim(p \wedge q)$ represents the statement *A car does not have a radio and a heater,* but $\sim p \wedge \sim q$ is *A car does not have a radio and does not have a heater.* If a car had a radio but not a heater, $\sim(p \wedge q)$ would be true but $\sim p \wedge \sim q$ would be false.

The statements $\sim(p \vee q)$ and $\sim p \vee \sim q$ also differ. In fact, $\sim(p \vee q)$ is equivalent to $\sim p \wedge \sim q$ and $\sim p \vee \sim q$ is the same as $\sim(p \wedge q)$.

Statements of the form *everyone has . . . , all are . . . , each is . . . ,* are negated by *some have not . . . , all are not . . . , each is not . . . .* To negate the statement *All the members of the Smith family have red hair,* you would have to change it to *At least one of the members of the Smith family does not have red hair.* Notice that the statement *No member of the Smith family has red hair* is *not* the negation.

Statements of the form *some are . . . , at least one is . . . ,* have negations of the form *none are . . . , no one is . . . , everyone is not. . . .* The negation of the statement *Some children have been spoiled by their parents,* is *No children have been spoiled by their parents.*

FIVE

WORDS FREQUENTLY APPEARING ON THE GMAT

In your preparation for the GMAT it is important that you become familiar with the meanings of as many words as possible. This is specially true for success on the Verbal Aptitude sections of the test, but it also necessary for better comprehension of Reading Recall and Business Judgment passages where a few key words may hold the meaning of an entire paragraph.

The two vocabulary lists presented here contain words that frequently appear on the GMAT and many terms that you may encounter in the course of the exam. The General Vocabulary List includes definitions of words that could appear anywhere in the exam, although their main application is in the Verbal Aptitude sections. The Glossary of Business Terms is a special list of basic business vocabulary designed to enhance your understanding of Business Judgment passages.

Study each list carefully to familiarize yourself with these words. Refer to these listings to check the meaning of any difficult words you may encounter in other parts of this guide.

General Vocabulary List

Abase—to humiliate, degrade
Abash—to bewilder, confound
Abate—to remove, lessen
Abdicate—to forsake, give up
Aberration—deviation
Abeyance—inactivity
Abhor—to detest, hate
Abject—degraded, miserable
Abjure—to recant, revoke
Abnegate—to deny, denounce
Abominate—to dislike
Abort—to be unsuccessful, fail to develop
Abrade—to scrape out
Abrogate—to abolish
Abscond—to bolt, decamp, flee
Absolve—to pardon
Abstemious—eating or drinking sparingly
Abstract—summary
Abstruse—profound, hidden, hard to understand
Accede—to consent
Accessory—accomplice
Acclivity—incline, rising slope
Accolade—honor, award
Accord—to grant, allow

Accost—to greet aggressively
Accretion—adhesion, concretion
Accrue—to accumulate
Acerbity—sharpness, bitterness
Acme—summit, peak
Acolyte—attendant, helper
Acrimonious—sharp, acrid
Actuate—to put into action
Adamant—immovable
Adduce—to give as proof
Adjudicate—to decide (a case)
Adjunct—auxiliary, appendage
Adjure—to state on oath
Admonish—to caution, warn
Adroit—skillful, clever
Adulation—flattery
Adulterate—to corrupt, contaminate
Advent—coming
Adventitious—accidental
Advocate—counsel, defender
Aegis—protection
Aesthetic—pertaining to beauty
Affability—politeness, courtesy
Affinity—relation, alliance
Affluence—wealth
Aggrandize—to increase in power
Agnostic—one who doubts the existence of God
Agrarian—relating to farming
Alacrity—willingness, agility
Albeit—although
Alchemy—chemistry of the middle ages
Alimentary—supplying food
Allay—to soothe, calm
Allegory—parable, fable
Allocate—to distribute
Allude—to insinuate, refer
Altercation—quarrel
Alternation—recurrence, succession
Altruism—unselfish devotion
Amalgamate—to combine, unite
Ambidextrous—using both hands equally well
Ameliorate—to amend, improve
Amenable—responsible, liable
Amenity—pleasantness
Amiable—pleasing, loving
Amorphous—shapeless
Anachronism—something misplaced in time
Analgesic—pain-reducing drug
Analogy—similarity, affinity
Anarchy—absence of government
Anathema—ban, curse
Anchorite—hermit
Ancillary—subordinate
Anecdote—tale, story
Animate—to inspire, encourage
Animosity—enmity, hatred
Annals—historical accounts
Anneal—to heat glass, metals, etc.
Annotator—commentator
Anomaly—abnormality, deviation
Antagonist—opponent
Antecede—to come before (in time or place)
Antedate—to assign a date earlier than the actual one
Anterior—front
Antimacassar—cover used to protect furniture
Antipathy—aversion, dislike
Antithesis—contrast, direct opposite
Aperture—opening
Apex—highest point
Aphorism—saying, adage
Apiary—place where bees are kept
Aplomb—self-confidence
Apochryphal—of questionable authenticity
Apogee—farthest orbit point from the earth
Apoplexy—sudden loss of consciousness
Apostasy—abandoning of faith
Apothecary—druggist
Apothegm—short, pithy statement
Appall—to terrify, shock
Appellation—name, title
Apposite—suitable, appropriate
Apprise—to inform
Approbation—approval, consent
Arbiter—arbitrator, judge
Archaic—no longer used
Archipelago—chain of islands
Archives—place where records are kept
Arduous—difficult
Argot—slang
Array—rank, order, finery
Arrears—in debt
Articulate—to speak or write clearly
Artifice—mastery, trickery
Asperity—acrimony, harshness
Aspersion—slander, false accusation
Assay—to analyze chemically
Asseverate—to state positively
Assiduity—care, diligence
Assimilate—to absorb
Assuage—to pacify, calm
Astral—starry
Astringent—contracting (tissues), severe
Astute—shrewd
Atheist—one who denies the existence of God
Atrophy—to waste away, deteriorate
Attenuate—to weaken
Attrition—a wearing away, weakening
Audacious—bold

Augment—to increase
Augur—to predict
August—majestic, noble
Auspice—protection
Auspicious—fortunate, favorable
Austere—rigid, severe
Authoritative—powerful, commanding
Autocratic—arrogant, dictatorial
Autonomy—self-government
Auxiliary—assistant, helping
Avarice—greed, cupidity
Aver—assert
Averse—unwilling
Aviary—place where birds are kept
Avidity—eagerness
Avoirdupois—weight
Avow—declare
Awry—crooked, bent
Axiomatic—principle accepted as self-evident

Badger—to harass, nag
Badinage—banter
Baleful—harmful, evil
Balm—something that soothes
Banal—meaningless, commonplace
Bandy—to exchange (words)
Bane—cause of harm
Barrister—court lawyer
Bedizen—to dress in a gaudy, vulgar manner
Beguile—to deceive
Belabor—to attack verbally, drag out
Bellicose—warlike
Beneficient—liberal, kind
Benign—gentle, mild
Berate—to scold
Bereft—bereaved, deprived of
Bestial—savage
Bestride—to mount
Bicameral—having two legislative chambers
Biennial—every two years
Bilious—bad-tempered
Biped—two-footed animal
Bivouac—encampment
Bland—mild
Blasé—indifferent
Blasphemy—profane abuse of anything sacred
Blatant—noisy, vociferous
Blazon—to adorn, proclaim
Bluster—to swagger, boast
Bogus—counterfeit
Boisterous—violent, furious
Bombast—pompous speech
Botch—to ruin
Bounty—generosity
Bourgeois—middle class
Bovine—ox or cow
Brandish—to wave menacingly
Bravado—pretense of bravery
Breech—lower part of the body
Brigand—robber, bandit
Broach—to start a discussion
Browbeat—to intimidate
Brusque—abrupt in manner
Bucolic—rustic
Buffoon—clown
Buoyancy—lightness, animation
Bureaucracy—government of specialized functions and hierarchy of officials
Burgeon—bud, sprout
Burnish—to polish
Butte—hill
Buttress—prop, protuberance

Cabal—intrigue, faction
Cache—hiding place
Cacophony—harsh sound
Cadence—measured movement
Cajole—to coax, flatter
Caldron—kettle
Calligraphy—penmanship
Callous—hard, obdurate
Callow—unfledged
Calumny—slander, defamation
Canard—hoax
Canker—ulcer
Cant—tilt, whining speech
Cantilever—supporting bracket
Canvass—to make a survey, solicit
Capacious—roomy, ample
Caper—frolic, mischievous act
Capitulate—to surrender
Caprice—whim, fancy
Captious—touchy, cross
Captivate—to charm, fascinate
Carnage—slaughter, massacre
Carniverous—flesh-eating
Carom—rebound
Carp—to complain constantly
Carrion—decaying flesh
Castigate—to punish
Casuistry—false reasoning
Cataclysm—violent change or upheaval
Catalyst—agent of change
Cathartic—purifying
Catholic—universal
Caustic—sarcastic, corrosive
Cavil—to quibble
Celerity—rapidity, velocity

Censorious—fault-finding
Censure—to criticize sharply
Centrifugal—moving away from center
Cephalic—of the head
Cerebration—thought process
Chafe—fret, irritate
Chaff—worthless material
Chagrin—embarrassment
Charlatan—faker
Charnel—place where corpses are deposited
Chary—discretely cautious
Chastise—to castigate, correct
Chattel—slave
Chauvinism—fanatical patriotism
Chicanery—deception
Chimerical—imaginary
Choleric—irascible, easily angered
Chronic—always present
Churlish—ill-bred
Circuitous—roundabout, tortuous
Circumlocution—evasion in speech
Circumspect—watchful, cautious
Circumvent—to avoid
Citadel—fortress
Civility—politeness, affability
Clairvoyant—able to perceive something not readily apparent
Clandestine—secret, hidden
Cloy—to overindulge with an initially pleasing thing
Coagulate—to thicken, clot
Coalesce—to unite, join forces
Coda—ending section distinct from the main body of a work
Coerce—to force
Cogent—forcible, convincing
Cogitate—to think seriously
Cognate—related
Cognizant—aware
Cohesion—a sticking together
Collate—to put together in proper order
Colligate—to group together
Collocate—to arrange in position
Colloquy—conversation, dialogue
Collusion—secret agreement to defraud
Colophon—inscription in a book
Colorable—plausible, ostensible
Comestible—edible
Commensurate—proportionate
Commodious—spacious
Commute—alter, exchange
Compatible—consistent
Compendious—brief, short
Compendium—abridgement, abstract
Compunction—uneasiness, remorse
Conclave—secret meeting
Concomitant—accompanying
Concupiscence—strong desire
Condign—appropriate
Condone—to overlook as unimportant
Conduce—to lead toward a desired end
Configuration—shape, arrangement
Confiscatory—seized by authority
Conflagration—destructive fire
Confute—to disprove, refute
Congeal—to change to a solid state
Congenital—existing from birth
Congruous—appropriate, in agreement
Coniferous—cone-bearing
Conjecture—guess, conclusion
Conjure—to summon solemnly
Connive—cooperate secretly
Connoisseur—expert, critic
Connote—suggest, imply
Conscript—to force into service, draft
Consecrate—to sanctify, dedicate
Consonance—harmony
Consort—associate, companion
Constellation—group of stars
Consternation—sudden confusion, panic
Constituency—voters in a district
Constrain—to restrict movement, limit
Constrict—to shrink
Consummate—to complete
Contemn—to despise, scorn
Contemptuous—scornful, insolent
Contentious—argumentative
Contiguous—adjacent, touching
Contingency—casualty, occurrence
Contravene—to contradict
Contrition—remorse, repentance
Contrivance—plan, scheme
Controvert—to debate, dispute
Contumely—rudeness
Contusion—bruise
Conundrum—riddle
Conversant—familiar with
Convivial—joyous, festal
Convoke—to assemble
Convulse—to shake violently, agitate
Copious—abundant
Corollary—inference, result
Corona—crown, luminous circle
Corporeal—pertaining to the body
Corpulent—fat, stout
Correlate—to be in mutual relation
Corrigible—amenable, tractable
Corroborate—to strengthen, confirm
Coterie—group

Countenance—facial expression, composure
Countermand—to cancel with a contrary order
Covenant—contract
Convert—clandestine, secret
Covet—to desire, aspire to
Cower—to cringe in fear
Cozen—to trick
Crag—steep projecting rock
Crass—grossly stupid
Credence—belief, faith
Credible—believable
Credulity—simplicity, gullibility
Crimp—to bend into shape, pinch together
Cruciate—cross-shaped
Crux—vital point
Cryptic—mysterious
Cudgel—club
Culmination—highest point, climax
Culpable—deserving blame
Cumbrous—unwieldy
Cupidity—avarice, greed
Curry—to seek favor by flattery
Cursory—hasty, superficial
Cynical—sarcastic, sneering
Cynosure—center of attraction

Dalliance—dawdling
Dank—chilly and wet
Dastard—coward
Dauntless—valiant, intrepid
Dearth—scarcity
Debacle—complete failure, fiasco
Debase—to degrade, lower
Debauch—to corrupt
Debility—weakness
Debonair—affable, jaunty
Decamp—to break camp, depart suddenly
Decant—to pour
Deciduous—shedding (leaves) annually
Declaim—speak, debate
Declaration—announcement
Declivity—descent, slope
Decorous—proper, in good taste
Decrepit—run-down, worn-out
Decry—censure
Deference—honor, respect
Definitive—explicit, conclusive
Defunct—no longer existing
Deign—to condescend
Deleterious—harmful
Delineate—to describe
Demean—to behave properly
Denigrate—to defame, belittle
Denizen—inhabitant
Denote—to stand for, mean
Denude—to strip, divest
Deposition—removal (from office), testimony
Depraved—sinful
Deprecate—to disapprove of
Depreciate—to lessen the value of
Depute—to appoint, entrust
Derogatory—disparaging
Descry—to discover, make known
Desecrate—to profane, abuse
Desiccate—to dry up
Desist—to cease, stop
Despicable—contemptible
Desultory—loose, rambling
Deterrent—constraint, preventative
Detritus—product of disintegration
Devious—rambling, errant, tricky
Diametric—opposite
Diaphanous—extremely delicate, insubstantial
Dichotomy—division into two parts
Dictum—positive statement
Didactic—instructive
Diffident—lacking confidence, reserved
Diffuse—to spread without restraint
Dilate—to stretch, widen
Dilatory—tardy, lagging
Dilettante—one who dabbles superficially
Diligent—industrious, assiduous
Diluvial—pertaining to floods
Discern—to observe, perceive
Discompose—to upset the order of
Disconcert—to confound, disturb
Disconsolate—sad, forlorn
Discord—disagreement
Discountenance—disapproval
Discursive—rambling
Disdain—to scorn
Disingenuous—without candor
Disparage—to belittle
Disparate—distinct in quality
Disputation—debate
Disseminate—to spread widely
Dissident—disagreeing
Dissimulate—to put on a false appearance
Dissipate—to scatter or use wastefully
Dissolute—morally loose
Dissonant—lacking harmony
Dissuade—to advise against
Distend—to stretch out
Distrait—absentminded, distracted
Distraught—mentally upset
Diverge—to branch off, deviate
Divers—various
Divest—to deprive, strip off

Doctrinate—impractical theorist
Dogmatic—arrogant stating of opinion
Doldrums—low spirits
Dole—something given sparingly
Doleful—dismal
Dolorous—mournful
Dolt—stupid person
Dotage—senility
Dour—stern, gloomy
Dowdy—shabby, styleless
Dregs—undesirable leftovers
Drivel—silly talk
Droll—funny, amusing
Dross—refuse, waste
Dubious—uncertain
Dubitable—open to doubt
Dupe—to deceive
Duplicity—deception
Duress—restraint, force

Ebony—hard durable wood, black
Ebullient—enthusiastic
Ecclesiastical—pertaining to the church
Echelon—formation of units or troops
Eclectic—made up of elements from a variety of sources
Ecology—study of the relationships in an environment
Ecumenical—general, worldwide
Edict—public announcement, decree
Edifice—large building
Edify—to enlighten
Educe—to bring forth
Effable—capable of being expressed
Efface—to wipe out, erase
Efficacious—effective
Effigy—image, crude likeness
Effluence—flowing out
Effrontery—impudence
Effulgent—illuminated
Effusive—highly emotional
Egocentric—self-centered
Egregious—flagrant
Egression—emergence
Electorate—voting body
Elicit—to cause a response
Elision—omission
Eloquent—pleasingly expressive
Elucidate—to make clear
Elusive—hard to grasp
Emaciate—to make thin
Emanate—to come out from
Embellish—to ornament
Embody—to make perceptible, personify
Embroil—involve in an argument
Emend—to correct or alter (as in a literary work)
Emissary—messenger
Emollient—soothing substance
Emolument—salary, compensation
Emulate—to rival or try to equal
Enclave—distinct unit surrounded by foreign territory
Encomium—glowing praise
Encroach—trespass
Encyclopedia—compendium of knowledge
Endemic—restricted to a given locality
Endogenous—originating from within
Enervate—to lessen the vitality of
Enfranchise—to give the right to vote
Engender—to bring into being
Engross—to take the entire attention of
Engulf—to swallow up
Enigmatic—hard to understand, puzzling
Enjoin—to impose by order, prohibit
Enmesh—to entangle
Enmity—hostility
Enormity—outrageous act
Ensconce—to conceal, settle snugly
Entity—something that exists independently
Entomology—study of insects
Entreat—to implore
Enunciate—to announce, pronounce clearly
Ephemeral—short-lived
Epic—long, narrative poem
Epicure—one who has discriminating tastes for foods and liquors
Epigram—terse, witty saying
Epilogue—closing section of a literary work
Epistle—letter
Epitaph—inscription
Epithet—word or phrase characterizing a person or thing
Epitome—ideal example, embodiment
Epoch—event or time that marks the start of a new period
Equable—uniform, even
Equanimity—composure
Equivocal—purposely ambiguous
Equivocate—to purposely deceive
Era—period of time marked by certain events
Ergo—therefore
Ersatz—artificial, substitute
Erudite—learned
Escapement—notched device regulating movement in a mechanism
Escarpment—steep slope between level areas
Eschew—to shun
Esculent—edible
Escutcheon—shield containing a coat of arms
Esoteric—limited to a chosen few
Esthetic—beautiful

Estival—pertaining to summer
Ethereal—airy
Etude—musical composition used for practice
Eulogy—speech in praise of a dead person
Euphemism—substitution of a less offensive word
Euphony—agreeable sounds
Euphoria—feeling of well-being
Evanescent—fading from sight
Evasion—avoidance
Evince—to show plainly
Evoke—to call forth, produce
Evolve—to develop gradually
Exacerbate—to aggravate
Exacting—making severe demands
Exclude—to bar
Excoriate—to strip the skin of
Exculpate—to free from blame
Execrable—detestable
Execrate—to curse
Exemplary—serving as a model
Exempt—to excuse from responsibility others are subject to
Exhort—to entreat, appeal urgently
Exhume—to dig up
Exigency—situation making extremely urgent demands
Exigent—urgent
Exiguous—scanty, meager
Exogenous—originating from outside
Exonerate—to clear from blame
Exorcise—to expel (an evil spirit)
Expatiate—to speak or write at length, wander
Expedite—to speed up
Expeditious—prompt
Expiate—to make amends
Expound—to state in detail
Expunge—to erase
Expurgate—to remove passages (from a book)
Exquisite—very beautiful, perfected
Extant—still existing
Extemporary—impromptu
Extemporize—to improvise
Extenuate—to lessen the seriousness of
Extirpate—to destroy completely
Extol—to laud
Extraneous—not pertinent to the whole
Extricate—to set free
Extrinsic—not essential
Extrude—to force out
Exude—to discharge
Exult—to rejoice

Fabricate—to manufacture, invent
Fabulous—fictitious
Facade—front or main face of a building
Facetious—lightly joking
Facile—easily done
Facilitate—to make easier
Facsimile—reproduction
Factious—producing dissention
Factitious—artificially produced
Factotum—general worker
Fallacious—tending to mislead
Fallible—capable of erring
Fallow—cultivated land not in use
Fastidious—hard to please, meticulous
Fatuous—foolish
Fawn—to court favor, grovel
Fealty—intense faithfulness
Feasible—possible
Feculent—impure
Fecund—fertile
Feign—to simulate, pretend
Felicitous—appropriate, pleasant
Fell—dangerous, cruel
Ferret—to search out
Fervid—ardent
Fervor—ardor, zeal
Festoon—decorative chain
Fetid—stinking
Fetish—an object believed to have magical powers
Fettle—condition, state of fitness
Fiasco—complete failure
Fickle—capricious
Figment—fabrication
Filament—fine thread
Filch—to pilfer
Finesse—skill
Fissure—cleft or crack
Flaccid—soft and limp
Flagitious—wicked
Flagrant—outrageous
Flail—implement for threshing grain
Flair—aptitude, attractive quality
Flamboyant—showy
Flaunt—to show off
Flex—to bend
Flinch—to draw back
Flippant—lacking proper respect
Florescence—flowering
Floriculture—care of ornamental plants
Flout—to mock or scoff
Fluctuate—to vary
Foible—minor weakness
Foment—to stir up
Foray—to plunder
Forensic—relating to court or public debate
Forerunner—predecessor, sign warning of something to follow

Forlorn—miserable
Formidable—dreadful, awesome
Fortitude—courage
Fortnight—two weeks
Fortuitous—by chance
Fractious—unruly
Fraught—laden
Fray—fight
Frenetic—wildly excited
Frugal—thrifty
Fruition—accomplishment
Fulminate—to explode, denounce
Fulsome—disgusting
Furtive—stealthy

Gainsay—to contradict
Gambol—to frolic
Gamut—entire range
Garble—to distort
Garish—showy, gaudy
Garrulous—talkative
Gastronomy—art of good eating
Gauntlet—glove (medieval), ordeal
Gelid—frozen
Genial—cordial
Genre—sort or type, category
Genus—class, group with similar characteristics
Germane—fitting
Germinate—to develop, sprout
Gestation—development, pregnancy
Gibber—to speak rapidly, chatter
Gibe—to scoff, deride
Gird—to encircle
Glib—superficial, unconvincing
Glut—to oversupply
Glutton—one who overindulges
Goad—to spur
Gourmet—expert on good food and drink
Gradient—slope
Grandeur—splendor
Gratuitous—free of charge
Gratuity—tip
Gregarious—sociable
Grimace—expression of pain
Grommet—metal ring
Grueling—very tiring
Guild—organization of persons with common interests
Guile—deceitful behavior
Guise—false pretense
Gyrate—to move in a circular fashion

Hackneyed—overused, trite
Haphazard—not planned, random
Harangue—long speech
Harass—to torment
Harbinger—forerunner
Haughty—extremely proud
Hauteur—disdainful pride
Havoc—great destruction
Hawser—strong rope
Heady—impetuous
Hearth—fireplace floor
Hegemony—dominance of authority
Heinous—hateful, evil
Heptagon—seven-sided polygon
Heresy—anti-religious thought
Hermetic—airtight
Heterodox—differing from the accepted standard
Heterogeneous—differing in structure, mixed
Hexapod—something with six legs
Hiatus—gap
Hibernal—pertaining to winter
Hierarchy—an ordering by rank or grade
Hinder—to thwart, impede
Histrionic—theatrical
Hoax—practical joke, trick
Holocaust—complete destruction
Homily—sermon
Homogeneous—uniform in structure
Homologous—corresponding in structure
Horology—science of measuring time
Horrendous—horrible
Hortative—exhorting, pleading
Horticulture—the art of growing flowers, plants, fruits
Huddle—to crowd together
Humus—fertilizer, organic part of soil
Hurtle—to speed
Husbandry—cultivation and care of plants and animals
Hybrid—of mixed origin
Hydrophobia—fear of water
Hyperbole—exaggeration
Hypothesis—assumption

Idiosyncrasy—peculiar mannerism
Idyllic—pleasing, simple, pastoral
Ignoble—mean, base
Ignominious—shameful, degrading
Illicit—unlawful
Illimitable—boundless
Illusory—deceptive
Imbibe—to absorb or drink
Imbroglio—confused situation
Imbue—to permeate
Immolate—to offer in sacrifice
Immutable—unchangeable
Impale—to pierce through
Impalpable—not understood, vague
Impasse—deadlock

Impassioned—ardent, fervent
Impeach—to accuse
Impeccable—flawless
Impecunious—having no money, poor
Imperceptible—slight, subtle
Imperious—domineering
Impertinent—rude
Impervious—not influenced
Impetuous—impulsive
Impious—lacking reverence
Implicit—implied, not apparent
Imply—to indicate by indirect statement
Importune—to urge persistently
Impromptu—without preparation
Impudence—insolence
Impugn—to challenge as false
Impunity—freedom from harm
Impute—to attribute (something bad) to another
Inadvertence—negligence, oversight
Inalienable—unable to be taken away
Inane—lacking sense
Inarticulate—unable to speak clearly
Incendiary—one who excites or agitates
Inception—beginning
Incessant—never ceasing
Inchoative—just begun, initial
Incipient—beginning to appear
Inclement—stormy
Inclusive—taking all factors into account
Incognito—disguised
Incongruous—unconforming, inconsistent
Inconsiderable—trivial, small
Inconspicuous—not readily apparent
Incorrigible—not able to be corrected, delinquent
Incredulous—skeptical
Increment—increase, addition
Inculpate—to incriminate
Incumbent—officeholder, obligatory
Indefatigable—tireless
Indigenous—native to
Indigent—poor
Indolent—lazy
Indurate—hardened
Ineffable—unspeakable, indescribable
Ineluctable—inevitable
Ineptitude—awkwardness, incompetence
Inert—without power to move or resist
Inexorable—unrelenting
Infamy—bad reputation
Inference—conclusion
Infernal—hellish, fiendish
Infinitesimal—immeasurably small
Infrastructure—basic framework of an organization
Infringe—to encroach upon
Ingenious—resourceful, inventive
Ingenuous—frank, naive
Ingratiate—to seek someone's favor
Inherent—belonging by nature
Inimical—hostile
Iniquitous—unjust
Injunction—court order, command
Innate—natural, existing from birth
Innocuous—harmless
Innuendo—hint, allusion
Inscrutable—enigmatic, mysterious
Insidious—treacherous
Insinuate—to suggest, hint at artfully
Insipid—dull, tasteless
Insolvent—bankrupt
Instigator—one who incites action
Insular—narrow-minded, limited
Insurgent—one who revolts against established authority
Intangible—incorporeal, vague
Intemperance—excessive indulgence
Interdict—to prohibit
Interment—burial
Interminable—endless
Internment—confinement (of enemies)
Interpolate—to change by inserting new material
Interstice—space, interval
Intractable—unruly, stubborn
Intransigent—refusing to compromise
Intrepid—fearless
Intrinsic—inherent
Introvert—to turn inward
Intuition—insight
Inundate—to overflow, overwhelm
Inure—habituate
Invective—denunciation
Inveigh—to complain bitterly
Inveigle—to trick, entice
Investiture—installation in office
Inveterate—firmly established
Invidious—offensive
Invincible—unconquerable
Inviolate—sacred
Irascible—easily angered
Ironical—contrary to what was expected, sarcastic
Isthmus—narrow strip of land
Iterate—to repeat over and over
Itinerant—traveling from place to place

Jaundice—yellow pigmentation of the skin
Jaunty—lively
Jettison—to throw overboard, discard as superfluous
Jocose—humorous
Jocund—cheerful
Jocular—playful, jolly

Jostle—to elbow, agitate
Judicious—showing sound judgment
Juggernaut—massive destructive force
Juridical—pertaining to law
Juxtapose—to put side by side

Kaleidoscopic—changing
Kindred—family relationship
Kinetic—active
Kismet—fate
Kith—friends
Knave—dishonest person
Kudos—credit for an achievement, praise

Labyrinth—maze
Lacerate—to mangle, tear
Laconic—concise
Lambaste—to scold, censure
Lampoon—satirical attack
Languid—weak, dull
Languish—to become weak
Languor—lack of vitality
Larcenous—thievish
Largess—generous giving
Lascivious—lustful
Lassitude—fatigue
Latent—hidden
Laudatory—expressing praise
Lethal—deadly
Lethargic—sluggish
Levity—lightness, frivolity
Lexicon—dictionary
Libation—ceremonial drinking
Licentious—morally unrestrained
Limpid—clear, transparent
Lineament—a distinctive feature
Lissome—nimble
Litany—prayer, chant
Lithe—flexible
Litigation—lawsuit
Livid—discolored by a bruise, enraged
Locution—style of speech
Loquacious—talkative
Lucid—shining, readily understood
Ludicrous—absurd
Lugubrious—affectedly mournful
Luminary—outstanding person
Lurid—sensational

Macabre—gruesome
Machination—evil plot
Macrocosm—entity representing on a larger scale, one of its smaller units
Madrigal—song, ballad
Magistrate—official who administers laws
Magnanimous—generous
Maladroit—awkward
Malefactor—evildoer
Malevolent—arising from an evil will
Malfeasance—wrongdoing
Malign—to slander
Malinger—to feign illness
Malleable—flexible, adaptable
Martinet—very strict disciplinarian
Masticate—to chew up
Maudlin—foolishly sentimental
Megalomania—illusions of grandeur
Meliorate—to make or become better
Mellifluous—flowing sweetly, smoothly
Ménage—household
Mendacious—untruthful
Mendicant—beggar
Menial—servile
Mercurial—changeable, fickle
Meretricious—falsely alluring, gaudy
Meritorious—deserving honor
Mesmerize—hypnotize
Metamorphosis—change of form
Metaphor—figure of speech using one idea in place of another to denote a likeness between the two
Mete—to allot
Meticulous—careful with details
Mettle—spirit, courage
Miasma—pervading corruptive atmosphere
Microcosm—a small unit that is the epitome of a larger entity
Mien—manner, appearance
Militate—to work (for or against)
Millenium—1000 years
Minion—favored person
Miscreant—villain
Misgiving—doubt
Misnomer—name wrongly applied
Missive—letter
Mitigate—to ease
Mnemonic—memory aid
Modicum—small portion
Modulate—to regulate
Mollify—to appease
Moot—debatable
Mordant—sarcastic
Mores—customs
Moribund—dying
Morose—gloomy
Motley—composed of many elements
Multifarious—diverse
Mundane—worldly
Munificent—generous, lavish

Myopia—nearsightedness
Myriad—very large number

Nadir—lowest point
Nape—back of the neck
Narcissism—self-love
Narrative—story, account
Nascent—coming into being
Nebulous—vague
Nefarious—very wicked
Nemesis—formidable rival, one who inflicts just punishment
Neology—use of an established word in a new way
Neophyte—beginner, convert
Nepotism—favoritism shown relatives
Nettle—irritate
Nexus—link, connection
Niggardly—stingy
Nocturnal—pertaining to night
Noisome—offensive, harmful to health
Nomenclature—system of names
Nonpareil—unequaled
Nonplussed—perplexed
Nostalgia—sentimental yearning for the past
Notorious—widely known
Noxious—harmful
Numismatic—monetary
Nuptial—pertaining to marriage
Nurture—train, rear

Obdurate—stubborn
Obeisance—gesture of respect
Obesity—stoutness, fatness
Obfuscate—to obscure
Objurgate—to denounce
Oblation—solemn offering
Oblique—evasive
Obloquy—widespread censure
Obsequious—servile
Obsolescent—falling into disuse
Obstreperous—noisy, unruly
Obstruct—to stop, close
Obtrude—to push out
Obtuse—stupid, blunt
Obviate—to prevent
Occidental—Western
Odious—disgusting
Odoriferous—giving off a smell
Officious—meddlesome
Olfactory—pertaining to smell
Oligarchy—government by a small group often for corrupt purposes
Ominous—threatening
Omnipotent—having unlimited power
Omnivorous—eating all sorts of food
Onerous—burdensome
Onus—burden
Opaque—not translucent
Opprobrious—disgraceful, infamous
Opulent—wealthy
Opus—work, composition
Orbit—revolving path
Ordinance—statute
Ordnance—artillery
Ordure—excrement
Ornate—showy
Ornery—obstinate
Ornithology—study of birds
Oscillate—to fluctuate between two points
Ossify—to change to bone
Ostensible—apparent
Ostentatious—showy
Ostracize—to banish
Overt—done openly
Overweening—arrogant

Palatable—agreeable to the senses
Pall—to lose effectiveness
Palliate—to reduce the intensity of
Pallid—pale
Palpable—obvious, easily perceived
Paltry—petty
Panacea—remedy for all maladies
Pandemic—widely spread
Parable—short story showing a moral
Paradigm—model, example
Paradox—a statement that seems contradictory but may be true in fact
Paragon—model of excellence
Paramount—highest in rank
Paraphernalia—personal belongings
Pariah—outcast
Parity—equality in value
Parody—farcical imitation
Paroxysm—sudden outburst
Parsimony—stinginess, thrift
Parsonage—pastor's dwelling
Pastoral—of shepherds, rural
Patent—evident
Pathos—something which arouses pity
Patrimony—property inherited from ancestors
Paucity—scarcity
Peculate—to embezzle
Pecuniary—involving money
Pedant—one who emphasizes trivial points of learning
Pejorative—worsening
Penchant—strong liking
Pendant—hanging object

Penitence—sorrow for sins
Penology—study of prisons and prison reform
Pensile—hanging
Penurious—stingy
Perambulate—to walk
Perdition—damnation
Perennial—enduring
Perfidy—treachery
Perforce—of necessity
Perfunctory—routine, superficial
Perigee—point of an orbit nearest the earth
Peripatetic—itinerant
Periphery—outside boundary
Periphrasis—using long phrasing instead of shorter expressions
Permeable—passable, penetrable
Permutation—change, alteration
Pernicious—destructive, fatal
Peroration—end of a speech
Perpetrate—carry out, commit
Perpetuate—cause to continue
Perquisite—something in addition to regular pay, tip, bonus
Personage—important person
Perspective—sense of proportion
Perspicacity—keen judgment
Perspicuous—easily understood
Pert—bold, cocky
Pertinent—relevant
Perturb—to upset, agitate
Peruse—to read carefully
Pervade—to spread throughout
Perverse—deviating from what is considered normal
Petulance—impatience
Phalanx—massed group of individuals
Philander—to court with no intention of marriage
Philistine—one governed by material rather than intellectual values
Philology—study of linguistics
Phlegmatic—sluggish
Phobia—persistent irrational fear
Picayune—of little value, petty
Piebald—marked with splotches of color, heterogeneous
Pillory—to scorn publicly
Piquant—agreeably stimulating, pungent
Pique—to offend, provoke
Piscatorial—pertaining to fish
Pithy—terse
Pixilated—amusingly eccentric
Placate—to appease
Placid—calm
Plaintive—melancholy
Plait—to braid, pleat
Platitude—trite remark
Plaudit—expression of approval
Plausible—seemingly reasonable
Plebiscite—popular vote
Plenary—full, complete
Plethora—overabundance
Plicate—folded lengthwise
Plumb—straight down, vertically
Ply—to use or practice diligently
Poach—to trespass
Poignant—pungent, touching the emotions
Polemic—involving dispute
Politic—prudent, expedient
Polity—political organization
Ponderous—unwieldy, dull
Pontificate—to orate, make dogmatic statements
Portend—to warn, foreshadow
Portentous—ominous
Posit—to postulate
Posterity—future generations
Postulate—hypothesis, axiom
Potable—suitable for drinking
Potpourri—mixture
Poultice—soft heated dressing applied to wounds
Pragmatic—practical, relating to fact
Prate—to chatter
Precarious—uncertain, risky
Precipitous—steep
Precipitate—hasty
Preclude—to shut out, prevent
Precursor—forerunner
Predacious—predatory
Predatory—tending to exploit others for one's own gain
Predicate—to affirm
Predilection—preconceived liking
Predispose—to make susceptible
Preeminent—outstanding, high-ranking
Preen—to dress up or adorn (oneself)
Premeditation—preplanning
Premise—statement forming the basis of an argument
Preponderate—to surpass in weight or power
Preposterous—absurd, ridiculous
Prerequisite—something needed for performing a function
Prescience—foreboding
Prescribe—to establish as a means of action
Presumptuous—too bold or forward
Pretentious—showy, making unjustified claims
Prevaricate—to evade the truth
Pristine—uncorrupted by society
Probity—integrity, honesty
Proclaim—to declare proudly
Proclivity—inclination
Prodigal—spendthrift
Prodigious—wonderous, enormous
Profane—irreligious

Proffer—to present for approval
Profligate—recklessly wasteful
Progeny—offspring
Prognosticate—to predict
Proliferate—to increase in number
Prolific—producing abundantly
Prolix—prolonged unduly
Prominent—noticeable, well-known
Promontory—high peak that overlooks lower land or water
Promulgate—to announce openly
Propensity—natural tendency
Propinquity—nearness
Propitiate—to appease
Propitious—favorable
Proponent—one in favor of
Propound—to present for discussion
Prorate—to divide proportionately
Prosaic—commonplace, dull
Proscribe—to outlaw, prohibit
Proselytize—to convert from one belief to another
Protagonist—main character in novel
Prototype—standard example
Provincial—having a limited outlook
Prurient—lustful, lewd
Puerile—childish, silly
Pulchritude—beauty
Punctilious—very exact
Pundit—learned person
Pungent—sharp sensation of taste and smell
Pugnacious—belligerent
Purloin—to steal
Purport—to give an appearance of, intend
Pusillanimous—lacking courage and resolve
Putative—assumed to exist
Putrefy—to rot
Pythonic—monstrous

Quadrant—one-quarter of a plane
Quaint—unusual, old-fashioned
Qualm—misgiving
Quandary—perplexed state
Querulous—complaining
Query—inquiry
Quiescent—quiet, still
Quintessence—perfect form
Quivering—shaking, trembling slightly
Quixotic—having highly romantic or chivalrous ideals

Raillery—playful teasing
Raiment—clothing
Rambunctious—boisterous
Ramification—offshoot, consequence
Rampant—widespread, without restraint
Ramshackle—loosely made, dilapidated
Rancor—ill will
Rankle—to cause resentment
Rapacious—greedy
Rapine—plunder
Ratification—formal approval
Raucous—rough sounding, boisterous
Ravenous—extremely eager for gratification
Recalcitrant—disobedient
Recant—to renounce
Recidivist—confirmed criminal
Reciprocal—complementary, mutually responsive
Recluse—hermit
Recondite—beyond ordinary understanding, concealed
Reconnoiter—to survey
Recreant—cowardly
Recrimination—countercharge
Rectitude—integrity
Recumbent—lying down
Redact—to edit
Redolent—fragrant
Redoubt—temporary fortification
Redress—to remedy, compensate
Redundant—superfluous, wordy
Refectory—dining hall
Referendum—popular vote on a measure submitted by a legislative body
Refractory—obstinate, unresponsive
Refute—to prove wrong
Refurbish—to renovate
Regale—to entertain
Regent—one who rules
Regicide—killing of a king
Regimen—system of diet, ruling system
Regressive—going backward
Relegate—to exile, to assign to a lower position
Reliquary—container for sacred objects
Remission—pardon, forgiveness, abatement
Remonstrate—to protest
Remunerate—to pay for work done, compensate
Renascent—reborn
Renegade—deserter, outcast
Renege—to go back on a promise
Renunciation—repudiation
Repast—meal
Repine—to long for
Replete—well filled
Reprehend—to criticize
Repression—stopping by force
Reprisal—act of retaliation
Reproach—disgrace, cause of blame
Reprobate—depraved, unprincipled
Reproof—rebuke, criticism
Repudiate—to refuse, reject, disown

Repugnant—distasteful, disliked
Requisite—requirement
Requital—suitable repayment
Rescind—to repeal, take back
Resilient—able to spring back into shape
Resplendent—dazzling
Restitution—restoration, refund
Restive—impatient
Resurgent—rising again
Resuscitate—revive
Retaliate—to get even
Reticence—silence, reserve
Retort—to make a witty reply
Retribution—just reward
Retroactive—extending to previous conditions
Retrograde—to go backward
Reverberate—to throw back, echo
Revile—to abuse verbally
Ribald—offensive, vulgar
Rife—widespread, abounding
Rift—opening, breach
Rigor—strictness
Risibility—laughter
Robust—healthy, strong
Rote—mechanical repetition or action
Rotund—rounded
Ruckus—noisy confusion
Rudiment—first principle, beginning of something
Ruminant—meditative
Ruminate—to meditate, ponder

Saccharine—overly sweet, affectedly agreeable
Sacrilege—desecration
Sagacious—shrewdly discerning
Salacious—lustful
Salient—conspicuous
Saline—salty
Sallow—dull greenish-yellow
Salubrious—wholesome
Salutary—curative
Salutatory—welcoming address
Sanctimony—pretended piety
Sanguine—confident, optimistic
Sapient—wise
Sardonic—scornful
Sartorial—pertaining to tailoring
Satiate—to satisfy, glut
Saturate—to soak, fill completely
Saturnine—sullen, sluggish
Savor—to relish, enjoy
Scabbard—sword sheath
Scathing—searing, blasting
Schematic—diagrammatic
Schism—split, difference of opinion
Scintilla—particle, trace
Scion—descendent
Scoff—derision
Scourge—whip, devastation
Scruple—small quantity, principle
Scrutinize—to examine closely
Scurrilous—coarse, vulgar
Secular—worldly, not religious
Sedition—rebellion
Sedulous—diligent
Semblance—appearance
Senescent—growing old
Sententious—given to moralistic expression
Sequester—to isolate
Serrate—having sawlike notches
Shallop—small, open boat
Shamble—to walk clumsily
Shunt—to turn to one side
Sibling—brother or sister
Sidle—move sidewise
Simile—figure of speech comparing two unlike things
Similitude—likeness
Simony—buying or selling of church pardons
Sinecure—easy job
Sinuous—bending, winding
Slothful—lazy
Sluice—artificial water channel
Sojourn—to remain somewhere temporarily
Solace—to comfort, console
Solicitous—showing care or concern
Soluble—able to be dissolved
Somatic—physical, of the body
Somnolent—sleepy, drowsy
Sonorous—full of sound, resonant
Sophistry—misleading but clever reasoning
Soporific—causing sleep
Sordid—dirty, ignoble
Spasmodic—intermittent
Spawn—to deposit eggs, bring forth
Specious—deceptively appealing
Specter—ghost
Sporadic—occasional
Spurious—false, not genuine
Staid—sedate
Stigma—mark of disgrace
Stilted—pompous
Stint—restriction
Stoicism—impassiveness, indifference
Stolid—showing little emotion
Stratagem—trick, device
Strategy—careful plan
Stricture—adverse criticism
Strident—harsh-sounding
Stultify—to appear foolish, impair

Stupor—loss of sensibility
Suave—polite, urbane
Subjoin—to append
Subjugate—to force to submit
Sublimate—to direct actions into more socially acceptable forms
Subservient—inferior, submissive
Subterfuge—deception used to evade something difficult or unpleasant
Subversive—destructive
Succinct—clearly and briefly stated
Succor—to help
Succulent—juicy
Suffuse—to overspread
Sully—to soil, stain
Sumptuous—lavish
Supercilious—haughty, contemptuous
Supernal—exalted, celestial
Supersede—to replace
Supervene—to happen additionally or unexpectedly
Supine—indolent, prone
Supple—flexible
Supplicate—to ask for humbly
Suppress—to keep from public knowledge
Surfeit—overindulgence
Surreptitious—acting in a secret and stealthy way
Surrogate—deputy, substitute
Sustenance—nourishment
Sycophant—self-serving flatterer
Syllogism—conclusion based on two premises
Synchronous—occurring simultaneously
Synopsis—summary
Synthesis—combining of elements to make a whole
Synthetic—man-made

Tacit—silent
Taciturn—tending toward silence
Tactic—means of accomplishing a purpose
Tactile—perceived by the sense of touch
Tantamount—equal in value
Tautology—needless repetition of an idea
Tawdry—gaudy, cheap
Taxonomy—classification (of plants and animals)
Temerity—foolish boldness
Temperate—moderate
Temporize—compromise
Tenacious—persistent, tough
Tenet—doctrine
Tenuous—unsubstantial, flimsy
Termagant—nagging woman
Terminus—end point
Terse—brief, to the point
Tertiary—third in order
Thespian—actor
Thrall—slave
Timorous—timid
Tirade—long, vehement speech or denunciation
Tithe—tenth part of something paid as a tax to a church
Titular—having a title without performing the functions involved
Tome—large book
Torpid—inactive, sluggish
Torrid—very hot
Toxic—pertaining to poison
Tractable—easily managed
Traduce—to slander
Tranquility—calmness, serenity
Transfuse—to transmit, imbue
Transgression—violation
Transitory—temporary
Translucent—permitting the passage of light
Transpire—to become known, happen
Transverse—placed crosswise
Travail—hard work
Travesty—ridiculous representation
Treble—to increase threefold
Tremulous—trembling
Trenchant—sharp, clear-cut
Trepidation—fear
Tribulation—misery, distress
Truculent—cruel, belligerent
Truncated—shortened, curtailed
Truncheon—club
Tumid—swollen, inflated
Tumultuous—violently turbulent
Turbid—muddy
Turgid—swollen
Turpitude—vileness
Tutelage—guardianship
Twit—to taunt

Ubiquitous—present everywhere simultaneously
Ulterior—lying beyond what is openly expressed
Umbrage—offense
Unctuous—oily, suave
Undaunted—determined in spite of adverse conditions
Undulate—to move in waves
Unerring—without fault
Ungainly—awkward, clumsy
Unmitigated—not lessened, absolute
Unobtrusive—not aggressive
Untenable—unable to be occupied or defended
Untoward—unfavorable
Upbraid—to scold, reproach
Uproarious—boisterous
Urbane—refined
Usurp—to take by force
Uxorial—pertaining to a wife

Vacillate—to show indecision
Vacuous—empty, stupid
Vagary—eccentric idea or action
Valorous—courageous
Vanguard—front part of a movement
Vapid—tasteless, flat
Variegated—marked with different colors
Vaunt—display boastfully
Vegetate—to lead an inactive life
Vehement—impassioned
Venal—open to corruption
Vendetta—extended bitter feud
Venerate—to show deep respect
Venial—excusable
Veracious—honest
Verbosity—wordiness
Verdant—green in color
Verisimilitude—truth
Verity—truth
Vermillion—bright red pigment
Vernacular—native language of a region
Versatile—able to change easily
Versification—metrical structure
Vertex—highest point
Vestige—trace
Viable—capable of living or functioning
Vicarious—experienced through the activity of another person
Vicissitude—changeability
Vilify—to defame
Vindicate—to clear from blame
Vindictive—wanting revenge
Virago—domineering woman
Viridity—greenness, naiveness
Virility—masculinity
Virulent—deadly, hateful
Viscous—sticky, lacking easy movement
Vitiate—to debase
Vitreous—pertaining to glass
Vituperate—to berate
Vivacious—spirited, lively
Vivid—vigorous, clear
Vixen—female fox
Vociferous—noisy
Volatile—quickly evaporating, explosive
Volition—act of determining
Voluble—talkative
Voracious—greedy
Votary—zealous follower
Votive—expressing a wish or vow
Vouchsafe—to grant

Waft—odor or sound carried through the air
Wan—pale
Wanton—reckless, immoral
Weal—well-being
Welter—confusion, turmoil
Wheedle—to coax
Whet—to arouse, stimulate
Windfall—unexpected gain
Wizened—dried up, withered
Wraith—ghost, apparition
Wrangle—to quarrel
Wroth—angry
Wry—twisted

Zany—fool, clown
Zealot—fanatic
Zenith—highest point
Zephyr—mild breeze

Glossary of Business Terms

Advertising—Any paid form of nonpersonal presentation and promotion of goods and services in such media as newspapers, magazines, television, radio, direct mail, and posters.

Amalgamation—The merger or consolidation of two corporations.

Amortization—A provision made in advance for the gradual liquidation of a future obligation by periodic charges against the capital account or by the creation of a money fund sufficient to meet the obligation when due.

Annuity—The payment or receipt of a fixed sum of money to a beneficiary at pre-determined, equal intervals of time.

Antitrust—Pertaining to legislation or procedures aimed at preventing or controlling monopoly power.

Arbitration—A procedure by which parties to a dispute allow a third party to mediate or decide the issue, the parties agreeing to abide by the decision.

Assets—The tangible or intangible properties of value owned by either a business or by an individual.

Balance of Payments—The "balance sheet" of a country's foreign transactions, basically reflecting the difference between payments made to and receipts from foreign nations over a given period of time.

Balance of Trade—A component of the balance of payments consisting of the residual between exports and imports.

Bankruptcy—A legal procedure used by one unable to meet his debts. After being declared bankrupt by a court, the bankrupt person surrenders his assets to the court for distribution to his creditors and is released from further liability on most debts.

Bear Market—A description of the stock market used when prices are generally going down.

Bond—A secured long-term obligation used to raise capital and promising to pay a specified sum at a set date(s) in the future.

Bond Market—A place to buy and sell bonds.

Bourgeoisie—The middle class.

Brand—A name, symbol, design, or term used to identify the product or service of a seller.

Broker—A selling agent who acts as intermediary between seller and buyer in negotiating a sale.

Bull Market—A description of the stock market used when the level of prices is generally rising.

Business—An economic unit that specializes in developing and distributing goods and/or services.

Capital—The money or other type of investments (goods, land, or equipment) used to produce other goods and/or services.

Capital Formation—The creation of capital goods. Capital formation comes from savings of individuals and businesses and may be used for business expansion, purchase of machinery and equipment, or on the labor force.

Capitalism—A term used synonymously with an economic system where the means of production and distribution are privately owned and where decisions as to what will be produced are made in the marketplace, with a high degree of consumer sovereignty.

Cartel—A contractual association of businesses where an agreement is made to divide markets, set prices, and determine promotion and other business activities.

Caveat Emptor—"Let the buyer beware."

Certificate—(see Notes and Certificates.)

Chain Store—A group of retail stores centrally owned and managed by one corporation.

Chattel—An article of tangible personal property.

Closed Shop—A company in which only union members are employed.

Collective Bargaining—The process by which representatives of labor and management seek to discuss, resolve, and settle their differences.

Commodity—An economic good that is the product of agriculture or mining.

Common Stock—A certificate of ownership in a corporation.

Communism—An economic system where the means of production are owned by the state. Decisions as to what to produce are made by a planning commission rather than directly by consumers.

Conglomerate—A corporation which has a wide diversification usually by acquiring other dissimilar industries or unrelated businesses through merger or purchase.

Consumer Cooperative—Goods produced by household consumers for consumption.

Consumers Group—A retail business owned and managed by consumers for their own use.

Consumer Sovereignty—The idea that consumers decide what goods and services will be produced.

Contract—A legally binding agreement between two or more parties which requires one party to perform a service in exchange for some form of consideration from the other party.

Corporation—A legal entity existing in law as if a single person with specific powers granted in a charter by a state or federal government. A major form of business organization made up of individuals to overcome the uncertain duration of a sole proprietorship or partnership.

Cost-of-Living Adjustment—An increase in wages according to provisions which are contained in some labor contracts or agreements and tied to increases in a cost-of-living index.

Currency—Something in circulation that has value and is used as a medium of exchange.

Current Assets—Assets of a short-term nature.

Debenture—An unsecured, long-term corporate obligation used to raise capital and promising to pay a specified sum at some future date.

Debt—Money, goods, or services owed to a creditor.

Deficit—The result of spending more than one's revenue, producing a loss in business operations.

Deflation—A decline of general price levels or a sharp decline in values.

Demand—The quantity of a good that will be bought at a given price.

Depreciation—The amount of capital lost by the wear and tear of equipment, buildings, and the like.

Devaluation—An official reduction in the exchange value of a currency by lowering its equivalency to some standard (e.g. gold) or some other medium of exchange.

Discount House—A retailing unit selling competitive goods below the "market" price.

Disposable Income—The income of an individual left after deducting taxes paid to federal, state, and local governments.

Duty—A tax on certain imports to prevent foreign products from having an advantage over domestic goods.

Economics—A system of abstract theories which attempts to explain the forces which govern the production, distribution, and consumption of goods and services.

Embargo—The governmental exclusion of certain foreign goods from entry into a country.

Entrepreneur—An individual who undertakes to assemble a business.

Equity—The money value of a property or interest in a property exclusive of claims against it.

Escrow—Property or money placed with a second person who holds it for a third person until the latter fulfills an obligation (as in a lease agreement).

Exports—Goods sold to another country or to businesses in other countries.

Expropriation—The take-over of individually-owned property by a government.

Fair Trade—The setting and maintaining of retail prices by the manufacturer or supplier of a product.

Fiscal Year—The year-long period used to delineate the administration of a business and its gains and losses. The beginning and end of the year correspond to the interests of the business, not the calendar.

Franchise—The licensing of retail establishments to operate according to an established pattern.

Free Trade—Trading between nations without tariffs or other trade barriers.

Goods and Services—The resources that businesses seek to develop and distribute, usually because the resources are scarce or in demand.

Gross National Product—The total value of all goods and services produced in a country during a given time period.

Gross Profit—The profit earned after deducting the cost of the goods sold, but before deducting other business expenditures.

Imports—Goods bought from a foreign country or from businesses in a foreign country.

Industrial Good—A good which is used primarily in the production of another good, e.g. electronic components as used in the manufacture of television sets.

Industrial Union—A labor union whose membership comprises workers from an entire industry.

Inflation—A chronic rise in the cost of living resulting from too much available money and credit in relation to the amount of goods and services existing.

Injunction—A court ruling that commands something to be done or restrains something from being done under penalty of law.

Inventory—A list of current assets such as property or goods.

Jobber—A term used synonymously with "wholesaler."

Laissez-Faire—"Let the people make or do what they choose." An attitude of governmental non-intervention in business affairs.

Liability—A debt owed by an individual to another or the equity of creditors in a business.

Lien—A charge upon real or personal property for the payment of a debt.

Management—The entrepreneurial function of a business enterprise; the coordination of the factors of production—land, labor, and capital.

Manufacturing—The process of adding value to basic materials by changing them into the form of goods.

Marginal Utility—An economic concept which relates the cost of a good to its degree of utility (or satisfaction) or availability (scarcity) at a given moment.

Market Area—The area over which goods and services are distributed.

Market Demand—The aggregate demand for a given good or service.

Marketing—The performance of business activities that direct the flow of goods and services from producer to consumer.

Marketing Research—The systematic gathering, recording, and analyzing of information pertaining to the marketing of a good or service.

Mediation—The introduction of a disinterested third party into the collective bargaining process for the purpose of offering non-binding suggestions for resolving the dispute.

Merchandising—The planning and supervision involved in the marketing of a good or service.

Merger—The combining of two independent businesses into one large business.

Middleman—A term used synonymously for "wholesaler."

Monopoly—A situation where there is only one supplier of a good or service.

Mortgage Bonds—A collateral bond on property which promises to pay by a lien on real property.

Net Income—The earnings of a business company after allowance for all expenses and taxes.

Notes and Certificates—Medium or short-term obligations which can be secured or unsecured.

Open Shop—A business enterprise where workers do not have to join a labor union.

Parity—The price at which agricultural goods would have to sell to give the farmer the same purchasing power as he possessed in a certain base year.

Partnership—A business of two or more persons that remains unincorporated.

Par Value—The stated (printed) value of a share of stock when issued.

Perquisite—A gift, bonus, or other benefit received in addition to a wage or salary.

Preferred Stock—A form of corporate ownership which has prior claims or assets over common stock; usually carries a fixed return.

Profit—The excess of revenue after all related expenses have been deducted.

Public Relations—The relations between a business enterprise and the public. Most large corporations have "public relations" departments that work to maintain a favorable public image distinct and separate from the company's advertising efforts.

Public Utility—An enterprise whose product or service is so important to the public that its operations, including the price it charges, are regulated by government.

Recession—A period of reduced economic activity, lack of economic growth, and high unemployment.

Resource—A natural source of material, wealth, or revenue.

Retailer—A business enterprise or individual who sells directly to the consumer.

Sales Forecast—An estimate of sales, in dollars or units, for a given period of time.

Short-Term—Refers to a time period usually of six months to a year.

Socialism—An economic system in which basic industries are owned and operated by the state.

Sole Proprietorship—A business with a single owner.

Specialty Goods—Goods purchased only occasionally; usually they are considered luxuries.

Speculative Buying—The purchasing of goods, commodities, or stock in the belief that the price or supply will change to one's economic advantage in the future.

Stagflation—Refers to a situation where the economy suffers from both inflation and recession (stagnation).

Standard of Living—A given level of wealth to which a person or group aspires.

Strike—A deliberate work stoppage by labor in an effort to force management to accede to union demands.

Subsidization—Aid or promotion of private industry with public funds.

Supply—The availability of a certain product and the changing quantities which will be available for sale as prices rise or fall.

Surety Bond—A bond which guarantees performance of a contract and protects against its nonperformance.

Surplus—The excess of a corporation's net worth over the par or stated value of its capital stock.

Tariff—A tax placed on imported goods.

Trademark—A name or mark pointing to the origin or ownership of goods to which it is applied. It is legally reserved for the exclusive use of the owner as maker or seller.

Ultimate Consumer—One who buys and/or uses goods for household consumption as distinguished from an industrial buyer.

Utility—The overall usefulness of a product to consumers. Utility together with scarcity determines the price of a product.

Utopia—An imaginative account of an ideal society.

Wholesaler—A business unit that buys goods in bulk from manufacturers for resale in smaller quantities to commercial, institutional, and government users.

Answer Sheet – Sample Test 1

Section I — Reading Recall

1. A B C D E
2. A B C D E
3. A B C D E
4. A B C D E
5. A B C D E
6. A B C D E
7. A B C D E
8. A B C D E
9. A B C D E
10. A B C D E
11. A B C D E
12. A B C D E
13. A B C D E
14. A B C D E
15. A B C D E
16. A B C D E
17. A B C D E
18. A B C D E
19. A B C D E
20. A B C D E
21. A B C D E
22. A B C D E
23. A B C D E
24. A B C D E
25. A B C D E
26. A B C D E
27. A B C D E
28. A B C D E
29. A B C D E
30. A B C D E

Section II — Mathematics

31. A B C D E
32. A B C D E
33. A B C D E
34. A B C D E
35. A B C D E
36. A B C D E
37. A B C D E
38. A B C D E
39. A B C D E
40. A B C D E
41. A B C D E
42. A B C D E
43. A B C D E
44. A B C D E
45. A B C D E
46. A B C D E
47. A B C D E
48. A B C D E
49. A B C D E
50. A B C D E
51. A B C D E
52. A B C D E
53. A B C D E
54. A B C D E
55. A B C D E
56. A B C D E
57. A B C D E
58. A B C D E
59. A B C D E
60. A B C D E
61. A B C D E
62. A B C D E
63. A B C D E
64. A B C D E
65. A B C D E
66. A B C D E
67. A B C D E
68. A B C D E
69. A B C D E
70. A B C D E
71. A B C D E
72. A B C D E
73. A B C D E
74. A B C D E
75. A B C D E
76. A B C D E
77. A B C D E
78. A B C D E
79. A B C D E
80. A B C D E
81. A B C D E
82. A B C D E
83. A B C D E
84. A B C D E
85. A B C D E

Section III — Verbal Aptitude

86. A B C D E
87. A B C D E
88. A B C D E
89. A B C D E
90. A B C D E
91. A B C D E
92. A B C D E
93. A B C D E
94. A B C D E
95. A B C D E
96. A B C D E
97. A B C D E
98. A B C D E
99. A B C D E
100. A B C D E
101. A B C D E
102. A B C D E
103. A B C D E
104. A B C D E
105. A B C D E
106. A B C D E
107. A B C D E
108. A B C D E
109. A B C D E
110. A B C D E
111. A B C D E
112. A B C D E
113. A B C D E
114. A B C D E
115. A B C D E
116. A B C D E
117. A B C D E
118. A B C D E
119. A B C D E
120. A B C D E
121. A B C D E
122. A B C D E
123. A B C D E
124. A B C D E
125. A B C D E

Section IV — Data Sufficiency

126. A B C D E
127. A B C D E
128. A B C D E
129. A B C D E
130. A B C D E
131. A B C D E
132. A B C D E
133. A B C D E
134. A B C D E
135. A B C D E
136. A B C D E
137. A B C D E
138. A B C D E
139. A B C D E
140. A B C D E

Section V — Business Judgment

141. A B C D E
142. A B C D E
143. A B C D E
144. A B C D E
145. A B C D E
146. A B C D E
147. A B C D E
148. A B C D E
149. A B C D E
150. A B C D E
151. A B C D E
152. A B C D E
153. A B C D E
154. A B C D E
155. A B C D E
156. A B C D E
157. A B C D E
158. A B C D E
159. A B C D E
160. A B C D E

Section VI — Mathematics

161. A B C D E
162. A B C D E
163. A B C D E
164. A B C D E
165. A B C D E
166. A B C D E
167. A B C D E
168. A B C D E
169. A B C D E
170. A B C D E
171. A B C D E
172. A B C D E
173. A B C D E
174. A B C D E
175. A B C D E
176. A B C D E
177. A B C D E
178. A B C D E
179. A B C D E
180. A B C D E
181. A B C D E
182. A B C D E
183. A B C D E
184. A B C D E
185. A B C D E
186. A B C D E
187. A B C D E
188. A B C D E
189. A B C D E
190. A B C D E
191. A B C D E
192. A B C D E
193. A B C D E
194. A B C D E
195. A B C D E

SIX
FIVE SAMPLE GMATs WITH ANSWERS AND ANALYSIS

Sample Test 1

Section I Reading Recall

TOTAL TIME: 35 minutes

Part A: TIME—15 minutes

DIRECTIONS: This part contains three reading passages. You are to read each one carefully. You will have fifteen minutes to study the three passages and twenty minutes to answer questions based on them. When answering the questions, you will *not* be allowed to refer back to the passages.

Passage 1:

The main burden of assuring that the resources of the federal government are well managed falls on relatively few of the five million men and women whom it employs. Under the department and agency heads there are 8,600 political, career, military, and foreign service executives—the top managers and professionals—who exert major influence on the manner in which the rest are directed and utilized. Below their level there are other thousands with assignments of some managerial significance, but we believe that the line of demarcation selected is the best available for our purposes in this attainment.

In addition to Presidential appointees in responsible posts, the 8,600 include the three highest grades under the Classification Act; the three highest grades in the postal field service; comparable grades in the foreign service; general officers in the military service; and similar classes in other special services and in agencies or positions excepted from the Classification Act.

There is no complete inventory of positions or people in federal service at this level. The lack may be explained by separate agency statutes and personnel systems, diffusion among so many special services, and absence of any central point (short of the President himself) with jurisdiction over all upper-level personnel of the government.

This Committee considers establishment and maintenance of a central inventory of these key people and positions to be an elementary necessity, a first step in improved management throughout the Executive Branch.

Top Presidential appointees, about 500 of them, bear the brunt of translating the philosophy and aims of the current administration into practical programs. This group includes the secretaries and assistant secretaries of cabinet departments, agency heads and their deputies, heads and members of boards and commissions with fixed terms, and chiefs and directors of major bureaus, divisions, and services. Appointments to many of these politically sensitive positions are made on recommendation by department or agency heads, but all are presumably responsible to Presidential leadership.

One qualification for office at this level is that there be no basic disagreement with Presidential political philosophy, at least so far as administrative judgments and actions are concerned. Apart from the bi-partisan boards and commissions, these men are normally identified with the political party of the President, or are sympathetic to it, although there are exceptions.

There are four distinguishable kinds of top Presidential appointees, including:

– Those whom the President selects at the outset to establish immediate and effective control over the government (e.g., Cabinet secretaries, agency heads, his own White House staff and Executive Office Personnel).
– Those selected by department and agency heads in order to establish control within their respective organizations (e.g.—assistant secretaries, deputies, assistants to, and major line posts in some bureaus and divisions).
– High-level appointees who—though often requiring clearance through political or interest group channels, or both—must have known scientific or technical competence (e.g.—the Surgeon General, the Commissioner of Education).
– Those named to residual positions traditionally filled on a partisan patronage basis.

These appointees are primarily regarded as policy makers and overseers of policy execution. In practice, however, they usually have substantial responsibilities in line management, often requiring a thorough knowledge of substantive agency programs.

Passage 2:

Under state fair trade acts, a producer or distributor of a good bearing his brand, trademark, or name can prescribe by contract either a minimum or stipulated resale price of that good, depending upon the particular state law. Prior to the passage of the fair trade laws, resale price maintenance agreements were considered illegal because such agreements by a producer with more than one distributor prevent price competition among those distributors. The effect is the same as if the distributors had combined and agreed to fix price.

In late 1963, forty states had fair trade laws; of these, twenty-three had "nonsigner" clauses. According to the nonsigner provision, all resellers are bound by the terms of the resale price maintenance contract signed by any *one* reseller. To be truly effective, a state fair trade law must contain a nonsigner provision; for unless the manufacturer has some control over the noncontracting price-cutter, there can be little effective control by the manufacturer over resale prices. In addition, in late 1963 special legislation in nine states made resale price maintenance with respect to alcoholic beverages either mandatory or subject to control by state liquor control agencies.

Not all branded goods are covered by the fair trade laws. Closeout sales are excepted. Exceptions are made in some of these laws on sales to colleges and libraries. Some make provisions to except damaged goods or those from which the brand or trade names have been removed or obliterated.

An obstacle to the success of fair trade is the fact that cut-price mail-order shipments of goods out of an area which has no fair trade law into a fair trade state cannot be prevented by an enforcement action under the fair trade law of the state into which the goods are shipped. For the buyer takes title to the goods in the location from which the goods are shipped. The mail-order business can thus be used to evade a state fair trade act. Likewise, an advertisement within a fair-trade state of cut prices of goods available in a non-fair-trade area has been judged not to be within the jurisdiction of the state fair trade law. Sales from within a fair-trade state to customers outside the state in a non-fair-trade area cannot, however, be made at cut prices.

Maintaining a fair-trade program is fraught with several legal problems. Responsibility for enforcement falls upon the producer or distributor, who must monitor and take legal action against the price-cutters. Legal enforcement must be continuous, vigorous, and effective; it cannot be selective. An assortment of marketing devices contrived by retailers to evade fair-trade prices, such as the granting of trading stamps in abnormally high volume or the placing of excessive value on the trade-in of durable consumer items, must be dealt with by court action. Further, utilization of fair trade prevents a manufacturer from itself selling in competition with those distributors, either wholesalers or retailers, who are governed by its fair-trade contracts, for the effect of such an arrangement is a horizontal agreement.

Passage 3:

U.S. trade with Eastern Europe has been small basically because of a determination, which was reflected in both government and business, that we did not want to engage in this kind of trade, that it was not in the national interest, not only for security reasons, but because of the whole antagonistic atmosphere that has prevailed over the last twenty-five years.

Many businessmen feel that this basic antagonism has very substantially disappeared. The Nixon Administration has been rather cautious in moving to any liberalization in terms of our legislative posture toward this area of the world. Surprisingly, Congress, particularly the Senate, has been pressing the Administration to do more.

The House has been tranquil on the subject, being content to follow the lead of the Senate and the Administration. In the Executive Branch, there is no question that in 1969 there was very sharp, very deep, and sometimes very bitter division as to what our policy should be. The President had said, rather ambivalently, that he favored liberalization of trade "at the appropriate time," thus allowing considerable room to maneuver. The issue first arose when the Export Control Act came up for renewal during 1969. The basic division was, of course, obvious within the Administration.

It is surprising that so many businessmen, when inquiring about license applications, are totally unaware of what happens when a major project is presented to the government — what steps it goes through before a decision is reached. It might be worthwhile to touch very briefly on this matter.

In the Executive Branch of government there are three basic interest groups, all of whom are deeply concerned with any major issue of economic activity in this area.

First, our defense establishment, which has responsibility for security and which interprets this responsibility very narrowly. It is not interested in any offsets or any balancing of trade. It considers itself a highly professional organization. In considering a project, it asks only whether our national security is jeopardized—there are no peripheral arguments. When the project has any real magnitude, when it makes a major contribution to the economic base of the host country, the answer from the defense establishment is that there is a security consideration and it therefore opposes the project.

On the other hand, the political group, which is centered in the State Department, is interested primarily in foreign relations. Here there is deep commitment to build east-west bridges and traditionally to support any activity that will facilitate or encourage broader trade.

Third, the Commerce Department has the responsibility both for expanding exports and for administering the Export Control Act. The Commerce Department feels that it factors these various elements and has a responsibility to the entire business community. It has a deep awareness that even if we in the United States do not authorize these transactions there is almost always comparable technology in other parts of the world. Further, the department feels that it is self-defeating to deny export license applications out of a transcendent concern for national security.

Usually, then, both the Commerce and the State Departments are in favor of approving such applications. When there is any division (there is a very strange rule of unanimity in government—that nothing can happen unless everybody is in agreement), the case moves to the White House where it often becomes involved in political byplay—whether concerned with oil in the Near East, prisoners of war in North Vietnam, or the SALT talks. However, major progress has been made in this area, particularly now that the National Security Council has advocated economic interests to a large degree and such interests in the White House have been transferred to the Council on International Economic Policy, whence it takes a separate route to the President.

If there is still time remaining, review the passages until all 15 minutes have elapsed.
Do not look at Part B until that time.

Part B: TIME—20 minutes

DIRECTIONS: Answer the following questions referring to information contained in the three passages you have just read. You may not turn back to those passages for assistance.

QUESTIONS TO

Passage 1:

1. According to the passage, about how many top managerial professionals work for the federal government?

   (A) five million
   (B) two million
   (C) twenty thousand
   (D) ten thousand
   (E) five thousand

2. No complete inventory exists of positions in the three highest levels of government service because

(A) no one bothered to count them
(B) computers cannot handle all the data
(C) separate agency personnel systems are used
(D) the President never requested such information
(E) the Classification Act prohibits a census

3. Top Presidential appointees translate the aims of the administration into

(A) action
(B) political decisions
(C) practical programs
(D) legislation
(E) fruition

4. Top Presidential appointees must be in agreement with the President's political philosophy in which of the following areas?

I. Administrative judgments
II. Administrative actions
III. Administrative policies

(A) I only
(B) III only
(C) I and II only
(D) II and III only
(E) I, II, and III

5. Applicants for Presidential appointments are usually identified with or are members of

(A) large corporations
(B) the foreign service
(C) government bureaus
(D) academic circles
(E) the President's political party

6. Appointees that are selected by the President include

(A) U.S. marshalls and attorneys
(B) military officers
(C) agency heads
(D) commissioners
(E) congressional committee members

7. Appointees usually have to possess expertise in

(A) line management
(B) military affairs
(C) foreign affairs
(D) strategic planning
(E) constitutional law

8. According to the passage, Presidential appointees are regarded primarily as

(A) highly competent individuals
(B) policy makers
(C) staff managers
(D) decision-makers
(E) career executives

9. Appointees selected by department and agency heads include

(A) military men
(B) cabinet secretaries
(C) assistant secretaries
(D) diplomats
(E) residual position holders

10. This passage might have been extracted from a book about all of the following subjects except

(A) public administration
(B) political science
(C) management
(D) government
(E) marketing

QUESTIONS TO

Passage 2:

11. Essentially fair trade legislation

(A) allows manufacturers to stipulate the resale price of a good
(B) allows manufacturers to bypass distributors in sales to retailers
(C) provides that manufacturers engage in fair and equal trade with distributors
(D) allows manufacturers to maintain a fair markup on their goods
(E) exempts resale items from anti-trust legislation

12. A "nonsigner clause" stipulates that

(A) all resellers who do not sign fair trade contracts are not bound by them
(B) all resellers are bound by the terms of the fair trade contract signed by one reseller
(C) resellers are not bound by law to sign fair trade contracts
(D) all branded goods are covered by the fair trade legislation
(E) "nonsigners" are exempt from the provisions of fair trade legislation

13. It can be inferred from the passage that fair trade laws would be most welcomed by

(A) discount stores
(B) wholesale distributors
(C) small-volume retailers
(D) supermarkets
(E) gasoline stations

14. An obstacle to the success of fair trade is that

(A) not all states have these laws
(B) not all resellers are bound by the laws
(C) cut-rate goods can be mailed from a non-fair-trade state
(D) manufacturers may not avail themselves of all privileges given by the legislation
(E) loss-leader selling is prohibited

15. Responsibility for enforcing fair trade falls on the

(A) state
(B) federal government
(C) courts
(D) manufacturer
(E) retailer

16. Some categories of goods are exempted from fair trade laws, such as

(A) pharmaceutical products
(B) alcoholic beverages
(C) imports
(D) closeout sales
(E) private label goods

17. At the time the passage was written, how many states had fair trade laws?

(A) all states
(B) about ten
(C) about twenty
(D) about thirty
(E) about forty

18. Retailers have used various methods to evade fair trade prices, such as

(A) refusing to comply with the law
(B) dealing with more than one supplier
(C) giving extra trading stamps
(D) giving extra discounts
(E) refusal to deal with the manufacturer

19. It is stated in the passage that fair trade laws are enacted by

(A) states
(B) the federal government
(C) local municipalities
(D) both states and the federal government
(E) both states and local municipalities

20. It can be inferred from the passage that fair trade

(A) stimulates competition among retailers
(B) stifles competition among retailers
(C) makes retailing less profitable
(D) exempts many goods from legislation
(E) is inexpensive to maintain and police

QUESTIONS TO

Passage 3:

21. U.S. trade with Eastern Europe has been small because

(A) the terms of trade were unfavorable to the U.S.
(B) the U.S. is anti-communist
(C) such trade was not in the national interest of the U.S.
(D) Eastern European goods are inferior
(E) Eastern European countries did not want U.S. goods

22. According to the passage, U.S.–Eastern European trade prospects seem

(A) favorable, because of Congressional approval
(B) favorable, because of Presidential approval
(C) doubtful, because of Congressional opposition
(D) doubtful, because of Administration opposition
(E) immediately possible

23. In matters of trade policy with Eastern Europe, the Executive Branch (in 1969) could be characterized as

(A) unanimously in favor
(B) favorably disposed
(C) uncertain
(D) divided
(E) against

24. The author states that the Defense Department considers trade prospects only in light of

(A) U.S. defense security
(B) their potential profitability
(C) their contribution to the host country
(D) their magnitude
(E) their cost

25. It is stated in the passage that the Export Control Act is administered by the

(A) State Department
(B) Defense Department
(C) Commerce Department
(D) National Security Council
(E) Executive Branch

26. With respect to U.S.–East European trade, it is inferred that the State Department

(A) favors more trade
(B) takes a cautious approach
(C) has a "wait-and-see" attitude
(D) is not in favor of more trade at this time
(E) will follow the lead of Congress

27. The positions of the Defense and Commerce Departments with respect to more U.S.–East European trade are

(A) similar to each other
(B) outdated
(C) opposed to each other
(D) self-defeating
(E) in agreement with the State Department

28. The positions of the State and Commerce Departments with respect to more U.S.–East European trade are

(A) similar to each other
(B) outdated
(C) opposed to each other
(D) self-defeating
(E) in agreement with the Defense Department

29. The Commerce Department feels that if the U.S. does not trade with Eastern European countries

(A) our foreign relations will be affected
(B) other countries will get this business
(C) our balance of payments will deteriorate
(D) our dollar reserves will shrink
(E) our technology lead with the rest of the world will deteriorate

30. When there is divided opinion in the Executive Branch as to the approval of export licenses, the case goes to the

(A) State Department
(B) Council on International Economic Policy
(C) National Security Council
(D) White House
(E) Commerce Department

If there is still time remaining, you may review the questions in this section only. You may not look at Part A or turn to any other section of the test.

Section II Mathematics

TIME: 75 minutes

DIRECTIONS: Solve each of the following problems; then indicate the correct answer on the answer sheet. [On the actual test you will be permitted to use any space available on the examination paper for scratch work.]

NOTE: A figure that appears with a problem is drawn as accurately as possible so as to provide information that may help in answering the question. Numbers in this test are real numbers.

31. If the length of a rectangle is increased by 20% and the width is decreased by 20%, then the area

(A) decreases by 20%
(B) decreases by 4%
(C) stays the same
(D) increases by 10%
(E) increases by 20%

32. The next number in the arithmetic progression 6,12,18, . . . is

(A) 12
(B) 18
(C) 24
(D) 30
(E) 36

33. If it is 250 miles from New York to Boston and 120 miles from New York to Hartford, what percentage of the distance from New York to Boston is the distance from New York to Hartford?

(A) 12
(B) 24
(C) 36
(D) 48
(E) 52

34. The lead in a mechanical pencil is 5 inches long. After pieces $\frac{1}{8}$ of an inch long, $1\frac{3}{4}$ inches long, and $1\frac{1}{12}$ inches long are broken off, how long is the lead left in the pencil?

(A) 2 in.
(B) $2\frac{1}{24}$ in.
(C) $2\frac{1}{12}$ in.
(D) $2\frac{1}{4}$ in.
(E) $2\frac{1}{2}$ in.

Use the following graph for questions 35–38.

Recent Changes in Gross National Product and its Components

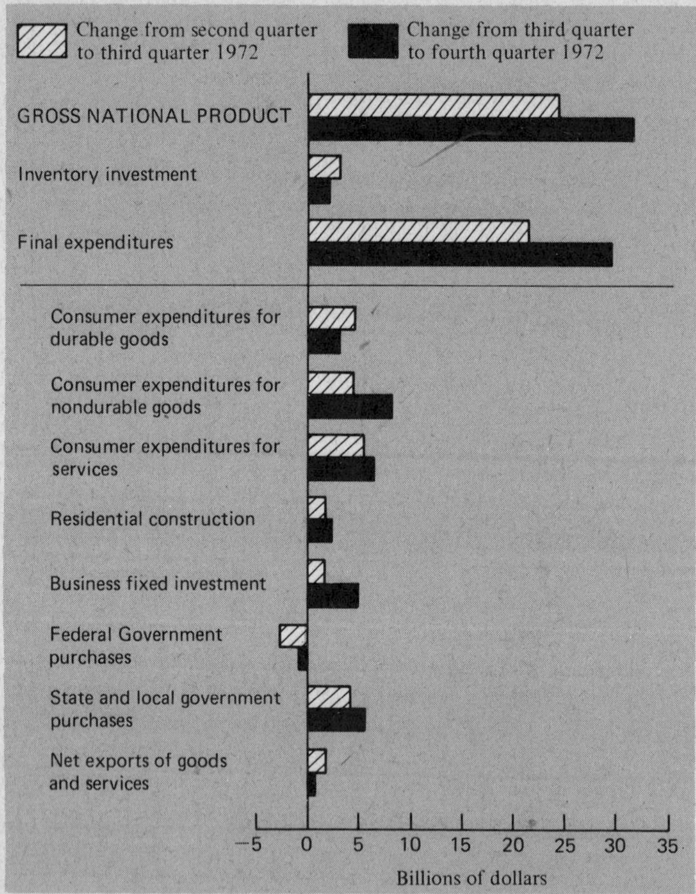

Source: United States Department of Commerce, Bureau of Economic Analysis.

35. The ratio of the change in Gross National Product to the change in Business fixed investment from the third quarter of 1972 to the fourth quarter of 1972 is about

(A) 1 to 4
(B) 4 to 1
(C) 6 to 1
(D) 9 to 1
(E) 10 to 1

36. Which of the following components of the Gross National Product increased the most between the second and third quarters of 1972?

(A) consumer expenditures for durable goods
(B) consumer expenditures for nondurable goods
(C) consumer expenditures for services
(D) residential construction
(E) business fixed investment

37. How many of the following categories decreased between the third and fourth quarters of 1972?
Inventory investment, Residential construction, Business fixed investment, Net exports of goods and services

(A) none
(B) 1
(C) 2
(D) 3
(E) 4

38. Which of the following statements about the Gross National Product and its components during 1972 can be inferred from the graph?

I. All the components increased between the second and third quarters of 1972.
II. Three of the components increased more than 10 billion dollars between the third and fourth quarters of 1972.
III. The Gross National Product increased by more than 45 billion dollars between the second and fourth quarters of 1972.

(A) I only
(B) III only
(C) I and II only
(D) II and III only
(E) I, II, and III

39. In 1968, Mr. Smith bought a car. In 1969 he purchased another car which cost 20% more than the car he bought in 1968. He paid a total of $4,400 for both cars. How much did he pay for the car he purchased in 1968?

(A) $1,800
(B) $2,000
(C) $2,200
(D) $2,400
(E) $2,600

40. It costs $1.00 each to make the first thousand copies of a record and it costs x dollars to make each subsequent copy. How many dollars will it cost to make 4800 copies of a record?

(A) 1,000
(B) 4800
(C) $4800x$
(D) $1000x + 3800$
(E) $1,000 + 3800x$

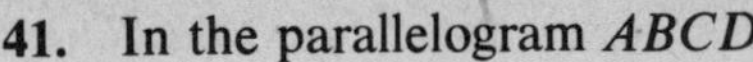

41. In the parallelogram *ABCD*

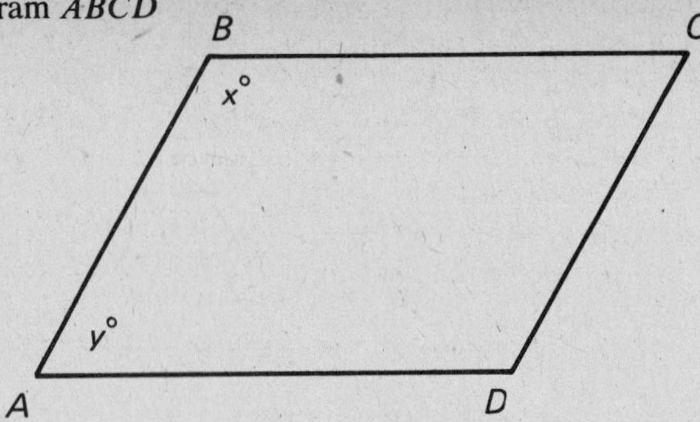

if $x = 2y$, then x is

(A) 40
(B) 60
(C) 90
(D) 120
(E) 150

42. If a worker makes 4 boxes of labels in $1\frac{2}{3}$ hours, how many boxes of labels can he make in 50 minutes?

(A) 2
(B) $2\frac{1}{3}$
(C) $2\frac{2}{3}$
(D) $2\frac{5}{6}$
(E) 3

43. If $x + y = 3$ and $y/x = 2$, then y is equal to

(A) 0
(B) $\frac{1}{2}$
(C) 1
(D) $\frac{3}{2}$
(E) 2

Use the following graph for questions 44–48.

National health expenditures and percent of gross national product, selected fiscal years 1950-72.

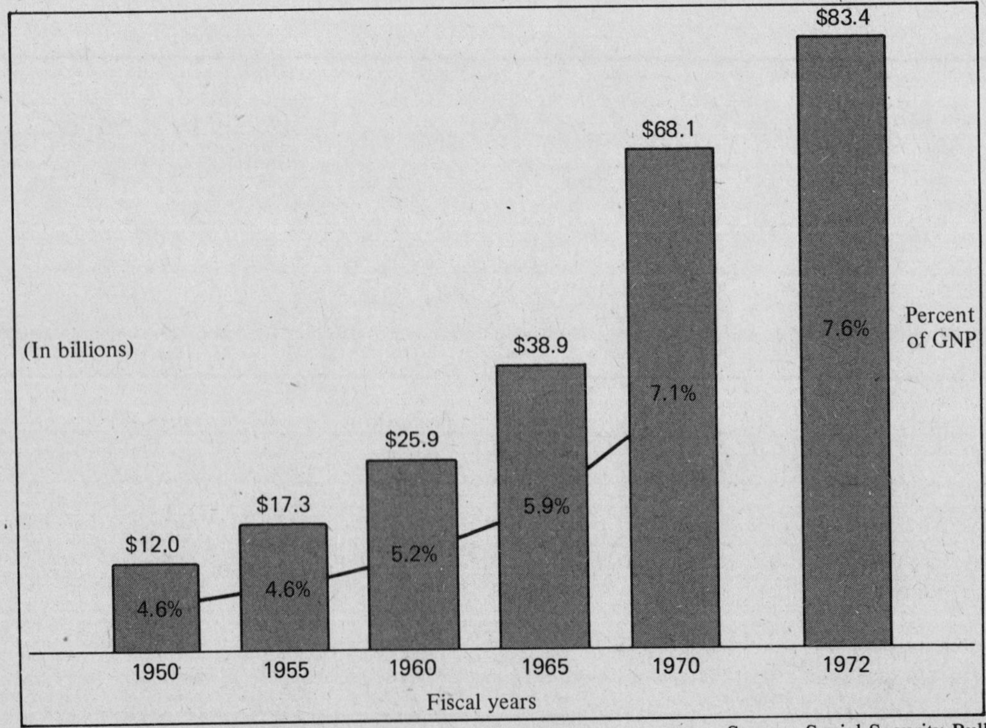

Source: Social Security Bulletin

44. The Gross National Product in 1950 was approximately

(A) $12 billion
(B) $68 billion
(C) $260 billion
(D) $405 billion
(E) $460 billion

45. In how many of the years shown on the graph were national health expenditures greater than $\frac{1}{20}$ of the Gross National Product?

(A) 1
(B) 2
(C) 3
(D) 4
(E) 5

46. Between 1950 and 1970 the amount spent on national health expenditures

(A) stayed about the same
(B) increased by about 75%
(C) increased by about 400%
(D) increased by about 500%
(E) increased by about 567%

47. Which of the following statements about national health expenditures and Gross National Product can be inferred from the graph?

I. The percentage of the Gross National Product used in national health expenditures increased during each of the successive 5 year periods shown.
II. In 1972, more than $\frac{3}{40}$ of the Gross National Product was spent on national health expenditures.
III. In 1969, 7% of the Gross National Product was spent on national health expenditures.

(A) I only
(B) II only
(C) I and III only
(D) II and III only
(E) I, II, and III

48. If retired people accounted for $\frac{1}{3}$ of all national health expenditures in 1970, and there were 20 million retired people in 1970, what was the average health expenditure for each retired person in 1970?

(A) $113
(B) $275
(C) $1,135
(D) $2,270
(E) $22,700

49. A store buys paper towels for $9.00 a carton, each carton containing 20 rolls. The store sells a roll of paper towels for 50¢. About what percent of the cost is the selling price of a roll of paper towels?

(A) 11
(B) 89
(C) 100
(D) 111
(E) 119

50. A history book weighs 2.4 pounds. 12 copies of the history book and 8 copies of an English book together weigh 42.8 pounds. How much will one copy of the English book weigh?

(A) 1 pound
(B) 1.4 pounds
(C) 1.75 pounds
(D) 2.88 pounds
(E) 14 pounds

51. A car goes 15 miles on a gallon of gas when it is driven at 50 miles per hour. When the car is driven at 60 miles per hour it only goes 80% as far. How far will it travel on a gallon of gas at 60 miles per hour?

(A) 12 miles
(B) 13.5 miles
(C) 16.5 miles
(D) 18.75 miles
(E) 20 miles

52. If $x + y = z$ and x and y are positive, then which of the following statements can be inferred?

I. $x < y$
II. $x < z$
III. $x < 2z$

(A) I only
(B) II only
(C) I and III only
(D) II and III only
(E) I, II, and III

53. How many cubes with sides of length 3 will fit into a cube with sides of length x?

(A) $9x^3$
(B) $27x^3$
(C) $\frac{27}{x^3}$
(D) $\frac{x^3}{9}$
(E) $\frac{x^3}{27}$

Use the following table for questions 54–59.

TABLE 2.—Composition of discouraged workers by reason for believing they cannot find a job, 1967–72
[Numbers in thousands]

Reason	1967	1968	1969	1970	1971	1972
Total	732	667	574	638	774	765
Job-market factors	383	371	311	437	537	540
Had looked but could not find job	168	161	161	244	300	300
Thinks no job available	215	210	150	193	237	240
Personal factors	349	297	263	201	236	226
Employers think too young or too old	216	171	139	105	112	111
Lacks education, skills, training	84	74	78	60	85	78
Other personal handicap	49	52	46	36	39	37
Percent distribution	100.0	100.0	100.0	100.0	100.0	100.0
Job-market factors	52.3	55.5	54.2	68.5	69.5	70.6
Had looked but could not find job	23.0	24.1	28.0	38.2	38.8	39.2
Thinks no job available	29.4	31.4	26.1	30.3	30.7	31.4
Personal factors	47.7	44.5	45.8	31.5	30.5	29.5
Employers think too young or too old	29.5	25.6	24.2	16.5	14.5	14.5
Lacks education, skills, training	11.5	11.1	13.6	9.4	11.0	10.2
Other personal handicap	6.7	7.8	8.0	5.6	5.0	4.8

NOTE: Because of rounding, sums of individual items may not equal totals.

Source: U.S. Department of Labor

54. In 1971 which of the following factors accounted for the largest number of discouraged workers?

(A) had looked but could not find a job
(B) thinks no job available
(C) employers think too young or too old
(D) lacks education, skills, training
(E) other personal handicaps

55. The ratio of those workers discouraged by job market factors to those discouraged by personal factors in 1972 is about

(A) 3 to 7
(B) 1 to 2
(C) 3 to 2
(D) 7 to 3
(E) 4 to 1

56. In what year were the least number of workers discouraged by other personal handicaps?

(A) 1967
(B) 1968
(C) 1969
(D) 1970
(E) 1971

57. Between which two years did the percentage of workers discouraged by personal factors decrease the most?

(A) 1967 to 1968
(B) 1968 to 1969
(C) 1969 to 1970
(D) 1970 to 1971
(E) 1971 to 1972

58. Which of the following statements about discouraged workers for 1967–1972 can be inferred from the table?

I. The number of workers discouraged by job market factors has always been greater than the number discouraged by personal factors.
II. The number of workers discouraged by personal factors has continually decreased.
III. $\frac{1}{5}$ of all the discouraged workers are over 60.

(A) I only
(B) II only
(C) I and II only
(D) I and III only
(E) I, II, and III

59. If you plot the number of discouraged workers in each year from 1967 to 1971 as a line graph, the shape of the line would most resemble a

(A) vee V
(B) horizontal line
(C) straight line which rises from left to right
(D) straight line which falls from left to right
(E) rectangle

60. If it costs x cents to produce a single sheet of paper for the first 800 sheets and if every subsequent sheet costs $x/15$ cents, how much will it cost to produce 5,000 sheets of paper?

(A) $800x$¢
(B) $1{,}080x$¢
(C) $1{,}400x$¢
(D) $2{,}430x$¢
(E) $3{,}500x$¢

61. If a ton of coal and 500 gallons of oil together cost $1,000 and 3 tons of coal and 300 gallons of oil cost $1,200, how much does a gallon of oil cost?

(A) $1.00
(B) $1.25
(C) $1.45
(D) $1.50
(E) $10.00

62. If a diameter of a circle is doubled, then the area of the circle is

(A) the same
(B) doubled
(C) tripled
(D) quadrupled
(E) quintupled

63. If in 1967, 1968, and 1969 a worker received 10% more in salary each year than he did the previous year, how much more did he receive in 1969 than in 1967?

(A) 10%
(B) 12%
(C) 19%
(D) 20%
(E) 21%

64. What is $(3^2)^3$?

(A) 27
(B) 81
(C) 263
(D) 720
(E) 729

Use the following graph for questions 65–69.

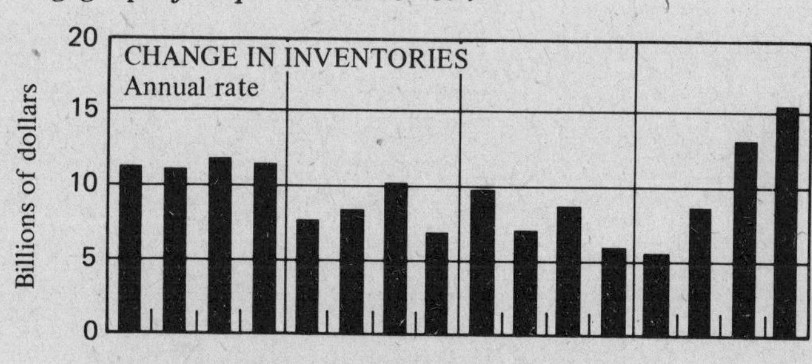

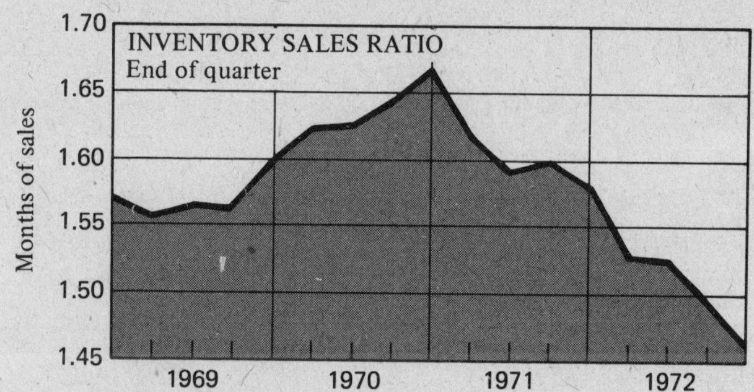

Note: Changes are from end of quarter to end of quarter.

Source: Federal Reserve Bank of New York

65. At the end of the third quarter of 1972, inventory was about x times monthly sales, where x is

(A) $\frac{2}{3}$
(B) 1
(C) $1\frac{1}{3}$
(D) $1\frac{1}{2}$
(E) 2

66. During 1972 the change in inventories

(A) increased almost arithmetically for the first three quarters
(B) totaled more than 60 billion dollars
(C) increased almost geometrically for the first three quarters
(D) increased an average of 14 billion dollars each quarter
(E) was greater than 10 billion dollars in every quarter

67. The smallest change in inventory was at the annual rate of about x dollars, where x equals

(A) $5\frac{1}{4}$ billion
(B) 7 billion
(C) 10 billion
(D) 20 billion
(E) 21 billion

68. Which of the following statements about change in inventories and inventory-sales ratios during 1969–1972 can be inferred from the graphs?

I. Change in inventories increases when the inventory-sales ratio increases.
II. The change in inventories changed the least from quarter to quarter in 1969 out of all the years shown.
III. The inventory-sales ratio had its maximum during 1971 in the last quarter.

(A) I only
(B) II only
(C) I and II only
(D) II and III only
(E) I, II, and III

69. If monthly sales were $50 billion in the third quarter of 1972, approximately how much were inventories worth during the third quarter of 1972?

(A) $45 billion
(B) $55 billion
(C) $60 billion
(D) $65 billion
(E) $75 billion

70. If triangle I and triangle II each have two pairs of corresponding angles that are equal, then

(A) the triangles are congruent
(B) the triangles are similar
(C) both triangles are isosceles
(D) both triangles are scalene
(E) both triangles are right triangles

71. How much simple interest will $1,000 earn in 21 months at an annual rate of 8%?

(A) $80
(B) $120
(C) $140
(D) $168
(E) $1,680

72. If factory A turns out a cars an hour and factory B turns out b cars every 2 hours, how many cars will both factories turn out in 8 hours?

(A) $a + b$
(B) $8a$
(C) $8b$
(D) $8a + 4b$
(E) $8a + 8b$

73. Two straight lines l and l' are intersected by a third straight line k. If the angles formed by k and l and k and l' are all right angles, then

(A) l and l' are parallel
(B) l and l' are identical
(C) l and l' intersect at 2 points
(D) l and l' will intersect in one and only one point
(E) none of the above is true

74. If John makes a box every 5 minutes and Tim takes 7 minutes to make a box, what will be the ratio of the number of boxes produced by John to the number of boxes produced by Tim if they work 5 hours and 50 minutes?

(A) 5 to 6
(B) 5 to 7
(C) 6 to 5
(D) 7 to 5
(E) 2 to 1

Use the following table for questions 75–78.

TABLE 19.—Selected characteristics of persons receiving or expecting to receive private pension from longest job: Percentage distribution of persons initially entitled to OASDHI retired-worker benefits, July 1969–June 1970 awards

Characteristic	Men		Women	
	Receiving private pension	Will receive private pension	Receiving private pension	Will receive private pension
Earnings				
Number reporting (in thousands)	97	58	29	21
Total percent	100	100	100	100
Under $5,000	7	7	41	40
5,000–5,999	8	9	21	17
6,000–6,999	13	14	13	13
7,000–7,999	16	15	9	13
8,000–8,999	12	14	6	7
9,000–9,999	10	9	3	2
10,000–14,999	22	18	5	6
15,000 or more	12	14	1	1
Median	*$8,490*	*$8,350*	*$5,440*	*$5,230*
Length of employment				
Number reporting (in thousands)	102	61	31	21
Total percent	100	100	100	100
Less than 10 years	1	3	2	5
10–14 years	4	6	11	14
15–19 years	11	13	20	20
20–24 years	14	15	19	20
25–29 years	17	18	15	17
30–34 years	14	11	9	8
35–39 years	14	9	10	7
40 years or more	25	25	14	9
Median	*31*	*29*	*24*	*23*

TABLE 19. *Cont.*

Characteristic	Men: Receiving private pension	Men: Will receive private pension	Women: Receiving private pension	Women: Will receive private pension
Occupation				
Number reporting (in thousands)	102	62	32	22
Total percent	100	100	100	100
Professional and technical workers	9	10	9	16
Managers and officials	11	12	5	3
Clerical and sales workers	13	12	47	37
Craftsmen	30	28	3	4
Operatives	30	27	30	32
Service and household workers	3	5	5	6
Laborers and foremen	5	7	1	1
Industry				
Number reporting (in thousands)	101	62	31	22
Total percent	100	100	100	100
Mining and construction	8	12	([1])	1
Manufacturing:				
Durable goods	37	30	20	14
Nondurable goods	24	21	26	28
Transportation and public utilities	15	12	14	5
Wholesale and retail trade	7	9	13	15
Finance, insurance, and real estate	6	6	10	8
Business and repair services	3	8	16	27
Other	1	1	1	2

[1] Less than 0.5 percent.

Source: Social Security Bulletin

75. Which income group has the largest percentage of women who will receive a private pension?

(A) Under $5,000
(B) $5,000–$5,999
(C) $6,000–$6,999
(D) $7,000–$7,999
(E) $9,000–$9,999

76. Approximately how many thousands of the women reporting among those receiving a private pension had earnings under $5,000?

(A) 11
(B) 12
(C) 21
(D) 40
(E) 41

77. Of the men reporting who will receive a private pension, how many had length of employment longer than the median length of employment for men who will receive a private pension?

(A) 6,760
(B) 11,000
(C) 25,000
(D) 27,450
(E) 29,300

78. Which of the following statements about workers who are receiving or expect to receive a private pension can be inferred from the table?

I. More than $\frac{1}{4}$ of the men worked in manufacturing durable goods.
II. More than $\frac{1}{5}$ of the men worked 45 years or longer.
III. More female than male professional and technical workers will receive a pension.

(A) I only
(B) II only
(C) I and II only
(D) II and III only
(E) I, II, and III

79. If a store sells $3\frac{1}{4}$ crates of lettuce on Monday, $2\frac{1}{6}$ on Tuesday, $4\frac{1}{2}$ on Wednesday, and $1\frac{2}{3}$ on Thursday, how many crates has the store sold altogether?

(A) 10
(B) $11\frac{1}{2}$
(C) $11\frac{7}{12}$
(D) $11\frac{3}{4}$
(E) $12\frac{1}{3}$

80. If $x + y > 4$ and $x < 3$, then $y > 1$ is true

(A) always
(B) only if $x < 0$
(C) only if $x > 0$
(D) only if $x = 0$
(E) never

81. If 50 apprentices can finish a job in 4 hours and 30 journeymen can finish the same job in $4\frac{1}{2}$ hours, how much of the job should be completed by 10 apprentices and 15 journeymen in one hour?

(A) $\frac{1}{9}$
(B) $\frac{29}{180}$
(C) $\frac{26}{143}$
(D) $\frac{1}{5}$
(E) $\frac{39}{121}$

82. If $x + y = 4$ and $3x + 2y = 11$, then $x - y$ is

(A) −2
(B) −1
(C) 1
(D) 2
(E) 3

83. What is the sum of $1 + 3 + 3^2 + 3^3 + \cdots + 3^9$?

(A) 3^9
(B) 3^{10}
(C) $\frac{1 - 3^{10}}{3}$
(D) $\frac{1 - 3^{10}}{1 - 3}$
(E) $\frac{1 - 3^9}{1 - 3}$

84. What is the area of a regular hexagon which is inscribed in a circle of radius 6 inches?

(A) $9\sqrt{3}$ sq. in.
(B) 36 sq. in.
(C) $48\sqrt{2}$ sq. in.
(D) $51\sqrt{5}$ sq. in.
(E) $54\sqrt{3}$ sq. in.

85. If 40% of all women are voters and 52% of the population are women, what percent of the population are women voters?

(A) 18.1
(B) 20.8
(C) 26.4
(D) 40
(E) 52

If there is still time remaining, you may review the questions in this section only. You may not turn to any other section of the test.

Section III Verbal Aptitude

TIME: 20 minutes

Antonyms

DIRECTIONS: For each question below, select the lettered word or phrase that comes closest to being *opposite* in meaning to the word appearing in capital letters. Be sure to consider all meanings carefully.

86. ABJURE: (A) injure (B) pledge (C) abdicate (D) realize (E) conjure

87. MITIGATE: (A) lose (B) transfer (C) intensify (D) abstain (E) extract

88. SPURIOUS: (A) soft (B) harmful (C) new (D) authentic (E) contradictory

89. TORRID: (A) wet (B) animated (C) cold (D) closed (E) even

90. CIRCUMSPECTION: (A) regret (B) humility (C) generosity (D) joy (E) recklessness

91. DESULTORY: (A) sad (B) methodical (C) rough (D) pleasant (E) contented

92. DISSONANCE: (A) heat (B) loudness (C) harmony (D) noise (E) disparity

93. INCREDULOUS: (A) irreligious (B) creditable (C) indifferent (D) believing (E) confused

94. OBDURATE: (A) unsusceptible (B) tender (C) right (D) intelligent (E) meager

95. UNGAINLY: (A) graceful (B) exceptional (C) winning (D) sensible (E) average

96. DISCERN: (A) observe (B) overlook (C) separate (D) include (E) disorganize

97. CONVIVIAL: (A) encouraging (B) unsociable (C) ignorant (D) tranquil (E) folksy

98. ALACRITY: (A) slowness (B) clarity (C) attractiveness (D) unfriendliness (E) culpability

99. PERFIDIOUS: (A) awkward (B) homely (C) faithful (D) comprehensible (E) ignorant

Word-Pair Relationships

DIRECTIONS: For each question below, determine the relationship between the pair of capitalized words and then select the lettered pair of words which have a similar relationship to the first pair.

100. COMPUTER : SLIDE RULE :: (A) car : driver (B) quadrant : teacher (C) reader : book (D) clock : sundial (E) solution : problem

101. BATTERY : FLASHLIGHT :: (A) sun : warmth (B) mercury : vapor (C) fertilizer : grass (D) tires : automobile (E) coal : furnace

102. MUFF : HANDS :: (A) helmet : head (B) polish : nails (C) glasses : eyes (D) anklet : legs (E) earring : ears

103. PHILATELIST : STAMPS :: (A) philanthropist : charity (B) entomologist : words (C) numismatist : medals (D) ornithologist : horticulture (E) government : taxes

104. PLACID : TRANQUILIZER :: (A) action : reaction (B) somnolent : sedative (C) cold : pill (D) run : frightened (E) traffic light : obey

105. MATURITY : INFANCY :: (A) culmination : inception (B) work : burden (C) applause : performance (D) seed : grass (E) foundation : building

106. FLORICULTURE : FLOWERS :: (A) gold : ore (B) bushel : grain (C) horticulture : raisins (D) cultivation : vegetables (E) arboriculture : trees

107. AVIARY : BIRDS :: (A) animals : zoo (B) money : bank (C) letters : post office (D) aquarium : fish (E) honey : bee-hive

108. MUSLIN : PLAIN :: (A) inlaid : tile (B) brocade : ornate (C) montage : colored (D) wool : decorated (E) linen : fragile

109. DISCOURSE : EPILOGUE :: (A) music : coda (B) speech : applause (C) stanza : poetry (D) sunset : dark (E) beginning : end

110. PLANE : PILOT :: (A) election : politician (B) conduct : police (C) radar : repairman (D) arms : captain (E) store : manager

111. DECADE : CENTURY :: (A) decibel : unit (B) decimeter : meter (C) decimal : equation (D) delineate : boundary (E) deuce : ace

112. MODEL : REALITY :: (A) blueprint : house (B) design : prototype (C) formula : chemical (D) hypothesis : theory (E) prognosis : diagnosis

Sentence Completions

DIRECTIONS: For each sentence below, select the lettered word or set of words which, when inserted in the sentence blanks, best complete the meaning of that sentence.

113. A ____ system depends upon the willingness of management to accept ____.

(A) business . . . payment (B) competitive . . . risks (C) socialist . . . dictatorship (D) communist . . . failures (E) patronage . . . bribes

114. With some exceptions, ____ generally have criticized advertising as ____.
(A) marketers . . . innocuous (B) consumers . . . helpful (C) economists . . . wasteful (D) businessmen . . . misleading (E) producers . . . ineffective

115. Attitudes are ____ to respond in an evaluative way toward objects.

(A) ways (B) bound (C) predispositions (D) believed (E) conditioned

116. The relationship between ____ and ____ has been closely studied.

(A) commodities . . . prices (B) research . . . development (C) advertising . . . sales (D) statistics . . . forecasting (E) commerce . . . inflation

117. The voters gave the winner a _____ without a _____.

(A) parade . . . permit (B) majority . . . plurality (C) victory . . . mandate (D) plebiscite . . . referendum (E) majority . . . election

118. Caveat emptor, let the _____ beware!

(A) traitor (B) populace (C) assembly (D) buyer (E) trespasser

119. The _____ received an emolument.

(A) farmer (B) wife (C) employee (D) prisoner (E) lawyer

120. In spite of heavy bombing, the bridge was _____.

(A) extant (B) palliated (C) tumified (D) collapsed (E) promulgated

121. The malingerer thought he could escape the _____.

(A) voyage (B) ballgame (C) work (D) party (E) election

122. Wars usually result from _____ among the parties involved.

(A) dissonance (B) doubt (C) prudence (D) disagreement (E) frustration

123. The _____ action of the participants led the referee to _____ the fight.

(A) belligerent . . . cancel (B) enthusiastic . . . begin (C) unwarranted . . . stop (D) inert . . . postpone (E) wild . . . enter

124. At the scene of the crime, the _____ was apprehended.

(A) victim (B) assailant (C) malefactor (D) observer (E) delinquent

125. Smoothness in the flow of _____ is an essential part of good _____ writing.

(A) supposition . . . newspaper (B) words . . . order (C) information . . . report (D) facts . . . novel (E) fiction . . . chronicle

If there is still time remaining, you may review the questions in this section only. You may not turn to any other section of the test.

Section IV Data Sufficiency

TIME: 15 minutes

DIRECTIONS: Each of the following problems has a question and two statements which are labeled (1) and (2). Use the data given in (1) and (2) together with other available information (such as the number of hours in a day, the definition of *clockwise,* mathematical facts, etc.) to decide whether the statements are *sufficient* to answer the question. Then fill in space

(A) if you can get the answer from (1) alone but not from (2) alone;

(B) if you can get the answer from (2) alone but not from (1) alone;

(C) if you can get the answer from (1) and (2) together, although neither statement by itself suffices;

(D) if statement (1) alone suffices *and* statement (2) alone suffices;

(E) if you cannot get the answer from statements (1) and (2) together, but need even more data.

All numbers used in this section are real numbers. A figure given for a problem is intended to provide information consistent with that in the question, but not necessarily with the additional information contained in the statements.

126. In triangle ABC, find x if $y = 40$.

(1) $AB = BC$
(2) $z = 100$

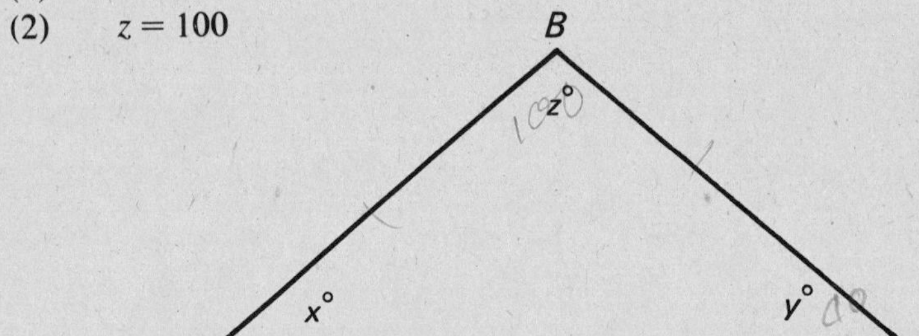

127. What is the area of the shaded part of the circle? O is the center of the circle.

(1) The radius of the circle is 4.
(2) x is 60.

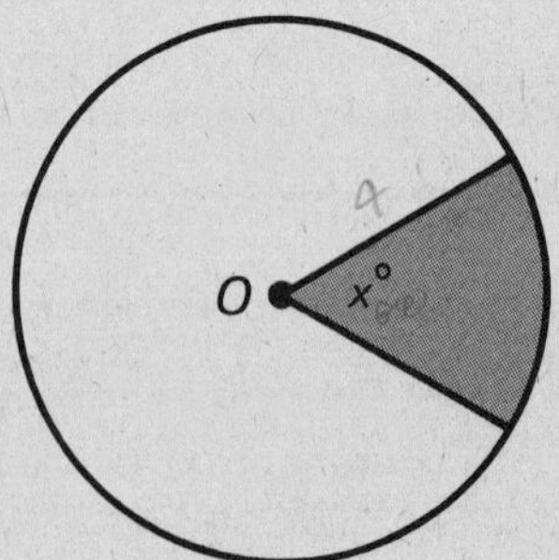

128. What was Mr. Kliman's income in 1970?

(1) His total income for 1968, 1969, and 1970 was $41,000.
(2) He made 20% more in 1969 than he did in 1968.

129. If l and l' are straight lines, find y.

(1) $x = 100$
(2) $z = 80$

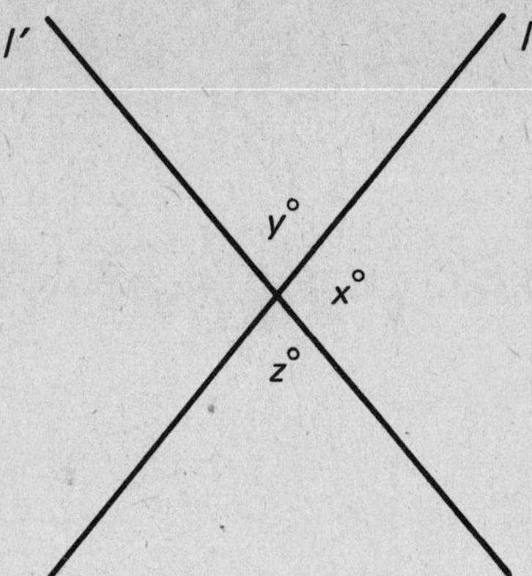

130. Fifty students have signed up for at least one of the courses German I and English I. How many of the 50 students are taking German I but not English I?

(1) 16 students are taking German I and English I.
(2) The number of students taking English I but not German I is the same as the number taking German I but not English I.

131. Is $ABCD$ a square?

(1) $AC = AB$
(2) $x = 90$

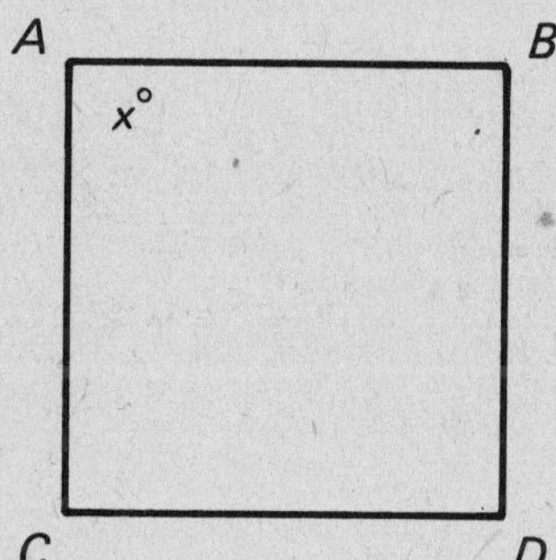

132. The XYZ Corporation has 7,000 employees. What is the average yearly wage of an employee of the XYZ Corporation?

(1) 4,000 of the employees are executives.
(2) The total amount the company pays in wages each year is \$77,000,000.

133. Is $x > y$?

(1) $(x + y)^2 > 0$
(2) x is positive

134. What is the area of the shaded region if both circles have radius 4 and O and O' are the centers of the circles?

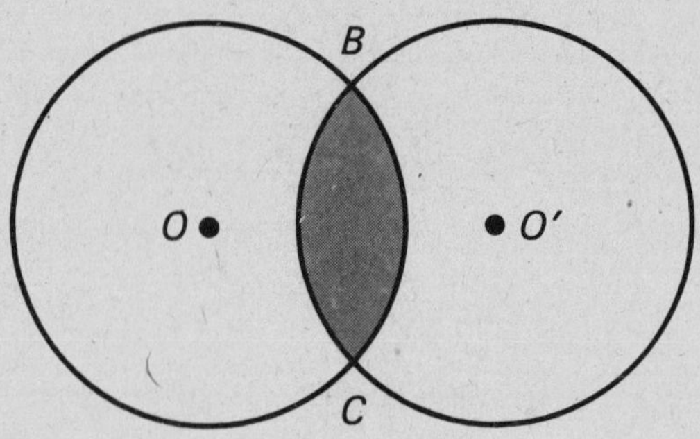

(1) The area enclosed by both circles is 29π.
(2) The line connecting O and O' is perpendicular to the line connecting B and C (B and C are the points where the two circles intersect).

135. How long will it take to travel from A to B? It takes 4 hours to travel from A to B and back to A.

(1) It takes 25% more time to travel from A to B than it does to travel from B to A.
(2) C is midway between A and B, and it takes 2 hours to travel from A to C and back to A.

136. l, l', and k are straight lines. Are l and l' parallel?

(1) $x = y$
(2) $y = z$

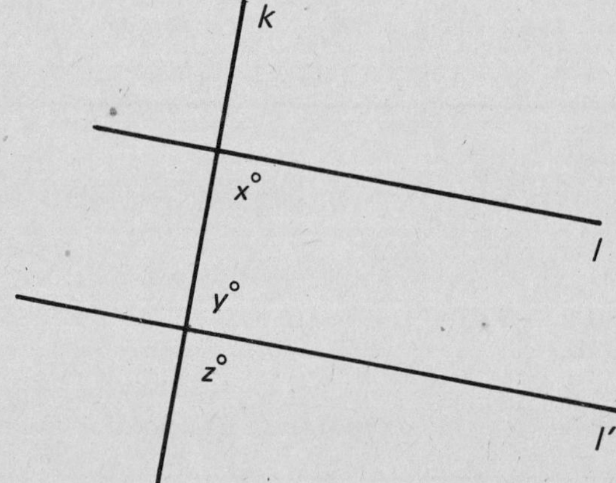

137. What is $x + y + z$?

(1) $x + y = 3$
(2) $x + z = 2$

138. How much cardboard will it take to make a rectangular box with a lid the length of whose base is 7 inches?

(1) The width of the box will be 5 inches.
(2) The height of the box will be 4 inches.

139. What is the profit on 15 boxes of detergent?

(1) The cost of a crate of boxes of detergent is $50.
(2) Each crate contains 100 boxes of detergent.

140. Which of the two figures, *ABCD* or *EFGH*, has the largest area?

(1) The perimeter of *ABCD* is longer than the perimeter of *EFGH*.
(2) *AC* is longer than *EG*.

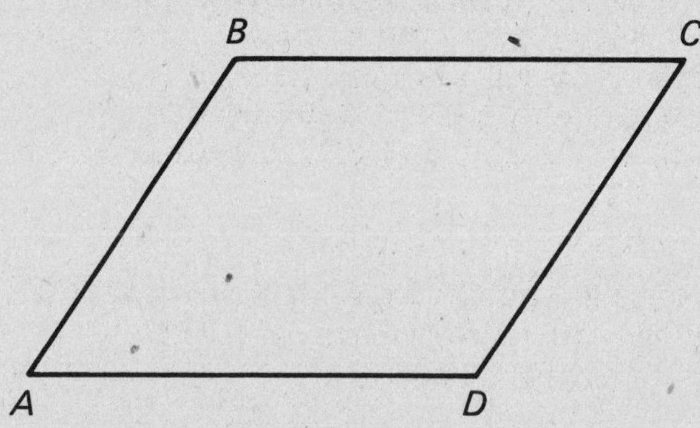

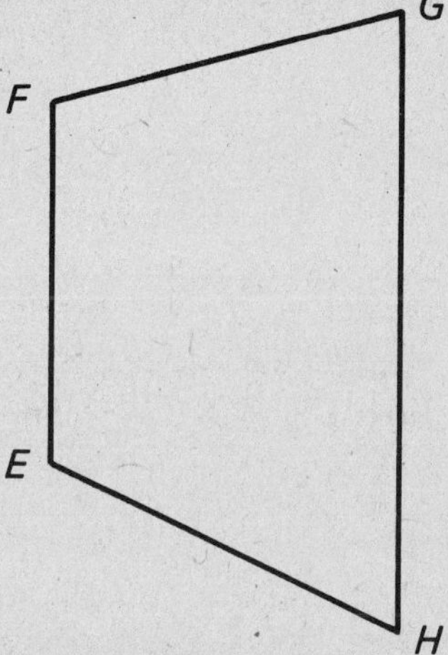

If there is still time remaining, you may review the questions in this section only. You may not turn to any other section of the test.

Section V Business Judgment

TIME: 35 minutes

DIRECTIONS: Read the following two passages. After you have completed each of them you will be asked to answer two sets of questions. The first of these, data evaluation, involves determining the importance of specific factors included in the passage. The second, data application, consists of general questions relating to the passage. When answering questions, you may consult the passage.

Passage 1:

Mr. Hesh came to Zaire this year straight from a four year assignment as Commercial Attaché in his country's embassy in Liberia. One of the first questions asked him came from executives of Zaire's small but growing textile industry and was about the possibility of expanding sales to the American market. They felt that if this were possible, many more people could be employed in this sector of industry, having a favorable effect on the country's economy.

"While I have been here only a short time," began Mr. Hesh, "I would certainly be prepared to say that everything I've seen indicates a tremendous future, particularly in the textile and small parts industries. Zaire has gone beyond the stage of manufacturing simple items, and is now moving into the more sophisticated goods."

Mr. Hesh has a great deal of confidence in Zaire inventiveness and offers as an example the pre-fab diner. "We sold you the manufacturing capability for this diner, and you are now producing a much better version and selling it back to us." He considers this legitimate and beneficial for an active trading relationship. Other Zaire goods and services that he feels are of particular interest for the American market are clothing and other textiles. Out of this line, but also in the area of creativity, is fashions for which he foresees an ever brighter future in America. Such unique services as those provided by the Institute for Literary Translations, which works largely on U.S. assignments, are another important Zaire export item.

Investments by American firms is another avenue of commercial relations that Mr. Hesh believes is going to increase.

Asked for his reaction to the proposed legislation to limit textile imports into the United States, Mr. Hesh said, "it looks as if the bill has a good chance of passing. Numerous members of Congress have spoken in support of the bill, and the Secretary of Commerce gave his support after a prolonged effort to solve the problem in other ways. It is unfortunate that his efforts were not successful. It is always preferable to solve such problems through negotiations rather than by unilateral actions, but certain countries were not willing to commit themselves to adequate restraints."

In light of Mr. Hesh's remarks, Zaire's textile executives were considering what the chances were to successfully penetrate the American textile market.

Data Evaluation Questions

DIRECTIONS: Evaluate each of the following factors used in decision-making which relate to the passage you have just read by selecting

(A) for a *Major Objective*—the result desired by the executive;

(B) for a *Major Factor*—a primary consideration, spelled out in the passage, that influences the decision;

(C) for a *Minor Factor*—a less important consideration in the decision;

(D) for a *Major Assumption*—a conclusion reached by the executive not necessarily supported by the factors present;

(E) for an *Unimportant Issue*—a consideration not directly related to the problem.

141. Expanding textile sales to the U.S.

142. Confidence in Zaire inventiveness

143. American investment in Zaire

144. Zaire is an African country

145. American trade protection

Data Application Questions

DIRECTIONS: Answer each of the following questions using information contained in the passage.

146. Expanding textile sales to the U.S. would

I. Decrease world textile prices
II. Increase profits in the textile industry
III. Increase employment in Zaire

(A) I only
(B) III only
(C) I and II only
(D) II and III only
(E) I, II, and III

147. According to the Commercial Attaché, Zaire manufactures

I. Mainly simple goods
II. Mostly cheap products
III. Some sophisticated goods

(A) I only
(B) III only
(C) I and II only
(D) II and III only
(E) I, II, and III

148. Mr. Hesh suggested that some products could be sold in the American market, such as

I. Heavy machinery
II. Clothing
III. Fashion design

(A) I only
(B) III only
(C) I and II only
(D) II and III only
(E) I, II, and III

149. According to the passage, the protectionist trade bill before the U.S. Congress would limit the importation of

I. Textiles
II. Machinery
III. Agricultural products

(A) I only
(B) III only
(C) I and II only
(D) II and III only
(E) I, II, and III

150. Goods other than textiles that Zaire might successfully sell in the U.S. market include

I. Small parts
II. Translations
III. Pre-fab diners

(A) I only
(B) III only
(C) I and II only
(D) II and III only
(E) I, II, and III

Passage 2:

For the past two years, Bennett Joseph, head of the regional firm R and S Packing Company, had been seriously considering the use of U.S. government grade labeling for its high-quality canned fruits and vegetables. Having enjoyed an excellent reputation for more than 30 years with the public, these canned goods under the trademark "Delish" were known throughout the area by distributors and consumers alike as some of the best.

The grade-labeling problem had come to the fore as the result of a new food supermarket chain called *Gaynes*. The new chain, a national organization, was making a depth penetration in the region by spending a sizeable portion of its large advertising and promotion budget for pushing its own private brands of frozen and canned fruits and vegetables. Its advertising emphasized that the public could find both grade and descriptive labeling on each package and can. The descriptive labels listed the type of food, the can size, the number of servings per can, the net contents, and the name and address of the chain.

Joseph had always paid careful attention to the descriptive labeling on R and S products but had been most reluctant to commit the company to the use of grade labeling. Joseph's reluctance was supported by the company's advertising and promotion manager and the production boss, who believed with him that grade labeling could hardly bring out the fresh flavor and taste upon which the company prided itself and had been able to capture through its own special heating, processing, and canning techniques.

A factor that seriously concerned Joseph in the use of grade labels on canned fruits and vegetables was the possible use of a high grade on one of the grading characteristics to offset a low score on another. This method could hardly help R and S, whose pack was known by distributors and consumers alike to be much better even than the highest grades of its competitors.

While Joseph was pondering this problem, he mulled over what he had read about grade labeling. In the first place, grading and labeling of canned foods had been developed to protect and help the consumer. Through the Department of Agriculture, federal standards had been set up for standardization, grading, and inspection work. To encourage voluntary use of these standards, the Department of Agriculture hired inspectors who carried out the federal inspection program at production periods. For canned fruits and vegetables, the grades were A, B, and C, which were based on such criteria as uniformity, succulence, and color—not flavor or food value.

Joseph certainly agreed that grade labeling could provide additional information for the consumer. R and S could also use it in company advertisements to supplement its own descriptive labels. But didn't everyone know about the taste and quality of R and S products? He also wondered what happened when a company using grade labeling saw the qualities of fruits and vegetables change from year to year. At one period, that quality might be high for most growers; it might also be low during another. Too, some factors that were very important in their effect on consumer choice could not be subjected to a grading discipline. For example, the range of individual tastes was impossible to standardize. Certainly taste, Joseph felt, should be just as important—perhaps more so—than the other, more tangible criteria used to grade canned goods.

Data Evaluation Questions

DIRECTIONS: Evaluate each of the following factors used in decision-making which relate to the passage you have just read by selecting

(A) for a *Major Objective*—the result desired by the executive;

(B) for a *Major Factor*—a primary consideration, spelled out in the passage, that influences the decision;

(C) for a *Minor Factor*—a less important consideration in the decision;

(D) for a *Major Assumption*—a conclusion reached by the executive not necessarily supported by the factors present;

(E) for an *Unimportant Issue*—a consideration not directly related to the problem.

151. Establishment of a new supermarket chain

152. Standardization of food products

153. Grade labeling of food products

154. Federal food standards

155. Continuing the R & S brand image

Data Application Questions

DIRECTIONS: Answer each of the following questions using information contained in the passage.

156. According to the passage, grade labeling was intended to

I. Increase the cost of canning
II. Increase competition
III. Protect and inform the consumer

(A) I only
(B) III only
(C) I and II only
(D) II and III only
(E) I, II, and III

157. R & S did not adopt grade labeling because

I. It had little reason to do so
II. The government did not require it
III. It was too expensive

(A) I only
(B) III only
(C) I and II only
(D) II and III only
(E) I, II, and III

158. Which of the following R & S employees had doubts about the efficacy of adopting grade labeling?

I. Bennett Joseph
II. The advertising manager
III. The production manager

(A) I only
(B) III only
(C) I and II only
(D) II and III only
(E) I, II, and III

159. Which government agency supervises the labeling program?

I. Department of Commerce
II. Department of Health
III. Department of Agriculture

(A) I only
(B) III only
(C) I and II only
(D) II and III only
(E) I, II, and III

160. Grading of fruits and vegetables was based on

I. Taste
II. Color
III. Uniformity

(A) I only
(B) III only
(C) I and II only
(D) II and III only
(E) I, II, and III

If there is still time remaining, you may review the questions in this section only.
You may not turn to any other section of the test.

Section VI Mathematics

TIME: 40 minutes

DIRECTIONS: Solve each of the following problems; then indicate the correct answer in the space provided. [On the actual test you will be permitted to use any space available on the examination paper for scratch work.]

NOTE: A figure that appears with a problem is drawn as accurately as possible so as to provide information that may help in answering the question. Numbers in this test are real numbers.

161. $^{15}/_{16} = x\%$ where x is

(A) 87.75
(B) 90
(C) 93.75
(D) 94.65
(E) 95

162. If it takes worker F 15 minutes to load a truck by himself and it takes worker S 20 minutes to load the same truck by himself, how long should it take worker F and worker S together to load the truck?

(A) $8^2/_3$ min.
(B) $8^4/_7$ min.
(C) $9^1/_2$ min.
(D) 10 min.
(E) $10^3/_4$ min.

163. A car traveling at 50 miles per hour increases its speed at the rate of 5 miles per hour each hour. How long will it take before the car reaches 65 miles per hour?

(A) 1 hr.
(B) 2 hr.
(C) $2^1/_2$ hr.
(D) 3 hr.
(E) 13 hr.

164. The Tarrytown factory produces 75 cars an hour when it is operating at 50% of its capacity. The Mahwah factory produces 100 cars an hour when it is operating at 80% of its capacity. What is the ratio of the production of the Tarrytown factory to the production of the Mahwah factory when they are both operating at full (100%) capacity?

(A) 3 to 4
(B) 5 to 6
(C) 7 to 8
(D) 6 to 5
(E) 4 to 3

165. If the average (arithmetic mean) of 5 integers is 7, what is the sum of the integers?

(A) 7
(B) 30
(C) 35
(D) 40
(E) 15,120

Use the following graphs for questions 166–169.

LABOUR COSTS IN INDUSTRY

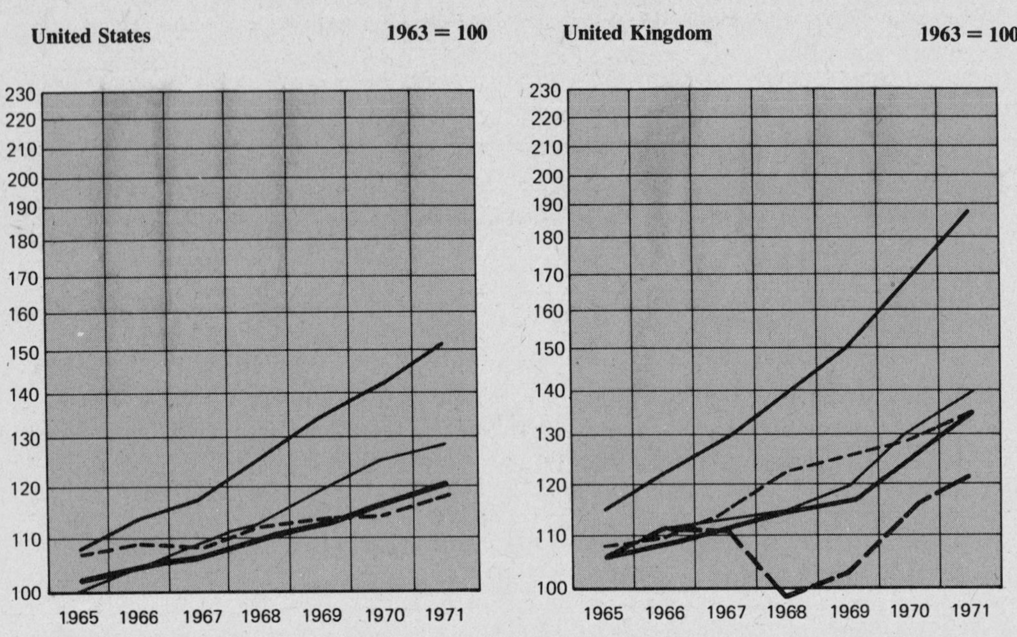

% change on preceding year

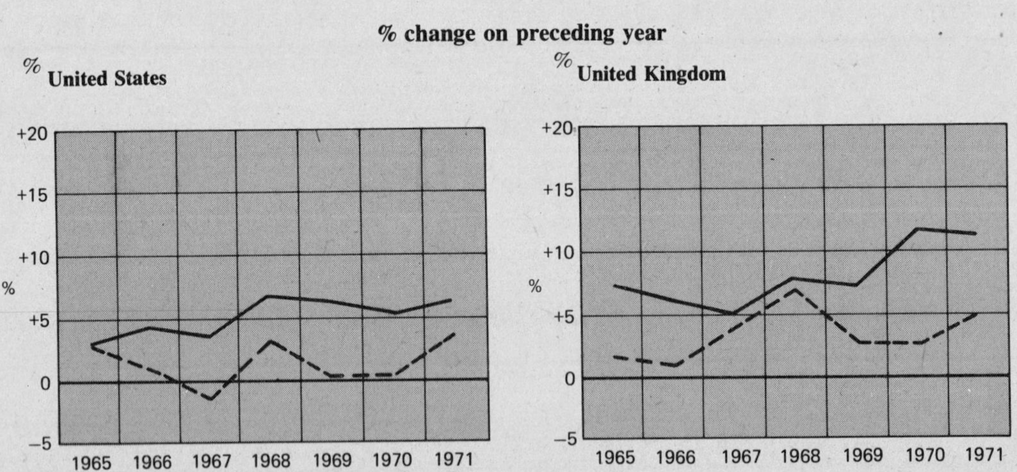

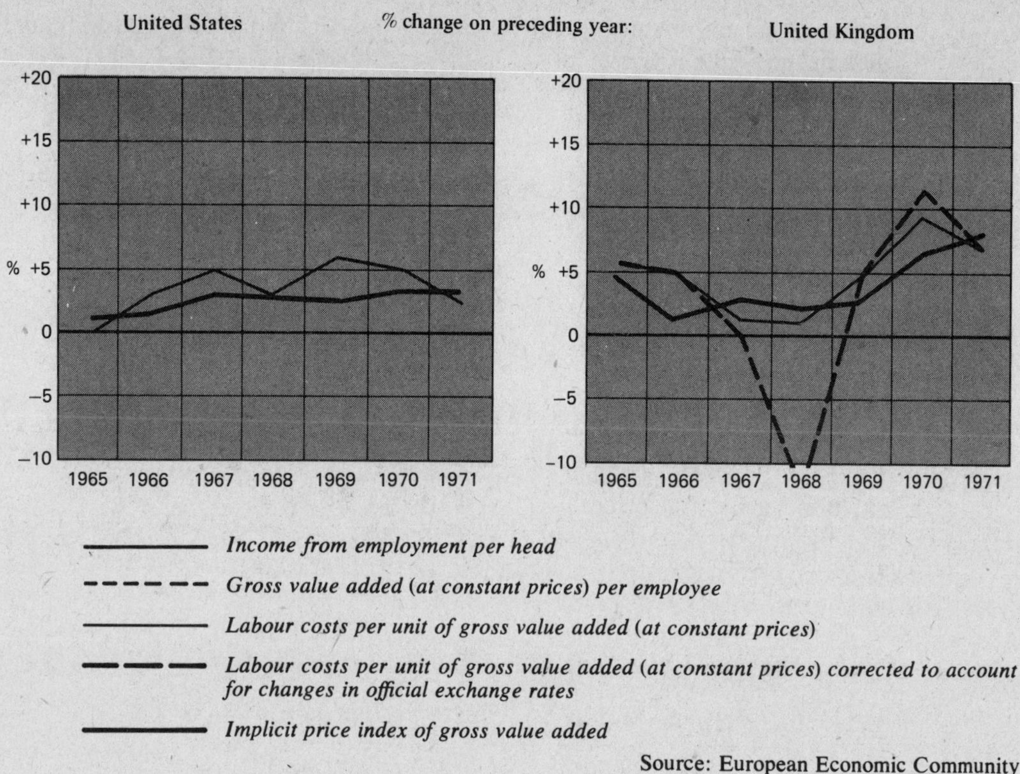

Source: European Economic Community

166. According to the passage, the one indicator that has increased at least 5% every year is

(A) income from employment per head in the United States
(B) income from employment per head in the United Kingdom
(C) gross value added per employee in the United States
(D) gross value added per employee in the United Kingdom
(E) implicit price index of gross value added in the United Kingdom

167. If income from employment per head in the United States had been 250 instead of 100 in 1963, then at the beginning of 1971 it would have been approximately

(A) 147
(B) 150
(C) 250
(D) 330
(E) 365

168. The difference between income from employment per head and labor costs per unit of gross value added (at constant prices) in the United States between 1965 and 1971 has

(A) decreased by 50%
(B) stayed about the same
(C) increased by about 90%
(D) more than doubled
(E) more than quadrupled

169. Which of the following statements about labor costs in industry between 1965 and 1971 can be inferred from the graphs?

I. Income from employment per head in 1965 was higher in the United Kingdom than in the United States.
II. The rate of increase of income from employment per head in the United Kingdom from 1963 to 1971 was greater than any other indicator shown.
III. Gross value added (at constant prices) per employee in the United States in 1970 was less than $\frac{6}{5}$ of its value in 1963.

(A) II only
(B) III only
(C) I and II only
(D) II and III only
(E) I, II, and III

170. The original price of a car is $3,000. The price is discounted 20% and then raised by 10%. What is the new price of the car?

(A) $2,400
(B) $2,640
(C) $2,700
(D) $2,760
(E) $2,800

Use the following table for questions 171–173.

GROSS INCOME	TAX
$10,000	$2,000
$12,000	$2,700
$14,000	$3,600
$16,000	$4,600
$18,000	$5,800
$20,000	$7,200

171. At what rate is a gross income of $10,000 taxed?

(A) 2%
(B) 10%
(C) 18%
(D) 20%
(E) 22%

172. If a person with a gross income of $10,000 receives $10,000 more in gross income, how much tax does he pay on the extra $10,000?

(A) $2,000
(B) $4,600
(C) $5,200
(D) $5,800
(E) $7,200

173. The taxes paid by 2 people, each with a gross income of $10,000, are what fraction of the tax paid by a person with a gross income of 20,000?

(A) $\frac{5}{18}$
(B) $\frac{23}{72}$
(C) $\frac{5}{9}$
(D) $\frac{27}{12}$
(E) $\frac{10}{9}$

174. If one pump can pump u cubic feet of water a minute and another pump can pump v cubic feet of water a minute, how many minutes will it take both pumps together to pump 50 cubic feet of water?

(A) $u + v$
(B) $50u + v$
(C) $50u + 50v$
(D) $\frac{50}{u} + v$
(E) $\frac{50}{u + v}$

175. The interior angles of a trapezoid are in the ratio 2 : 4 : 5 : 7. How many degrees is the smallest interior angle of the trapezoid?

(A) 10
(B) 20
(C) 30
(D) 40
(E) 45

176. What is $9/7$ divided by $5/6$?

(A) $5/6$
(B) $15/14$
(C) $27/24$
(D) $10/7$
(E) $54/35$

Use the graph and table below for questions 177–180.

UNDER 19
$11.5 Billion

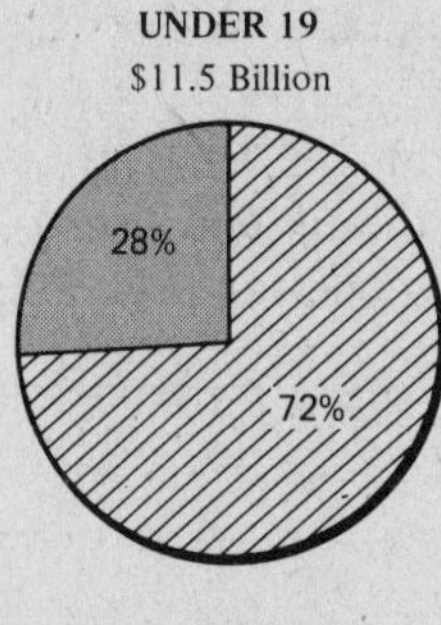

19-64
$40.7 Billion

26%
74%

65 AND OVER
$19.8 Billion

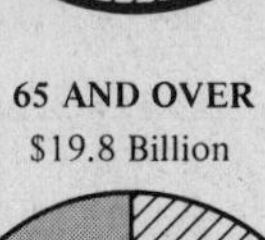

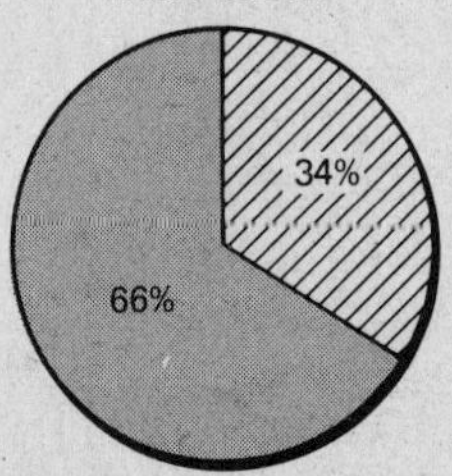

Distribution of public funds for Personal Health Care

Age	Percentage distribution		
	Total	Federal funds	State and local funds
All ages	100.0	66.3	33.7
Under 19	100.0	57.9	42.1
19–64	100.0	51.2	48.8
65 and over	100.0	80.8	19.2

Source: Social Security Bulletin

177. Which of the following categories accounts for the largest amount of personal health care expenditures?

(A) private, under 19
(B) public, under 19
(C) private, 19 to 64
(D) public, 65 and over
(E) private, 65 and over

178. Approximately how much is spent from federal funds for health care of people 65 and over?

(A) \$9 billion
(B) \$10.5 billion
(C) \$12 billion
(D) \$13.2 billion
(E) \$19.8 billion

179. The ratio of the amount of money taken from public sources for health care for those between 19 and 64 and those 65 and over is about

(A) $\frac{1}{2}$
(B) $\frac{3}{4}$
(C) $\frac{7}{8}$
(D) $\frac{4}{3}$
(E) $\frac{2}{1}$

180. Which of the following statements about expenditures for personal health care during the fiscal year 1972 can be inferred from the graphs and table?

I. More than $\frac{1}{7}$ of the total expenditures for personal health care were spent for the under 19 group.
II. The expenditures from private sources for the under 19 group were higher than the expenditures from private sources for the 65 and over group.
III. The group which accounted for the largest expenditure of state and local funds was the 19 to 64 group.

(A) I only
(B) II only
(C) I and II only
(D) II and III only
(E) I, II, and III

Use the graph below for questions 181–182.

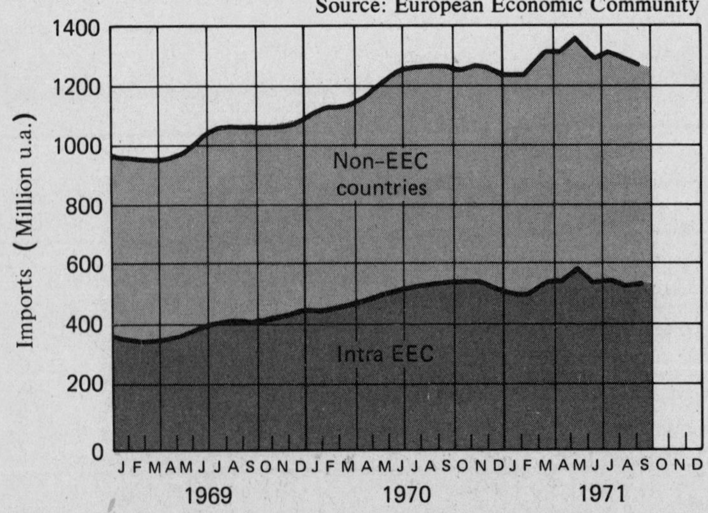

181. The maximum value of imports from non-EEC countries during the time shown on the graph was about

(A) 590
(B) 600
(C) 700
(D) 750
(E) 1350

182. During the time shown, imports from non-EEC countries divided by total imports have been roughly

(A) $\frac{1}{4}$
(B) $\frac{1}{2}$
(C) 1
(D) $\frac{3}{2}$
(E) 2

183. The total weekly wages paid to 15 workers was $1,800. Five of the workers earned $180 each that week. What was the average weekly wage for the remaining 10 workers?

(A) $50
(B) $90
(C) $100
(D) $105
(E) $110

184. If the two sides of a right triangle adjacent to the right angle have lengths of 5 and 12 respectively, then the length of the side opposite the right angle is

(A) 5
(B) 10
(C) 13
(D) 15
(E) 17

Use the table below for questions 185–187.

SPEED of a car over a 3 hour period

Time since start (in minutes)	30	60	90	105	120	150	180
Speed at time (in mph)	50	55	60	62.5	67.5	65	60

185. How fast was the car traveling $2\frac{1}{2}$ hours after the start?

(A) 60 mph
(B) 62.5 mph
(C) 65 mph
(D) 67.5 mph
(E) 70 mph

186. During the last hour of the time period shown on the table, the speed of the car

(A) decreased by 10 mph
(B) decreased by 7.5 mph
(C) decreased by 5 mph
(D) decreased by 2.5 mph
(E) stayed the same

187. Which of the following statements about the speed of the car during the 3 hour period can be inferred from the table?

I. The average speed was 60 mph.
II. The car slowed down during the fifth half-hour of the time period.
III. The slowest speed the car traveled at was 50 mph.

(A) II only
(B) III only
(C) I and III only
(D) II and III only
(E) I, II, and III

188. If John makes 4 baskets in an hour and Allison makes 6 baskets in an hour and ten minutes, how many baskets will they make together in two hours?

(A) 8
(B) $10\frac{1}{4}$
(C) $12\frac{3}{7}$
(D) $15\frac{6}{11}$
(E) $18\frac{2}{7}$

189. If the sum of four consecutive integers is 26, what is their product?

(A) 210
(B) 336
(C) 840
(D) 1,680
(E) 2,964

190. If $x^2 + 3x - 4 = 0$, then x is either 1 or

(A) -4
(B) -1
(C) 0
(D) 3
(E) 4

Use the graph below for questions 191–193.

Source: Department of Commerce, Bureau of the Census.

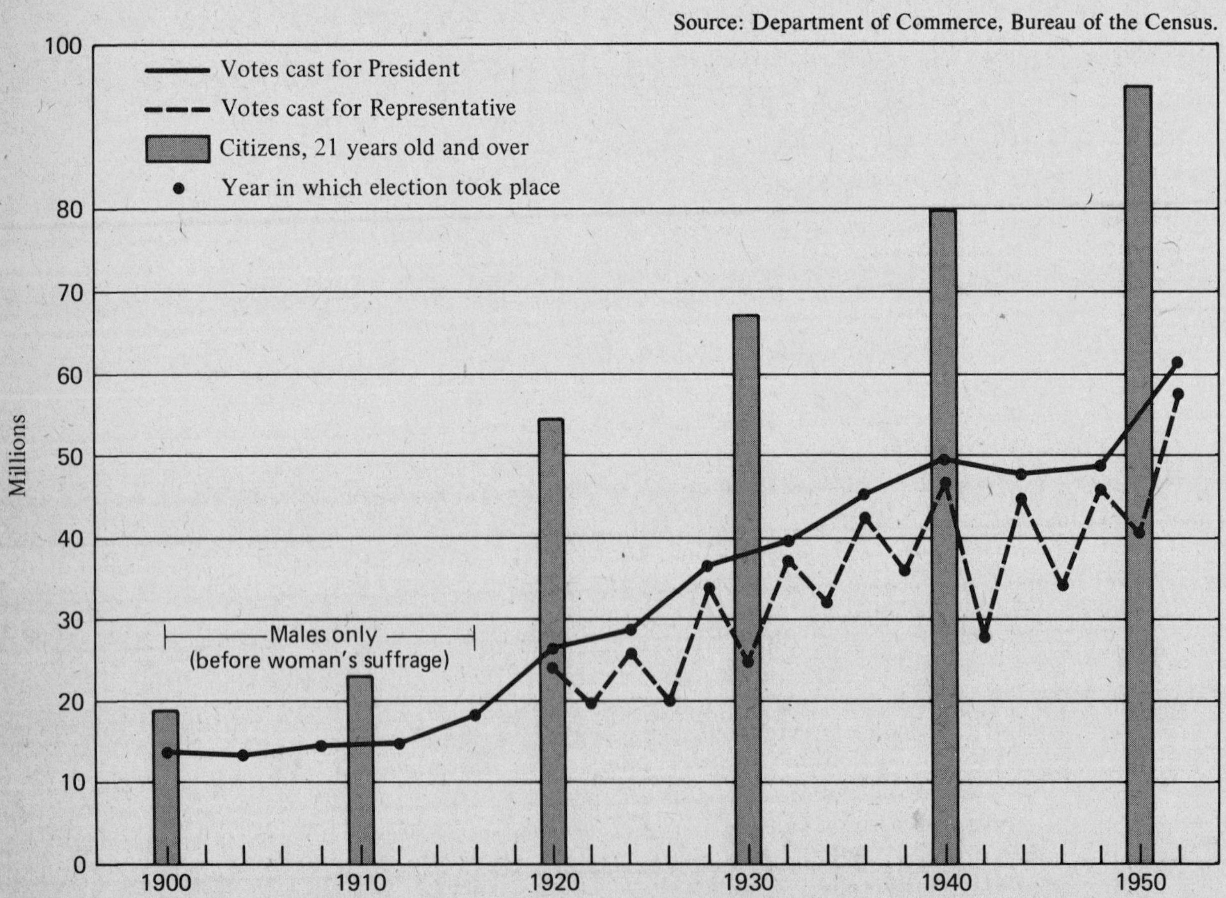

191. About how many million votes were cast for president in the 1948 election?

(A) 45
(B) 49
(C) 51
(D) 58
(E) 62

192. In the 1940 election, the proportion of citizens 21 years old and over who voted for president was

(A) $\frac{3}{8}$
(B) $\frac{1}{2}$
(C) $\frac{5}{8}$
(D) $\frac{7}{8}$
(E) $\frac{9}{8}$

193. The election with the smallest number of voters for representatives between 1931 and 1951 was

(A) 1932
(B) 1938
(C) 1942
(D) 1944
(E) 1946

194. If $x + y = 2$ and $y > 3$, then

(A) $x < -1$
(B) $x > -1$
(C) $x < 0$
(D) $x > 0$
(E) $x = 3$

195. How much is $\frac{2}{3}$ of $\frac{5/2}{3/4}$?

(A) $\frac{2}{3}$
(B) $\frac{5}{4}$
(C) $\frac{9}{5}$
(D) $\frac{20}{9}$
(E) 5

If there is still time remaining, you may review the questions in this section only.
You may not turn to any other section of the test.

Answers

Section I Reading Recall

1. **(D)**
2. **(C)**
3. **(C)**
4. **(C)**
5. **(E)**
6. **(C)**
7. **(A)**
8. **(B)**
9. **(C)**
10. **(E)**
11. **(A)**
12. **(B)**
13. **(C)**
14. **(C)**
15. **(D)**
16. **(D)**
17. **(E)**
18. **(C)**
19. **(A)**
20. **(B)**
21. **(C)**
22. **(A)**
23. **(D)**
24. **(A)**
25. **(C)**
26. **(A)**
27. **(C)**
28. **(A)**
29. **(B)**
30. **(D)**

Section II Mathematics

(Numbers in parentheses indicate the section in the Mathematics Review where material concerning the question is discussed.)

31. **(B)** (I–4)
32. **(C)** (II–6)
33. **(D)** (I–4)
34. **(B)** (I–2)
35. **(C)** (IV–4, II–5)
36. **(C)** (IV–4)
37. **(A)** (IV–4)
38. **(B)** (IV–4)
39. **(B)** (I–4, II–2)
40. **(E)** (II–3)
41. **(D)** (III–5)
42. **(A)** (II–5)
43. **(E)** (II–2)
44. **(C)** (IV–4)
45. **(D)** (IV–4)
46. **(E)** (IV–4)
47. **(B)** (IV–4)
48. **(C)** (IV–4, I–7)
49. **(D)** (I–4)
50. **(C)** (II–3)
51. **(A)** (II–3)
52. **(D)** (II–7)
53. **(E)** (III–8)
54. **(A)** (IV–1)
55. **(D)** (IV–1, II–5)
56. **(D)** (IV–1)
57. **(C)** (IV–1)
58. **(A)** (IV–1)
59. **(A)** (IV–1)
60. **(B)** (II–3)
61. **(D)** (II–2)
62. **(D)** (III–6)
63. **(E)** (I–4)
64. **(E)** (I–8)
65. **(D)** (IV–4, II–5)
66. **(A)** (IV–4)
67. **(A)** (IV–4)
68. **(B)** (IV–3, IV–4)
69. **(E)** (IV–3, II–5)
70. **(B)** (III–4)
71. **(C)** (I–4)
72. **(D)** (II–1)
73. **(A)** (III–1)
74. **(D)** (II–5)
75. **(A)** (IV–1)
76. **(B)** (IV–1)
77. **(D)** (IV–1)
78. **(A)** (IV–1)
79. **(C)** (I–2)
80. **(A)** (II–7)
81. **(B)** (II–3)
82. **(D)** (II–2)
83. **(D)** (II–6)
84. **(E)** (III–3, III–6, III–7)
85. **(B)** (II–4)

Section III Verbal Aptitude

86. (B)
87. (C)
88. (D)
89. (C)
90. (E)
91. (B)
92. (C)
93. (D)
94. (B)
95. (A)
96. (B)
97. (B)
98. (A)
99. (C)
100. (D)
101. (E)
102. (A)
103. (C)
104. (B)
105. (A)
106. (E)
107. (D)
108. (B)
109. (A)
110. (E)
111. (B)
112. (A)
113. (B)
114. (C)
115. (C)
116. (C)
117. (C)
118. (D)
119. (C)
120. (A)
121. (C)
122. (D)
123. (C)
124. (B)
125. (C)

Section IV Data Sufficiency

126. (D)
127. (C)
128. (E)
129. (D)
130. (C)
131. (E)
132. (B)
133. (E)
134. (A)
135. (A)
136. (C)
137. (E)
138. (C)
139. (E)
140. (E)

Section V Business Judgment

141. (A)
142. (C)
143. (E)
144. (E)
145. (D)
146. (B)
147. (B)
148. (D)
149. (A)
150. (A)
151. (B)
152. (C)
153. (B)
154. (B)
155. (A)
156. (B)
157. (A)
158. (E)
159. (B)
160. (D)

Section VI Mathematics

(Numbers in parentheses indicate the section in the Mathematics Review where material concerning the question is discussed.)

161. (C) (I–4)
162. (B) (II–3)
163. (D) (II–3)
164. (D) (II–5, I–4)
165. (C) (I–7)
166. (B) (IV–3)
167. (E) (IV–3)
168. (D) (IV–3)
169. (D) (IV–3)
170. (B) (I–4)
171. (D) (I–4)
172. (C) (IV–1)
173. (C) (I–2)
174. (E) (II–3)
175. (D) (III–5, II–5)
176. (E) (I–2)
177. (C) (IV–2)
178. (B) (IV–2)
179. (B) (IV–2, I–5)
180. (E) (IV–2)
181. (D) (IV–5)
182. (B) (IV–5)
183. (B) (I–7)
184. (C) (III–4)
185. (C) (IV–1)
186. (B) (IV–1)
187. (A) (IV–1)
188. (E) (I–2)
189. (D) (I–7)
190. (A) (II–2)
191. (B) (IV–3)
192. (C) (IV–3, IV–4)
193. (C) (IV–4)
194. (A) (II–7)
195. (D) (I–2)

Analysis

Section I   Reading Comprehension

1. **(D)** Note that the question asks "about how many" which requires an approximate figure. Of all the alternative answers, (D) comes closest to the 8,600 employees given in paragraph 1.

2. **(C)** See paragraph 3, lines 1 and 2.

3. **(C)** See paragraph 5, line 1: "Top Presidential appointees, . . . bear the brunt of translating the philosophy and aims of the current administration into practical programs."

4. **(C)** See paragraph 6, line 1: ". . . there be no basic disagreement with Presidential political philosophy, at least so far as administrative judgments and actions are concerned."

5. **(E)** See paragraph 6, last line.

6. **(C)** See paragraph 7: "Those whom the President selects. . . ." and following.

7. **(A)** See paragraph 8: ". . . they usually have substantial responsibilities in basic management."

8. **(B)** Paragraph 8, line 1: "These appointees are primarily regarded as policy makers. . . ."

9. **(C)** See paragraph 7: "Those selected by department and agency heads . . ." and following.

10. **(E)** Alternatives (B) through (D) are definitely acceptable, leaving (E) as the only possible answer.

11. **(A)** See paragraph 1.

12. **(B)** See paragraph 2: ". . . all resellers are bound by the terms of the . . . contract. . . ."

13. **(C)** This is inferred throughout the passage.

14. **(C)** See paragraph 4, line 1.

15. **(D)** Paragraph 5: "Responsibility for enforcement falls upon the producer or distributor. . . ."

16. **(D)** See paragraph 3: "Closeout sales are excepted."

17. **(E)** This is found in paragraph 2, line 1.

18. **(C)** See paragraph 5: ". . . granting of trading stamps in abnormally high volume. . . ."

19. **(A)** See paragraph 2, line 1.

20. **(B)** These laws stifle competition because retailers cannot compete on a price basis.

21. **(C)** See paragraph 1, line 1.

22. **(A)** See paragraph 2: "Congress, particularly the Senate, has been pressing the Administration to do more" to liberalize East-West trade.

23. **(D)** See paragraph 3: ". . . there is no question that in 1969 there was very sharp, very deep, and sometimes very bitter division. . . ."

24. **(A)** See paragraph 6: ". . . it asks only whether our national security is jeopardized. . . ."

25. **(C)** See paragraph 8, line 1.

26. **(A)** This is found in paragraph 7.

27. **(C)** The Defense Department (in paragraph 6) takes a dim view toward such trade expansion, while the Commerce Department favors it (in paragraphs 8 and 9).

28. **(A)** Both are in favor. See paragraph 9, line 1: ". . . both the Commerce and State Departments are in favor. . . ."

29. **(B)** See paragraph 8: ". . . if we in the United States do not authorize these transactions there is almost always comparable technology in other parts of the world," i.e., other nations will obtain this trade.

30. **(D)** See paragraph 9: "When there is any division . . . the case moves to the White House. . . ."

Section II Mathematics

31. **(B)** Let L be the original length and W the original width. The new length is 120% of L which is $(1.2)L$; the new width is 80% of W which is $(.8)W$. The area of a rectangle is length times width, so the original area is LW and the new area is $(1.2)(L)(.8)W$ or $(.96)LW$. Since the new area is 96% of the original area, the area has decreased by 4%.

32. **(C)** The progression is arithmetical; since $12 - 6 = 6$ and $18 - 12 = 6$, each term is 6 more than the previous term. Therefore, the term after 18 is $18 + 6$ which equals 24.

33. **(D)** The distance from New York to Hartford divided by the distance from New York to Boston is $\frac{120}{250}$ or .48, and $.48 = 48\%$.

34. **(B)** The amount broken off is $\frac{1}{8} + 1\frac{3}{4} + 1\frac{1}{12}$ inches. Since $\frac{1}{8} + 1\frac{3}{4} + 1\frac{1}{12} = \frac{3}{24} + \frac{42}{24} + \frac{26}{24} = \frac{71}{24}$ and the lead was 5 inches long to begin with, the amount left $= 5 - \frac{71}{24} = \frac{120}{24} - \frac{71}{24} = \frac{49}{24} = 2\frac{1}{24}$ inches.

35. **(C)** The solid bars denote change from the third to the fourth quarter of 1972. Business fixed investment increased by about $5 billion and Gross National Product increased by about $31 billion. Therefore, the ratio is 31 to 5 which is about 6 to 1.

36. **(C)** The striped bars denote change from the second to the third quarter of 1972. The category, consumer expenditures for services, extends the furthest to the right among the given categories so it increased the most.

37. **(A)** For all the categories cited, the solid bars extend to the right. Therefore, they all increased between the third and fourth quarters of 1972.

38. **(B)**

STATEMENT I is not true since federal government expenditures decreased (the striped bar extends to the left) between the second and third quarters of 1972.

STATEMENT II can't be inferred since only final expenditures increased more than $10 billion between the third and fourth quarters of 1972.

STATEMENT III is true. The striped bar (change from the second to the third quarter) is beyond $20 billion and the solid bar (change from the third to the fourth quarter) is beyond $25 billion. Therefore, the total change in Gross National Product from the second to the fourth quarter is greater than 20 + 25 or 45 billion dollars.

So only STATEMENT III can be inferred from the graph.

39. **(B)** Let x dollars be the amount he paid for the 1968 car; then he paid 120% of x or $(1.2)x$ for the 1969 car. Therefore, he paid a total of $x + (1.2)x$ or $(2.2)x$ for both cars. Since we know he paid a total of $4,400 for both cars, we have $(2.2)x = \$4{,}400$. Thus $x = \frac{\$4{,}400}{2.2} = \$2{,}000$; so he paid $2,000 for the 1968 car.

40. **(E)** The first 1,000 copies cost $1 each; so altogether they will cost $1,000. The remaining 3,800 copies (4,800 − 1,000) cost x dollars each; so their cost is $\$3{,}800x$. Therefore, the total cost of all 4,800 copies is $\$1{,}000 + \$3{,}800x$.

41. **(D)** Since the interior angles in a parallelogram on the same side are supplementary, $x + y = 180$. Therefore, $3y = 180$, $y = 60$, and $x = 120$.

42. **(A)** Since $1\frac{2}{3}$ hours is 100 minutes, 50 minutes is $\frac{1}{2}$ of $1\frac{2}{3}$ hours. Therefore, he should make half as much in 50 minutes as he does in $1\frac{2}{3}$ hours. Since he made 4 boxes in $1\frac{2}{3}$ hours, he makes 2 boxes in 50 minutes.

43. **(E)** Since $\frac{y}{x} = 2$, $y = 2x$. Therefore, $x + y = x + 2x = 3x$ which equals 3. So $3x = 3$, which means $x = 1$. Thus, $y = 2$ because $y = 2x$.

44. **(C)** 4.6% of the Gross National Product in 1950 was \$12 billion. Therefore, the Gross National Product in 1950 is $\frac{\$12 \text{ billion}}{.046} =$ \$260.9 billion. You can save time by using the fact that 4.6% is close to 5% which equals $\frac{1}{20}$; an estimate for the Gross National Product in 1950 is (\$12 billion) (20) or \$240 billion. Since the only answer near \$240 billion is \$260 billion, \$260 billion is the answer.

45. **(D)** $\frac{1}{20}$ is 5%. National health expenditures were greater than $\frac{1}{20}$ of the Gross National Product in 1960, 1965, 1970, and 1972.

46. **(E)** The amount spent on national health expenditures in 1950 was \$12 billion; in 1970, \$68.1 billion was spent. Since $(5\frac{2}{3})(12) = 68$, the amount increased by a factor of about $5\frac{2}{3}$ which is $566\frac{2}{3}\%$. Therefore, it increased by about 567%.

47. **(B)**

In both 1950 and 1955 the percentage was 4.6%, so the percentage did not increase. Therefore, STATEMENT I is not true.

$\frac{3}{40} = 7.5\%$, and since 7.6% of the Gross National Product was spent on national health expenditures in 1972, STATEMENT II is true.

The graph gives no information about 1969, so STATEMENT III cannot be inferred from the graph.

Therefore, only STATEMENT II can be inferred from the graph.

48. **(C)** In 1970, $\frac{1}{3}$ of national health expenditures was $\frac{1}{3}$ of \$68.1 billion, which is \$22.7 billion. If there were 20 million retired people in 1970, the per capita expenditure was $\frac{\$22.7 \text{ billion}}{20 \text{ million}}$ which equals \$1,135.

49. **(D)** Since there are 20 rolls in a carton and a carton costs \$9, each roll costs $\frac{1}{20}$ of \$9 which is 45¢. The roll sells for 50¢, so the selling price divided by the cost is $\frac{50}{45} = \frac{10}{9}$ which is about 111%. (or divide the total income by the total cost: $\frac{20 \times .50}{9} = \frac{10}{9} = 111\%$.)

50. **(C)** 12 copies of the history book weigh (12)(2.4) or 28.8 pounds. Since the total weight of the books is 42.8 pounds, the weight of the English books is 42.8 − 28.8 or 14 pounds. Therefore, each English book weighs $\frac{14}{8}$ or 1.75 pounds.

51. **(A)** Let x be the number of miles the car travels on a gallon of gas when driven at 60 miles an hour. Then 80% of 15 is x; so $\frac{4}{5} \cdot 15 = x$ and $x = 12$.

52. **(D)**

STATEMENT I cannot be inferred since if $x = 2$ and $y = 1$, then x and y are positive but x is not less than y.

STATEMENT II is true since $x + y = z$ and y is positive so $x < z$.

STATEMENT III is true. z is positive since it is the sum of two positive numbers and so $z < 2z$. Since we know $x < z$ and $z < 2z$, then $x < 2z$.

Therefore, only STATEMENTS II and III can be inferred.

53. **(E)** The volume of a cube is s^3 where s is the length of a side of the cube. So the cube with sides of length x has volume x^3, and a cube with sides of length 3 has volume $3^3 = 27$. Therefore, $\frac{x^3}{27}$ is the number of cubes with sides of length 3 which will fit into a cube with sides of length x.

54. **(A)** There were 300,000 discouraged workers in the "had looked but could not find job" category in 1971. All the other categories had less than 300,000.

55. (D) It is easier to use the percentages to find the ratio. Those discouraged by job market factors were 70.6% and those discouraged by personal factors were 29.5%. So the ratio is 70.6 to 29.5 which is about 70 to 30 or 7 to 3.

56. (D) The row "other personal handicap" has 36 in 1970 and 36 is the smallest entry in that row. Therefore, 1970 was the year in which the least number of workers were discouraged by other personal handicaps.

57. (C) In 1969 the percentage was 45.8 and it dropped to 31.5 in 1970. Therefore, it dropped 14.3% between 1969 and 1970; the change between any other two successive years shown on the graph was always less than 5%.

58. (A)

STATEMENT I can be inferred from the table since the percentage discouraged by job market factors was larger than 50% in each year while that for personal factors is less.

STATEMENT II cannot be inferred since the number of workers discouraged by personal factors increased from 201,000 in 1970 to 236,000 in 1971. (Don't read the percentages for STATEMENT II.)

STATEMENT III cannot be inferred since there is no data given about the age of the discouraged workers.

Therefore, only STATEMENT I can be inferred.

59. (A) The line graph has a minimum in 1969; it decreases from 1967 to 1969 and increases from 1969 to 1971.

60. (B) The first 800 sheets cost $800x$ ¢. The remaining 4,200 sheets cost $\frac{x}{15}$ ¢ apiece which comes to $(4{,}200)\left(\frac{x}{15}\right)$¢ or $280x$ ¢. Therefore, the total cost of the 5,000 sheets of paper is $800x$ ¢ + $280x$ ¢, which is $1{,}080x$ ¢.

61. (D) Let C be the cost of a ton of coal, and let G be the cost of a gallon of oil. Translating the statements into equations, we have

$$C + 500G = \$1{,}000$$
$$3C + 300G = \$1{,}200.$$

Subtract the second equation from three times the first equation and the result is $1{,}200\ G = \$1{,}800$. Therefore, $G = \$1.50$.

62. (D) The area of a circle is πr^2 where r is the radius of the circle. The diameter of a circle is $2r$; so if the diameter is doubled the radius is doubled. If the radius is doubled, then the square of the radius is quadrupled $[(2r)^2 = 4r^2]$. So the area of the circle is quadrupled.

63. (E) Let S denote the worker's salary in 1967. In 1968 he received 110% of S which is $(1.1)S$, and in 1969 he received 110% of $(1.1)S$ which is $(1.1)(1.1)S$ or $1.21\ S$. Therefore, he received 21% more in 1969 than he did in 1967.

64. (E) Since $3^2 = 9$, $(3^2)^3 = 9^3$ and $9^3 = 9 \times 9 \times 9 = 729$.

65. (D) The inventory-sales ratio was about 1.5 at the end of the third quarter of 1972; so inventory was about 1.5 of monthly sales and $1.5 = 1\frac{1}{2}$.

66. (A) A quick way to check whether or not a set of values is increasing arithmetically is to see whether the values lie on a straight line which rises from left to right. The first three quarters have values which almost lie on a rising straight line.

67. (A) The units are in terms of the annual rate, so just check the height of the lowest bar (*don't* multiply by 4). In the first quarter of 1972, the bar was just a little bit above an annual rate of 5 billion dollars.

68. (B)

STATEMENT I is false since in 1972 the line graph decreased while the bar graph increased.

STATEMENT II can be inferred. In 1969 all the bars are nearly the same height, and the change from quarter to quarter is the difference in the height of adjacent columns. In all the other years, there is much more of a difference between adjacent columns.

STATEMENT III is false since at the end of 1970, the line graph is higher (above 1.65) than it is at the end of 1971 (about 1.58).

Therefore, only STATEMENT II can be inferred from the graph.

69. **(E)** The inventory-sales ratio was about 1.5 in the third quarter of 1972. Therefore, if monthly sales were $50 billion in the third quarter of 1972, inventories were about (1.5)(50) or $75 billion during the third quarter of 1972.

70. **(B)** If two pairs of corresponding angles of the triangles are equal, then the third angles must be equal since the sum of the three angles of a triangle is 180°. Since all the pairs of corresponding angles are equal, the triangles are similar. Since there is no information about the sides or about the relation of the angles within a triangle, (A), (C), (D),and (E) are not necessarily true.

71. **(C)** Interest = (amount) (time) (annual rate). So the interest is ($1,000) ($1\frac{3}{4}$) (.08) or ($1,000) (.14) or $140.00. (Note that we translate the time into years since we are given the annual interest rate.)

72. **(D)** Factory A turns out $8a$ cars in 8 hours. Since factory B turns out b cars in 2 hours, it turns out $4b$ cars in 8 hours. Therefore, the total is $8a + 4b$.

73. **(A)** If the corresponding angles formed by a transversal with two lines are equal, then the lines are parallel.

74. **(D)** In 35 minutes John makes 7 boxes and Tim makes 5. The required ratio, 7 to 5, is constant no matter how long they work.

75. **(A)** 40% of the women who will receive a pension are in the under $5,000 category.

76. **(B)** There were 29,000 women reporting who received a private pension. 41% of these women had earnings under $5,000. Since (.41) (29,000) = 11,890, there are about 12,000 women receiving a private pension who reported earnings under $5,000.

77. **(D)** The median length of employment was 29 years for those men who will receive a private pension. 45% = 11% + 9% + 25% of the men reporting who will receive a private pension worked 30 or more years. Therefore, 45% worked longer than the median. 61,000 men will receive a private pension, so (.45) (61,000) = 27,450 of the men reporting worked longer than the median length of employment.

78. **(A)**

STATEMENT I is true. The men are divided into two categories, those receiving a pension and those who will receive a pension. In the first category 37% worked in manufacturing durable goods, and in the second category 30% worked in manufacturing durable goods, so at least 30% of the total manufactured durable goods; 30% is greater than $\frac{1}{4}$.

STATEMENT II cannot be inferred since we know only how many worked over 40 years; we have no data on how many worked over 45 years.

STATEMENT III is not true. Although a higher percentage of women than of men expect to receive a pension in the professional and technical category, there are more men reporting than women. In fact, there are (.16) (22,000) women; this is less than the (.10) (62,000) men in the category.

Therefore, we can infer only STATEMENT I.

79. **(C)** The total number of crates sold is $3\frac{1}{4} + 2\frac{1}{6} + 4\frac{1}{2} + 1\frac{2}{3}$ which is equal to $\frac{39}{12} + \frac{26}{12} + \frac{54}{12} + \frac{20}{12} = \frac{139}{12} = 11\frac{7}{12}$. A shorter method would be to add the integral parts of each of the numbers $3 + 2 + 4 + 1 = 10$. Next add the fractional parts $\frac{1}{4} + \frac{1}{6} + \frac{1}{2} + \frac{2}{3}$. Using 12 as a common denominator you get $\frac{(3 + 2 + 6 + 8)}{12}$ which is $\frac{19}{12} = 1\frac{7}{12}$. Therefore, the answer is $10 + 1\frac{7}{12} = 11\frac{7}{12}$.

80. **(A)** If $x + y$ exceeds 4 and x is less than 3, it is clear that y must exceed 1.

81. **(B)** Since 10 is $\frac{1}{5}$ of 50, the 10 apprentices should do $\frac{1}{5}$ as much work as 50 apprentices. 50 apprentices did the job in 4 hours, so in 1 hour 50 apprentices will do $\frac{1}{4}$ of the job.

Therefore, 10 apprentices should do $\frac{1}{5}$ of $\frac{1}{4} =$ $\frac{1}{20}$ of the job in an hour.

Since 15 is $\frac{1}{2}$ of 30, 15 journeymen will do half as much work as 30 journeymen. The 30 journeymen finished the job in $4\frac{1}{2}$ hours, so in 1 hour they will do $\frac{2}{9}$ of the job. Therefore, 15 journeymen will do $\frac{1}{2}$ of $\frac{2}{9} = \frac{1}{9}$ of the job in an hour.

So both groups will do $\frac{1}{20} + \frac{1}{9} = \frac{9}{180} + \frac{20}{180} =$ $\frac{29}{180}$ of the job in an hour.

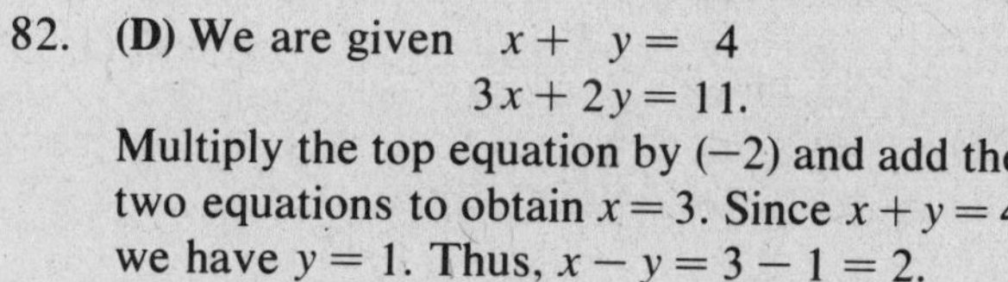

82. (D) We are given $x + y = 4$
$3x + 2y = 11.$
Multiply the top equation by (−2) and add the two equations to obtain $x = 3$. Since $x + y = 4$ we have $y = 1$. Thus, $x - y = 3 - 1 = 2$.

83. (D) The number is the sum of the geometric progression $a + ar + ar^2 + \ldots + ar^n$ with $a = 1$, $r = 3$, and $n = 9$. The sum of such a geometric progression is $\frac{a(1 - r^{n+1})}{1 - r}$, so the sum is

$$\frac{(1)(1 - 3^{9+1})}{1 - 3} = \frac{1 - 3^{10}}{1 - 3}.$$

OR

Let $S = 1 + 3 + 3^2 + \ldots + 3^9$
then $-3S = -3 - 3^2 - \ldots - 3^9 - 3^{10}$
and $(1 - 3)S = 1 - 3^{10}$,
with $S = \frac{1 - 3^{10}}{1 - 3}$.

84. (E) As indicated by the figure, the hexagon can be divided into 6 equilateral triangles with sides 6 inches long. The altitude of any of these triangles is $3\sqrt{3}$ inches long. So the area of each triangle is $(\frac{1}{2})(3\sqrt{3})(6)$ or $9\sqrt{3}$ square inches. Therefore, the area of the hexagon is $6 \cdot 9\sqrt{3}$ which equals $54\sqrt{3}$ square inches.

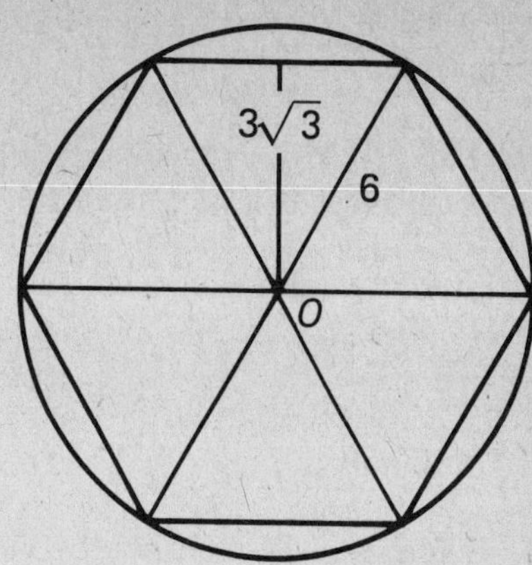

85. (B) 40% of the 52% of the population who are women are voters. So (.40) (.52) = .2080 = 20.8% of the population are women voters.

Section III Verbal Aptitude

86. (B) ABJURE: recant, revoke. *Antonym:* pledge

87. (C) MITIGATE: alleviate, abate. *Antonym:* intensify

88. (D) SPURIOUS: counterfeit, false. *Antonym:* authentic

89. (C) TORRID: hot, scorching. *Antonym:* cold

90. (E) CIRCUMSPECTION: watchfulness, caution. *Antonym:* recklessness

91. (B) DESULTORY: rambling, superficial. *Antonym:* methodical

92. (C) DISSONANCE: discord, lack of agreement. *Antonym:* harmony

93. (D) INCREDULOUS: skeptical, doubtful. *Antonym:* believing

94. (B) OBDURATE: callous, insensible. *Antonym:* tender

95. (A) UNGAINLY: clumsy, awkward. *Antonym:* graceful

96. **(B)** DISCERN: observe, perceive. *Antonym:* overlook

97. **(B)** CONVIVIAL: sociable, hospitable. *Antonym:* unsociable

98. **(A)** ALACRITY: willingness, quickness. *Antonym:* slowness

99. **(C)** PERFIDIOUS: faithless, insidious. *Antonym:* faithful

100. **(D)** A slide rule is a kind of computer. A sundial is a kind of clock.

101. **(E)** A battery powers a flashlight. Coal powers a furnace.

102. **(A)** A muff covers the hands. A helmet covers the head.

103. **(C)** Both are hobbyists. A philatelist collects stamps. A numismatist collects medals. Note that a government (E) collects taxes, but not as a hobby!

104. **(B)** A tranquilizer makes one placid. A sedative makes one somnolent.

105. **(A)** Maturity is the opposite of infancy. Culmination is the opposite of inception.

106. **(E)** Floriculture is the raising of flowers. Arboriculture is the raising of trees.

107. **(D)** An aviary is a bird haven or large cage. An aquarium is a fish tank or tanks.

108. **(B)** Muslin is a plain cloth. Brocade is an ornate cloth.

109. **(A)** An epilogue is at the end of a discourse. A coda is a final passage of a music piece.

110. **(E)** A pilot has responsibility for running a plane. A manager is responsible for running a store.

111. **(B)** A decade is a tenth part of a century. A decimeter is a tenth part of a meter.

112. **(A)** A model is a framework of reality or a real situation. A blueprint is a model of a house.

113. **(B)** Risks necessarily go along with competition.

114. **(C)** The word criticized implies a negative such as wasteful. Neither businessmen nor producers are apt to be critical as they continue to use advertising.

115. **(C)** Predispositions, or inclinations.

116. **(C)** Economists and marketers are interested in determining the effect that advertising has on sales.

117. **(C)** A winner can gain a victory without a mandate, interpreted as a majority of all the voters. The other alternatives have little or no meaning in context.

118. **(D)** Caveat Emptor, Latin for let the buyer beware.

119. **(C)** Emolument means a salary.

120. **(A)** Still standing; existing.

121. **(C)** malingerer means someone who shirks work.

122. **(D)** contains the best *meaning*.

123. **(C)** Alternatives (A), (B), and (E) have no meaning in context; a referee would not postpone a scheduled fight owing to the participants' ineptness, but he might stop the fight if the participants' behavior was unwarranted, e.g., fighting in an unsportsmanlike manner.

124. **(B)** has the most *meaning*.

125. **(C)** Alternatives (A), (B), (D), and (E) are illogical.

Section IV Data Sufficiency

126. **(D)** (1) alone is sufficient, since if two sides of a triangle are equal, the angles opposite the equal sides are equal. Since $AB = BC$ then $x = y$, so $x = 40$. (2) alone is sufficient

since the sum of the angles of a triangle is 180°. Therefore, if $z=100$ and $y=40$, x must equal $180-100-40=40$. Therefore, each statement alone is sufficient.

127. **(C)** (1) tells us the area of the circle is $\pi 4^2 = 16\pi$. Since there are 360° in the whole circle, (2) tells us that the shaded area is $^{60}/_{360}$ or $^1/_6$ of the area of the circle. Thus, using both (1) and (2), we can answer the question, but since we need both the radius of the circle and the value of x, neither of them alone is sufficient. Therefore, the answer is (C).

128. **(E)** Using (1) we can find the income for 1970 if we know the income for 1968 and 1969, but (1) gives no more information about the inçome for 1968 and 1969. If we also use (2) we can get the income in 1969 if we know the income for 1968, but we still can't determine the income for 1968. Therefore, both together are not sufficient.

129. **(D)** Since a straight line forms an angle of 180° and l' is a straight line, we know $x+y=180$. If we use (1) we get $y=80$, so (1) alone is sufficient. When two straight lines intersect, the vertical angles are equal. So $y=z$; thus if we use (2) we have that $y=80$. Therefore, (2) alone is sufficient. Thus, each statement alone is sufficient.

130. **(C)** In the figure, x denotes the number taking German I but not English I, and y the number taking English I but not German I. From (1) we know that $x+16+y=50$; from (2), $x=y$. Neither statement alone can be solved for x, but both together are sufficient (and yield $x=17$).

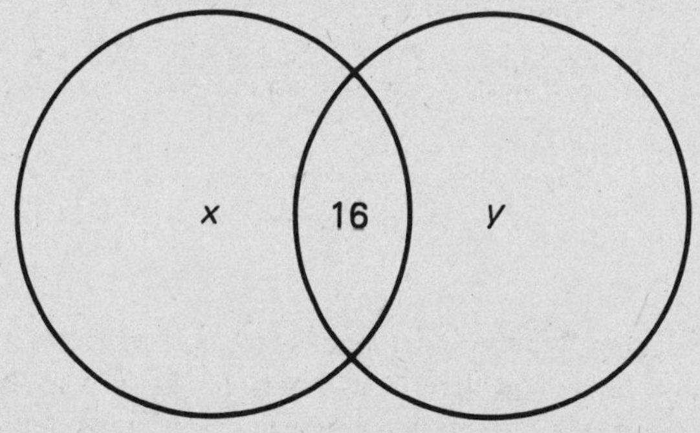

131. **(E)** (1) alone is not sufficient because it only says two sides are equal; in a square all four sides are equal. Even if we use (2) we don't know if $ABCD$ is a square since *all* angles have to be right angles in a square. Therefore, both statements together are insufficient.

132. **(B)** The average yearly wage per employee is the total amount of wages divided by the number of employees. So (2) alone is sufficient since it gives the total amount of wages and we are given the number of employees. (1) alone is not sufficient, since (1) by itself does not tell us the total wages. Therefore, the answer is (B).

133. **(E)** Since the square of any nonzero number is positive, (1) says $x+y \neq 0$ or $x \neq -y$. So (1) alone is not sufficient. If we also assume (2), we know only that x is positive and unequal to $-y$, not whether x is greater than or less than y. Thus (1) and (2) together are insufficient.

134. **(A)** Since the circles both have radius 4, the figure $OBO'C$ is a rhombus (each side is a radius) and the diagonals BC and OO' (of a rhombus) are perpendicular. So (2) does not give any new information, and is thus not sufficient alone. (1) alone is sufficient. The area of each circle is 16π since the radius of each circle is 4. If there were no shaded area, the area enclosed by both circles would be $16\pi + 16\pi = 32\pi$. Since the area enclosed by both circles is 29π, the shaded area is $32\pi - 29\pi$ or 3π. So (1) alone is sufficient but (2) alone is insufficient.

135. **(A)** Let x be the time it takes to travel from A to B and let y be the time it takes to travel from B to A. We know $x+y=4$. (1) says x is 125% of y or $x = {}^5/_4 y$. So using (1) we have $x + {}^5/_4 x = 4$ which we can solve for x. Thus, (1) alone is sufficient. (2) alone is not sufficient since we need information about the relation of x to y to solve the problem and (2) says nothing about the relation between x and y. Therefore, (1) alone is sufficient but (2) alone is insufficient.

136. **(C)** (1) alone is insufficient. If x and y were right angles,(1) would imply that l and l' are

parallel, but if x and y are not right angles, (1) would imply that l and l' are not parallel. (2) alone is not sufficient since it gives information only about l' and says nothing about the relation of l and l'. (1) and (2) together give $x = z$ which means that l and l' are parallel. Therefore, (1) and (2) together are sufficient but neither alone is sufficient.

137. **(E)** If we use (1), we have $x + y + z = 3 + z$, but we have no information about z, so (1) alone is insufficient. If we use (2) alone, we have $x + y + z = y + 2$, but since we have no information about y, (2) alone is insufficient. If we use both (1) and (2), we obtain $x + y + z = y + 2 = 3 + z$. We can also add (1) and (2) to obtain $2x + y + z = 5$, but we can't find the value of $x + y + z$ without more information. So the answer is (E).

138. **(C)** We need to know the surface area of the box. Since each side is a rectangle, we know the surface area will be $2LW + 2LH + 2HW$ where H is the height of the box, L is the length, and W is the width. We are given that $L = 7$, so to answer the question we need H and W. Since (1) gives only the value of W and (2) gives only the value of H, neither alone is sufficient. But both (1) and (2) together are sufficient.

139. **(E)** The profit is the selling price minus the cost, so to answer the question we need to know both the selling price and the cost of 15 boxes of detergent. Since (1) and (2) give information only about the cost but no information about the selling price, both statements together are insufficient.

140. **(E)** (1) alone is not sufficient. A four-sided figure can have both larger perimeter and smaller area than another four-sided figure, or it could have larger perimeter and larger area. (2) alone is also insufficient since the length of one diagonal does not determine the area of a four-sided figure. (1) and (2) together are also insufficient, as shown by the figure.

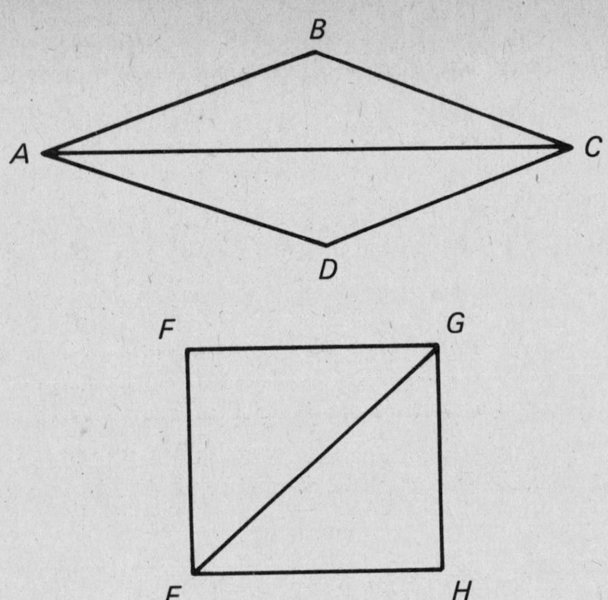

(1) and (2) are both satisfied and the area of $EFGH$ is larger than $ABCD$. But (1) and (2) could still be satisfied and the area of $ABCD$ be larger than the area of $EFGH$; so the answer is (E).

Section V Business Judgment

141. **(A)** Expanding sales to the U.S. is the objective of Zaire's textile executives.

142. **(C)** Confidence in Zaire's inventiveness, while potentially beneficial, was a minor factor in the executive's immediate search for ways to penetrate the American market.

143. **(E)** That American companies might invest in Zaire was of no immediate concern to the textile executives, although conceivably it might benefit them in the future.

144. **(E)** That Zaire is an African country had no influence on the decision or the decision makers.

145. **(D)** The consequences of and probability that restrictive legislation might be passed by the American Congress was considered

by Mr. Hesh and the textile executives. The assumption seemed to be that such legislation would pass.

146. **(B)** The only one of the three mentioned in the passage was III.

147. **(B)** Zaire industry had progressed from the manufacture of simple items to sophisticated goods. See paragraph 2.

148. **(D)** Both clothing and fashion design. See paragraph 3.

149. **(A)** Only textiles. See paragraph 5.

150. **(A)** The question states "might" sell, i.e., it is a conditional possibility. Zaire industry has *already* successfully sold translations and pre-fabricated diners to the United States.

151. **(B)** The establishment of a new supermarket chain in the R & S market area and its use of grade labeling was a major factor considered by Joseph in his decision to adopt (or not) the practice.

152. **(C)** The fact that the government's program would standardize grading was a minor factor related to the consideration of whether or not to adopt the practice.

153. **(B)** Grade labeling was a major factor considered by R & S in determining the consequences of their adoption on the future sale of their products.

154. **(B)** Federal food standards were also a major factor in the decision.

155. **(A)** In deciding whether to adopt grade labeling, Mr. Joseph's major consideration was what effect it would have on consumer acceptance of his products. Since R & S already enjoyed a high reputation, Joseph did not want to take any action that would jeopardize it.

156. **(B)** See the last paragraph. It is clear that grade labeling was intended to help the consumer identify brands by level of quality.

157. **(A)** R & S management felt that it enjoyed a good reputation as canners of high quality canned fruits and vegetables. Already having this favorable brand image, there was little reason to adopt grade labeling.

158. **(E)** All three. See the third paragraph.

159. **(B)** The Department of Agriculture. See paragraph 5.

160. **(D)** Taste was not a consideration in the Department of Agriculture's labeling procedure. See paragraph 5.

Section VI Mathematics

161. **(C)** $\frac{15}{16} = .9375$ which is 93.75%.

162. **(B)** Worker F loads $\frac{1}{15}$ of the truck in a minute and worker S loads $\frac{1}{20}$ of the truck in a minute. Therefore, working together they load $\frac{1}{15} + \frac{1}{20} = \frac{7}{60}$ of the truck in a minute. So it will take them $\frac{60}{7} = 8\frac{4}{7}$ minutes to load the truck.

163. **(D)** Since the car accelerates its speed 5 mph, at the end of each hour it will be traveling 5 mph faster than it was at the beginning of the hour. The car was traveling 50 mph to begin with so it has to be traveling 15 mph faster to go 65 mph. Therefore, it will take $\frac{15}{5} = 3$ hours to reach a speed of 65 mph.

164. **(D)** Since 75 cars an hour is $50\% = \frac{1}{2}$ of its capacity, the Tarrytown factory will produce $75 \times 2 = 150$ cars an hour at full capacity. 100 cars an hour is $80\% = \frac{4}{5}$ of the capacity of the Mahwah factory, so at full

capacity it will produce $100 \times \frac{5}{4} = 125$ cars an hour. Therefore, the Tarrytown production at full capacity divided by the Mahwah production at full capacity is $\frac{150}{125} = \frac{6}{5}$ or a ratio of 6 to 5.

165. **(C)** The average is the sum of the 5 integers divided by 5. Since the average is 7, the sum of the 5 integers is $5 \times 7 = 35$.

166. **(B)** The solid black line which represents income from employment per head in the United Kingdom is the only line which never drops below 5%. Therefore, it is the only indicator which has increased by at least 5% every year.

167. **(E)** When income from employment per head in the United States was 100 in 1963, it was about 146 at the beginning of 1971. If it was 250 in 1963 and x at the beginning of 1971, then $\frac{146}{100} = \frac{x}{250}$ so $x = 365$.

168. **(D)** The difference between the solid black line (income from employment) and the solid red line (labor cost per unit of gross value) in the United States was about 8 in 1965. By 1971 it was more than 20 but less than 30. Therefore, it more than doubled, but it did not quadruple.

169. **(D)**

STATEMENT I cannot be inferred since the graphs only compare the later values in the U.S. to earlier values in the U.S. There is no information which compares the value of any of the indicators in the U.S. and U.K. (For example, if the value of income from employment per head in 1963 was twice as high in the U.S. as in the U.K., then the value would still be higher in the U.S. in 1971 although it increased at a higher *rate* between 1963 and 1971 in the U.K.)

STATEMENT II can be inferred since in 1963 *all* indicators were at 100 and only income from employment per head in the U.K. had gone over 160 by 1971.

STATEMENT III can be inferred since $\frac{6}{5}$ of $100 = 120$ and the black dotted line never went over 120 in 1970.

Therefore, only STATEMENTS II and III can be inferred from the graph.

170. **(B)** After the 20% discount, the price of the car is 80%, which is .8 of \$3,000, or \$2,400. If the price is now raised by 10%, then the price is raised by .1 of \$2,400, or \$240. Therefore, the final price is \$2,400 + \$240 = \$2,640.

171. **(D)** The tax on a gross income of \$10,000 is \$2,000. Since $\frac{2{,}000}{10{,}000} = .2 = 20\%$, the rate of taxation is 20%.

172. **(C)** The tax on \$20,000 is \$7,200 and the tax on \$10,000 is 2,000. Therefore, he will pay \$7,200 − \$2,000 or \$5,200 tax on the extra \$10,000.

173. **(C)** Each person with an income of \$10,000 pays \$2,000 in taxes, so together they pay \$4,000 in taxes. The tax on \$20,000 is \$7,200, so the fraction is $\frac{\$4{,}000}{\$7{,}200} = \frac{40}{72} = \frac{10}{18} = \frac{5}{9}$.

174. **(E)** Working together both pumps pump $(u + v)$ cubic feet of water per minute, so it will take $\frac{50}{u + v}$ minutes to pump 50 cubic feet of water.

175. **(D)** A trapezoid can be divided into 2 triangles by connecting any two opposite vertices, so the sum of the interior angles is 360°. Since $2 + 4 + 5 + 7 = 18$ and $\frac{360}{18} = 20$, the angles are 40°, 80°, 100°, and 140°. Therefore, the smallest angle is 40°.

176. **(E)** $\frac{9/7}{5/6}$ is equal to $\frac{9}{7} \times \frac{6}{5} = \frac{54}{35}$.

177. **(C)** Since the largest percentage is 74%, and the largest amount spent is by the 19 to 64 age group, the amount spent by the 19 to 64 age group from private sources is larger than the amount spent in any of the other categories.

178. **(B)** \$19.8 billion is spent on health care for those 65 and over, and 66% of that comes from public sources. The table tells us that for people 65 and over, 80.8% of the public sources are federal funds. So (.66) (.808) (19.8) billion is spent from federal funds on health care for those 65 and over. To save time notice that .66 is about $\frac{2}{3}$ and .808 is about $\frac{4}{5}$, so the answer is about $\frac{2}{3} \times \frac{4}{5} \times$ (19.8 billion) which is $\frac{8 \times 6.6}{5}$ billion $= \frac{52.8}{5} =$ \$10.56 billion.

179. **(B)** 26% is about $\frac{1}{4}$, so about $\frac{1}{4}$ of the \$40.7 billion of the 19 to 64 group comes from public funds. This is about \$10.2 billion. 66% is about $\frac{2}{3}$, so about $\frac{2}{3}$ of the \$19.8 billion of the 65 and over group comes from public sources. Therefore, about \$13.2 billion comes from public sources, so the ratio is $\frac{10.2}{13.2}$, or about $\frac{3}{4}$.

180. **(E)**

The total expenditure for health care is (11.5 + 40.7 + 19.8) billion = \$72 billion. \$11.5 billion was spent for the under 19 group. Since 11.5 is more than $\frac{1}{7}$ of 72, STATEMENT I is true.
STATEMENT II is true since 72% of 11.5 is more than 34% of 19.8.

STATEMENT III is also true. The under 19 group gets 42.1% of 28% of 11.5 billion from state and local funds, the 19 to 64 group gets 19.2% of 66% of 19.8 billion from state and local groups, and the 65 and over group gets 19.2% of 6% of 19.8 billion from state and local group. It is obvious that the under 19 groups gets less than the 19 to 64 group. Since $\frac{1}{2}$ of $\frac{1}{4}$ of 40.7 is much larger than $\frac{1}{5}$ of $\frac{2}{3}$ of 20, we can see that the 19 to 64 group gets the most from state and local funds.

Therefore, STATEMENTS I, II, and III all can be inferred.

181. **(D)** Imports from non-EEC countries are denoted by the striped area which is the *difference* between the two lines. This difference was the largest in V (the fifth month) of 1971 when total imports were about 1350 and imports from the EEC were about 600. So the maximum was about 1350 − 600 or 750.

182. **(B)** Since the striped area represents about one half the total import area of the graph, the answer is $\frac{1}{2}$.

183. **(B)** Since 5 of the workers earned \$180 each, those 5 workers earned a total of \$900. The total for all 15 workers was \$1,800, so the remaining 10 workers earned a total of \$1,800 − \$900 = \$900. Therefore, the average weekly wage of the 10 remaining workers is $\frac{1}{10}$ of \$900 which is \$90.

184. **(C)** Using the Pythagorean theorem, we can determine that the square of the length of the side opposite the right angle is equal to $5^2 + 12^2$ which equals 169. Since the square root of 169 is 13, the side has length 13.

185. **(C)** Since $2\frac{1}{2}$ hours is equal to 150 minutes, you must look in the column with time equal to 150. $2\frac{1}{2}$ hours after it started, the car was traveling at 65 mph.

186. **(B)** At the end of 2 hours (120 minutes) the speed was 67.5 mph and at the end of 3 hours (180 minutes) the speed of the car was 60 mph. Therefore, the speed decreased by 7.5 mph during the last hour of the 3-hour period shown on the table.

187. **(A)**

STATEMENT I cannot be inferred since we need to know how far the car traveled in the three hours to find its average speed.

STATEMENT II is true because at the beginning of the fifth half hour (120 minutes) the car was going 67.5 mph but at the end of the fifth half hour (150 minutes) the car was going 65 mph. Since 65 mph is slower than 67.5 mph, the car must have slowed down during the fifth half hour.

STATEMENT III cannot be inferred because the table only gives the speed of the car at certain times during the 3 hours. The car may have started out going 0 miles per hour.

Therefore, only STATEMENT II can be inferred from the table.

188. **(E)** Since John makes 4 baskets in 1 hour, he will make 8 in 2 hours. Since Allison makes 6 baskets in 1 hr. 10 min. $\left(\frac{7}{6}\text{ of an hour}\right)$, she makes 1 basket in $\frac{7}{36}$ of an hour, and she will make $\frac{2}{7/36} = 2 \times \frac{36}{7} = \frac{72}{7} = 10\frac{2}{7}$ in 2 hours. Therefore, together they will make $18\frac{2}{7}$ baskets in 2 hours.

189. **(D)** The average of the four integers is $\frac{1}{4}$ of 26 which is $6\frac{1}{2}$, so the integers should include 6 and 7. If you add 5, 6, 7, and 8, the result is 26, so the four integers are 5, 6, 7, and 8. The product of $5 \times 6 \times 7 \times 8 = 30 \times 56 = 1{,}680$.

190. **(A)** Factor $x^2 + 3x - 4$ into $(x - 1)(x + 4)$. $x^2 + 3x - 4$ is equal to 0 only if $x - 1$ or $x + 4$ is equal to 0. Therefore, $x^2 + 3x - 4 = 0$ only when $x = 1$ or $x = -4$.

191. **(B)** The solid line denoting presidential votes was just below the 50 million mark in 1948.

192. **(C)** About 50 million of the 80 million citizens 21 years old or over voted for president in 1940. Therefore, the proportion is about $\frac{50 \text{ million}}{80 \text{ million}}$ which is $\frac{5}{8}$.

193. **(C)** Between 1931 and 1951 the only election in which the dotted line (representatives) was below 30 was in 1942.

194. **(A)** Since $x + y = 2$, this implies that $x = 2 - y$. If $y > 3$, then $2 - y$ is < -1, so $x < -1$.

195. **(D)** $\frac{5/2}{3/4} = \frac{5}{2} \times \frac{4}{3} = \frac{10}{3}$, so $\frac{2}{3}$ of $\frac{10}{3}$ is $\frac{2}{3} \times \frac{10}{3} = \frac{20}{9}$.

Evaluating Your Score

Tabulate your score for each section of Sample Test 1 according to the directions on pages 3–4 and record the results in the Self-scoring Table below. Then find your rank for each score on the Self-scoring Scale and record it in the appropriate blank.

Self-scoring Table

PART	SCORE	RANK
1		
2		
3		
4		
5		
6		

Self-scoring Scale

ACHIEVEMENT

PART	POOR	FAIR	GOOD	EXCELLENT
1	0–15	16–21	22–25	26–30
2	0–29	30–40	41–47	48–55
3	0–20	21–28	29–34	35–40
4	0–7	8–10	11–12	13–15
5	0–10	11–14	15–16	17–20
6	0–18	19–25	26–30	31–35

Study again the Review sections covering material in Sample Test 1 for which you had a rank of FAIR or POOR. Then go on to Sample Test 2.

Answer Sheet – Sample Test 2

Section I — Reading Recall

1. A B C D E
2. A B C D E
3. A B C D E
4. A B C D E
5. A B C D E
6. A B C D E
7. A B C D E
8. A B C D E
9. A B C D E
10. A B C D E
11. A B C D E
12. A B C D E
13. A B C D E
14. A B C D E
15. A B C D E
16. A B C D E
17. A B C D E
18. A B C D E
19. A B C D E
20. A B C D E
21. A B C D E
22. A B C D E
23. A B C D E
24. A B C D E
25. A B C D E
26. A B C D E
27. A B C D E
28. A B C D E
29. A B C D E
30. A B C D E

Section II — Mathematics

31. A B C D E
32. A B C D E
33. A B C D E
34. A B C D E
35. A B C D E
36. A B C D E
37. A B C D E
38. A B C D E
39. A B C D E
40. A B C D E
41. A B C D E
42. A B C D E
43. A B C D E
44. A B C D E
45. A B C D E
46. A B C D E
47. A B C D E
48. A B C D E
49. A B C D E
50. A B C D E
51. A B C D E
52. A B C D E
53. A B C D E
54. A B C D E
55. A B C D E
56. A B C D E
57. A B C D E
58. A B C D E
59. A B C D E
60. A B C D E
61. A B C D E
62. A B C D E
63. A B C D E
64. A B C D E
65. A B C D E
66. A B C D E
67. A B C D E
68. A B C D E
69. A B C D E
70. A B C D E
71. A B C D E
72. A B C D E
73. A B C D E
74. A B C D E
75. A B C D E
76. A B C D E
77. A B C D E
78. A B C D E
79. A B C D E
80. A B C D E
81. A B C D E
82. A B C D E
83. A B C D E
84. A B C D E
85. A B C D E

Section III — Verbal Aptitude

86. A B C D E
87. A B C D E
88. A B C D E
89. A B C D E
90. A B C D E
91. A B C D E
92. A B C D E
93. A B C D E
94. A B C D E
95. A B C D E
96. A B C D E
97. A B C D E
98. A B C D E
99. A B C D E
100. A B C D E
101. A B C D E
102. A B C D E
103. A B C D E
104. A B C D E
105. A B C D E
106. A B C D E
107. A B C D E
108. A B C D E
109. A B C D E
110. A B C D E
111. A B C D E
112. A B C D E
113. A B C D E
114. A B C D E
115. A B C D E
116. A B C D E
117. A B C D E
118. A B C D E
119. A B C D E
120. A B C D E
121. A B C D E
122. A B C D E
123. A B C D E
124. A B C D E
125. A B C D E

Section IV — Data Sufficiency

126. A B C D E
127. A B C D E
128. A B C D E
129. A B C D E
130. A B C D E
131. A B C D E
132. A B C D E
133. A B C D E
134. A B C D E
135. A B C D E
136. A B C D E
137. A B C D E
138. A B C D E
139. A B C D E
140. A B C D E

Section V — Business Judgment

141. A B C D E
142. A B C D E
143. A B C D E
144. A B C D E
145. A B C D E
146. A B C D E
147. A B C D E
148. A B C D E
149. A B C D E
150. A B C D E
151. A B C D E
152. A B C D E
153. A B C D E
154. A B C D E
155. A B C D E
156. A B C D E
157. A B C D E
158. A B C D E
159. A B C D E
160. A B C D E

Section VI — Mathematics

161. A B C D E
162. A B C D E
163. A B C D E
164. A B C D E
165. A B C D E
166. A B C D E
167. A B C D E
168. A B C D E
169. A B C D E
170. A B C D E
171. A B C D E
172. A B C D E
173. A B C D E
174. A B C D E
175. A B C D E
176. A B C D E
177. A B C D E
178. A B C D E
179. A B C D E
180. A B C D E
181. A B C D E
182. A B C D E
183. A B C D E
184. A B C D E
185. A B C D E
186. A B C D E
187. A B C D E
188. A B C D E
189. A B C D E
190. A B C D E
191. A B C D E
192. A B C D E
193. A B C D E
194. A B C D E
195. A B C D E

Sample Test 2

Section I Reading Recall

TOTAL TIME: 35 minutes

Part A: TIME—15 minutes

DIRECTIONS: This part contains three reading passages. You are to read each one carefully. You will have fifteen minutes to study the three passages and twenty minutes to answer questions based on them. When answering the questions, you will *not* be allowed to refer back to the passages.

Passage 1:

Viewed in historical perspective, the multinational corporation has demonstrated surprising vitality and flexibility in adjusting to economic and political changes. It has, in fact, demonstrated not only great tenacity in surviving but also an ability to expand, even when governments have attempted to suppress its growth.

In the United States, multinational corporations go back to the 1850's. They grew rapidly, and by 1900 about one-half of the then-existing 50 largest corporations had significant overseas operating interests, including manufacturing and distribution outlets. This growth continued through the 1920's but it slackened in the 1930's as a result of the world-wide depression. The new element that emerged during the 1940's was not the concept of the multinational enterprise, with its perception of a common corporate strategy, but the capability of having the management of that strategy take place at a common nerve center based on a flow of common information.

Until the 1930's, most countries paid little attention to the capacity of multinational corporations for moving across international boundaries; except for purposes of trade, no reasons existed for imposing restrictions at their boundaries. By the mid 1930's, however, Lord Keynes had demonstrated that it was possible to pursue maximum income and full employment objectives within national boundaries. As nations began to articulate national goals and priorities, they were confronted by entities that could move across boundaries, institute policies, and undertake activities which could frustrate these efforts. Governments discovered that international corporations by their activities abroad had demonstrated the porosity of such boundaries.

This apparent conflict between the multinational corporation with its supranational point of view and the nation-state with its national economic concerns and special interest groups has given rise to a host of economic and political problems. These must be resolved if the potential inherent in multinational enterprise is to be utilized for promoting world welfare. For both its adherents and opponents acknowledge that the multinational corporation is here to stay and will probably grow in the future. What is at issue at this juncture is the degree of freedom that should be allowed or the nature and extent of regulation that should be imposed on its present operations and future growth in order to make it better serve often divergent national interests.

In the last 15 years two events have focused public attention here and abroad on the activities of U.S. multinational corporations. One was the massive influx of American capital into Europe, especially into the Common Market countries. This investment produced an economic revolution in management and technology; stimulated a massive upsurge in income, employment and trade; and resulted in a vast improvement in living standards. As a direct consequence, the EEC countries became potent competitors of the United States in our own as well as in foreign markets within relatively few years.

The impact of this movement has been dramatically portrayed by the French journalist-politician Servan-Schreiber in his book *The American Challenge*. While accurately depicting the relative backwardness and inefficiencies of European entrepreneurs which he felt could be overcome by emulating American managerial techniques, he laid excessive emphasis on the extent to which U.S. multinational companies were buying into European industry. American firms were thus acquiring dominant control over the high technology sectors of the European economy on which it depended for future growth. He neglected, however, to counterbalance these observations with the benefits conferred on European industry through the influx of highly efficient U.S. management and technology which went far toward closing the managerial and technology gaps and enhancing the competitive position of European industry. As *Fortune* noted recently, Servan-Schreiber appeared to miss the main point which is that not only U.S. business but business *everywhere* is outgrowing national boundaries; an economic infrastructure is evolving which is laying the basis for a world economic and political community.

The second event was the persistent deficit in the U.S. balance of payments during much of the past two decades. This was a deliberate U.S. policy during the early 1950's to promote European recovery from the Second World War. It permitted trade discrimination against the United States to allow the building of export markets and to bring about a more equitable distribution of the world's monetary reserves. The persistence of this deficit after 1960, however, led to rising concern in the United States and abroad. For these deficits led to massive outflows of gold, a large accumulation of short-term claims on the United States held mainly by Europe and Japan and, in 1971, the appearance of a series of monthly deficits in our merchandise trade accounts for the first time since 1893.

Passage 2:

Indian management is undergoing a process of change, both intellectually and operationally. This change is partly indigenous inasmuch as it pertains to the changing cultural and political orientation of the people, and it is partly foreign inasmuch as the economy of the country shows a *basic* direction towards the utilization of foreign techniques and concepts of business in achieving the desired growth pattern. The dual nature of change which is characterizing the modern managerial behavior in India is a significant example of "cultural fusion" and "international integration." Judged in this manner, the identity of Indian management appears to be primarily eclectic in nature and essentially adaptive in substance.

The discipline of comparative management provides the framework for comparing managerial systems through several variables and models. It enables the analyst to compare (and contrast) the history and practice of administration in two separate regions, hypothesizing about the similarities and divergences. This is an interesting and novel aid for the manager, as it permits him to see his performance in a comparative setting and cross-cultural perspective. However, in the history and practice of Indian management, the effectiveness of this research methodology is questionable, at least in the immediate time span. The processes of transition and fusion through which management is currently passing in India preclude the possibility of effective utilization of the research and conceptual models based upon the assumptions and hypotheses derived from the discipline of comparative management. Management is in a state of great flux in India, addressing itself in a number of different *directions* simultaneously, and also molding itself according to a number of different structures at the same time. All the four sectors, namely, the Public, Private, Family and Foreign—functioning in the Indian context—have not organized their contents and actions in a rigid fashion with the result that they are malleable and supple enough to experiment with practically anything. Various new innovations and experiments that are being made by Indian industry and the Government are signs of this fluid state of behavior in the body of Indian management. Unless this flexibility is transformed into something positively identifiable, it would be futile to apply comparative techniques for the study of Indian managerial processes.

Another reason for the present inadequacy of the comparative framework for the analysis of Indian management is the existence of various "norms" of managerial behavior functioning simultaneously in the same areas, and also reflecting in the actions of the same executives on different occasions. When there is such a great degree of diversity both in management's actions and patterns, what will the comparative management analyst accept as being the "normal" managerial action and reaction in India, for the purposes of comparing them with the "norms" in other countries and cultures? The diversities in income, population mix, and living habits, in addition to the more fundamental items such as the language, religion, caste, and educational level lead to the existence of differing, and at times mutually contradictory, behavior patterns and managerial actions in the Indian business scene. It has also been noted that the Indian manager is capable of exercising his decision-making in a number of different time-periods simultaneously. These considerations suggest the solid existence of quite a few different managerial patterns in India. It is therefore impossible to isolate any single one from them as being typically representative of the Indian administrative practice.

Passage 3:

The first and decisive step in the expansion of Europe overseas was the conquest of the Atlantic Ocean. That the nation to achieve this should be Portugal was the logical outcome of her geographical position and her history. Placed on the extreme margin of the old, classical Mediterranean world and facing the untraversed ocean, Portugal could adapt and develop the knowledge and experience of the past to meet the challenge of the unknown. Some centuries of navigating the coastal waters of Western Europe and Northern Africa had prepared Portuguese seamen to appreciate the problems which the Ocean presented and to apply and develop the methods necessary to overcome them. From the seamen of the Mediterranean, particularly those of Genoa and Venice, they had learned the organization and conduct of a mercantile marine, and from Jewish astronomers and Catalan mapmakers the rudiments of navigation. Largely excluded from a share in Mediterranean commerce at a time when her increasing and vigorous population was making heavy demands on her resources, Portugal turned southwards and westwards for opportunities of trade and commerce. At this moment of national destiny it was fortunate for her that in men of the calibre of Prince Henry, known as the Navigator, and King John II she found resolute and dedicated leaders.

The problems to be faced were new and complex. The conditions for navigation and commerce in the Mediterranean were relatively simple, compared with those in the western seas. The landlocked Mediterranean, tideless and with a climatic regime of regular and well-defined seasons, presented few obstacles to sailors who were the heirs of a great body of sea lore garnered from the experiences of many centuries. What hazards there were, in the form of sudden storms or dangerous coasts, were known and could be usually anticipated. Similarly the Mediterranean coasts, though they might be for long periods in the hands of dangerous rivals, were described in sailing directions or laid down on the portolan charts drawn by Venetian, Genoese and Catalan cartographers. Problems of determining positions at sea, which confronted the Portuguese, did not arise. Though the Mediterranean seamen by no means restricted themselves to coastal sailing, the latitudinal extent of the Mediterranean was not great, and voyages could be conducted from point to point on compass bearings; the ships were never so far from land as to make it necessary to fix their positions in latitude by astronomical observations. Having made a landfall on a bearing, they could determine their precise position from prominent landmarks, soundings or the nature of the sea bed, after reference to the sailing directions or charts.

By contrast, the pioneers of ocean navigation faced much greater difficulties. The western ocean which extended, according to the speculations of the cosmographers, through many degrees of latitude and longitude, was an unknown quantity, but certainly subjected to wide variations of weather and without known bounds. Those who first ventured out over its waters did so without benefit of sailing directions or traditional lore. As the Portuguese sailed southwards, they left behind them the familiar constellations in the heavens by which they could determine direction and the hours of the night, and particularly the pole-star from which by a simple operation they could determine their latitude. Along the unknown coasts they were threatened by shallows, hidden banks, rocks and contrary winds and currents, with no knowledge of convenient shelter to ride out storms or of very necessary watering places. It is little wonder that these pioneers dreaded the thought of being forced on to a lee shore or of having to choose between these inshore dangers and the unrecorded perils of the open sea.

If there is still time remaining, review the passages until all 15 minutes have elapsed.
Do not look at Part B until that time.

Part B: TIME—20 minutes

DIRECTIONS: Answer the following questions pertaining to information contained in the three passages you have just read. You may not turn back to those passages for assistance.

QUESTIONS TO

Passage 1:

1. According to the passage, the multinational corporation

   (A) is headquartered in more than one country
   (B) has more than one nationality
   (C) employs nationals of several countries
   (D) has foreign investors
   (E) is not defined in the passage

2. In the United States, multinational corporations date back to the

   (A) 1700's
   (B) 1800's
   (C) 1850's
   (D) 1900's
   (E) end of W.W. II

3. The book written by Servan-Schreiber and quoted in the passage is entitled

(A) *European Fortune*
(B) *The American MNC's*
(C) *European Industry*
(D) *The American Challenge*
(E) *The Multinational Challenge*

4. Servan-Schreiber's attitude toward American multinational corporations was that he

(A) welcomed them
(B) felt American firms would contribute to EEC economic development
(C) claimed American companies were gaining control over European industry
(D) welcomed the competition they would bring to Europe
(E) thought American firms were too large for European markets

5. Lord Keynes had demonstrated that it was possible to pursue

(A) maximum income and full employment objectives within national boundaries
(B) freedom of trade between countries
(C) a common corporate strategy beyond national boundaries
(D) activities which would frustrate the operations of multinational corporations
(E) expansionary fiscal policies

6. The conflict between multinational corporations and nation states has been partly attributed to

(A) the ability of a multinational corporation to avoid paying taxes in more than two countries
(B) multinational corporations bound only by international law
(C) multinational corporations taking a supranational point of view
(D) different political systems of various countries
(E) the porosity of national boundaries

7. One major event that has focused public attention on the activities of U.S. multinational corporations in the past 15 years has been

(A) their fast growth
(B) the massive influx of American capital into Europe
(C) the growth of nationalism abroad
(D) the introduction of advanced technology by these companies
(E) the efficiency with which they operate

8. American investment in Europe has resulted in all of the following except

(A) increased income in these countries
(B) an improvement of technology
(C) the introduction of modern management techniques
(D) increased employment and trade
(E) increased political tensions

9. The U.S. balance of payments deficit after 1960 was partly caused by

(A) America's help in promoting European recovery after the Second World War
(B) trade discrimination against the United States
(C) a more equitable distribution of the world's monetary reserves
(D) massive outflows of gold from the U.S.
(E) a decline in U.S. exports to Europe

10. The passage probably appeared in

(A) a literary journal
(B) Servan-Schreiber's book
(C) a management journal
(D) an economic journal
(E) a marketing journal

QUESTIONS TO

Passage 2:

11. According to the author, comparative management methodology in the study of Indian management is

(A) effective in the long-run
(B) effective in the short-run
(C) questionable in the long-run
(D) questionable in the short-run
(E) of no conceivable use at all

12. In what area is Indian management undergoing a change?

(A) intellectual
(B) social
(C) technological
(D) organizational
(E) political

13. Management in India can be categorized as being in a state of

(A) stability
(B) uncertainty
(C) retrenchment
(D) change
(E) permissiveness

14. According to the author, there are four sectors of management: Public, Private, Foreign, and

(A) Domestic
(B) Family
(C) Native
(D) Government
(E) Caste

15. Differences in language, religion, education, and caste have led to what sort of managerial actions?

(A) contradictory
(B) deleterious
(C) consensus decision-making
(D) eclectic
(E) ineffective

16. Comparative management can be best expressed as a study of

(A) Indian management
(B) Western management
(C) managerial systems of two or more countries
(D) comparative settings
(E) managerial processes

17. Managerial behavior in India can be described as

(A) inefficient
(B) following "normal" patterns
(C) exhibiting a great degree of diversity
(D) inflexible
(E) unresponsive to change

18. Which of the following is described by the author as descriptive of Indian administrative practice?

(A) rapid decision-making
(B) Western oriented
(C) too much reliance on the British system
(D) lacking an indigenous frame of reference
(E) there is no one pattern which can be called typically Indian

19. Which of the following sectors function in a flexible fashion?

I. Public
II. Private
III. Foreign

(A) I only
(B) III only
(C) I and II only
(D) II and III only
(E) I, II, and III

20. The comparative management approach

(A) limits the manager's ability to judge his performance
(B) is unique in its methodology
(C) hypothesizes about similarities and differences between management systems
(D) analyzes the history of management
(E) uses the model building approach

QUESTIONS TO

Passage 3:

21. Before the expansion of Europe overseas could take place

(A) vast sums of money had to be raised
(B) an army had to be recruited
(C) the Atlantic Ocean had to be conquered
(D) ships had to be built
(E) seamen had to be trained

22. One of Portugal's leaders, known as the Navigator, was in reality

(A) Christopher Columbus
(B) King John II
(C) a Venetian
(D) Prince Henry
(E) Prince Paul

23. Portugal was adept at exploring unknown waters because she possessed all of the following except

(A) a navy
(B) past experience
(C) experienced navigators
(D) experienced mapmakers
(E) extensive trade routes

24. In addition to possessing the necessary resources for exploration, Portugal was the logical country for this task because of her

(A) wealth
(B) navigational experience
(C) geographical position
(D) prominence
(E) ability

25. The Portuguese learned navigational methods and procedures from all of the following except

(A) Jews
(B) Catalans
(C) Genoese
(D) Venetians
(E) Aegeans

26. Mediterranean seamen generally kept close to shore because

(A) they were afraid of pirates
(B) they feared being forced to a lee shore
(C) they lacked navigational ability
(D) they feared running into storms
(E) the latitudinal extent of the Mediterranean was not great

27. Hazards such as sudden storms and dangerous coasts were

(A) predictable risks
(B) unknown risks
(C) unknown to the area
(D) a major threat to exploration
(E) no threat to navigation

28. Sailing close to the coast enabled seamen to

(A) reach their destination faster
(B) navigate without sailing directions
(C) determine their positions from landmarks
(D) determine their longitude and latitude
(E) avoid dangerous shoals

29. According to the passage, ocean navigators faced many difficulties except which of the following?

(A) latitude and longitude were largely unknown
(B) sailing directions were incomplete
(C) astronomical bearings were more difficult to make
(D) coastal water depths were unknown
(E) ships were unseaworthy

30. According to the passage, Portugal was induced to explore to her south and west owing to her desire for

(A) conquest
(B) colonization of these areas
(C) opportunities for commerce and trade
(D) entering the slave trade
(E) "getting there first"

If there is still time remaining, you may review the questions in this section only. You may not look at Part A or turn to any other section of the test.

Section II Mathematics

TIME: 75 minutes

DIRECTIONS: Solve each of the following problems; then indicate the correct answer on the answer sheet. [On the actual test you will be permitted to use any space available on the examination paper for scratch work.]

NOTE: A figure that appears with a problem is drawn as accurately as possible so as to provide information that may help in answering the question. Numbers in this test are real numbers.

31. A toy originally cost $10.00. The toy was offered for sale at 110% of the cost. After a month the price was discounted 10% and the toy was sold. The toy sold for

(A) $9.00
(B) $9.52
(C) $9.90
(D) $10.00
(E) $11.00

32. Of the numbers 7, 9, 11, 13, 29, 33, how many are prime numbers?

(A) none
(B) 3
(C) 4
(D) 5
(E) all

33. A factory has 50 workers. Each worker makes $1/5$ of a yard of cloth in 20 minutes. How many yards of cloth will the factory produce in one hour?

(A) 25
(B) 30
(C) $32\frac{1}{2}$
(D) 35
(E) 50

Use the following table for questions 34–37.

Average weekly hours and average overtime hours of production workers in manufacturing industries, New York State

Industry	Average weekly hours		Average weekly overtime hours		Overtime hours as per cent of total hours	
	Nov. 1972	Nov. 1971	Nov. 1972	Nov. 1971	Nov. 1972	Nov. 1971
All manufacturing	40.1	39.5	3.3	2.7	8.2	6.8
Durable goods	41.8	40.9	3.8	2.9	9.1	7.1
Ordnance and accessories	42.3	40.9	4.5	2.4	10.6	5.9
Lumber and wood products, exc. furniture	41.0	39.9	3.9	2.9	9.4	7.2
Furniture and fixtures	40.4	40.1	3.3	2.7	8.3	6.8
Stone, clay and glass products	40.7	39.8	3.7	3.6	9.0	9.1
Primary metal industries	41.7	40.8	3.6	3.2	8.6	7.7
Fabricated metal products	41.7	40.9	3.7	3.0	8.9	7.4
Machinery, except electrical	43.6	41.5	5.2	3.0	11.8	7.3
Electrical machinery, equipment and supplies	41.0	40.3	3.1	2.4	7.7	6.0
Transportation equipment	42.4	41.6	4.1	3.3	9.8	8.0
Instruments; photographic and optical goods	41.7	41.2	3.0	2.6	7.2	6.3
Nondurable goods	38.7	38.4	2.9	2.5	7.4	6.6
Food and kindred products	41.7	40.7	4.3	3.8	10.3	9.3
Tobacco manufactures						
Textile mill products	40.8	40.5	4.4	3.7	10.7	9.2
Apparel and other finished fabric products	35.2	35.3	1.3	1.3	3.6	3.6
Paper and allied products	43.1	42.9	4.4	4.3	10.1	10.1
Printing, publishing and allied industries	38.0	37.6	3.6	3.0	9.4	7.9
Chemicals and allied products	42.7	42.5	3.3	3.1	7.8	7.3
Petroleum refining and related industries						
Rubber and miscellaneous plastics products						
Leather and leather products	38.2	38.0	1.8	1.6	4.8	4.3
Miscellaneous manufacturing industries	39.2	39.2	2.9	2.4	7.5	6.0

Source: New York State Department of Labor

34. Which of the following industries had the most average weekly overtime hours in November 1972?

(A) Ordnance and accessories
(B) Furniture and fixtures
(C) Machinery, except electrical
(D) Food and kindred products
(E) Paper and allied products

35. In November 1972, in how many of the industries shown on the table was the average of weekly hours less than 40?

(A) 1
(B) 2
(C) 3
(D) 4
(E) 5

36. In how many of the industries shown did the average of weekly hours decrease between November 1971 and November 1972?

(A) none
(B) 1
(C) 2
(D) 3
(E) 4

37. The average of weekly hours in all manufacturing during November 1971 was

(A) 38.1
(B) 39.5
(C) 40.1
(D) 40.9
(E) 41.8

38. Which of the following triangles has the largest area?

(A) an equilateral triangle whose sides have length 3, 3, 3
(B) an isosceles triangle whose sides have length 4, 4, $3\frac{1}{2}$
(C) an equilateral triangle whose sides have length 4, 4, 4
(D) an isosceles triangle whose sides are 3, 3, 4
(E) all of the above

39. In a certain town 40% of the people have brown hair, 25% have brown eyes, and 10% have both brown hair and brown eyes. What percentage of the people in the town have neither brown hair nor brown eyes?

(A) 35
(B) 40
(C) 45
(D) 50
(E) 55

40. A company issues 100,000 shares of stock. In 1960 each of the shares was worth $9.50. In 1970 each share was worth $13.21. How much more were the 100,000 shares worth in 1970 than in 1960?

(A) $37,000
(B) $37,010
(C) $37,100
(D) $371,000
(E) $371,100

41. A worker's daily salary varies each day. In one week he worked five days. His daily salaries were $40.62, $41.35, $42.00, $42.50, and $39.53. What was his average daily salary for the week?

(A) $40.04
(B) $40.89
(C) $41.04
(D) $41.20
(E) $206.00

Use the following graph for questions 42–44.

Source: New York State Department of Labor

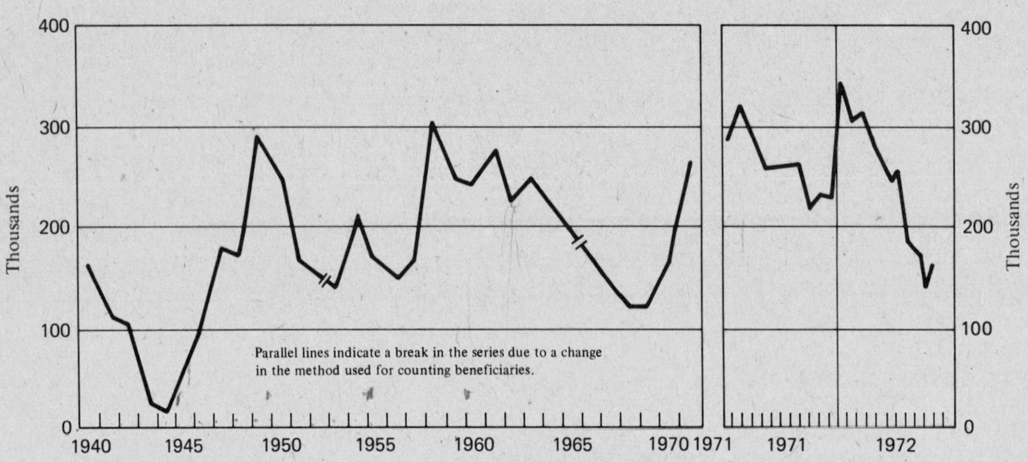

42. Between 1940 and 1970 the largest number of beneficiaries at any time was approximately

(A) 300
(B) 325
(C) 3,000
(D) 30,000
(E) 300,000

43. In what year between 1940 and 1970 was the largest number of beneficiaries served?

(A) 1948
(B) 1956
(C) 1957
(D) 1959
(E) 1960

44. Which of the following conclusions can be deduced from the graph?

I. The number of beneficiaries was under 100,000 for a longer period of time than it exceeded 300,000 (for the years covered by the graph).
II. More people were employed in 1944 than in 1956.
III. The number of beneficiaries declined from 1962 to 1965.

(A) only I
(B) only III
(C) I and III only
(D) II and III only
(E) I, II, and III

45. One dozen eggs and ten pounds of apples are currently the same price. If the price of a dozen eggs rises by 10% and the price of a pound of apples goes up by 2%, how much more will it cost to buy a dozen eggs and ten pounds of apples?

(A) 6%
(B) 10%
(C) 12%
(D) 20%
(E) 30%

46. Find x when $x + y = 4$, and $2y = 6$

(A) 1
(B) $\frac{3}{2}$
(C) -2
(D) -3
(E) -1

47. If 10 rats can eat 30 pounds of corn in a week, how many pounds of corn will 3 rats eat in a week?

(A) 3
(B) 9
(C) 10
(D) 12
(E) 13

48. How much bigger is the area of a triangle with sides of length 3, 4, and 5 miles, than the area of a square whose sides are 2 miles long?

(A) 1 square mile
(B) 2 square miles
(C) 4 square miles
(D) 6 square miles
(E) 8 square miles

49. A person has $10,000 invested in a company. If the investment is worth $\frac{1}{2}$ as much at the end of each year as it is at the beginning of the year, in how many years will it be worth less than $1,000?

(A) 1
(B) 2
(C) 3
(D) 4
(E) 5

50. A worker is paid $2.50 an hour for the first 8 hours he works each day. He is paid one and a half of the regular rate for any time he works over 8 hours in a day. How long does he have to work to make $27.50 in a day?

(A) 8 hours
(B) 9 hours
(C) $9\frac{1}{2}$ hours
(D) 10 hours
(E) 11 hours

Use the following graph for questions 51–55.

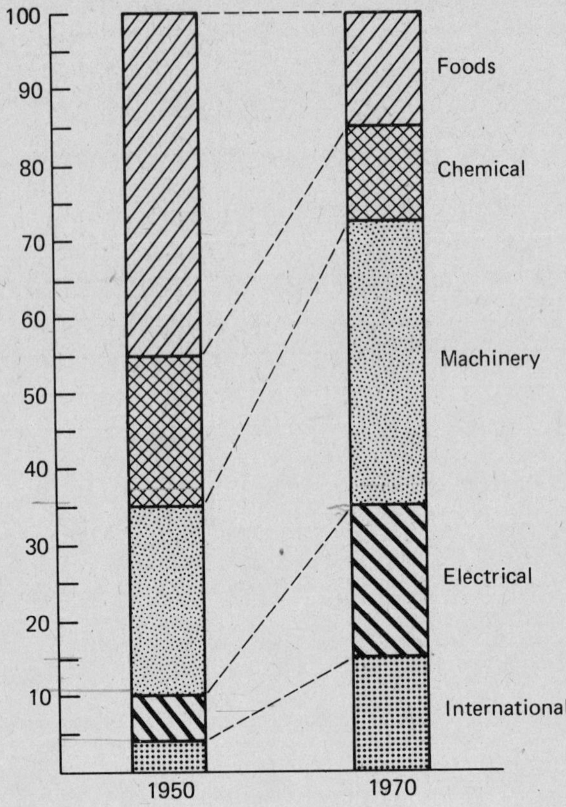

51. For what percentage of the total sales did foods account in 1950?

(A) 15%
(B) 20%
(C) 25%
(D) 30%
(E) 45%

52. Which category showed the greatest increase in its percentage of total sales from 1950 to 1970?

(A) Foods
(B) Chemical
(C) Machinery
(D) Electrical
(E) International

53. Which category accounted for the second largest amount of sales in 1970?

(A) Foods
(B) Chemical
(C) Machinery
(D) Electrical
(E) International

54. Which of the following statements can be deduced from the graph?

I. The income from food sales declined from 1950 to 1970.
II. If total income from sales in 1970 was $1,000,000,000.00, then sales income from international sales in 1970 was about $15,000,000.00.
III. Foods accounted for more sales than all the other categories combined in 1950.

(A) None
(B) only I
(C) only II
(D) I and II only
(E) I, II, and III

55. If sales income doubled from 1950 to 1970, then income from foods in 1970 is what fraction of income from foods in 1950?

(A) $\frac{1}{3}$
(B) $\frac{2}{3}$
(C) 1
(D) $1\frac{1}{3}$
(E) 2

56. If 25 men can unload a truck in 1 hour and 30 minutes, how long should it take 15 men to unload the truck?

(A) 2 hours
(B) $2\frac{1}{4}$ hours
(C) $2\frac{1}{3}$ hours
(D) $2\frac{1}{2}$ hours
(E) 3 hours

57. A car gets 20 miles per gallon of gas when it travels at 50 miles per hour. The car gets 12% fewer miles to the gallon at 60 miles per hour. How far can the car travel at 60 miles per hour on 11 gallons of gas?

(A) 193.6 miles
(B) 195.1 miles
(C) 200 miles
(D) 204.3 miles
(E) 220 miles

58. If the radius of a circle is increased by 5%, then the area of the circle is increased by

(A) .5%
(B) 2.5%
(C) 5%
(D) 10.25%
(E) 25%

59. Feathers cost $500 a ton for the first 12 tons and $(500 − *x*) a ton for any tons over 12. What is *x*, if it costs $10,000 for 30 tons of feathers?

(A) 270.00
(B) 277.00
(C) 277.70
(D) 277.78
(E) 280.00

60. If $x + y = 2$, and $3x + y = 4$ what is $x - y$?

(A) −2
(B) 0
(C) 2
(D) 4
(E) 5

Use the table for questions 61–64.

Federal Reserve Reciprocal Currency Arrangements
March 9, 1973
In millions of dollars

Institution	Amount of facility
Austrian National Bank	200
National Bank of Belgium	600
Bank of Canada	1,000
National Bank of Denmark	200
Bank of England	2,000
Bank of France	1,000
German Federal Bank	1,000
Bank of Italy	1,250
Bank of Japan	1,000
Bank of Mexico	130
Netherlands Bank	300
Bank of Norway	200
Bank of Sweden	250
Swiss National Bank	1,000
Bank for International Settlements:	
Swiss francs-dollars	600
Other authorized European currencies-dollars	1,000
Total	11,730

Source: Federal Reserve Bank of New York

61. How many institutions have more than one billion dollars in reciprocal currency arrangements?

(A) 2
(B) 3
(C) 6
(D) 7
(E) 8

62. Which institution has the smallest amount of reciprocal currency arrangements?

(A) Austrian National Bank
(B) National Bank of Denmark
(C) Bank of England
(D) Bank of Mexico
(E) Bank of Norway

63. What is the average amount of reciprocal currency arrangements of the institutions?

(A) $782
(B) $800
(C) $750,000,000
(D) $782,000,000
(E) $800,000,000

64. Which conclusions can be inferred from the table?

I. No institution has more than 20% of the total reciprocal currency arrangements.
II. None of the institutions has less than 2% of the total.
III. The Bank of Italy has ten times as much in reciprocal currency arrangements as the Bank of Mexico.

(A) only I
(B) only II
(C) I and II only
(D) II and III only
(E) I, II, and III

65. A grocer buys cereal at \$5 a case. Each case contains 40 boxes. He sells a box of cereal for 20¢. How much profit does he make on each case of cereal?

(A) \$2.00
(B) \$3.00
(C) \$3.40
(D) \$5.00
(E) \$8.00

66. The angles of a triangle are in the ratio 2:3:4. The largest angle in the triangle is

(A) 30°
(B) 50°
(C) 70°
(D) 75°
(E) 80°

67. Mr. Maceli pays 15% tax on his weekly income of \$200. How much tax will he pay in a year?

(A) \$300
(B) \$1,230
(C) \$1,560
(D) \$1,650
(E) \$1,730

68. If a car cost \$2,500 in 1967 and the same model car cost \$3,360 in 1973, by what percentage did the price of the car increase between 1967 and 1973?

(A) 20
(B) 25.6
(C) 29.3
(D) 31.4
(E) 34.4

69. What is the ratio of $\frac{1}{6}$ to $\frac{4}{5}$?

(A) $\frac{1}{6}$
(B) $\frac{2}{15}$
(C) $\frac{5}{24}$
(D) $\frac{3}{15}$
(E) $\frac{4}{15}$

70. Find the area of the trapezoid *ABCD*. *AB* = *CD* = 5, *BC* = 10, *AD* = 16, and *BE* is an altitude of the trapezoid.

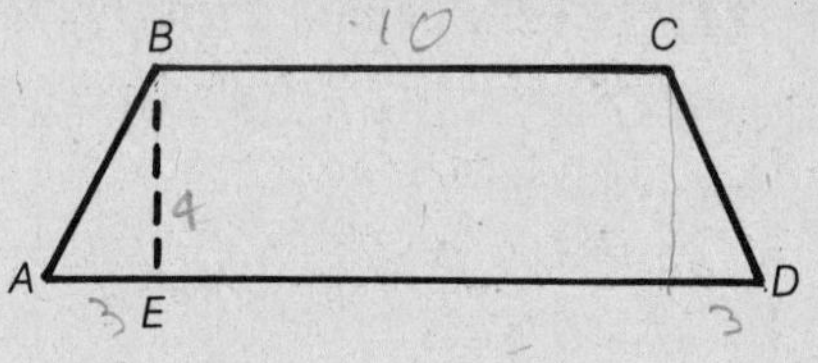

(A) 50
(B) 52
(C) 64
(D) 80
(E) 160

71. How much simple interest will you have to pay if you borrow \$650 for 6 months at an annual interest rate of 8%?

(A) \$26.00
(B) \$26.50
(C) \$34.00
(D) \$40.00
(E) \$52.00

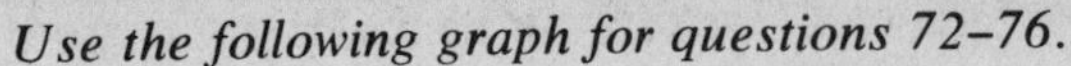

Use the following graph for questions 72–76.

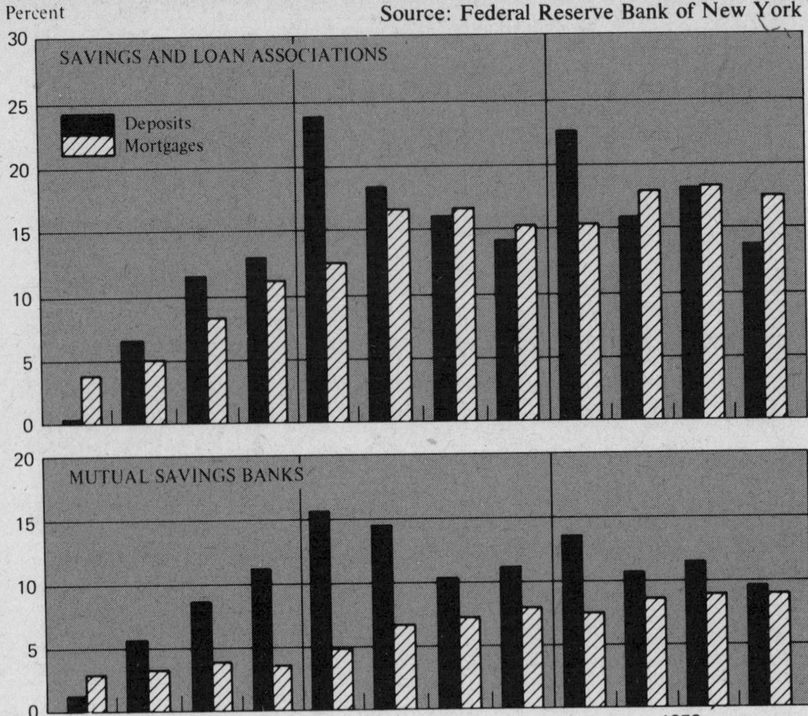

Note: Mutual savings bank mortgage statistics for the fourth quarter of 1972 are based on October and November data.

72. During how many quarters were deposits higher than 15% in savings and loan associations?

(A) 5
(B) 6
(C) 7
(D) 8
(E) 9

73. In savings and loan associations, the largest ratio of deposits to mortgages was about

(A) 1 to 2
(B) 1 to 1
(C) 1.5 to 1
(D) 2 to 1
(E) 3 to 1

74. For the time shown, mortgage lending was at the maximum for savings and loan associations during the

(A) 4th quarter 1970
(B) 2nd quarter 1971
(C) 2nd quarter 1972
(D) 3rd quarter 1972
(E) 4th quarter 1972

75. The deposits in mutual savings banks decreased the most between the

(A) first and second quarters of 1970
(B) fourth quarter of 1970 and first quarter of 1971
(C) second and third quarters of 1971
(D) first and second quarters of 1972
(E) third and fourth quarters of 1972

76. Which of the following statements are true?

I. In every year shown, mortgages are higher in the 3rd quarter than they are in the first quarter.
II. Deposits were higher than mortgages in every quarter since the second quarter of 1970.
III. Deposits have been higher for savings and loan associations than for mutual savings banks in each quarter shown.

(A) I only
(B) III only
(C) I and II only
(D) I and III only
(E) I, II, and III

77. If x is greater than 2, which of the following statements are true?

I. x is negative.
II. x is positive.
III. $2x$ is greater than or equal to x.
IV. x^2 is greater than or equal to x.

(A) III only
(B) IV only
(C) I and III only
(D) I, III, and IV only
(E) II, III, and IV only

78. A man walks around the outside of a square field. The area of the field is 144 square yards. How far did the man walk?

(A) 12 yards
(B) 24 yards
(C) 48 yards
(D) 100 yards
(E) 144 yards

79. At 1 A.M. a car is traveling at 50 miles per hour. The driver accelerates so that at the end of each hour he is traveling 10% faster than he was at the beginning of the hour. How many miles per hour is the car traveling by 3 A.M.?

(A) 55
(B) 60
(C) 60.5
(D) 61.5
(E) 120

80. If a stock average was at 531.54 and it fell 12%, what is the new stock average?

(A) 435.25
(B) 464.72
(C) 466.7
(D) 467.76
(E) 468.59

81. A worker is digging a ditch. He gets 2 assistants who work $\frac{2}{3}$ as fast as he does. If all 3 work on a ditch they should finish it in what fraction of the time that the worker takes working alone?

(A) $\frac{3}{7}$
(B) $\frac{1}{2}$
(C) $\frac{3}{4}$
(D) $\frac{4}{3}$
(E) $\frac{7}{3}$

82. Mr. Jones decides to paint the ceiling and walls of his storage room. (The storage room has no windows.) The room is 15 ft. long, 12 ft. wide, and 8 ft. high. How many gallons of paint will he need, if he can paint 36 square feet with one gallon of paint?

(A) 12
(B) $12\frac{2}{3}$
(C) 15
(D) 17
(E) $25\frac{1}{3}$

Use this table for questions 83–85.

TABLE 1.—Basic data 1970

	Community	Germany	France	Italy	Netherlands	Belgium	Luxembourg
Total area ('000 sq. km.)	1 167.5	248.5	551.2	301.2	33.5	30.5	2.6
Total population ('000)	188 147	61 547	50 705	53 486	13 032	9 676	339.2
Density of population per sq. km.	161	248	92	178	389	317	130.5
Numbers in employment ('000)	74 196	27 204	20 473	18 956	4 678	3 842	143.6
Numbers in employment, breakdown by main sector (%):							
Agriculture	13	8.8	14.2	19.4	7.3	4.6	10.9
Industry	44	48.7	40.6	43.3	41.2	42.8	46.3
Services	44	42.5	45.2	37.3	51.5	52.6	42.8
Share of gross domestic product (%):							
Agriculture	.	4.1	6.0	10.3	6.2	4.5	4.1
Industry	.	51.7	48.2	40.5	42.0	42.6	56.9
Services	.	44.2	45.8	49.2	51.8	52.9	39.0
In % of gross domestic product:							
Private consumers' expenditure	.	55.7	58.8	63.9	56.8	60.4	55.7
Public current expenditure on goods and services	.	15.7	12.1	12.7	16.1	14.0	10.8
Gross fixed asset formation	.	26.5	25.8	21.2	26.3	22.1	25.6
Total exports	.	23.2	16.0	20.2	48.3	44.4	83.2
Total imports	.	21.6	15.8	19.6	49.6	42.1	72.6

Source: European Economic Community

83. Which country has the greatest percentage of its employees in the agricultural sector of its economy?

(A) Germany
(B) France
(C) Italy
(D) Netherlands
(E) Belgium

84. The population of Germany is roughly what percentage of the total population of the Community?

(A) 30%
(B) 32%
(C) 33%
(D) 34%
(E) 35%

85. In how many countries is the percentage of employees engaged in services less than the percentage engaged in services overall for the Community?

(A) 1
(B) 2
(C) 3
(D) 4
(E) 5

If there is still time remaining, you may review the questions in this section only. You may not turn to any other section of the test.

Section III Verbal Aptitude

TIME: 20 minutes

Antonyms

DIRECTIONS: For each question below, select the lettered word or phrase that comes closest to being *opposite* in meaning to the word appearing in capital letters. Be sure to consider all meanings carefully.

86. CONTRITION: (A) anger (B) expansion (C) renunciation (D) reprobation (E) disbelief

87. EXONERATE: (A) condemn (B) denounce (C) verify (D) repent (E) expunge

88. ARRAY: (A) disorder (B) circle (C) place (D) notation (E) army

89. SALIENT: (A) pleasant (B) mountainous (C) inconspicuous (D) tentative (E) prominent

90. LASCIVIOUS: (A) laudable (B) viscous (C) vicious (D) chaste (E) prolific

91. PIQUANT: (A) colorful (B) clever (C) bland (D) loud (E) sad

92. SUBTERFUGE: (A) terror (B) openness (C) degradation (D) insurgence (E) carnage

93. TEMERITY: (A) wisdom (B) caution (C) malice (D) strength (E) beauty

94. EPHEMERAL: (A) permanent (B) quick (C) impetuous (D) earthy (E) metaphysical

95. TENACIOUS: (A) resilient (B) staunch (C) fickle (D) lively (E) austere

96. AVIDITY: (A) generosity (B) redundancy (C) speed (D) avariciousness (E) sluggishness

97. CHIMERICAL: (A) real (B) somber (C) soft (D) numerical (E) troublesome

98. COGNIZANT: (A) honest (B) ignorant (C) lucid (D) optimistic (E) afraid

99. FACETIOUS: (A) serious (B) facile (C) jaunty (D) obstinate (E) partial

Word-Pair Relationships

DIRECTIONS: For each question below, determine the relationship between the pair of capitalized words and then select the lettered pair of words which have a similar relationship to the first pair.

100. WINTER : SNOW :: (A) summer : heat (B) spring : rain (C) cold : ice (D) field : grass (E) river : water

101. FIRE : SMOKE :: (A) car : accident (B) pill : relief (C) war : death (D) police : arrest (E) energy : battery

102. VOLT : ELECTRICITY :: (A) inch : foot (B) metric : kilometer (C) letter : alphabet (D) oxygen : water (E) ocean : wave

103. WEIGHT : SCALE :: (A) distance : miles (B) height : ruler (C) liquid : quart (D) wheat : bushel (E) coal : ton

104. DECLARATION : AFFIRMATION :: (A) proclaim : predict (B) proclamation : ratification (C) protestation : plebiscite (D) expression : dictum (E) dogmatize : attest

105. NEED : MOTIVATION :: (A) enemy : war (B) careless : accident (C) hunger : food (D) unfulfillment : frustration (E) repression : dictator

106. CIGARETTE : TOBACCO :: (A) house : termites (B) cigar : filter (C) milk : bottle (D) coffee : caffeine (E) shoes : socks

107. POVERTY : WEALTH :: (A) master : servant (B) pilot : plane (C) conductor : train (D) warden : jail (E) needy : welfare

108. CLANDESTINE : SURREPTITIOUSLY :: (A) subversive : secretly (B) annihilate : willingly (C) plan : devotedly (D) material : corporeally (E) subjugate : rationally

109. AIR PRESSURE : BAROMETER :: (A) sound : photometer (B) meteorologist : weather (C) altitude : altimeter (D) doctor : pulse (E) mechanic : motor

110. AXIOMATIC : SELF-EVIDENT :: (A) law : divine (B) abstract : understood (C) dogmatic : asserted (D) asserted : true (E) believed : loved

111. BANDIT : ROBBERY :: (A) army : tactics (B) treason : traitor (C) designer : art (D) roadmap : driver (E) canal : builder

112. SUSPICIOUS : CONFIDING :: (A) cautious : bold (B) fearful : inferior (C) industrious : assiduous (D) torpid : apathetic (E) indifferent : uncertain

Sentence Completions

DIRECTIONS: For each sentence below, select the lettered word or set of words which, when inserted in the sentence blanks, best complete the meaning of that sentence.

113. It looked as if there might be a _____ in the negotiations.

(A) upswing (B) breakthrough (C) resolution (D) agreement (E) expiation

114. Controls will be retained over areas of the _____ that have been highly _____.

(A) economy . . . inflationary (B) population . . . prolific (C) demonstrators . . . unobtrusive (D) country . . . suspicious (E) battlefield . . . predacious

115. It is assumed by some that one _____ is not necessarily a _____.

(A) phrase . . . sentence (B) battle lost . . . defeat (C) primary . . . victory (D) misfortune . . . failure (E) default . . . step backward

116. By her actions, the country found herself ____ to a full-scale economic war.

(A) a precursor (B) bound (C) committed (D) outdistanced (E) plicated

117. Another term for ____ is ____.

(A) truck . . . trailer (B) democracy . . . republic (C) communism . . . socialism (D) household . . . family (E) residence . . . domicile

118. Many market surveys are ____ because the ____ was inadequate.

(A) expensive . . . design (B) unreliable . . . sample size (C) worthless . . . conclusion (D) unnecessary . . . objective (E) disregarded . . . hypothesis

119. For some people their ____ state of mind prevents them from flying.

(A) physiological (B) rational (C) morbid (D) prodigious (E) perfidious

120. According to some, ____ is our sole protection from nuclear attack.

(A) destruction (B) deterrence (C) condemnation (D) vengeance (E) punishment

121. Protectionists attempt to ____ foreign trade barriers.

(A) establish (B) remove (C) reduce (D) acknowledge (E) destroy

122. Uneasy rests the ____ that ____ the crown.

(A) man . . . covets (B) government . . . seizes (C) head . . . wears (D) person . . . steals (E) king . . . bears

123. Uniformity carries with it the seeds of ____.

(A) mediocrity (B) disaster (C) diversity (D) temptation (E) moderation

124. The establishment of a stricter ____ for prisoners ____ the guards.

(A) system . . . startled (B) regimen . . . pleased (C) command . . . annoyed (D) sanction . . . vexed (E) circumspection . . . disturbed

125. In the ____ he was a dilettante rather than a ____.

(A) arts . . . professional (B) game . . . spectator (C) government . . . bureaucrat (D) sport . . . player (E) party . . . amateur

If there is still time remaining, you may review the questions in this section only.
You may not turn to any other section of the test.

Section IV Data Sufficiency

TIME: 15 minutes

DIRECTIONS: Each of the following problems has a question and two statements which are labeled (1) and (2). Use the data given in (1) and (2) together with other available information (such as the number of hours in a day, the definition of *clockwise,* mathematical facts, etc.) to decide whether the statements are *sufficient* to answer the question. Then fill in space

(A) if you can get the answer from (1) alone but not from (2) alone;

(B) if you can get the answer from (2) alone but not from (1) alone;

(C) if you can get the answer from (1) and (2) together, although neither statement by itself suffices;

(D) if statement (1) alone suffices *and* statement (2) alone suffices;

(E) if you cannot get the answer from statements (1) and (2) together, but need even more data.

All numbers used in this section are real numbers. A figure given for a problem is intended to provide information consistent with that in the question, but not necessarily with the additional information contained in the statements.

126. ABC is a triangle inscribed in circle $AOCB$. Is AC a diameter of the circle $AOCB$?

(1) Angle x is a right angle.
(2) The length of AB is $\frac{3}{4}$ the length of BC.

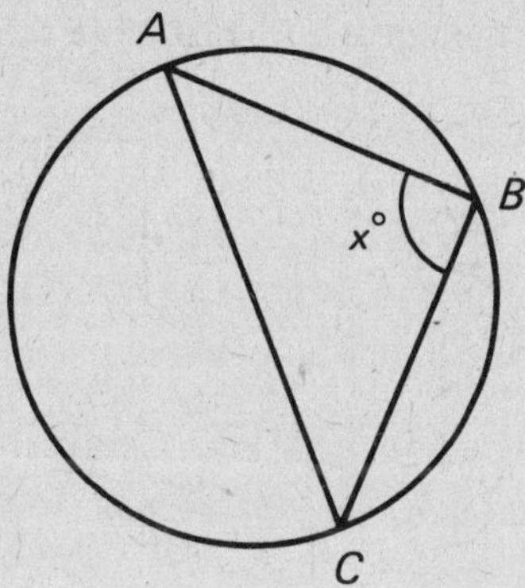

127. A cylindrical tank has a radius of 10 feet and its height is 20 feet. How many gallons of a liquid can be stored in the tank?

(1) A gallon of the liquid occupies about .13 cubic feet of space.
(2) The diameter of the tank is 20 feet.

128. How many books are on the bookshelf?

(1) The average weight of each book is 1.2 pounds.
(2) The books and the bookshelf together weigh 34 pounds.

129. Is the triangle ABC congruent to the triangle DEF? Angle x is equal to angle y.

(1) AB is equal to DE.
(2) BC is equal to EF.

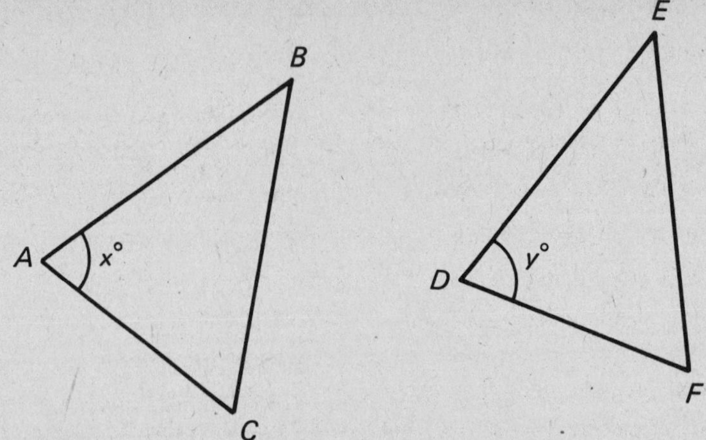

130. A plane flies over New York City. What is its speed in miles per hour?

(1) The plane is flying in a circle.
(2) The plane is flying at the speed of $\frac{1}{9}$ mile per second.

131. Mr. Carpenter wants to build a room in the shape of a rectangle. The area of the floor will be 32 square feet. What is the length of the floor?

(1) The length of the floor will be twice the width of the floor.
(2) The width of the floor will be 4 feet less than the length of the floor.

132. Do the rectangle *ABCD* and the square *EFGH* have the same area?

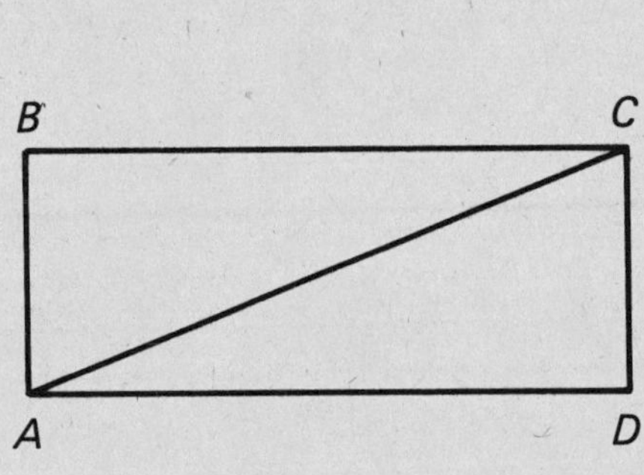

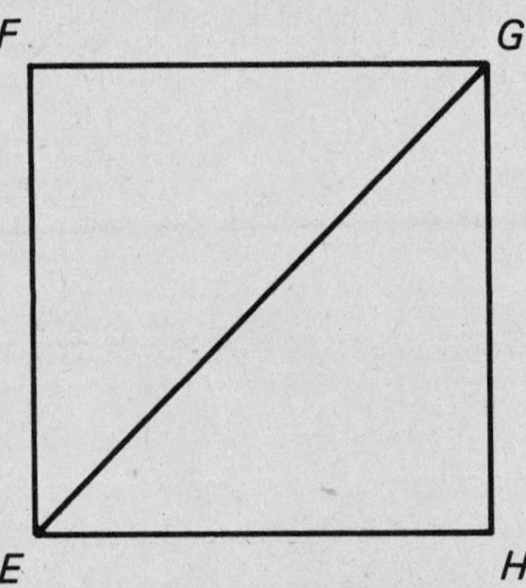

(1) $AC = EG$, $AB = \frac{1}{2} EH$
(2) The area of triangle *ABC* is not equal to the area of triangle *EFG*.

133. How much does Susan weigh?

(1) Susan and Joan together weigh 250 pounds.
(2) Joan weighs twice as much as Susan.

134. Two different holes, hole *A* and hole *B*, are put in the bottom of a full water tank. If the water drains out through the holes, how long before the tank is empty?

(1) If only hole *A* is put in the bottom, the tank will be empty in 24 minutes.
(2) If only hole *B* is put in the bottom, the tank will be empty in 42 minutes.

135. Find $x + y$

(1) $x - y = 6$
(2) $2x - 2y = 12$

136. C is a circle with center D and radius 2. E is a circle with center F and radius R. Are there any points which are on both E and C?

(1) The distance from D to F is $1 + R$.
(2) $R = 3$.

137. Mr. Parker made $20,000 in 1967. What is Mr. Parker's average yearly income for the three years 1967 to 1969?

(1) He made 10% more in each year than he did in the previous year.
(2) His total combined income for 1968 and 1969 was $46,200.

138. Is angle x a right angle?

(1) $y = z$
(2) $(AC)^2 + (CB)^2 = (AB)^2$

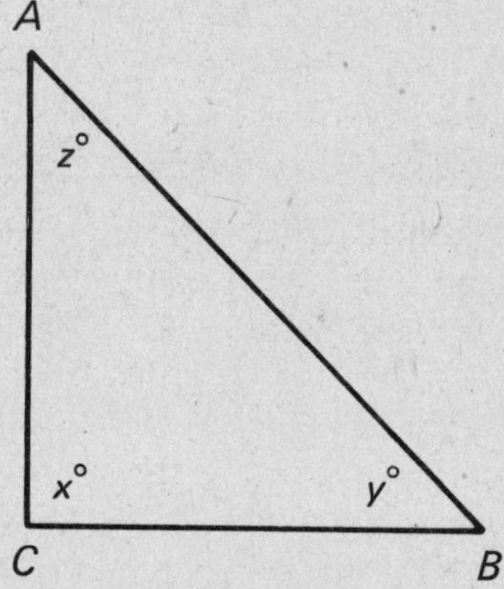

139. John and Paul are standing together on a sunny day. John's shadow is 10 feet long. Paul's shadow is 9 feet long. How tall is Paul?

(1) John is 6 feet tall.
(2) John is standing 2 feet away from Paul.

140. Is x greater than y?

(1) x^2 is greater than y^2
(2) $x + 3$ is greater than $y + 2$

If there is still time remaining, you may review the questions in this section only.
You may not turn to any other section of the test.

Section V Business Judgment

TIME: 35 minutes

DIRECTIONS: Read the following two passages. After you have completed each of them you will be asked to answer two sets of questions. The first of these, data evaluation, involves determining the importance of specific factors included in the passage. The second, data application, consists of general questions relating to the passage. When answering questions, you may consult the passage.

Passage 1:

The Climax Corporation manufactures a line of major electrical appliances distributed through sixty wholesalers, many of whom are company owned. Retailers carry competitive lines, but wholesalers do not; portable appliances move to market through nonexclusive distributors.

The company presently depends on wholesalers to provide service either directly or through supervision of retailers' service departments. When the warranty is involved, the manufacturer furnishes the parts and the wholesaler the labor. Retailers who perform the service function are given a larger discount than are those who return the goods to the wholesaler to fulfill the guarantee.

Home office officials are currently questioning the adequacy of the service thus rendered either under the terms of the warranty or independently. Typical retailers, it was alleged, carry several brands and, in general, do not have competent service personnel. The result is that the blame for the defect is passed back to the manufacturer. This, said the sales manager, is a major consideration. Others believed that reduction of service costs would follow centralizing the entire operation in the hands of a relatively few factory service branches or in carefully trained service personnel employed by a relatively few widely distributed wholesalers. Costs would be thus reduced, and, at the same time, the quality of service rendered would be enhanced, it was claimed.

The product service manager argued that more money should be spent on training retail sales service personnel. Retailers like to render service, he claimed, since it helps to bring traffic into their stores and thus is profitable. A third possibility explored was the promotion of good service by concerns who service but do not sell appliances.

During the conference, the rise of the discount house was discussed. It was thought to be a phenomenon partly based on the realization that good independent service can be secured in most markets and for most appliances. There may be an exception in the case of TV sets, it was admitted, since it is common to find great resentment as to quality of service and delay in meeting calls.

The subsequent discussion raised questions as to the validity of the policy of requiring the retailer to give free service time under the terms of the guarantee. Often owners expect to receive this service free, even though they bought the appliance elsewhere. Some company officials believed that the company should pay dealers for their time costs when they enable the company to make good on its guarantee. One executive pointed out, during a heated discussion on this point, that at least one major automobile company now pays its dealers for making repairs under the warranty.

About this time the sales manager read about a consumer survey that found that the average owner gave little thought to service availability when buying an appliance, except perhaps in the case of TV sets. But when trouble arises, the owner expected the maker to "stand behind his product" and not fall back on any excuse as to costs or time involved, limitations which are found in the normal warranty.

Data Evaluation Questions

DIRECTIONS: Evaluate each of the following factors used in decision-making which relate to the passage you have just read by selecting

(A) for a *Major Objective*—the result desired by the executive;

(B) for a *Major Factor*—a primary consideration, spelled out in the passage, that influences the decision;

(C) for a *Minor Factor*—a less important consideration in the decision;

(D) for a *Major Assumption*—a conclusion reached by the executive not necessarily supported by the factors present;

(E) for an *Unimportant Issue*—a consideration not directly related to the problem.

141. Training retail service personnel

142. The rise of the discount house

143. Typical retailers do not have competent service personnel

144. Adequacy of service demanded by consumers

145. Centralizing the service operation

Data Application Questions

DIRECTIONS: Answer each of the following questions using information contained in the passage.

146. Under Climax Corporation's current warranty, which agency repairs defective appliances?

I. Wholesaler
II. Retailer
III. Manufacturer

(A) I only
(B) III only
(C) I and II only
(D) II and III only
(E) I, II, and III

147. Which of the following reasons are given by executives of Climax Corporation to reconsider their service system?

I. Retailers do not have competent service personnel
II. Climax's service system is revised annually
III. The customers were not utilizing the service

(A) I only
(B) III only
(C) I and II only
(D) II and III only
(E) I, II, and III

148. Some executives believed that if service were centralized

I. Quality of service would be improved
II. Service costs would decrease
III. Fewer call-backs would occur

(A) I only
(B) III only
(C) I and II only
(D) II and III only
(E) I, II, and III

149. According to the passage, buyers of appliances at the time of purchase regard service availability

I. As an important factor
II. As a minor factor
III. As an unimportant issue

(A) I only
(B) III only
(C) I and II only
(D) II and III only
(E) I, II, and III

150. According to the passage, retailers like to service appliances because it

I. Brings traffic to the store
II. Is profitable
III. Keeps them busy

(A) I only
(B) III only
(C) I and II only
(D) II and III only
(E) I, II, and III

Passage 2:

Sam Hoe's small furniture factory was doing more business than ever before and had a solid backlog of orders that ensured continuous production. Its profits, however, had not kept pace with production. Rising machinery, lumber, and hardware costs, higher wages, and higher operating expenses all combined to eat into profits. Mr. Hoe was concerned about this situation and had thought about raising prices on many of his products. This was not practical at the present, however, because the prices of most items had been increased within the last six months. Among various alternatives, he had considered opening an outlet to retail his own products.

The Hoe Company had been established when Sam's father had started a small woodworking shop in his garage twenty years before. When Sam had come into the business about five years later, the shop had been moved to a warehouse on the outskirts of town. At that time, much of the space was used for storage of materials and finished goods. Through the next ten years more and more of the storage area had been taken over for equipment and work space; therefore an additional storage building had been constructed next to the original building. The payroll had grown to twenty craftsmen, who were supervised by a production manager. Mr. Hoe and one bookkeeper did the purchasing, accounting and sales work.

The shop, located in a city of 25,000 people, had begun on a special order custom basis, selling mainly to local residents. Through the years a standard line of tables and chairs had been developed, which now accounted for 78 percent of sales. Most of the standard line furniture was sold through four wholesalers to retail furniture stores in a five state area. Two outlets in the city, a department store and a large furniture showroom, bought directly from the factory. Although most orders for custom made items came from within the state, a few came from states from all areas of the country.

In examining his sales and profit records for the past two years, Mr. Hoe found that while sales had increased steadily, profits showed only a very slight increase over the preceding year. Further study showed that while the sale of custom made merchandise netted a consistently good profit, standard items, sold on a slimmer margin, lost money in some cases. Rising material costs and more rigid specifications and demands from large retail purchasers had both contributed to the problem. Unfortunately, the number of orders for custom work had to be limited, for top craftsmen were in short supply and much of this work demanded highly skilled cabinetmakers.

Discussing the situation with his production manager, Mr. Hoe commented, "Sam, what would you think about opening a retail showroom here? The way I see it, our standard items are popular and almost sell themselves. There's plenty of room since we added the new building, and fixing up a nice-looking showroom shouldn't be too difficult or expensive. If we cut out the retailer's margin and split it between the customer and ourselves, we can cut prices—or hold them steady, anyway—and still make a decent profit. What do you say?"

Data Evaluation Questions

DIRECTIONS: Evaluate each of the following factors used in decision-making which relate to the passage you have just read by selecting

(A) for a *Major Objective*—the result desired by the executive;

(B) for a *Major Factor*—a primary consideration, spelled out in the passage, that influences the decision;

(C) for a *Minor Factor*—a less important consideration in the decision;

(D) for a *Major Assumption*—a conclusion reached by the executive not necessarily supported by the factors present;

(E) for an *Unimportant Issue*—a consideration not directly related to the problem.

151. Higher operating expenses

152. Increased demand for furniture

153. Storage space

154. Employs 20 craftsmen

155. A retail showroom

Data Application Questions

DIRECTIONS: Answer each of the following questions using information contained in the passage.

156. Although production at Sam Hoe's factory was increasing steadily

I. Employee morale was low
II. Prices were fluctuating
III. Profits increased only slightly

(A) I only
(B) III only
(C) I and II only
(D) II and III only
(E) I, II, and III

157. Sam Hoe considered a price increase for his goods, but decided against it because

I. Competition was too intense
II. His father was against it
III. He had had a general price increase within the past six months

(A) I only
(B) III only
(C) I and II only
(D) II and III only
(E) I, II, and III

158. Most of Sam Hoe's furniture sales were generated by

I. Custom pieces
II. Standard line items
III. American colonial lines

(A) I only
(B) III only
(C) I and II only
(D) II and III only
(E) I, II, and III

159. Sam Hoe wanted to increase his output of custom items and

I. Was constrained from doing so because of a labor shortage
II. Scheduled an expansion of his factory space
III. Received encouragement from his production manager

(A) I only
(B) III only
(C) I and II only
(D) II and III only
(E) I, II, and III

160. Mr. Hoe's furniture was sold mainly to

I. Areas throughout the United States
II. Local residents
III. A five state area

(A) I only
(B) III only
(C) I and II only
(D) II and III only
(E) I, II, and III

If there is still time remaining, you may review the questions in this section only.
You may not turn to any other section of the test.

Section VI Mathematics

TIME: 40 minutes

DIRECTIONS: Solve each of the following problems; then indicate the correct answer on the answer sheet. [On the actual test you will be permitted to use any space available on the examination paper for scratch work.]

NOTE: A figure that appears with a problem is drawn as accurately as possible so as to provide information that may help in answering the questions. Numbers in this test are real numbers.

161. What is the next number in the geometric progression 4, 12, 36?

(A) 44
(B) 60
(C) 72
(D) 108
(E) 144

162. An angle of x degrees has the property that its complement is equal to $1/6$ of its supplement where x is

(A) 30
(B) 45
(C) 60
(D) 63
(E) 72

163. If a company makes a profit of $250 on sales of $1,900, the profit was approximately what percentage of sales?

(A) 10%
(B) 12%
(C) 13%
(D) 15%
(E) 17%

164. Which of the following numbers is the least common multiple of the numbers 2, 3, 4, and 5?

(A) 12
(B) 24
(C) 30
(D) 40
(E) 60

Use the following graph for questions 165–167.

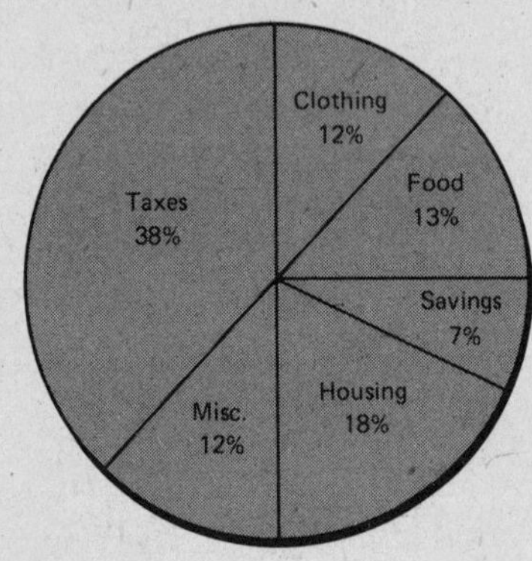

The income of the Walker family for 1972 was $23,352.

165. About how much did the Walkers spend on housing and clothing in 1972?

(A) $700
(B) $6,900
(C) $7,000
(D) $7,200
(E) $70,000

166. The ratio of the amount the Walkers paid in taxes to the amount they spent on food is about

(A) 1 to 3
(B) 2 to 1
(C) $2\frac{1}{2}$ to 1
(D) 3 to 1
(E) 4 to 1

167. Which of the following statements about the Walkers' budget for 1972 can be inferred from the graph?

I. Taxes cost more than any two other categories combined.
II. There are 3 categories which account for more than the average of all the categories.
III. Each category cost more than $1,500 in 1972.

(A) I only
(B) III only
(C) I and II only
(D) I and III only
(E) I, II, and III

168. In a sample of car owners, 30% owned a Chevrolet, 25% owned a Ford, and 48% owned neither a Ford nor a Chevrolet. How many car owners in the sample owned both a Ford and a Chevrolet?

(A) none
(B) 3%
(C) 4%
(D) 52%
(E) 55%

169. If the altitude of a triangle increases by 5% and the base of the triangle increases by 7%, by what percent will the area of the triangle increase?

(A) 3.33%
(B) 5%
(C) 6%
(D) 12%
(E) 12.35%

170. A shipping firm charges 2¢ a pound for the first 20 pounds of package weight and 1.5¢ for each pound or fraction of a pound over 20 pounds of package weight. How much will it charge to ship a package which weighs 23½ pounds?

(A) 6¢
(B) 40¢
(C) 45¢
(D) 46¢
(E) 52¢

171. If paper costs 1¢ a sheet, and a buyer gets a 2% discount on all the paper he buys after the first 1,000 sheets, how much will it cost to buy 5,000 sheets of paper?

(A) $49.20
(B) $50.00
(C) $3,920.00
(D) $4,920.00
(E) $5,000.00

172. Tom's salary is 150% of John's salary. John's salary is 80% of Steve's salary. What is the ratio of Steve's salary to Tom's salary?

(A) 1 to 2
(B) 2 to 3
(C) 5 to 6
(D) 6 to 5
(E) 5 to 4

Use the following table for questions 173–176.

Unemployment insurance beneficiaries by age, education and average number of weeks compensated second quarter, 1972

Age	Beneficiaries	Education: 8 years or less	Education: 9–11 years	Education: 12 years or more	Education: Unknown	Average number of weeks compensated during quarter
Total	499,300	144,800	110,500	216,100	27,900	6.9
Under 25	80,700	7,200	14,300	55,200	4,000	7.3
25–44	189,800	45,000	42,700	91,000	11,100	6.7
45–64	191,300	71,400	47,400	61,400	11,100	6.6
65 and over	37,500	21,200	6,100	8,500	1,700	7.8

Source: New York State Department of Labor

173. About what percentage of the beneficiaries are between 25 and 44 years old?

(A) 18
(B) 19
(C) 23
(D) 36
(E) 38

174. Which of the following categories had the most beneficiaries?

(A) Under 25
(B) 25 to 44
(C) 45 to 64
(D) 8 years or less of education
(E) 12 years or more of education

175. Approximately how many weeks of compensation were paid to beneficiaries during the quarter shown on the table?

(A) 500,000
(B) 1,550,000
(C) 2,600,000
(D) 3,000,000
(E) 3,450,000

176. Which of the following statements about unemployment insurance beneficiaries during the second quarter of 1972 can be inferred from the table?

I. You are more likely to be unemployed if you have 12 years or more of education than if you have 9 to 11 years of education.
II. Beneficiaries 65 or over received more compensation than beneficiaries under 65.
III. The average length of compensation for beneficiaries 65 or over was longer than the average length of compensation for beneficiaries under 65.

(A) none
(B) I only
(C) III only
(D) I and II only
(E) I, II, and III

177. A driver is taking a 5 hour trip. If he travels 135 miles in the first 3 hours, how far will he have to drive in the final 2 hours in order to average 50 miles an hour for the entire trip?

(A) 50 miles
(B) 55 miles
(C) 110 miles
(D) 115 miles
(E) 165 miles

178. If it takes 50 workers 4 hours to dig a sewer, how long should it take 30 workers to dig the same sewer?

(A) 2 hrs., 24 min.
(B) 5 hrs., 12 min.
(C) 6 hrs., 12 min.
(D) 6 hrs., 20 min.
(E) 6 hrs., 40 min.

179. If hamburger costs 98¢ a pound and the price goes up 7%, how much will a pound of hamburger then cost?

(A) $1.02
(B) $1.04
(C) $1.05
(D) $1.06
(E) $10.48

180. Dictionaries weigh 6 pounds each and a set of encyclopedias weighs 75 pounds. 20 dictionaries are shipped in each box. 2 sets of encyclopedias are shipped in each box. A truck is loaded with 98 boxes of dictionaries and 50 boxes of encyclopedias. How much does the truck's load weigh?

(A) 588 pounds
(B) 7,500 pounds
(C) 11,750 pounds
(D) 19,260 pounds
(E) 22,840 pounds

181. Mary is paid $600 a month on her regular job. During July in addition to her regular job, she makes $400 from a second job. Approximately what percentage of her annual income does Mary make in July?

(A) 8
(B) $8\frac{1}{3}$
(C) $12\frac{1}{2}$
(D) 13
(E) 14

Use the following graph for questions 182–186.

Source: Social Security Bulletin

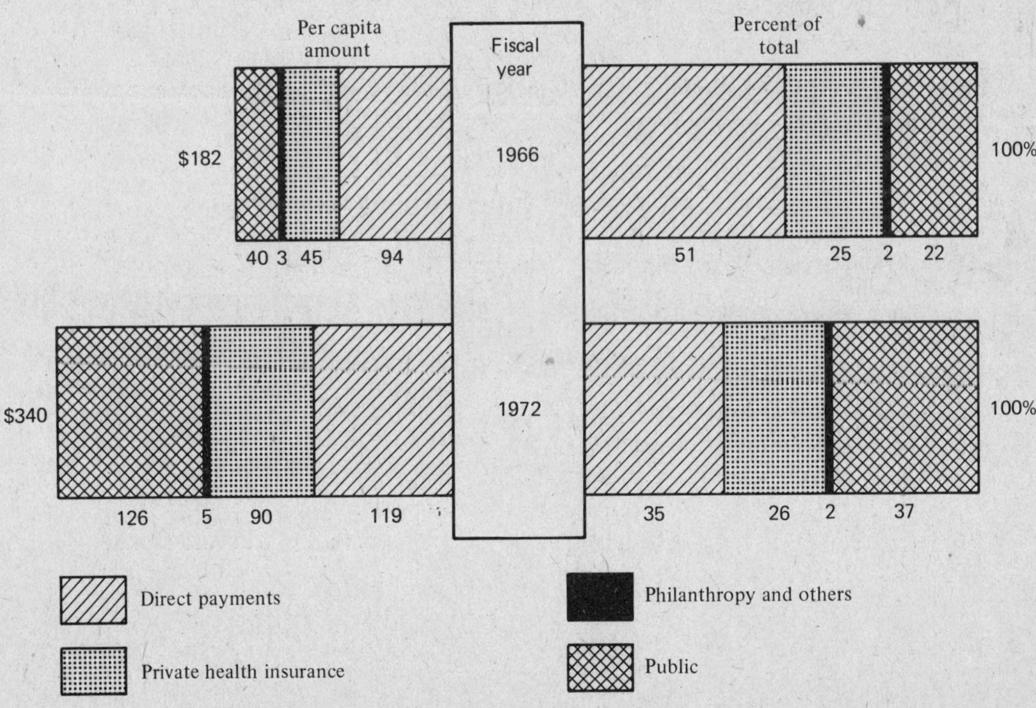

182. The per capita amount spent on personal health care between 1966 and 1972

(A) decreased by about 50%
(B) stayed about the same
(C) increased by about $\frac{1}{3}$
(D) almost doubled
(E) almost tripled

183. The percentage of personal health care expenditures paid for by private health insurance between 1966 and 1972

(A) decreased by 5%
(B) stayed about the same
(C) increased by 10%
(D) increased by 50%
(E) almost doubled

184. According to the graph, the personal health care expenditures from all sources in 1972 for an average family with 5 members were

(A) $200
(B) $470
(C) $630
(D) $910
(E) $1,700

185. What percentage of the personal health care expenditures for a family of 5 came from public funds in 1972?

(A) 22
(B) 26
(C) 37
(D) 51
(E) 175

186. Which of the following statements about personal health care expenditures can be inferred from the graph?

I. The amount per capita paid by direct payment declined from 1966 to 1972.
II. The amount per capita paid by private health insurance doubled between 1966 and 1972.
III. Hospitals cost more in 1972 than they did in 1966.

(A) II only
(B) III only
(C) I and III only
(D) I and II only
(E) I, II, and III

187. If the area of a triangle with base S is equal to the area of a square with side S, then the altitude of the triangle is

(A) $\frac{1}{2}S$
(B) S
(C) $2S$
(D) $3S$
(E) $4S$

188. A train travels at an average speed of 20 mph through urban areas, 50 mph through suburban areas, and 75 mph through rural areas. If a trip consists of traveling half an hour through urban areas, $3\frac{1}{2}$ hours through suburban areas, and 3 hours through rural areas, what is the train's average speed for the entire trip?

(A) 50 mph
(B) $53\frac{2}{7}$ mph
(C) $54\frac{3}{7}$ mph
(D) $58\frac{4}{7}$ mph
(E) $59\frac{2}{7}$ mph

189. $(x - y)(y + 3)$ is equal to

(A) $x^2 - 3y + 3$
(B) $xy - 3y + y^2$
(C) $xy - y^2 - 3y + 3x$
(D) $xy - 3y + y^2 + 3x$
(E) $y^2 - 3y + 3x - xy$

190. If $x < y$, $y < z$, and $z > w$, which of the following statements is always true?

(A) $x > w$
(B) $x < z$
(C) $y = w$
(D) $y > w$
(E) $x < w$

191. A box of nuts and bolts costs 53¢. How much would 10 boxes cost if they were sold at a 10% loss?

(A) 47¢
(B) 48¢
(C) $4.70
(D) $4.77
(E) $4.80

192. What is the ratio of $\frac{2}{3}$ to $\frac{5}{4}$?

(A) $\frac{1}{4}$
(B) $\frac{10}{12}$
(C) $\frac{8}{15}$
(D) $\frac{20}{6}$
(E) $\frac{2}{7}$

Use the following graph for questions 193–195.

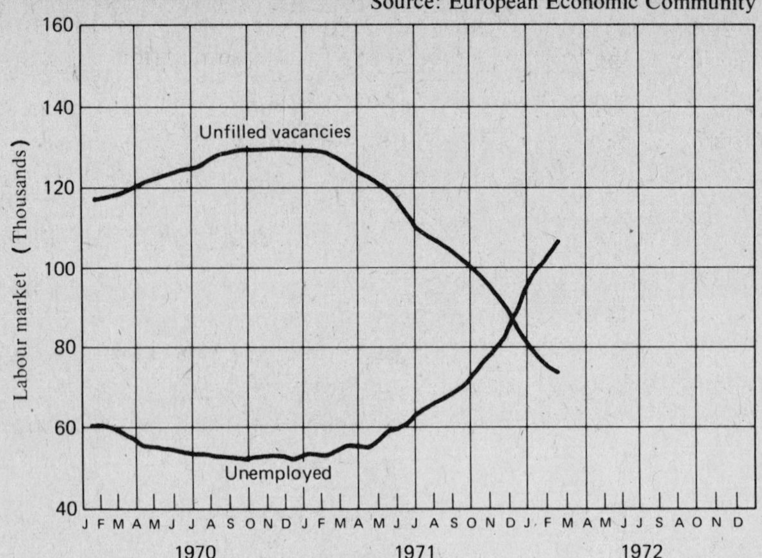

193. When were the unfilled vacancies equal to the number of unemployed?

(A) September 1970
(B) July 1971
(C) September 1971
(D) December 1971
(E) January 1972

194. About how many persons were unemployed when the unfilled vacancies were equal to the number of unemployed?

(A) 80,000
(B) 83,000
(C) 86,000
(D) 92,000
(E) 100,000

195. There were more people unemployed than there were unfilled vacancies during x of the months shown where x is

(A) 1
(B) 3
(C) 5
(D) 7
(E) 9

If there is still time remaining, you may review the questions in this section only.
You may not turn to any other section of the test.

Answers

Section I Reading Recall

1. **(E)**
2. **(C)**
3. **(D)**
4. **(C)**
5. **(A)**
6. **(C)**
7. **(B)**
8. **(E)**
9. **(A)**
10. **(D)**
11. **(D)**
12. **(A)**
13. **(D)**
14. **(B)**
15. **(A)**
16. **(C)**
17. **(C)**
18. **(E)**
19. **(E)**
20. **(C)**
21. **(C)**
22. **(D)**
23. **(E)**
24. **(C)**
25. **(E)**
26. **(E)**
27. **(A)**
28. **(C)**
29. **(E)**
30. **(C)**

Section II Mathematics

(Numbers in parentheses indicate the section in the Mathematics Review where material concerning the question is discussed.)

31. **(C)** (I–4)
32. **(C)** (I–1)
33. **(B)** (II–3)
34. **(C)** (IV–1)
35. **(D)** (IV–1)
36. **(B)** (IV–1)
37. **(B)** (IV–1)
38. **(C)** (III–4, III–7)
39. **(C)** (II–4)
40. **(D)** (II–3)
41. **(D)** (I–7)
42. **(E)** (IV–3)
43. **(C)** (IV–3)
44. **(C)** (IV–3)
45. **(A)** (I–4)
46. **(A)** (II–2)
47. **(B)** (II–5)
48. **(B)** (III–7)
49. **(D)** (II–6)
50. **(D)** (I–2)
51. **(E)** (IV–4)
52. **(D)** (IV–4)
53. **(D)** (IV–4)
54. **(A)** (IV–4)
55. **(B)** (IV–4, I–2)
56. **(D)** (II–3)
57. **(A)** (I–4, II–3)
58. **(D)** (I–4, II–7)
59. **(D)** (II–3)
60. **(B)** (II–2)
61. **(B)** (IV–1)
62. **(D)** (IV–1)
63. **(D)** (IV–1, I–7)
64. **(A)** (IV–1)
65. **(B)** (II–3)
66. **(E)** (II–5, III–4)
67. **(C)** (I–4)
68. **(E)** (I–4)
69. **(C)** (I–2, II–5)
70. **(B)** (III–7)
71. **(A)** (I–4)
72. **(B)** (IV–4)
73. **(D)** (IV–4, II–5)
74. **(D)** (IV–4)
75. **(C)** (IV–4)
76. **(A)** (IV–4)
77. **(E)** (II–7)
78. **(C)** (III–7)
79. **(C)** (I–4)
80. **(D)** (I–4)
81. **(A)** (II–3)
82. **(D)** (III 7, III–8)
83. **(C)** (IV–1)
84. **(C)** (IV–1)
85. **(C)** (IV–1)

Section III Verbal Aptitude

86. **(D)**	96. **(A)**	106. **(D)**	116. **(C)**
87. **(A)**	97. **(A)**	107. **(A)**	117. **(E)**
88. **(A)**	98. **(B)**	108. **(A)**	118. **(B)**
89. **(C)**	99. **(A)**	109. **(C)**	119. **(C)**
90. **(D)**	100. **(B)**	110. **(C)**	120. **(B)**
91. **(C)**	101. **(C)**	111. **(B)**	121. **(A)**
92. **(B)**	102. **(A)**	112. **(A)**	122. **(C)**
93. **(B)**	103. **(B)**	113. **(B)**	123. **(A)**
94. **(A)**	104. **(B)**	114. **(A)**	124. **(B)**
95. **(C)**	105. **(D)**	115. **(B)**	125. **(A)**

Section IV Data Sufficiency

126. **(A)**	130. **(B)**	134. **(C)**	138. **(B)**
127. **(A)**	131. **(D)**	135. **(E)**	139. **(A)**
128. **(E)**	132. **(D)**	136. **(A)**	140. **(E)**
129. **(E)**	133. **(C)**	137. **(D)**	

Section V Business Judgment

141. **(B)**	146. **(C)**	151. **(B)**	156. **(B)**
142. **(C)**	147. **(A)**	152. **(B)**	157. **(B)**
143. **(B)**	148. **(C)**	153. **(C)**	158. **(A)**
144. **(D)**	149. **(B)**	154. **(E)**	159. **(A)**
145. **(B)**	150. **(C)**	155. **(A)**	160. **(D)**

Section VI Mathematics

(Numbers in parentheses indicate the section in the Mathematics Review where material concerning the question is discussed.)

161. **(D)** (II–6)	173. **(E)** (IV–1, I–5)	185. **(C)** (IV–4, I–4)
162. **(E)** (III–1, II–2)	174. **(E)** (IV–1)	186. **(A)** (IV–4)
163. **(C)** (I–4)	175. **(E)** (IV–1, I–7)	187. **(C)** (III–7)
164. **(E)** (I–1)	176. **(C)** (IV–1)	188. **(D)** (I–7)
165. **(C)** (IV–2)	177. **(D)** (II–3)	189. **(C)** (II–1)
166. **(D)** (IV–2, II–5)	178. **(E)** (II–3)	190. **(B)** (II–7)
167. **(D)** (IV–2)	179. **(C)** (I–4)	191. **(D)** (I–4)
168. **(B)** (II–4)	180. **(D)** (II–3)	192. **(C)** (I–2, II–5)
169. **(E)** (III–7, I–4)	181. **(D)** (I–4)	193. **(D)** (IV–3)
170. **(D)** (II–3)	182. **(D)** (IV–4)	194. **(C)** (IV–3)
171. **(A)** (I–4)	183. **(B)** (IV–4)	195. **(B)** (IV–3)
172. **(C)** (II–3, II–5)	184. **(E)** (IV–4)	

Analysis

Section I Reading Recall

1. **(E)** Although the multinational corporation was described as having the capacity to move across international boundaries (see paragraph 3), no specific definition of such a company was given in the passage.

2. **(C)** See paragraph 2.

3. **(D)** See paragraph 6.

4. **(C)** See paragraph 6: "American firms were thus acquiring dominant control over the high technology sectors of the European economy on which it depended for future growth."

5. **(A)** See paragraph 3: ". . . Lord Keynes had demonstrated that it was possible to pursue maximum income and full employment objectives within national boundaries.

6. **(C)** See paragraph 4.

7. **(B)** See paragraph 5.

8. **(E)** All are mentioned in paragraph 5.

9. **(A)** See the last paragraph. The deficit after 1960 was largely caused by factors not mentioned in the passage, such as large military expenditures abroad and foreign aid. However, the passage did mention one initial cause during the 1950's, i.e., the promotion of European recovery.

10. **(D)** The subject matter of the passage deals with the effects of multinational corporations on nation-state economies; thus, it could appear in an economic journal.

11. **(D)** See paragraph 2: ". . . the effectiveness of this research methodology is questionable, at least in the immediate time span," i.e., the short-run.

12. **(A)** See paragraph 1, first line.

13. **(D)** See paragraph 2: "Management is in a great state of flux in India. . . ."

14. **(B)** See paragraph 2.

15. **(A)** See the last paragraph: "The diversities . . . lead to the existence of differing, and at times mutually contradictory, behavior patterns and managerial actions."

16. **(C)** See paragraph 2: "It enables the analyst to compare (and contrast) . . . in two separate regions . . ." (i.e., countries); also, see paragraph 3 where the author writes about the comparative analyst comparing "norms" in other countries and cultures.

17. **(C)** See paragraph 3: ". . . there is such a great degree of diversity."

18. **(E)** See especially the last paragraph. Throughout the passage, the author stresses that there are a number of "norms" of managerial behavior in India and cross-cultural fusion of ideas from within and from the west. This line of thinking would rule out alternatives (B) through (D). As for (A), it is not mentioned in the passage.

19. **(E)** See paragraph 2: "All the four sectors . . . have not organized their contents and actions in a rigid fashion . . . they are malleable. . . . ," i.e., flexible.

20. **(C)** See paragraph 2: "It enables the analyst to compare . . . hypothesizing about the similarities and divergences."

21. **(C)** See paragraph 1, line 1: "The first and decisive step in the expansion of Europe overseas was the conquest of the Atlantic Ocean."

22. **(D)** See paragraph 1: ". . . in men of the calibre of Prince Henry, known as the Navigator. . . ."

23. **(E)** In paragraph 1, the sentence starting "Portugal could adapt and develop the knowledge and experience of the past to meet the challenge of the future . . . ," meets answer (B); also in this paragraph there is mention of experienced Portuguese seamen and a mercantile marine (A), rudiments of navigation (C), and mapmakers (D). Since extensive trade routes are never mentioned, the correct answer is (E).

24. **(C)** Portugal was the logical nation for this task because of her "geographical position and her history." Wealth (A) and navigational experience (B) are resources in context with the question, while (D) and (E) are vague.

25. **(E)** See paragraph 1.

26. **(E)** See paragraph 2: Seamen kept close to shore because ". . . the latitudinal extent of the Mediterranean was not great, and voyages could be conducted from point to point on compass bearings," not because of the other reasons given in the question.

27. **(A)** Predictable risks. See paragraph 2: ". . . hazards . . . in the form of sudden storms or dangerous coasts, were known and could be usually anticipated."

28. **(C)** In paragraph 2: "Having made a landfall on a bearing, they could determine their precise position from prominent landmarks. . . ."

29. **(E)** These are given in paragraph 3.

30. **(C)** See paragraph 1: ". . . her increasing and vigorous population was making heavy demands on her resources, Portugal turned southwards and westwards for opportunities of trade and commerce."

Section II Mathematics

31. **(C)** The toy was originally offered at ($1.10)($10.00) or $11.00. This price was discounted by (.10)($11.00) which equals $1.10. So the toy was sold for $11.00 − $1.10 or $9.90.

32. **(C)** 3 divides 9 evenly and 3 divides 33 evenly, so 9 and 33 are not primes. 7, 11, 13, and 29 have no divisors except 1 and themselves, so they are all primes. Thus, the set of numbers contains 4 prime numbers.

33. **(B)** Each worker makes $\frac{1}{5}$ of a yard in 20 minutes. So 50 workers will make $(\frac{1}{5})(50)$, 10 yards in 20 minutes. 20 minutes is $\frac{1}{3}$ of an hour, so the factory produces 3×10 or 30 yards in an hour.

34. **(C)** The third column gives the average of weekly overtime hours for November 1972; machinery, except electrical, is the only category with over 5 hours.

35. **(D)** Look in the first column. Only the apparel, printing, leather, and miscellaneous industries show less than 40 hours. Be careful not to include nondurable goods for which there is an average of *all* such industries.

36. **(B)** If the average of weekly hours decreased, then the entry in the second column is larger than the entry in the first column. This is true only for apparel. Notice that the miscellaneous category did not decrease, it stayed the same.

37. **(B)** Look in column two in the row headed "All manufacturing." Do not bother to find the average of all the entries; it will waste time.

38. **(C)** The area in (A) is clearly less than that in (C). So (A) and (E) are eliminated. Since each of the other triangles has a side of length 4, use that side as the base in the area formula. Whichever triangle has the largest altitude will have the largest area. (C) will have a larger altitude than either (B) or (D) since the sides of (C) beside the base are longer.

39. **(C)** Since 10% have both brown eyes and brown hair, and 25% have brown eyes, 15% of the people have brown eyes but do not have brown hair. Thus, 40% + 15% or 55% of the people have brown eyes or brown hair or both. Therefore, 100% − 55% or 45% of the people have neither brown eyes nor brown hair.

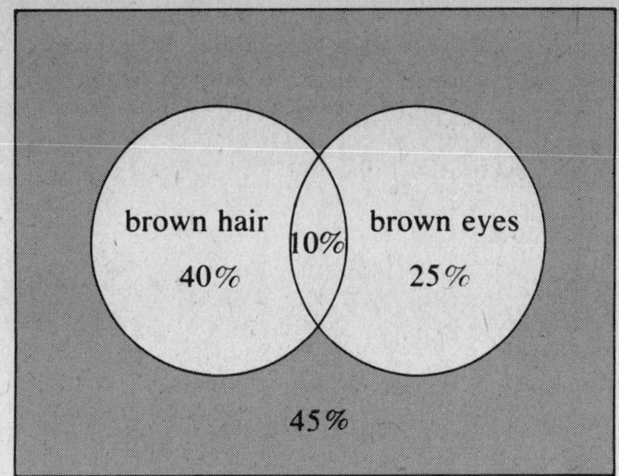

40. **(D)** Each share is worth \$13.21 − \$9.50 or \$3.71 more in 1970 than it was in 1960. So 100,000 shares are worth (\$3.71)(100,000) or \$371,000.00 more in 1970 than they were in 1960.

41. **(D)** Add up all the daily wages for the week: \$40.62 + 41.35 + 42.00 + 42.50 + 39.53 = \$206.00. Divide \$206.00 by 5 to get the average daily wage, \$41.20.

42. **(E)** The graph gives the number of thousands; so 300 corresponds to 300,000. There were more beneficiaries in 1971 and 1972, but the question asked for the largest number of beneficiaries between 1940 and 1970.

43. **(C)** If you have trouble figuring out the scale, start at one end and work through the graph. Thus, if you start at 1940, which is the first mark, you can see that the graph hit 300,000 for the year 1957.

44. **(C)**

STATEMENT I is true since the number was under 100,000 for the years 1942, 1943, 1944, and 1945, but was over 300,000 only during 1957 and for fewer than 12 months in 1971–1972.

STATEMENT II is false since the graph does not say anything about the number of people employed, only about the number receiving unemployment insurance.

STATEMENT III is true since if a line were drawn between the points on the graph for 1962 and 1965, it would fall.

45. **(A)** If the price of a pound of apples rises 2%, then the price of ten pounds of apples rises 2%. This is because the percentage change is the same for any amount sold. Since a dozen eggs and ten pounds of apples currently cost the same, each costs one half of the total price. Therefore, one half of the total is increased by 10% and the other half is increased by 2%, so the total price is increased by $\frac{1}{2}(10\%) + \frac{1}{2}(2\%) = 6\%$.

46. **(A)** $2y = 6$, so $y = 3$. Therefore, $x + 3 = 4$; so $x = 1$.

47. **(B)** Each rat eats $\frac{1}{10}$ of 30 pounds or 3 pounds in a week. Therefore, 3 rats will eat 3×3 pounds or 9 pounds.

48. **(B)** The area of the triangle is $\frac{1}{2}(a \cdot b)$ where the base is a and the altitude b. Since $3^2 + 4^2 = 5^2$, the triangle is a right triangle. So if 4 is the length of the base, 3 is the length of the altitude. Thus, the area of the triangle is $\frac{1}{2} \cdot 3 \cdot 4$ or 6 square miles. The area of the square is 2^2 or 4 square miles. The area of the triangle is thus 2 square miles larger than the area of the square.

49. **(D)** At the end of the first year, he will have $\frac{1}{2}$(\$10,000); at the end of the second year $\frac{1}{2} \cdot \frac{1}{2}(10,000)$; at the end of n years he will have $(\frac{1}{2})^n$(\$10,000). Therefore, we want to find the value of n so that $(\frac{1}{2})^n$ is less than $\frac{1}{10}$ (since $\frac{1}{10}$(\$10,000) = \$1,000). $(\frac{1}{2})^2 = \frac{1}{4}$, $(\frac{1}{2})^3 = \frac{1}{8}$, $(\frac{1}{2})^4 = \frac{1}{16}$. So after 4 years his investment will be worth less than \$1,000.

50. **(D)** If he works 8 hours, he makes (8)(\$2.50) or \$20.00. For any time worked over 8 hours he makes (1.5)(\$2.50) or \$3.75 an hour. So find x, the number of hours, such that (\$3.75)x = \$27.50 − \$20.00 or \$7.50. Therefore, $x = 2$, and the total number of hours is 8 + 2 or 10.

51. **(E)** Each line indicates 5% of sales. In 1950 (the left column) food sales use up 9 lines; so food sales were $9 \cdot 5\%$ or 45%.

52. **(D)** Electrical sales went from 5% to 19%, an increase of 14%. Machinery increased from 26% to 38%, an increase of 12%. International sales increased from 4% to 15%, an increase of 11%. The others decreased.

53. **(D)** In 1970 (right column), machinery had the largest percentage and electrical sales were second in percentage.

54. **(A)**

The graph gives no information about the monetary value of sales. Even though the percentage of sales of food was less in 1970 than in 1950, their monetary value might have been greater. Therefore, STATEMENT I can not be inferred from the graph.

STATEMENT II is false; international sales were 15% of the total in 1970; 15% of $1,000,000,000 is $150,000,000, not $15,000,-000.

STATEMENT III is false because food sales were 45% in 1950; the other categories add up to 55%.

55. **(B)** In 1950, food sales were 45% or $\frac{9}{20}$ of total sales. In 1970, food sales were 15% or $\frac{3}{20}$ of total sales. Since total income doubled between 1950 and 1970, $\frac{3}{20}$ of the 1970 total is $\frac{3}{20} \cdot 2$ or $\frac{3}{10}$ of the 1950 total. So the ratio of food income in 1970 to that in 1950 is $\frac{3/10}{9/20}$ or $\frac{3}{10} \times \frac{20}{9}$ or $\frac{2}{3}$.

56. **(D)** Each man does $\frac{1}{25}$ of the job in $1\frac{1}{2}$ hours. Thus, 15 men will do $\frac{15}{25}$ or $\frac{3}{5}$ of the job in $1\frac{1}{2}$ hours. So 15 men will complete the job in $\frac{5}{3} \cdot \frac{3}{2} = \frac{5}{2} = 2\frac{1}{2}$ hours. Another method gives $\frac{15}{25} = \frac{3/2}{x}$ where x is the time 15 men will take to complete the job. Therefore, $15x = \frac{3}{2} \cdot 25 = \frac{75}{2}$ so $x = \frac{5}{2} = 2\frac{1}{2}$.

57. **(A)** The car gets 100% − 12% or 88% of 20 miles to the gallon at 60 miles per hour. Thus, the car gets (.88)(20) or 17.6 miles to the gallon at 60 mph. Therefore, it can travel (11)(17.6) or 193.6 miles.

58. **(D)** The area of a circle is πr^2. If the radius is increased by 5%, then the new radius is 1.05 times the old radius. So the new area is $\pi(1.05r)^2 = \pi(1.1025)r^2$. Since the area of the new circle is 1.1025 times the area of the old, it has increased by 10.25%.

59. **(D)** The first 12 tons cost (12)($500) or $6,000. When you purchase 30 tons, you are buying 18 tons in addition to the first 12 tons costing additionally $\$(500 - x)(18)$. Since $10,000 − $6,000 = $4,000, we get $\$9{,}000 - 18x = \$4{,}000$, and $18x = \$5{,}000$. So $x = 277.78$.

60. **(B)** Subtract $x + y = 2$ from $3x + y = 4$; the result is $2x = 2$. So $x = 1$; then $y = 1$ since $x + y = 2$. Therefore, $x - y = 0$.

61. **(B)** One thousand million is a billion. The Bank of England and the Bank of Italy have over a thousand million. Also the Bank for International Settlements has 1,600 million. (It is shown divided into two categories, but the question asks for the *number* of institutions.)

62. **(D)** The Bank of Mexico has 130 million; all the other institutions have 200 million or more.

63. **(D)** The total is 11,730 million and there are 15 institutions, so the average is 11,730/15 million or 782,000,000.

64. **(A)**

STATEMENT I is true since 20% of 11,730 is 2,346, and since all the institutions have less than 2,100.

STATEMENT II is false since 2% of 11,730 is 234.60 and since many institutions have 200 or less.

STATEMENT III is false since 10 times 130 is 1,300, which is larger than 1,250.

65. **(B)** He sells a case for 40(20¢) or \$8.00. Since he pays \$5 a case, his profit is \$8.00 − \$5.00 or \$3.00.

66. **(E)** The sum of the angles of a triangle is 180°. Let x be the number of degrees in the largest angle; then the other angles are $\frac{1}{2}x$ and $\frac{3}{4}x$ degrees. Therefore, $\frac{1}{2}x + \frac{3}{4}x + x = \frac{9}{4}x = 180°$, so $x = 80°$.

67. **(C)** He pays (.15)(\$200) or \$30 in taxes a week. So he pays (52)(\$30.00) or \$1,560.00 a year.

68. **(E)** The price of the model increased by \$3,360 − \$2,500 or by \$860. Since it cost \$2,500 in 1967 and 860/2500 = 86/250 = .344, the percentage of increase was 34.4%.

69. **(C)** The ratio of $\frac{1}{6}$ to $\frac{4}{5} = \frac{1}{6}/\frac{4}{5} = \frac{1}{6} \cdot \frac{5}{4} = \frac{5}{24}$.

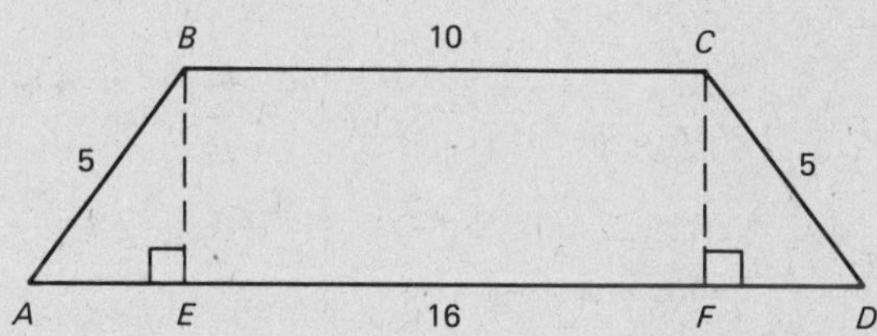

70. **(B)** If we draw $CF \perp AD$, then $\triangle ABE \cong \triangle DCF$ and $AE = FD = 3$. Then $BE = 4$. Thus the area of the trapezoid, which equals the product of the altitude and the average of the bases, equals $(4)(\frac{1}{2})(10 + 16) = 52$.

71. **(A)** Interest = principal × annual rate × time. The principal is \$650.00; the annual rate is 8%; the time is 6 months or $\frac{1}{2}$ year. Thus, the interest = (\$650)(.08)($\frac{1}{2}$) = (\$650)(.04) = \$26.00.

72. **(B)** Look at the black columns in the top graph. Put your pencil on the 15% indicator at each side of the graph, and just count the black columns above your pencil. Each mark on the horizontal scale represents one quarter of a year.

73. **(D)** In the first quarter of 1971, deposits were about 24%, and mortgages were 12%. So the ratio was about 2 to 1. In every other quarter, the bars are more nearly the same height.

74. **(D)** The striped column (mortgages) is highest for the third quarter of 1972. Use your pencil to check nonadjacent columns.

75. **(C)** Look at the black columns in the bottom graph. (A) and (B) are incorrect since deposits increased between those quarters. Of the remaining answers the height of the column dropped the most from the second quarter of 1971 to the third quarter of 1971. (Use your pencil to measure the difference in heights between adjacent columns.)

76. **(A)**

STATEMENT I is true since the striped bar is higher for the third quarter of each year than it is for the first quarter.

STATEMENT II is false; the striped bar is higher than the black bar for the fourth quarter of 1972 for savings and loan associations.

STATEMENT III is false since the black bar is higher for the first quarter of 1970 in the bottom graph (mutual savings banks) than it is in the top graph (savings and loan associations).

77. **(E)**

Since x is greater than 2 and 2 is greater than 0, x is greater than 0. Therefore, STATEMENT I is false but STATEMENT II is true.

If we add x to each side of the inequality $x > 0$ we obtain $x + x > x + 0$, so $2x > x$. Therefore, STATEMENT III is true.

Since x is greater than 2 which is greater than 1, we know $x > 1$. Multiply the inequality by x (x is positive so the inequality is preserved); the result is $x^2 > x$, so STATEMENT IV is true.

Therefore, STATEMENTS II, III, and IV are true.

78. **(C)** Since the field is a square, the area = $(\text{side})^2 = 144$ square yards. Thus, the side must have length $\sqrt{144}$ or 12 yards. Since the man walked around all 4 sides, he walked 4×12 or 48 yards.

79. **(C)** At 2 A.M. the car is traveling (.10)50 or 5.0 mph faster than at 1 A.M. So at 2 A.M. the car is traveling at 55 mph. At 3 A.M. the car is traveling (.10)55 or 5.5 mph faster than at 2 A.M. Therefore, the car is traveling 60.5 mph at 3 A.M.

80. **(D)** It falls (.12)(531.54) or 63.78. So it is now at 531.54 − 63.78 or 467.76, where we have rounded up.

OR

It falls 12% so it will be 88% of 531.54 which equals (.88)(531.54) or 467.76.

81. **(A)** Since each assistant does $^2/_3$ as much as the worker, all 3 will accomplish $1 + 2(^2/_3)$ or $^7/_3$ as much as the worker by himself. So they will finish the job in $1 \div {^7/_3}$ or $^3/_7$ as much time as it would take the worker by himself.

82. **(D)** The ceiling is 15 ft. long and 12 ft. wide. So the area of the ceiling is (15)(12) = 180 sq. ft. Two walls are 15 ft. long and 8 ft. high, so the area of each of those walls is (8)(15) = 120 square feet. The other two walls are 12 ft. wide and 8 ft. high. So the area of each of those walls is (8)(12) = 96 square ft. Therefore, the area to be painted is 180 + 2(120) + 2(96) or 612 square feet. Therefore, the amount of paint needed is $^{612}/_{36} = {^{102}/_6} = 17$ gallons.

83. **(C)** Look in the fifth row of figures; Italy has 19.4% in agriculture. This is higher than each of the other entries in the row.

84. **(C)** The population of Germany is 61,547,000, and the population of the entire Community is 188,147,000. So 61,547,000/188,147,000 = 61,547/188,147 = .3271 = 32.7% which rounds off to 33%. (Notice you must carry out the division beyond two decimal places, because the third decimal place can affect the second.)

85. **(C)** Look in the seventh row of figures. The Community has 44% of its employees in services, and Germany (42.5), Italy (37.3) and Luxembourg (42.8) have fewer than 44% in services.

Section III Verbal Aptitude

86. **(D)** CONTRITION: remorse, repentance. *Antonym:* reprobation

87. **(A)** EXONERATE: absolve, acquit. *Antonym:* condemn

88. **(A)** ARRAY: arrangement, apparel. *Antonym:* disorder

89. **(C)** SALIENT: notable, conspicuous. *Antonym:* inconspicuous

90. **(D)** LASCIVIOUS: lewd, lustful. *Antonym:* chaste

91. **(C)** PIQUANT: pungent, savory. *Antonym:* bland

92. **(B)** SUBTERFUGE: evasion, subtlety. *Antonym:* openness

93. **(B)** TEMERITY: audacity, nerve. *Antonym:* caution

94. **(A)** EPHEMERAL: of short duration. *Antonym:* permanent

95. **(C)** TENACIOUS: steadfast, persistent. *Antonym:* fickle

96. **(A)** AVIDITY: eagerness, greed. *Antonym:* generosity

97. **(A)** CHIMERICAL: existing in fantasy, imaginary. *Antonym:* real

98. **(B)** COGNIZANT: sensible, aware. *Antonym:* ignorant

99. **(A)** FACETIOUS: pleasant, jocose. *Antonym:* serious

100. **(B)** Snow in winter is the antithesis of rain in spring. Note that heat is associated with summer, but does not have the same relationship as the above two sets.

101. **(C)** Fires produce smoke as wars cause death. You cannot have one without the other. Pills sometimes produce relief but not always; and in any event, relief is a positive result. The correct sets are negative occurrences.

102. **(A)** A volt is a measure (actually of electromagnetic force) of electricity; an inch is part of or a measure of a foot.

103. **(B)** Weight is measured by a device called a scale as height can be measured by a device called a ruler.

104. **(B)** The relationship here is one of synonyms. Declaration and proclamation, affirmation and ratification are synonyms.

105. **(D)** A need triggers motivation in a person as an unfulfilled need leads to frustration. Both sets have in common the behavior of an individual. Note that in (C), hunger is a need which triggers some sort of motivation (activity) which has the objective of obtaining food. Food is the object, not the motivation or behavior.

106. **(D)** A cigarette contains tobacco as coffee contains caffeine. Both are integral parts of the products.

107. **(A)** The relationship is one of opposites. The opposite of poverty is wealth as the opposite of master is servant.

108. **(A)** Something that is clandestine is done surreptitiously. Something that is subversive is done secretly.

109. **(C)** Air pressure is measured by a barometer; altitude is measured by an altimeter.

110. **(C)** Something that is axiomatic is self-evident. Something that is dogmatic is asserted without proof.

111. **(B)** A bandit commits robbery. A traitor commits treason.

112. **(A)** A person who is suspicious is not usually confiding. A person who is cautious is not usually bold.

113. **(B)** is the only alternative that makes sense.

114. **(A)** While the first words in the sets (A) through (E) fit the sentence, only the second word of (A) makes any sense.

115. **(B)** Another possibility is (D), but (B) has better meaning.

116. **(C)** Alternatives (A), (D) and (E) plicated (folded) do not have meaning in the context; (C) is superior to (B).

117. **(E)** Alternatives (A), (B) and (C) are incorrect, i.e., the two terms are not the same. Likewise with (D), a household may contain one individual and not a family.

118. **(B)** A small sample size can render a survey unreliable; an inadequate design (A) will not necessarily make a survey expensive. The other alternatives should have been eliminated owing to their unsound assumptions.

119. **(C)** Physiological means physical, not a state of mind. Rational means sensible. Prodigious means great, and perfidious means evil.

120. **(B)** Alternatives (D) and (E) are too general; (A) and (C) have little meaning; (B) is specific and in context.

121. **(A)** Protectionists attempt to curb imports and thus impede foreign trade. They are "protecting" their home economy.

122. **(C)** This is a well known proverb.

123. **(A)** The implication is that uniformity results in a lack of innovation and thus leads to

mediocrity. Whether it leads to disaster (B) or moderation (E) is unknown, but certainly uniformity cannot lead to diversity (C). Finally, (D) does not have meaning.

124. **(B)** Certainly, prison guards would not react according to the other alternatives, e.g., they would not be "annoyed" at a stricter command or "vexed" at stronger sanctions.

125. **(A)** A dilettante is one who dabbles in the arts.

Section IV Data Sufficiency

126. **(A)**

STATEMENT (1) alone is sufficient. If angle x is a right angle, then AOC is a semi-circle. Therefore, AC is a diameter.

STATEMENT (2) alone is insufficient. There are many (an infinite number) triangles we can inscribe in the circle such that $AB = \frac{3}{4}BC$. Not all of these will have AC as a diameter.

Therefore, STATEMENT (1) alone is sufficient, but STATEMENT (2) alone is not sufficient.

127. **(A)**

To find how many gallons the tank will hold, we need to calculate the volume of the tank and then divide this by the volume of one gallon of the liquid. Therefore, STATEMENT (1) alone is sufficient.

STATEMENT (2) alone is not sufficient (note that it gives no further information about the tank). We need to know how much space a gallon of the liquid occupies.

Therefore, STATEMENT (1) alone is sufficient, but STATEMENT (2) alone is not.

128. **(E)**

STATEMENT (1) alone is not sufficient. We still need the total weight of the books; then we can divide by the average weight to obtain the number of books.

STATEMENT (2) tells us how much the books and the bookshelf together weigh, but we don't know how much the books weigh.

So STATEMENTS (1) and (2) together are not sufficient.

129. **(E)**

STATEMENT (1) alone is not sufficient, since many noncongruent triangles can have a side and an angle which are equal.

By the same reasoning, STATEMENT (2) alone is not sufficient.

STATEMENTS (1) and (2) together are not sufficient. For two triangles to be congruent, they must have two pairs of corresponding sides and the included angles equal. For example, the following two triangles satisfy STATEMENTS (1) and (2) and angle x = angle y but they are not congruent.

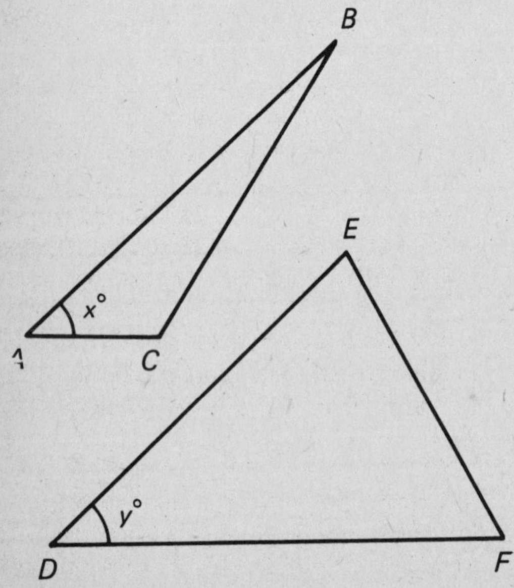

Therefore, STATEMENTS (1) and (2) together are not sufficient.

130. **(B)**

STATEMENT (2) alone is sufficient, since we can multiply $\frac{1}{9}$ by (60×60) to obtain the speed in mph.

STATEMENT (1) alone is not sufficient, because the plane's flying in a circle gives us no information about the exact speed of the plane.

So STATEMENT (2) alone is sufficient, but STATEMENT (1) alone is not.

131. **(D)**

STATEMENT (1) alone is sufficient. If L = the length of the floor, then STATEMENT (1) says the width is $\frac{1}{2}L$. The area of the floor is length times width or $(L)(\frac{1}{2}L)$ or $\frac{1}{2}L^2$. Since the area is equal to 32 square feet, we have $\frac{1}{2}L^2 = 32$ so $L^2 = 64$ and $L = 8$ feet.

STATEMENT (2) alone is sufficient. Let W = the width of the floor. Then STATEMENT (2) says $W = L - 4$. So the area is $L(L-4)$ or $L^2 - 4L$ which equals 32. Therefore, L satisfies $L^2 - 4L - 32 = 0$, and since $L^2 - 4L - 32 = (L-8)(L+4)$, $L^2 - 4L - 32 = 0$ if and only if $L = 8$ or $L = -4$. Since $L = -4$ has no meaning for the problem, $L = 8$.

So STATEMENT (1) alone is sufficient, and STATEMENT (2) alone is sufficient.

132. **(D)** We have to determine whether $(AB)(BC)$ which is the area of the rectangle $ABCD$ is equal to $(EH)^2$ which is the area of the square $EFGH$.

STATEMENT (1) alone is sufficient. Since ABC is a right triangle, $BC = \sqrt{(AC)^2 - (AB)^2}$, and using STATEMENT (1) we have $BC = \sqrt{(EG)^2 - \frac{1}{4}(EH)^2}$. Using the fact that $EFGH$ is a square, we know $(EG)^2 = 2(EH)^2$, so we can express BC in terms of EH. Using STATEMENT (1) we can express AB as $\frac{1}{2}EH$, so $(AB)(BC)$ can be expressed as a multiple of $(EH)^2$. Notice that to answer the question you don't have to actually set up the equation. If you work it out you will find that the area of $ABCD$ is $\frac{\sqrt{7}}{4}(EH)^2$, so the areas are not equal. *Don't* waste time carrying out the extra work on the test.

STATEMENT (2) alone is sufficient since the diagonal of a rectangle divides the rectangle into two congruent triangles. Therefore, the area of $ABCD$ is equal to the area of $EFGH$ if and only if the area of ABC is equal to the area of EFG.

133. **(C)**

STATEMENT (2) says $J = 2S$, where J = Joan's weight and S = Susan's weight. But since we don't know Joan's weight, STATEMENT (2) alone is not sufficient.

STATEMENT (1) says $J + S = 250$; so if we use STATEMENT (2) we have $2S + S = 250$ or $S = \frac{250}{3} = 83\frac{1}{3}$. But STATEMENT (1) alone is not sufficient. If we use only STATEMENT (1), we don't know how much Joan weighs.

Therefore, STATEMENTS (1) and (2) together are sufficient, but neither statement alone is sufficient.

134. **(C)**

In each minute, hole A drains $\frac{1}{24}$ of the tank according to STATEMENT (1). Since we have no information about B, STATEMENT (1) alone is not sufficient.

In each minute, hole B drains $\frac{1}{42}$ of the tank according to STATEMENT (2), but STATEMENT (2) gives no information about hole A. So STATEMENT (2) alone is not sufficient.

If we use STATEMENTS (1) and (2), then both holes together will drain $\frac{1}{24} + \frac{1}{42}$ or $\frac{7+4}{6 \times 28}$ or $\frac{11}{168}$ of the tank each minute. Therefore, it will take $\frac{168}{11}$ or $15\frac{3}{11}$ minutes for the tank to be empty. So STATEMENTS (1) and (2) together are sufficient, but neither statement alone is sufficient.

135. **(E)** STATEMENTS (1) and (2) are equivalent, since $x - y = 6$ if and only if $2x - 2y = 2(x-y) = 2 \cdot 6 = 12$. Each statement tells us only what $x - y$ is, and we have no other information. Therefore, each statement alone is insufficient. But since the two statements are the same, even together they are not sufficient.

136. **(A)**

STATEMENT (2) alone is not sufficient, since we must know how close the circles are and we know only the radius of each circle.

STATEMENT (1) alone is sufficient. The centers of the two circles are closer than the sum of the radii. (So we can form a triangle with DF as one side and the two other sides with length 2 and R respectively; but this means that the third vertex of the triangle will be on both circle E and circle C.)

So STATEMENT (1) alone is sufficient, but STATEMENT (2) alone is not sufficient.

137. **(D)** It is sufficient to be able to find his total income for the years 1967 through 1969 since we divide the total income by 3 to obtain the average income.

STATEMENT (1) alone is sufficient. Since we know his income for 1967, we can find his income in 1968 and 1969 by using STATEMENT (1). Therefore, we can find the total income.

STATEMENT (2) alone is sufficient. Add the combined income from 1968 and 1969 to the income from 1967 (which is given), and we have the total income.

Therefore, STATEMENTS (1) and (2) are each sufficient.

138. **(B)**

STATEMENT (1) alone is not sufficient. $y = z$ does not imply $x = 90°$. For example, in an equilateral triangle, $x = y = z$ and $x = 60°$.

STATEMENT (2) alone is sufficient. Pythagoras' theorem says x is a right angle if and only if $(AC)^2 + (BC)^2 = (AB)^2$.

139. **(A)**

STATEMENT (1) alone is sufficient. If $P =$ Paul's height, then we can write a proportion $\frac{P}{6} = \frac{9}{10}$ since their shadows are proportional to their heights. $\left[\text{Thus, } P = \frac{54}{10} = 5.4 \text{ feet.}\right]$

STATEMENT (2) alone is not sufficient. The distance they are apart does not give us any information about their heights.

Therefore, STATEMENT (1) alone is sufficient, but STATEMENT (2) alone is not sufficient.

140. **(E)**

STATEMENT (1) alone is not sufficient. Note that $4 = (-2)^2 > 1 = (-1)^2$ but $-2 < -1$.

STATEMENT (2) alone is not sufficient. If $x + 3$ is greater than $y + 2$, then x can be less than y or greater than y. For example, $\frac{1}{2}$ is greater than 0, and $\frac{1}{2} + 3$ is greater than $0 + 2$. However, $\frac{1}{2}$ is less than 1, while $\frac{1}{2} + 3$ is greater than $1 + 2$.

STATEMENTS (1) and (2) together are not sufficient. For example, $-\frac{1}{2}$ is less than $\frac{1}{4}$, $-\frac{1}{2} + 3$ is greater than $2 + \frac{1}{4}$, and $(-\frac{1}{2})^2 = \frac{1}{4}$ is greater than $\frac{1}{16} = (\frac{1}{4})^2$. Also, $\frac{1}{4}$ is less than 2, $(\frac{1}{4})^2$ is less than 2^2, and $2 + 3$ is greater than $\frac{1}{4} + 2$. So STATEMENTS (1) and (2) together are not sufficient.

Section V Business Judgment

141. **(B)** The major decision to be made by the executives of Climax Corporation is whether to maintain their present service operation, or if not, what alternative would be best. In this question, the training of retail service personnel is a *Major Factor* in making that decision; it was suggested by the product service manager that more money be spent on such training. It is not a *Major Objective* because no decision has been made that more training is the answer to their problem. It is obviously not the only answer.

142. **(C)** The rise of the discount house is a *Minor Factor* to be considered only because consumers who buy appliances at such stores do so under the realization that discount houses do not have service facilities. The question, of course, is why consumers do buy appliances at discount stores when they know the dealers do not provide service.

143. **(B)** The fact that typical (i.e., the average) retailers do not have competent service personnel is a, if not *the, Major Factor* in making a decision about Climax's service system. The other important factor, of course, is whether consumers really expect service facilities in each retail store.

144. **(D)** The adequacy of service demanded by consumers is a *Major Assumption* that must be examined before a decision about service can be made. In simple terms, how much service do consumers really want? Where do they want this service—from retailers, wholesalers, the manufacturer? In several places in the passage, some concern about this problem is expressed. See the discussion about discount stores and TV sets.

145. **(B)** Centralizing the service operation is a *Major Factor* or consideration. It is not an objective because no decision as to the final form of the operation has been made.

146. **(C)** In paragraph two, it is stated that repairs are made either by retailers or wholesalers. In the case of wholesalers, the manufacturer supplies the parts, the wholesaler the labor.

147. **(A)** The adequacy of service rendered by retailers was given as the major reason for the review of Climax's service operation. It was felt that present service was inadequate owing to the lack of competent service personnel among retailers.

148. **(C)** See paragraph 3. The sales manager and others believed that if the service operation were centralized, its quality would increase while its costs would decrease.

149. **(B)** According to the results of the consumer survey quoted in paragraph 7, consumers did not pay much attention to the availability of service at the *time of purchase*.

150. **(C)** See paragraph 4. Retailers like to service appliances because of the profit and store traffic generated.

151. **(B)** The major decision to be made by Sam Hoe is whether to open a retail showroom for the sale of his custom line. He felt that this strategy might be a solution to his major problem of a declining profit position. If he could retail his own products, he felt that his profit margin would be improved. Therefore, the fact of higher operating expenses was a *Major Factor* in making his decision.

152. **(B)** The increased demand for furniture which Sam Hoe had experienced was a *Major Factor* leading him to consider opening a retail showroom.

153. **(C)** Storage space is an *Unimportant Issue* in making the decision; it bears no direct relation to the manufacture and sale of furniture in this problem.

154. **(E)** Mr. Hoe's workshop employed 20 craftsmen but this fact wouldn't affect the opening of a showroom. It is an *Unimportant Issue*.

155. **(A)** Sam's major decision is whether to open a retail showroom or not. This is the *Major Objective*. See the explanation in answer 151 above.

156. **(B)** See paragraphs 1 and 4. Profits were not increasing at the same rate as production. The other factors were not mentioned.

157. **(B)** See paragraph 1. Sam did consider a price increase, but did not take any action of the sort since he had recently raised prices of most items during the past six months.

158. **(A)** See paragraph 3. Custom furniture accounted for 78 percent of sales.

159. **(A)** See paragraph 4. Demand for Sam's custom line of furniture was increasing, but he had to limit his output owing to a shortage of skilled craftsmen.

160. **(D)** See paragraph 3. Most of Mr. Hoe's standard line was sold in a five-state area, while most of his custom made items were sold within the state. Only a few items of the latter category were sold throughout the country.

Section VI Mathematics

161. **(D)** Since $\frac{12}{4} = 3 = \frac{36}{12}$, the ratio of one term to the previous term is 3. So if x is the next term, $\frac{x}{36} = 3$ and $x = 3(36) = 108$.

162. **(E)** The complement of x is an angle of $90 - x$ degrees, and the supplement of x is an angle of $180 - x$ degrees. Thus, we have $90 - x = \frac{1}{6}(180 - x) = 30 - \frac{1}{6}x$, so $60 = \frac{5}{6}x$ or $x = 72$.

163. **(C)** The profit was $250 on sales of $1,900, so the ratio of profit to sales is $\frac{250}{1{,}900} = \frac{25}{190}$ which is approximately .132 or about 13%.

164. **(E)** Since 4 is a multiple of 2, the least common multiple of 3, 4, and 5 will be the least common multiple of 2, 3, 4, and 5. 3, 4, and 5 have no common factors so the least common multiple is $3 \cdot 4 \cdot 5 = 60$.

165. **(C)** Housing and clothing accounted for 30% of the budget. Therefore, they cost (.30) ($23,352) = $7,005.60, which is about $7,000.

166. **(D)** They spent 38% on taxes and 13% on food, so the ratio is 38 to 13, which is almost 3 to 1, since 3 times 13 is 39. (You don't have to find the amounts they spent on taxes and food. The ratio of these amounts will be the same as the ratio of the percentages and you will waste time calculating the amounts.)

167. **(D)**

STATEMENT I is true. If we add the percentages of any two other categories we get less than 38.

STATEMENT II is not true. Since there are 6 categories, the average is $16\frac{1}{4}$%, and only taxes and housing have percentages higher than $16\frac{1}{4}$.

STATEMENT III is true. Every category cost at least 7% of $23,352. Therefore, each category cost at least $1,634.64, which is greater than $1,500.

168. **(B)** Since 48% own neither a Ford nor a Chevrolet, the remaining 52% must own a Ford or a Chevrolet or both. 30% own a Chevrolet and 25% own a Ford, so since 30% + 25% = 55%, there must be 55% − 52% = 3% who own both a Ford and a Chevrolet.

169. **(E)** Area = ½(altitude)(base). The increased altitude is (1.05) altitude and the increased base is (1.07) base. Therefore, the increased area is ½(1.05)(1.07)(altitude)(base). So the increased area is (1.1235) area. Thus, the area has increased by 12.35%.

170. **(D)** The first 20 pounds cost $20 \cdot 2¢ = 40¢$. The package weighs $3\frac{1}{2}$ pounds more than 20 pounds, so there are 3 pounds and one fraction of a pound over 20 pounds. The weight over 20 pounds will cost $4 \cdot (1.5)¢ = 6¢$. Therefore, the total cost will be 46¢.

171. **(A)** Since 5,000 − 1,000 = 4,000, there are 4,000 sheets which will be discounted. The 4,000 sheets cost 4,000¢ or $40.00 before the discount, so they will cost (.98)($40.00) or $39.20 after the 2% discount. The first 1,000 sheets cost 1¢ each so they cost 1,000¢ or $10.00. Therefore, the total cost of the 5,000 sheets will be $49.20.

172. **(C)** Let T be Tom's salary, J be John's salary, and S be Steve's salary, then the given information is $T = (1.5)J$ and $J = (.8)S$. Changing to fractions we get $T = \frac{3}{2}J$ and $J = \frac{4}{5}S$ so $S = \frac{5}{4}J$. Therefore, $\frac{S}{T} = \frac{5}{4}J/\frac{3}{2}J = \frac{5}{4}/\frac{3}{2} = \frac{5}{4}\cdot\frac{2}{3} = \frac{5}{6}$. The ratio is 5 to 6.

173. **(E)** There are 499,300 beneficiaries and 189,800 of these are between 25 and 44. So the percentage is about 190,000/500,000 = 38%. (You should save time by using 190,000 and 500,000 instead of dividing 189,800 by 499,300.)

174. **(E)** There were 216,000 with 12 years or more of education. All the other categories had less than 200,000.

175. **(E)** The average number of weeks of compensation was 6.9. So about (6.9)(500,000) = 3,450,000 weeks of compensation were paid to the beneficiaries. (Since you only need an approximate solution, use 500,000 instead of 499,300.)

176. **(C)**

STATEMENT I can not be inferred since there is no data about the *total* number of people in each category. Also, the table only gives information on the number of people receiving unemployment insurance. There may be unemployed people who are not beneficiaries.

STATEMENT II can not be inferred since we have no data on how much compensation is received, only information about how long it is received.

STATEMENT III can be inferred. The average length of compensation was 7.8 weeks for those over 65. Every other category had an average length of compensation less than 7.8 weeks, so the average of those under 65 must be less than 7.8 weeks.

177. **(D)** If the average speed is 50 mph, then in 5 hours the driver will travel $5 \cdot 50$ miles or 250 miles. He traveled 135 miles in the first 3 hours, so he needs to travel $250 - 135 = 115$ miles in the final 2 hours.

178. **(E)** 30 workers are $\frac{3}{5}$ of 50 workers, so it should take the 30 workers $\frac{5}{3}$ as long as the 50 workers. Therefore, the 30 workers should take $\frac{5}{3} \cdot 4 = \frac{20}{3} = 6\frac{2}{3}$ hours $= 6$ hours and 40 minutes.

179. **(C)** If the price goes up 7%, then the new price will be 107% of the old price. Therefore, a pound of hamburger will cost (1.07) (98)¢ = 105¢ = $1.05.

180. **(D)** Each box of dictionaries weighs $6 \times 20 = 120$ pounds. Each box of encyclopedias weighs $2 \times 75 = 150$ pounds. So the load weighs $98 \times 120 + 50 \times 150 = 19{,}260$ pounds.

181. **(D)** Mary makes $600 a month on her regular job. Therefore, she receives $600 · 12 = $7,200 a year from her regular job. Her only other income is $400. So her total yearly income is $7,600. She makes $600 + $400 = $1,000 during July, so she makes 1,000/7,600 = $\frac{5}{38}$ which is about .13 of her annual income during July. Therefore, Mary makes about 13% of her annual income in July.

182. **(D)** The per capita amount has gone up from $182 to $340. Since $360 = 2 \times 180$, the amount has almost doubled.

183. **(B)** Look at the right hand side of the graph for percentages. Percentage paid by private health insurance was 25% in 1966 and 25% in 1972, so the percentage has stayed about the same.

184. **(E)** The per capita amount in 1972 was $340, so for 5 people the amount would be 5 × $340 = $1,700.

185. **(C)** In 1972, the percentage from public funds per capita was 37%. So the percentage for 5 people would still be 37%. (The amount but not the percentage changes if you have more people.)

186. **(A)**

STATEMENT I is false since direct payments increased from $94 per capita to $119 per capita.

STATEMENT II is true, since private health insurance paid $45 per capita in 1966 and $90 per capita in 1972.

STATEMENT III can not be inferred since there is no information given about hospitals.

187. **(C)** The area of the triangle is ½(altitude) (base) = ½ (altitude)S. The area of the square is S^2. Therefore, ½S(altitude) = S^2, so the altitude must be $2S$.

188. **(D)** The train will average 50 mph for 3½ hours, 75 mph for 3 hours and 20 mph for half an hour. So the distance of the trip is $(3\frac{1}{2})(50) + (3)(75) + (\frac{1}{2})(20) = 175 + 225 + 10 = 410$ miles. The trip takes 7 hours. Therefore, the average speed is $410/7 = 58\frac{4}{7}$ mph.

189. **(C)**
$$\begin{aligned}(x - y)(y + 3) &= x(y + 3) - y(y + 3)\\ &= xy + 3x - y^2 - 3y\\ &= xy - y^2 - 3y + 3x\end{aligned}$$

190. **(B)** If $x < y$ and $y < z$, then $x < z$. All the other statements may be true but are not always true.

191. **(D)** The 10 boxes cost 10 × 53¢ = $5.30. They are sold for 90% of the cost, if the loss is 10%. Therefore, they are sold for (.90) ($5.30) = $4.77.

192. **(C)** The ratio is $\frac{2}{3} / \frac{5}{4}$ which is equal to $\frac{2}{3} \cdot \frac{4}{5} = \frac{8}{15}$.

193. **(D)** The two lines crossed in December 1971, so unfilled vacancies were equal to unemployed in December 1971.

194. **(C)** The two lines crossed about ⅓ of the way between 80 and 100, so 86,000 is the best approximation. (Sometimes you can use the rings around the eraser to estimate values between the marks on a scale.)

195. **(B)** The unemployed was above the unfilled vacancies line only during December 1971, January 1972, and February 1972.

Evaluating Your Score

Tabulate your score for each section of Sample Test 2 according to the directions on pages 3–4 and record the results in the Self-scoring Table below. Then find your rank for each score on the Self-scoring Scale and record it in the appropriate blank.

Self-scoring Table

PART	SCORE	RANK
1		
2		
3		
4		
5		
6		

Self-scoring Scale

	ACHIEVEMENT			
PART	POOR	FAIR	GOOD	EXCELLENT
1	0–15	16–21	22–25	26–30
2	0–29	30–40	41–47	48–55
3	0–20	21–28	29–34	35–40
4	0– 7	8–10	11–12	13–15
5	0–10	11–14	15–16	17–20
6	0–18	19–25	26–30	31–35

Study again the Review sections covering material in Sample Test 2 for which you had a rank of FAIR or POOR. Then go on to Sample Test 3.

Answer Sheet — Sample Test 3

Section I — Reading Recall

1. A B C D E
2. A B C D E
3. A B C D E
4. A B C D E
5. A B C D E
6. A B C D E
7. A B C D E
8. A B C D E
9. A B C D E
10. A B C D E
11. A B C D E
12. A B C D E
13. A B C D E
14. A B C D E
15. A B C D E
16. A B C D E
17. A B C D E
18. A B C D E
19. A B C D E
20. A B C D E
21. A B C D E
22. A B C D E
23. A B C D E
24. A B C D E
25. A B C D E
26. A B C D E
27. A B C D E
28. A B C D E
29. A B C D E
30. A B C D E

Section II — Mathematics

31. A B C D E
32. A B C D E
33. A B C D E
34. A B C D E
35. A B C D E
36. A B C D E
37. A B C D E
38. A B C D E
39. A B C D E
40. A B C D E
41. A B C D E
42. A B C D E
43. A B C D E
44. A B C D E
45. A B C D E
46. A B C D E
47. A B C D E
48. A B C D E
49. A B C D E
50. A B C D E
51. A B C D E
52. A B C D E
53. A B C D E
54. A B C D E
55. A B C D E
56. A B C D E
57. A B C D E
58. A B C D E
59. A B C D E
60. A B C D E
61. A B C D E
62. A B C D E
63. A B C D E
64. A B C D E
65. A B C D E
66. A B C D E
67. A B C D E
68. A B C D E
69. A B C D E
70. A B C D E
71. A B C D E
72. A B C D E
73. A B C D E
74. A B C D E
75. A B C D E
76. A B C D E
77. A B C D E
78. A B C D E
79. A B C D E
80. A B C D E
81. A B C D E
82. A B C D E
83. A B C D E
84. A B C D E
85. A B C D E

Section III — Verbal Aptitude

86. A B C D E
87. A B C D E
88. A B C D E
89. A B C D E
90. A B C D E
91. A B C D E
92. A B C D E
93. A B C D E
94. A B C D E
95. A B C D E
96. A B C D E
97. A B C D E
98. A B C D E
99. A B C D E
100. A B C D E
101. A B C D E
102. A B C D E
103. A B C D E
104. A B C D E
105. A B C D E
106. A B C D E
107. A B C D E
108. A B C D E
109. A B C D E
110. A B C D E
111. A B C D E
112. A B C D E
113. A B C D E
114. A B C D E
115. A B C D E
116. A B C D E
117. A B C D E
118. A B C D E
119. A B C D E
120. A B C D E
121. A B C D E
122. A B C D E
123. A B C D E
124. A B C D E
125. A B C D E

Section IV — Data Sufficiency

126. A B C D E
127. A B C D E
128. A B C D E
129. A B C D E
130. A B C D E
131. A B C D E
132. A B C D E
133. A B C D E
134. A B C D E
135. A B C D E
136. A B C D E
137. A B C D E
138. A B C D E
139. A B C D E
140. A B C D E

Section V — Business Judgment

141. A B C D E
142. A B C D E
143. A B C D E
144. A B C D E
145. A B C D E
146. A B C D E
147. A B C D E
148. A B C D E
149. A B C D E
150. A B C D E
151. A B C D E
152. A B C D E
153. A B C D E
154. A B C D E
155. A B C D E
156. A B C D E
157. A B C D E
158. A B C D E
159. A B C D E
160. A B C D E

Section VI — Mathematics

161. A B C D E
162. A B C D E
163. A B C D E
164. A B C D E
165. A B C D E
166. A B C D E
167. A B C D E
168. A B C D E
169. A B C D E
170. A B C D E
171. A B C D E
172. A B C D E
173. A B C D E
174. A B C D E
175. A B C D E
176. A B C D E
177. A B C D E
178. A B C D E
179. A B C D E
180. A B C D E
181. A B C D E
182. A B C D E
183. A B C D E
184. A B C D E
185. A B C D E
186. A B C D E
187. A B C D E
188. A B C D E
189. A B C D E
190. A B C D E
191. A B C D E
192. A B C D E
193. A B C D E
194. A B C D E
195. A B C D E

Sample Test 3

Section I Reading Recall

TOTAL TIME: 35 minutes

Part A: TIME—15 minutes

DIRECTIONS: This part contains three reading passages. You are to read each one carefully. You will have fifteen minutes to study the three passages and twenty minutes to answer questions based on them. When answering the questions, you will *not* be allowed to refer back to the passages.

Passage 1:

With Friedrich Engels, Karl Marx in 1848 published the *Communist Manifesto,* calling upon the masses to rise and throw off their economic chains. His maturer theories of society were later elaborated in his large and abstruse work *Das Capital.* Starting as a non-violent revolutionist, he ended life as a major social theorist more or less sympathetic with violent revolution, if such became necessary in order to change the social system which he believed to be frankly predatory upon the masses.

On the theoretical side, Marx set up the doctrine of surplus value as the chief element in capitalistic exploitation. According to this theory, the ruling classes no longer employed military force primarily as a means to plundering the people. Instead, they used their control over employment and working conditions under the bourgeois capitalistic system for this purpose, paying only a bare subsistence wage to the worker while they appropriated all surplus values in the productive process. He further taught that the strategic disadvantage of the worker in industry prevented him from obtaining a fairer share of the earnings by bargaining methods and drove him to revolutionary procedures as a means to establishing his economic and social rights. This revolution might be peacefully consummated by parliamentary procedures if the people prepared themselves for political action by mastering the materialistic interpretation of history and by organizing politically for the final event. It was his belief that the aggressions of the capitalist class would eventually destroy the middle class and take over all their sources of income by a process of capitalistic absorption of industry—a process which has failed to occur in most countries.

With minor exceptions, Marx's social philosophy is now generally accepted by left-wing labor movements in many countries, but rejected by centrist labor groups, especially those in the United States. In Russia and other Eastern European countries, however, Socialist leaders adopted the methods of violent revolution because of the opposition of the ruling classes. Yet, many now hold that the present Communist regime in Russia and her satellite countries is no longer a proletarian movement based on Marxist social and political theory, but a camouflaged imperialistic effort to dominate the world in the interest of a new ruling class.

It is important, however, that those who wish to approach Marx as a teacher should not be "buffaloed" by his philosophic approach. They are very likely to in these days, because those most interested in propogating the ideas of Marx, the Russian Bolsheviks, have swallowed down his Hegelian philosophy along with his science of revolutionary engineering, and they look upon us irreverent peoples who presume to meditate social and even revolutionary problems without making our obeisance to the mysteries of Dialectic Materialism, as a species of unredeemed and well-nigh unredeemable barbarians. They are right in scorning our ignorance of the scientific ideas of Karl Marx and our indifference to them. They are wrong in scorning our distaste for having practical programs presented in the form of systems of philosophy. In that we simply represent a more progressive intellectual culture than that in which Marx received his education—a culture farther emerged from the dominance of religious attitudes.

Passage 2:

The basic character of our governmental and political institutions conditions the federal budgetary system. The working relationships between branches, and between the elements within each branch, are intricate, subtle, and in continuous change—affected by partisan politics, personalities, social forces, and public opinion. A few landmark stages in the evolution of the present system provide perspective.

In 1789 Alexander Hamilton, as the first Secretary of the Treasury, affirmed and successfully established a position of strong executive leadership in matters of public finance. His proposals on revenues, banking, and the assumption of prior debts of both national and state governments were based on his philosophy that federal fiscal policies should be designed to encourage economic growth. However, Hamilton's successors, and the Presidents under whom they served, did not follow his concept of executive responsibility for "plans of finance."

Partly through default, Congress took charge of all phases of fiscal policy. At the outset, each chamber was so small that coherent initiative was possible. (The first House had some 60 members—about the number of its present Appropriations Committee.) Spending estimates, considered in Committee of the Whole in 1789, were later referred to the Committee on Ways and Means. In 1865 expenditures were assigned to a new Appropriations Committee while revenues remained with the Ways and Means Committee. In 1885 most spending proposals were subdivided among the legislative committees so that appropriation bills came to be handled by numerous committees (14 in the House and 15 in the Senate), each dealing directly with the departments. The presidential role was minimal.

By the turn of the century there was a clear need for reform in financial management. At all levels of government, officials spent money on activities "as authorized by law" and in line with "appropriations" made by legislative bodies—usually after committee consideration. Other officials collected taxes and fees under various unrelated statutes. Such a system—or lack-of-system—worked within reason as long as governments had little to do. But as government activities grew, becoming more technical and closely interrelated, this lack-of-system bogged down.

Several factors played a part in the eventual breakthrough. In the first decade of the twentieth century, an "executive budget" came into successful use by some cities and states. President Taft's Commission on Efficiency and Economy prepared an illustrative federal budget which—while rejected by Congress—commanded broad public support. The more advanced methods developed by European governments came to American attention. World War I precipitated accounting chaos, with an aftermath of scandal. The need for new and better methods was established beyond dispute.

The Budget and Accounting Act of 1921 placed direct responsibility for preparation and execution of the federal budget upon the President, making a unified federal budget possible for the first time. The Act set up two new organizational units, the General Accounting Office (GAO) and the Bureau of the Budget. GAO is headed by the Comptroller General, appointed by the President *with* senate approval for a 15-year term, and is regarded as primarily a congressional rather than an executive resource. The Bureau, under a Director appointed by the President *without* senate confirmation and serving at his pleasure, has from its inception been the President's chief reliance in budgetary and related matters.

Passage 3:

In describing the Indians of the various sections of the United States at different stages in their history, some of the factors which account for their similarity amid difference can be readily accounted for, others are difficult to discern.

The basic physical similarity of the Indians from Alaska to Patagonia is explained by the fact that they all came originally from Asia by way of the Bering Strait and the Aleutian Islands into Alaska and then southward. They came in different waves, the earliest around 25,000 years ago, the latest probably not long before America was discovered by Europeans. Because these people all came from Asia and were therefore drawn from the same pool of Asiatic people, they tended to look alike. But since the various waves of migration crossed into Alaska at widely separated times, there were differences among them in their physical characteristics.

There were also differences in cultural equipment. The earliest arrivals are known to science only through their simple tools of chipped stone and bone. Despite their limited technical equipment, some of the New Mexico Indians were very successful big game hunters. Twenty-five thousand years ago they were hunting the wooly mammoth, the giant bison, the ground sloth and the camel, all characteristic animals of the closing phases of the last ice age.

After their arrival from Asia in various waves across the Bering Strait, the early peoples in the Americas slowly spread southward into the vast empty spaces of the two continents. A group of people moving slowly down the Mackenzie River valley east of the Rockies into the general region of Southern Alberta, then eastward across the northern prairies reaching the wooded country around the upper Mississippi and the Western Great Lakes, then in a southeastward movement following the Mississippi valley until some final settlement was reached in the Gulf states, would encounter a wide variety of physical environments. At various stages of such wanderings they would have to evolve methods of coping with the cold, barren, tundra country of northern Canada; the prairies, cold, treeless but well stocked with large game; then later thc completely different flora and fauna of the Minnesota-Wisconsin-Illinois area, thickly forested and well watered and providing an abundance of small game and wild vegetable foods; then the semi-tropical character of the lower Mississippi country as they neared the Gulf of Mexico. Since such a migration would be spread over many centuries, the modification of whatever basic culture they had on their arrival from Asia would be very slow. Yet the end result would be completely different from their original culture. It would also be different from the final culture of a closely allied group who became separated from them early in their wanderings and whose movements led them into different types of country. In its final form, the culture of this second group would have little in common with that of the first except perhaps a continuing resemblance in language and in physical type.

If there is still time remaining, review the passages until all 15 minutes have elapsed.
Do not look at Part B until that time.

Part B: TIME—20 minutes

DIRECTIONS: Answer the following questions pertaining to information contained in the three passages you have just read. You may not turn back to those passages for assistance.

QUESTIONS TO

Passage 1:

1. According to Marx, the chief element in capitalist exploitation was the doctrine of

(A) just wages
(B) the price system
(C) surplus value
(D) predatory production
(E) subsistence work

2. Which of the following books did Marx author or co-author?

I. *Communist Manifesto*
II. *Das Capital*
III. *Political Taxation*

(A) I only
(B) III only
(C) I and II only
(D) II and III only
(E) I, II, and III

3. According to the passage, Marx started his philosophical life as a

(A) social theorist
(B) believer in non-violent revolution
(C) believer in violent revolution
(D) follower of Hegel
(E) follower of Engels

4. According to the passage, Marx ended his life as

I. A believer in non-violent revolution
II. Accepting violent revolution
III. A social theorist

(A) I only
(B) III only
(C) I and II only
(D) II and III only
(E) I, II, and III

5. The author holds that the present Communist regime in Russia can best be categorized as a(n)

(A) proletarian movement
(B) socialist government
(C) imperialistic state
(D) revolutionary government
(E) social democracy

6. One of Marx's theories mentioned in the passage is called

(A) Dialectic Materialism
(B) Hegelian Socialism
(C) Social Engineering
(D) Materialistic Value
(E) Countervailing Power

7. Marx's social philosophy is now generally accepted by

(A) centrist labor groups
(B) most labor unions
(C) left-wing labor unions
(D) only those in Communist countries
(E) only those in Russia

8. It can be concluded that the author of the passage is

(A) sympathetic to Marx's ideas
(B) unsympathetic to Marx's ideas
(C) uncritical of Marx's interpretation of history
(D) a believer in Hegelian philosophy
(E) a Lenenist-Marxist

9. Which of the following classes did Marx believe should control the economy?

(A) working class
(B) upper class
(C) middle class
(D) lower class
(E) capitalist class

10. According to Marx, a social and economic revolution could take place through

I. Parliamentary procedures
II. Political action
III. Violent revolution

(A) I only
(B) III only
(C) I and II only
(D) II and III only
(E) I, II, and III

QUESTIONS TO

Passage 2:

11. Alexander Hamilton's philosophy was that federal fiscal policies should

(A) be expansionary
(B) encourage economic growth
(C) be determined by Congress
(D) encourage a balanced budget
(E) be determined by the President

12. Hamilton's successors

I. Followed his economic philosophy of "plans of finance"
II. Followed his social philosophy
III. Did not follow his philosophy of strong executive leadership

(A) I only
(B) III only
(C) I and II only
(D) II and III only
(E) I, II, and III

13. Looking at the history of U.S. fiscal management, spending estimates were *first* considered by the

I. Committee of the Whole
II. Appropriations Committee
III. Ways and Means Committee

(A) I only
(B) III only
(C) I and II only
(D) II and III only
(E) I, II, and III

14. At the turn of the century, there was need for

(A) strong executive leadership
(B) a new finance committee
(C) more Congressional interest in finance
(D) overall reform of financial management
(E) more financial legislation

15. The "executive budget" was first used

(A) by Alexander Hamilton
(B) in the 19th century
(C) in the first decade of the 20th century
(D) by President Eisenhower
(E) by President Truman

16. President Taft's federal budget was

(A) based on procedures used by some European governments
(B) enthusiastically accepted by Congress
(C) a failure
(D) rejected by Congress
(E) vilified by the public

17. In 1921, the responsibility for preparation and execution of the federal budget fell upon the

(A) President
(B) Congress
(C) Bureau of Accounts
(D) House of Representatives
(E) Senate

18. In the General Accounting Office, the Comptroller General is

(A) appointed by the President
(B) appointed by the President without Senate approval
(C) appointed by the President with Senate approval
(D) a civil service employee
(E) an elected official

19. The Director of the Budget is

(A) appointed by the President
(B) appointed by the President with Senate approval
(C) appointed by the President without Senate approval
(D) a civil service employee
(E) an elected official

20. The working relationships between government branches are affected by all of the following except

(A) partisan politics
(B) personalities
(C) social forces
(D) public opinion
(E) the military

QUESTIONS TO

Passage 3:

21. According to the passage, Indians who migrated to what is now the United States originated in

(A) Asia
(B) Africa
(C) South America
(D) Alaska
(E) Patagonia

22. Physical differences among Indians who migrated to Alaska can be accounted for by the fact that they came

(A) from different places
(B) from different tribes
(C) at different times
(D) from different races
(E) to different places

23. It is estimated that Indians first came to what is now the United States about

(A) 5,000 years ago
(B) 10,000 years ago
(C) 15,000 years ago
(D) 25,000 years ago
(E) 50,000 years ago

24. The intent of the author is to expound on the Indians'

(A) cultural background
(B) eating habits
(C) technical abilities
(D) migration patterns
(E) physical characteristics

25. According to the passage, the southernmost area reached by the Indians was the

(A) northern prairies
(B) upper Mississippi
(C) Great Lakes
(D) Mackenzie River valley
(E) Gulf States

26. Which of the following Indians were noted for their hunting prowess?

(A) Mississippi
(B) Bering
(C) Mackenzie
(D) New Mexico
(E) Patagonia

27. Although the Indians' culture underwent change, what characteristics remained fairly stable?

I. Language
II. Physical type
III. Technical abilities

(A) I only
(B) III only
(C) I and II only
(D) II and III only
(E) I, II, and III

28. Which animals were hunted by the Indians when they first migrated to the Americas?

I. Bison
II. Wooly mammoth
III. Camel

(A) I only
(B) III only
(C) I and II only
(D) II and III only
(E) I, II, and III

29. According to the author, some of the Indians were

(A) extremely intelligent
(B) bi-lingual
(C) slow to adjust to new environments
(D) largely a farming people
(E) successful big game hunters

30. The passage most likely was written by a(n)

(A) economist
(B) historian
(C) educator
(D) social scientist
(E) anthropologist

If there is still time remaining, you may review the questions in this section only. You may not look at Part A or turn to any other section of the test.

Section II Mathematics

TIME: 75 minutes

DIRECTIONS: Solve each of the following problems; then indicate the correct answer on the answer sheet. [On the actual test you will be permitted to use any space available on the examination paper for scratch work.]

NOTE: A figure that appears with a problem is drawn as accurately as possible so as to provide information that may help in answering the question. Numbers in this test are real numbers.

31. A borrower pays 6% interest on the first \$500 he borrows and $5\frac{1}{2}$% on the part of the loan in excess of \$500. How much interest will the borrower have to pay on a loan of \$5,500?

(A) \$275
(B) \$280
(C) \$302.50
(D) \$305
(E) \$330

32. If $2x - y = 4$, then $6x - 3y$ is

(A) 4
(B) 6
(C) 8
(D) 10
(E) 12

33. The next number in the arithmetical progression 5, 11, 17, . . . is

(A) 18
(B) 22
(C) 23
(D) 28
(E) 33

Use the following graph for questions 34–36.

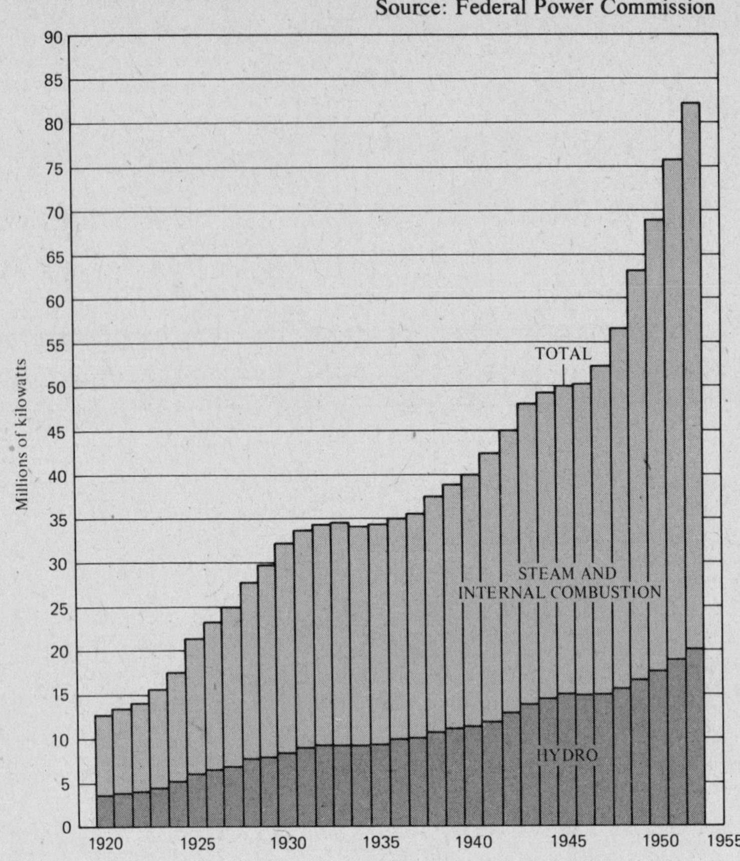

34. In what year did the installed capacity first reach 50 million kilowatts?

(A) 1939
(B) 1944
(C) 1945
(D) 1947
(E) 1950

35. In 1952, the installed capacity of steam and internal combustion plants was about x times the installed capacity of the hydro plants where x is

(A) ½
(B) 1
(C) 2
(D) 3
(E) 4

36. Which of the following statements about the installed capacity of electric utility generating plants between 1920 and 1952 can be inferred from the graph?

I. In the period 1930–39, there was less of an increase in capacity than in either of the periods 1920–1929 or 1940–1949.
II. More than ⅕ of the capacity in 1925 was produced by hydro plants.
III. The increase in capacity in kilowatts between 1945 and 1952 was greater than the increase between 1925 and 1945.

(A) I only
(B) II only
(C) I and III only
(D) II and III only
(E) I, II, and III

A warehouse has 20 packers. Each packer can load $\frac{1}{8}$ of a box in 9 minutes. How many boxes can be loaded in $1\frac{1}{2}$ hours by all 20 packers?

(A) $1\frac{1}{4}$
(B) $10\frac{1}{4}$
(C) $12\frac{1}{2}$
(D) 20
(E) 25

In Motor City 90% of the population owns a car, 15% owns a motorcycle, and everybody owns a car or motorcycle or both. What percent of the population owns a motorcycle but not a car?

(A) 5
(B) 8
(C) 9
(D) 10
(E) 15

Use the following table for questions 39–40.

TABLE 2.—Children under 18 years old, by age group, type of family, labor force status of mother, and race, March 1972

Type of family, labor force status of mother, and race	Number of children (thousands)		
	Under 18 years	Under 6 years	6 to 17 years
Total children	65,255	19,235	46,020
Mother in labor force	25,762	5,607	20,155
Husband-wife family	56,625	17,173	39,452
Mother in labor force	21,722	4,838	16,884
Mother not in labor force	34,903	12,335	22,568
Female family head	7,924	1,977	5,947
Mother in labor force	4,040	769	3,271
Mother not in labor force	3,884	1,208	2,676
Other male family head	706	85	621
White children, total	56,303	16,603	39,700
Mother in labor force	21,539	4,495	17,044
Husband-wife family	50,796	15,409	35,387
Mother in labor force	18,799	4,031	14,768
Mother not in labor force	31,997	11,378	20,619
Female family head	4,967	1,130	3,837
Mother in labor force	2,740	464	2,276
Mother not in labor force	2,227	666	1,561
Other male family head	540	64	476
Negro children, total	8,093	2,345	5,748
Mother in labor force	3,855	999	2,856
Husband-wife family	5,078	1,504	3,574
Mother in labor force	2,609	707	1,902
Mother not in labor force	2,469	797	1,672
Female family head	2,855	821	2,034
Mother in labor force	1,246	292	954
Mother not in labor force	1,609	529	1,080
Other male family head	160	20	140

Source: Social Security Bulletin

39. Approximately how many children between the ages of 6 to 17 did not have mothers in the labor force in 1972?

(A) 20,000,000
(B) 26,000,000
(C) 28,000,000
(D) 30,000,000
(E) 46,000,000

40. Roughly x percent of the Negro children under 6 years of age had mothers in the labor force, where x is

(A) 30
(B) 35
(C) 40
(D) 50
(E) 55

41. A chair originally cost $50.00. The chair was offered for sale at 108% of its cost. After a week the price was discounted 10% and the chair was sold. The chair was sold for

(A) $45.00
(B) $48.60
(C) $49.00
(D) $49.40
(E) $54.00

42. A worker is paid x dollars for the first 8 hours he works each day. He is paid y dollars per hour for each hour he works in excess of 8 hours. During one week he works 8 hours on Monday, 11 hours on Tuesday, 9 hours on Wednesday, 10 hours on Thursday, and 9 hours on Friday. What is his average daily wage in dollars for the five day week?

(A) $x + \frac{7}{5}y$
(B) $2x + y$
(C) $\frac{5x + 8y}{5}$
(D) $x + 2y$
(E) $5x + 7y$

43. What is the area of a rectangular field which is 25 yards wide and 50 yards long?

(A) 625 square yards
(B) 1,000 square yards
(C) 1,250 square yards
(D) 1600 square yards
(E) 2,500 square yards

Use the chart below for questions 44–47.

Source: Department of Commerce, Bureau of the Census

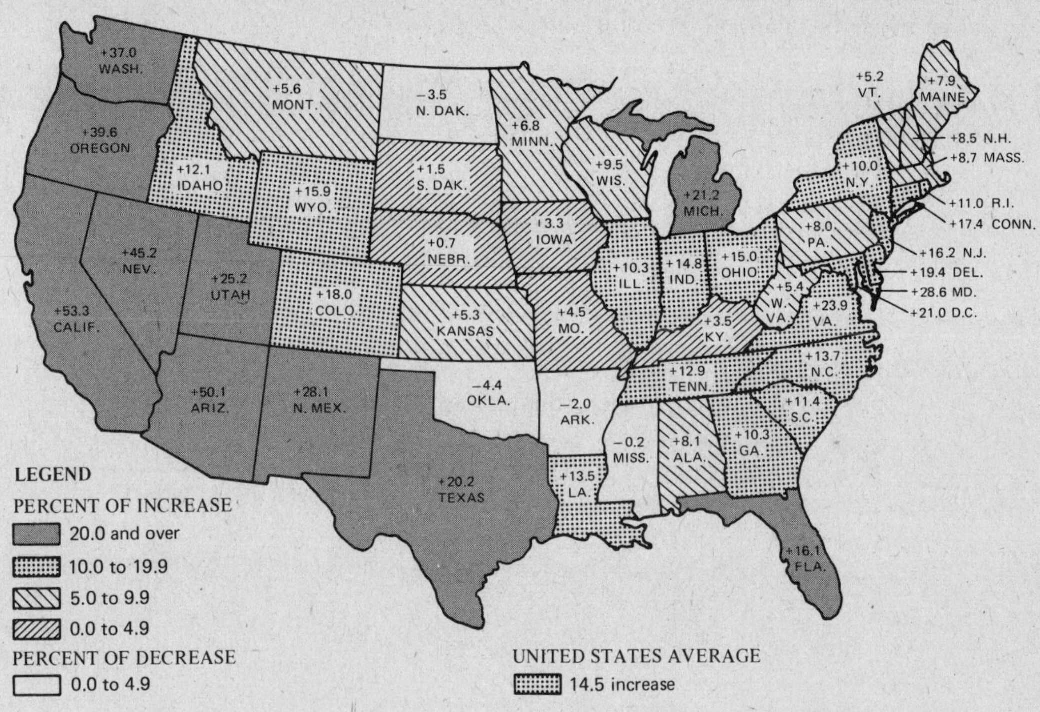

44. Which state had the largest percentage of increase in population between 1940 and 1950?

(A) Arizona
(B) Arkansas
(C) California
(D) Florida
(E) Maine

45. How many states had population decreases between 1940 and 1950?

(A) 1
(B) 2
(C) 3
(D) 4
(E) 5

46. If the population of the United States in 1940 was 100 million, then the population of the United States in 1950 was approximately

(A) 100 million
(B) 105 million
(C) 110 million
(D) 115 million
(E) 120 million

47. Which of the following statements about population changes between 1940 and 1950 can be inferred from the graph?

I. Exactly 6 states had population increases of $\frac{1}{3}$ or more.
II. The number of people living in Oregon in 1950 was larger than the number of people living in Washington.
III. The population of Nebraska was larger in 1950 than it was in 1940.

(A) I only
(B) III only
(C) I and III only
(D) II and III only
(E) I, II and III

48. If 12 apples cost 63¢, how much should 4 apples cost?

(A) 19¢
(B) 21¢
(C) 25¢
(D) 31¢
(E) 32¢

49. A car costs $2,500 when it is brand new. At the end of each year it is worth $\frac{4}{5}$ of what it was at the beginning of the year. What is the car worth when it is 3 years old?

(A) $1,000
(B) $1,200
(C) $1,280
(D) $1,340
(E) $1,430

Use the following table for questions 50–52.

Type of vehicle	*Cost of fuel for 500-mile trip*
Automobile	$15
Motorcycle	$ 5
Bus	$20
Truck	$50
Airplane	$70

50. What is the cost of fuel for a 300-mile trip by automobile?

(A) $5
(B) $9
(C) $12
(D) $15
(E) $30

51. If the wages of a bus driver for a 500-mile trip are $70, and the only costs for a bus are the fuel and the driver's wages, how much should a bus company charge to charter a bus and driver for a 500-mile trip in order to obtain 120% of the cost?

(A) $24
(B) $90
(C) $94
(D) $104
(E) $108

52. If 3 buses, 4 automobiles, 2 motorcycles, and one truck each make a 500-mile trip, what is the average fuel cost per vehicle?

(A) $5
(B) $15
(C) $18
(D) $20
(E) $24

53. If $x + 2y = 2x + y$, then $x - y$ is equal to

(A) 0
(B) 2
(C) 4
(D) 5
(E) none of the preceding

54. 15% of the families in state x have an income of $25,000 or more. $^2/_3$ of the families with income of $25,000 or more in state x own a boat. What fraction of the families own a boat and have an income of $25,000 or more in state x?

(A) $^1/_{15}$
(B) $^1/_{12}$
(C) $^1/_{10}$
(D) $^4/_{21}$
(E) $^9/_{40}$

55. If the angles of a triangle are in the ratio 1:2:2, then the triangle

(A) is isosceles
(B) is obtuse
(C) is a right triangle
(D) is equilateral
(E) has one angle greater than 80°

Use the following graphs for questions 56–60.

U.S. Department of Commerce, Bureau of Economic Analysis

BY MAJOR CATEGORIES

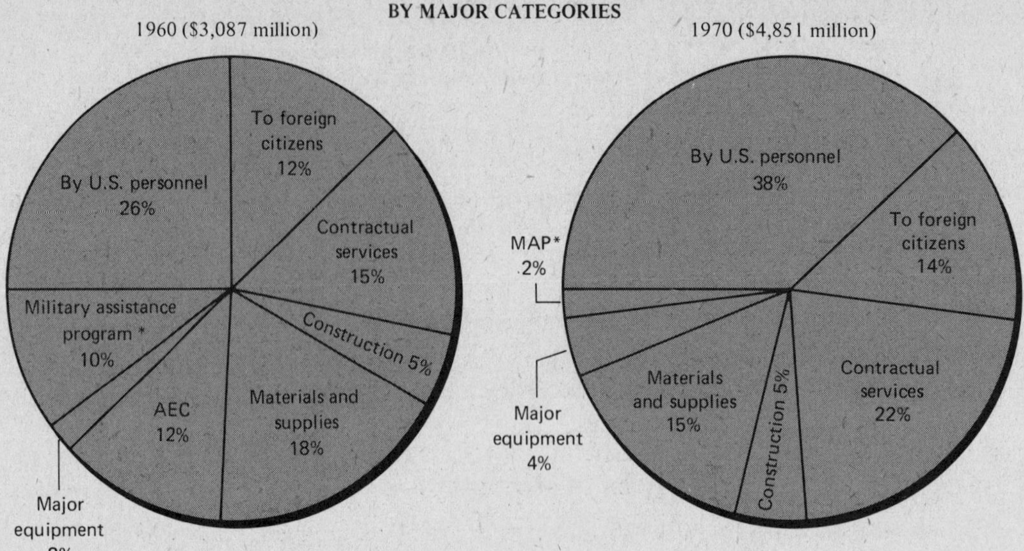

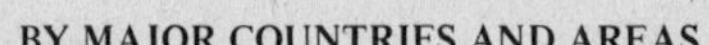

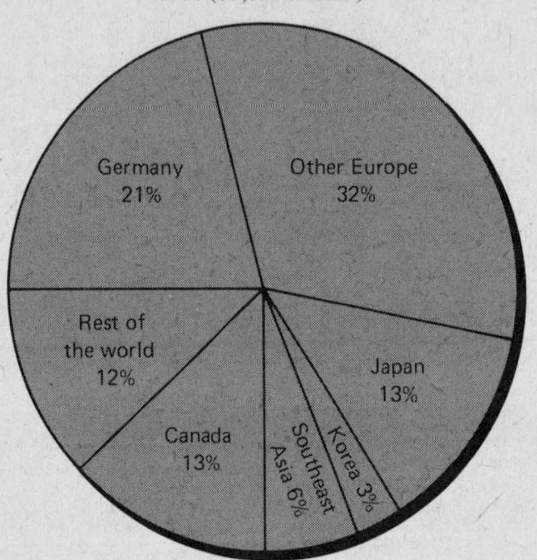

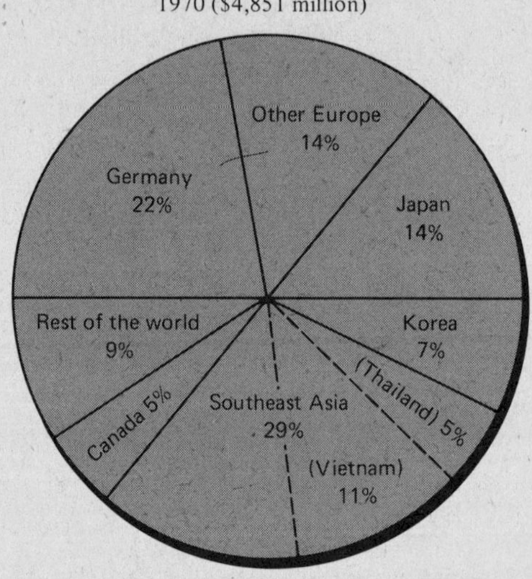

* Includes NATO Infrastructure

56. In 1970, $\$x$ was spent in Canada for defense where x is about

(A) 200 million
(B) 230 million
(C) 240 million
(D) 250 million
(E) 260 million

57. In 1960, what fraction of defense expenditures was used in all for the Military Assistance Program, AEC, and materials and supplies?

(A) $^3/_{10}$
(B) $^7/_{20}$
(C) $^{39}/_{100}$
(D) $^2/_5$
(E) $^{11}/_{25}$

58. Which of the following countries received the least amount of defense expenditures in 1970?

(A) Germany
(B) Japan
(C) Vietnam
(D) Korea
(E) Thailand

59. If $\frac{5}{7}$ of the defense expenditures in Europe other than Germany was spent in Spain, about how much was spent in Spain in 1970?

(A) \$308 million
(B) \$485 million
(C) \$550 million
(D) \$750 million
(E) \$1,200 million

60. Which of the following statements about direct expenditures abroad for goods and services can be inferred from the graphs?

I. In both 1960 and 1970, more than $\frac{1}{5}$ of the expenditures was spent in Germany.
II. The total amount of expenditures increased by more than $\frac{1}{3}$ between 1960 and 1970.
III. More than $\frac{2}{5}$ of the total expenditures for 1960 and 1970 together was spent by U.S. personnel.

(A) I only
(B) II only
(C) I and II only
(D) II and III only
(E) I, II, and III

61. If a car travels at a constant rate of 60 miles per hour, how long will it take to travel 255 miles?

(A) $3\frac{3}{4}$ hours
(B) 4 hours
(C) $4\frac{1}{8}$ hours
(D) $4\frac{1}{4}$ hours
(E) $4\frac{1}{2}$ hours

62. A car travels 15 miles on a gallon of gas but after a tune-up the car uses only $\frac{3}{4}$ as much gas as before. How many miles will the car travel on a gallon of gas after the tune-up?

(A) 15
(B) $16\frac{1}{2}$
(C) $17\frac{1}{2}$
(D) $18\frac{2}{3}$
(E) 20

63. Successive discounts of 20% and 15% are equal to a single discount of

(A) 30%
(B) 32%
(C) 34%
(D) 35%
(E) 36%

Use the following graphs for questions 64–67.

Source: Social Security Bulletin

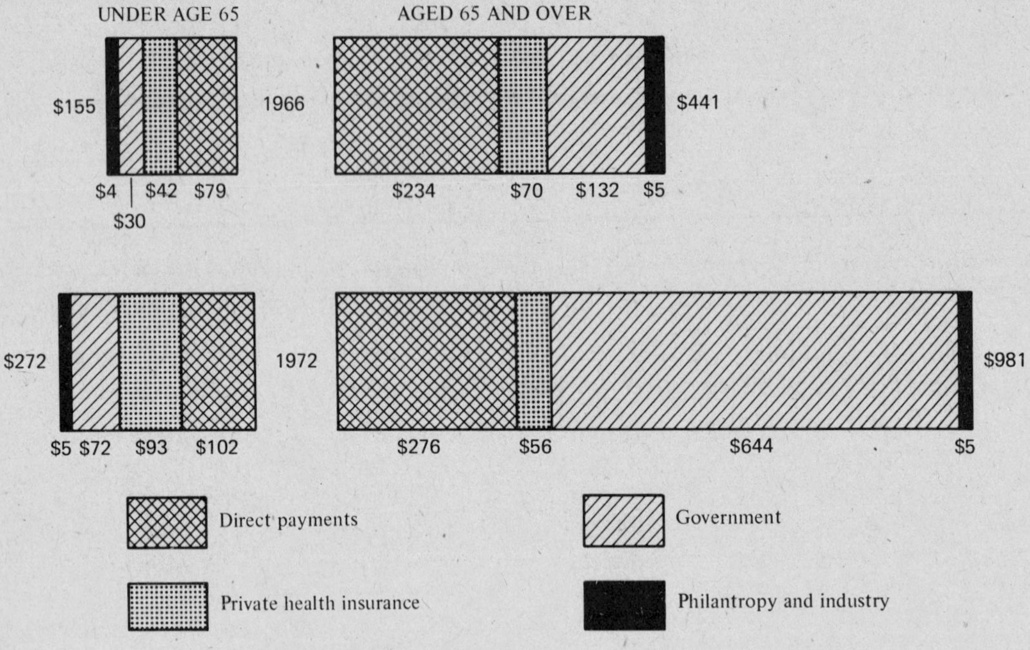

64. If there were about 20 million people 65 and over in 1966, how much did the government spend on personal health care for people aged 65 and over in 1966?

(A) $26 million
(B) $264 million
(C) $2 billion
(D) $2.640 billion
(E) $3.6 billion

65. Between 1966 and 1972, the per capita amount spent by the government on personal health care for those under age 65 increased by $x\%$ where x is

(A) 100
(B) 120
(C) 200
(D) 220
(E) 240

66. In 1972, the fraction contributed by philanthropy and industry towards expenditures for personal health care for those aged 65 and over was about

(A) $\frac{1}{500}$
(B) $\frac{1}{196}$
(C) $\frac{1}{99}$
(D) $\frac{1}{88}$
(E) $\frac{2}{101}$

67. Which of the following statements about expenditures for personal health care between 1966 and 1972 can be inferred from the graphs?

I. The total amount spent for those aged 65 and over in 1972 was more than 3 times as much as the total amount spent on those under 65.
II. Between 1966 and 1972, the amount spent per capita by those aged 65 and over increased in each of the four categories (direct payments, government, private health insurance, philanthropy).
III. The government paid more than ½ of the amount of expenditures for those aged 65 and over in 1972.

(A) I only
(B) II only
(C) III only
(D) I and III only
(E) II and III only

68. Oranges cost $1.00 for a crate containing 20 oranges. If oranges are sold for 6¢ each, what percent of the selling price is the profit?

(A) 5%
(B) 10%
(C) $16\frac{2}{3}$%
(D) 20%
(E) 25%

69. A hen lays $7\frac{1}{2}$ dozen eggs during the summer. There are 93 days in the summer and it costs $10 to feed the hen for the summer. How much does it cost in food for each egg produced?

(A) 10¢
(B) $11\frac{1}{9}$¢
(C) $12\frac{3}{13}$¢
(D) $13\frac{1}{13}$¢
(E) 15¢

70. If the diameter of a circle has length d, the radius length r, and the area equals a, then which of the following statements are true?

I. $a = \pi d^2$
II. $d = 2r$
III. $\frac{a}{d} = \pi \frac{r}{2}$

(A) only II
(B) I and II only
(C) I and III only
(D) II and III only
(E) I, II, and III

Use the following graph for questions 71–74.

Source: Social Security Bulletin

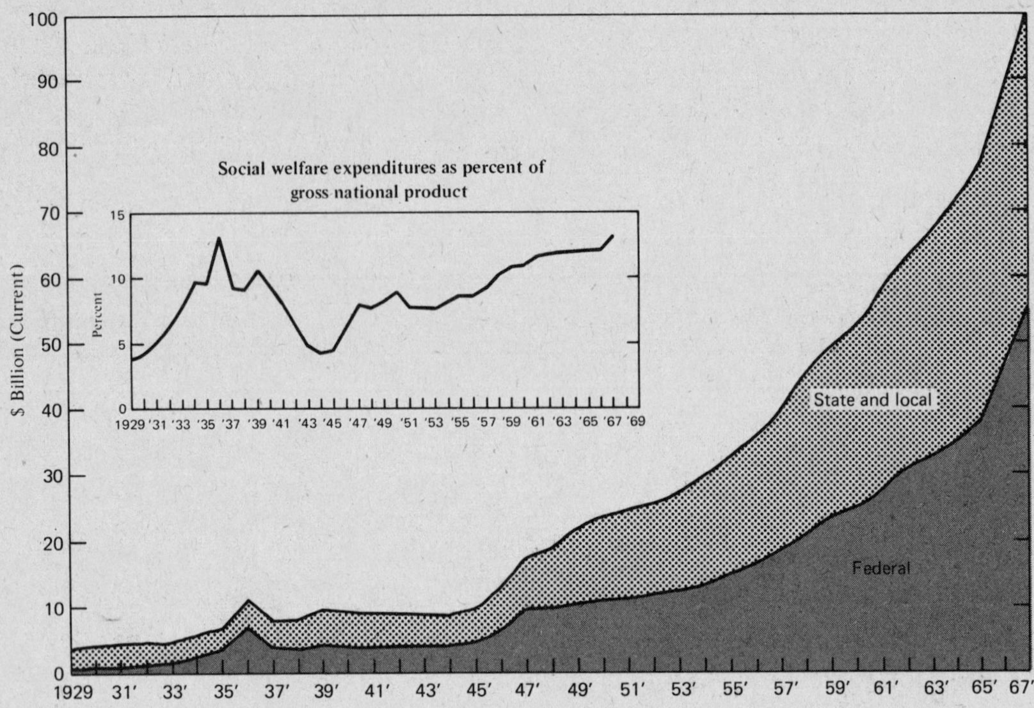

71. During the period from 1929 to 1944 in what year were social welfare expenditures the highest?

(A) 1933
(B) 1935
(C) 1936
(D) 1939
(E) 1944

72. The Gross National Product in 1958 was about

(A) $100 billion
(B) $200 billion
(C) $300 billion
(D) $450 billion
(E) $600 billion

73. In 1957, the federal government spent about x times as much as state and local governments on social welfare, where x is

(A) $\frac{1}{4}$
(B) $\frac{1}{2}$
(C) 1
(D) 2
(E) 3

74. Which of the following statements about social welfare expenditures can be inferred from the graph?

I. The percentage of Gross National Product spent on social welfare decreased between 1939 and 1943.
II. The state and local governments never spent more than $60 billion on social welfare in any of the years between 1929 and 1967.
III. Between 1929 and 1933, the state and local government spent more on social welfare than did the federal government.

(A) I only
(B) II only
(C) I and III only
(D) II and III only
(E) I, II, and III

75. If hose *A* can fill up a tank in 20 minutes, and hose *B* can fill up the same tank in 15 minutes, how long will it take for the hoses together to fill up the tank?

(A) 5 minutes
(B) $7\frac{1}{2}$ minutes
(C) $8\frac{4}{7}$ minutes
(D) $9\frac{2}{7}$ minutes
(E) 12 minutes

76. If 5 men take 2 hours to dig a ditch, how long will it take 12 men to dig the ditch?

(A) 45 minutes
(B) 50 minutes
(C) 54 minutes
(D) 60 minutes
(E) 84 minutes

Use the following table for questions 77–79.

Car Production at Plant T for One Week

	Number of cars produced	*Total daily wages*
MONDAY	900	$30,000
TUESDAY	1200	$40,000
WEDNESDAY	1500	$52,000
THURSDAY	1400	$50,000
FRIDAY	1000	$32,000

77. What was the average number of cars produced per day for the week shown?

(A) 1,000
(B) 1,140
(C) 1,180
(D) 1,200
(E) 1,220

78. What was the average cost in wages per car produced for the week?

(A) $25
(B) $26
(C) $29
(D) $32
(E) $34

79. Which of the following statements about the production of cars and the wages paid for the week can be inferred from the table?

I. $\frac{1}{4}$ of the cars were produced on Wednesday.
II. More employees came to the plant on Friday than on Monday.
III. $\frac{2}{5}$ of the days accounted for $\frac{1}{2}$ the wages paid for the week.

(A) I only
(B) II only
(C) I and II only
(D) I and III only
(E) I, II, and III

80. How many rectangular plots 40 yards long by 30 yards wide can be obtained from a field which is a square with sides 1200 yards long?

(A) 100
(B) 120
(C) 1000
(D) 1200
(E) 14000

81. A train travels from Cleveland to Toledo in 2 hours and 10 minutes. If the distance from Cleveland to Toledo is 150 miles, then the average speed of the train is about

(A) 60 mph
(B) 66 mph
(C) 70 mph
(D) 72 mph
(E) 75 mph

82. If $x > 2$ and $y > -1$, then

(A) $xy > -2$
(B) $-x < 2y$
(C) $xy < -2$
(D) $-x > 2y$
(E) $x < 2y$

83. What is the area of the rectangle $ABCD$, if the length of AC is 5 and the length of AD is 4?

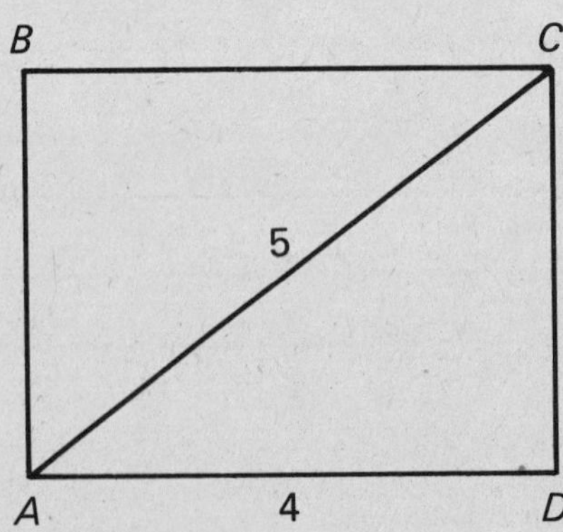

(A) 3
(B) 6
(C) 12
(D) 15
(E) 20

84. If electricity costs k¢ an hour, heat $\$d$ an hour, and water w¢ an hour, how much will all three cost for 12 hours?

(A) $12(k+d+w)$¢

(B) $\$(12k+12d+12w)$

(C) $\$(k+100d+w)$

(D) $\$\left(12k+\frac{12d}{100}+12w\right)$

(E) $\$(.12k+12d+.12w)$

85. If $x=y=2z$ and $x \cdot y \cdot z=256$, then x equals

(A) 2

(B) $2\sqrt[3]{2}$

(C) 4

(D) $4\sqrt[3]{2}$

(E) 8

If there is still time remaining, you may review the questions in this section only. You may not turn to any other section of the test.

Section III Verbal Aptitude

TIME: 20 minutes

Antonyms

DIRECTIONS: For each question below, select the lettered word or phrase that comes closest to being *opposite* in meaning to the word appearing in capital letters. Be sure to consider all meanings carefully.

86. ABSTRUSE: (A) detested (B) detained (C) obvious (D) tight (E) rebuilt

87. COAGULATE: (A) strengthen (B) release (C) plunge (D) dissipate (E) prepare

88. PROCLIVITY: (A) proposition (B) propensity (C) aversion (D) activity (E) delay

89. TACIT: (A) late (B) open (C) implied (D) skilled (E) indiscreet

90. VORACIOUS: (A) bellicose (B) powerful (C) generous (D) inclined (E) stoic

91. SAGACIOUS: (A) fat (B) stupid (C) happy (D) unwelcome (E) irrational

92. RETICENT: (A) repellent (B) related (C) communicative (D) truthful (E) repetitious

93. FECUND: (A) barren (B) timid (C) sinister (D) determined (E) awful

94. FURTIVE: (A) active (B) expected (C) open (D) abetting (E) fearful

95. INCLEMENT: (A) incipient (B) inevitable (C) new (D) kind (E) contrary

96. NOTORIOUS: (A) wicked (B) enigmatic (C) respected (D) open (E) political

97. DILATE: (A) expand (B) contract (C) remedy (D) include (E) concentrate

98. BOISTEROUS: (A) peaceful (B) undaunted (C) covert (D) auspicious (E) fatal

99. ECLECTIC: (A) agnostic (B) dogmatic (C) habitual (D) incisive (E) impulsive

Word-Pair Relationships

DIRECTIONS: For each question below, determine the relationship between the pair of capitalized words and then select the lettered pair of words which have a similar relationship to the first pair.

100. SAMPLE : UNIVERSE :: (A) plan : research (B) individual : population (C) mathematics : statistics (D) element : electron (E) tactic : strategy

101. CARBOHYDRATES : OBESITY :: (A) aversion : regression (B) sugar : cavities (C) pressure : burst (D) hostility : war (E) sick : hospital

102. PROMISE : FULFILL :: (A) pawn : redeem (B) pledge : surfeit (C) plan : action (D) commit : hedge (E) abrogate : release

103. ADDICTED : DEDICATED :: (A) infected : supporter (B) fanatic : enthusiast (C) disease : chronic (D) injected : permanent (E) habit : continuous

104. RECALL : REMEMBER :: (A) falsification : forgery (B) behave : action (C) construct : terminate (D) cigarette : tobacco (E) pipe : stem

105. ABUNDANCE : LUXURY :: (A) developed : growing (B) humble : unpretentious (C) poverty : indigence (D) pilot : plane (E) reserved : suppressed

106. STAMP : LETTER :: (A) words : telegram (B) coin : telephone (C) gasoline : automobile (D) road : toll (E) profession : license

107. FUEL : PIPES :: (A) air : lungs (B) food : stomach (C) wood : trees (D) cars : freeway (E) power : generator

108. EXEMPTION : EXCLUSION :: (A) debarment : prevention (B) immunity : isolation (C) forgive : condone (D) discharge : elimination (E) enclosure : open

109. INDIGENOUS : FOREIGN :: (A) indifferent : interested (B) resident : visitor (C) native : extraneous (D) part : whole (E) outsider : inhabitant

110. EFFICACIOUS : LACKING :: (A) efficient : incompetent (B) effective : effortless (C) missing : missive (D) trial : failure (E) attempt : error

111. EIGHT : OCTAVE :: (A) top : bottom (B) centimeter : meter (C) fifth : quart (D) thousand : millenium (E) foot : yard

112. THROW : TARGET :: (A) aim : hit (B) dive : water (C) tactic : objective (D) movement : destination (E) laughter : joy

Sentence Completions

DIRECTIONS: For each sentence below, select the lettered word or set of words which, when inserted in the sentence blanks, best complete the meaning of that sentence.

113. We strongly favor fair ____ to victims of manufacturing defects.

(A) play (B) compensation (C) probity (D) consultations (E) instructions

114. The ____ of a man might well be measured by his ____ of himself.

(A) worth . . . opinion (B) weight . . . estimation (C) education . . . value (D) value . . . picture (E) ability . . . judgment

115. It was the practice in a certain country for the President to offer a full ____ to some prisoners on the national holiday.

(A) restitution (B) amnesty (C) acquittal (D) pardon (E) clemency

116. Police, prepared for a long ____, held a(n) ____ on the street.

(A) discussion . . . council (B) seige . . . meeting (C) time . . . gathering (D) intercession . . . suspect (E) strike . . . assembly

117. The meeting between the two was ____ with ____ significance.

(A) begun . . . extraneous (B) complicated . . . no (C) fraught . . . historical (D) ended . . . reciprocal (E) broken off . . . little

118. It was not a(n) ____ beginning for the railroad as two trains ____.

(A) early . . . were late (B) bad . . . were on time (C) auspicious . . . collided (D) inadequate . . . stalled (E) plausible . . . failed

119. Some ____ of why he does not think that to be their ____ came in the subject he discussed.

(A) indication . . . intention (B) example . . . inversion (C) part . . . machine (D) mention . . . conversation (E) foreboding . . . posture

120. The best ____ is that he thinks he has ____ of time.

(A) story . . . plenty (B) explanation . . . run out (C) part . . . lost control (D) solution . . . arrived (E) estimate . . . want

121. It was the first time since the ____ effort to ____ an accord last year.

(A) prohibitory . . . announce (B) reciprocal . . . purchase (C) abortive . . . reach (D) last . . . convey (E) pessimistic . . . abrogate

122. Like the United States, England was forced by economic events to embrace a program of ____ restraints despite past pronouncements espousing less ____.

(A) financial . . . interference (B) voluntary . . . optimism (C) compulsory . . . intervention (D) literary . . . control (E) temporary . . . freedom

123. To say that a study is synthetic and ____ is to say that it is ____.

(A) general . . . theoretical (B) timely . . . insipid (C) biased . . . reliable (D) absolute . . . accurate (E) dated . . . extemporary

124. People who are loquacious are also called ____.

(A) lazy (B) independent (C) talkative (D) eloquent (E) tormented

125. The development of agriculture and that of industry act and react on each other; they are complementary and not _____.

(A) redundant (B) concentrated (C) associated (D) competitive (E) organized

If there is still time remaining, you may review the questions in this section only. You may not turn to any other section of the test.

Section IV Data Sufficiency

TIME: 15 minutes

DIRECTIONS: Each of the following problems has a question and two statements which are labeled (1) and (2). Use the data given in (1) and (2) together with other available information (such as the number of hours in a day, the definition of *clockwise,* mathematical facts, etc.) to decide whether the statements are *sufficient* to answer the question. Then fill in space

(A) if you can get the answer from (1) alone but not from (2) alone;

(B) if you can get the answer from (2) alone but not from (1) alone;

(C) if you can get the answer from (1) and (2) together, although neither statement by itself suffices;

(D) if statement (1) alone suffices *and* statement (2) alone suffices;

(E) if you cannot get the answer from statements (1) and (2) together, but need even more data.

All numbers used in this section are real numbers. A figure given for a problem is intended to provide information consistent with that in the question, but not necessarily with the additional information contained in the statements.

126. Is x greater than y?

(1) $3x = 2k$
(2) $k = y^2$

127. Is $ABCD$ a parallelogram?

(1) $AB = CD$
(2) AB is parallel to CD.

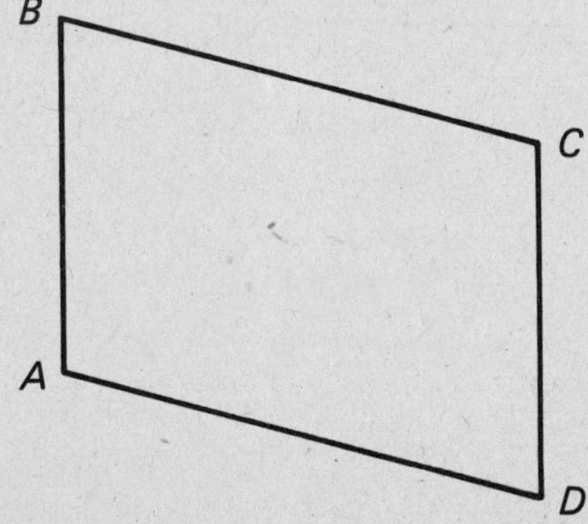

128. What was Mr. Smith's combined income for the years 1965–1970? In 1965 he made \$10,000.

(1) His average yearly income for the years 1965–1970 was \$12,000.
(2) In 1970, his income was \$20,000.

129. How much profit did Walker's Emporium make selling dresses?

(1) Each dress cost \$10.
(2) 600 dresses were sold.

130. k is a positive integer. Is k a prime number?

(1) No integer between 2 and $\sqrt{k}$ inclusive divides k evenly.
(2) No integer between 2 and $\frac{k}{2}$ inclusive divides k evenly, and k is greater than 5.

131. The towns A, B, and C lie on a straight line. C is between A and B. The distance from A to B is 100 miles. How far is it from A to C?

(1) The distance from A to B is 25% more than the distance from C to B.
(2) The distance from A to C is $\frac{1}{4}$ of the distance from C to B.

132. Is AB perpendicular to CD?

(1) $AC = BD$
(2) $x = y$

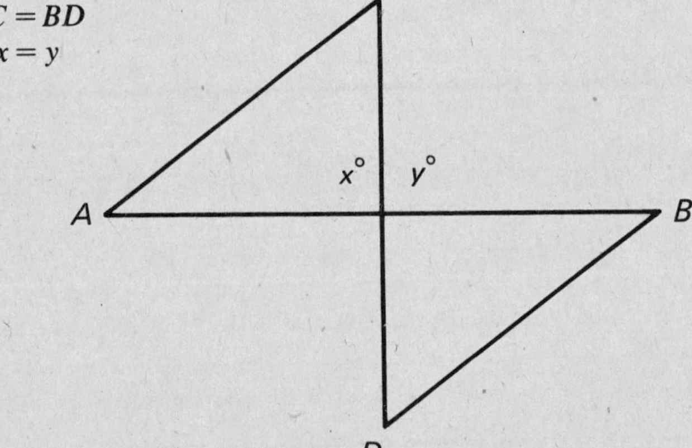

133. What is the value of $x - y$?

(1) $x + 2y = 6$
(2) $x = y$

134. The number of eligible voters is 100,000. How many eligible voters voted?

(1) 63% of the eligible men voted.
(2) 67% of the eligible women voted.

135. If $z=50$, find the value of x.

(1) $RS=ST$
(2) $x+y=60$

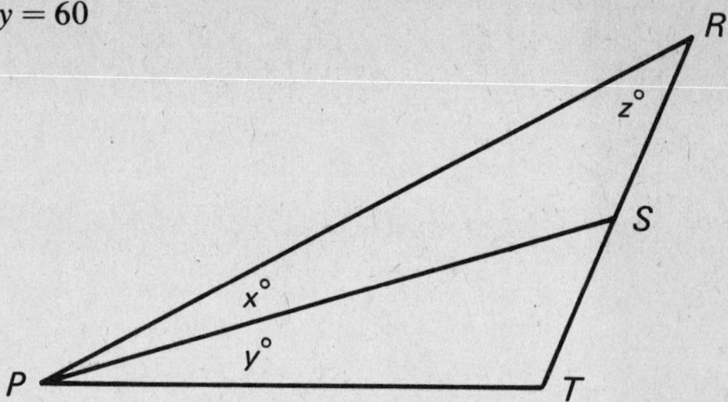

136. How much was the original cost of a car which sold for $2300?

(1) The car was sold for a discount of 10% from its original cost.
(2) The sales tax was $150.

137. The hexagon *ABCDEF* is inscribed in the circle with center *O*. What is the length of *AB?*

(1) The radius of the circle is 4 inches.
(2) The hexagon is a regular hexagon.

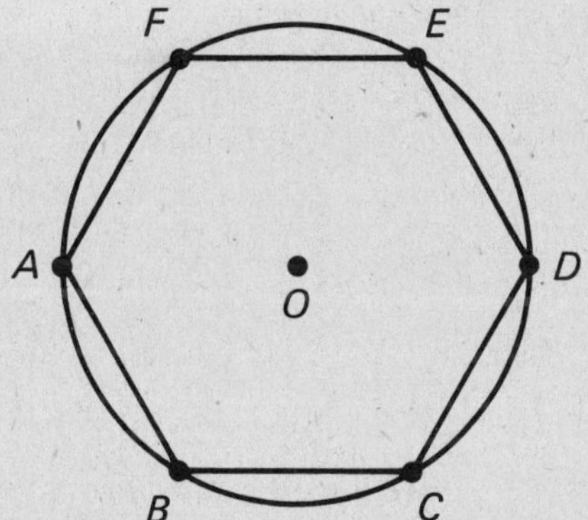

138. How many rolls of wallpaper are necessary to cover the walls of a room whose floor and ceiling are rectangles 12 feet wide and 15 feet long?

(1) A roll of wallpaper covers 20 square feet.
(2) There are no windows in the walls.

139. What is the average daily wage of a worker who works five days? He made $80 the first day.

(1) The worker made a total of $400 for the first four days of work.
(2) The worker made 20% more each day then he did on the previous day.

140. Is ABC a right triangle? $AB = 5$; $AC = 4$.

(1) $BC = 3$
(2) $AC = CD$

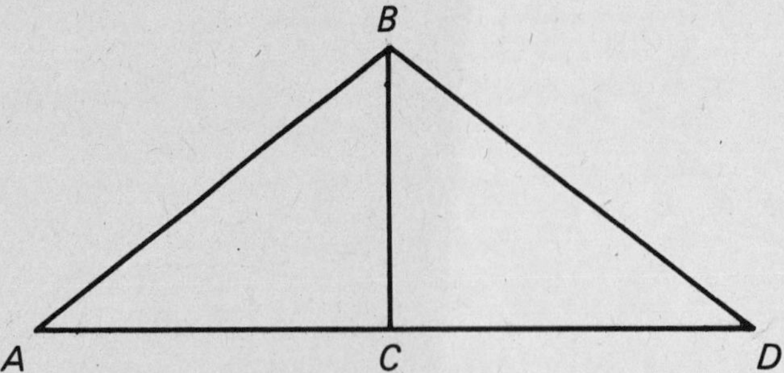

If there is still time remaining, you may review the questions in this section only. You may not turn to any other section of the test.

Section V Business Judgment

TIME: 35 minutes

DIRECTIONS: Read the following two passages. After you have completed each of them you will be asked to answer two sets of questions. The first of these, data evaluation, involves determining the importance of specific factors included in the passage. The second, data application, consists of general questions relating to the passage. When answering questions, you may consult the passage.

Passage 1:

In 1967 Mr. Ed Sim, a chemical engineer, began experimenting in his spare time with a new formula for processing fresh orange juice. By 1970 he had perfected the process to such an extent that he was ready to begin production in a small way. His process enabled him to extract 18 percent more juice from oranges than was typically extracted by a pressure juicer of the type currently used in cafes. His process also removed some of the bitterness which got into the juice from the peelings when oranges were squeezed without peeling them.

Since many of the better quality restaurants preferred to serve fresh orange juice instead of canned or frozen juice, Mr. Sim believed he could find a ready market for his product. Another appeal of his product would be that he could maintain more consistent juice flavor than haphazard restaurant juicing usually produced.

Mr. Sim patented the process and then started production. Since his capital was limited, he began production in a small building which previously had been a woodworking shop. Mr. Sim, with the help of his brother, marketed the juice through local restaurants. The juice was distributed in glass jugs which proved to be rather expensive because of high breakage. The new product was favorably accepted by the public, and the business proved to be a success.

Mr. Sim began to receive larger and more frequent orders from his customers and their business associates. In 1972 he quit his regular job in order to devote full time to his juice business. He soon reached his capacity because of his inability to cover personally a larger area with his pickup truck. Advertising was on a small scale because of limited funds. Faced with these problems of glass jug breakage, advertising and limited distribution, Mr. Sim approached a regional food distributor for a solution. Mr. Sim was offered a plan whereby the distributor would advertise and distribute the product on the basis of 25 percent of gross sales. The distributor would assist Mr. Sim in securing a loan from the local bank to expand production.

Before he had an opportunity to contact the bank to borrow money, Mr. Sim was introduced to Mr. Bernie Lubo, a plastics engineer, who produced plastic containers. Mr. Sim mentioned his own problems in the expansion of his business. Mr. Lubo wanted to finance expanded juice production with the understanding that plastic containers would be used for marketing the orange juice. He would lend the money interest free, but he was to receive 40 percent of the net profits for the next ten years. Distribution and advertising were to be done through a local broker for 25 percent of gross sales. The principal on Mr. Lubo's invested money was to be repaid by Mr. Sim on a basis of 10 percent of his share of the profits. Mr. Lubo was to retain an interest in the profits of the firm until the loan was repaid, or at least for ten years.

Data Evaluation Questions

DIRECTIONS: Evaluate each of the following factors used in decision-making which relate to the passage you have just read by selecting

(A) for a *Major Objective*—the result desired by the executive;

(B) for a *Major Factor*—a primary consideration, spelled out in the passage, that influences the decision;

(C) for a *Minor Factor*—a less important consideration in the decision;

(D) for a *Major Assumption*—a conclusion reached by the executive not necessarily supported by the factors present;

(E) for an *Unimportant Issue*—a consideration not directly related to the problem.

141. Cost of securing a loan

142. High breakage of glass jugs

143. Business expansion

144. Public acceptance of the product

145. General economic trends

Data Application Questions

DIRECTIONS: Answer each of the following questions using information contained in the passage.

146. A major appeal of Mr. Sim's product was its

I. Ability to extract more juice
II. Removing the bitterness of juice
III. Utilization of orange peels

(A) I only
(B) III only
(C) I and II only
(D) II and III only
(E) I, II, and III

147. Which of the following reasons were given for the need to expand Mr. Sim's business?

I. High breakage of glass jugs
II. Production reached capacity
III. Larger and more frequent orders received

(A) I only
(B) III only
(C) I and II only
(D) II and III only
(E) I, II, and III

148. According to the expansion plan suggested by the food distributor, the distributor would

I. Advertise the product
II. Loan money to Mr. Sim
III. Receive 50 percent of gross sales

(A) I only
(B) III only
(C) I and II only
(D) II and II only
(E) I, II, and III

149. According to Mr. Lubo's plan, he offered Mr. Sim a(n)

I. Interest free loan
II. Distribution channel
III. Free use of plastic containers

(A) I only
(B) III only
(C) I and II only
(D) II and III only
(E) I, II, and III

150. Which of the following prevented immediate expansion of Mr. Sim's business?

I. He could not acquire a patent
II. His product was more expensive than frozen orange juice
III. He lacked expansion capital

(A) I only
(B) III only
(C) I and II only
(D) II and III only
(E) I, II, and III

Passage 2:

Speculations and prophecies are not the sort of thing Mr. Gage deals in. "I deal in facts," he said, "and one of the outstanding facts of the Congo's relationship with the United States is that the Congo is an old and good client of the U.S. This can be substantiated by another fact," he noted, "which is that in the first 20 years or so of our existence we have exceeded a deficit trading account with America of some $1 billion.

Despite the fact that the Congo's exports to the United States will no doubt increase, Mr. Gage believes that his country's trade deficit will also increase. "The U.S. is a tough market, in which the Congo has to face stiff competition both in the area of prices from such low wage countries as Taiwan and Korea, and in quality from such distinguished competitors as Italy, France and, of course, America itself. We have to compete with the quality suppliers by offering more sophisticated goods."

Another problem which must be faced is the business recession in the United States and the demand by some labor unions and Congressmen for legislation restricting the import of goods. Although such legislation is not given much chance of passage, some increase in protectionist sentiment might develop, effectively reducing exports to the United States. With these facts in mind, Mr. Gage, the Congo's Trade Minister, seriously began considering alternative strategies for his country's export efforts.

The first strategy was expanding the Congo's promotional effort in the United States. At present, the Congo spends about $50,000 in all sorts of promotional activities, mainly in leaflets and brochures sent to importers and large retail chains. While it is known that the advertising appropriation figure is a moderate one for a country of the Congo's size, it is not known what the effect of the promotion has been. Since it is difficult to judge the effectiveness of promotion of this kind, some have suggested to the Minister that the Congo open a trade center in the United States where its goods could be exhibited on a permanent basis. Such a center could also be the focal point for the preparation and dissemination of promotional material. Opponents of such a measure claim that such a center would be prohibitive in cost and offer no guarantee that the investment will produce a satisfactory return. Moreover, the critics state that until the Congo produces more sophisticated goods of better quality, it is useless to try and compete with domestic U.S. producers. The Congo should concentrate on the sale of specialized goods which are not produced in large quantities in the U.S. As to what goods should be sold in the U.S., a survey of the market was suggested.

Data Evaluation Questions

DIRECTIONS: Evaluate each of the following factors used in decision making which relate to the passage you have just read by selecting

(A) for a *Major Objective*—the result desired by the executive;

(B) for a *Major Factor*—a primary consideration, spelled out in the passage, that influences the decision;

(C) for a *Minor Factor*—a less important consideration in the decision;

(D) for a *Major Assumption*—a conclusion reached by the executive not necessarily supported by the factors present;

(E) for an *Unimportant Issue*—a consideration not directly related to the problem.

151. Reducing the Congo's trade deficit

152. The business recession in the U.S.

153. The Congo is an old client of the U.S.

154. Competition from Italy and France

155. Impending trade legislation in the U.S.

Data Application Questions

DIRECTIONS: Answer each of the following questions using information contained in the passage.

156. Protectionist legislation in the United States

I. Would reduce U.S. imports
II. Is not given much chance of passage
III. Would restrict U.S. exports

(A) I only
(B) III only
(C) I and II only
(D) II and III only
(E) I, II, and III

157. With regard to the Congo's promotional campaign in the United States, the Trade Minister

I. Praised its success
II. Suggested increasing the budget
III. Was not sure how effective the promotion really was

(A) I only
(B) III only
(C) I and II only
(D) II and III only
(E) I, II, and III

158. To increase the Congo's exports to the United States, it was suggested that

I. Product prices be increased
II. A trade center be opened in the United States
III. Only specialized goods be sold in the United States

(A) I only
(B) III only
(C) I and II only
(D) II and III only
(E) I, II, and III

159. Those demanding passage of restrictionist trade legislation in the United States include

I. Congressmen
II. Labor unions
III. Business groups

(A) I only
(B) III only
(C) I and II only
(D) II and III only
(E) I, II, and III

160. Which trade strategy did the Congo's Trade Minister consider?

I. Increasing the promotional effort in the United States
II. Opening a trade center in the United States
III. Increasing the quality of goods sold in the United States

(A) I only
(B) III only
(C) I and II only
(D) II and III only
(E) I, II, and III

If there is still time remaining, you may review the questions in this section only. You may not turn to any other section of the test.

Section VI Mathematics

TIME: 40 minutes

DIRECTIONS: Solve each of the following problems; then indicate the correct answer on the answer sheet. [On the actual test you will be permitted to use any space available on the examination paper for scratch work.]

NOTE: A figure that appears with a problem is drawn as accurately as possible so as to provide information that may help in answering the question. Numbers in this test are real numbers.

161. If a bus can travel 15 miles on a gallon of gas, how many gallons of gas will it use to travel 200 miles?

(A) 10
(B) $12\frac{1}{2}$
(C) $13\frac{1}{3}$
(D) 15
(E) $20\frac{1}{5}$

162. If $x < 3$ and $y > 3$, then $x < y$

(A) always
(B) only if $y > 0$
(C) only if $x > 0$
(D) never
(E) sometimes

Use the following graph for questions 163–166.

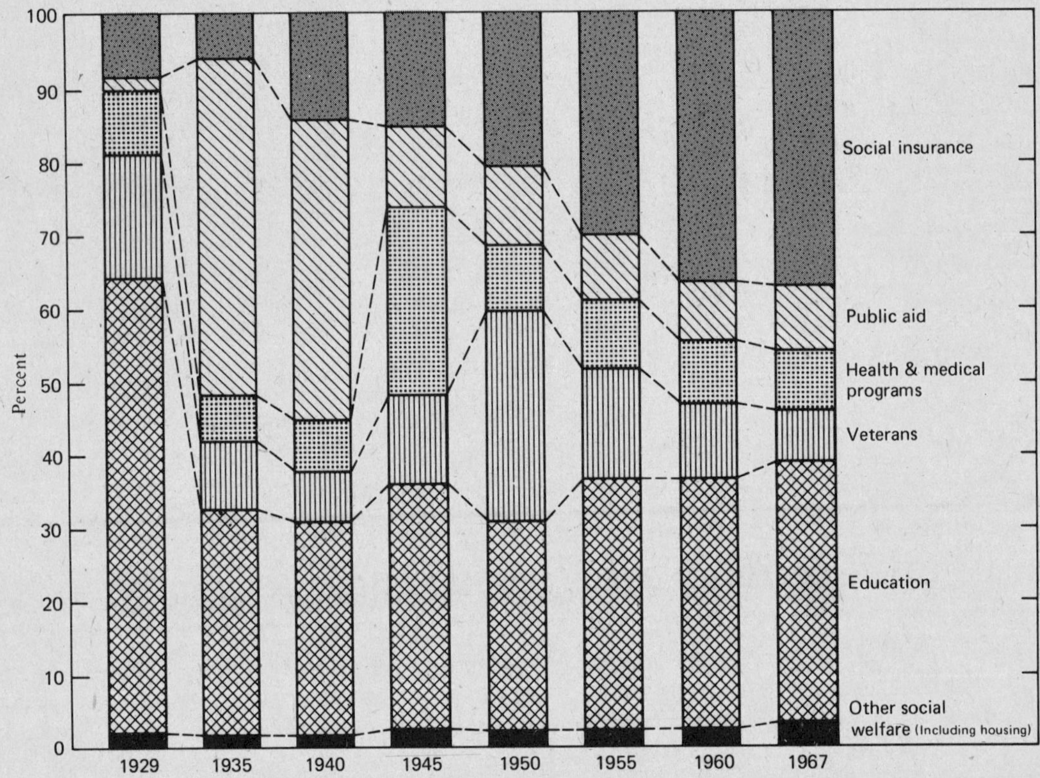

163. In 1940 which category received the largest amount of social welfare expenditures?

(A) social insurance
(B) public aid
(C) health & medical programs
(D) veterans
(E) education

164. Between 1950 and 1967, which category had the largest decrease in its percentage of social welfare expenditures?

(A) social insurance
(B) public aid
(C) veterans
(D) education
(E) other social welfare

165. If \$50 billion was spent on social welfare in 1929, approximately how much was spent on veterans programs in 1929?

(A) \$5 billion
(B) \$8 billion
(C) \$11 billion
(D) \$14 billion
(E) \$20 billion

166. Which of the following statements about social welfare expenditures can be inferred from the graph?

I. More money was spent on education in 1929 than in 1960.
II. The percentage devoted to social insurance increased between 1945 and 1967.
III. In 1935, education received more than all the other categories.

(A) I only
(B) II only
(C) I and II only
(D) I and III only
(E) I, II, and III

167. If the radius of a cylinder is increased by 10% and the height of the cylinder is increased by 20%, then the volume of the cylinder is increased by

(A) 21%
(B) 32%
(C) 32.4%
(D) 44%
(E) 45.2%

168. A tank contains 10 gallons of water. If a pump takes $15 - \frac{x}{10}$ minutes to pump one gallon of water out of the tank, how many minutes will it take for the pump to empty the tank?

(A) x
(B) $15 - 10x$
(C) $150 - 10x$
(D) $150 - x$
(E) $15 - 10x$

169. A company makes a profit of 6% on its first \$1,000 of sales each day, and 5% on all sales in excess of \$1,000 for that day. How many dollars in profit will the company make in a day when sales are \$6,000?

(A) \$250
(B) \$300
(C) \$310
(D) \$320
(E) \$360

Use the following graphs for questions 170–173.

Source: Department of Commerce, Bureau of the Census

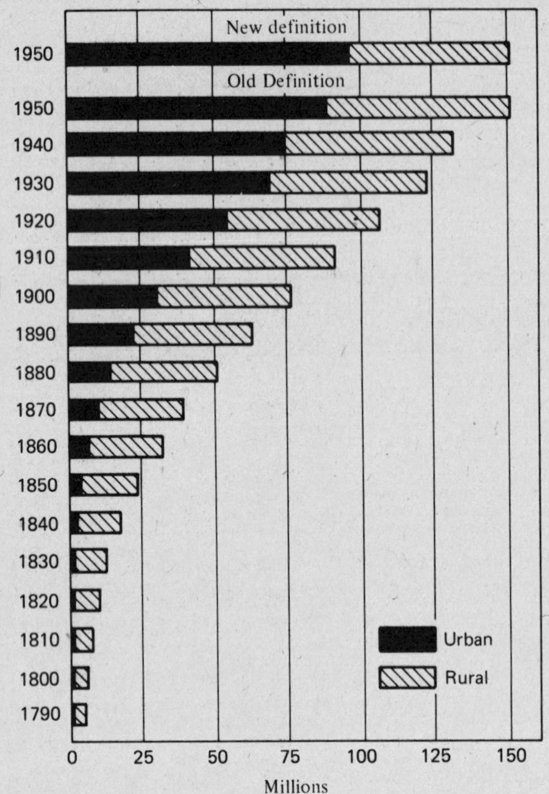

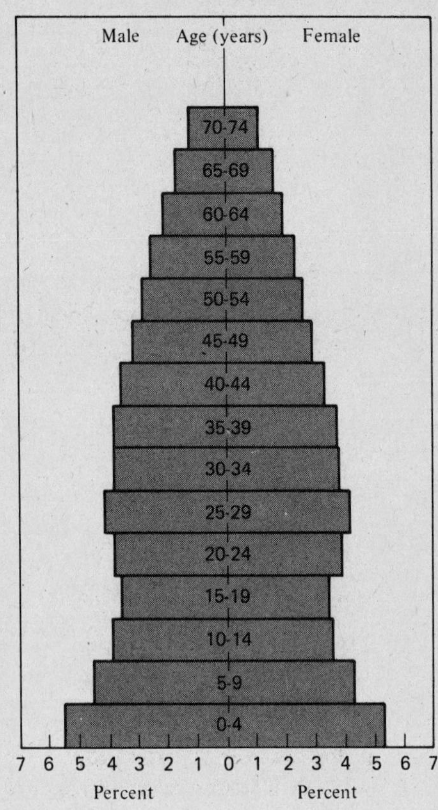

170. In 1950, approximately how many people were there in the United States 4 years old or younger?

(A) 7.5 million
(B) 10 million
(C) 12.5 million
(D) 16.5 million
(E) 20 million

171. Between which two censuses did the population of the U.S. increase the most?

(A) 1870–1880
(B) 1890–1900
(C) 1910–1920
(D) 1930–1940
(E) 1940–1950

172. In 1940, approximately what percentage of the population was classified as urban?

(A) 50
(B) 60
(C) 70
(D) 75
(E) 80

173. Which of the following conclusions about the population of the United States can be inferred from the graphs?

I. There were more people over 15 years old than under 15 years of age in 1950.
II. There were more males under 20 years of age in 1950 than there were people classified as rural in 1940.
III. The population of the United States in 1900 was more than three times as large as it was in 1850.

(A) I only
(B) III only
(C) I and III only
(D) II and III only
(E) I, II, and III

174. If 15 men working independently and at the same rate can manufacture 27 baskets in an hour, how many baskets would 45 men working independently and at the same rate manufacture in 40 minutes?

(A) 27
(B) 35
(C) 40
(D) 54
(E) 81

175. If one elevator can lift 2 tons in 5 minutes and another elevator can lift 3 tons in 7 minutes, how many minutes will it take to lift 20 tons using both elevators?

(A) 12
(B) $16\frac{4}{7}$
(C) $18\frac{3}{26}$
(D) 21
(E) $24\frac{4}{29}$

Use the following chart for questions 176–178.

ANALYSIS OF EXPENSES (In Dollars)

	Mon.	*Tues.*	*Wed.*	*Thurs.*	*Fri.*
TRANSPORTATION:					
FARE	75.00				
TOLLS					
PARKING		3.00	2.00		
TAXI	4.00				4.00
MEALS:					
BREAKFAST	1.50	2.50	1.50		2.00
LUNCH	3.50	3.00	2.50	3.00	4.00
DINNER	6.00	7.50	5.00	6.00	5.50
LODGING:	15.00	15.00	15.00	15.00	15.00

176. How much was spent for lodging and transportation?

(A) $75
(B) $88
(C) $153
(D) $163
(E) $175

177. What was the average daily expenditure for meals during the five days shown?

(A) $10
(B) $10.40
(C) $10.70
(D) $11.05
(E) $11.25

178. The greatest amount of money was spent on

(A) Monday
(B) Tuesday
(C) Wednesday
(D) Thursday
(E) Friday

179. If $x - 3y = 2$, then $9y - 3x$ is equal to

(A) −6
(B) −2
(C) 2
(D) 6
(E) 12

180. A bank charges 10% interest on the first $2,000 of a loan and 8% interest on all of the loan in excess of $2,000. What percentage will the interest be on a loan of $10,000?

(A) 8.2%
(B) 8.4%
(C) 8.5%
(D) 9.0%
(E) 9.6%

Use the following charts for questions 181–184.

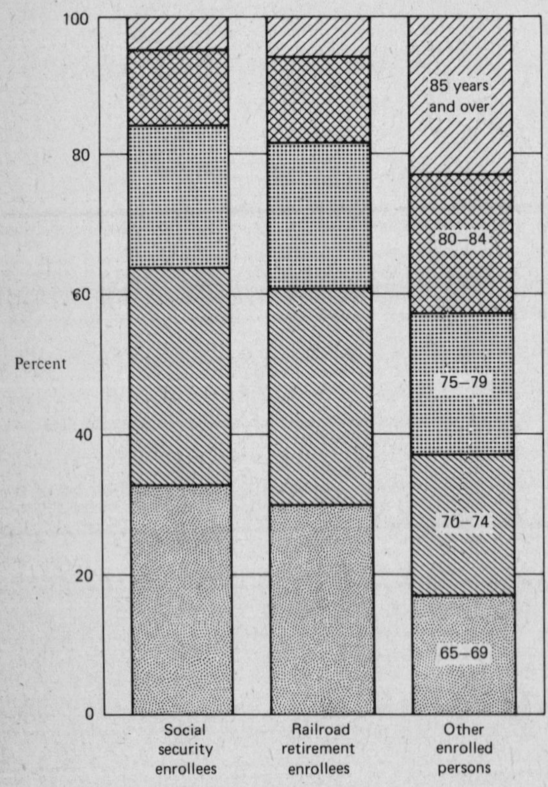

Characteristic	All enrolled persons	Persons entitled to social security benefits	Persons entitled to railroad retirement benefits	Other enrolled persons
Total number (in thousands)........	18,859	15,856	821	2,446
Age:				
Percent..................	100.0	100.0	100.0	100.0
65–69................	31.2	33.4	30.4	17.3
70–74................	29.5	31.0	30.3	20.1
75–79................	20.6	20.6	21.6	20.3
80–84................	11.9	10.6	12.1	20.2
85 and over.........	6.8	4.5	5.6	22.0
Sex:				
Percent..................	100.0	100.0	100.0	100.0
Men....................	42.8	45.3	48.4	24.2
Women..............	57.2	54.7	51.6	75.8
Race:				
Number reporting (in thousands)...	18,227	15,848	795	1,848
Percent..................	100.0	100.0	100.0	100.0
White.................	92.3	93.2	92.2	84.4
Nonwhite............	7.7	6.8	7.8	15.6

Source: Social Security Bulletin

181. Approximately how many people who are entitled to social security benefits are in the age group 65–69?

(A) 5,000,000
(B) 5,300,000
(C) 5,600,000
(D) 6,000,000
(E) 6,500,000

182. The ratio of men to women in the category of other enrolled persons is about

(A) 1 to 3
(B) 1 to 2
(C) 2 to 3
(D) 3 to 1
(E) 4 to 1

183. Which of the following statements about enrollees in the hospital insurance program can be inferred from the charts?

I. There are more enrollees 85 and over entitled to social security benefits than enrollees aged 85 and over in the other enrolled persons category.
II. More than 9 times as many whites are enrolled as nonwhites.
III. More than $\frac{1}{3}$ of all enrollees are in the age category 65–69.

(A) II only
(B) III only
(C) I and II only
(D) II and III only
(E) I, II, and III

184. If 50% of all retired people were enrolled in the hospital insurance program on July 1, 1966, how many retired people were there on July 1, 1966?

(A) 36,000
(B) 37,718
(C) 37,634,000
(D) 37,718,000
(E) 38,518,000

185. A truck originally was priced at $6,800. It was discounted 10% and a month later was discounted 15% more, and sold. How much was the truck sold for?

(A) $5,100
(B) $5,152
(C) $5,198
(D) $5,202
(E) $5,248

186. A field is rectangular and its width is $\frac{1}{3}$ as long as its length. What is the area of the field if the length of the field is 120 yards?

(A) 480 square yards
(B) 2,400 square yards
(C) 4,800 square yards
(D) 5,000 square yards
(E) 7,200 square yards

187. If the price of steak is currently $1.00 a pound, and the price triples every 6 months, how long will it be until the price of steak is $81.00 a pound?

(A) 1 year
(B) 2 years
(C) $2\frac{1}{2}$ years
(D) 13 years
(E) $13\frac{1}{2}$ years

Use the following table for questions 188–190.

TABLE 2.—Key indicators

	% change by volume on preceding year					Volume indices (1963 = 100)
	1966	**1967**	**1968**	**1969**	**1970**	**1969**
Gross Community product	+ 4.3	+3.2	+ 6.0	+ 7.3	+ 5.4	144
Industrial production	+ 5.0	+1.3	+ 8.9	+11.9	+ 6.3	154
Visible imports	+ 7.1	+0.8	+11.6	+12.6	+21.1	184
Private customers' expenditure	+ 4.7	+3.7	+ 4.9	+ 7.0	+ 6.4	143
Gross fixed asset formation	+ 4.5	+1.0	+ 7.4	+ 9.6	+ 8.2	152
Visible exports	+ 8.3	+7.6	+13.5	+ 7.5	+ 9.3	188
Intra-Community visible trade	+11.0	+5.7	+19.5	+22.5	+12.4	245
Gross product per capita	+ 3.4	+2.6	+ 5.4	+ 6.4	+ 4.5	135

Source: European Economic Community

188. Which indicator increased most in volume between 1963 and 1969?

(A) gross community product
(B) visible imports
(C) visible exports
(D) intra-community visible trade
(E) gross product per capita

189. The only year in which no indicator increased by $\frac{1}{10}$ of its volume for the preceding year was

(A) 1966
(B) 1967
(C) 1968
(D) 1969
(E) 1970

190. The average percentage change by volume on the preceding year for gross community product over the 5 years 1966–1970 was

(A) 5%
(B) 5.24%
(C) 5.33%
(D) 5.78%
(E) 6.02%

191. The next number in the sequence 1, 4, 9, 16, 25, . . . is

(A) 32
(B) 35
(C) 36
(D) 39
(E) 42

192. If $\frac{x}{y} = \frac{2}{3}$, then $\frac{y^2}{x^2}$ is

(A) $\frac{4}{9}$
(B) $\frac{2}{3}$
(C) $\frac{3}{2}$
(D) $\frac{9}{4}$
(E) $\frac{5}{2}$

193. An employer pays 3 workers *X*, *Y*, and *Z* a total of \$610 a week. *X* is paid 125% of the amount *Y* is paid and 80% of the amount *Z* is paid. How much does *X* make a week?

(A) \$150
(B) \$175
(C) \$180
(D) \$195
(E) \$200

194. What is the maximum number of points of intersection of two circles which have unequal radii?

(A) none
(B) 1
(C) 2
(D) 3
(E) infinite

195. If the area of a rectangle is equal to the area of a square, then the perimeter of the rectangle

(A) is ½ the perimeter of the square
(B) equal to the perimeter of the square
(C) equal to twice the perimeter of the square
(D) equal to the square root of the perimeter of the square
(E) none of the above

If there is still time remaining, you may review the questions in this section only.
You may not turn to any other section of the test.

Answers

Section I Reading Recall

1. **(C)**
2. **(C)**
3. **(B)**
4. **(D)**
5. **(C)**
6. **(A)**
7. **(C)**
8. **(B)**
9. **(A)**
10. **(E)**
11. **(B)**
12. **(B)**
13. **(A)**
14. **(D)**
15. **(C)**
16. **(D)**
17. **(A)**
18. **(C)**
19. **(C)**
20. **(E)**
21. **(A)**
22. **(C)**
23. **(D)**
24. **(D)**
25. **(E)**
26. **(D)**
27. **(C)**
28. **(E)**
29. **(E)**
30. **(E)**

Section II Mathematics

(Numbers in parentheses indicate the section in the Mathematics Review where material concerning the question is discussed.)

31. **(D)** (I–4)
32. **(E)** (II–2)
33. **(C)** (II–6)
34. **(C)** (IV–4)
35. **(D)** (IV–4)
36. **(E)** (IV–4)
37. **(E)** (II–5)
38. **(D)** (II–4)
39. **(B)** (IV–1)
40. **(C)** (IV–1)
41. **(B)** (I–4)
42. **(A)** (II–3)
43. **(C)** (III–7)
44. **(C)** (IV–1)
45. **(D)** (IV–1)
46. **(D)** (IV–1, I–4)
47. **(C)** (IV–1)
48. **(B)** (II–5)
49. **(C)** (II–6)
50. **(B)** (II–7)
51. **(E)** (I–4)
52. **(C)** (I–7)
53. **(A)** (II–2)
54. **(C)** (I–2)
55. **(A)** (III–4)
56. **(C)** (IV–2)
57. **(D)** (IV–2)
58. **(E)** (IV–2)
59. **(B)** (IV–2)
60. **(C)** (IV–2)
61. **(D)** (II–3)
62. **(E)** (I–2)
63. **(B)** (I–4)
64. **(D)** (IV–5)
65. **(E)** (IV–5)
66. **(B)** (IV–5)
67. **(C)** (IV–5)
68. **(C)** (I–4)
69. **(B)** (I–2)
70. **(D)** (III–6, III–7)
71. **(C)** (IV–3)
72. **(D)** (IV–3)
73. **(C)** (IV–3)
74. **(E)** (IV–3)
75. **(C)** (II–3)
76. **(B)** (II–3)
77. **(D)** (IV–1, I–7)
78. **(E)** (IV–1, I–7)
79. **(D)** (IV–1)
80. **(D)** (III–7)
81. **(C)** (II–3)
82. **(B)** (II–7)
83. **(C)** (III–4, III–7)
84. **(E)** (II–3)
85. **(E)** (II–2)

Section III Verbal Aptitude

86. **(C)**
87. **(D)**
88. **(C)**
89. **(B)**
90. **(C)**
91. **(B)**
92. **(C)**
93. **(A)**
94. **(C)**
95. **(D)**
96. **(C)**
97. **(B)**
98. **(A)**
99. **(B)**
100. **(B)**
101. **(B)**
102. **(C)**
103. **(B)**
104. **(A)**
105. **(C)**
106. **(B)**
107. **(A)**
108. **(B)**
109. **(C)**
110. **(A)**
111. **(D)**
112. **(B)**
113. **(B)**
114. **(A)**
115. **(D)**
116. **(B)**
117. **(C)**
118. **(C)**
119. **(A)**
120. **(B)**
121. **(C)**
122. **(C)**
123. **(A)**
124. **(C)**
125. **(D)**

Section IV Data Sufficiency

126. **(E)**
127. **(C)**
128. **(A)**
129. **(E)**
130. **(D)**
131. **(D)**
132. **(B)**
133. **(B)**
134. **(E)**
135. **(E)**
136. **(A)**
137. **(C)**
138. **(E)**
139. **(B)**
140. **(A)**

Section V Business Judgment

141. **(B)**
142. **(C)**
143. **(A)**
144. **(D)**
145. **(E)**
146. **(C)**
147. **(D)**
148. **(A)**
149. **(A)**
150. **(B)**
151. **(A)**
152. **(B)**
153. **(C)**
154. **(C)**
155. **(D)**
156. **(C)**
157. **(B)**
158. **(D)**
159. **(C)**
160. **(E)**

Section VI Mathematics

(Numbers in parentheses indicate the section in the Mathematics Review where material concerning the question is discussed.)

161. **(C)** (I–2)
162. **(A)** (II–7)
163. **(B)** (IV–5)
164. **(C)** (IV–5)
165. **(B)** (IV–5)
166. **(B)** (IV–5)
167. **(E)** (III–8, I–4)
168. **(D)** (II–3)
169. **(C)** (I–4)
170. **(D)** (IV–4)
171. **(E)** (IV–4)
172. **(B)** (IV–4)
173. **(C)** (IV–4)
174. **(D)** (II–5)
175. **(E)** (II–3)
176. **(D)** (IV–1)
177. **(C)** (I–7)
178. **(A)** (IV–1)
179. **(A)** (II–2)
180. **(B)** (I–4)
181. **(B)** (IV–1)
182. **(A)** (II–5, I–5)
183. **(C)** (IV–1)
184. **(D)** (I–4)
185. **(D)** (I–4)
186. **(C)** (III–7, II–3)
187. **(B)** (II–6)
188. **(D)** (IV–1)
189. **(B)** (I–4)
190. **(B)** (I–7)
191. **(C)** (II–6)
192. **(D)** (I–2, I–8)
193. **(E)** (II–3)
194. **(C)** (III–6)
195. **(E)** (III–7)

Analysis

Section I Reading Recall

1. **(C)** See paragraph 2, line 1.

2. **(C)** See paragraph 1.

3. **(B)** See paragraph 1: "Starting as a non-violent revolutionist. . . ."

4. **(D)** See paragraph 1: ". . . he ended life as a major social theorist . . . sympathetic with violent revolution. . . ."

5. **(C)** See paragraph 3: ". . . Russia . . . is no longer a proletarian movement . . . but a camouflaged imperialistic effort. . . ."

6. **(A)** See paragraph 4.

7. **(C)** See paragraph 3: Of course it is accepted by those in (D) and (E), but also by those in (C).

8. **(B)** This can be deduced from the last paragraph.

9. **(A)** See paragraph 2.

10. **(E)** All these are mentioned in paragraph 1.

11. **(B)** See paragraph 2: ". . . fiscal policies should be designed to encourage economic growth."

12. **(B)** See paragraph 2: They did not.

13. **(A)** See paragraph 3: The Committee of the Whole.

14. **(D)** See paragraph 4, line 1.

15. **(C)** See paragraph 5: "In the first decade of the twentieth century, an 'executive budget' came into successful use. . . ."

16. **(D)** See paragraph 5: It was rejected.

17. **(A)** See paragraph 6, line 1: The responsibility was given by the Budget and Accounting Act of 1921.

18. **(C)** See paragraph 6.

19. **(C)** See paragraph 6.

20. **(E)** See paragraph 1: All factors but (E) are relevant.

21. **(A)** See paragraph 2.

22. **(C)** See paragraph 2: They came at different times.

23. **(D)** See paragraph 2.

24. **(D)** Paragraphs 2 and 4 especially mention the various points of migration which the Indians reached.

25. **(E)** See paragraph 4.

26. **(D)** See paragraph 3: ". . . the New Mexico Indians were very successful big game hunters."

27. **(C)** See the last line of paragraph 4.

28. **(E)** All these are given in paragraph 3.

29. **(E)** See paragraph 3.

30. **(E)** Certainly, alternatives (A) and (C) do not correspond to the contents of the passage, while (B) and (D) are too general. The main point in the passage is the migration of Indians, their cultures, and their acclimation to new surroundings. These subjects are in the domain of the anthropologist.

Section II Mathematics

31. **(D)** Since he pays 6% on the first \$500, this equals (.06)(500) or \$30 interest on the first \$500. He is borrowing \$5,500 which is \$5,000 in excess of the first \$500. Thus, he also pays $5\frac{1}{2}$% of \$5,000, which is (.055)(5,000) or \$275.00. Therefore, the total interest is \$305.

32. **(E)** $6x - 3y$ is $3(2x - y)$. Since $2x - y = 4$, $6x - 3y = 3 \cdot 4$ or 12.

33. **(C)** The progression is arithmetic and $11 - 5 = 6 = 17 - 11$, so every term is 6 more than the previous term. Therefore, the next term after 17 is $17 + 6$ or 23.

34. **(C)** The bar first touched 50 in 1945.

35. **(D)** In 1952, hydro plants had about 21 million kilowatts, while the total capacity was about 84 million kilowatts. Therefore, the capacity of the steam and internal combustion plants in 1952 was about (84 − 21) or 63 million kilowatts. Since $\frac{63}{21} = 3$, x is 3.

36. **(E)**

    STATEMENT I is true since the graph is almost horizontal between 1930 and 1939, whereas it rises between 1920 and 1929 and between 1940 and 1949.

    Since the total capacity in 1952 was less than 25 million kilowatts and the capacity of the hydro plants in 1925 was more than 5 million kilowatts, STATEMENT II can be inferred.

    STATEMENT III is also true. Between 1925 and 1945, the capacity went from about 22 million to about 50 million kilowatts, which is an increase of about 28 million kilowatts. However, the capacity in 1952 was about 84 million kilowatts, so the increase between 1945 and 1952 was about 34 million kilowatts.

    Therefore, STATEMENTS I, II, and III can all be inferred from the graph.

37. **(E)** Since each packer loads $\frac{1}{8}$ of a box in 9 minutes, the 20 packers will load $\frac{20}{8}$ or $2\frac{1}{2}$ boxes in 9 minutes. There are 90 minutes in $1\frac{1}{2}$ hours; so the 20 packers will load $10 \times 2\frac{1}{2}$ or 25 boxes in $1\frac{1}{2}$ hours.

38. **(D)** The entire population can be divided into three nonoverlapping parts: owns both a car and a motorcycle, owns a car but not a motorcycle, and owns a motorcycle but not a car. If we denote these categories by A, B, and C respectively, we know that $A + B + C = 100\%$. Also, since $A + B$ consists of all the people who own a car, we have $A + B = 90\%$. Therefore, C must be 10%. But C is the category of people who own a motorcycle but do not own a car.

39. **(B)** The total number of children between 6 and 17 in 1972 was about 46,000,000 and of these 20,155,000 had mothers in the labor force. Therefore, about 46,000,000 minus 20,000,000, or 26,000,000, did not have mothers in the labor force.

40. **(C)** There were 2,345,000 Negro children under 6, of whom 999,000 had mothers in the labor force. $\frac{999{,}000}{2{,}345{,}000}$ is about $\frac{1{,}000{,}000}{2{,}350{,}000}$ or $\frac{100}{235}$, which is roughly $\frac{5}{12}$. $\frac{5}{12} = 5 \times 8\frac{1}{3}\% = 41\frac{2}{3}\%$.

41. **(B)** Since 108% of \$50 = (1.08)(50) = \$54, the chair was offered for sale at \$54.00. It was sold for 90% of \$54 since there was a 10% discount. Therefore, the chair was sold for (.9)(\$54) or \$48.60.

42. **(A)** Here's a table of the hours worked:

	Mon.	Tues.	Wed.	Thurs.	Fri.	Wages for week
	8	8	8	8	8	$5x$
excess over 8 hrs	0	3	1	2	1	$(0+3+1+2+1)y = 7y$.

The average daily wage equals $\frac{(5x + 7y)}{5}$, or $x + \frac{7}{5}y$.

43. **(C)** The area of a rectangle is length times width; so the area of the field is 50×25 square yards or 1,250 square yards.

44. **(C)** California's population increased by 53.3%.

45. **(D)** Arkansas, Mississippi, North Dakota, and Oklahoma had decreases in population.

46. **(D)** The population of the United States increased by 14.5% between 1940 and 1950. So if the population was 100 million in 1940, it would have been 114.5 million in 1950. Therefore, the correct answer is 115 million.

47. **(C)**

STATEMENT I is true. $\frac{1}{3}$ is $33\frac{1}{3}\%$ and only California, Arizona, Florida, Nevada, Oregon, and Washington had population increases of more than $33\frac{1}{3}\%$.

STATEMENT II cannot be inferred since the graph tells us only that the *percentage* increase in Oregon's population was larger than the *percentage* increase in Washington's population. There is no information about the number of people living in each state.

STATEMENT III is true because Nebraska's population increased by .7%.

Therefore, only STATEMENTS I and III can be inferred from the graph.

48. **(B)** Since 4 is $\frac{1}{3}$ of 12, 4 apples cost $\frac{1}{3}$ of 63¢, which is 21¢.

49. **(C)** Let x_n be what the car is worth after n years. Then we know $x_0 = \$2,500$ and $x_{n+1} = \frac{4}{5}\, x_n$. So $x_1 = \frac{4}{5} \times 2,500$, which is \$2,000, x_2 is $\frac{4}{5} \times 2,000$, which is 1,600, and finally x_3 is $\frac{4}{5} \times 1,600$, which is 1,280. Therefore, the car is worth \$1,280 at the end of three years.

OR

$x_3 = \frac{4}{5}x_2 = \frac{4}{5}(\frac{4}{5}x_1) = (\frac{4}{5})(\frac{4}{5})(\frac{4}{5}x_0) = \frac{64}{125}x_0$. $(\frac{64}{125})2500 = 1280$.

50. **(B)** Since 300 miles is $\frac{3}{5}$ of 500 miles, it should cost $\frac{3}{5}$ of \$15 to travel 300 miles by automobile. Therefore, the cost is \$9.

51. **(E)** Since the only costs are \$20 for fuel and \$70 for the drivers wages, the total cost is \$90. Therefore, the company should charge 120% of \$90, which is (1.2)(\$90) or \$108.00.

52. **(C)** The total fuel cost will be $3 \cdot 20 + 4 \cdot 15 + 2 \cdot 5 + 1 \cdot 50$, which is \$180. Since there are 10 vehicles, the average fuel cost is 180/10 or \$18 per vehicle.

53. **(A)** Since $x + 2y = 2x + y$, we can subtract $x + 2y$ from each side of the equation and the result is $0 = x - y$.

54. **(C)** $\frac{2}{3}$ of the 15% of the families with income over \$25,000 own boats. Since $\frac{2}{3}$ of 15% = 10%, $\frac{1}{10}$ of the families own boats and have an income of \$25,000 or more.

55. **(A)** The angles are in the ratio of 1:2:2, so 2 angles are equal to each other, and both are twice as large as the third angle of the triangle. Since a triangle with two equal angles must have the sides opposite equal, the triangle is isosceles. (Using the fact that the sum of the angles of a triangle is 180°, you can see that the angles of the triangle are 72°, 72° and 36°, so only (A) is true.)

56. **(C)** In 1970, total expenditures were \$4,851 million, of which 5% was spent in Canada; so x is 5% of \$4,851 million, or \$242.55 million. Therefore, the correct answer is about 240 million.

57. **(D)** In 1960, the military assistance program used 10%, the AEC 12%, and materials and supplies 18%. So all together the three programs received (10 + 12 + 18)% or 40% of defense expenditures; 40% = $\frac{2}{5}$.

58. **(E)** Thailand received 5% of defense expenditures in 1970.

59. **(B)** Since 14% was spent in "other Europe" in 1970, $\frac{5}{7}$ of 14% or 10% was spent in Spain in 1970. Thus, 10% of \$4,851 million, or about \$485 million, was spent in Spain in 1970.

60. **(C)**

STATEMENT I can be inferred since $\frac{1}{5}$ = 20% and in both years more than 20% was spent in Germany.

The expenditures for 1970 were \$4,851 million and for 1960 \$3,087 million; so the expenditures increased by \$(4,851 − 3,087) million or \$1,764 million. Since \$1,764 million is more than $\frac{1}{3}$ of \$3,087 million, STATEMENT II can be inferred from the graph.

STATEMENT III is false. $\frac{2}{5}$ = 40%; U.S. personnel spent 26% in 1960 and 38% in 1970, so it is impossible for U.S. personnel to have spent 40% of the total for 1960 and 1970.

Therefore, only STATEMENTS I and II can be inferred from the graphs.

61. **(D)** The car travels at 60 mph; so the time to travel 255 miles is $\frac{255}{60}$ hours. Since $\frac{255}{60} = 4\frac{15}{60} = 4\frac{1}{4}$, it takes $4\frac{1}{4}$ hours.

62. **(E)** After the tune-up, the car will travel 15 miles on $\frac{3}{4}$ of a gallon of gas. So it will travel $\frac{15}{3/4}$ or $\frac{4}{3} \times 15$ or 20 miles on one gallon of gas.

63. **(B)** The price after a discount of 20% is 80% of P, the original price. After another 15% discount, the price is 85% of 80% of P or (.85)(.80) P, which equals $.68P$. Therefore, after the successive discounts, the price is 68% of what it was originally, which is the same as a single discount of 32%.

64. **(D)** Since the government spent $132 per capita on personal health care for people aged 65 and over in 1966, the total expenditure by the government was $(20)(132) million, which is $2,640 million, or $2.640 billion.

65. **(E)** In 1966, the government spent $30 per capita on people under 65; by 1972 the per capita amount for those under 65 was $72. Therefore, since $\frac{72}{30} = 2\frac{12}{30} = 2\frac{2}{5} = 240\%$, the correct answer is (E).

66. **(B)** In 1972, philanthropy and industry contributed $5 out of the $981 per capita spent on personal health care for those aged 65 and over. Therefore, the fraction is $\frac{5}{981}$, which is about $\frac{5}{980} = \frac{1}{196}$.

67. **(C)**

STATEMENT I cannot be inferred since the graph gives only per capita amounts. The total amount will also depend on the number of people in each group.

STATEMENT II is false since private health insurance decreased from $70 to $56 per capita.

STATEMENT III is true since $644 is more than ½ of $981.

Therefore, only STATEMENT III can be inferred from the graphs.

68. **(C)** Since there are 20 oranges in a crate, a crate of oranges is sold for 20 × 6¢ or $1.20. A crate of oranges costs $1.00; so the profit on a crate is $1.20 − $1.00 or $.20. Therefore, the rate of profit $= \frac{.20}{1.20} = \frac{1}{6} = 16\frac{2}{3}\%$.

69. **(B)** $7\frac{1}{2}$ dozen is $\frac{15}{2} \times 12 = 90$, so during the summer the hen lays 90 eggs. The food for the summer costs $10, so the cost in food per egg is $\frac{\$10}{90} = \frac{\$1}{9} = 11\frac{1}{9}$¢.

70. **(D)**

STATEMENT I is not true since the diameter is not equal to the radius and the area of the circle is πr^2.

STATEMENT II is true since the length of a diameter is twice the length of a radius.

STATEMENT III is true since $a = \pi r^2 = \pi r(d/2) = \pi(r/2)d$. Therefore, $a/d = \pi(r/2)$.

Therefore, only STATEMENTS II and III are true.

71. **(C)** The graph was highest in 1935.

72. **(D)** In 1958 about 10% of the Gross National Product was spent on social welfare and about $45 billion on social welfare. Therefore, the Gross National Product was about $450 billion.

73. **(C)** The federal government spent about $20 billion in 1957, and the total was about $40 billion. Therefore, the state and local governments spent about $20 billion. So the federal government and state and local governments spent about the same amount.

74. **(E)**

STATEMENT I is true since the graph giving the percentage of Gross National Product falls from 1939 to 1943.

STATEMENT II is true since the state and local expenditures have never reached $50 billion (½ of the height of the whole scale).

STATEMENT III is true because the state and local portion is greater than the federal government portion between 1929 and 1933.

Therefore, STATEMENTS I, II and III can all be inferred from the graph.

75. (C) Since hose A takes 20 minutes to fill the tank, it fills up $\frac{1}{20}$ of the tank each minute. Since hose B fills up the tank in 15 minutes, it fills up $\frac{1}{15}$ of the tank each minute. Therefore, hose A and hose B together will fill up $\frac{1}{20}+\frac{1}{15}$ or $\frac{3+4}{60}$ or $\frac{7}{60}$ of the tank each minute. Thus, it will take $\frac{60}{7}$ or $8\frac{4}{7}$ minutes to fill the tank.

76. (B) If T is the amount of time it takes for 12 men to dig the ditch, then $T = \frac{5}{12}$ of $2 = \frac{5}{6}$ of an hour. Therefore, the 12 men will take 50 minutes.

77. (D) The total number of cars produced was $900 + 1200 + 1500 + 1400 + 1000$ or 6,000. So the average per day is $\frac{6{,}000}{5}$ or 1,200 cars per day.

78. (E) There were 6,000 cars produced and the total wages paid for the week was (\$30,000 + \$40,000 + \$52,000 + \$50,000 + \$32,000) or \$204,000. Therefore, the average cost in wages per car $= \frac{\$204{,}000}{6{,}000} = \$34$.

79. (D)

STATEMENT I is true since the total number of cars produced was 6,000 and $\frac{1}{4}$ of 6,000 is 1,500.

STATEMENT II cannot be inferred since there is no data about the number of employees. Even though some employees are paid more than others, there may be fewer employees present who receive higher wages.

STATEMENT III is true since \$102,000 was paid on Wednesday and Thursday and \$102,000 is $\frac{1}{2}$ of the weekly total of \$204,000.

Therefore, only STATEMENTS I and III can be inferred from the graph.

80. (D) The area of the field is $(1200)^2$ or 1,440,000 square yards. The area of each plot is 40×30 or 1200 square yards. Therefore, the number of plots $= \frac{1{,}440{,}000}{1{,}200} = 1{,}200$.

81. (C) The train travels 150 miles in 2 hours and 10 minutes which is $2\frac{1}{6}$ hours. Therefore, the average speed is $\frac{150}{2\frac{1}{6}} = 150 \times \frac{6}{13} = \frac{900}{13} = 69\frac{3}{13}$ or about 70 miles per hour.

82. (B) Since $x > 2$, then $-x < -2$; but $y > -1$ implies $2y > -2$. Therefore, $-x < -2 < 2y$ so $-x < 2y$. None of the other statements is always true. (A) is false if x is 5 and $y = -\frac{1}{2}$; (C) is false if $x = 3$ and $y = -\frac{1}{2}$; (D) is false if $x = 3$ and $y = 3$, and (E) is false if $x = 3$ and $y = -\frac{1}{2}$.

83. (C) Since $ABCD$ is a rectangle, all angles are right angles. The area of a rectangle is length times width; and the length of AD is 4. Using the Pythagorean theorem we have $4^2 + (\text{width})^2 = 5^2$, so the $(\text{width})^2$ is $25 - 16 = 9$. Therefore, the width is 3, and the area is $4 \times 3 = 12$.

84. (E) The electricity costs $12k$¢ for 12 hours, the heat costs $\$12d$ for 12 hours, and the water costs $12w$¢ for 12 hours. So the total is $12k$¢ $+ \$12d + 12w$¢ or $\$.12k + \$12d + \$.12w$ which is $\$(.12k + 12d + .12w)$.

85. (E) Since $x = 2z$ and $y = 2z$, $x \cdot y \cdot z = (2z)(2z)(z) = 4z^3$; but $x \cdot y \cdot z = 256$ so $4z^3 = 256$. Therefore, $z^3 = 64$ and z is 4; so $x = 8$.

Section III Verbal Aptitude

86. (C) ABSTRUSE: profound, enigmatic. *Antonym:* obvious

87. (D) COAGULATE: mix, thicken. *Antonym:* dissipate

88. (C) PROCLIVITY: tendency, propensity. *Antonym:* aversion

89. **(B)** TACIT: implied, silent. *Antonym:* open

90. **(C)** VORACIOUS: greedy, ravenous. *Antonym:* generous

91. **(B)** SAGACIOUS: discerning, wise. *Antonym:* stupid

92. **(C)** RETICENT: reserved, secretive. *Antonym:* communicative

93. **(A)** FECUND: fertile, productive. *Antonym:* barren

94. **(C)** FURTIVE: sly, stealthy. *Antonym:* open

95. **(D)** INCLEMENT: severe, cruel. *Antonym:* kind

96. **(C)** NOTORIOUS: infamous, well-known. *Antonym:* respected

97. **(B)** DILATE: expand, stretch. *Antonym:* contract

98. **(A)** BOISTEROUS: violent, loud. *Antonym:* peaceful

99. **(B)** ECLECTIC: selecting what appears best from various doctrines. *Antonym:* dogmatic

100. **(B)** A sample (as in a survey) is part of the universe. An individual is part of a population.

101. **(B)** Carbohydrates may cause obesity. Sugar may cause cavities.

102. **(C)** One fulfills a promise, whereas action carries out a plan.

103. **(B)** One who is addicted gives himself up habitually, e.g. for food, for a cause, etc.; dedicated is a milder form of the same behavior. A similar relationship is held between a fanatic and an enthusiast.

104. **(A)** Recall and remember are synonyms as are falsification and forgery. Behave and action are related in the same manner, but grammatically different. The correct grammatical form would be: behave : act.

105. **(C)** Again, the relationship is one of synonyms. Abundance : luxury :: poverty : indigence.

106. **(B)** A stamp is payment for sending a letter (using the mails), while a coin is payment for using a pay telephone.

107. **(A)** Fuel flows through pipes as air flows through lungs.

108. **(B)** Exemption and immunity both mean to free someone from an obligation, while exclusion and isolation mean a refusal to admit someone.

109. **(C)** Indigenous is an antonym of foreign, as native is an antonym of extraneous. While other alternatives are also antonyms, e.g., outsider : inhabitant, only (C) has the same meaning as indigenous : foreign. Note that (E) might have been acceptable if it were written inhabitant : outsider.

110. **(A)** Efficacious (adequate) is the opposite of lacking as efficient is an antonym of incompetent.

111. **(D)** An octave consists of eight notes; a millenium is a thousand years.

112. **(B)** As one throws to "hit" a target, one dives to "hit" a certain spot in the water.

113. **(B)** Alternative (B) clearly has the most substance and meaning.

114. **(A)** Alternatives (C) and (E) can be ruled out, because one does not judge ability by subjective factors. Alternatives (D) and (B) do not make sense in the context.

115. **(D)** Alternatives (A) and (C) are incorrect because their meaning is not clear, and prisoners are not "acquitted" once they have been sentenced to a prison term. Alternative (E), clemency (leniency), is also unclear; i.e., what form does clemency take? Amnesty (B) is usually only granted to political prisoners, but in any case, it also means pardon, which is alternative (D).

116. **(B)** The police would hardly hold a council or assembly on the street for purposes of a

strike or a discussion, but they would more likely meet to discuss a seige.

117. **(C)** All the first word fill-ins are acceptable, but (C) has the most meaning when both words are used.

118. **(C)** Alternative (D) might be acceptable, but (C) has more meaning.

119. **(A)** In alternatives (B) through (D), only the first word fill-ins have meaning.

120. **(B)** has the most meaning.

121. **(C)** An effort is not pessimistic (or optimistic) as in (E), nor prohibitory (A). Alternative (B) hardly makes sense; and one does not convey an accord (D).

122. **(C)** The term "financial" restraints is too implicit; (B) and (E) are unclear; and (D) has little meaning.

123. **(A)** Terms such as "insipid" and "absolute" are not used to refer to studies. In (E), if a study is dated (old), it cannot be extemporary (timely).

124. **(C)** Loquacious means talkative.

125. **(D)** If they are complementary, they are *not* competitive.

Section IV Data Sufficiency

126. **(E)**

Since STATEMENT (1) describes only x and STATEMENT (2) describes only y, both are needed to get an answer. Using STATEMENT (2), STATEMENT (1) becomes $3x = 2k = 2y^2$, so $x = \frac{2y^2}{3}$. However, this is not sufficient, since if $y = -1$ then $x = 2/3$ and x is greater than y, but if $y = 1$ then again $x = 2/3$ but now x is less than y.

Therefore, STATEMENTS (1) and (2) together are not sufficient.

127. **(C)**

$ABCD$ is a parallelogram if AB is parallel to CD and BC is parallel to AD. STATEMENT (2) tells you that AB is parallel to CD, but this is not sufficient since a trapezoid has only one pair of opposite sides parallel. Thus, STATEMENT (2) alone is not sufficient.

STATEMENT (1) alone is not sufficient since a trapezoid can have the two nonparallel sides equal.

However, using STATEMENTS (1) and (2) together we can deduce that BC is parallel to AD, since the distance from BC to AD is equal along two different parallel lines.

128. **(A)**

STATEMENT (1) alone is sufficient. The average is the combined income for 1965–1970 divided by 6 (the number of years). Therefore, the combined income is 6 times the average yearly income.

STATEMENT (2) alone is not sufficient since there is no information about his income for the years 1966–1969.

129. **(E)**

To find the profit, we must know the selling price of the dress as well as its cost. STATEMENTS (1) and (2) together are not sufficient, since there is no information about the selling price of the dresses.

130. **(D)**

k is a prime if none of the integers 2, 3, 4, . . . up to $k - 1$ divide k evenly. STATEMENT (1) alone is sufficient since if k is not a prime then $k = (m)(n)$ where m and n must be integers less than k. But this means either m or n must be less than or equal to $\sqrt{k}$, since if m and n are both larger than $\sqrt{k}$, $(m)(n)$ is larger than $(\sqrt{k})(\sqrt{k})$ or k. So STATEMENT (1) implies k is a prime.

STATEMENT (2) alone is also sufficient, since if $k = (m)(n)$ and m and n are both larger than $\frac{k}{2}$, then $(m)(n)$ is greater than $\frac{k^2}{4}$; but $\frac{k^2}{4}$ is greater than k when k is larger than 5. Therefore, if no integer between 2 and $\frac{k}{2}$ inclusive divides k evenly, then k is a prime.

131. **(D)**

Since we are given the fact that 100 miles is the distance from A to B, it is sufficient to find the distance from C to B. This is because 100 minus the distance from C to B is the distance from A to C. STATEMENT (1) says that 125% of the distance from C to B is 100 miles. Thus, we can find the distance from C to B, which is sufficient. Since the distance from A to C plus the distance from C to B is the distance from A to B, we can use STATEMENT (2) to set up the equation 5 times the distance from A to C equals 100 miles.

Therefore, STATEMENTS (1) and (2) are each sufficient.

132. **(B)**

STATEMENT (1) alone is not sufficient. If the segment AC is moved further away from the segment BD, then the angles x and y will change. So STATEMENT (1) does not ensure that CD and AB are perpendicular.

STATEMENT (2) alone is sufficient. Since AB is a straight line, $x + y$ equals 180. Thus, if $x = y$, x and y both equal 90 and AB is perpendicular to CD. So the correct answer is (B).

133. **(B)**

STATEMENT (2) alone is sufficient, since $x=y$ implies $x-y=0$.

STATEMENT (1) alone is not sufficient. An infinite number of pairs satisfy STATEMENT (1), for example, $x = 2$, $y = 2$, for which $x-y=0$, or $x=4$, $y=1$, for which $x-y=3$.

134. **(E)**

Since there is no information on how many of the eligible voters are men or how many are women, STATEMENTS (1) and (2) together are not sufficient.

135. **(E)**

We need to find the measure of angle PSR or of angle PST. Using STATEMENT (2), we can find angle PTR, but STATEMENT (1) does not give any information about either of the angles needed.

136. **(A)**

STATEMENT (1) is sufficient since it means 90% of the original cost is $2300. Thus, we can solve the equation for the original cost.

STATEMENT (2) alone is insufficient, since it gives no information about the cost.

137. **(C)**

Draw the radii from O to each of the vertices. These lines divide the hexagon into six triangles. STATEMENT (2) says that all the triangles are congruent since each of their pairs of corresponding sides is equal. Since there are 360° in a circle, the central angle of each triangle is 60°. And, since all radii are equal, each angle of the triangle equals 60°. Therefore, the triangles are equilateral, and AB is equal to the radius of the circle. Thus, if we assume STATEMENT (1), we know the length of AB. Without STATEMENT (1), we can't find the length of AB.

Also, STATEMENT (1) alone is not sufficient, since AB need not equal the radius unless the hexagon is regular.

138. **(E)**

We need to know the area of the walls. To find the area of the walls, we need the distance from the floor to the ceiling. Since neither STATEMENT (1) nor (2) gives any information about the height of the room, together they are not sufficient.

139. **(B)**

STATEMENT (2) alone is sufficient, since we know $80 was the amount the worker made the first day. We can use STATEMENT (2) to find his pay for each day thereafter and then find the average daily wage.

STATEMENT (1) alone is not sufficient, since there is no way to find out how much the worker made on the fifth day.

140. **(A)**

STATEMENT (1) alone is sufficient. Since $3^2 + 4^2 = 5^2$, ABC is a right triangle by the Pythagorean theorem.

STATEMENT (2) alone is not sufficient since you can choose a point D so that $AC = CD$ for *any* triangle ABC.

Section V Business Judgment

141. **(B)** The cost of securing a loan is a *Major Factor* in making the decision; that is, the expansion of his business.

142. **(C)** The high breakage of glass jugs is a *Minor Factor* relating to which company to use in securing a loan.

143. **(A)** The issue of business expansion is clearly the *Major Objective* of Mr. Sim.

144. **(D)** Public acceptance of the product is a *Major Assumption* which has led Mr. Sim to expand his business.

145. **(E)** General economic conditions were an *Unimportant Issue* bearing upon Mr. Sim's decision to expand, and were not mentioned in the passage. Whether Mr. Sim considered such factors in his decision is an unknown.

146. **(C)** See paragraph 1: Among the major appeals of Mr. Sim's product were its ability to extract 18 percent more juice than conventional means, and the removal of bitterness from the peelings.

147. **(D)** See paragraph 4: Mr. Sim needed to expand his business because he had reached production capacity and could not fill the growing demand for his product.

148. **(A)** See paragraph 4: Among the alternatives listed in this question, only the first, the promise to advertise the product, was given by the distributor.

149. **(A)** See paragraph 5: Among the alternatives listed in the question, only the first, an interest free loan, was offered by Mr. Lubo.

150. **(B)** See paragraph 3: Mr. Sim had a patent; whether his product was more expensive than the use of frozen orange juice was not an issue. Of most importance, he lacked expansion capital.

151. **(A)** See paragraph 1: The *Major Objective* of the Congo was to provide a viable means by which its $1 billion trade deficit with the United States could be reduced.

152. **(B)** A *Major Factor* considered by Mr. Gage, the Congo's Trade Minister, in determining alternative trade strategies was the business recession in the United States at the time. This, of course, would affect the sale of Congo goods.

153. **(C)** That the Congo is an old client of the United States only means that reciprocal trade relations have been good. As such, it has led to a large trade deficit which the Congo is trying—unsuccessfully to date—to correct. However, it is a *Minor Factor,* related solely to the problem.

154. **(C)** Competition from Italy and France is a *Minor Factor,* relating to the problem of how to penetrate the United States market.

155. **(D)** Impending trade legislation in the United States is a *Major Assumption* which might be weighed by the decision maker, in this case Mr. Gage, when considering the alternative trade strategies suggested for the Congo.

156. **(C)** See paragraph 3: Protectionist trade legislation, the objective of which would be to restrict U.S. imports, was not given much chance of passage.

157. **(B)** Paragraph 4 states that it is difficult to measure the effectiveness of such promotion, ergo, the Trade Minister could not really make an evaluation.

158. **(D)** Both alternatives II and III are given in paragraph 4.

159. **(C)** See paragraph 3: Business groups were not mentioned.

160. **(E)** See paragraph 4: All three alternatives were considered by the Trade Minister.

Section VI Mathematics

161. **(C)** The amount of gas needed for a bus to travel 200 miles if the bus travels 15 miles on a gallon is $\frac{200}{15}$ or $13\frac{1}{3}$ gallons.

162. **(A)** Since x is less than 3 and y is greater than 3, we have $x < 3 < y$, so $x < y$. Therefore, the correct answer is always.

163. **(B)** In 1940, public aid received about 40% (between 45% and 85%) of the social welfare expenditures. Education only received about 30%, and all the other categories received less than 30%.

164. **(C)** The percentage received by veterans was only about 1/5 as much in 1967 as in 1950. Public aid's percentage decreased slightly and the percentage received by the other categories increased.

165. **(B)** In 1929 about 16% of social welfare expenditures were received by veterans programs. 16% of \$50 billion is \$8 billion.

166. **(B)**

STATEMENT I cannot be inferred because the graph only gives percentages, not the amount spent on each program.

STATEMENT II can be inferred. In fact, the percentage devoted to social insurance increased from about 15% in 1945 to almost 40% in 1967.

STATEMENT III is not true. Education received about 30% of the expenditures in 1935, so all the others combined received about 70%.

Therefore, only STATEMENT II can be inferred from the graph.

167. **(E)** The volume of a cylinder is $\pi r^2 h$ where r is the radius and h is the height of the cylinder. After the increases, the volume will be $\pi(1.10r)^2(1.20)h$, which is $(1.1)^2(1.2)\pi r^2 h$. So the new volume has increased by $(1.2)(1.1)^2$ which equals 1.452. Therefore, the volume has increased by 45.2%.

168. **(D)** The time required to pump 10 gallons of water out of the tank is $(10)\left(15 - \frac{x}{10}\right)$ which equals $150 - x$ minutes.

169. **(C)** The profit is 6% of \$1,000 plus 5% of \$6,000 − \$1,000 which is (.06)(\$1,000) + (.05)(\$5,000). Therefore, the profit equals \$60 + \$250 which is \$310.

170. **(D)** According to the graph on the left, the population of the U.S. in 1950 was about 150 million and according to the graph on the right, about 10% of the population was 4 years old or younger in 1950. Therefore, about 10% of 150 million or 15 million were 4 years old or younger in 1950.

171. **(E)** The population increased by almost 20 million between 1940 and 1950.

172. **(B)** In 1940, the total population was about 130 million. 75 million were classified as urban. Therefore, since $\frac{75}{125} = .6$, the answer is about 60%.

173. **(C)**

STATEMENT I is true since less than 30% of the population was under 15 in 1950.

STATEMENT II is false. In 1940 there were more than 50 million people classified as rural, but less than 20% of the population in 1950 consisted of males under 20. Since 20% of the 1950 population is 30 million, STATEMENT II is false.

STATEMENT III is true because in 1850 the population was less than 25 million, but by 1900 the population was greater than 75 million.

Therefore, only STATEMENTS I and III can be inferred from the graphs.

174. **(D)** Since the number of baskets manufactured in an hour is proportional to the number of workers, $\frac{15}{45} = \frac{27}{x}$, where x is the number of baskets manufactured by 45 men in an hour. Therefore, x is 81. Since 40 minutes is $\frac{2}{3}$ of an hour, 45 men will make $\frac{2}{3}$ of 81 or 54 baskets in 40 minutes.

175. **(E)** The first elevator lifts $\frac{2}{5}$ of a ton per minute and the second elevator lifts $\frac{3}{7}$ of a ton per minute, so both elevators together will lift $\frac{2}{5} + \frac{3}{7} = \frac{29}{35}$ of a ton per minute. Therefore, using both elevators it will take $\frac{20}{29/35} =$

$\frac{35}{29} \times 20 = \frac{700}{29}$ or $24\frac{4}{29}$ minutes to lift 20 tons.

176. **(D)** It costs $15 a night for lodging, so the total amount spent on lodging was 5 times $15 or $75.00. The total amount spent on transportation was $75 + $4 + $3 + $2 + $4 or $88. Therefore, $75 + $88 = $163 was spent on lodging and transportation.

177. **(C)** The average daily amount for meals will be the total expenditure for meals divided by 5. The total spent on meals for each day was $11, $13, $9, $9 and $11.50, so $53.50 was the expenditure for meals. Therefore, the daily average was $\frac{\$53.50}{5} = \$10.70$.

178. **(A)** Since the $75 fare appears on Monday, you should be able to quickly check that the most money was spent on Monday.

179. **(A)** Since $9y - 3x$ is $(-3)(x - 3y)$, $9y - 3x$ is equal to $(-3)(2)$ which is -6.

180. **(B)** The interest on a loan of $10,000 will be 10% of $2,000 + 8% of $8,000 which is $200 + $640 or $840. Since $\frac{840}{10{,}000}$ is .084, the interest is 8.4% of $10,000.

181. **(B)** There are 15,856 thousand people entitled to social security benefits and 33.4% are in the age group. Since 33.4% is approximately $\frac{1}{3}$, approximately 5,300,000 are in the 65–69 age group.

182. **(A)** 24.2% of the people in the category of other enrolled persons are men and 75.8% are women. The ratio of 24.2 to 75.8 is about 1 to 3 since $3 \cdot 25 = 75$.

183. **(C)**

STATEMENT I is true since 6.8% of 18,859,-000 is more than 22% of 2,446,000.

STATEMENT II is true. 92.3% of the people are white and 7.7% are nonwhite and 92.3 is more than 9 times 7.7.

STATEMENT III is not true because only 31.2% of all enrollees are in the 65–69 age group and $\frac{1}{3}$ is $33\frac{1}{3}$%.

Therefore, only STATEMENTS I and II can be inferred.

184. **(D)** There were 18,859 thousand people enrolled. Since 50% = $\frac{1}{2}$, 18,859 thousand people is $\frac{1}{2}$ the number of retired people. Therefore, there were 37,718,000 retired people on July 1, 1966.

185. **(D)** After the first discount the truck was selling for 90% of $6,800, which is $6,120. The selling price of the truck was 85% of $6,120, which is $5,202.

186. **(C)** Since the width is $\frac{1}{3}$ of the length and the length is 120 yards, the width of the field is 40 yards. The area of a rectangle is length times width, so the area of the field is 120 yards times 40 yards, which is 4,800 square yards.

187. **(B)** The price will be $3.00 a pound 6 months from now and $9.00 a pound a year from now. The price is a geometric progression of the form $\$3^j$ where j is the number of 6 month periods which have passed. Since $3^4 = 81$, after 4 six month periods, the price will be $81.00 a pound. Therefore, the answer is two years, since 24 months is 2 years.

188. **(D)** The volume index for Intra-community visible trade was 245 for 1969 compared to 100 in 1963. All the other categories had a volume index of 100 in 1963, but their volume index was less than 245 in 1969. So Intra-community visible trade increased the most between 1963 and 1969.

189. **(B)** $\frac{1}{10}$ is 10% and 1967 is the only year where each indicator has less than +10%.

190. **(B)** The gross community product had percentage changes of 4.3, 3.2, 6.0, 7.3, 5.4 in each of the years. Therefore, the average change is $\frac{1}{5}$ of $(4.3 + 3.2 + 6.0 + 7.3 + 5.4)$, which is $\frac{1}{5}$ of (26.2) or 5.24%.

191. **(C)** 1 is 1^2, 4 is 2^2, 9 is 3^2, 16 is 4^2 and 25 is 5^2, so the next number in the sequence will be 6^2 which is 36.

192. **(D)** Since $\frac{x}{y} = \frac{2}{3}$, $\frac{y}{x}$, which is the reciprocal

of $\frac{x}{y}$, must be equal to $\frac{3}{2}$. Also, $\frac{y^2}{x^2}$ is equal to $\left(\frac{y}{x}\right)^2$, so $\frac{y^2}{x^2}$ is equal to $\frac{9}{4}$.

193. (E) X is paid 125%, or $5/4$ of Y's salary, so Y makes $4/5$ of what X makes. X makes 80% or $4/5$ of Z's salary, so Z makes $5/4$ of what X makes. Thus, the total salary of X, Y, and Z is the total of X's salary, $4/5$ of X's salary and $5/4$ X's salary. Therefore, the total is $61/20$ of X's salary. Since the total of the salaries is \$610, X makes $20/61$ of \$610, or \$200.

194. (C) Since the radii are unequal, the circles cannot be identical, thus (E) is incorrect. If two circles intersect in 3 points they must be identical, so (D) is also incorrect. Two different circles can intersect in 2 points without being identical, so (C) is the correct answer.

195. (E) Let L be the length and W be the width of the rectangle, and let S be the length of a side of the square. It is given that $LW = S^2$. A relation must be found between $2L + 2W$ and $4S$. It is possible to construct squares and rectangles so that (A), (B), (C), or (D) is false, so (E) is correct. For example, if the rectangle is a square, then the two figures are identical and (A), (C) and (D) are false. If the rectangle is not equal to a square, then the perimeter of the rectangle is smaller than the perimeter of the square, so (B) is also false.

Evaluating Your Score

Tabulate your score for each section of Sample Test 3 according to the directions on pages 3–4 and record the results in the Self-scoring Table below. Then find your rank for each score on the Self-scoring Scale and record it in the appropriate blank.

Self-scoring Table

PART	SCORE	RANK
1		
2		
3		
4		
5		
6		

Self-scoring Scale

	ACHIEVEMENT			
PART	POOR	FAIR	GOOD	EXCELLENT
1	0–15	16–21	22–25	26–30
2	0–29	30–40	41–47	48–55
3	0–20	21–28	29–34	35–40
4	0– 7	8–10	11–12	13–15
5	0–10	11–14	15–16	17–20
6	0–18	19–25	26–30	31–35

Study again the Review sections covering material in Sample Test 3 for which you had a rank of FAIR or POOR. Then go on to Sample Test 4.

Answer Sheet — Sample Test 4

Section I — Reading Recall

1.A B C D E
2.A B C D E
3.A B C D E
4.A B C D E
5.A B C D E
6.A B C D E
7.A B C D E
8.A B C D E
9.A B C D E
10.A B C D E
11.A B C D E
12.A B C D E
13.A B C D E
14.A B C D E
15.A B C D E
16.A B C D E
17.A B C D E
18.A B C D E
19.A B C D E
20.A B C D E
21.A B C D E
22.A B C D E
23.A B C D E
24.A B C D E
25.A B C D E
26.A B C D E
27.A B C D E
28.A B C D E
29.A B C D E
30.A B C D E

Section II — Mathematics

31.A B C D E
32.A B C D E
33.A B C D E
34.A B C D E
35.A B C D E
36.A B C D E
37.A B C D E
38.A B C D E
39.A B C D E
40.A B C D E
41.A B C D E
42.A B C D E
43.A B C D E
44.A B C D E
45.A B C D E
46.A B C D E
47.A B C D E
48.A B C D E
49.A B C D E
50.A B C D E
51.A B C D E
52.A B C D E
53.A B C D E
54.A B C D E
55.A B C D E
56.A B C D E
57.A B C D E
58.A B C D E
59.A B C D E
60.A B C D E
61.A B C D E
62.A B C D E
63.A B C D E
64.A B C D E
65.A B C D E
66.A B C D E
67.A B C D E
68.A B C D E
69.A B C D E
70.A B C D E
71.A B C D E
72.A B C D E
73.A B C D E
74.A B C D E
75.A B C D E
76.A B C D E
77.A B C D E
78.A B C D E
79.A B C D E
80.A B C D E
81.A B C D E
82.A B C D E
83.A B C D E
84.A B C D E
85.A B C D E

Section III — Verbal Aptitude

86.A B C D E
87.A B C D E
88.A B C D E
89.A B C D E
90.A B C D E
91.A B C D E
92.A B C D E
93.A B C D E
94.A B C D E
95.A B C D E
96.A B C D E
97.A B C D E
98.A B C D E
99.A B C D E
100.A B C D E
101.A B C D E
102.A B C D E
103.A B C D E
104.A B C D E
105.A B C D E
106.A B C D E
107.A B C D E
108.A B C D E
109.A B C D E
110.A B C D E
111.A B C D E
112.A B C D E
113.A B C D E
114.A B C D E
115.A B C D E
116.A B C D E
117.A B C D E
118.A B C D E
119.A B C D E
120.A B C D E
121.A B C D E
122.A B C D E
123.A B C D E
124.A B C D E
125.A B C D E

Section IV — Data Sufficiency

126. A B C D E
127. A B C D E
128. A B C D E
129. A B C D E
130. A B C D E
131. A B C D E
132. A B C D E
133. A B C D E
134. A B C D E
135. A B C D E
136. A B C D E
137. A B C D E
138. A B C D E
139. A B C D E
140. A B C D E

Section V — Business Judgment

141. A B C D E
142. A B C D E
143. A B C D E
144. A B C D E
145. A B C D E
146. A B C D E
147. A B C D E
148. A B C D E
149. A B C D E
150. A B C D E
151. A B C D E
152. A B C D E
153. A B C D E
154. A B C D E
155. A B C D E
156. A B C D E
157. A B C D E
158. A B C D E
159. A B C D E
160. A B C D E

Section VI — Mathematics

161. A B C D E
162. A B C D E
163. A B C D E
164. A B C D E
165. A B C D E
166. A B C D E
167. A B C D E
168. A B C D E
169. A B C D E
170. A B C D E
171. A B C D E
172. A B C D E
173. A B C D E
174. A B C D E
175. A B C D E
176. A B C D E
177. A B C D E
178. A B C D E
179. A B C D E
180. A B C D E
181. A B C D E
182. A B C D E
183. A B C D E
184. A B C D E
185. A B C D E
186. A B C D E
187. A B C D E
188. A B C D E
189. A B C D E
190. A B C D E

Sample Test 4

Section I Reading Recall

TOTAL TIME: 35 minutes

Part A: TIME – 15 minutes

DIRECTIONS: This part contains three reading passages. You are to read each one carefully. You will have fifteen minutes to study the three passages and twenty minutes to answer questions based on them. When answering the questions, you will *not* be allowed to refer back to the passages.

Passage 1:

Youthful rebellion is more dramatic now than in prior generations because the source of values—or the sense of what is important in life—comes not from one's parents but from one's peer group. Past generations largely adopted the values and goals of their parents. They were what David Reisman, in his book *The Lonely Crowd,* called "inner-directed people." Parental values were programmed into the children, and these values acted as guides or decision rules when difficult decisions of any kind had to be made by the children in later life. Reisman demonstrated that newer generations were what he termed "other-directed" people or people that adopt or assimilate the values, not of their parents, but of their contemporaries—friends, neighbors, and associates. High mobility and a host of other factors enable a person to come into close contact with a continuous stream of new people and new values to assimilate.

In the middle and late sixties, a large number of people became 17 and 18 years old—and "other directed." Also, a large percentage of these people (almost 50 percent) went to college, had free time, assumed very few responsibilities, possessed large discretionary income, and became impressionable to new ideas and movements. The emotional honesty revolution found expression; the youth of America almost instantaneously became identified as radicals who were challenging long established social and political institutions. Many of the young people found identity with these causes and became intoxicated with them, confusing many other people and some popular writers as to what it all meant.

The historical significance of population changes is well known to economists. Some of them argue that a growing population is a source of continued economic expansion because it creates a need for more automobiles, home furnishings, gasoline, clothing and so on. The economic consequences are thought to be profitable markets for these goods, increased investment in manufacturing facilities, and an expanding labor market. Other economists argue that increasing population leads to declining productivity, increased depletion of forests, and the exhaustion of important mineral products such as oil, coal, and iron.

Sociologists are also deeply involved with population problems—especially those that involve the composition of populations. A population of mixed racial composition that gains in percentage points gives impetus to minority problems, and problems of racial discrimination become more apparent. A dense population causes the development of large cities with problems of poverty, traffic congestion, housing, slums, and crime.

From a socio-economic viewpoint, just as the turbulence of the sixties was predictable, certain happenings in the seventies are predictable. As early as 1955, it was apparent that there would be a large group of 17 to 21 year olds by 1965 and that a significant percentage would be enrolled in colleges and universities. It was also apparent that the age composition of the population would become more heavily weighted at the younger age groups. This, in turn, would cause a strong downward shift in the average age of the population and, more importantly, a large percentage of the shift would come within a five year period.

Many events such as those associated with the Freedom Riders and Vietnam could not have been predicted, but the changing age composition was sure to have a dramatic, predictable influence upon our society and economy. Therefore, the behavior of certain segments of our society can be predicted by analyzing population dynamics.

Passage 2:

Much as an electrical lamp transforms electrical energy into heat and light, the visual "apparatus" of a human being acts as a transformer of light into sight. Light projected from a source or reflected by an object enters the cornea and lens of the eyeball. The energy is transmitted to the retina of the eye whose rods and cones are activated.

The stimuli are transferred by nerve cells to the optic nerve and then to the brain. Man is a binocular animal, and the impressions from his two eyes are translated into sight—a rapid, compound analysis of the shape, form, color, size, position, and motion of the things he sees.

Photometry is the science of measuring light. The illuminating engineer and designer employ photometric data constantly in their work. In all fields of application of light and lighting, they predicate their choice of equipment, lamps, wall finishes, colors of light and backgrounds, and other factors affecting the luminous and environmental pattern to be secured, in great part from data supplied originally by a photometric laboratory. Today, extensive tables and charts of photometric data are used widely, constituting the basis for many details of design.

Although the lighting designer may not be called upon to do the detailed work of making measurements or plotting data in the form of photometric curves and analyzing them, an understanding of the terms used and their derivation form valuable background knowledge.

The perception of color is a complex visual sensation, intimately related to light. The apparent color of an object depends primarily upon four factors: its ability to reflect various colors of light, the nature of the light by which it is seen, the color of its surroundings, and the characteristics and state of adaptation of the eye.

In most discussions of color, a distinction is made between white and colored objects. White is the color name most usually applied to a material that diffusely transmits a high percentage of all the hues of light. Colors that have no hue are termed neutral or achromatic colors. They include white, off-white, all shades of gray, down to black.

All colored objects selectively absorb certain wave-lengths of light and reflect or transmit others in varying degrees. Inorganic materials, chiefly metals such as copper and brass, reflect light from their *surfaces*. Hence we have the term "surface" or "metallic" colors, as contrasted with "body" or "pigment" colors. In the former, the light reflected from the surface is often tinted.

Most paints, on the other hand, have body or pigment colors. In these, light is reflected from the surface without much color change, but the body material absorbs some colors and reflects others; hence, the diffuse reflection from the body of the material is colored but often appears to be overlaid and diluted with a "white" reflection from the glossy surface of the paint film. In paints and enamels, the pigment particles, which are usually opaque, are suspended in a vehicle such as oil or plastic. The particles of a dye, on the other hand, are considerably finer and may be described as coloring matter in solution. The dye particles are more often transparent or translucent.

Passage 3:

The international economy has undergone a remarkable transformation in the past decade. For many years after World War II, import quotas, discriminatory trade practices, and exchange restrictions on all forms of international payments characterized the bulk of international transactions. Though further progress needs to be made, much of this restrictive legacy has now been swept away. This transformation culminated in the formal acceptance by the major European countries in early 1961 of the currency convertibility requirements of the International Monetary Fund. It is a notable achievement and has far-reaching implications for the U.S. economy and U.S. economic policy.

Among the factors facilitating this development has been a massive redistribution of the world's gold and foreign exchange reserves. At the end of 1948, the United States held 71 percent of the free world's monetary gold stock; by June 1962, the U.S. share had fallen to 40 percent. During the same period, Western Europe's share grew from 15 percent to 44 percent. In addition, foreign official holdings of liquid dollar assets rose by nearly $9 billion. This redistribution ended the excessive concentration of reserves which had been brought about by the political upheavals in Europe in the 1930's, World War II, and the requirements of postwar reconstruction. In achieving balance of payments surpluses which rebuilt reserves, continental European countries gained greater freedom of action to promote economic expansion and to reduce restrictions on international transactions.

The redistribution of reserves was brought about partly through deficits in the international payments of the United States, which led to large transfers of gold and liquid dollar assets to Europe. These U.S. payments deficits have persisted beyond the point where they improve the distribution of the world's monetary reserves. Indeed, continuing large payments deficits by the United States could create doubts about the stability of the dollar and threaten the efficient operation of the international payments system. As a result, the U.S. Government has had to pay close and constant attention to the net financial outcome of its transactions, and those of its citizens, with the rest of the world. Important measures have been taken to improve the payments position of the United States, and domestic economic policy has been framed with attention to the balance of payments and the position of the dollar.

The relaxation of many restrictions on trade and payments and the redistribution of world reserves have not been the only factors transforming the world economy. The progress of the European Economic Community (EEC) toward a rapidly growing, unified, tariff-free market encompassing six European countries—and possibly more in the future—has already profoundly altered world economic relationships. The EEC offers a domestic market broadly comparable to the United States and an import market even larger. Liberal access to this market will be vital to future foreign trade; exclusion by restrictive import tariffs or other barriers could seriously affect the trade and economic development of many countries of the free world.

It is now generally acknowledged that the responsibility of the industrial nations for providing capital and technical knowledge to other countries for economic development requires more than the occasional and sporadic efforts made before the mid-1950's. Systematic economic development of the low-income parts of the free world—within a span of time that is very short by historical standards—has become a major objective of western foreign policy. Carrying out this gigantic task will require considerable transfers of capital and technical skill. It will result in large shifts in the structure of world production and trade and will require substantial adjustments in both advanced and developing countries.

These developments have one common characteristic: they bring countries economically closer together. They tend to integrate the free world economy. Markets will become more unified, competition will be keener, and differences among nations in techniques of production will diminish. Substantial progress toward our foreign economic objectives will be made, but new challenges for economic policy, national and international, will arise.

If there is still time remaining, review the passages until all 15 minutes have elapsed.
Do not look at Part B until that time.

Part B: TIME—20 minutes

DIRECTIONS: Answer the following questions pertaining to information contained in the three passages you have just read. You may not turn back to those passages for assistance.

QUESTIONS TO

Passage 1:

1. According to David Reisman, older generations of people are

(A) value oriented
(B) goal oriented
(C) inner-directed
(D) other-directed
(E) peer group oriented

2. Reisman's book is entitled

(A) *Youthful Rebellion*
(B) *The Generation Gap*
(C) *Changing Values*
(D) *The Lonely Crowd*
(E) *The American Past*

3. One of the largest age groups in the sixties was the

(A) 12–13 year olds
(B) 17–18 year olds
(C) 21–25 year olds
(D) 30–35 year olds
(E) over 35 year olds

4. A growing population is a source of all the following except

(A) increased economic problems
(B) resource depletion
(C) increased demand for goods and services
(D) efficient utilization of resources
(E) economic growth

5. Concerning the effect of population growth, economists

(A) are not certain as to what it means
(B) cannot predict what the effects will be
(C) are unanimous in their assessment of its effect on the economy
(D) are divided in their assessment of its effect on the economy
(E) take a Malthusian point of view

6. Sociologists study population characteristics, especially

(A) growth
(B) composition
(C) productivity
(D) needs
(E) identity

7. The major subject of the passage is about

(A) David Reisman's book
(B) youthful rebellion
(C) population dynamics
(D) the emotional honesty rebellion
(E) socio-economic patterns

8. From the passage it can be inferred that rebellion of youth in the sixties came about because

I. Young people comprised a major part of the population
II. The values and goals of young people have changed
III. Young people are more radical than in earlier times

(A) I only
(B) III only
(C) I and II only
(D) II and III only
(E) I, II, and III

9. According to the passage, the youth of the sixties took their values from

(A) their parents
(B) their peers
(C) the very rich
(D) existing social-political institutions
(E) university professors

10. Which of the following best illustrates the author's estimation of the largest single age group in the 1970's?

(A) 17–18 year olds
(B) 21–25 year olds
(C) 30–35 year olds
(D) over 35 year olds
(E) no estimation was made

QUESTIONS TO

Passage 2:

11. Light projected from a source enters the eyeball through the

(A) cornea
(B) retina
(C) rods
(D) cones
(E) brain

12. Photometry is the science of

(A) studying sight
(B) color configurations
(C) light projection
(D) light and motion
(E) measuring light

13. According to the passage, lighting engineers need *not*

(A) plot photometric curves
(B) understand photometric techniques
(C) utilize photometric data
(D) have mathematical expertise
(E) be college graduates

14. The color black is an example of a

(A) surface color
(B) organic color
(C) achromatic color
(D) diffuse color
(E) pigment color

15. The reflection of light wave-lengths is accomplished by

(A) all colors
(B) selective colors
(C) surface colors
(D) achromatic colors
(E) pigment colors

16. Inorganic materials reflect light from their

(A) hues
(B) body
(C) surface
(D) pigment
(E) compounds

17. Paint would be an example of a substance containing

(A) inorganic material
(B) surface colors
(C) body colors
(D) metallic colors
(E) enamels

18. The perception of color is

(A) a photometric phenomenon
(B) activated by the brain
(C) a complex visual sensation
(D) light reflected by a source
(E) energy transmitted from the retina

19. The subject of the passage is concerned with the

I. Transmission of light
II. Color perception
III. Photometry

(A) I only
(B) III only
(C) I and II only
(D) II and III only
(E) I, II, and III

20. This passage could have been culled from a

(A) business journal
(B) popular magazine
(C) lighting manual
(D) designer's manual
(E) medical textbook

QUESTIONS TO

Passage 3:

21. In early 1961, major European countries agreed to a plan of

(A) economic reform
(B) exchange restrictions
(C) currency convertibility
(D) international transactions
(E) common accounting procedures

22. The United States' holdings of the free world's gold stock during the period 1948 to 1962

(A) increased from 61 to 80 percent
(B) increased from 40 to 71 percent
(C) decreased from 71 to 50 percent
(D) decreased from 71 to 40 percent
(E) decreased from 71 to 30 percent

23. During 1948 to 1962, Western Europe's holdings of the world's gold stock

(A) decreased from 25 to 15 percent
(B) decreased from 44 to 15 percent
(C) increased from 15 to 24 percent
(D) increased from 15 to 35 percent
(E) increased from 15 to 44 percent

24. The redistribution of the free world's gold and foreign exchange reserves was brought about partly by the

(A) end of World War II
(B) International Monetary Fund
(C) growth of the EEC
(D) relaxation of trade restrictions
(E) deficits in the United States' international payments

25. The altering of world economic relationships has been caused by the

I. Relaxation of trade and payment restrictions
II. Redistribution of world gold and exchange reserves
III. Growth of the European Economic Community

(A) I only
(B) III only
(C) I and II only
(D) II and III only
(E) I, II, and III

26. The domestic market size of the EEC countries is

(A) as large as all free world countries' markets
(B) larger than the domestic market of the United States
(C) about the size of the domestic market of the United States
(D) smaller than the domestic market of the United States
(E) comparable to all Western European countries combined

27. According to the passage, a major objective of Western European foreign policy is the

(A) encouragement of world trade
(B) removal of trade restrictions
(C) strengthening the International Monetary Fund
(D) economic development of low-income countries
(E) strengthening of the western alliance

28. If, as the passage states, free world economies will become integrated, which of the following is likely to occur?

(A) markets will become unified
(B) trade will increase
(C) economic policy problems will decrease
(D) political objectives will standardize
(E) monetary systems will become uniform

29. Continuing large deficits in the international payments of the United States could affect the

I. Economies of low-income countries
II. Stability of the dollar
III. International payments system

(A) I only
(B) III only
(C) I and II only
(D) II and III only
(E) I, II, and III

30. According to the passage, United States domestic economic policy has been framed with attention to

(A) world trade
(B) the U.S. balance of payments
(C) trade restrictions
(D) taxation policy
(E) inflation

If there is still time remaining, you may review the questions in this section only. You may not look at Part A or turn to any other section of the test.

Section II Mathematics

TIME: 75 minutes

DIRECTIONS: Solve each of the following problems; then indicate the correct answer on the answer sheet. [On the actual test you will be permitted to use any space available on the examination paper for scratch work.]

NOTE: A figure that appears with a problem is drawn as accurately as possible so as to provide information that may help in answering the question. Numbers in this test are real numbers.

31. If 64% of the students in a class got a grade of C and there are 200 students in the class, how many students in the class received a grade of C?

(A) 64
(B) 118
(C) 124
(D) 128
(E) 164

32. If $2x + y = 10$ and $x = 3$, what is $x - y$?

(A) -4
(B) -1
(C) 0
(D) 1
(E) 7

Use the following graphs for questions 33–35.

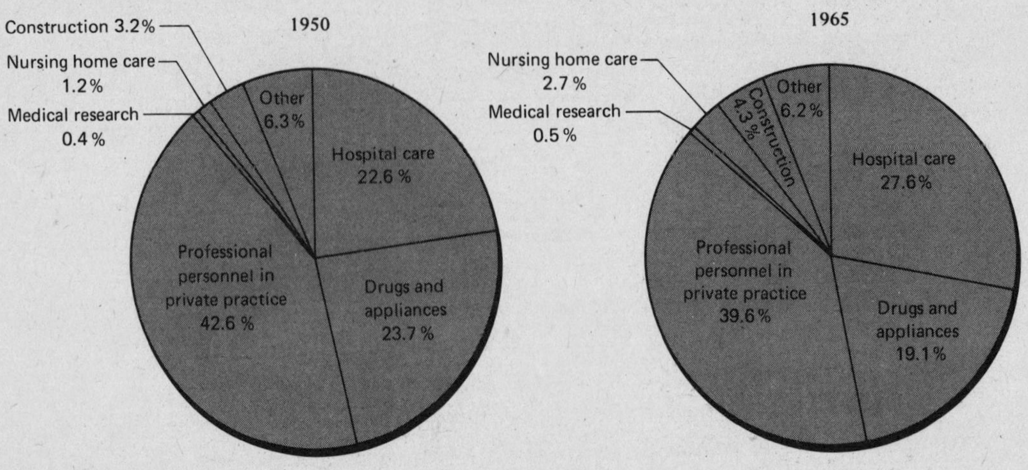

33. In 1965, about x times as much was spent on hospital care as on drugs and appliances, where x equals

(A) $\frac{2}{3}$
(B) 1
(C) $1\frac{1}{2}$
(D) 2
(E) 3

34. In 1950, medical research, construction, and other items received about what fraction of private health expenditures?

(A) $\frac{1}{16}$
(B) $\frac{1}{10}$
(C) $\frac{1}{8}$
(D) $\frac{1}{7}$
(E) $\frac{2}{11}$

35. Which of the following statements about private health expenditures in 1950 and 1965 can be inferred from the graphs?

I. In 1950, hospital care received more than 7 times as much as construction.
II. More money was spent on professional personnel in private practice in 1950 than in 1965.
III. In 1950, more than $\frac{3}{8}$ of the total private health expenditures was spent on professional personnel in private practice.

(A) I only
(B) III only
(C) I and II only
(D) I and III only
(E) I, II, and III

36. If a worker can pack $\frac{1}{6}$ of a carton of canned food in 15 minutes and there are 40 workers in a factory, how many cartons should be packed in the factory in $1\frac{2}{3}$ hours?

(A) 33
(B) $40\frac{2}{9}$
(C) $43\frac{4}{9}$
(D) $44\frac{4}{9}$
(E) $45\frac{2}{3}$

37. Potatoes cost 15¢ a pound. If the price of potatoes rises by 10%, how much will 10 pounds of potatoes cost?

(A) 17¢
(B) $1.50
(C) $1.60
(D) $1.65
(E) $1.70

38. A truck driver must complete a 180-mile trip in 4 hours. If he averages 50 miles an hour for the first three hours of his trip, how fast must he travel in the final hour?

(A) 30 mph
(B) 35 mph
(C) 40 mph
(D) 45 mph
(E) 50 mph

Questions 39–42 refer to the table on page 450.

39. How many countries had an annual quota of more than 10,000 between 1936 and 1952?

(A) 1
(B) 2
(C) 3
(D) 4
(E) 5

40. The ratio of the annual quota for Northern and Western Europe to the annual quota for Southern and Eastern Europe was approximately

(A) 2 to 1
(B) 3 to 1
(C) 4 to 1
(D) 5 to 1
(E) 6 to 1

41. Between 1946 and 1950, the second largest number of quota immigrants was admitted from

(A) Germany
(B) Great Britain and Northern Ireland
(C) Ireland
(D) Italy
(E) Poland

42. The quota for a nationality was 2% of the foreign born of that nationality who were residing in the U.S. in 1910. Approximately how many people born in Greece were residents of the U.S. in 1910?

(A) 10,000
(B) 15,000
(C) 25,000
(D) 100,000
(E) 150,000

No. 104.—Annual quotas allotted and quota immigrants admitted, by quota country or region: years ending June 30, 1936 to 1952

Quota country or region	Annual quota 1936–1952	Quota immigrants admitted						
		1936–1940	1941–1945	1946–1950	1949	1950	1951	1952
All countries	154,277	203,330	80,879	502,828	113,046	197,460	156,547	194,247
Europe	150,572	199,792	78,202	494,713	111,443	195,671	154,759	192,754
Northern and western Europe	125,853	127,414	49,388	259,802	59,578	69,366	47,026	73,302
Belgium	1,304	1,435	2,001	5,252	1,270	979	991	1,103
Denmark	1,181	1,188	761	4,738	1,109	1,101	1,082	1,183
France	3,086	3,438	3,850	13,937	2,997	3,187	2,900	2,935
Germany	25,957	93,910	21,723	78,855	12,819	31,511	14,637	35,453
Great Britain and Northern Ireland	65,721	14,551	14,885	96,430	23,543	17,194	15,369	20,368
Iceland	100	25	98	376	68	88	96	95
Ireland	17,853	4,298	1,043	24,950	8,505	6,444	3,810	3,819
Luxembourg	100	81	218	335	94	74	59	103
Netherlands	3,153	2,816	2,043	12,458	2,991	3,067	3,102	3,032
Norway	2,377	1,966	926	9,170	2,303	2,179	2,248	2,333
Sweden	3,314	1,556	627	7,692	2,376	1,876	1,360	1,554
Switzerland	1,707	2,150	1,213	5,609	1,503	1,666	1,372	1,324
Southern and eastern Europe	24,719	72,378	28,814	234,911	51,865	126,305	107,733	119,452
Austria	1,413	978	....	11,460	1,327	6,153	1,361	2,236
Bulgaria	100	423	153	439	65	177	231	330
Czechoslovakia	2,874	9,833	3,316	13,771	3,255	4,058	3,870	5,398
Estonia	116	309	151	7,444	1,716	5,387	2,230	1,366
Finland	569	1,526	628	2,248	497	518	556	494
Greece	310	1,795	1,237	1,348	426	285	3,638	5,621
Hungary	869	4,735	1,360	7,818	1,445	4,054	5,079	7,331
Italy	5,677	16,943	1,244	23,003	5,207	5,861	4,325	5,901
Latvia	236	735	443	21,714	3,534	17,439	11,220	4,999
Lithuania	386	1,428	646	19,326	6,452	11,774	4,568	3,330
Poland	6,524	18,189	10,602	88,957	21,462	50,692	45,766	42,665
Portugal	440	1,656	1,523	2,080	462	426	384	388
Rumania	291	2,028	1,233	3,844	699	2,019	2,042	5,184
Spain	252	1,236	1,118	881	194	197	286	256
Turkey	226	1,030	723	1,370	177	697	401	374
U.S.S.R. (Russia)	2,798	5,362	3,531	19,545	3,710	10,854	14,019	15,269
Yugoslavia	938	3,171	779	8,486	976	5,359	7,411	17,265
Other southern and eastern Europe	700	1,001	127	1,177	261	355	346	1,045
Asia	1,905	2,249	1,582	5,133	1,003	1,173	1,341	1,085
Africa	1,200	355	440	1,516	328	328	272	253
Pacific	600	934	655	1,466	272	288	175	155

Source: Statistical abstract of U.S. 1953

43. If a triangle has base B and the altitude of the triangle is twice the base, then the area of the triangle is

(A) $\frac{1}{2}AB$
(B) AB
(C) $\frac{1}{2}B^2$
(D) B^2
(E) $2B$

44. If the product of two numbers is 10 and the sum of the two numbers is 7, then the larger of the two numbers is

(A) −2
(B) 2
(C) 3
(D) $4\frac{1}{4}$
(E) 5

45. Oranges cost $\$x$ a bag for the first 100 bags a store buys from a wholesaler. All bags bought in addition to the first 100 get a discount of 10%. How much does it cost to buy 150 bags of oranges from the wholesaler?

(A) \$100
(B) $\$140x$
(C) $\$145x$
(D) $\$150x$
(E) $\$100x + \$50$

Use the following graph for questions 46–48.

Source: 1963 Census of Business, U.S. Department of Commerce, Bureau of the Census

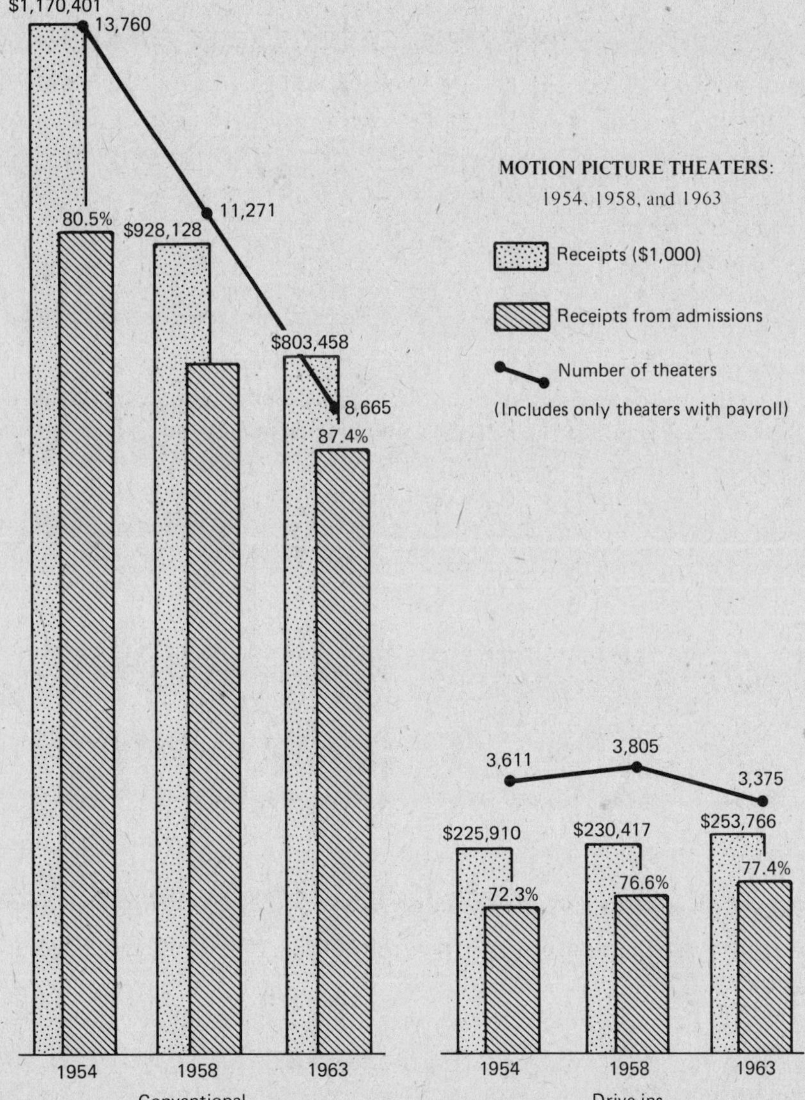

46. Which of the following obtained the largest amount in receipts from admissions?

(A) conventional-1954
(B) conventional-1958
(C) conventional-1963
(D) drive-ins-1958
(E) drive-ins-1963

47. If the average admission price was $1.00 in 1954, about how many people attended movies in a conventional theater in 1954?

(A) 600,000
(B) 750,000
(C) 925,000
(D) 1,050,000
(E) 930,000,000

48. Which of the following statements about motion picture theaters can be inferred from the graph?

I. The total number of movie theaters (conventional and drive-ins) was higher in 1954 than in 1958 or in 1963.
II. The percentage of receipts derived from admissions has increased in each category in each time interval shown on the graph.
III. The receipts of conventional motion picture theaters in 1963 were more than triple the receipts of drive-ins in 1963.

(A) I only
(B) III only
(C) I and III only
(D) II and III only
(E) I, II, and III

49. If the lengths of the two sides of a right triangle adjacent to the right angle are 8 and 15 respectively, then the length of the side opposite the right angle is

(A) $\sqrt{258}$
(B) 15.8
(C) 16
(D) 17
(E) 17.9

50. A store sells a baseball glove for $10.20 and makes a profit of 20%. How much did the baseball glove cost the store?

(A) $8.30
(B) $8.50
(C) $8.92
(D) $9.15
(E) $9.65

51. It costs x¢ each to print the first 600 copies of a newspaper. It costs $\left(x - \frac{y}{10}\right)$¢ for every copy after the first 600. How much does it cost to print 1,500 copies of the newspaper?

(A) $1500x$¢
(B) $150y$¢
(C) $(1500x - 90y)$¢
(D) $\$(150x - 9y)$
(E) $\$15x$

52. If the side of a square increases by 40%, then the area of the square increases by

(A) 16%
(B) 40%
(C) 96%
(D) 116%
(E) 140%

Use the following graph for questions 53–56.

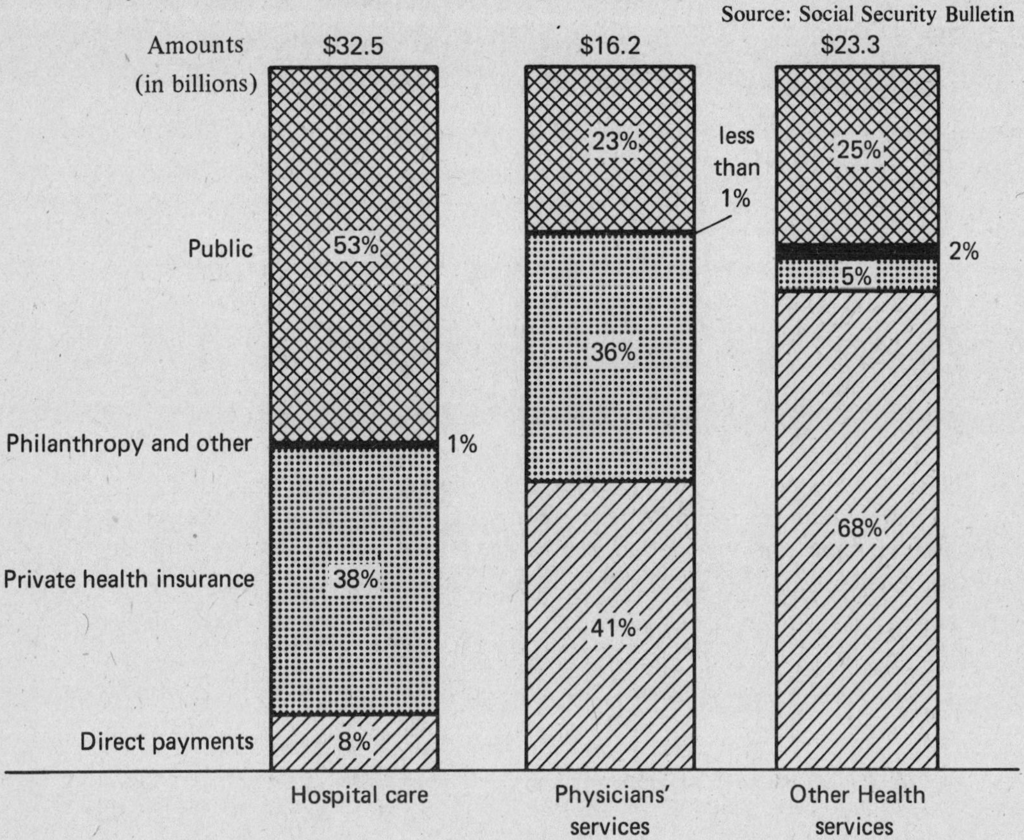

53. The ratio of the amount spent on hospital care to the amount spent on physicians' services in the fiscal year 1972 was approximately

(A) 1 to 2
(B) 2 to 1
(C) 8 to 3
(D) 3 to 1
(E) 7 to 2

54. The amount paid in direct payments for physicians' services was about

(A) $5 billion
(B) $5.8 billion
(C) $6 billion
(D) $6.5 billion
(E) $7 billion

55. If the population was 216 million, what was the per capita expenditure on personal health care in the fiscal year 1972?

(A) $3.33
(B) $300
(C) $322½
(D) $330⅛
(E) $333⅓

56. Which of the following statements about personal health care expenditures in the fiscal year 1972 can be inferred from the graph?

I. The greatest amount of public funds are spent for other health services.
II. More than \$25 billion of public funds were spent on personal health care needs in fiscal year 1972.
III. More than $^2/_5$ of the amount spent for physician's services came from private health insurance.

(A) II only
(B) III only
(C) I and II only
(D) II and III only
(E) I, II, and III

57. If 28 cartons of soda cost \$21.00, then 7 cartons of soda should cost

(A) \$5.25
(B) \$5.50
(C) \$6.40
(D) \$7.00
(E) \$10.50

58. Plane P takes off at 2 A.M. and flies at an average speed of x mph. Plane Q takes off at 3:30 A.M. and flies the same route as P but travels at an average speed of y mph. Assuming that y is greater than x, how many hours after 3:30 A.M. will plane Q overtake plane P?

(A) $\frac{3}{2}x$ hrs.
(B) $\frac{3}{2}$ hrs.
(C) $\frac{3}{2y}$ hrs.
(D) $\frac{3x}{2(y-x)}$ hrs.
(E) $\frac{3x}{2(y-x)}$ hrs.

59. A worker is paid \$20 for each day he works, and he is paid proportionately for any fraction of a day he works. If during one week he works $^1/_8$, $^2/_3$, $^3/_4$, $^1/_3$, and 1 full day, what are his total earnings for the week?

(A) \$40.75
(B) \$52.50
(C) \$54
(D) \$57.50
(E) \$58.25

Use the following table for questions 60–61.

DISTRIBUTION OF TEST SCORES IN A CLASS

Number of Students	*Number of Correct Answers*
10	36 to 40
16	32 to 35
12	28 to 31
14	26 to 27
8	0 to 25

60. What percent of the class answered 32 or more questions correctly?

(A) 20
(B) 26
(C) $32\frac{1}{2}$
(D) $43\frac{1}{3}$
(E) 52

61. The number of students who answered 28 to 31 questions correctly is x times the number who answered 25 or fewer correctly, where x is

(A) $\frac{2}{3}$
(B) 1
(C) $\frac{3}{2}$
(D) $\frac{7}{4}$
(E) 2

62. If the product of 3 consecutive integers is 210, then the sum of the two smaller integers is

(A) 5
(B) 11
(C) 12
(D) 13
(E) 18

63. Cereal costs $\frac{1}{3}$ as much as bacon. Bacon costs $\frac{5}{4}$ as much as eggs. Eggs cost what fraction of the cost of cereal?

(A) $\frac{5}{12}$
(B) $\frac{5}{4}$
(C) $\frac{5}{3}$
(D) $\frac{12}{5}$
(E) $\frac{4}{5}$

64. A truck gets 15 miles per gallon of gas when it is empty. When the truck is full, it travels only 80% as far on a gallon of gas as when empty. How many gallons will the loaded truck use to travel 80 miles?

(A) $5\frac{1}{3}$
(B) 6
(C) $6\frac{1}{3}$
(D) $6\frac{2}{3}$
(E) $6\frac{3}{4}$

Questions 65–68 refer to the graphs on pages 456 and 457.

65. In each year the category which provided the most receipts was

(A) individual income tax
(B) national defense
(C) corporation income taxes
(D) employment taxes
(E) interest on public debt

66. Between the end of 1945 and 1952, the amount of money spent on national defense

(A) decreased by about 87%
(B) decreased by about 43%
(C) decreased by about 25%
(D) increased by about 25%
(E) increased by about 300%

67. The percentage of government expenditures allocated to the category "all other" in 1950 was about

(A) 15
(B) 20
(C) 25
(D) 30
(E) 35

68. Which of the following statements can be inferred from the graphs?

I. More money was collected in corporation income taxes in 1946 than in 1947.
II. The total receipts of the federal government increased each year between 1945 and 1950.
III. The federal government spent less in 1948 than in any of the other years between 1946 and 1952.

(A) I only
(B) III only
(C) I and II only
(D) I and III only
(E) II and III only

EXPENDITURES OF THE FEDERAL GOVERNMENT, BY MAJOR CLASSIFICATIONS: YEARS ENDING JUNE 30, 1945 TO 1952

Source: Treasury Department

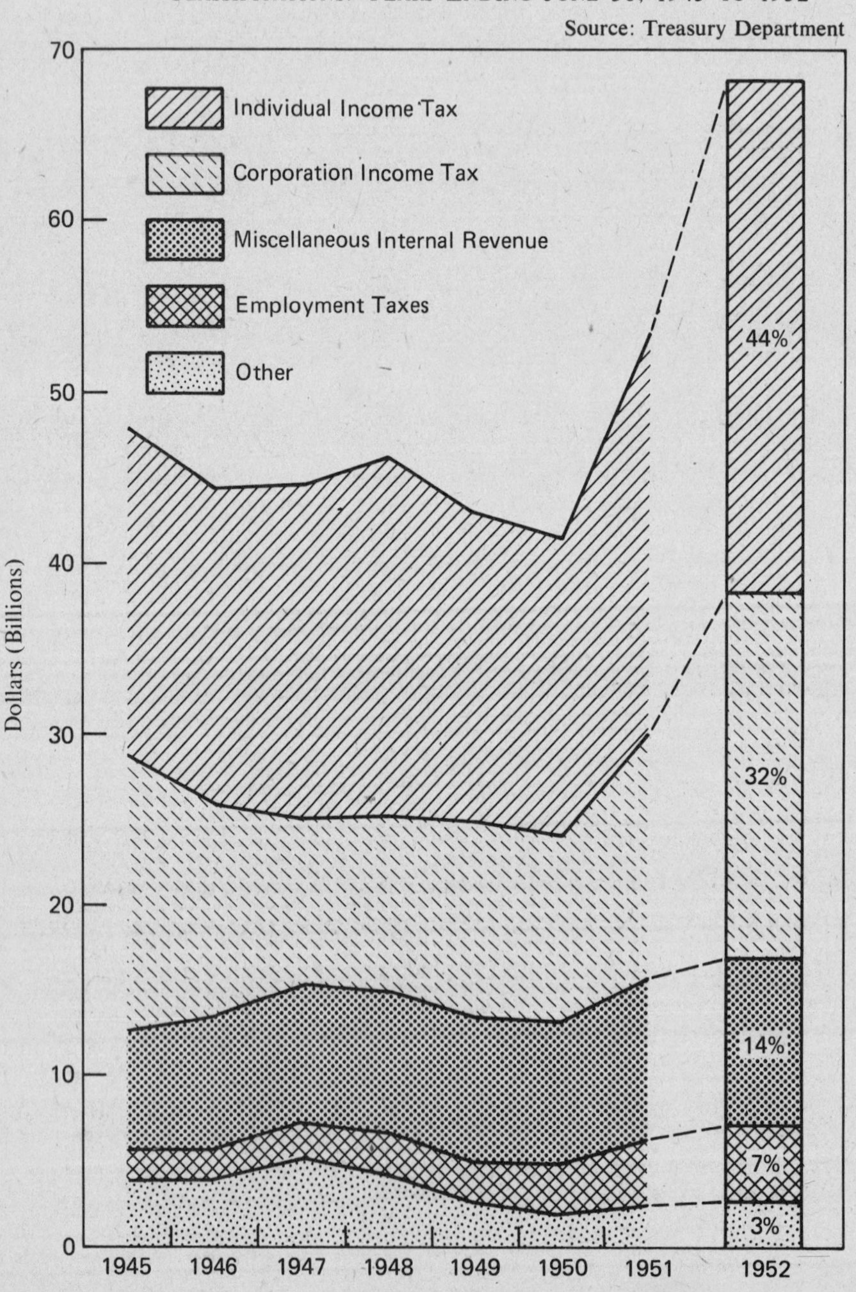

TOTAL RECEIPTS OF THE FEDERAL GOVERNMENT, BY MAJOR SOURCES: YEARS ENDING JUNE 30, 1945 TO 1952

Source: Treasury Department

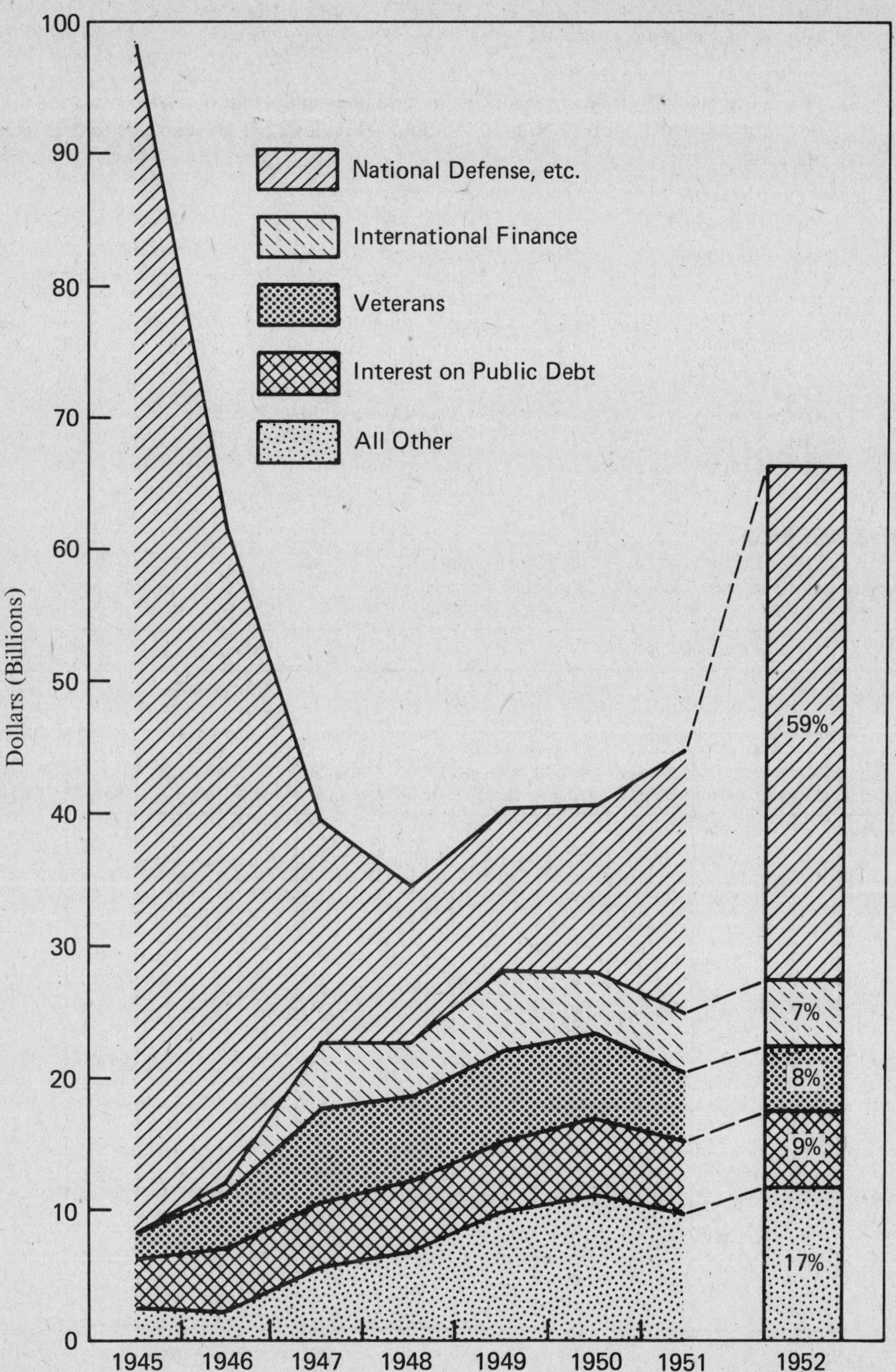

69. If x and y are negative numbers, which of the following statements are always true?

I. $x - y$ is negative. II. $-x$ is positive III. $(-x)(-y)$ is positive.

(A) I only
(B) II only
(C) I and II only
(D) II and III only
(E) I and III only

70. A car travels at 70 miles an hour for the first hour and a half of a trip. After the first $1\frac{1}{2}$ hours the car travels at 50 miles an hour. How long will the car take to drive 200 miles?

(A) $1\frac{1}{2}$ hours
(B) 2 hours
(C) $2\frac{3}{5}$ hours
(D) $3\frac{1}{5}$ hours
(E) $3\frac{2}{5}$ hours

71. A manufacturer makes books at a cost of $\$x$ each for the first 1,000 copies. The second thousand copies cost $\$(x - 2y)$ each. How much will it cost to make 1,600 copies of a book?

(A) $\$1600x$
(B) $\$160x + \$120y$
(C) $\$1600x + \$1200y$
(D) $\$1600x - \$1200y$
(E) $\$16{,}000x - \$1200y$

Use the following table for questions 72–74.

Consumer and Wholesale Price Indexes, annual averages and changes, 1951–72
[1967 = 100]

Year	Consumer prices						Wholesale prices					
	All items		Commodities		Services		All commodities		Farm products, processed foods and feeds		Industrial commodities	
	Index	Percent change	Index	Percent change	Index	Percent change	Index	Percent change	Index	Percent change	Index	Percent change
1951	77.8	7.9	85.9	9.0	61.8	5.3	91.9	11.4	106.9	13.8	86.1	10.4
1952	79.5	2.2	87.0	1.3	64.5	4.4	88.6	−2.7	102.7	−3.9	84.1	−2.3
1953	80.1	.8	86.7	−.3	67.3	4.3	87.4	−1.4	96.0	−6.5	84.8	.8
1954	80.5	.5	85.9	−.9	69.5	3.3	87.6	.2	−95.7	−.3	85.0	.2
1955	80.2	−.4	85.1	−.9	70.9	2.0	87.8	.2	91.2	−4.7	86.9	2.2
1956	81.4	1.5	85.9	.9	72.7	2.5	90.7	3.3	90.6	−.7	90.8	4.5
1957	84.3	3.6	88.6	3.1	75.6	4.0	93.3	2.9	93.7	3.4	93.3	2.8
1958	86.6	2.7	90.6	2.3	78.5	3.8	94.6	1.4	98.1	4.7	93.6	.3
1959	87.3	.8	90.7	.1	80.8	2.9	94.8	.2	93.5	−4.7	95.3	1.8
1960	88.7	1.6	91.5	.9	83.5	3.3	94.9	.1	93.7	.2	95.3	.0
1961	89.6	1.0	92.0	.5	85.2	2.0	94.5	−.4	93.7	.0	94.8	−.5
1962	90.6	1.1	92.8	.9	86.8	1.9	94.8	.3	94.7	1.1	94.8	.0
1963	91.7	1.2	93.6	.9	88.5	2.0	94.5	−.3	93.8	−1.0	94.7	−.1
1964	92.9	1.3	94.6	1.1	90.2	1.9	94.7	.2	93.2	−.6	95.2	.5
1965	94.5	1.7	95.7	1.2	92.2	2.2	96.6	2.0	97.1	4.2	96.4	1.3
1966	97.2	2.9	98.2	2.6	95.8	3.9	99.8	3.3	103.5	6.6	98.5	2.2
1967	100.0	2.9	100.0	1.8	100.0	4.4	100.0	.2	100.0	−3.4	100.0	1.5
1968	104.2	4.2	103.7	3.7	105.2	5.2	102.5	2.5	102.4	2.4	102.5	2.5
1969	109.8	5.4	108.4	4.5	112.5	6.9	106.5	3.9	108.0	5.5	106.0	3.4
1970	116.3	5.9	113.5	4.7	121.6	8.1	110.4	3.7	111.6	3.3	110.0	3.8
1971	121.3	4.3	117.4	3.4	128.4	5.6	113.9	3.2	113.8	2.0	114.0	3.6
1972	125.3	3.3	120.9	3.0	133.3	3.8	119.1	4.6	122.4	7.6	117.9	3.4

Source: U.S. Bureau of Labor Statistics

72. Wholesale prices for all commodities were the lowest in

(A) 1951
(B) 1952
(C) 1953
(D) 1954
(E) 1955

73. Of the six categories shown on the table, how many have increased every year between 1951 and 1972?

(A) none
(B) 1
(C) 2
(D) 3
(E) 4

74. The index of consumer prices on all items has increased by about x percent from 1951 to 1972, where x is

(A) 25
(B) 50
(C) 60
(D) 90
(E) 125

75. If $\frac{1}{3} < x$, then

(A) x is greater than 1
(B) x is greater than 3
(C) $\frac{1}{x}$ is greater than 3
(D) $\frac{1}{x}$ is less than 3
(E) all of the above statements are true

76. $\frac{1}{3} + \frac{2}{7} = \frac{x}{42}$ where x is

(A) $\frac{13}{21}$
(B) 13
(C) 21
(D) 24.5
(E) 26

77. If $r + x + y + z = 12$ and x is less than 6, then at least k of the numbers r, x, y, and z must be positive, where k is

(A) 0
(B) 1
(C) 2
(D) 3
(E) 4

Use the following table for questions 78–81.

Source: 1963 Census of Business, U.S. Department of Commerce, Bureau of the Census

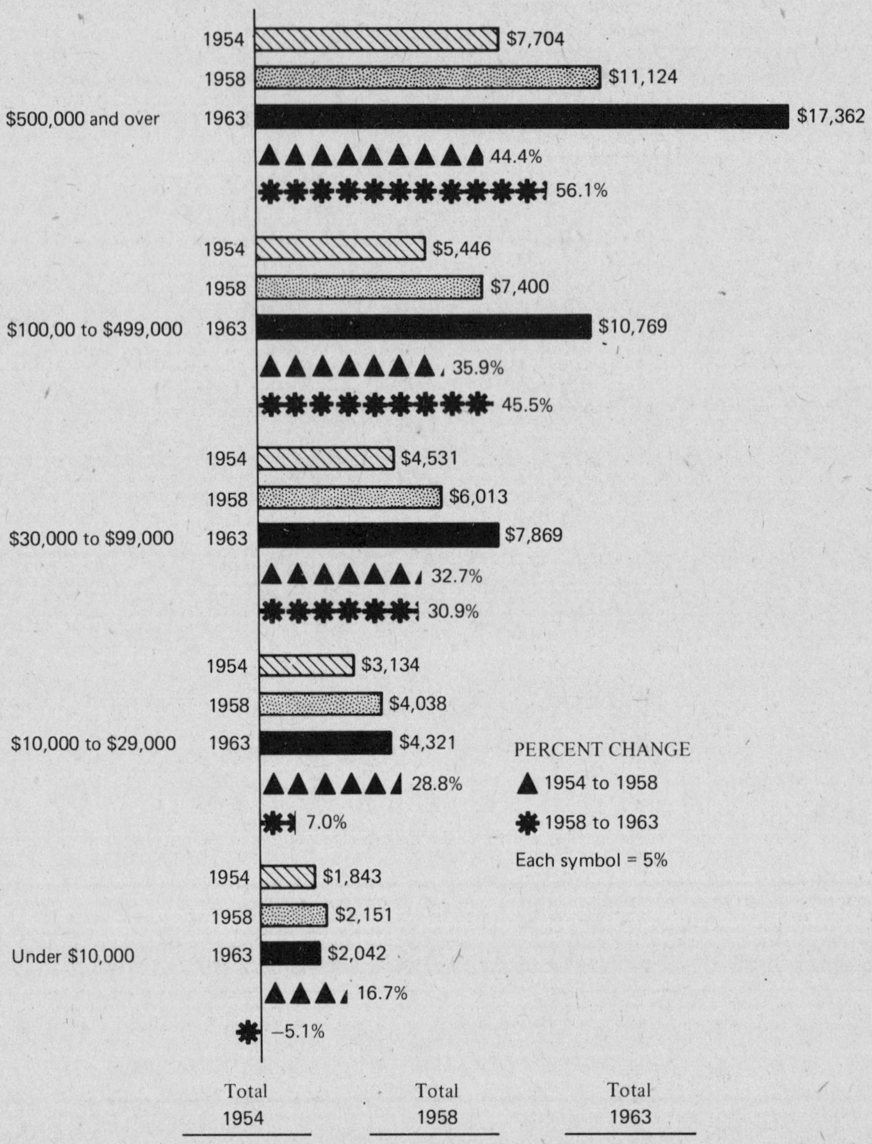

78. The ratio of total receipts for 1963 to total receipts for 1954 was approximately

(A) 1 to 3
(B) 1 to 2
(C) 3 to 2
(D) 2 to 1
(E) 3 to 1

79. Which category of establishment had the greatest percentage of increase in receipts between 1958 and 1963?

(A) $500,000 and over
(B) $100,000 to $499,000
(C) $30,000 to $99,000
(D) $10,000 to $29,000
(E) Under $10,000

80. The percent of total receipts in 1954 which came from establishments whose receipts were $30,000 to $99,000 was about

(A) 10
(B) 20
(C) 30
(D) 40
(E) 50

81. Which of the following statements can be inferred from the graph?

I. The receipts have increased during each time period for all five categories of establishment.
II. More than $\frac{1}{4}$ of the establishments had receipts of $500,000 or more in 1963.
III. More than 20% of the total receipts in 1963 came from establishments with receipts between $100,000 and $499,000.

(A) III only
(B) I and II only
(C) I and III only
(D) II and III only
(E) I, II, and III

82. If the radius of a sphere is increased by a factor of 2, then the volume of the sphere is increased by a factor of

(A) 1
(B) 2
(C) 4
(D) 6
(E) 8

83. Successive discounts of 10% and 15% are equivalent to a simple discount of

(A) 11.5%
(B) 16.5%
(C) 20%
(D) 23.5%
(E) 25%

84. How many rectangular tiles 4 inches wide and 6 inches long are necessary to cover the floor of a square room with sides 12 feet long?

(A) 6
(B) 60
(C) 144
(D) 576
(E) 864

85. If the two sides of a right triangle adjacent to the right angle have lengths $n-1$ and $2\sqrt{n}$, then the length of the side of the triangle opposite the right angle is

(A) $n-1$
(B) $4\sqrt{n}$
(C) $4n$
(D) $\sqrt{n^2+2n}$
(E) $n+1$

If there is still time remaining, you may review the questions in this section only.
You may not turn to any other section of the test.

Section III Verbal Aptitude

TIME: 20 minutes

Antonyms

DIRECTIONS: For each question below, select the lettered word or phrase that comes closest to being *opposite* in meaning to the word appearing in capital letters. Be sure to consider all meanings carefully.

86. ABETTOR: (A) criminal (B) instigator (C) proponent (D) antagonist (E) gambler

87. INTERDICT: (A) compose (B) allow (C) compel (D) reduce (E) solicit

88. PEDANTIC: (A) swift (B) brave (C) efficient (D) modest (E) proud

89. SATIATE: (A) reduce (B) recover (C) stint (D) envelop (E) overcome

90. PLAINTIVE: (A) exultant (B) complaining (C) defendant (D) stubborn (E) thoughtful

91. POIGNANT: (A) inflated (B) dull (C) simple (D) exact (E) wise

92. INSIDIOUS: (A) treacherous (B) sadistic (C) ungrateful (D) sincere (E) proliferate

93. INSIPID: (A) hasty (B) secret (C) widespread (D) gullible (E) intense

94. FLIPPANT: (A) gregarious (B) grave (C) fluent (D) cherished (E) distorted

95. OSTENTATIOUS: (A) modest (B) beguiled (C) defiant (D) arrogant (E) violent

96. SATURNINE: (A) dry (B) honest (C) cheerful (D) planetary (E) wicked

97. SANGUINE: (A) mistaken (B) distrustful (C) hopeful (D) ruthless (E) uneven

98. ABASEMENT: (A) elevation (B) sublimation (C) bewilderment (D) lowering (E) habitation

99. CALUMNY: (A) disaster (B) accusation (C) degradation (D) vindication (E) surrender

Word-Pair Relationships

DIRECTIONS: For each question below, determine the relationship between the pair of capitalized words and then select the lettered pair of words which have a similar relationship to the first pair.

100. SLOPE : SKI :: (A) tracks : train (B) road : car (C) pool : swim (D) hill : slide (E) floor : dance

101. REASONING : SOLUTION :: (A) deduce : discover (B) infer : rational (C) problem : hypothesis (D) experiment : law (E) assert : posit

102. AUTO : SPEEDOMETER :: (A) camera : film (B) line : turnstile (C) tremor : seismograph (D) music : phonograph (E) census : people

103. LANDSCAPE : PORTRAIT :: (A) gardener : artist (B) symphony : conductor (C) meteorologist : scientist (D) concerto : sonata (E) scene : still-life

104. POETRY : SONNET :: (A) chorus : refrain (B) music : rhythm (C) verse : stanza (D) music : concerto (E) stage : drama

105. RETALIATION : REPRISAL :: (A) reciprocate : revenge (B) return : exchange (C) counter : retribution (D) prevoke : react (E) oppose : resist

106. PRODIGAL : INSOLVENCY :: (A) opulent : loss (B) default : abscond (C) arrears : nullify (D) thrifty : resources (E) sumptuous : solvent

107. MAPLE : TREE :: (A) flower : plant (B) sedan : automobile (C) seeds : vegetables (D) disease : illness (E) problem : solution

108. CIRCUIT : STRAIGHT :: (A) manual : automatic (B) necessity : urgency (C) road : path (D) belief : superstition (E) ethical : rules

109. OBSERVANT : RELIGION :: (A) conductor : train (B) teacher : students (C) doctor : medicine (D) soldier : army (E) ethical : rules

110. THIEF : INCARCERATION :: (A) addict : rehabilitate (B) performance : cancellation (C) disease : immunization (D) robber : apprehension (E) illness : cure

111. WALK : RUN :: (A) swim : race (B) trot : gallop (C) glide : fly (D) slide : slip (E) push : shove

112. MONOLOGUE : PLAY :: (A) speech : convention (B) address : audience (C) solo : concert (D) performance : execution (E) dialogue : encore

Sentence Completions

DIRECTIONS: For each sentence below, select the lettered word or set of words which, when inserted in the sentence blanks, best complete the meaning of that sentence.

113. The bare ____ give little idea of its ____.

(A) facts . . . interpretation (B) contents . . . excellence (C) inferior . . . warmth (D) terrain . . . beauty (E) details . . . success

114. All his efforts to ____ the economy were ____, so he gave up in disgust.

(A) cool . . . to no avail (B) boost . . . successful (C) improve . . . efficacious (D) control . . . deceptive (E) plan . . . futile

115. Because the teacher failed to announce the ____, his students exhibited considerable ____.

(A) exam . . . consternation (B) recess . . . pleasure (C) substitution . . . delight (D) time . . . ambivalence (E) punishment . . . sadness

116. In order to ____ the research, a number of ____ activities had to be taken.

(A) complete . . . nebulous (B) undertake . . . sequential (C) cancel . . . indefinite (D) discharge . . . volatile (E) test . . . provisional

117. A person who is an editor, might also be called a(n) ____.

(A) topographer (B) lexicographer (C) author (D) phonographer (E) stenographer

118. The awesome experiment proved ____ to mankind.

(A) horrendous (B) tolerant (C) salutary (D) nebulous (E) accurate

119. The judge's ____ was that the accused should be ____.

(A) opinion . . . educated (B) sentence . . . freed (C) attitude . . . unfettered (D) verdict . . . incarcerated (E) belief . . . myopic

120. The announcement of price controls injected ____ into the investment atmosphere.

(A) funds (B) capital (C) arrogance (D) irreverence (E) doubt

121. A writer who succeeds in publishing many books may be called ____.

(A) wealthy (B) profound (C) avaricious (D) prolific (E) effective

122. The witness's story was suspect and was regarded with ____.

(A) incredulity (B) credence (C) congruity (D) inaction (E) attention

123. The "energy crisis" must be ____ before we can solve it.

(A) discovered (B) contrived (C) probed (D) wrestled (E) stressed

124. The committee is still examining the ____ amid ____ concern.

(A) report . . . mounting (B) controversy . . . averred (C) bill . . . elusive (D) hoax . . . impartial (E) ouster . . . biased

125. Unlike his phlegmatic co-worker, he was ____.

(A) relieved (B) healthy (C) alert (D) calm (E) nervous

If there is still time remaining, you may review the questions in this section only.
You may not turn to any other section of the test.

Section IV Data Sufficiency

TIME: 15 minutes

DIRECTIONS: Each of the following problems has a question and two statements which are labeled (1) and (2). Use the data given in (1) and (2) together with other available information (such as the number of hours in a day, the definition of *clockwise,* mathematical facts, etc.) to decide whether the statements are *sufficient* to answer the question. Then fill in space

(A) if you can get the answer from (1) alone but not from (2) alone;

(B) if you can get the answer from (2) alone but not from (1) alone;

(C) if you can get the answer from (1) and (2) together, although neither statement by itself suffices;

(D) if statement (1) alone suffices *and* statement (2) alone suffices;

(E) if you cannot get the answer from statements (1) and (2) together, but need even more data.

All numbers used in this section are real numbers. A figure given for a problem is intended to provide information consistent with that in the question, but not necessarily with the additional information contained in the statements.

126. A piece of wood 5 feet long is cut into three smaller pieces. How long is the longest of the three pieces?

(1) One piece is 2 feet, 7 inches long.
(2) One piece is 7 inches longer than another piece and the third piece is 5 inches long.

127. *AC* is a diameter of the circle. *ACD* is a straight line. What is the value of x?

(1) $AB = BC$
(2) $x = 2y$

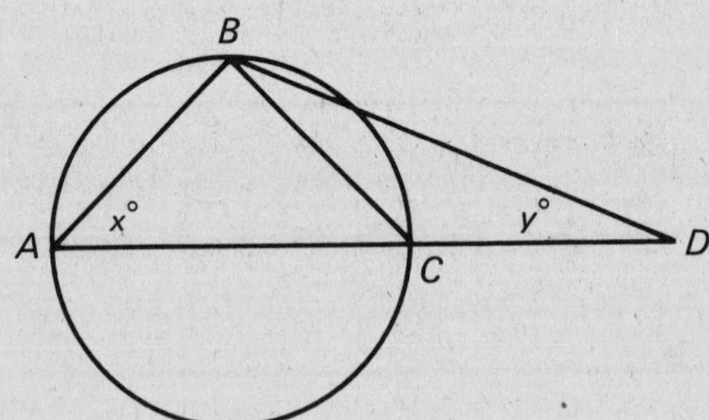

128. What is the value of y?

(1) $x + 2y = 6$
(2) $y^2 - 2y + 1 = 0$

129. Two pipes, A and B, empty into a reservoir. Pipe A can fill the reservoir in 30 minutes by itself. How long will it take for pipe A and pipe B together to fill up the reservoir.

(1) By itself, pipe B can fill the reservoir in 20 minutes.
(2) Pipe B has a larger cross-sectional area than pipe A.

130. AB is perpendicular to CO. Is A or B closer to C?

(1) OA is less than OB.
(2) $ACBD$ is not a parallelogram.

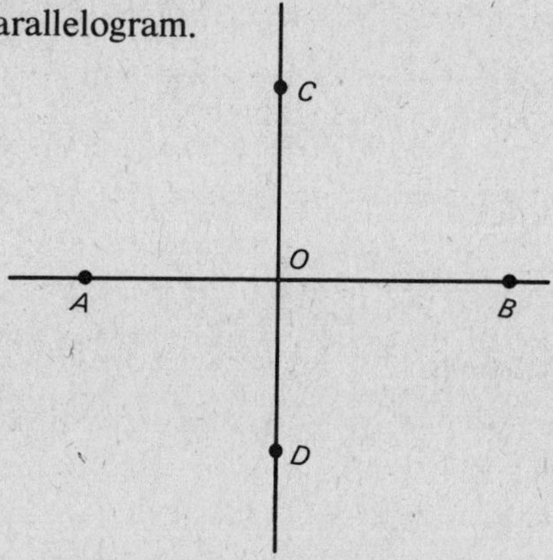

131. Is xy greater than 1? x and y are both positive.

(1) x is less than 1.
(2) y is greater than 1.

132. Does $x = y$?

(1) $z = u$
(2) $ABCD$ is a parallelogram.

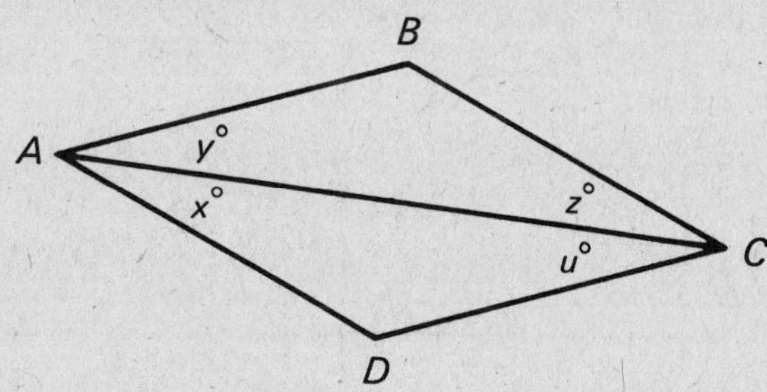

133. Train T leaves town A for town B and travels at a constant rate of speed. At the same time train S leaves town B for town A and also travels at a constant rate of speed. Town C is between A and B. Which train is traveling faster?

(1) Train S arrives at town C before train T.
(2) C is closer to A than to B

134. Does $x = y$?

(1) BD is perpendicular to AC.
(2) AB is equal to BC.

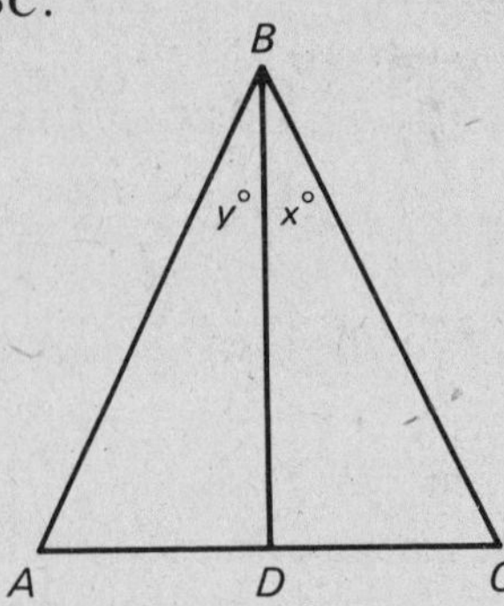

135. What is the value of $x + y$?

(1) $x - y = 4$
(2) $3x + 3y = 4$

136. Did the XYZ Corporation have higher sales in 1968 or in 1969?

(1) In 1968 the sales were twice the average (arithmetic mean) of the sales in 1968, 1969, and 1970.
(2) In 1970, the sales were three times those in 1969.

137. AB and CD are both chords of the circle with center O. Which is longer, AB or CD?

(1) Arc AEB is smaller than arc CFD.
(2) The area of the circular segment $CAEBD$ is larger than the area of circular segment $ACFDB$.

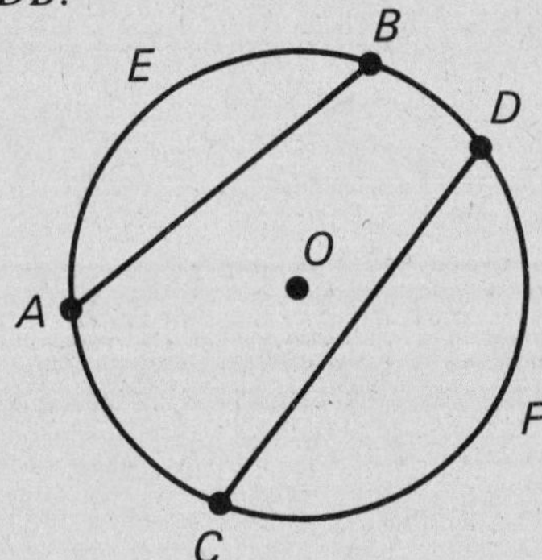

138. Is $ABCD$ a square?

(1) BC is perpendicular to AD.
(2) $BE = EC$.

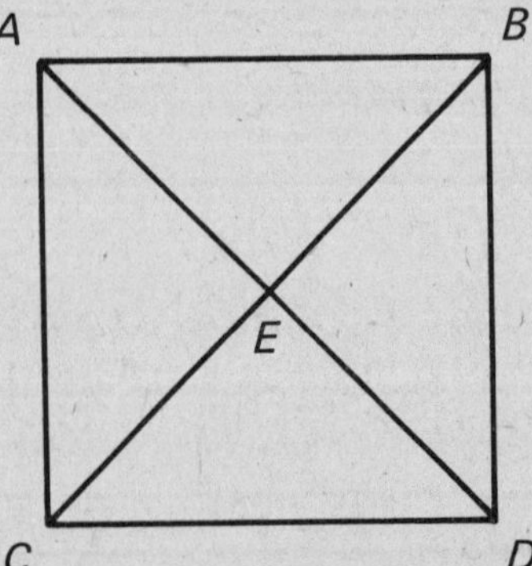

139. k is an integer. Is k divisible by 12?

(1) k is divisible by 4.
(2) k is divisible by 3.

140. How far is it from A to B?

(1) It is 15 miles from A to C.
(2) It is 25 miles from C to B.

If there is still time remaining, you may review the questions in this section only. You may not turn to any other section of the test.

Section V Business Judgment

TIME: 35 minutes

DIRECTIONS: Read the following two passages. After you have completed each of them you will be asked to answer two sets of questions. The first of these, data evaluation, involves determining the importance of specific factors included in the passage. The second, data application, consists of general questions relating to the passage. When answering questions, you may consult the passage.

Passage 1:

The unclear economic situation into which the economy of this developing country has drifted has caused considerable uneasiness to both local industrialists and their employees, and to present and potential foreign investors. The seemingly firm course set by the now nearly defunct price-wage-tax restraint has faltered. As a result, the ABC Corporation was reconsidering its previous plans to invest in the country. Its management cited some of the following reasons for its decision to reevaluate its investment plans.

The chain of events which started with the government's apparent decision on a policy of economic slowdown via an increase of taxes has resulted in an unprecedented wave of price rises in the form of an additional cost of living allowance. That the business community will not accede to these requests has been hinted at by the Manufacturer's Association.

Compounding the current situation is the perennial tightness of capital and the galloping interest rates, which are from 17 to 18 percent; though "regular" clients can receive credit at 15 to 15 $\frac{1}{2}$ percent.

One positive result of all of this may be an increase in the relative profitability of exports which are heavily supported by the government. Efforts to increase exports and foreign investments are in full swing as the various committees of the Investment Board bring their influence to bear. Nevertheless, foreign investors have proved cautious at this stage and are not rushing to transfer dollars to this country while the economic situation still seeks direction.

Some firm helmsmanship is required at this juncture on the part of government leaders, who must guide both industry and labor into an era of social peace and economic development. At the same time they seek a solution to the many economic and social problems facing the country.

Data Evaluation Questions

DIRECTIONS: Evaluate each of the following factors used in decision-making which relate to the passage you have just read by selecting

(A) for a *Major Objective*—the result desired by the executive;

(B) for a *Major Factor*—a primary consideration, spelled out in the passage, that influences the decision;

(C) for a *Minor Factor*—a less important consideration in the decision;

(D) for a *Major Assumption*—a conclusion reached by the executive not necessarily supported by the factors present;

(E) for an *Unimportant Issue*—a consideration not directly related to the problem.

141. Poor economic situation

142. ABC Corporation's investment plans

143. Economic slowdown

144. Foreign companies are reluctant to invest

145. Government efforts to increase foreign investment

Data Application Questions

DIRECTIONS: Answer each of the following questions using information contained in the passage.

146. The economic slowdown was caused by

I. A lack of foreign investment
II. Militant labor unions
III. Government economic policy

(A) I only
(B) III only
(C) I and II only
(D) II and III only
(E) I, II and III

147. Despite the economic situation, the government

I. Remained optimistic
II. Continued to waste capital
III. Encouraged foreign investment

(A) I only
(B) III only
(C) I and II only
(D) II and III only
(E) I, II, and III

148. The government's economic policy had resulted in increased

I. Taxes
II. Prices
III. Investment

(A) I only
(B) III only
(C) I and II only
(D) II and III only
(E) I, II, and III

149. A positive result of the government's economic policy was an increase in

I. Wages
II. Foreign investment
III. Relative profitability of exports

(A) I only
(B) III only
(C) I and II only
(D) II and III only
(E) I, II, and III

150. The additional cost of living allowance resulted in

I. Inflation
II. Lower wages
III. Social unrest

(A) I only
(B) III only
(C) I and II only
(D) II and III only
(E) I, II, and III

Passage 2:

The home office of the Hiram Insurance Company was divided into several departments, each consisting of over 200 persons. This problem concerns Department K, which employs mostly skilled men.

Almost every man within the department works without direct supervision, although each is under the general supervision of a section head. Each employee has definite duties to perform and definite lines of responsibility. These duties do not necessarily follow any definite sequence throughout the day, although the work must be completed on schedule.

The head of Department K retired, and no qualified successor was available in the department. Finally the management hired a man from another company. This man had satisfactory over-all qualifications, but his experience was in a position which was different from the one to which he was appointed. In general, the employees opposed selection of the new department head, because they felt some of their own number were qualified.

Shortly after becoming head of the department, the new executive issued a directive through his assistant that effective immediately each employee within the department would account for his time hour for hour throughout the working day. Each person would give this time report to his section head, who would in turn send a report to the department head.

The reaction was immediate and negative. A majority of the working force were intelligent men of high caliber who had been with the Hiram Insurance Company from ten to thirty years. Their judgment on utilization of time during the day had seldom before been questioned. The younger employees and those who had been with the organization only a short time took the attitude, "I will not observe the directive. I will resign first." The older men, and those who had only a few years until retirement, took a strongly negative attitude toward the directive, refusing to accept it for its apparent lack of reason. They argued that they never had reported their time, that other departments did not now have to report time, and that Department K would not become an exception to the rule.

The section heads had no recourse other than to report to the new department head that the men refused to co-operate with the directive. The department head threatened to tender his resignation to his superior, the vice-president, effective at once.

The president of the Hiram Insurance Company received word of the trouble from the vice-president. The president immediately intervened and supposedly settled the matter by soothing hot tempers with a diplomatic speech to the section heads. He then dropped the matter completely. The department head felt then that he was left with no recourse but to require compliance with his directive. Many employees still did not report their time, and their section heads asked the department head what should be done.

Data Evaluation Questions

DIRECTIONS: Evaluate each of the following factors used in decision-making which relate to the passage you have just read by selecting

(A) for a *Major Objective*—the result desired by the executive;

(B) for a *Major Factor*—a primary consideration, spelled out in the passage, that influences the decision;

(C) for a *Minor Factor*—a less important consideration in the decision;

(D) for a *Major Assumption*—a conclusion reached by the executive not necessarily supported by the factors present;

(E) for an *Unimportant Issue*—a consideration not directly related to the problem.

151. Department K head and subordinate relations

152. The work force was of high caliber

153. The company has several departments

154. Employees have no direct supervision

155. The head of Department K retired

Data Application Questions

DIRECTIONS: Answer each of the following questions using information contained in the passage.

156. According to the passage, which of the following employees threatened to resign?

I. The new department head
II. Section heads
III. The vice-president

(A) I only
(B) III only
(C) I and II only
(D) II and III only
(E) I, II, and III

157. A new department head was needed because the previous one

I. Was fired
II. Was promoted
III. Retired

(A) I only
(B) III only
(C) I and II only
(D) II and III only
(E) I, II, and III

158. The president's talk to section heads

I. Solved the company's problem
II. Soothed "hot tempers"
III. Delayed a solution

(A) I only
(B) III only
(C) I and II only
(D) II and III only
(E) I, II, and III

159. Department K personnel refused to accept time reports because

I. They resented the new department head
II. Other departments did not have time reports
III. They never had to report time before

(A) I only
(B) III only
(C) I and II only
(D) II and III only
(E) I, II, and III

160. It can be inferred from the passage that the department head's difficulties with his subordinates was due to

I. A lack of communication
II. His promotion from outside the company
III. His poor mannerisms

(A) I only
(B) III only
(C) I and II only
(D) II and III only
(E) I, II, and III

Section VI Reading Recall

TOTAL TIME: 35 minutes

Part A: TIME – 15 minutes

DIRECTIONS: This part contains three reading passages. You are to read each one carefully. You will have fifteen minutes to study the three passages and twenty minutes to answer questions based on them. When answering the questions, you will *not* be allowed to refer back to the passages.

Passage 1:

Literature is at once the most intimate and the most articulate of the arts. It cannot impart its effect through the senses or the nerves as the other arts can; it is beautiful only through the intelligence; it is the mind speaking to the mind; until it has been put into absolute terms, of an invariable significance, it does not exist at all. It cannot awaken this emotion in one, and that in another; if it fails to express precisely the meaning of the author, if it does not say *him,* it says nothing, and is nothing. So that when a poet has put his heart, much or little, into a poem, and sold it to a magazine, the scandal is greater than when a painter has sold a picture to a patron, or a sculptor has modelled a statue to order. These are artists less articulate and less intimate than the poet; they are more exterior to their work; they are less personally in it; they part with less of themselves in the dicker. It does not change the nature of the case to say that Tennyson and Longfellow and Emerson sold the poems in which they couched the most mystical messages their genius was charged to bear mankind. They submitted to the conditions which none can escape;

but that does not justify the conditions, which are none the less the conditions of hucksters because they are imposed upon poets. If it will serve to make my meaning a little clearer, we will suppose that a poet has been crossed in love, or has suffered some real sorrow, like the loss of a wife or child. He pours out his broken heart in verse that shall bring tears of sacred sympathy from his readers, and an editor pays him a hundred dollars for the right of bringing his verse to their notice. It is perfectly true that the poem was not written for these dollars, but it is perfectly true that it was sold for them. The poet must use his emotions to pay his provision bills; he has no other means; society does not propose to pay his bills for him. Yet, and at the end of the ends, the unsophisticated witness finds the transaction ridiculous, finds it repulsive, finds it shabby. Somehow he knows that if our huckstering civilization did not at every moment violate the eternal fitness of things, the poet's song would have been given to the world, and the poet would have been cared for by the whole human brotherhood, as any man should be who does the duty that every man owes it.

The instinctive sense of the dishonor which money-purchase does to art is so strong that sometimes a man of letters who can pay his way otherwise refuses pay for his work, as Lord Byron did, for a while, from a noble pride, and as Count Tolstoy has tried to do, from a noble conscience. But Byron's publisher profited by a generosity which did not reach his readers; and the Countess Tolstoy collects the copyright which her husband foregoes; so that these two eminent instances of protest against business in literature may be said not to have shaken its money basis. I know of no others; but there may be many that I am culpably ignorant of. Still, I doubt if there are enough to affect the fact that Literature is Business as well as Art, and almost as soon. At present business is the only human solidarity; we are all bound together with that chain, whatever interests and tastes and principles separate us.

Passage 2:

It is impossible to measure the importance of Edison by adding up the specific inventions with which his name is associated. Far-reaching as many of them have been in their effect on modern civilization, the total effect of Edison's career surpasses the sum of them all. He did not merely make the incandescent lamp and the phonograph and innumerable other devices practicable for general use; it was given to him to demonstrate the power of applied science so concretely, so understandably, so convincingly that he altered the mentality of mankind. In his lifetime, largely because of his successes, there came into widest acceptance the revolutionary conception that man could by the use of his intelligence invent a new mode of living on this planet; the human spirit, which in all previous ages had regarded the conditions of life as essentially unchanging and beyond man's control, confidently, and perhaps somewhat naively, adopted the conviction that anything could be changed and everything could be controlled.

The idea of progress is in the scale of history a very new idea. It seems first to have taken possession of a few minds in the seventeenth and eighteenth centuries as an accompaniment of the great advances in pure science. It gained greater currency in the first half of the nineteenth century when industrial civilization began to be transformed by the application of steam power. But these changes, impressive as they were, created so much human misery by the crude and cruel manner in which they were exploited that all through the century men instinctively feared and opposed the progress of machines, and of the sciences on which they rested. It was only at the end of the century, with the perfecting of the electric light bulb, the telephone, the phonograph, and the like, that the ordinary man began to feel that science could actually benefit him. Edison supplied the homely demonstrations which inspired the popular acceptance of science, and clinched the popular argument, which had begun with Darwin, about the place of science in man's outlook on life.

Thus he became the supreme propagandist of science and his name the great symbol of an almost blind faith in its possibilities. . . . [Y]ears ago, [in 1900] when I was a schoolboy, the ancient conservatism of man was still the normal inheritance of every child. We began to have electric lights, and telephones, and to see horseless carriages, but our attitude was a mixture of wonder, fear and doubt. Perhaps these things would work. Perhaps they would not explode. Today every schoolboy not only takes all the existing inventions as much for granted as we took horses and dogs for granted, but, also, he is entirely convinced that all other desirable things can and will be invented. In my youth the lonely inventor who could not obtain a hearing was still the stock figure of the imagination. Today the only people who are not absolutely sure that television is perfected are the inventors themselves. No other person played so great a part as Edison in this change in human expectation, and, finally, by the cumulative effect of his widely distributed inventions plus a combination of the modern publicity technique and the ancient myth-making faculty of men, he was lifted in the popular imagination to a place where he was looked upon not only as the symbol but the creator of a new age.

Passage 3:

Unemployment is an important index of economic slack and lost output, but it is much more than that. For the unemployed person, it is often a damaging affront to human dignity and sometimes a catastrophic blow to family life. Nor is this cost distributed in proportion to ability to bear it. It falls most heavily on the young, the semiskilled and unskilled, the Negro, the older worker, and the underemployed person in a low income rural area who is denied the option of securing more rewarding urban employment. Especially serious is the discouragement, disillusion, and bitterness generated among young people, entering the labor market for the first time, when the economy leaves them without opportunities of finding employment.

The concentrated incidence of unemployment among specific groups in the population means far greater costs to society than can be measured simply in hours of involuntary idleness or dollars of income lost. The extra costs include disruption of the careers of young people, increased juvenile delinquency, and perpetuation of conditions which breed racial discrimination in employment and otherwise deny equality of opportunity.

There is another and more subtle cost. The social and economic strains of prolonged underutilization create strong pressures for cost increasing solutions. The longer the economic slack continues, the more difficult it is to resist the efforts of its victims to claim, often quite plausibly, prosperity comes out of undercapacity output. On the side of labor, prolonged high unemployment leads to "share-the-work" pressures for shorter hours, intensifies resistance to technological change and to rationalization of work rules, and, in general, increases incentives for restrictive and inefficient measures to protect existing jobs. On the side of business, the weakness of markets leads to attempts to raise prices to cover high average overhead costs and to pressures for protection against foreign and domestic competition. On the side of agriculture, higher prices are necessary to achieve income objectives when urban and industrial demand for foods and fibers is depressed and lack of opportunities for jobs and higher incomes in industry keep people on the farm. In all these cases, the problems are real and the claims understandable. But the solutions suggested raise costs and promote inefficiency. By no means the least of the advantages of full utilization will be a diminution of these pressures. They will be weaker, and they can be more firmly resisted in good conscience, when markets are generally strong and job opportunities are plentiful.

The demand for labor is derived from the demand for the goods and services which labor participates in producing. Thus, unemployment will be reduced to 4 percent of the labor force only when the demand for the myriad of goods and services—automobiles, clothing, food, haircuts, electric generators, highways, and so on—is sufficiently great in total to require the productive efforts of 96 percent of the civilian labor force.

Although many goods are initially produced as materials or components to meet demands related to the further production of other goods, all goods (and services) are ultimately destined to satisfy demands that can, for convenience, be classified into four categories: consumer demand, business demand for new plants and machinery and for additions to inventories, net export demand of foreign buyers, and demand of government units, Federal, state, and local. Thus gross national product (GNP), our total output, is the sum of four major components of expenditure; personal consumption expenditures, gross private domestic investment, net exports, and government purchases of goods and services.

The primary line of attack on the problem of unemployment must be through measures which will expand one or more of these components of demand. Once a satisfactory level of employment has been achieved in a growing economy, economic stability requires the maintenance of a continuing balance between growing productive capacity and growing demand. Action to expand demand is called for not only when demand actually declines and a recession appears but even when the rate of growth of demand falls short of the rate of growth of capacity.

If there is still time remaining, review the passages until all 15 minutes have elapsed.
Do not look at Part B until that time.

Part B: TIME—20 minutes
DIRECTIONS: Answer the following questions pertaining to information contained in the three passages you have just read. You may not turn back to those passages for assistance.

QUESTIONS TO

Passage 1:

161. The author implies that writers are

(A) incompetent businessmen
(B) not sufficiently paid for their work
(C) greedy
(D) hucksters
(E) profiting against their will

162. A possible title which best expresses the meaning of the passage would be

(A) "The Man of Letters As A Man of Business"
(B) "Literature and the Arts"
(C) "Progress in Literature"
(D) "Poets and Writers"
(E) "The State of the Arts"

163. The author laments the fact that Tennyson, Longfellow, and Emerson

(A) wrote mystical poems
(B) had to sell their poetry
(C) were not appreciated in their time
(D) were prolific poets
(E) wrote emotional poetry

164. The passage states that authors such as Tennyson "submitted to the conditions which none can escape." What conditions is the author of the passage referring to?

(A) an unappreciative audience
(B) a materialistic society
(C) the fact that writers had to sell their work to survive
(D) authors wrote for an esoteric audience
(E) authors wrote what the public wanted

165. According to the author, Lord Byron

(A) refused payment for his work
(B) combined business with literature
(C) did not copyright his work
(D) was well known in the business community
(E) founded a school for aspiring writers

166. The author of the passage implies that

(A) society should subsidize artists and writers
(B) writers should rebel against the business system
(C) more writers should follow the example set by Lord Byron
(D) writers should only accept remuneration that will provide them with a basic standard of living
(E) writers should not attempt to change society

167. The author of the passage proposes that writers and artists

(A) make the best out of a bad situation
(B) attempt to induce society to change its values
(C) withhold their work until they gain recognition
(D) adopt the principles of commercialism
(E) adopt the value system of society

168. By accepting payment for works of literature or art, its creators are

I. Writing and painting solely for monetary gain
II. Justifying the practice of art
III. Exchanging their work for remuneration

(A) I only
(B) III only
(C) I and II only
(D) II and III only
(E) I, II, and III

169. The passage asserts that painters and sculptors are

I. Less committed than poets
II. More apt to reject monetary rewards than poets
III. Less articulate and intimate than poets

(A) I only
(B) III only
(C) I and II only
(D) II and III only
(E) I, II, and III

170. The passage would likely appear in a

(A) business journal
(B) educational journal
(C) literary journal
(D) legal journal
(E) financial journal

QUESTIONS TO

Passage 2:

171. According to the passage, Edison was the inventor of the

I. Incandescent lamp
II. Phonograph
III. Electric typewriter

(A) I only
(B) III only
(C) I and II only
(D) II and III only
(E) I, II, and III

172. It may be inferred that the year the passage was written is near

(A) 1700
(B) 1850
(C) 1900
(D) 1930
(E) 1950

173. The author states that today everyone

I. Expects more than they get
II. Takes all inventions for granted
III. Believes that almost anything can be invented

(A) I only
(B) III only
(C) I and II only
(D) II and III only
(E) I, II, and III

174. According to the passage, the importance of Edison can be measured by

(A) the sum total of his inventions
(B) the economic contributions of his inventions
(C) the total number of his patents
(D) his demonstration of the power of applied science
(E) the fact that so many remember his name

175. In the seventeenth and eighteenth centuries, progress was

(A) accepted without reservation
(B) somewhat suspect
(C) a new idea
(D) exploited by the ruling classes
(E) non-existent

176. In the first half of the nineteenth century, progress

I. Was indirectly responsible for human exploitation
II. Gained greater acceptance
III. Was widely applied

(A) I only
(B) III only
(C) I and II only
(D) II and III only
(E) I, II, and III

177. According to the passage, Edison and Darwin both

(A) had a desire to improve prediction in science
(B) took action to win popular acceptance of science
(C) had a goal to improve the living standards of mankind
(D) had an impoverished childhood
(E) were inventors

178. The author of the passage states that before Edison's contributions to science, the general belief was that conditions of life were

I. Static
II. Beyond man's control
III. Regressive

(A) I only
(B) III only
(C) I and II only
(D) II and III only
(E) I, II, and III

179. It can be inferred that the author of the passage treats progress as being

(A) over-emphasized by modern publicity techniques
(B) a necessary evil
(C) historically exploiting the masses
(D) solely in the debt of Edison
(E) something that is now taken for granted

180. It can be inferred that the passage deals with the subject of

I. History
II. Biography
III. Electricity

(A) I only
(B) III only
(C) I and II only
(D) II and III only
(E) I, II, and III

QUESTIONS TO

Passage 3:

181. According to the passage, unemployment is an index of

(A) over-utilization of capacity
(B) economic slack and lost output
(C) diminished resources
(D) the employment rate
(E) undercapacity

182. While unemployment is damaging to many, it falls most heavily upon all except the

(A) Negro
(B) semiskilled
(C) unskilled
(D) underemployed
(E) white middle class

183. The cost to society of unemployment can be measured by all except

(A) lost incomes
(B) idleness
(C) juvenile delinquency
(D) disruption of careers
(E) the death rate

184. Serious unemployment leads labor groups to demand

(A) more jobs by having everyone work shorter hours
(B) higher wages to those employed
(C) "no fire" policies
(D) cost cutting solutions
(E) higher social security payments

185. According to the passage, a typical business reaction to a recession is to press for

(A) higher unemployment insurance
(B) protection against imports
(C) government action
(D) restrictive business practices
(E) restraint against union activity

186. The demand for labor is

(A) a derived demand
(B) declining
(C) about 4 percent of the total work force
(D) underutilized
(E) dependent upon technology

187. Gross national product (**GNP**) is a measure of

(A) personal consumption
(B) net exports
(C) domestic investment
(D) government purchases of goods and services
(E) our total output

188. According to the passage, a satisfactory level of unemployment is

(A) 85 percent of the civilian work force
(B) 90 percent of the civilian work force
(C) 4 percent unemployment
(D) 2 percent unemployment
(E) no unemployment

189. Unemployment can be reduced if

I. Domestic investment increases
II. Exports from the U.S. increase
III. Personal consumption expenditures increase

(A) I only
(B) III only
(C) I and II only
(D) II and III only
(E) I, II, and III

190. Which of the following best describes the context of the passage you have just read?

I. Costs of unemployment
II. Demand and unemployment
III. Structural unemployment

(A) I only
(B) III only
(C) I and II only
(D) II and III only
(E) I, II, and III

If there is still time remaining, you may review the questions in this section only.
You may not look at Part A or turn to any other section of the test.

Answers

Section I Reading Recall

1. **(C)**
2. **(D)**
3. **(B)**
4. **(D)**
5. **(D)**
6. **(B)**
7. **(C)**
8. **(D)**
9. **(B)**
10. **(E)**
11. **(A)**
12. **(E)**
13. **(A)**
14. **(C)**
15. **(A)**
16. **(C)**
17. **(C)**
18. **(C)**
19. **(E)**
20. **(C)**
21. **(C)**
22. **(D)**
23. **(E)**
24. **(E)**
25. **(E)**
26. **(C)**
27. **(D)**
28. **(A)**
29. **(D)**
30. **(B)**

Section II Mathematics

(Numbers in parentheses indicate the section in the Mathematics Review where material concerning the question is discussed.)

31. **(D)** (I–4)
32. **(B)** (II–2)
33. **(C)** (IV–2)
34. **(B)** (IV–2)
35. **(D)** (IV–2)
36. **(D)** (II–3)
37. **(D)** (I–4)
38. **(A)** (I–7)
39. **(C)** (IV–1)
40. **(D)** (IV–1)
41. **(E)** (IV–1)
42. **(B)** (IV–1)
43. **(D)** (III–7)
44. **(E)** (II–2)
45. **(C)** (I–4)
46. **(A)** (IV–4)
47. **(E)** (IV–4)
48. **(E)** (IV–3, IV–4)
49. **(D)** (III–4)
50. **(B)** (I–4)
51. **(C)** (II–3)
52. **(C)** (I–4, III–7)
53. **(B)** (IV–5)
54. **(D)** (IV–5)
55. **(E)** (IV–5, I–7)
56. **(A)** (IV–5)
57. **(A)** (II–6)
58. **(E)** (II–3)
59. **(D)** (I–2)
60. **(D)** (I–4)
61. **(C)** (II–3)
62. **(B)** (I–1)
63. **(D)** (I–2)
64. **(D)** (I–4)
65. **(A)** (IV–5)
66. **(B)** (IV–5)
67. **(C)** (IV–5)
68. **(D)** (IV–5)
69. **(D)** (I–6)
70. **(E)** (II–3)
71. **(D)** (II–3)
72. **(C)** (IV–1)
73. **(B)** (IV–1)
74. **(C)** (IV–1)
75. **(D)** (II–7)
76. **(E)** (I–2)
77. **(B)** (I–6, II–7)
78. **(D)** (IV–4)
79. **(A)** (IV–4)
80. **(B)** (IV–4)
81. **(A)** (IV–4)
82. **(E)** (III–8)
83. **(D)** (I–4)
84. **(E)** (III–7)
85. **(E)** (III–4)

Section III Verbal Aptitude

86. **(D)**	96. **(C)**	106. **(D)**	116. **(B)**
87. **(B)**	97. **(B)**	107. **(B)**	117. **(C)**
88. **(D)**	98. **(A)**	108. **(A)**	118. **(C)**
89. **(C)**	99. **(D)**	109. **(C)**	119. **(D)**
90. **(A)**	100. **(D)**	110. **(C)**	120. **(E)**
91. **(B)**	101. **(A)**	111. **(B)**	121. **(B)**
92. **(D)**	102. **(C)**	112. **(C)**	122. **(A)**
93. **(E)**	103. **(A)**	113. **(B)**	123. **(C)**
94. **(B)**	104. **(D)**	114. **(E)**	124. **(A)**
95. **(A)**	105. **(A)**	115. **(A)**	125. **(C)**

Section IV Data Sufficiency

126. **(D)**	130. **(A)**	134. **(C)**	138. **(E)**
127. **(A)**	131. **(E)**	135. **(B)**	139. **(C)**
128. **(B)**	132. **(C)**	136. **(A)**	140. **(E)**
129. **(A)**	133. **(C)**	137. **(D)**	

Section V Business Judgment

141. **(B)**	146. **(B)**	151. **(A)**	156. **(A)**
142. **(A)**	147. **(B)**	152. **(C)**	157. **(B)**
143. **(B)**	148. **(C)**	153. **(E)**	158. **(D)**
144. **(C)**	149. **(B)**	154. **(B)**	159. **(E)**
145. **(E)**	150. **(A)**	155. **(B)**	160. **(C)**

Section VI Reading Recall

161. **(E)**	169. **(B)**	177. **(B)**	185. **(B)**
162. **(A)**	170. **(C)**	178. **(C)**	186. **(A)**
163. **(B)**	171. **(C)**	179. **(E)**	187. **(E)**
164. **(C)**	172. **(E)**	180. **(C)**	188. **(C)**
165. **(A)**	173. **(D)**	181. **(B)**	189. **(E)**
166. **(A)**	174. **(D)**	182. **(E)**	190. **(C)**
167. **(A)**	175. **(C)**	183. **(E)**	
168. **(B)**	176. **(C)**	184. **(A)**	

Analysis

Section I Reading Recall

1. **(C)** See paragraph 1: Older generations are inner directed, adopting the values of their parents.

2. **(D)** See paragraph 1: *The Lonely Crowd.*

3. **(B)** In paragraph 2 it is stated that "In the middle and late sixties a large number of people became 17 and 18 years old. . . ."

4. **(D)** See paragraph 3: Only (D) is not a result of a growing population.

5. **(D)** See paragraph 3: Some economists believe that an increasing population is a source of economic expansion while others believe it to cause environmental degradation.

6. **(B)** See paragraph 4: One area of concern to sociologists is the composition of population.

7. **(C)** Practically the entire passage deals with the socio-economic problems of population.

8. **(D)** The passage states that young people—17 and 18 year olds—were larger in number (see paragraph 2.) A "larger number" does not infer that young people comprised a "major part" of the population. It so happens that the 17 and 18 year old group was the largest single age group in the population during 1965, but comprised only a small part of the total population. That young people were more radical is the effect of changing attitudes and values.

9. **(B)** See paragraph 1: They were other directed and took their values from their peers.

10. **(E)** No prediction was made; age structures were given for the 1960's only.

11. **(A)** See paragraph 1: "Light projected from a source . . . enters the cornea and lens of the eyeball."

12. **(E)** See paragraph 3, line 1.

13. **(A)** See paragraph 4: "Lighting designers may not be called upon to do . . . photometric curves. . . ."

14. **(C)** See paragraph 6: "Colors that have no hue are termed neutral or achromatic colors. They include . . . black."

15. **(A)** See paragraph 7: "All colored objects selectively absorb certain wave lengths of light and reflect. . . ."

16. **(C)** See paragraph 7.

17. **(C)** See paragraph 8: According to the passage, most paints have body or pigment colors.

18. **(C)** See paragraph 5, line 1.

19. **(E)** The first five paragraphs treat the subject of light transmission; paragraph 3 discusses photometry and paragraphs five through eight concern color perception.

20. **(C)** Alternative (D) might seem plausible as an answer because the passage partly deals with lighting design. However, (D) does not specify what *sort* of designer's manual. Alternative (C) is the most logical in this case.

21. **(C)** See paragraph 1 where it is stated that the agreement for currency convertibility in 1961 was a notable achievement and had important implications for the U.S. economy.

22. **(D)** See paragraph 2: At the end of 1948, the U.S. held 71 percent of the free world's gold stock; by 1962 its share had fallen to 40 percent.

23. **(E)** See paragraph 2: During the period 1948 to 1962, Western Europe's share of gold stock grew from 15 to 44 percent.

24. **(E)** See paragraph 3: "The redistribution of reserves was brought about partly through deficits in the international payments of the United States. . . ."

25. **(E)** All are given in paragraph 4.

26. **(C)** See paragraph 4: "The EEC offers a domestic market broadly comparable to the [domestic market of the] United States. . . ."

27. **(D)** The idea of help for low-income countries is given in paragraph 5.

28. **(A)** See the last paragraph. The only alternative mentioned is that "markets will become more unified."

29. **(D)** See paragraph 3: ". . . continuing large payments deficits by the United States could create doubts about the stability of the dollar and threaten the efficient operation of the international payments system."

30. **(B)** Much of the passage is given over to the problem of the United States balance of payments, but see especially paragraph 3: ". . . domestic economic policy has been framed with attention to the balance of payments and the position of the dollar."

Section II Mathematics

31. **(D)** 64% of 200 is (.64)(200), which equals 128. Therefore, 128 students received a grade of C.

32. **(B)** Since $x = 3$, $2x + y = 6 + y$; so $6 + y = 10$ and $y = 4$. Therefore, $x - y = 3 - 4 = -1$.

33. **(C)** In 1965, 27.6% was spent on hospital care and 19.1% was spent on drugs and appliances. Note that $1\frac{1}{2}$ times 19.1 = 28.65.

34. **(B)** Medical research received .4%, construction 3.2%, and other items 6.3%; so together they received .4% + 3.2% + 6.3%, which is equal to 9.9%. 9.9% is almost 10%, which equals $\frac{1}{10}$.

35. **(D)**

STATEMENT I is true, since (7)(3.2) equals 22.4, which is less than 22.6.

STATEMENT II cannot be inferred because no information is given about the amounts of money spent. The *percentage* expended for professional personnel was higher in 1950 than in 1965; but if the total spent in 1965 was enough larger than in 1950, the *amount* spent in 1965 could have been larger than that spent in 1950.

STATEMENT III is true, since $\frac{3}{8}$ is equal to 37.5%.

Therefore, only STATEMENTS I and III can be inferred from the graphs.

36. **(D)** Since 15 minutes is $\frac{1}{4}$ of an hour, each worker can pack $4 \times \frac{1}{6}$ or $\frac{2}{3}$ of a case an hour. The factory has 40 workers, so they should pack $40 \times \frac{2}{3}$ or $\frac{80}{3}$ cases each hour. Therefore, in $1\frac{2}{3}$ or $\frac{5}{3}$ hours the factory should pack $\left(\frac{5}{3} \times \frac{80}{3}\right)$, which equals $\frac{400}{9}$ or $44\frac{4}{9}$ cases.

37. **(D)** If potatoes cost 15¢ a pound, then 10 pounds will cost $1.50. If the price increases by 10%, then 10 pounds of potatoes will cost 110% of $1.50, which is $1.65.

38. **(A)** Since the truck driver averaged 50 miles per hour for the first three hours, he traveled 3 × 50 or 150 miles during the first three hours. Since he needs to travel 180 − 150 miles in the final hour, he should drive at 30 mph.

39. **(C)** Only Germany, Great Britain and Northern Ireland, and Ireland had quotas in excess of 10,000.

40. **(D)** The annual quota for Northern and Western Europe was 125,853, and the annual quota for Southern and Eastern Europe was 24,719. The ratio of 125,000 to 25,000 is 5 to 1.

41. **(E)** Great Britain and Northern Ireland had the largest number, and Poland the second

largest number of quota immigrants between 1946 and 1950.

42. **(B)** The quota for Greece was 310, so 2% of the residents of the U.S. in 1910 who were born in Greece equals 310. Therefore, 50 × 310 or 15,500 is the total number of residents of the U.S. in 1910 born in Greece.

43. **(D)** The area of a triangle is $\frac{1}{2}$ the base times the altitude. The altitude is $2B$, so the area is $(\frac{1}{2})(B)(2B)$ or B^2.

44. **(E)** If we denote the two numbers by x and y, then $xy = 10$ and $x + y = 7$. Then x is $7 - y$ and $(7 - y)y = 7y - y^2 = 10$ or $y^2 - 7y + 10 = 0$. But $y^2 - 7y + 10$ equals $(y - 5)(y - 2)$; so the two numbers are 5 and 2. The correct answer can be selected quickly by inspection of the choices.

45. **(C)** Since the first 100 bags cost $\$x$ each, the total cost of the first 100 bags is $\$100x$. Since the remaining 50 bags are discounted 10%, each bag costs 90% of $\$x$ or $\$(.90)x$ and the 50 bags cost $\$45x$. Thus, the total cost is $\$145x$.

46. **(A)** In 1954, conventional theaters received 80.5% of their receipts from admissions. 80% of $1,170,401,000 is more than $936,000,000, which exceeds the total receipts for any of the other categories.

47. **(E)** Since the average price in 1954 was $1, simply find the amount received from admissions by conventional theaters in 1954. About 80% of receipts came from admissions, and (.8)($1,170,000,000) is $936,000,000. (Notice that receipts are given in thousands of dollars.)

48. **(E)**

STATEMENT I is true because 1954 is the only year shown when there were more than 17,000 theaters.

STATEMENT II is true. The percentage derived from receipts in conventional theaters increased from 80.5% to 85.5% to 87.4%. The percentage of drive-in receipts from admissions increased from 72.3% to 76.6% to 77.4%.

STATEMENT III is true, because 3 times $253,766,000 is less than $803,458,000.

Therefore, STATEMENTS I, II, and III can be inferred from the graphs.

49. **(D)** According to the Pythagorean theorem, the length squared equals $8^2 + 15^2$, which is 289. So the length of the side opposite the right angle is 17.

50. **(B)** The store made a profit of 20%; so the store sold the glove for 120% of what the glove cost. If C is the cost of the glove, 120% of $C = \$10.20$, or $\frac{6}{5}C = \$10.20$. Therefore, $C = \frac{5}{6}$ of $10.20, which is $8.50.

51. **(C)** The first 600 copies cost a total of $600x$¢. There are 1,500 − 600 or 900 copies after the first 600, each of which costs $\left(x - \frac{y}{10}\right)$¢; so the 900 copies cost $900\left(x - \frac{y}{y}\right)$¢, which equals $(900x - 90y)$¢. Therefore, the total cost is $(1500x - 90y)$¢.

52. **(C)** If s is the original side of the square, then s^2 is the area of the original square. The side of the increased square is 140% of s or $(1.4)s$. Therefore, the area of the increased square is $(1.4s)^2$ or $1.96s^2$, which is 196% of the original area. Thus, the area has increased by 96%.

53. **(B)** $32.5 billion was spent on hospital care and $16.2 billion on physicians' services in 1972. The ratio of 32.5 to 16.2 is almost exactly 2 to 1.

54. **(D)** 40% of 16 billion is 6.4 billion. (Save time by estimating.)

55. **(E)** The total amount spent was 32.5 + 16.2 + 23.3 or $72 billion. If the population was 216 million, then the per capita expenditure = $\frac{\$72,000,000,000}{216,000,000,000} = \frac{\$1,000}{3} = \$333\frac{1}{3}$.

56. **(A)**

STATEMENT I is false. 53% of $32.5 billion is spent on hospital care, and this amount is more than 25% of $23.3 billion, which was spent on other health services.

STATEMENT II is true. Estimate quickly by taking ($\frac{1}{2}$ of 32) + ($\frac{1}{4}$ of 16) + ($\frac{1}{4}$ of 23), which is more than 25. This is much faster than finding the exact amount.

STATEMENT III is false, since only 36% comes from private health insurance and 36% is less than 40%, which equals ⅖.

Therefore, only STATEMENT II can be inferred from the graph.

57. **(A)** If P is the price of 7 cartons, then $\frac{7}{28}=\frac{P}{21}$, so $P=\frac{1}{4}$ of \$21, which is \$5.25.

58. **(E)** Plane P will travel $\frac{3}{2}$ of an hour before Q takes off, so it will be $\frac{3x}{2}$ miles away at 3:30 A.M. Let t denote the number of hours after 3:30 A.M. it takes Q to overtake P. By then P has flown $tx+\frac{3x}{2}$ miles and Q has flown ty miles. We want the value of t, where $ty = tx + \frac{3x}{2}$, or $t(y-x) = \frac{3x}{2}$. Therefore, $t = \frac{3x}{2(y-x)}$.

59. **(D)** Note that $\left(\frac{2}{3}+\frac{1}{3}\right)$ equals 1 full day, and that $\left(\frac{1}{8}+\frac{3}{4}\right)$ is shy $\frac{1}{8}$ of being 1 full day. So he works $2\frac{7}{8}$ days altogether.

$$\left(2\frac{7}{8}\right)(20)=\left(\frac{23}{8}\right)(20)=\frac{460}{8}=\$57.50.$$

60. **(D)** There were 26 (16 + 10) students who answered 32 or more questions correctly. Since the total number of students is 60, and $\frac{26}{60}=.43\frac{1}{3}$, $43\frac{1}{3}\%$ of the class answered 32 or more questions correctly.

61. **(C)** 12 students had scores of 28 to 31, and 8 scores of 25 or less; so $8x=12$ and $x=\frac{12}{8}=\frac{3}{2}$.

62. **(B)** The product of 3 consecutive integers is of the form $(x-1)(x)(x+1)$ and a good approximation to this is x^3. Since $6^3 = 216$, a good guess for x is 6, 6 is correct since $5\times 6\times 7 = 210$. Therefore, the sum of the two smaller integers is 5 + 6 or 11.

63. **(D)** Let C, B, and E denote the cost of cereal, bacon, and eggs respectively. Then $C=\frac{1B}{3}$ and $B=\frac{5E}{4}$, or $E=\frac{4B}{5}$. Therefore, $E=\frac{4B}{5}$ and $B=3C$; so we conclude that $E=\left(\frac{4}{5}\right)3C=\frac{12C}{5}$.

64. **(D)** Since 80% of 15 is 12, the loaded truck travels 12 miles on a gallon of gas. Therefore, it will use $\frac{80}{12}$ or $6\frac{8}{12}$ or $6\frac{2}{3}$ gallons of gas to travel 80 miles.

65. **(A)** Consider only the figure at the left.

66. **(B)** At the end of 1945, the amount spent on national defense was about 80 − 10 or \$70 billion. In 1952, about \$40 billion was spent on national defense. Since the amount decreased by \$30 billion, it decreased by $^{30}/_{70}$ or $^{3}/_{7}$, which is about 43%.

67. **(C)** In 1950, the total expenditures were \$40 billion. The category "all other" received \$10 billion in 1950, so "all other" received about $^{10}/_{40}$ or 25% of total government expenditures in 1950.

68. **(D)**

STATEMENT I is true, since the band which denotes corporation income taxes is wider in 1946 than in 1947.

STATEMENT II is false, since the top line on the receipts graph falls between 1945 and 1950.

STATEMENT III is true, since the top line on the expenditures graph is lower in 1948 than at any other time between 1945 and 1952.

Therefore, only STATEMENTS I and III can be inferred from the graph.

69. **(D)**

STATEMENT I is not always true. For example, if $x=-2$ and $y=-4$, then $x-y=2$, which is not negative.

STATEMENT II is true. If x is negative, then $-x$ is always positive.

STATEMENT III is true. Since x and y are negative, $-x$ and $-y$ are positive and the product of two positive numbers is positive.

Therefore, only STATEMENTS II and III are always true.

70. **(E)** In the first $1\frac{1}{2}$ hours, the car will travel $\frac{3}{2} \times 70$ or 105 miles. In order to travel a total of 200 miles the car has 95 miles left. At a speed of 50 miles per hour it will take $\frac{95}{50}$ or $1\frac{9}{10}$ hours to travel 95 miles. Therefore, the total traveling time necessary to travel 200 miles is $1\frac{1}{2} + 1\frac{9}{10}$, which equals $3\frac{4}{10}$ or $3\frac{2}{5}$ hours.

71. **(D)** The first 1,000 copies will cost $\$1{,}000x$. There are 600 copies after the first thousand, each costing $\$(x - 2y)$, so all 600 cost $\$600x - \$1200y$. Therefore, the cost of 1,600 copies is $\$1600x - \$1200y$.

72. **(C)** The lowest value was 87.4 in 1953.

73. **(B)** Look at the percent changes. If there are any negative signs the category did not increase every year, since it decreased when the percent change was negative. Therefore, only consumer prices for services has increased every year.

74. **(C)** The index on all items was 77.8 in 1951 and 125.3 in 1972. Since 125 is $1\frac{2}{3}$ of 75, the index increased by about 60%.

75. **(D)** If $\frac{1}{3} < x$, then since inverting positive numbers reverses inequalities, $\frac{1}{1/3} > \frac{1}{x}$. Since $\frac{1}{1/3} = 3$, 3 is greater than $\frac{1}{x}$ or $\frac{1}{x}$ is less than 3. (x is positive since it is greater than $\frac{1}{3}$.)

76. **(E)** $\frac{1}{3} = \frac{14}{42}$ and $\frac{2}{7} = \frac{12}{42}$, so $\frac{1}{3} + \frac{2}{7} = \frac{26}{42}$. Therefore, $x = 26$.

77. **(B)** Since 12 is positive, one of the numbers must be positive because the sum of negative numbers is negative. If r is 13, then $x = 0$, $y = -1$, and $z = 0$ satisfy $r + x + y + w = 12$ and $x < 6$.

78. **(D)** Total receipts in 1963 were \$42,363 million, and total receipts in 1954 were \$22,658 million. Since $\frac{42}{21} = \frac{2}{1}$, the correct answer is 2 to 1.

79. **(A)** Between 1958 and 1963, receipts increased 56.1% in establishments whose receipts were \$500,000 and over, all the other categories increasing by less than 50%.

80. **(B)** In 1954, the receipts from establishments in the category \$30,000 to \$99,000 were \$4,531 million. The total receipts for 1954 were \$22,658 million. Since 5 times 4,531 is 22,655, $\frac{4{,}531}{22{,}658}$ is about .2 or 20%.

81. **(A)**

STATEMENT I is false, since the receipts from establishments with receipts of \$10,000 or under declined from 1958 to 1963.

STATEMENT II cannot be inferred, since there is no information about the number of establishments.

STATEMENT III is true. More than \$10,000 million in receipts came from establishments with receipts between \$100,000 and \$499,-000. The total receipts for 1963 were \$42,363 million. Since 20% = $\frac{1}{5}$ and 5 times 10 is 50 (which is greater than 42), STATEMENT III is true.

Therefore, only STATEMENT III can be inferred from the table.

82. **(E)** The volume of a sphere of radius r is $\frac{4}{3}\pi r^3$. If r is replaced by $2r$, the volume $= \frac{4}{3}\pi(2r)^3 = \frac{4}{3}\pi 8r^3 = 8\left(\frac{4}{3}\pi r^3\right)$, so the volume has increased by a factor of 8.

83. **(D)** The price of an object which costs C is $C(1 - d)$, where d is the discount. Therefore, the price of something after successive dis-

counts of 10% and 15% = $C(1-10\%)(1-15\%) = C(90\%)(85\%)$, which is $C(76.5\%)$. So $1-d = 76.5\%$ and the successive discount is equivalent to a single discount of 100% − 76.5%, which equals 23.5%.

Another method for solving the problem would be to calculate the discount on an item which costs \$100. After the 10% discount the item would cost \$100(.90) = \$90 and the second discount would be \$(90)(.15) = \$13.50. The final cost would be \$90 − \$13.50 = \$76.50. Therefore, the discount was \$23.50, so the rate of discount is $\frac{23.50}{100} = 23.5\%$.

84. (E) The area of the room is 12^2 or 144 square feet. The area of a tile $= \frac{1}{3} \times \frac{1}{2} = \frac{1}{6}$ of a square foot since the area of a rectangle is length times width. The number of tiles necessary $= 144 \div \frac{1}{6} = 6 \times 144 = 864$ tiles.

Notice that we changed all the measurements into feet. We can also do the problem by changing all measurements into inches, but the multiplication and division would take more time.

85. (E) According to the Pythagorean theorem, the length of the hypotenuse, the side opposite the right angle, is the square root of $(n-1)^2 + (2\sqrt{n})^2$, which is $n^2 - 2n + 1 + 4n$ or $n^2 + 2n + 1$. This equals $(n+1)^2$. Therefore, the answer is $\sqrt{(n+1)^2}$, which is $n+1$.

Section III Verbal Aptitude

86. (D) ABETTOR: accomplice, instigator. *Antonym:* antagonist

87. (B) INTERDICT: inhibit, prohibit. *Antonym:* allow

88. (D) PEDANTIC: pedagogical, learned. *Antonym:* modest

89. (C) SATIATE: satisfy, surfeit. *Antonym:* stint

90. (A) PLAINTIVE: mournful, sad. *Antonym:* exultant

91. (B) POIGNANT: severe, sharp. *Antonym:* dull

92. (D) INSIDIOUS: treacherous, sly. *Antonym:* sincere

93. (E) INSIPID: dull, tasteless. *Antonym:* intense

94. (B) FLIPPANT: glib, pert. *Antonym:* grave

95. (A) OSTENTATIOUS: boastful, showy. *Antonym:* modest

96. (C) SATURNINE: reserved, sluggish. *Antonym:* cheerful

97. (B) SANGUINE: trustful, confident. *Antonym:* distrustful

98. (A) ABASEMENT: fall, degradation. *Antonym:* elevation

99. (D) CALUMNY: defamation, slander. *Antonym:* vindication

100. (C) One skis on a slope as one swims in a pool. Alternative (E) might seem acceptable, but it is not as functionally close as the other two pairs, i.e. related to sports activity. Alternatives (A), (B), and (D) do not have the same meaning.

101. (A) As one arrives at a solution through reasoning, one makes a discovery through deduction. None of the other alternatives has the same meaning.

102. (C) A speedometer measures the speed of an automobile, while a seismograph measures the strength of an earthquake. None of the other alternatives has the same function or meaning, except (E), where the order is incorrect.

103. (A) A gardener creates a landscape as an artist creates a portrait.

104. (D) A sonnet (or poem) is a part of (or an example of) poetry as a concerto is a piece

of (or an example of) music. While drama may be part of the stage (E), the meaning is not the same. Other alternatives do not possess similar meaning or function.

105. **(A)** Alternative (A) has the same meaning, order, and function.

106. **(D)** If one is prodigal (wasteful), it may lead to insolvency, just as being thrifty builds up resources. Other alternatives do not exemplify the same function.

107. **(B)** A maple is a *type* of tree as a sedan is a *type* of automobile.

108. **(A)** The relationship is one of *opposites*. Straight is an antonym of circuit, as automatic is an antonym of manual.

109. **(C)** An observant person practices his religion; a doctor practices medicine.

110. **(C)** A thief may be stopped by incarcerating him, as a disease may be stopped by immunization. Alternative (A) would be acceptable except that the part of speech is incorrect; the correct form would be: addict : rehabilitation.

111. **(B)** A person runs faster than he walks (same basic function of movement), and a horse gallops faster than he trots.

112. **(C)** A monologue is a performance by one actor in a play, whereas a solo is played by one instrumentalist in a concert.

113. **(B)** Alternative (B) has the most logic and meaning; alternative (D) is a possibility, but it is not grammatically correct: "The bare terrain give. . . ."

114. **(E)** Here again, logic and meaning are important. Alternatives (B), (C), and (D) are illogical and (A) has little meaning.

115. **(A)** Alternatives (B) and (E) are illogical, and the meaning of (C) and (D) is unclear.

116. **(B)** Alternatives (A), (C), (D), and (E) are illogical. (B) has the most meaning; to complete the research, a number of sequential (or successive) activities had to be taken.

117. **(C)** Alternative (C) has the most meaning. A topographer makes maps, a lexicographer compiles dictionaries, a stenographer and phonographer write in shorthand.

118. **(C)** If the experiment was awesome (full of wonder), then it most likely proved salutary (beneficial) to mankind.

119. **(D)** Alternatives (A), (B), (C), and (E) are illogical; e.g., in (B) an accused cannot be sentenced and freed by the same act.

120. **(E)** Alternatives (A) and (B) are illogical, while (C) and (D) have no meaning at all.

121. **(B)** He may be called wealthy (A), but he certainly would be called prolific (B). Whether alternatives (D) and (E) would apply is questionable at best.

122. **(A)** If the story was suspect, it certainly was not regarded with credence (B) and congruity (C). Alternatives (D) and (E) have no meaning.

123. **(C)** If it is a crisis, it must have been discovered (A); alternative (B) is illogical; (D) and (E) have little meaning.

124. **(A)** Alternatives (B) through (E) have no meaning and are illogical.

125. **(C)** If he was not phlegmatic (sluggish), he must have been alert (C).

Section IV Data Sufficiency

126. **(D)**

STATEMENT (1) alone is sufficient. 2 feet 7 inches is more than half of 5 feet, so the piece which is 2 feet 7 inches long must be longer than the other two pieces put together.

STATEMENT (2) alone is sufficient. Since one piece is 5 inches long, the sum of the lengths of the remaining two pieces is 4 feet, 7 inches. Since one piece is 7 inches longer than the other, $L + (L + 7 \text{ in.}) = 4 \text{ ft. } 7 \text{ in.}$, where L is the length of the smaller of the two remaining pieces. Solving the equation yields $L + 7$ in. as the length of the longest piece.

127. **(A)** Since AC is a diameter, angle ABC is inscribed in a semicircle and is therefore a right angle.

STATEMENT (1) alone is sufficient since it implies the two other angles in the triangle must be equal. Since the sum of the angles of a triangle is 180°, we can deduce that $x = 45$.

STATEMENT (2) alone is not sufficient. There is no information about the angle ABD; so STATEMENT (2) cannot be used to find the angles of triangle ABD.

128. **(B)**

STATEMENT (2) alone is sufficient. $y^2 - 2y + 1$ equals $(y - 1)^2$, so the only solution to $(y - 1)^2 = 0$ is $y = 1$.

STATEMENT (1) alone is not sufficient. $x + 2y = 6$ implies $y = 3 - \frac{x}{2}$, but there is no data given about the value of x.

129. **(A)**

STATEMENT (1) alone is sufficient. Pipe A fills up $\frac{1}{30}$ of the reservoir per minute. STATEMENT (1) says pipe B fills up $\frac{1}{20}$ of the reservoir per minute, so A and B together fill up $\frac{1}{20} + \frac{1}{30}$ or $\frac{5}{60}$ or $\frac{1}{12}$ of the reservoir. Therefore, together pipe A and pipe B will take 12 minutes to fill the reservoir.

STATEMENT (2) alone is not sufficient. There is no information about how long it takes pipe B to fill the reservoir.

130. **(A)**

STATEMENT (1) alone is sufficient. Draw the lines AC and BC; then AOC and BOC are right triangles, since AB is perpendicular to CO. By the Pythagorean theorem, $(AC)^2 = (AO)^2 + (CO)^2$ and $(BC)^2 = (OB)^2 + (CO)^2$; so if AO is less than OB, then AC is less than BC.

STATEMENT (2) alone is not sufficient. There is no restriction on where the point D is.

131. **(E)**

STATEMENTS (1) and (2) together are not sufficient. If $x = \frac{1}{2}$ and $y = 3$, then xy is greater than 1, but if $x = \frac{1}{2}$ and $y = \frac{3}{2}$, then xy is less than 1.

132. **(C)**

STATEMENT (1) alone is not sufficient. By choosing B and D differently we can have either $x = y$ or $x \neq y$ and still have $z = u$.

STATEMENT (2) alone is not sufficient. It implies that $x = z$ and $y = u$, but gives no information to compare x and y. STATEMENTS (1) and (2) together, however, yield $x = y$.

133. **(C)**

STATEMENT (1) alone is not sufficient. If town C were closer to B, even if S were going slower than T, S could arrive at C first. But if you also use STATEMENT (2), then train S must be traveling faster than train T, since it is further from B to C than it is from A to C.

So STATEMENTS (1) and (2) together are sufficient.

STATEMENT (2) alone is insufficient since it gives no information about the trains.

134. **(C)**

STATEMENT (2) alone is not sufficient, since D can be any point if we assume only STATEMENT (2).

STATEMENT (1) alone is not sufficient. Depending on the position of point C, x and y can be equal or unequal. For example, in both of the following triangles BD is perpendicular to AC.

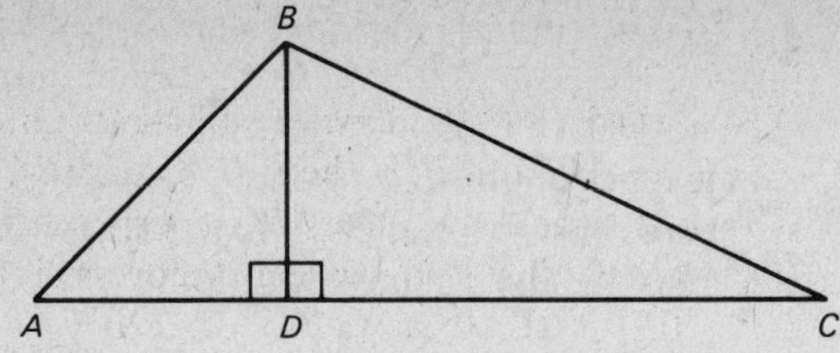

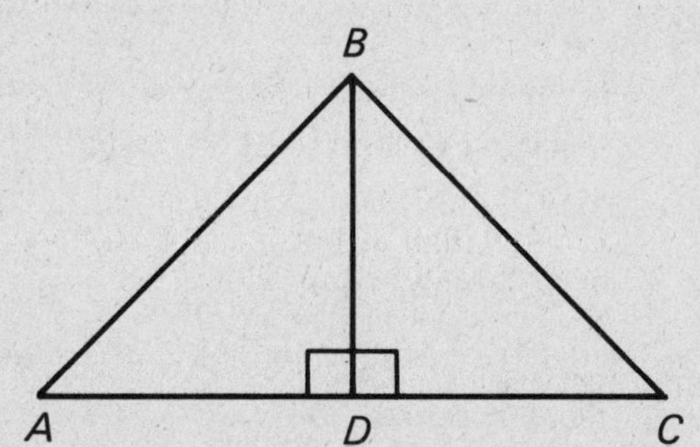

If STATEMENTS (1) and (2) are both true, then $x = y$. The triangles ABD and BDC are both right triangles with two pairs of corresponding sides equal; the triangles are therefore congruent and $x = y$.

135. **(B)**

STATEMENT (2) alone is sufficient, since $3x + 3y$ is $3(x + y)$. (Therefore, if $3x + 3y = 4$, then $x + y = 4/3$.)

STATEMENT (1) alone is not sufficient, since you need another equation besides $x - y = 4$ to find the values of x and y.

136. **(A)**

STATEMENT (1) alone is sufficient. We know that the total of sales for 1968, 1969, and 1970 is three times the average and that sales in 1968 were twice the average. Then the total of sales in 1969 and 1970 was equal to the average. Therefore, sales were less in 1969 than in 1968.

STATEMENT (2) alone is insufficient, since it does not relate sales in 1969 to sales in 1968.

137. **(D)**

Since the length of the arc of the circle is proportional to the length of the chord connecting the endpoints, STATEMENT (1) alone is sufficient.

STATEMENT (2) alone is sufficient, since the areas of the circular segments are proportional to the squares of the lengths of the chord.

138. **(E)**

STATEMENTS (1) and (2) together are not sufficient, since the points A and D can be moved and STATEMENTS (1) and (2) still be satisfied.

139. **(C)**

STATEMENT (1) alone is not sufficient, since 24 and 16 are both divisible by 4 but only 24 is divisible by 12.

STATEMENT (2) alone is not sufficient, since 24 and 15 are divisible by 3 but 15 is not divisible by 12.

STATEMENT (1) implies that $k = 4m$ for some integer m. If you assume STATEMENT (2), then since k is divisible by 3, either 4 or m is divisible by 3. Since 4 is not divisible by 3, m must be. Therefore, $m = 3j$, where j is some integer and $k = 4 \times 3j$ or $12j$. So k is divisible by 12. Therefore, STATEMENTS (1) and (2) together are sufficient.

140. **(E)**

STATEMENTS (1) and (2) together are not sufficient, because there is no information about the location of C relative to the locations of A and B.

Section V Business Judgment

141. **(B)** The poor economic situation was a *Major Factor* leading to the ABC Corporation's reconsidering its investment plans.

142. **(A)** The *Major Objective* or result sought by the company was another look at its previous decision to invest.

143. **(B)** The economic slowdown was a *Major Factor* in the company's decision to reconsider.

144. **(C)** That other foreign companies were also reluctant to invest was a *Minor Factor* entering into ABC's decision to invest.

145. **(E)** That the government sought to attract foreign investment was an *Unimportant Issue* to ABC. Its major concern was the state of the economy and the effect on its plans.

146. **(B)** See paragraph 2: The economic slowdown was caused by deliberate government action.

147. **(B)** See paragraph 4: The government still encouraged foreign investment.

148. **(C)** See paragraph 2: Government economic policy resulted in increased prices and taxes.

149. **(B)** See paragraph 4: Only the relative profitability of exports was a positive consequence of the government's economic policy.

150. **(A)** See paragraph 2: The cost of living allowance (paid to workers) led to higher wage costs and directly to higher prices.

151. **(A)** This case illustrates problems of company discipline and inter-executive relationships. It is replete with miscues on the part of the new department head as well as top management. The major problem is not whether subordinates in Department K will accede to their supervisors' requests to fill out time sheets but whether their relationships with the new department head are not irreparably damaged. This, then, is the *Major Objective;* a restoration of discipline in Department K.

152. **(C)** That the employees are of high caliber is a *Minor Factor* with regard to the issue of discipline, although it might have been a more important factor in the original decision to demand that time sheets be used.

153. **(E)** That the company has several departments certainly has no bearing on the issues at hand and is an *Unimportant Issue.*

154. **(B)** Apparently the fact employees worked without any *direct* supervision strongly motivated them against the acceptance of any procedure that would change the status quo. This is in effect what the new department head's directive would do.

155. **(B)** Another major grievance of the employees was that management went outside the company to hire a replacement for the retired department head. This is certainly a *Major Factor* that top management should have considered more carefully before making their decision—and now that it has been made—a solution must be found.

156. **(A)** See paragraph 6: The new department head threatened to resign.

157. **(B)** See paragraph 3: The head of Department K retired.

158. **(D)** While the passage states (in paragraph 3) that the president's talk soothed "hot tempers," it is clear that it also delayed a decision of what to do next. Many employees still did not report their time, and presumably the new department head's threat to resign still stood.

159. **(E)** See paragraph 5: All of these are given. Employees resented the new department head because he was hired from outside the company; they never had to fill out time sheets and neither did other departments.

160. **(C)** We know nothing about his mannerisms; but his communication with subordinates leaves something to be desired. Apparently he did not consult with them before issuing his directive.

Section VI Reading Recall

161. **(E)** This expression is found throughout the passage, e.g.: in paragraph 1: ". . . when a poet has put his heart . . . into a poem, and sold it to a magazine, the scandal is greater. . . ."

162. **(A)** The passage treats the problem of the poet or writer who must "sell" his works to survive; therefore he acts like a businessman.

163. **(B)** See paragraph 1: They sold their poetry, i.e. "submitted to the conditions which none can escape."

164. **(C)** See paragraph 1: ". . . the poem was not written for these dollars, but it is perfectly true that it was sold for them."

165. **(A)** See paragraph 2: Lord Byron refused payment for his work (although others gained monetarily from it).

166. **(A)** This is implied in paragraph 1: ". . . the poet would have been cared for by the whole human brotherhood, as any man should be who does the duty that every man owes it."

167. **(A)** The author proposes that until society changes its value system (which he does not foresee) the artist and writer must compromise as best they can with the existing system without, however, debasing their work.

168. **(B)** See paragraph 1: By exchanging their work for money does not mean that it was "written for these dollars," even though it was "sold for them." Moreover, the act of selling for gain "does not justify the conditions" or reality of the situation.

169. **(B)** See paragraph 1: "These are artists less articulate and less intimate than the poet. . . ."

170. **(C)** The main idea expressed in the passage is that of the dilemma faced by the writer who must support himself solely through his writing. Even though it is implied that the artist or writer is forced to be a businessman of sorts by circumstances, the author's message is directed more to those in the literary world (or interested in literature). The passage, therefore, would most likely appear in a literary journal or book (as it actually did).

171. **(C)** Both are specifically mentioned in paragraph 1.

172. **(E)** The author was a schoolboy in 1900. As there is mention of television, it must have been written after 1950.

173. **(D)** See paragraph 3: "Today every schoolboy not only takes all the existing inventions as much for granted, . . . also, he is entirely convinced that all other desirable things can and will be invented."

174. **(D)** See paragraph 1: "It is impossible to measure the importance of Edison by adding up the specific inventions with which his name is associated. . . . It was given to him to demonstrate the power of applied science. . . ."

175. **(C)** See paragraph 2, line 1: "The idea of progress is in the scale of history a very new idea. It seems to have taken possession of a few minds in the seventeenth and eighteenth centuries. . . ."

176. **(C)** See paragraph 2: ". . . these changes [brought about by progress] created so much human misery. . . ." And, above in the same paragraph: "It [progress] gained greater currency in the first half of the nineteenth century. . . ."

177. **(B)** This is stated in the last sentence of paragraph 2.

178. **(C)** See paragraph 1: ". . . the human spirit, which in all previous ages had regarded the conditions of life as essentially unchanging and beyond man's control. . . ."

179. **(E)** The main idea of the passage was to show Edison's role as a popularizer of progress and what it stood for. It was not the intention of the author to make his own value judgment of progress. Progress was taken for granted.

180. **(C)** While the passage deals with the life of a well known inventor (biography) of some years ago (history) who invented the light bulb, the latter was the only connection with electricity as a subject.

181. **(B)** See paragraph 1, line 1: "Unemployment is an important index of economic slack and lost output. . . ."

182. **(E)** See paragraph 1: "It falls most heavily on the young, the semiskilled [B] and unskilled [C], the Negro [A], the older worker, and the underemployed worker [D]."

183. **(E)** See paragraph 2: In the first line are included the costs of involuntary idleness (B) and income lost (A), followed by (C) and (D) in the next sentence.

184. **(A)** See paragraph 3: "On the side of labor, prolonged high unemployment leads to 'share-the-work' pressures for shorter hours. . . .", i.e., if workers are employed fewer hours, there will be "more jobs."

185. **(B)** In paragraph 3: "On the side of business, the weakness of markets [i.e. a recession] leads to pressures for protection against foreign . . . competition," i.e., protection against imports. (A) was not mentioned, (C) is too vague, and (D) was implied by "protection against . . . domestic competition" but is also vague.

186. **(A)** See paragraph 4: "The demand for labor is derived from the demand for the goods and services which labor participates in producing."

187. **(E)** See paragraph 5: GNP is a measure of the total goods and services produced, "our total output." It consists of the components in (A), (B), (C),and (D).

188. **(C)** Mention was made in paragraph 4 of reducing unemployment to a level of 4 percent (employment of 96 percent of the civilian work force), and it can be inferred that this figure constitutes a "satisfactory level" of unemployment.

189. **(E)** See paragraph 6, line 1: "The primary line of attack on the problem of unemployment must be through measures which will expand one or more of these components of demand," referring to the components of GNP listed in paragraph 5, which are (I), (II),and (III).

190. **(C)** The cost of unemployment is the subject of the first three paragraphs, while the subject of demand and unemployment is discussed in paragraphs 4 and 5. Structural unemployment is not discussed in the passage.

Evaluating Your Score

Tabulate your score for each section of Sample Test 4 according to the directions on pages 3–4 and record the results in the Self-scoring Table below. Then find your rank for each score on the Self-scoring Scale and record it in the appropriate blank.

Self-scoring Table

PART	SCORE	RANK
1		
2		
3		
4		
5		
6		

Self-scoring Scale

	ACHIEVEMENT			
PART	POOR	FAIR	GOOD	EXCELLENT
1	0–15	16–21	22–25	26–30
2	0–29	30–40	41–47	48–55
3	0–20	21–28	29–34	35–40
4	0– 7	8–10	11–12	13–15
5	0–10	11–14	15–16	17–20
6	0–15	16–21	22–25	26–30

Study again the Review sections covering material in Sample Test 4 for which you had a rank of FAIR or POOR. Then go on to Sample Test 5.

Answer Sheet – Sample Test 5

Section I — Reading Recall

1. A B C D E
2. A B C D E
3. A B C D E
4. A B C D E
5. A B C D E
6. A B C D E
7. A B C D E
8. A B C D E
9. A B C D E
10. A B C D E
11. A B C D E
12. A B C D E
13. A B C D E
14. A B C D E
15. A B C D E
16. A B C D E
17. A B C D E
18. A B C D E
19. A B C D E
20. A B C D E
21. A B C D E
22. A B C D E
23. A B C D E
24. A B C D E
25. A B C D E
26. A B C D E
27. A B C D E
28. A B C D E
29. A B C D E
30. A B C D E

Section II — Mathematics

31. A B C D E
32. A B C D E
33. A B C D E
34. A B C D E
35. A B C D E
36. A B C D E
37. A B C D E
38. A B C D E
39. A B C D E
40. A B C D E
41. A B C D E
42. A B C D E
43. A B C D E
44. A B C D E
45. A B C D E
46. A B C D E
47. A B C D E
48. A B C D E
49. A B C D E
50. A B C D E
51. A B C D E
52. A B C D E
53. A B C D E
54. A B C D E
55. A B C D E
56. A B C D E
57. A B C D E
58. A B C D E
59. A B C D E
60. A B C D E
61. A B C D E
62. A B C D E
63. A B C D E
64. A B C D E
65. A B C D E
66. A B C D E
67. A B C D E
68. A B C D E
69. A B C D E
70. A B C D E
71. A B C D E
72. A B C D E
73. A B C D E
74. A B C D E
75. A B C D E
76. A B C D E
77. A B C D E
78. A B C D E
79. A B C D E
80. A B C D E
81. A B C D E
82. A B C D E
83. A B C D E
84. A B C D E
85. A B C D E

Section III — Verbal Aptitude

86. A B C D E
87. A B C D E
88. A B C D E
89. A B C D E
90. A B C D E
91. A B C D E
92. A B C D E
93. A B C D E
94. A B C D E
95. A B C D E
96. A B C D E
97. A B C D E
98. A B C D E
99. A B C D E
100. A B C D E
101. A B C D E
102. A B C D E
103. A B C D E
104. A B C D E
105. A B C D E
106. A B C D E
107. A B C D E
108. A B C D E
109. A B C D E
110. A B C D E
111. A B C D E
112. A B C D E
113. A B C D E
114. A B C D E
115. A B C D E
116. A B C D E
117. A B C D E
118. A B C D E
119. A B C D E
120. A B C D E
121. A B C D E
122. A B C D E
123. A B C D E
124. A B C D E
125. A B C D E

Section IV — Data Sufficiency

126. A B C D E
127. A B C D E
128. A B C D E
129. A B C D E
130. A B C D E
131. A B C D E
132. A B C D E
133. A B C D E
134. A B C D E
135. A B C D E
136. A B C D E
137. A B C D E
138. A B C D E
139. A B C D E
140. A B C D E

Section V — Business Judgment

141. A B C D E
142. A B C D E
143. A B C D E
144. A B C D E
145. A B C D E
146. A B C D E
147. A B C D E
148. A B C D E
149. A B C D E
150. A B C D E
151. A B C D E
152. A B C D E
153. A B C D E
154. A B C D E
155. A B C D E
156. A B C D E
157. A B C D E
158. A B C D E
159. A B C D E
160. A B C D E

Section VI — Mathematics

161. A B C D E
162. A B C D E
163. A B C D E
164. A B C D E
165. A B C D E
166. A B C D E
167. A B C D E
168. A B C D E
169. A B C D E
170. A B C D E
171. A B C D E
172. A B C D E
173. A B C D E
174. A B C D E
175. A B C D E
176. A B C D E
177. A B C D E
178. A B C D E
179. A B C D E
180. A B C D E
181. A B C D E
182. A B C D E
183. A B C D E
184. A B C D E
185. A B C D E

Sample Test 5

Section I Reading Recall

TOTAL TIME: 35 minutes

Part A: TIME—15 minutes

DIRECTIONS: This part contains three reading passages. You are to read each one carefully. You will have fifteen minutes to study the three passages and twenty minutes to answer questions based on them. When answering the questions, you will *not* be allowed to refer back to the passages.

Passage 1:

The United States economy made progress in reducing unemployment and moderating inflation. On the international side, this year was much calmer than last. Nevertheless, continuing imbalances in the pattern of world trade contributed to intermittent strains in the foreign exchange markets. These strains intensified to crisis proportions, precipitating a further devaluation of the dollar.

The domestic economy expanded in a remarkably vigorous and steady fashion. After a few lingering doubts about the strength of consumer demand in the opening weeks, the vitality of the expansion never came again into serious question. The resurgence in consumer confidence was reflected in the higher proportion of incomes spent for goods and services and the marked increase in consumer willingness to take on installment debt. A parallel strengthening in business psychology was manifested in a stepped-up rate of plant and equipment spending and a gradual pickup in outlays for inventory. Confidence in the economy was also reflected in the strength of the stock market and in the stability of the bond market, where rates showed little net change over the year as a whole despite the vigorous economic upturn. On several occasions during the year, the financial markets responded to shifting appraisals of the outlook for peace in Vietnam. For the year as a whole, consumer and business sentiment benefited from rising public expectations that a resolution of the conflict was in prospect and that East-West tensions were easing.

The underpinnings of the business expansion were to be found in part in the stimulative monetary and fiscal policies that had been pursued. Moreover, the restoration of sounder liquidity positions and tighter management control of production efficiency had also helped lay the groundwork for a strong expansion. In addition, the economic policy moves made by the President had served to renew optimism on the business outlook while boosting hopes that inflation would be brought under more effective control. Finally, of course, the economy was able to grow as vigorously as it did because sufficient leeway existed in terms of idle men and machines.

The United States balance of payments deficit declined sharply. Nevertheless, by any other test, the deficit remained very large, and there was actually a substantial deterioration in our trade account to a sizable deficit, almost two thirds of which was with Japan. It was to be expected that the immediate effect of devaluation would be a worsening in our trade accounts, with the benefits coming only later. While the overall trade performance proved disappointing, there are still good reasons for expecting the delayed impact of devaluation to produce in time a significant strengthening in our trade picture. Given the size of the Japanese component of our trade deficit, however, the outcome will depend importantly on the extent of the corrective measures undertaken by Japan. Also important will be our own efforts in the United States to fashion internal policies consistent with an improvement in our external balance.

The underlying task of public policy for the year ahead—and indeed for the longer run—remained a familiar one: to strike the right balance between encouraging healthy economic growth and avoiding inflationary pressures. With the economy showing sustained and vigorous growth, and with the currency crisis highlighting the need to improve our competitive posture internationally, the emphasis seemed to be shifting to the problem of inflation. The Phase Three program of wage and price restraint can contribute to dampening inflation. Unless productivity growth is unexpectedly large, however, the expansion of real output must eventually begin to slow down to the economy's larger run growth potential if generalized demand pressures on prices are to be avoided. Indeed, while the unemployment rates of a bit over five percent were still too high, it seems doubtful whether the much lower rates of four percent and below often cited as appropriate definitions of full employment do in fact represent feasible goals for the United States economy—unless there are improvements in the structure of labor and product markets and public policies influencing their operation. There is little doubt that overall unemployment rates can be brought down to four percent or less, for a time at least, by sufficient stimulation of aggregate demand. However, the resultant inflationary pressures have in the past proved exceedingly difficult to contain. After a point, moreover, it is questionable just how much, if any, additional reduction in unemployment can be permanently "bought" by accepting a stepped-up rate of inflation.

Passage 2:

These huge waves wreak terrific damage when they crash on the shores of distant lands or continents. Under a perfectly sunny sky and from an apparently calm sea, a wall of water may break twenty or thirty feet high over beaches and waterfronts, crushing houses and drowning unsuspecting residents and bathers in its path.

How are these waves formed? When a submarine earthquake occurs, it is likely to set up a tremendous amount of shock, disturbing the quiet waters of the deep ocean. This disturbance travels to the surface and forms a huge swell in the ocean many miles across. It rolls outward in all directions, and the water lowers in the center as another swell looms up. Thus, a series of concentric swells are formed similar to those made when a coin or small pebble is dropped into a basin of water. The big difference is in the size. Each of the concentric rings of basin water traveling out toward the edge is only about an inch across and less than a quarter of an inch high. The swells in the ocean are sometimes nearly a mile wide and rise to several multiples of ten feet in height.

Many of us have heard about these waves, often referred to by their Japanese name of "tsunami." For ages they have been dreaded in the Pacific, as no shore has been free from them. An underwater earthquake in the Aleutian Islands could start a swell that would break along the shores and cause severe damage in the southern part of Chile in South America. These waves travel hundreds of miles an hour, and one can understand how they would crash as violent breakers when caused to drag in the shallow waters of a coast.

Nothing was done about tsunamis until after World War II. In 1947 a particularly bad submarine earthquake took place south of the Aleutian Islands. A few hours later, people bathing in the sun along the quiet shores of Hawaii were dashed to death and shore-line property became a mass of shambles because a series of monstrous, breaking swells crashed along the shore and drove far inland. Hundreds of lives were lost in this catastrophe, and millions upon millions of dollars' worth of damage was done.

Hawaii (at that time a territory) and other Pacific areas then asked the U.S. Coast and Geodetic Survey to attempt to forecast these killer waves. With the blessing of the government, the Coast and Geodetic Survey initiated a program in 1948 known as the Seismic Seawave Warning System, using the earthquake-monitoring facilities of the agency, together with the world seismological data center, to locate submarine earthquakes as soon as they might occur. With this information they could then tell how severe a submarine earthquake was and could set up a tracking chart, with the center over the area of the earthquake, which would show by concentric time belts the rate of travel of the resulting wave. This system would indicate when and where, along the shores of the Pacific, the swells caused by the submarine earthquakes would strike.

Passage 3:

It is indisputable that in order to fulfill its many functions, water should be clean and biologically valuable. The costs connected with the provision of biologically valuable water for food production with the maintenance of sufficiently clean water, therefore, are primarily production costs. Purely "environmental" costs seem to be in this respect only costs connected with the safeguarding of cultural, recreational and sports functions which the water courses and reservoirs fulfill both in nature and in human settlements.

The problems of the atmosphere resemble those of water only partly. So far, the supply of air has not been deficient as was the case for water, and the dimensions of the air-shed are so vast that a number of people still hold the opinion that air need not be economized. However, scientific forecasts have shown that the time may be already approaching when clear and biologically valuable air will become problem No. 1.

Air being ubiquitous, people are particularly sensitive towards any reduction in the quality of the atmosphere, the increased contents of dust and gaseous exhalations, and particularly towards the presence of odors. The demand for purity of atmosphere, therefore, emanates much more from the population itself than from the specific sectors of the national economy affected by a polluted or even biologically aggressive atmosphere.

The households' share in atmospheric pollution is far bigger than that of industry which, in turn, further complicates the economic problems of atmospheric purity. Some countries have already collected positive experience with the reconstruction of whole urban sectors on the basis of new heating appliances based on the combustion of solid fossil fuels; estimates of the economic consequences of such measures have also been put forward.

In contrast to water where the maintenance of purity would seem primarily to be related to the costs of production and transport, a far higher proportion of the costs of maintaining the purity of the atmosphere derive from environmental considerations. Industrial sources of gaseous and dust emissions are well known and classified; their location can be accurately identified which makes them controllable. With the exception, perhaps, of the elimination of sulphur dioxide, technical means and technological processes exist which can be used for the elimination of all excessive impurities of the air from the various emissions.

Atmospheric pollution caused by the private property of individuals (their dwellings, automobiles, etc.) is difficult to control. Some sources such as motor vehicles are very mobile, and they are thus capable of polluting vast territories. In this particular case, the cost of anti-pollution measures will have to be borne, to a considerable extent, by individuals, whether in the form of direct costs or indirectly in the form of taxes, dues, surcharges, etc.

The problem of noise is a typical example of an environmental problem which cannot be solved passively, i.e., merely by protective measures, but will require the adoption of active measures, i.e., direct interventions at the source. The costs of a complete protection against noise are so prohibitive as to make it unthinkable even in the economically most developed countries. At the same time it would not seem feasible, either economically or politically, to force the population to carry the costs of individual protection against noise, for example, by reinforcing the sound insulation of their homes. A solution of this problem probably cannot be found in the near future.

If there is still time remaining, review the passages until all 15 minutes have elapsed.
Do not look at Part B until that time.

Part B: TIME—20 minutes

DIRECTIONS: Answer the following questions pertaining to information contained in the three passages you have just read. You may not turn back to those passages for assistance.

QUESTIONS TO

Passage 1:

1. The passage was most likely published in a

(A) popular magazine
(B) general newspaper
(C) science journal
(D) financial journal
(E) textbook

2. The passage deals with the economy of

(A) Japan
(B) Europe
(C) North America
(D) the United States
(E) New York State

3. Confidence in the economy was expressed by all of the following except

(A) a strong stock market
(B) a stable bond market
(C) increased installment debt
(D) increased plant and equipment expenditures
(E) rising interest rates

4. Public confidence in the economy resulted in part from which of the following occurrences?

   I. Possible peace in Vietnam
   II. Reduction in East-West tensions
   III. An entente with China

   (A) I only
   (B) III only
   (C) I and II only
   (D) II and III only
   (E) I, II, and III

5. Business expansion for the period under review was caused by

   (A) stimulative monetary and fiscal policies
   (B) rising interest rates
   (C) increased foreign trade
   (D) price and wage controls
   (E) Phase I

6. Most of the trade deficit in the balance of payments was attributed to which country?

   (A) United Kingdom
   (B) Japan
   (C) Germany
   (D) France
   (E) South America

7. Part of the public policy task—as outlined in the passage—is to

   (A) cut consumer spending
   (B) prevent balance of payments deficits
   (C) devalue the dollar
   (D) avoid inflationary pressures
   (E) increase the balance of trade

8. The Phase Three program contained

   (A) higher income taxes
   (B) reduced government spending
   (C) devaluation of the dollar
   (D) productivity measures
   (E) wage and price controls

9. The passage implies that the unemployment rate

   (A) cannot be reduced
   (B) can be reduced to below 4 percent
   (C) can be reduced to below 5 percent
   (D) can be reduced to below 6 percent
   (E) may or may not be reduced

10. The passage states that the unemployment rate at the time the article was written was

   (A) 6 percent
   (B) a little over 5 percent
   (C) 5 percent
   (D) a little over 4 percent
   (E) 4 percent

QUESTIONS TO

Passage 2:

11. The main subject of the passage is

(A) the Japanese
(B) Hawaii
(C) waves
(D) underwater earthquakes
(E) early warning systems

12. The waves discussed in the passage usually occur during

(A) stormy weather
(B) clear weather
(C) cold temperatures
(D) deep swells
(E) the night

13. The waves discussed in the passage are referred to as

I. Tsunami
II. Killer waves
III. Submarines

(A) I only
(B) III only
(C) I and II only
(D) II and III only
(E) I, II, and III

14. It is believed that the waves are caused by

(A) seismatic conditions
(B) concentric time belts
(C) atmospheric conditions
(D) underwater earthquakes
(E) storms

15. The width of the waves is often

(A) five feet
(B) ten feet
(C) one mile
(D) 5 miles
(E) more than thirty feet

16. The U.S. Coast and Geodetic Survey set up a program to

I. Prevent submarine earthquakes
II. Locate submarine earthquakes
III. Determine the severity of submarine earthquakes

(A) I only
(B) III only
(C) I and II only
(D) II and III only
(E) I, II, and III

17. Nothing was done about the waves until

(A) death occurred
(B) after World War I
(C) a solution was found
(D) millions of dollars worth of damage was incurred in Hawaii
(E) 1937

18. The movement of the waves has been tracked at

(A) 30 miles an hour
(B) 40 miles an hour
(C) 50 miles an hour
(D) 100 miles an hour
(E) more than a hundred miles an hour

19. According to the passage, the waves occurred in the area of the

(A) Eastern U.S. seaboard
(B) Pacific
(C) Argentina
(D) Western Europe
(E) Asia

20. Given present wave-tracking systems, scientists can forecast all of the following except

(A) the severity of underwater earthquakes
(B) the wave's rate of travel
(C) when a wave will strike
(D) where a wave will strike
(E) the height of the wave

QUESTIONS TO

Passage 3:

21. The passage discusses which of the following environmental areas?

I. Noise
II. Water
III. Air

(A) I only
(B) III only
(C) I and II only
(D) II and III only
(E) I, II, and III

22. According to the passage, problems of the atmosphere resemble those of water

(A) completely
(B) only partly
(C) only in certain countries
(D) only where pollution occurs
(E) in developing countries

23. Scientific forecasts have shown that clear and biologically valuable air may soon become

(A) extant
(B) extinct
(C) problem No. 1
(D) cheaper to produce
(E) economically feasible

24. According to the passage, which of the following contributes most to atmospheric pollution?

(A) industry
(B) production
(C) households
(D) mining
(E) waste disposal

25. The maintenance of pure water is determined by

I. Production costs
II. Transport costs
III. Research costs

(A) I only
(B) III only
(C) I and II only
(D) II and III only
(E) I, II, and III

26. New heating appliances were developed to prevent damage to the

(A) atmosphere
(B) environment
(C) water supply
(D) power supply
(E) economy

27. According to the passage, atmospheric pollution caused by private property is

(A) easy to control
(B) impossible to control
(C) difficult to control
(D) decreasing
(E) negligible

28. The problem of noise can be solved through

I. Active measures
II. Passive measures
III. Tax levies

(A) I only
(B) III only
(C) I and II only
(D) II and III only
(E) I, II, and III

29. According to the passage, the costs of some anti-pollution measures will have to be borne by individuals because

(A) individuals partly cause pollution
(B) governments do not have adequate resources
(C) industry is not willing to bear their share
(D) individuals are more easily taxed than producers
(E) individuals demand production which causes pollution

30. Complete protection against noise

(A) may be forthcoming in the near future
(B) is impossible to achieve
(C) may have prohibitive costs
(D) is possible only in developed countries
(E) has been achieved in some countries

If there is still time remaining, you may review the questions in this section only. You may not look at Part A or turn to any other section of the test.

Section II Mathematics

TIME: 75 minutes

DIRECTIONS: Solve each of the following problems; then indicate the correct answer on the answer sheet. [On the actual test you will be permitted to use any space available on the examination paper for scratch work.]

NOTE: A figure that appears with a problem is drawn as accurately as possible so as to provide information that may help in answering the question. Numbers in this test are real numbers.

31. A trip takes 6 hours to complete. After traveling $\frac{1}{4}$ of an hour, $1\frac{3}{8}$ hours, and $2\frac{1}{3}$ hours, how much time is necessary to complete the trip?

(A) $2\frac{1}{12}$ hours
(B) 2 hours, $2\frac{1}{2}$ minutes
(C) 2 hours, 5 minutes
(D) $2\frac{1}{8}$ hours
(E) 2 hours, $7\frac{1}{2}$ minutes

32. If a stock average was 500 points at the beginning of a week and 400 points at the end of the same week, by what percent has it decreased during the week?

(A) 20
(B) 22
(C) 25
(D) 27
(E) 30

Use the following graph for questions 33–36.

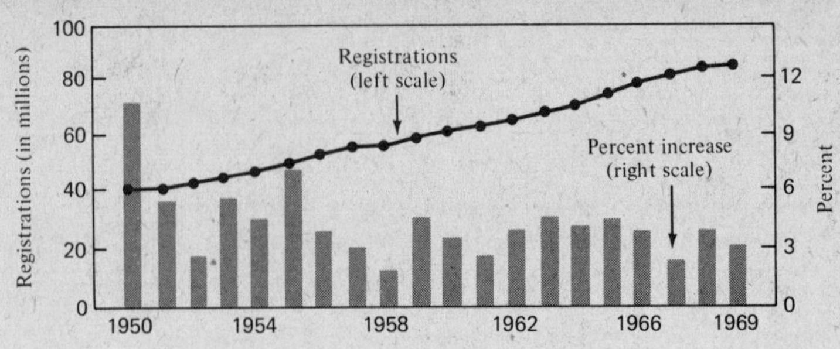

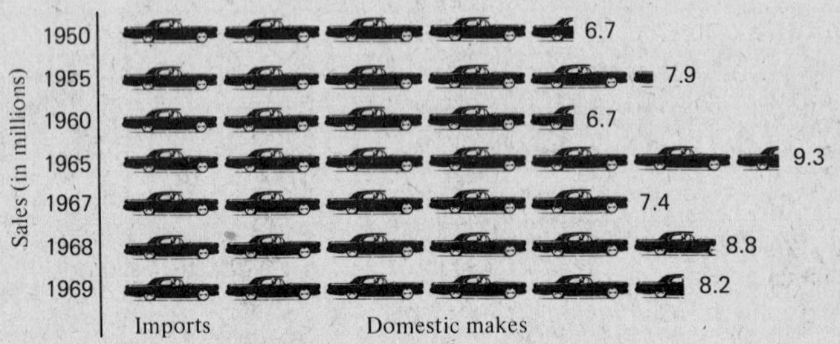

33. Of the years shown, the year which showed the greatest percent increase in passenger car registrations was

(A) 1950
(B) 1955
(C) 1965
(D) 1968
(E) 1969

34. In the pictograph representing new car sales, one car represents sales of about

(A) 1 million
(B) 1.5 million
(C) 2 million
(D) 2.5 million
(E) 3 million

35. In 1950, there were about x million passenger cars registered, where x equals

(A) 7
(B) 20
(C) 40
(D) 60
(E) 70

36. Which of the following statements about passenger car registrations and new car sales can be inferred from the graphs?

I. In 1955, the increase in passenger car registration was greater than 40%.
II. Between 1950 and 1969, the number of passenger cars registered roughly doubled.
III. In each year between 1950 and 1969, at least 5 million new cars were sold.

(A) I only
(B) II only
(C) III only
(D) I and II only
(E) I, II, and III

37. A car wash can wash 8 cars in 18 minutes. At this rate, how many cars can the car wash wash in 3 hours?

(A) 13
(B) 40.5
(C) 80
(D) 125
(E) 405

38. If the ratio of the areas of 2 squares is 2:1, then the ratio of the perimeters of the squares is

(A) 1:2
(B) $1:\sqrt{2}$
(C) $\sqrt{2}:1$
(D) 2:1
(E) 4:1

Use the following table for questions 39–41.

Life insurance in force in the United States by type and geographic division

Amount in 1972
(000,000 Omitted)

Division	Ordinary	Group	Industrial	Credit	Total
New England	$ 53,174	$ 38,159	$ 1,309	$ 5,849	$ 98,491
Middle Atlantic	167,331	131,721	5,820	16,233	321,105
East North Central	175,636	139,388	7,274	21,453	343,751
West North Central	71,614	43,087	1,489	8,859	125,049
South Atlantic	119,431	90,520	11,990	19,126	241,067
East South Central	41,552	30,940	5,166	7,913	85,571
West South Central	75,470	48,904	4,697	11,917	140,988
Mountain	35,529	21,419	524	4,960	62,432
Pacific	108,806	86,562	1,706	12,457	209,531
United States	$848,543	$630,700	$39,975	$108,767	$1,627,985

Percent change 1962–1972

Division	Ordinary	Group	Industrial	Credit	Total
New England	+104.7%	+195.7%	−48.4%	+176.9%	+126.3%
Middle Atlantic	+ 82.8	+169.3	−25.7	+163.1	+107.9
East North Central	+110.9	+194.1	− 8.8	+202.0	+135.8
West North Central	+118.6	+226.5	−15.7	+177.6	+145.6
South Atlantic	+158.6	+251.8	+29.1	+220.7	+176.6
East South Central	+151.9	+240.7	+31.7	+213.5	+167.2
West South Central	+141.6	+235.1	+22.9	+209.1	+163.5
Mountain	+140.4	+235.9	− 0.8	+185.9	+166.6
Pacific	+132.0	+179.3	−13.0	+132.6	+145.9
United States	+118.1%	+201.5%	+ 0.9%	+186.1%	+140.8%

Source: Institute of Life Insurance

39. The ratio of the amount of credit life insurance to the amount of ordinary life insurance in the Pacific region in 1972 was about

(A) 1 to 10
(B) 1 to 9
(C) 1 to 8
(D) 1 to 1
(E) 8 to 1

40. The region which had the largest amount of industrial life insurance in 1972 was

(A) Middle Atlantic
(B) East North Central
(C) South Atlantic
(D) East South Central
(E) Pacific

41. How many of the categories of life insurance shown had a greater percentage increase from 1962 to 1972 than the percent change in total life insurance from 1962 to 1972?

(A) 0
(B) 1
(C) 2
(D) 3
(E) 4

42. In Leesville, 70% of the cars have whitewall tires and 25% of the cars are air-conditioned. If 20% of the cars are air-conditioned and have whitewall tires, what percentage of the cars have neither air-conditioning nor whitewall tires?

(A) 5
(B) 10
(C) 15
(D) 20
(E) 25

43. A company issued 100,000 shares of stock. In 1970, each share of stock was worth $122.50. In 1973, each share of the stock was worth $111.10. How much less were the 100,000 shares worth in 1973 than in 1970?

(A) $114,000
(B) $1,100,040
(C) $1,140,000
(D) $114,000,000
(E) $1,140,000,000

44. A worker's daily salary varies each day. In one week he worked five days. His daily salaries were $51.90, $52.20, $49.80, $51.50, and $50.60. What was his average daily wage for the week?

(A) $50.80
(B) $51.20
(C) $51.50
(D) $51.60
(E) $255.00

Questions 45 and 46 refer to the graph on page

45. The ratio of deaths from heart disease to deaths from cancer in 1969 was about

(A) 2 to 3
(B) 3 to 2
(C) 2 to 1
(D) 9 to 4
(E) 3 to 1

46. The number of people who died in all accidents in 1969 was roughly

(A) 56,000
(B) 100,000
(C) 112,000
(D) 125,000
(E) 560,000

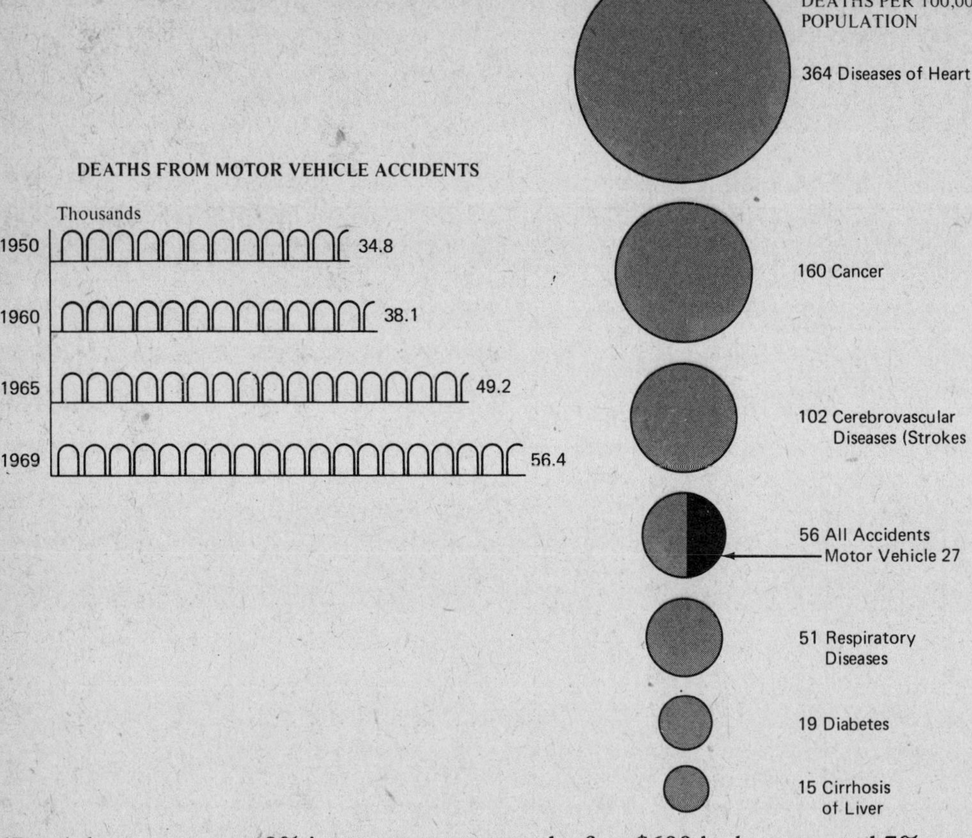

47. A borrower pays 8% interest per year on the first \$600 he borrows and 7% per year on the part of the loan in excess of \$600. How much interest will the borrower pay on a loan of \$6,000 for 1 year?

(A) \$378
(B) \$420
(C) \$426
(D) \$436
(E) \$480

48. If $3x - 2y = 8$, then $4y - 6x$ is:

(A) −16
(B) −8
(C) 8
(D) 16
(E) none of these

Questions 49–51 refer to the table on page 000.

49. Which country among those shown had the third largest length of railroad?

(A) Argentina
(B) Brazil
(C) Canada
(D) Mexico
(E) United States

50. Which country had the most kilometers per area of railroad track?

(A) Argentina
(B) Canada
(C) Cuba
(D) Jamaica
(E) Peru

51. Between 1953 and 1965, passenger kilometers in Paraguay

(A) decreased by about 70%
(B) decreased by about 40%
(C) decreased by about 20%
(D) increased by about 20%
(E) increased by about 40%

Railroads: Length, Passengers, and Freight

	Year	Length (kilometers)	Length (miles)	Km. per area (1000 km.)	Km. per 1000 persons	Passenger kilometers (millions)	
						1953	1965
MEXICO	1968	19 749	12 271	10.04	0.42	2 987	3 882
COSTA RICA	1967	951	600	18.65	0.60	51	[7]–
EL SALVADOR	1966	513	318	24.43	0.17	–	–
GUATEMALA	1965	958	595	8.79	0.22	[0]–	–
HONDURAS	1967	1 005	624	8.10	0.43	–	–
NICARAGUA	1964	403	250	2.90	0.25	118	51
PANAMA	1966	650	403	8.55	0.51	–	–
Total, Central America		4 480	2 790	–	–	–	–
BARBADOS		–	–	–	–	–	–
CUBA	1963	5 122	3 233	44.54	0.71	–	822
DOMINICAN REPUBLIC	1966	560	347	11.67	0.15	–	–
HAITI	1964	254	157	9.07	0.06	–	–
JAMAICA	1967	330	205	30.00	0.18	43	54
TRINIDAD and TOBAGO	1967	13	8	2.54	0.01	–	–
Total, Caribbean		–	–	–	–	–	–
ARGENTINA	1965	40 180	24 966	14.47	1.78	13 564	12 829
BOLIVIA	1968	3 524	2 189	3.21	0.75	–	220
BRAZIL	1968	32 054	19 917	3.77	0.36	11 593	16 684
CHILE	1967	10 136	6 298	13.39	1.11	1 789	2 411
COLOMBIA	1966	3 435	2 134	3.02	0.18	668	513
ECUADOR	1964	1 154	717	4.26	0.23	106	52
GUYANA	1968	127	78	0.59	0.18	–	75
PARAGUAY	1969	441	274	1.08	0.19	60	35
PERU	1966	2 620	1 628	2.05	0.22	282	236
URUGUAY	1966	2 762	1 716	14.77	1.00	–	–
VENEZUELA	1964	484	300	0.54	0.06	21	44
Total, South America		96 917	60 217	–	–	–	–
Total, REPUBLICS		–	–	–	–	–	–
Comparison							
Canada	1967	69 472	43 168	7.53	3.40	4 805	4 287
UNITED STATES	1967	336 823	209 292	35.97	1.69	50 983	28 090

SOURCES:

PAU, IASI, *America en Cifras 1970*, Tables 333–01 and 333–03.
U.N., *Statistical Yearbook 1970*, Table 147.
University of California, *Cuba 1968: Supplement to the Statistical Abstract of Latin America*, Table 66.

Source: Statistical Abstract of Latin America 1970

52. It costs 10¢ a mile to fly and 12¢ a mile to drive. If you travel 200 miles, flying x miles of the distance and driving the rest, then the cost of the trip in dollars is

(A) 20
(B) 24
(C) $24 - 2x$
(D) $24 - .02x$
(E) $2400 - 2x$

53. If two identical rectangles R_1 and R_2 form a square when placed next to each other, and the length of R_1 is x times the width of R_1, then x is

(A) 1
(B) $\frac{3}{2}$
(C) $\frac{5}{4}$
(D) 2
(E) 3

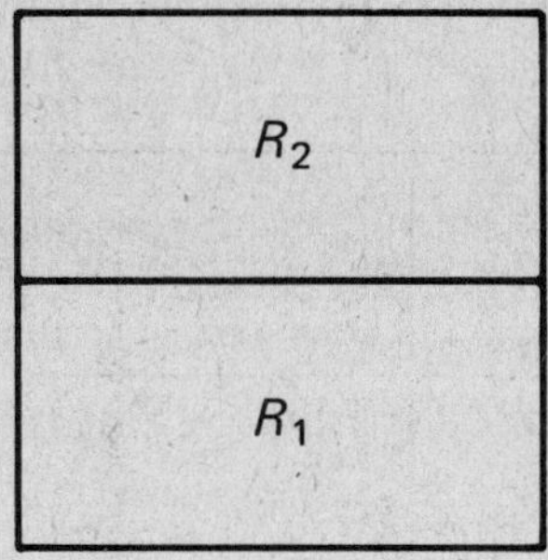

54. If the area of a square increases by 69%, then the side of the square increases by

(A) 13%
(B) 30%
(C) 39%
(D) 69%
(E) 130%

Use the following graph for questions 55–57.

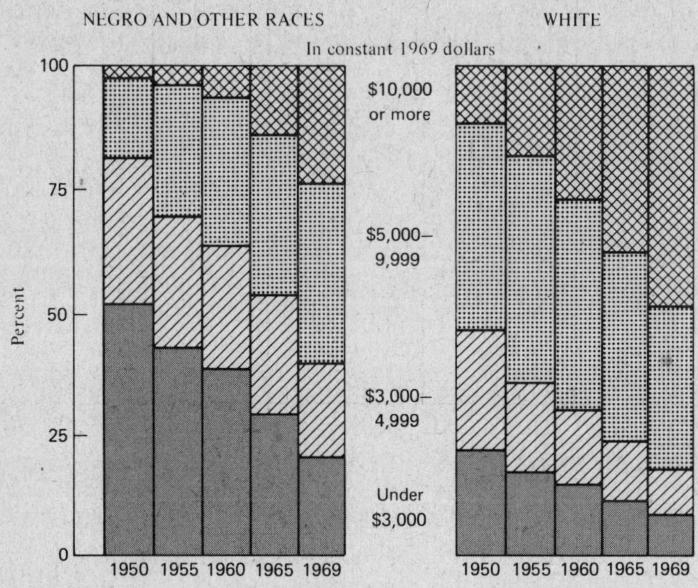

55. Which of the following income groups contained the largest number of white families in 1950?

(A) under \$3,000
(B) \$3,000–4,999
(C) \$5,000–9,999
(D) \$10,000–19,999
(E) \$20,000 or more

56. In 1969, the ratio of the number of white families with income of more than $5,000 to the number of white families with income of less than $5,000 was about

(A) 1 to 2
(B) 1 to 1
(C) 2 to 1
(D) 3 to 1
(E) 4 to 1

57. Which of the following statements can be inferred from the graphs?

I. There were more white families than Negro families in 1965.
II. Between 1950 and 1969, the percentage of families in the category "Negro and other races" with income under $3,000 decreased by more than 50%.
III. The average income of a white family in 1969 was more than $3,000.

(A) only I
(B) only II
(C) only I and III
(D) only II and III
(E) I, II, and III

58. A used car dealer sells a car for $1,380 and makes a 20% profit. How much did the car cost the dealer?

(A) $1,100
(B) $1,120
(C) $1,150
(D) $1,180
(E) $1,560

59. If $x < z$ and $x < y$, which of the following statements are always true?

I. $y < z$
II. $x < yz$
III. $x < y + z$

(A) only I
(B) only II
(C) only III
(D) II and III only
(E) I, II, and III

Use the following table for questions 60–62.

Distribution of Work Hours in a Factory

Numbers of Workers		*Number of Hours Worked*
20		45–50
15		40–44
25		35–39
16		30–34
4		0–29
80	TOTAL	3100

60. What percentage worked 40 or more hours?

(A) 18.75
(B) 25
(C) $33\frac{1}{3}$
(D) 40
(E) 43.75

61. The number of workers who worked from 40 to 44 hours is x times the number who worked up to 29 hours, where x is

(A) $\frac{15}{16}$
(B) $3\frac{3}{4}$
(C) 4
(D) 5
(E) $6\frac{1}{4}$

62. Which of the following statements can be inferred from the table?

I. The average number of hours worked per worker is less than 40.
II. At least 3 worked more than 48 hours.
III. More than half of all the workers worked more than 40 hours.

(A) I only
(B) II only
(C) I and II only
(D) I and III only
(E) I, II, and III

63. A truck traveling at 70 miles per hour uses 30% more gasoline to travel a certain distance than it does when it travels at 50 miles per hour. If the truck can travel 19.5 miles on a gallon of gasoline at 50 miles per hour, how far can the truck travel on 10 gallons of gasoline at a speed of 70 miles per hour?

(A) 130
(B) 140
(C) 150
(D) 175
(E) 195

64. $\frac{2}{5}+\frac{1}{3}=\frac{x}{30}$, where x is

(A) 4
(B) 7
(C) 11
(D) 16
(E) 22

65. How many squares with sides $\frac{1}{2}$ inch long are needed to cover a rectangle which is 4 feet long and 6 feet wide?

(A) 24
(B) 96
(C) 3,456
(D) 13,824
(E) 14,266

Use the following graph for questions 66–69.

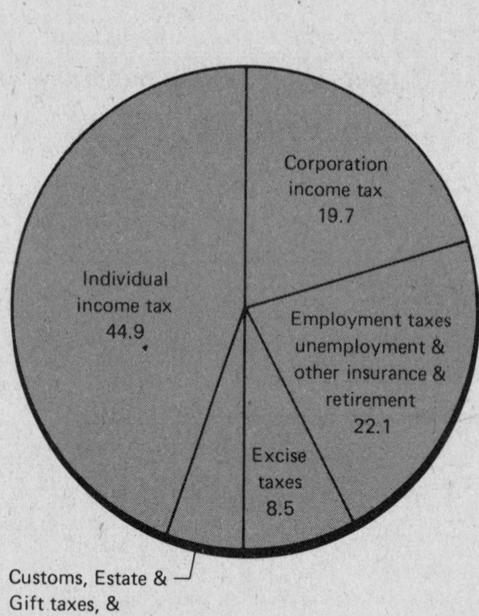

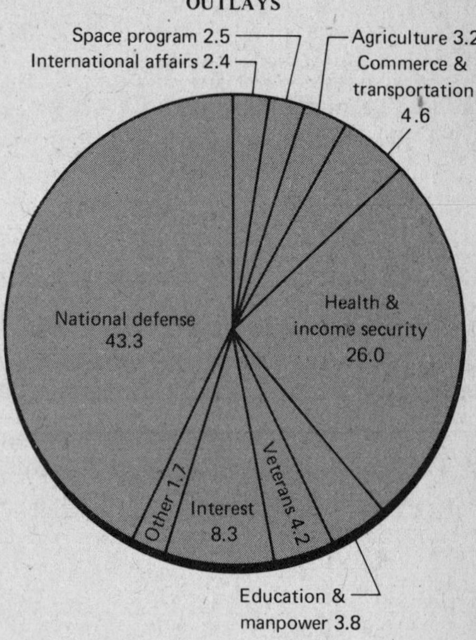

66. If the annual average receipts from the corporation income tax during the years 1967–1970 equal x, then the average annual receipts during this period were about

(A) $\frac{x}{4}$
(B) x^2
(C) $3x$
(D) $5x$
(E) x^5

67. The average annual combined outlay for veterans, education and manpower, and health and income security was roughly what fraction of the average annual outlays?

(A) $\frac{1}{4}$
(B) $\frac{1}{3}$
(C) $\frac{2}{5}$
(D) $\frac{1}{2}$
(E) $\frac{2}{3}$

68. What category received the second smallest average annual outlay during 1967–1970?

(A) excise taxes
(B) other
(C) veterans
(D) space program
(E) international affairs

69. If $\frac{5}{8}$ of the average annual outlays for agriculture was spent in the western U.S., what percentage of average annual outlays was spent on agriculture in the western U.S.?

(A) $\frac{5}{8}$
(B) 1
(C) $1\frac{1}{4}$
(D) 2
(E) 3.2

70. The next number in the geometric progression 5,10,20 . . . is

(A) 25
(B) 30
(C) 35
(D) 40
(E) 50

71. Eggs cost 8¢ each. If the price of eggs increases by $\frac{1}{8}$, how much will a dozen eggs cost?

(A) 90¢
(B) $1.08
(C) $1.10
(D) $1.12
(E) $1.18

72. A trapezoid *ABCD* is formed by adding the isosceles right triangle *BCE* with base 5 inches to the rectangle *ABED* where *DE* is t inches. What is the area of the trapezoid in square inches?

(A) $5t + 12.5$
(B) $5t + 25$
(C) $2.5t + 12.5$
(D) $(t + 5)^2$
(E) $t^2 + 25$

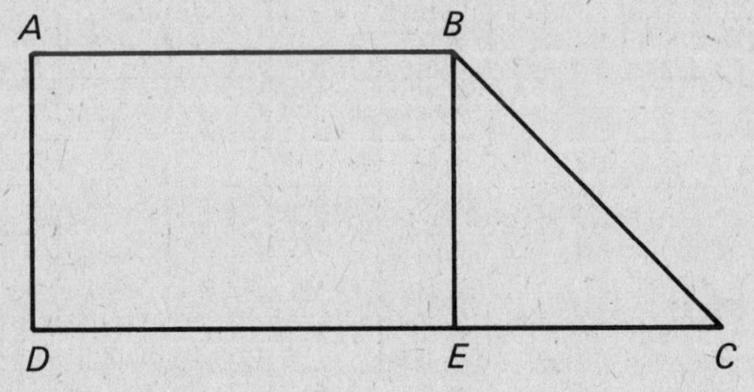

A B
D E C

73. A manufacturer of jam wants to make a profit of $75 when he sells 300 jars of jam. It costs 65¢ each to make the first 100 jars of jam and 55¢ each to make each jar after the first 100. What price should he charge for the 300 jars of jam?

(A) $75
(B) $175
(C) $225
(D) $240
(E) $250

Use the following table for questions 74–77.

Prices of major trade commodities: 1962–1971

Commodity	Unit of measure	Country	Percent of world exports	1962	1966	1967	1968	1969	1970	1971
BEEF (Frozen)	100 pounds	Argentina	46	16.08	25.57	20.82	28.02	25.26	33.06	39.27
(Corned)	100 pounds	Argentina		32.86	38.90	40.17	41.42	39.75	39.27	39.99
(Frozen)	100 pounds	Uruguay	5	16.37	24.82	23.72	22.59	22.14	25.07	31.25M
(Preserved)	100 pounds	Uruguay		33.99	31.25	36.93	41.58	39.91	34.90	–
CACAO	100 pounds	Brazil	7	19.54	20.45	23.56	27.58	40.61	29.42	–
COFFEE	100 pounds	Brazil	40	29.67	34.31	31.83	31.72	31.47	42.97	–
	100 pounds	Colombia	16	38.22	44.58	39.99	40.41	38.41	50.09	47.33M
	100 pounds	Guatemala	4	37.05	41.63	38.14	36.10	–	47.96	44.52
	100 pounds	El Salvador	4	32.90	41.85	36.63	35.69	35.56	46.12	44.97
COPPER	100 pounds	Canada	12	29.31	46.91	46.16	48.42	50.63	63.07	47.05
	100 pounds	Chile	29	29.36	42.54	–	–	–	–	–
COTTON	100 pounds	Brazil	5	23.65	21.35	21.75	23.97	19.99	–	–
	100 pounds	Mexico	9	23.24	23.44	24.08	24.46	24.02	26.25	–
	100 pounds	United States	29	28.33	25.11	24.82	25.62	24.17	25.52	26.91M
HIDES	100 pounds	Argentina	16	–	–	–	–	–	–	–
LEAD	100 pounds	Canada	8	7.14	11.77	10.15	10.32	11.71	10.05	10.73M
	100 pounds	Mexico	16	9.06	10.97	11.34	10.65	12.25	13.60	13.47Sa
	100 pounds	Peru	9	5.14	10.30	9.25	8.68	10.03	13.21	–
LINSEED OIL	100 pounds	Argentina	–	10.09	7.83	7.53	8.47	9.30	9.21	8.90F
	100 pounds	Uruguay	–	11.41	7.58	6.82	8.51	8.96	8.58	8.10F
NEWSPRINT	Short ton	Canada	47	114.60	114.90	118.60	122.80	127.00	131.5	134.3M
PETROLEUM	Barrel	Colombia	1	2.49	2.01	1.96	1.97	1.96	1.88	2.09M
	Barrel	United States	15	–	–	–	–	–	–	–
QUEBRACHO	100 pounds	Argentina	82	5.74	7.51	7.44	7.88	8.71	9.75	10.12F
	100 pounds	Paraguay	18	6.21	7.17	7.22	7.46	7.94	9.08	9.69M
SISAL	100 pounds	Haiti	1	8.00	6.91	5.13	5.20	5.75	–	–
SUGAR	100 pounds	Dominican Republic	8	5.03	5.82	5.73	6.16	6.37	6.65	5.90
TIN	100 pounds	Bolivia	15	112.20	161.20	150.80	142.60	155.10	164.40	158.0M
WHEAT	Bushel	Argentina	4	1.67	1.51	1.61	1.56	1.61	1.49	1.60F
	Bushel	Canada	28	1.87	1.84	1.96	1.87	1.78	1.67	1.79M
	Bushel	United States	48	1.81	1.69	1.74	1.68	1.64	1.58	1.72M
WOOL	100 pounds	Argentina	9	37.70	34.80	36.00	34.61	35.90	34.50	30.2F
ZINC	100 pounds	Canada	36	9.05	12.11	11.13	10.98	11.26	11.97	11.76M
	100 pounds	Mexico	19	9.20	11.43	11.52	10.86	10.91	12.04	–

SOURCES:

IMF, *International Financial Statistics*, Vol. 23, No. 12, December 1970, and Vol. 24, August 1971.

NOTES:

1. Data given in current U.S. dollars. Unit values are derived from trade statistics of countries listed and are not wholesale prices of the commodity.

Source: Statistical Abstract of Latin America 1970

74. For how many different commodities did the countries shown account for more than 50% of the world's exports between 1962 and 1971?

(A) 1
(B) 2
(C) 3
(D) 4
(E) 5

75. The price per barrel of petroleum paid to Colombia in 1970 was about what percentage of the price per barrel in 1962?

(A) 70%
(B) 75%
(C) 79%
(D) 81%
(E) 125%

76. For how many of the commodities was the price received in 1970 less than that in 1962 in at least one country?

(A) 1
(B) 2
(C) 3
(D) 4
(E) 5

77. Which commodity yielded the most income for each unit of measure in 1970?

(A) Canadian copper
(B) Canadian newsprint
(C) Bolivian tin
(D) Colombian coffee
(E) Mexican zinc

78. A roofer can finish a roof in 7 hours by himself. If he hires two assistants who each work $2/3$ as fast as he does, how long will it take the three of them together to finish a roof?

(A) 2 hrs.
(B) $2\frac{1}{3}$ hrs.
(C) 3 hrs.
(D) $3\frac{1}{2}$ hrs.
(E) $3\frac{2}{3}$ hrs.

79. If a stock average was 1000 at the end of Monday's trading and it declined by 10% each day, what was the average at the end of Thursday's trading?

(A) 700
(B) 720
(C) 724
(D) 729
(E) 730

Questions 80–82 refer to the graph on page 000.

80. In 1970 the total amount of funds used for research and development was roughly x times the amount used in 1957, where x is

(A) 50%
(B) 100%
(C) 150%
(D) 200%
(E) 250%

81. The total amount of research and development funds used first exceeded $15 billion in

(A) 1958
(B) 1959
(C) 1960
(D) 1961
(E) 1963

82. Which of the following statements can be inferred from the graph?

I. The amount of funds used for research and development increased every year between 1957 and 1970.
II. The amount of funds used for research and development more than doubled between 1958 and 1968.
III. Of the five categories shown, the most funds used have been for research and development performed by universities and funded by the federal government.

(A) I only
(B) II only
(C) I and II only
(D) II and III only
(E) I, II, and III

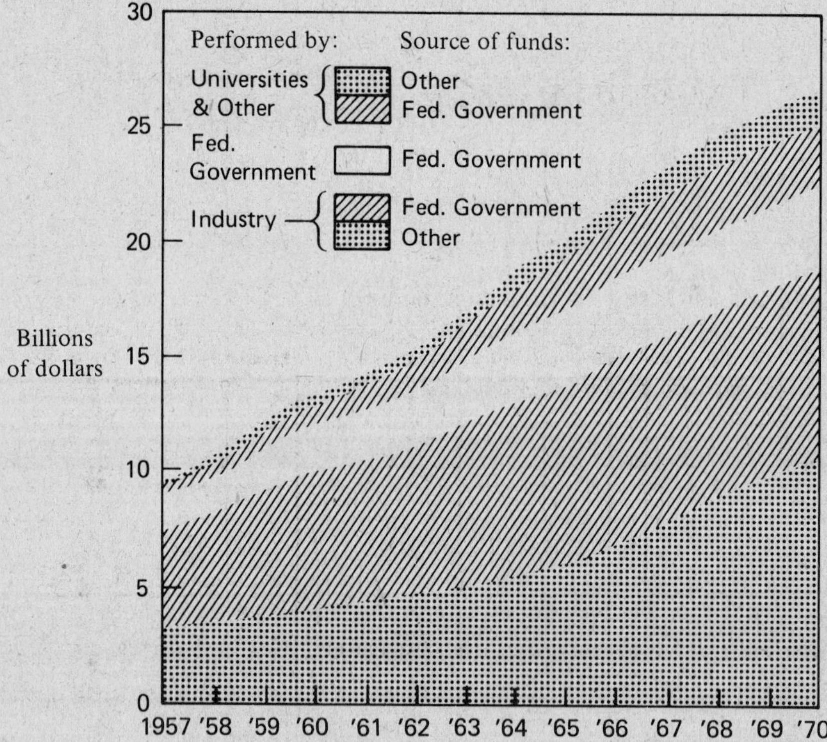

83. A farmer walks around the outside of a rectangular field at a constant speed. It takes him twice as long to walk the length of the field as it takes him to walk the width of the field. If he walked 300 yards when he walked around the field, what is the area of the field in square yards?

(A) 5,000
(B) 15,000
(C) 20,000
(D) 25,000
(E) 30,000

84. A company makes a profit of 7% selling goods which cost $2,000; it also makes a profit of 6% selling a machine which cost the company $5,000. How much total profit did the company make on both transactions?

(A) $300
(B) $400
(C) $420
(D) $440
(E) $490

85. If $\frac{x}{y} = \frac{3}{z}$, then $9y^2$ equals

(A) $\frac{x^2}{9}$
(B) x^3z
(C) x^2z^2
(D) $3x^2$
(E) $\left(\frac{1}{9}\right)x^2z^2$

If there is still time remaining, you may review the questions in this section only. You may not turn to any other section of the test.

Section III Verbal Aptitude

TIME: 20 minutes

Antonyms

DIRECTIONS: For each question below, select the lettered word or phrase that comes closest to being *opposite* in meaning to the word appearing in capital letters. Be sure to consider all meanings carefully.

86. SEDITIOUS: (A) incendiary (B) orderly (C) sedate (D) proper (E) quaint

87. REDOLENT: (A) enthusiastic (B) propitious (C) agreeable (D) fetid (E) unsure

88. PUERILE: (A) savory (B) aromatic (C) mature (D) sterile (E) weak

89. ABATE: (A) deter (B) proceed (C) deny (D) increase (E) animate

90. ACERBITY: (A) reluctance (B) weakness (C) lassitude (D) acidity (E) sweetness

91. ACTUATE: (A) dismiss (B) dissuade (C) demote (D) deny (E) denigrate

92. IRRESOLUTE: (A) resolved (B) determined (C) unsound (D) sensitive (E) defensible

93. FRACTIOUS: (A) delicate (B) solid (C) agreeable (D) liberal (E) wholesome

94. ADMONITION: (A) countenance (B) evasion (C) deposition (D) declaration (E) denial

95. ENMITY: (A) affection (B) security (C) approbation (D) ire (E) preponderance

96. ARTIFICE: (A) opening (B) skill (C) honesty (D) reality (E) cupidity

97. CONDUCE: (A) confide (B) direct (C) confirm (D) counteract (E) disprove

98. DEBILITY: (A) credibility (B) strength (C) waste (D) lucidity (E) simplicity

99. CONJURE: (A) propose (B) upset (C) deprecate (D) erect (E) consult

Word-Pair Relationships

DIRECTIONS: For each question below, determine the relationship between the pair of capitalized words and then select the lettered pair of words which have a similar relationship to the first pair.

100. AVIARY : ARBORETUM :: (A) animals : zoo (B) money : bank (C) letters : post office (D) dovecote : greenhouse (E) honey : beehive

101. CONVICT : PRISON :: (A) student : school (B) exile : banishment (C) juvenile delinquent : orphanage (D) prisoner : court (E) expectancy : closure

102. WATER : FLOOD :: (A) rain : river (B) wind : sleet (C) snow : blizzard (D) calm : severe (E) summer : winter

103. PENITENCE : OBDURACY :: (A) pensive : thoughtless (B) vacuous : empty (C) reward : award (D) happy : ecstatic (E) problem : solution

104. FORTITUDE : RESOLUTION :: (A) timidity : weakness (B) heroic : dastardly (C) medal : bravery (D) poem : poet (E) plan : execution

105. TAPE MEASURE : MEASUREMENT :: (A) scientist : observation (B) electricity : power (C) dictator : ruler (D) car : highway (E) hypothesis : theory

106. VOICE : AMPLIFIER :: (A) musician : instrument (B) wind : velocity (C) runner : distance (D) automobile : accelerator (E) shipment : expediter

107. PHLEGMATIC : ENERGETIC :: (A) perfidious : faithful (B) fissure : split (C) canvas : composition (D) forfeiture : confiscation (E) flagrant : atrocious

108. MURDER : GENOCIDE :: (A) accident : assault (B) attack : war (C) wind : tornado (D) stultify : invigorate (E) scanty : overdone

109. NEBULOUS : CLARIFICATION :: (A) trite : obscure (B) erroneous : emendation (C) abhor : hostile (D) accusation : investigation (E) break : accord

110. CLANDESTINE : SURREPTITIOUS :: (A) secret : subversive (B) annihilate : extirpate (C) plan : deviate (D) material : corporeal (E) subjugator : emancipator

111. AMALGAMATE : UNITED :: (A) conglomeration : assortment (B) organize : arranged (C) oscillate : display (D) dissipate : anticipated (E) trial : lawyer

112. EXORCISM : INCANTATION :: (A) confrontation : pandemonium (B) petition : candidate (C) devotion : prayer (D) neology : libation (E) incarcerate : cajole

Sentence Completions

DIRECTIONS: For each sentence below, select the lettered word or set of words which, when inserted in the sentence blanks, best complete the meaning of that sentence.

113. The ____ sources are so polluted that employees dare not ____ it.

(A) water . . . drink (B) air . . . imbibe (C) river . . . swim (D) energy . . . tap (E) atmospheric . . . test

114. The throbbing ____ of 20 ____ poured forth the music of Vivaldi, Mozart, and Bach.

(A) soliloquy . . . voices (B) singing . . . musicians (C) sonority . . . stringed instruments (D) hum . . . recorders (E) motion . . . horns

115. More ____ would be seen as a step toward eventual resumption of diplomatic relations.

(A) animosity (B) incentives (C) embargoes (D) trade (E) lobbying

116. That the ____ know their plight is clear from the way they dart in different ____ to find an exit.

(A) participants . . . ways (B) victims . . . directions (C) birds . . . holes (D) animals . . . corners (E) rescuers . . . avenues

117. The theories of the two anthropologists look ____ opposed.

(A) reliably (B) possibly (C) academically (D) diametrically (E) accedingly

118. The ____ received an emolument.

(A) farmer (B) wife (C) employee (D) prisoner (E) invalid

119. The method of popular decision has been called a ____ or a(n) ____.

(A) success . . . failure (B) mistake . . . affirmation (C) plebiscite . . . referendum (D) dictatorship . . . monarchy (E) myth . . . reality

120. Tax reduction will increase the ____ and ____ of consumers.

(A) savings . . . returns (B) mobility . . . gregariousness (C) spending . . . inflation (D) income . . . purchasing power (E) leisure time . . . consumption

121. Muskrats are of the ____ food chain.

(A) staple (B) forest (C) carnivorous (D) lemming (E) wild

122. It is the ____ attention to this dimension which makes the report so important.

(A) unflinching (B) inceptive (C) fortuitous (D) dubious (E) redolent

123. The story itself is ____ simple.

(A) incongruously (B) lugubriously (C) circuitously (D) abstrusely (E) inscrutably

124. He never stopped talking; he was ____.

(A) silent (B) loquacious (C) pedantic (D) eccentric (E) restrained

125. For some people, their ____ state of mind prevents them from flying.

(A) physiological (B) morbid (C) psychological (D) prodigious (E) perfidious

If there is still time remaining, you may review the questions in this section only. You may not turn to any other section of the test.

Section IV Data Sufficiency

TIME: 15 minutes

DIRECTIONS: Each of the following problems has a question and two statements which are labeled (1) and (2). Use the data given in (1) and (2) together with other available information (such as the number of hours in a day, the definition of *clockwise,* mathematical facts, etc.) to decide whether the statements are *sufficient* to answer the question. Then fill in space

(A) if you can get the answer from (1) alone but not from (2) alone;

(B) if you can get the answer from (2) alone but not from (1) alone;

(C) if you can get the answer from (1) and (2) together, although neither statement by itself suffices;

(D) if statement (1) alone suffices *and* statement (2) alone suffices;

(E) if you cannot get the answer from statements (1) and (2) together, but need even more data.

All numbers used in this section are real numbers. A figure given for a problem is intended to provide information consistent with that in the question, but not necessarily with the additional information contained in the statements.

126. Are two triangles congruent?

(1) Both triangles are right triangles.
(2) Both triangles have the same perimeter.

127. Is x greater than zero?

(1) $x^4 - 16 = 0$
(2) $x^3 - 8 = 0$

128. If both conveyer belt A and conveyer belt B are used, they can fill a hopper with coal in one hour. How long will it take for conveyer belt A to fill the hopper without conveyer belt B?

(1) Conveyer belt A moves twice as much coal as conveyer belt B.
(2) Conveyer belt B would take 3 hours to fill the hopper without belt A.

129. A fly crawls around the outside of a circle once. A second fly crawls around the outside of a square once. Which fly travels further?

(1) The diagonal of the square is equal to the diameter of the circle.
(2) The fly crawling around the circle took more time to complete his journey than the fly crawling around the square.

130. How much did it cost the *XYZ* Corporation to insure its factory from fire in 1972?

(1) It cost $5,000 for fire insurance in 1971.
(2) The total amount the corporation spent for fire insurance in 1970, 1971, and 1972 was $18,000.

131. Is y larger than 1?

(1) y is larger than 0.
(2) $y^2 - 4 = 0$.

132. A worker is hired for 6 days. He is paid $2 more for each day of work than he was paid for the preceding day of work. How much was he paid for the first day of work?

(1) His total wages for the 6 days were $150.
(2) He was paid 150% of his first day's pay for the sixth day.

133. A car originally sold for $3,000. After a month, the car was discounted x%, and a month later the car's price was discounted y%. Is the car's price after the discounts less than $2,600?

(1) $y = 10$
(2) $x = 15$

134. What is the value of a?

(1) $a = f$
(2) $a = b$

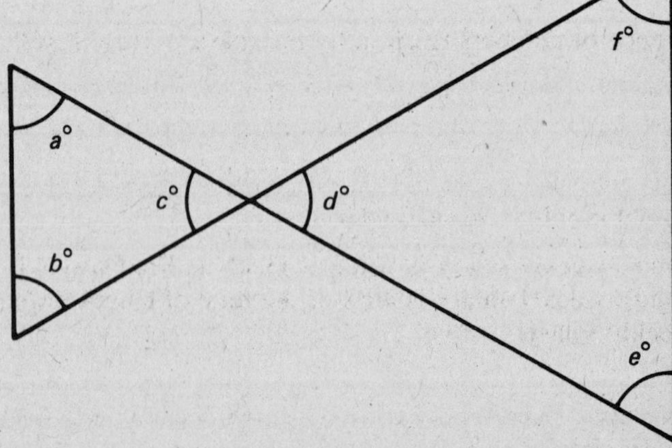

135. In triangle ABC, find z if $AB = 5$ and $y = 40$.

(1) $BC = 5$
(2) The bisector of angle B is perpendicular to AC.

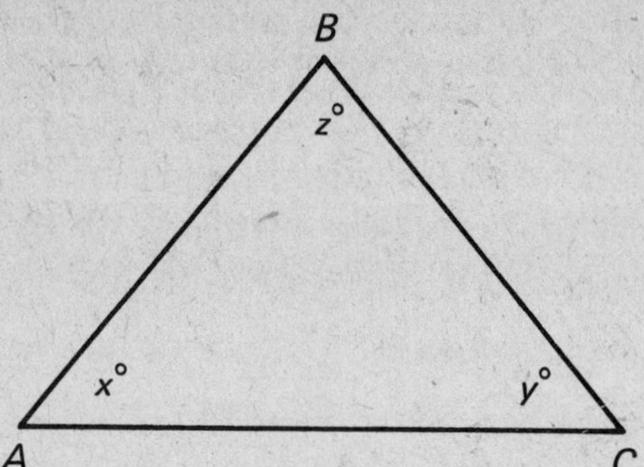

136. How much cardboard will it take to make an open cubical box with no top?

(1) The area of the bottom of the box is 4 square feet.
(2) The volume of the box is 8 cubic feet.

137. How many books are on a bookshelf?

(1) The total weight of all the books on the bookshelf is 40 pounds.
(2) The average weight of the books on the bookshelf is 2.5 pounds.

138. Is the figure $ABCD$ a rectangle?

(1) $x = 90$
(2) $AB = CD$

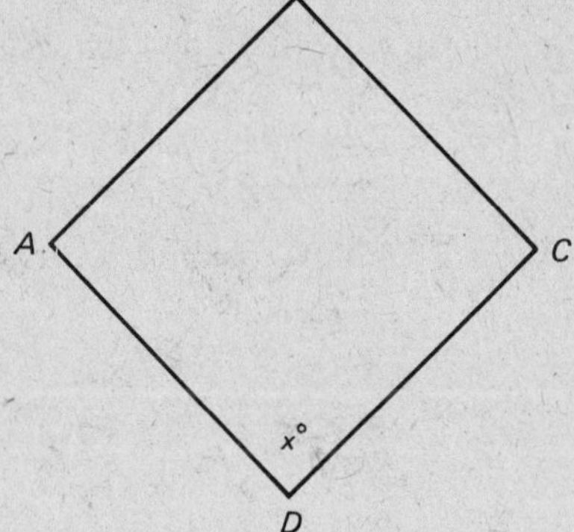

139. A sequence of numbers is given by the rule $a_n = (a_{n-1})^2$. What is a_5?

(1) $a_1 = -1$
(2) $a_3 = 1$

140. How much is John's weekly salary?

(1) John's weekly salary is twice as much as Fred's weekly salary.
(2) Fred's weekly salary is 40% of the total of Chuck's weekly salary and John's weekly salary.

If there is still time remaining, you may review the questions in this section only. You may not turn to any other section of the test.

Section V Business Judgment

TIME: 35 minutes

DIRECTIONS: Read the following two passages. After you have completed each of them you will be asked to answer two sets of questions. The first of these, data evaluation, involves determining the importance of specific factors included in the passage. The second, data application, consists of general questions relating to the passage. When answering questions, you may consult the passage.

Passage 1:

The success of the Abco Corporation in the investment-conscious country of Korea had recently been the subject of a government inquiry.

The Abco Corporation, along with a local leather merchant and a well-known American shoe machinery manufacturer constructed a shoe manufacturing plant in Korea. Government support for the enterprise was given because of high unemployment in the country, but despite the fact that there was at that time surplus shoe production—most factories having large excess capacities and underworked labor forces. It was known that Abco had promised the government, among others to (1) give employment to hundreds of workers, (2) to reduce the price of shoes by some 30 percent and (3) to export more than half their output.

In return for these promises, Abco received the following concessions from the government:

(1) Land was given the company on a lease basis for a period of 99 years rent free.
(2) A government owned contracting firm built the factory at low-subsidized prices.
(3) The company received loans at very low interest rates for an extended period of time. These loans could be renewed at company request at lower than the prevailing interest rate.
(4) The government trained workers at the plant at no expense to the company.

Within five years the company was thrown into bankruptcy hearings. The government was asked by both the company management and workers to grant the company an additional one million dollar loan so that some 300 employees would not lose their jobs during a time of high unemployment. Also, the Board of Directors stated that if the government would not agree to their request for a loan, the company should be purchased by the government for an "agreed" price, rather than let the hearings commence. Upon investigation, however, the government learned that the Abco Corporation had kept none of its original promises. For one, shoe prices at the factory were not lower than any of its competitors. As for exports, not only had the company failed to reach its promised goal of 50 percent, but as of the hearings, its exports for a five year period only amounted to 5 percent of total output. In light of these developments, the government established a special commercial committee to resolve this state of affairs.

Data Evaluation Questions

DIRECTIONS: Evaluate each of the following factors used in decision-making which relate to the passage you have just read by selecting

(A) for a *Major Objective*—the result desired by the executive;

(B) for a *Major Factor*—a primary consideration, spelled out in the passage, that influences the decision;

(C) for a *Minor Factor*—a less important consideration in the decision;

(D) for a *Major Assumption*—a conclusion reached by the executive not necessarily supported by the factors present;

(E) for an *Unimportant Issue*—a consideration not directly related to the problem.

141. Employment for shoe workers

142. High unemployment in the country

143. Excess shoe-manufacturing capacity

144. More loans for Abco

145. Investment incentives

Data Application Questions

DIRECTIONS: Answer each of the following questions using information contained in the passage.

146. Abco management desired that the company

I. Go into bankruptcy
II. Be purchased by its workers
III. Be purchased by the government

(A) I only
(B) III only
(C) I and II only
(D) II and III only
(E) I, II, and III

147. Although the government approved the Abco operation

I. Shoe manufacturers had excess capacity
II. World shoe prices had declined
III. Consumers were buying fewer shoes

(A) I only
(B) III only
(C) I and II only
(D) II and III only
(E) I, II, and III

148. Of all the promises given Abco by the government, which of the following were fulfilled?

I. Exportation of 50 percent of output
II. Lower shoe prices
III. Employment of hundreds of workers

(A) I only
(B) III only
(C) I and II only
(D) II and III only
(E) I, II, and III

149. It can be inferred from the passage that the failure of the company was due to

I. Poor management
II. Inflation
III. Too many competitors in the shoe industry

(A) I only
(B) III only
(C) I and II only
(D) II and III only
(E) I, II, and III

150. The government's decision to help establish Abco can be described as

I. Optimistic
II. Myopic
III. Fortuitous

(A) I only
(B) III only
(C) I and II only
(D) II and III only
(E) I, II, and III

Passage 2:

Norris Products Company, located in Pontiac, Michigan, produces small mechanical parts for the automobile industry. The firm sells both to automobile manufacturers and to individual car owners. It maintains an active research department and has always been a leader in product development. Mr. Joe Doran is director of product development and has five subordinates.

Management of the Norris Company believes that research has been worthwhile because several new products have been invented and patented by the laboratory and then put into regular production. Some of these products did not sell and were discontinued, but these failures were more than offset by the profits earned by those products which have been successful. Investigation discloses that 45 percent of the firm's present dollar volume of sales comes from products developed in its laboratory within the last ten years.

At a recent meeting of the Management Board (all top officials) Mr. Doran told about a new type of control for private airplanes, which he discovered quite by accident while working on an automobile steering problem. Mr. Doran is an avid aviation fan and owns his own plane; it was therefore natural for him to "find" this aircraft application as he worked on an automobile problem. He has applied for a Norris Company patent on the device. He feels that the device will be an overnight sales success and urges that it be produced immediately and placed on the market. The other officials, including Mr. Norris, even though they respect highly the ability of Mr. Doran, are of the opinion that the firm should manufacture only automobile parts and accessories. They argue that, even though they could produce the item, their marketing channels are keyed to automobile products and therefore it would take a great deal of added money to develop new and divergent sales contacts. It is their contention that the new idea should be either sold outright or an arrangement made by which they would collect royalties on sales for letting another concern (most likely a firm already in the aircraft business) use the idea.

Mr. Doran's retort is, "Remember the wagon manufacturers? They didn't want to enter the automobile business, and what happened to them!"

Data Evaluation Questions

DIRECTIONS: Evaluate each of the following factors used in decision-making which relate to the passage you have just read by selecting

(A) for a *Major Objective*—the result desired by the executive;

(B) for a *Major Factor*—a primary consideration, spelled out in the passage, that influences the decision;

(C) for a *Minor Factor*—a less important consideration in the decision;

(D) for a *Major Assumption*—a conclusion reached by the executive not necessarily supported by the factors present;

(E) for an *Unimportant Issue*—a consideration not directly related to the problem.

151. Channels of distribution

152. Expertise in the aircraft industry

153. A product discovered by accident

154. Mr. Doran applied for a Norris Co. patent

155. Production capability for the new product

Data Application Questions

DIRECTIONS: Answer each of the following questions using information contained in the passage.

156. According to the passage, the Norris Company sells

I. Laboratory equipment
II. Safety controls
III. Small mechanical parts

(A) I only
(B) III only
(C) I and II only
(D) II and III only
(E) I, II, and III

157. Joe Doran's product idea should be

I. Developed by his company
II. Sold to another company
III. Licensed under a royalty agreement

(A) I only
(B) III only
(C) I and II only
(D) II and III only
(E) I, II, and III

158. Joe Doran's new product idea was developed

I. By "accident"
II. In the Norris Company laboratory
III. Over a ten year period

(A) I only
(B) III only
(C) I and II only
(D) II and III only
(E) I, II, and III

159. Management of the Norris Company was reluctant to process Joe Doran's idea because the company lacked

I. Production facilities
II. Experience in the aircraft industry
III. Distribution channels to reach the aircraft market

(A) I only
(B) III only
(C) I and II only
(D) II and III only
(E) I, II, and III

160. Mr. Doran feels his product idea will be an "overnight sales success." On what basis does he hold to that belief?

I. A thorough research of the market
II. Past experience in the industry
III. Intuition

(A) I only
(B) III only
(C) I and II only
(D) II and III only
(E) I, II, and III

If there is still time remaining, you may review the questions in this section only. You may not turn to any other section of the test.

Section VI Data Sufficiency

TIME: 25 minutes

DIRECTIONS: Each of the following problems has a question and two statements which are labeled (1) and (2). Use the data given in (1) and (2) together with other available information (such as the number of hours in a day, the definition of *clockwise*, mathematical facts, etc.) to decide whether the statements are *sufficient* to answer the question. Then fill in space

(A) if you can get the answer from (1) alone but not from (2) alone;

(B) if you can get the answer from (2) alone but not from (1) alone;

(C) if you can get the answer from (1) and (2) together, although neither statement by itself suffices;

(D) if statement (1) alone suffices *and* statement (2) alone suffices;

(E) if you cannot get the answer from statements (1) and (2) together, but need even more data.

All numbers used in this section are real numbers. A figure given for a problem is intended to provide information consistent with that in the question, but not necessarily with the additional information contained in the statements.

161. Find $x + 2y$.

(1) $x + y = 4$
(2) $2x + 4y = 12$

162. Is angle x a right angle?

(1) $x = 2y$
(2) $y = 1.5z$

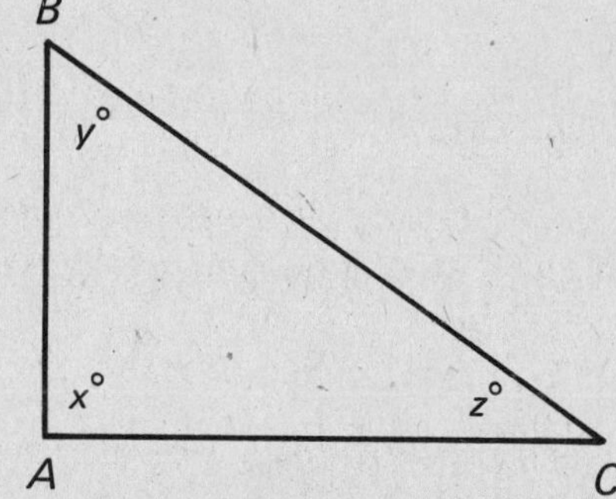

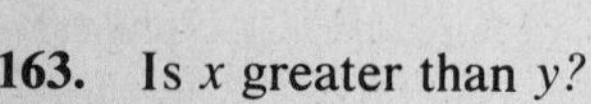

163. Is x greater than y?

(1) $x = 2k$
(2) $k = 2y$

164. How much profit did Toyland make selling 65 dolls if each doll costs $8?

(1) The amount the dolls sold for was $750.
(2) The dolls cost $7 each last year.

165. 50% of the people in Teetown have blue eyes and blond hair. What percent of the people in Teetown have blue eyes but do not have blond hair?

(1) 70% of the people in Teetown have blond hair.
(2) 60% of the people in Teetown have blue eyes.

166. The pentagon *ABCDE* is inscribed in the circle with center *O*. How many degrees is angle *ABC*?.

(1) The pentagon *ABCDE* is a regular pentagon.
(2) The radius of the circle is 5 inches.

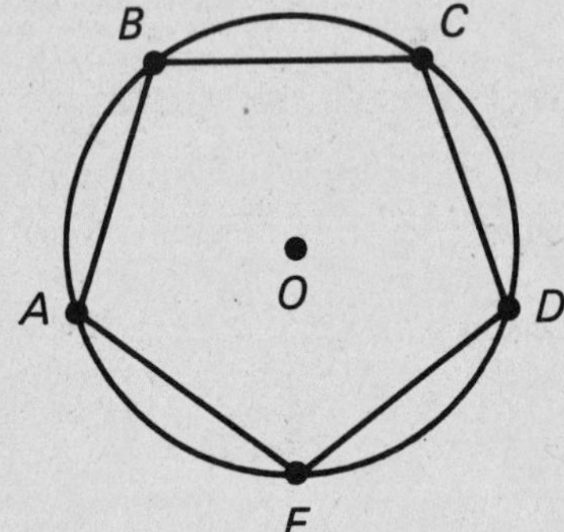

167. What is the area of the circle with center *O*? (*AB* and *DE* are straight lines)

(1) $DE = 5$ inches
(2) $AB = 7$ inches

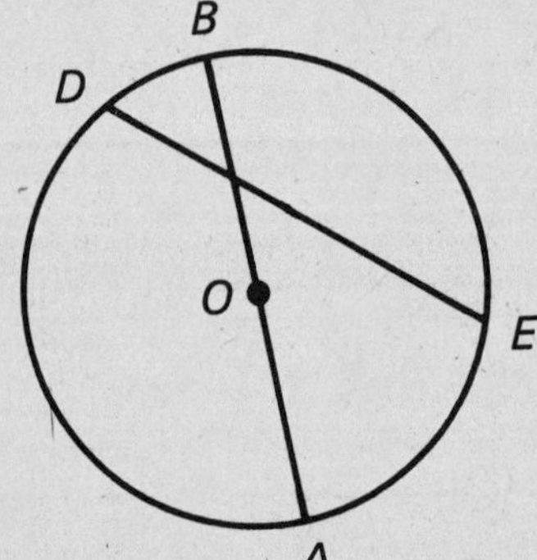

168. What is the taxable income of the Kell family in 1973? The taxable income of the Kell family in 1971 was $10,000.

(1) The Kell family had taxable income of $12,000 in 1972.
(2) The total taxable income of the Kell family for the three years 1971, 1972, and 1973 was $34,000.

169. A piece of string 6 feet long is cut into three smaller pieces. How long is the longest of the three pieces?

(1) Two pieces are the same length.
(2) One piece is 3 feet, 2 inches long.

170. If a group of 5 craftsmen take 3 hours to finish a job, how long will it take a group of 4 apprentices to do the same job?

(1) An apprentice does $\frac{2}{3}$ as much work as a craftsman.
(2) The 5 craftsmen and the 4 apprentices working together will take $1\frac{22}{23}$ hours to finish the job.

171. Is $\frac{1}{x}$ greater than $\frac{1}{y}$?

(1) x is greater than 1.
(2) x is less than y.

172. AB intersects CD at point O. Is AB perpendicular to CD? $AC = AD$.

(1) Angle CAD is bisected by AO.
(2) $BC = AD$

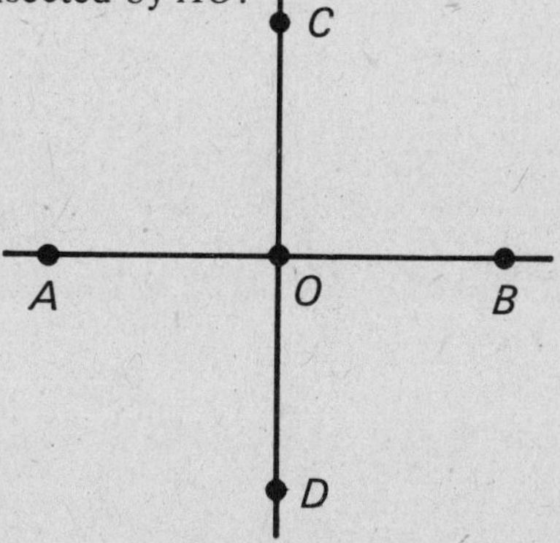

173. Plane X flies at r miles per hour from A to B. Plane Y flies at S miles per hour from B to A. Both planes take off at the same time. Which plane flies at a faster rate? Town C is between A and B.

(1) C is closer to A than it is to B.
(2) Plane X flies over C before plane Y.

174. What is the value of $x + y$?

(1) $2x + y = 4$
(2) $x + 2y = 5$

175. What is the area of the circular section AOB? A and B are points on the circle which has O as its center.

(1) Angle $AOB = 36°$
(2) $OB = OA$

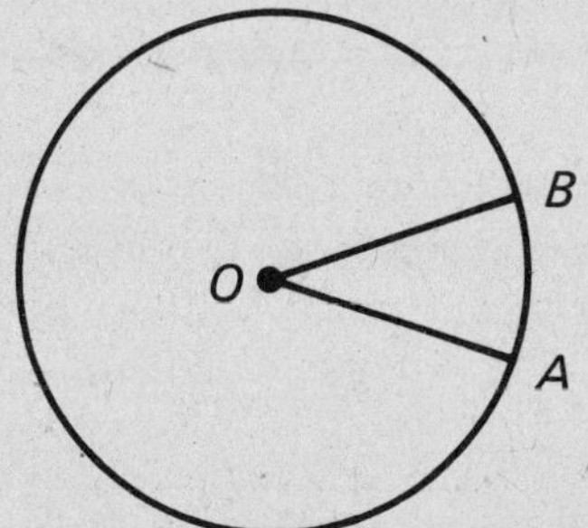

176. k is an integer. Is k divisible by 8?

(1) k is divisible by 4.
(2) k is divisible by 16.

177. How much is the average salary of the 30 assembly workers? The foreman is paid a salary of \$12,000.

(1) The total salary paid to the assembly workers and the foreman is \$312,000.
(2) The foreman's salary is 120% of the average salary of the assembly workers.

178. How far is it from town A to town B? Town C is 12 miles east of town A.

(1) Town C is south of town B.
(2) It is 9 miles from town B to town C.

179. How many vinyl squares with sides 5 inches long will be needed to cover the rectangular floor of a room?

(1) The floor is 10 feet long.
(2) The floor is 5 feet wide.

180. Mary must work 15 hours to make in wages the cost of a set of luggage. How many dollars does the set of luggage cost?

(1) Jim must work 12 hours to make in wages the cost of the set of luggage.
(2) Jim's hourly wage is 125% of Mary's hourly wage.

181. What is the value of x?

(1) $\frac{x}{y} = 3$
(2) $x - y = 9$

182. Is DE parallel to AB?

(1) The triangles DEC and ABC are similar.
(2) $CE = EB$

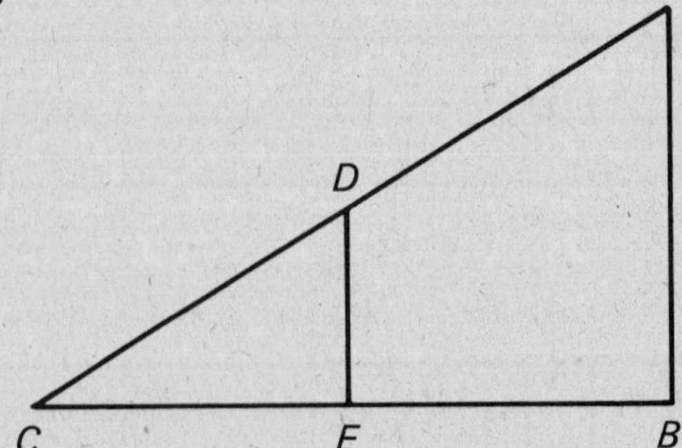

183. How many of the numbers x and y are positive? Both x and y are less than 20.

(1) x is less than 5.
(2) $x + y = 24$

184. What is the value of x? $PS = SR$.

(1) $y = 30$
(2) $PQ = QR$

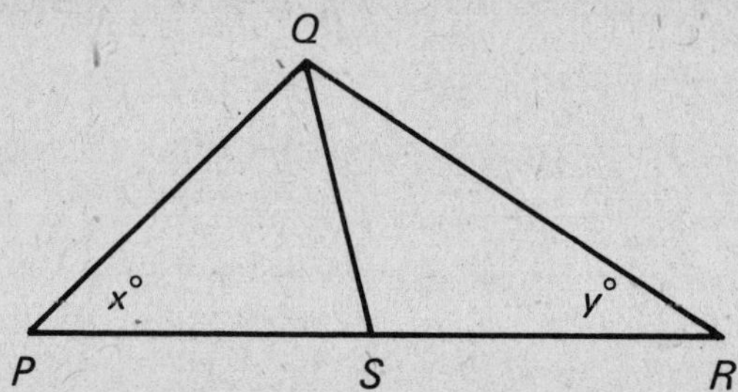

185. How much does the first volume of a 5 volume work weigh?

(1) The first 3 volumes weigh 4 pounds.
(2) The second, third and fourth volumes weigh a total of $3\frac{1}{2}$ pounds.

If there is still time remaining, you may review the questions in this section only.
You may not turn to any other section of the test.

Answers

Section I Reading Recall

1. **(D)**
2. **(D)**
3. **(E)**
4. **(C)**
5. **(A)**
6. **(B)**
7. **(D)**
8. **(E)**
9. **(E)**
10. **(B)**
11. **(C)**
12. **(B)**
13. **(C)**
14. **(D)**
15. **(C)**
16. **(D)**
17. **(D)**
18. **(E)**
19. **(B)**
20. **(E)**
21. **(E)**
22. **(B)**
23. **(C)**
24. **(C)**
25. **(C)**
26. **(A)**
27. **(C)**
28. **(C)**
29. **(A)**
30. **(C)**

Section II Mathematics

(Numbers in parentheses indicate the section in the Mathematics Review where material concerning the question is discussed.)

31. **(B)** (I–2)
32. **(A)** (I–4)
33. **(A)** (IV–4)
34. **(B)** (IV–4)
35. **(C)** (IV–3)
36. **(B)** (IV–3, IV–4)
37. **(C)** (II–5)
38. **(C)** (II–5, III–7)
39. **(B)** (IV–1)
40. **(C)** (IV–1)
41. **(C)** (IV–1)
42. **(E)** (II–4)
43. **(C)** (I–3)
44. **(B)** (I–7)
45. **(D)** (IV–1)
46. **(C)** (IV–4)
47. **(C)** (I–4)
48. **(A)** (II–2)
49. **(A)** (IV–1)
50. **(C)** (IV–1)
51. **(B)** (IV–1)
52. **(D)** (II–1)
53. **(D)** (III–5)
54. **(B)** (III–7, I–4)
55. **(C)** (IV–5)
56. **(E)** (IV–5)
57. **(D)** (IV–5)
58. **(C)** (I–4)
59. **(C)** (II–7)
60. **(E)** (I–4)
61. **(B)** (II–2)
62. **(A)** (IV–1)
63. **(C)** (I–4, II–3)
64. **(E)** (I–2)
65. **(D)** (III–7)
66. **(D)** (IV–2)
67. **(B)** (IV–2)
68. **(E)** (IV–2)
69. **(D)** (IV–2)
70. **(D)** (II–6)
71. **(B)** (I–2)
72. **(A)** (III–7)
73. **(E)** (II–3)
74. **(E)** (IV–1)
75. **(B)** (IV–1)
76. **(E)** (IV–1)
77. **(C)** (IV–1)
78. **(C)** (II–3)
79. **(D)** (I–4)
80. **(E)** (IV–5)
81. **(D)** (IV–5)
82. **(C)** (IV–5)
83. **(A)** (III–7)
84. **(D)** (I–4)
85. **(C)** (II–2)

Section III Verbal Aptitude

86. (B)
87. (D)
88. (C)
89. (D)
90. (E)
91. (B)
92. (B)
93. (C)
94. (A)
95. (A)
96. (C)
97. (D)
98. (B)
99. (C)
100. (D)
101. (B)
102. (C)
103. (A)
104. (A)
105. (B)
106. (E)
107. (A)
108. (C)
109. (B)
110. (B)
111. (B)
112. (C)
113. (A)
114. (C)
115. (D)
116. (B)
117. (D)
118. (C)
119. (C)
120. (D)
121. (C)
122. (A)
123. (B)
124. (B)
125. (C)

Section IV Data Sufficiency

126. (E)
127. (B)
128. (D)
129. (A)
130. (E)
131. (C)
132. (D)
133. (B)
134. (E)
135. (D)
136. (D)
137. (C)
138. (E)
139. (D)
140. (E)

Section V Business Judgment

141. (A)
142. (B)
143. (E)
144. (C)
145. (E)
146. (B)
147. (A)
148. (B)
149. (B)
150. (C)
151. (A)
152. (B)
153. (E)
154. (E)
155. (B)
156. (B)
157. (E)
158. (A)
159. (D)
160. (B)

Section VI Data Sufficiency

161. (B)
162. (C)
163. (E)
164. (A)
165. (B)
166. (A)
167. (B)
168. (C)
169. (B)
170. (D)
171. (C)
172. (A)
173. (E)
174. (C)
175. (E)
176. (B)
177. (D)
178. (C)
179. (C)
180. (E)
181. (C)
182. (A)
183. (B)
184. (C)
185. (E)

Analysis

Section I Reading Recall

1. **(D)** This is clearly a subject dealing with the economy and economic policy. Note that (E) is too vague; an economic *policy* textbook might have been a correct answer.

2. **(D)** The United States is mentioned in paragraphs 1, 4, and 5.

3. **(E)** All of the others are given in paragraph 2.

4. **(C)** See paragraph 2: "... consumer and business sentiment benefited from rising public expectations that a resolution of the conflict [Vietnam] was in prospect and that East-West tensions were easing." The reference to the stock market response to possible peace in Vietnam is not an issue because of "shifting" appraisals, i.e., pessimism followed by downturns in the stock averages.

5. **(A)** See paragraph 3, line 1: "The underpinnings of the business expansion were to be found in part in the stimulative monetary and fiscal policies that had been pursued."

6. **(B)** See paragraph 4: "... there was actually a substantial deterioration in our trade account to a sizable deficit, almost two thirds of which was with Japan."

7. **(D)** See paragraph 5, line 1: Only (D) was mentioned.

8. **(E)** See paragraph 5, sentence 2: "The Phase Three program of wage and price restraint can contribute to dampening inflation."

9. **(E)** Paragraph 5 is obscure as to how much unemployment can be reduced. First, it states "... it seems doubtful whether the much lower rates of four percent and below often cited ... do in part represent feasible goals. . . ." Further on the paragraph reads "There is little doubt that overall unemployment rates can be brought down to 4 percent or less, for a time at least. . . ."

10. **(B)** See paragraph 5: "... while the unemployment rates of a bit over 5 percent. . . ."

11. **(C)** The subject is about killer waves which are *caused* by underwater earthquakes (D).

12. **(B)** See paragraph 1: "Under a perfectly sunny sky and from an apparently calm sea. . . ."

13. **(C)** Tsunami is the Japanese name (paragraph 3) and the term "killer" waves is mentioned in paragraph 5.

14. **(D)** See paragraph 2, line 1: "How are these waves formed? When a submarine earthquake occurs. . . ."

15. **(C)** See paragraph 2: "The swells in the ocean are sometimes nearly a mile wide. . . ."

16. **(D)** See paragraph 5: "... the Coast and Geodetic Survey initiated a program ... to locate submarine earthquakes [and] tell how severe a submarine earthquake was. . . ."

17. **(D)** See paragraph 4.

18. **(E)** See paragraph 3: "These waves travel hundreds of miles an hour. . . ."

19. **(B)** See paragraph 3.

20. **(E)** All are mentioned in paragraph 5, except for the height of the wave.

21. **(E)** See paragraphs 1, 2, and 6: The passage deals with the problems of all three.

22. **(B)** See paragraph 2, line 1: "The problems of the atmosphere resemble those of water only partly."

23. **(C)** This is stated in paragraph 2.

24. **(C)** See paragraph 3: "The households' share in atmospheric pollution is far bigger than that of industry. . . ." The key word in the question is "most."

25. **(C)** Maintenance is determined by both production *and* transportation costs. Although paragraph 1 states that the maintenance of clean water is "primarily" one of production costs, paragraph 4 states that this problem is "related to the costs of production and transport. . . ."

26. **(A)** This is discussed in paragraph 3 in context with atmospheric pollution.

27. **(C)** See paragraph 5, line 1: "Atmospheric pollution caused by the private property of individuals . . . is difficult to control."

28. **(C)** See paragraph 6: Both active and passive resources. No mention is made of levying taxes.

29. **(A)** See paragraph 5: "*In this particular case,* the cost of anti-pollution measures will have to be borne to a considerable extent by individuals." "In this particular case" refers to the situation also described in the paragraph where pollution is caused by the private property of individuals.

30. **(C)** See paragraph 6: While noise abatement is not impossible to achieve, the "costs of a complete protection against noise are so prohibitive. . . ."

Section II Mathematics

31. **(B)** The time needed to complete the trip is $\left(6 - \frac{1}{4} - 1\frac{3}{8} - 2\frac{1}{3}\right)$ hours. This equals $6 - (1 + 2) - \left(\frac{1}{4} + \frac{3}{8} + \frac{1}{3}\right) = 3 - \frac{6 + 9 + 8}{24} = 3 - \frac{23}{24} = 2\frac{1}{24} = 2$ hours $2\frac{1}{2}$ minutes.

32. **(A)** The average has decreased by 500 − 400 or 100 points during the week, so the percentage of decrease is 100/500 or 20%.

33. **(A)** The bars in the upper figure give percent increase; the highest bar corresponds to the year 1950.

34. **(B)** The total sales of a year divided by the number of cars in the pictograph for any year will give the number of sales that a single car represents. In 1950, sales were 6.7 million, and there were about $4\frac{1}{2}$ cars in the pictograph. $6.7 \div \frac{9}{2} = 6.7 \times \frac{2}{9} \approx 6.3 \times \frac{2}{9} \approx 1.4$ (where $\approx$ denotes "approximately").

35. **(C)** The dots on the line graph and the right-hand scale give registrations. In 1950, there were about 40 million passenger cars registered.

36. **(B)**

STATEMENT I is not true, since percentage is indicated by the right scale, not by the left scale.

STATEMENT III cannot be inferred, since there are many years between 1950 and 1969 for which no sales figures are given.

STATEMENT II is true, since registrations were about 40 million in 1950 and they increased to about 80 million by 1969.

So only STATEMENT II can be inferred from the graphs.

37. **(C)** Since there are 180 minutes in 3 hours, then $\frac{x}{8} = \frac{180}{18}$, where x is the number of cars washed in 3 hours. Therefore, $x = 8 \times 10 = 80$.

38. **(C)** If s and t denote the sides of the two squares, then $s^2 : t^2 = 2 : 1$, or $\frac{s^2}{t^2} = \frac{2}{1}$. Thus $\left(\frac{s}{t}\right)^2 = \frac{2}{1}$ and $\frac{s}{t} = \frac{\sqrt{2}}{1}$.

39. (B) In the Pacific region, the amount of credit life insurance was \$12,457,000,000 and the amount of ordinary life insurance \$108,806,000,000. Therefore, the ratio is about $\frac{12}{108}$ which equals $\frac{1}{9}$ or 1 to 9.

40. (C) Only the South Atlantic region had more than \$10,000,000,000 in industrial life insurance in 1972.

41. (C) The percent change for total life insurance was 140.8%, so only group (201.5%) and credit (186.1%) had a greater percentage of increase from 1962 to 1972.

42. (E) The Venn diagram indicates the answer immediately. The region outside both circles denotes neither whitewall tires nor air-conditioning.

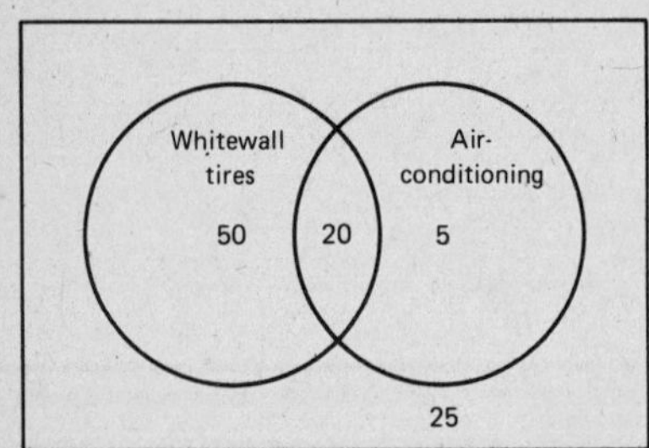

43. (C) Each share was worth \$122.50 − \$111.10 or \$11.40 less in 1973 than it was in 1970. Therefore, the 100,000 shares were worth 100,000 × \$11.40 or \$1,140,000 less in 1973 than in 1970.

44. (B) Add up the daily wages to get the total wages for the week. \$51.90 + 52.20 + 49.80 + 51.50 + 50.60 = \$256.00. Divide \$256.00 by 5 to get the average daily wage, \$51.20.

45. (D) The exact ratio is $\frac{364}{160}$ or $\frac{91}{40}$, which is about 9 to 4.

46. (C) $\frac{27}{50}$ of all accident deaths occurred in motor vehicle accidents, and there were 56,400 motor vehicle deaths in 1969. So the number of accidental deaths is $56{,}400 \times \frac{56}{27}$. Since you need only an approximate answer and $\frac{56}{27}$ is about 2, 112,800 is a good approximation.

47. (C) The interest on the first \$600 is (.08)(\$600) or \$48.00 for a year. There is \$5,400 of the loan in excess of \$600; so he must pay (.07)(5,400) or \$378.00 interest for the year on the \$5,400. Therefore, the interest for one year will be \$48 + \$378 or \$426.

48. (A) $4y - 6x = -2(3x - 2y) = -2(8) = -16$.

49. (A) Argentina had 40,180 kilometers of railroad which is third after the United States and Canada.

50. (C) Check the column headed Km. per area. The largest entry in the column is 44.54, for Cuba.

51. (B) In 1953, there were 60 million passenger kilometers in Paraguay and in 1965 35 million, so passenger kilometers decreased by 25 million. $\frac{25}{60} = \frac{5}{12} = 41\frac{2}{3}\%$. Therefore, the decrease was about 40%.

52. (D) Since the total distance is 200 miles, of which you fly x miles, you drive $(200 - x)$ miles. Therefore, the cost is $10x + (200 - x)12$, which is $10x - 12x + 2400$ or $2400 - 2x$ cents. The answer in dollars is obtained by dividing by 100, which is $(24 - .02x)$ dollars.

53. (D) Since the sides of the square equal the length of the rectangles, which is twice the width, the length of R_1 is 2 times its width.

54. (B) If A_1 denotes the increased area and A the original area, then $A_1 = 1.69A$, since A_1 is A increased by 69%. Thus, $s_1^2 = A_1 = 1.69A = 1.69s^2$, where s_1 is the increased side and s the original side. Since the square root of 1.69 is 1.3, we have $s_1 = 1.3s$ so s is increased by .3 or 30%.

55. **(C)** The \$5,000–9,999 income group is the only group which contained more than 30% of the white families in 1950.

56. **(E)** In 1969, about 80% of the white families had incomes of over \$5,000, and about 20% of the white families had incomes of less than \$5,000. Therefore, the ratio is about 80 to 20 or 4 to 1.

57. **(D)**

STATEMENT I can not be inferred since the graphs do not give any information about the number of white or Negro families.

STATEMENT II can be inferred since over 50% of the families in the category "Negro and other races" had an income of \$3,000 or less, while in 1969 fewer than 25% of these families had an income of \$3,000 or less; so the percentage decreased by more than $\frac{1}{2}$ or 50%.

STATEMENT III can be inferred, since about 50% of the white families had incomes of \$10,000 or more in 1969. Therefore, the average income would be at least \$5,000, even if the other 50% had no income.

Therefore, STATEMENTS II and III can be inferred from the graph, but STATEMENT I can not.

58. **(C)** Since the dealer made a profit of 20%, he sold the car for 120% of what the car cost. Thus, if C is the cost of the car, 120% of C = \$1,380 or $(\frac{6}{5})C$ = \$1,380. Therefore, $C = \frac{5}{6}$ of \$1,380, which is \$1,150.

59. **(C)**

STATEMENT I is not always true. For example, 1 is less than 5 and 1 is less than 6, but 6 is not less than 5.

STATEMENT II is not always true, since $\frac{3}{8} < \frac{1}{2}$ and $\frac{3}{8} < \frac{2}{3}$ but $\frac{3}{8}$ is not less than $(\frac{1}{2})(\frac{2}{3}) = \frac{1}{3}$.

Since STATEMENT III is always true, (C) is the correct answer.

60. **(E)** The total number of workers is 80, and 35 of them work 40 or more hours. Therefore, $\frac{35}{80} = .4375 = 43.75\%$.

61. **(B)** 15 people worked 40 to 44 hours, and 4 worked up to 29 hours. So $4x = 15$, which means $x = \frac{15}{4} = 3\frac{3}{4}$.

62. **(A)**

STATEMENT I can be inferred, since the average number of hours worked is $\frac{3100}{80} = 38\frac{3}{4}$ which is less than 40.

STATEMENT II can not be inferred, since there is no information about the number of workers who worked over 48 hours.

STATEMENT III is not true, since there are only 35 workers who worked 40 or more hours.

63. **(C)** The truck uses 30% more gasoline to travel the same distance at 70 mph than it does at 50 mph. Therefore, the truck requires 130% of a gallon of gasoline, which is 1.3 gallons, to travel 19.5 miles at 70 mph. So the truck will travel (10/1.3)(19.5) or 150 miles on 10 gallons of gas at 70 mph.

64. **(E)** Convert $\frac{2}{5}$ and $\frac{1}{3}$ into fractions with denominators of 30. Since $\frac{2}{5} = \frac{12}{30}$ and $\frac{1}{3} = \frac{10}{30}$, $\frac{2}{5} + \frac{1}{3} = \frac{12}{30} + \frac{10}{30} = \frac{22}{30}$, and x is equal to 22.

65. **(D)** The area of the rectangle is $4 \times 6 = 24$ square feet. Since 1 square foot is 144 square inches, the area of the rectangle is 3,456 square inches. Each square has an area of $(\frac{1}{2})^2$ or $\frac{1}{4}$ square inches. Therefore, the number of squares needed $= 3{,}456 \div \frac{1}{4} = 3{,}456 \times 4 = 13{,}824$.

66. **(D)** The corporation income tax accounted for 19.7% of all average annual receipts for the years 1967–1970. Since 19.7% is about 20% or $\frac{1}{5}$, the average annual receipts were about 5 times the average annual receipts from the corporation income tax. Therefore, the answer is $5x$.

67. **(B)** Veterans received 4.2%, education and manpower 3.8%, and health and income security 26% of the average annual outlays; so together the three categories received 4.2% + 3.8% + 26% or 34%. Since $\frac{1}{3}$ is $33\frac{1}{3}\%$, 34% is roughly $\frac{1}{3}$.

68. **(E)** International affairs received 2.4% which is more than "others" (1.7%) but less than every other category on the graph.

69. **(D)** Since $^5/_8$ of 3.2% = 5 × .4% = 2.0%, the correct answer is (D).

70. **(D)** $\frac{10}{5} = 2 = \frac{20}{10}$, so the ratio of successive terms of the progression is 2. Therefore, the term which follows 20 is 2 times 20 or 40.

71. **(B)** Since $^1/_8$ of 8¢ is 1¢, each egg will cost 8¢ + 1¢ or 9¢ after the price has increased. The price of a dozen eggs will be 12 × 9¢ or $1.08.

72. **(A)** The area of trapezoid *ABCD* equals the area of rectangle *ABED*, which is $t \times 5$ (since $BE = BC = 5$), plus the area of triangle *BEC*, which is $\frac{(5 \times 5)}{2}$. The answers is thus $5t + 12.5$.

73. **(E)** The selling price of the jars should equal cost + $75. The cost of making 300 jars = (100)65¢ + (200)55¢ = $65 + $110 = $175. So the selling price should be $175 + $75 or $250.

74. **(E)** The countries shown accounted for more than 50% of world exports in beef (51%), coffee (64%), quebracho (100%), wheat (80%), and zinc (55%).

75. **(B)** In 1962 the price was $2.49, and in 1970 the price was $1.88; so the percentage is $\frac{1.88}{2.49}$. We can divide 249 into 188, but it is faster to divide 250 into 188. $\frac{188}{250}$ is about 75%.

76. **(E)** The price dropped in linseed oil, cotton, petroleum, wheat and wool. Notice that for some commodities not all countries had prices which dropped but at least one country did.

77. **(C)** Bolivian tin received $164.40 per 100 pounds in 1970.

78. **(C)** Since each assistant does $^2/_3$ as much as the roofer, all 3 will accomplish 1 + 2($^2/_3$) or $^7/_3$ as much as the roofer by himself. So they will finish the job in 7 ÷ $^7/_3$ or 3 hours.

79. **(D)** At the end of Tuesday it would be 1,000 − 100 or 900, since 10% of 1,000 = 100. At the end of Wednesday, it would be 810 or 900 − 90, and after Thursday's trading the stock average would be 810 − 81 or 729.

80. **(E)** In 1957, about $10 billion was spent on research and development; in 1970, more than $25 billion was spent. $\frac{25}{10} = 250\%$.

81. **(D)** The top of the graph is higher than 15 billion in 1961.

82. **(C)**

STATEMENT I can be inferred since the top of the graph is always rising.

STATEMENT II can also be inferred, since the amount of funds used in 1958 was less than $12 billion while the amount in 1968 was more than $24 billion.

STATEMENT III is not true, since the strip which denotes research and development performed by universities and others and funded by the federal government is narrower than many of the other categories so less was spent in that category.

83. **(A)** Since it takes twice as long to walk the length as the width, $l = 2w$ where l is the length and w the width. The perimeter equals $2l + 2w = 3l = 300$ yards, so the length is 100 yards and the width is 50 yards. Therefore, the area is 50 × 100 = 5,000 square yards.

84. **(D)** The company's profit = (2,000)(.07) + (5,000)(.06) = $140 + $300 = $440.

85. **(C)** Since $\frac{x}{y} = \frac{3}{z}$, $xz = 3y$ and $9y^2 = (3y)^2$; so $9y^2 = (xz)^2 = x^2z^2$.

Section III Verbal Aptitude

86. **(B)** SEDITIOUS: factious, rebellious. *Antonym:* orderly

87. **(D)** REDOLENT: odorous, fragrant. *Antonym:* fetid

88. **(C)** PUERILE: youthful, juvenile. *Antonym:* mature

89. **(D)** ABATE: lessen, reduce. *Antonym:* increase

90. **(E)** ACERBITY: sharpness, acrimony. *Antonym:* sweetness

91. **(B)** ACTUATE: move, instigate. *Antonym:* dissuade

92. **(B)** IRRESOLUTE: undetermined, vacillating. *Antonym:* determined

93. **(C)** FRACTIOUS: petulant, testy. *Antonym:* agreeable

94. **(A)** ADMONITION: warning, caution. *Antonym:* countenance

95. **(A)** ENMITY: animosity, hostility. *Antonym:* affection

96. **(C)** ARTIFICE: trick, delusion. *Antonym:* honesty

97. **(D)** CONDUCE: lead, contribute. *Antonym:* counteract

98. **(B)** DEBILITY: languor, weakness. *Antonym:* strength

99. **(C)** CONJURE: entreat, adjure. *Antonym:* deprecate

100. **(D)** An aviary is a place where birds are kept while an arboretum is a place for plants. Dovecote and greenhouse have the same relationship.

101. **(B)** A convict is sentenced to prison; an exile is sentenced to banishment.

102. **(C)** A flood is a compounded state (extreme form) of water. A blizzard and snow have the same relationship.

103. **(A)** The relationship is one of opposites. Penitence is an antonym of obduracy. The same relationship holds for pensive and thoughtless.

104. **(A)** The relationship is one of synonyms. Fortitude is a synonym of resolution as is timidity of weakness.

105. **(B)** A tape measure is an instrument used to provide measurement and electricity is the instrument used to provide power.

106. **(E)** An amplifier enlarges the voice as an expediter speeds a shipment.

107. **(A)** The relationship is one of antonyms. Perfidious is an antonym of faithful.

108. **(C)** Genocide is an extreme form of murder, as a tornado is an extreme form of wind.

109. **(B)** A clarification is the opposite of nebulous, while emendation is the opposite of erroneous.

110. **(B)** The relationship is one of antonyms. Annihilate is the opposite of extirpate.

111. **(B)** The relationship is one of synonyms. Amalgamate and united are the same, as are organize and arranged.

112. **(C)** An incantation is recited during exorcism while a prayer is recited during devotion.

113. **(A)** Air is not imbibed (B), neither do the other alternatives fit the meaning of the sentence.

114. **(C)** Recorders do not "hum" (D); a soliloquy is a rendering by one person, while musicians do not sing (B).

115. **(D)** While incentives (B) might be a logical alternative, trade (D) is more specific.

116. **(B)** Victims has the most meaning in the context of plight.

117. **(D)** Diametrically or "directly" opposed.

118. **(C)** Emolument means salary. A farmer who receives a salary is also an employee, but not vice-versa.

119. **(C)** A plebiscite calls on the "plebs" or common people for a vote of confidence. A referendum is the referring of questions,

e.g., "the right of 18 year olds to vote" to most or all of the citizens for a decision by vote.

120. **(D)** Tax reductions increase (real) income and raise purchasing power.

121. **(C)** Carnivorous or flesh-eating.

122. **(A)** It certainly is not fortuitous (accidental) nor dubious (unclear).

123. **(B)** Lugubriously or mournfully simple. It is not incongruously (incompatible), abstrusely (complex) nor inscrutably (latent).

124. **(B)** If he continued talking, he was loquacious (very talkative).

125. **(C)** Alternative (B) might seem plausible, but (C) is more inclusive; it covers those which fit in category (B).

Section IV Data Sufficiency

126. **(E)**

A triangle with sides of lengths 3, 4, and 5 is a right triangle since $3^2 + 4^2 = 5^2$, and its perimeter is 12. A triangle with sides of lengths 2, $4\frac{4}{5}$, and $5\frac{1}{5}$ also has a perimeter of 12. And since $2^2 + (4\frac{4}{5})^2 = (5\frac{1}{5})^2$, it too is a right triangle. Therefore, two triangles can satisfy STATEMENTS (1) and (2) yet not be congruent. On the other hand, any pair of congruent right triangles satisfy STATEMENTS (1) and (2). Thus, STATEMENTS (1) and (2) together are not sufficient to answer the question.

127. **(B)**

$x^3 - 8 = 0$ has only $x = 2$ as a real solution. And 2 is greater than 0, so STATEMENT (2) alone is sufficient.

Since $x = 2$ and $x = -2$ are both solutions of $x^4 - 16 = 0$, STATEMENT (1) alone is not sufficient.

128. **(D)**

STATEMENT (1) is sufficient since it implies that conveyer belt A loads $\frac{2}{3}$ of the hopper while conveyer belt B loads only $\frac{1}{3}$ with both working. Since conveyer belt A loads $\frac{2}{3}$ of the hopper in a hour, it will take $1 \div \frac{2}{3}$ or $1\frac{1}{2}$ hours to fill the hopper by itself.

STATEMENT (2) is also sufficient since it implies that conveyer belt B fills $\frac{1}{3}$ of the hopper in 1 hour. Thus, conveyer belt A loads $\frac{2}{3}$ in one hour, and that means conveyer belt A will take $1\frac{1}{2}$ hours by itself.

129. **(A)** The first fly will travel a distance equal to the circumference of the circle which is π times the diameter. The second fly will travel $4s$ where s is the length of a side. Since the diagonal of a square has length $\sqrt{2}S$, the second fly will travel $4/\sqrt{2}$ times the diagonal of the square. Therefore, (1) alone is sufficient, since $4/\sqrt{2} = 4\sqrt{2}/2 = 2\sqrt{2}$ which is less than π. (2) alone is not sufficient, since one fly might have crawled faster than the other.

130. **(E)** Using (1) and (2) together, it is only possible to determine the total amount paid for fire insurance in 1970 and 1972. Since no relation is given between the amounts paid in 1970 and 1972, there is not enough information to determine the cost in 1972.

131. **(C)** (2) alone is not sufficient since both $y = 2$ and $y = -2$ satisfy $y^2 - 4 = 0$. (1) alone is not sufficient, since $\frac{1}{2}$ is larger than 0 but less than 1 while 3 is larger than 0 and larger than 1. The only solution of $y^2 - 4 = 0$ which is larger than 0 is 2 which is larger than 1. Therefore, (1) and (2) are sufficient.

132. **(D)** Let $\$x$ be the amount he was paid the first day. Then he was paid $x + 2$, $x + 4$, $x + 6$, $x + 8$, and $x + 10$ dollars for the succeeding days. (1) alone is sufficient, since the total he was paid is $(6x + 30)$ dollars, and we can solve $6x + 30 = 150$ (to find that he was paid \$20 for the first day). (2) alone is also sufficient. He was paid $\$(x + 10)$ on the sixth day, so (2) means that $(1.5)x = x + 10$ (which is the same as $x = 20$).

133. **(B)** Since 85% of \$3,000 is \$2,550, (2) alone is sufficient. (1) alone is not sufficient, since

if x were 5% (1) would tell us the price of the car is less than \$2,600. But if x were 1%, (1) would imply that the price of the car is greater than \$2,600.

134. **(E)** Vertical angles are equal, so $c = d$. Since the sum of the angles in a triangle is 180°, $a + b + c = d + e + f$ which means $a + b = e + f$. If we use (1) and (2), we have $a + a = e + a$ so $e = a$. And we know the triangles are similar. However this does not give any information about the value of a, since any two similar triangles can be made to satisfy conditions (1) and (2). Therefore, (1) and (2) together are not sufficient.

135. **(D)** (1) alone is sufficient since $BC = AB$ implies $x = y = 40$. Since the sum of the angles in a triangle is 180°, z must equal 100. (2) alone is sufficient. Let D be the point where the bisector of angle B meets AC. Then according to (2), triangle BDC is a right triangle. Since angle y is 40°, the remaining angle in triangle BDC is 50° and equals $\frac{1}{2}z$, so $z = 100$.

136. **(D)** Since there is a bottom and 4 sides, each a congruent square, the amount of cardboard needed will be $5e^2$ where e is the length of an edge of the box. So we need to find e. (1) alone is sufficient. Since the area of the bottom is e^2, (1) means $e^2 = 4$ with $e = 2$ feet. (2) alone is also sufficient. Since the volume of the box is e^3. (2) means $e^3 = 8$ and $e = 2$ feet.

137. **(C)** The average weight of the books is the total weight of all the books divided by the number of books on the shelf. Thus (1) and (2) together are sufficient. (Solve $2.5 = {}^{40}/_{x}$ for x, the number of books on the shelf.) (1) alone is not sufficient, nor is (2) alone sufficient.

138. **(E)** If $ABCD$ has the pairs of opposite sides equal and each angle is 90°, then it is a rectangle. But there are many quadrilaterals which have two opposite sides equal with one angle a right angle. For example, the figure has $AB = DC$ and $x = 90$, but it is not a rectangle. Therefore, (1) and (2) together are insufficient.

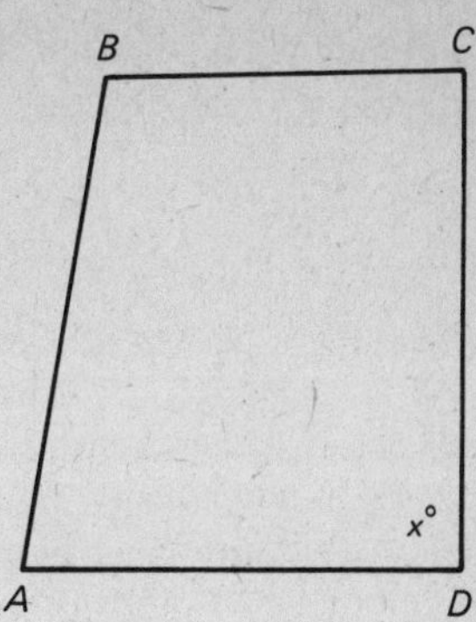

139. **(D)** (2) alone is sufficient, since if $a_3 = 1$ then $a_4 = (a_3)^2 = 1^2 = 1$; then $a_5 = (a_4)^2 = 1^2 = 1$. (1) alone is also sufficient. If $a_1 = -1$ then $a_2 = (a_1)^2 = 1$, and $a_3 = (a_2)^2 = 1$, but $a_3 = 1$ is given by (2) which we know is sufficient.

140. **(E)** Let J, F and C stand for the weekly salaries of John, Fred, and Chuck. (1) says $J = 2F$ and (2) says $F = .4(C + J)$. Since there is no information given about the values of C or F, we cannot deduce the value of J. Therefore, (1) and (2) together are insufficient.

Section V Business Judgment

141. **(A)** Employment for workers (and shoe laborers in particular) was the *Major Objective* of the government in making a decision to encourage the establishment of Abco.

142. **(B)** See paragraph 2: High unemployment in the country was a *Major Factor* in approving the enterprise.

143. **(E)** Excess shoe manufacturing capacity *should* have been a major factor in making the decision, but according to the passage, apparently was considered to be an *Unimportant Issue*.

144. **(C)** That Abco needed more capital to continue in operation was a symptom of its

failure and not a cause; therefore, a *Minor Factor* in the government decision to help continue its operation.

145. **(E)** Investment incentives *were* a major factor in Abco's decision to establish in Korea, but do not figure in the government's current decision.

146. **(B)** See paragraph 4: Abco wanted the government to bail them out at an "agreed" price.

147. **(A)** Only the fact of excess capacity was mentioned.

148. **(B)** See paragraph 4: Abco did manage to employ some 300 workers.

149. **(B)** Whether the company suffered from poor management is unknown. However, since there was excess capacity in the industry, this is the same as too many competitors.

150. **(C)** Based on the facts, the government was optimistic in its assessment that Abco could succeed in such an industry and certainly myopic not to have realized the consequences of some obvious indicators, e.g., the over-supply of shoes.

151. **(A)** The major reason why management initially rejected Dorn's idea was because they lacked distribution channels to the aviation industry.

152. **(B)** Knowledge of the aircraft industry is a *Major Factor* and secondary to the lack of distribution channels.

153. **(E)** How the product idea was discovered is an *Unimportant Issue* in the decision of how to *exploit* it.

154. **(E)** Again, it is how to *exploit* the idea that is important.

155. **(B)** Production capability is as important as marketing ability. However, the passage states that the company has production capability (paragraph 3), so marketing ability still remains the number one concern.

156. **(B)** See paragraph 1: Small mechanical parts.

157. **(E)** All three alternatives are discussed in the passage.

158. **(A)** See paragraph 3: "he discovered quite by accident. . . ."

159. **(D)** Both reasons lead to management's cautious approach as discussed above.

160. **(B)** The passage makes no mention of any market research performed to test the marketability of the proposed product. Also we know the firm had no experience in the aviation industry.

Section VI Data Sufficiency

161. **(B)**

STATEMENT (2) alone is sufficient. $2x+4y = 2(x+2y)$, so if $2x+4y=12$ then $2(x+2y)=12$ and $x+2y=6$.

STATEMENT (1) alone is insufficient. If you only use STATEMENT (1) then you can get $x+2y = x+y+y = 4+y$ but there is no information on the value of y.

162. **(C)**

Since the sum of the angles in a triangle is 180°, $x+y+z=180$. Using STATEMENT (1) alone we have $2y+y+z = 3y+z = 180$, which is insufficient to determine y or x.

Using STATEMENT (2) alone we have $x + 1.5z + z = x + 2.5z = 180$, which is not sufficient to determine x or z.

However, if we use both STATEMENTS (1) and (2) we obtain $3y+z=4.5z+z=5.5z=180$, so $z = \frac{2}{11}$ of 180. Now $y = \frac{3}{2}$ of z, so $y = \frac{3}{11}$ of 180, and $x = \frac{6}{11}$ of 180. Therefore, x is not a right angle and STATEMENTS (1) and (2) are sufficient.

163. **(E)**

Since STATEMENT (1) only describes x and STATEMENT (2) only describes y both are needed to get an answer. Using STATEMENT (2), STATEMENT (1) becomes $x = 2k = 2 \cdot 2y = 4y$, so $x = 4y$. However, this is not sufficient, since if $y = -1$ then $x = -4$ and -4 is less than -1, but if $y = 1$ then $x = 4$ and x is greater than y.

164. **(A)**

If each doll costs \$8, then 65 dolls will cost 8 × \$65 = \$520. Using STATEMENT (1), the profit is selling price minus cost = \$750 − \$520 = \$230, so STATEMENT (1) alone is sufficient.

STATEMENT (2) alone is not sufficient since you need to know what price the dolls sell for to find the profit.

165. **(B)**

STATEMENT (2) alone is sufficient. 60% of the people have blue eyes and 50% of the people have blue eyes and blond hair, so 60% − 50% = 10% of the people have blue eyes but do not have blond hair.

STATEMENT (1) alone is not sufficient. Using STATEMENT (1) alone we can only find out how many people have blond hair and do not have blue eyes, in addition to what is given.

166. **(A)**

The sum of the angles of the pentagon are 540°. (The sum of the angles of a polygon with n sides which is inscribed in a circle is $(n - 2)180°$.) STATEMENT (1) alone is sufficient. If the polygon is regular, all angles are equal and so angle ABC is $\frac{1}{5}$ of 540° or 108°.

STATEMENT (2) alone is insufficient because the radius of the circle does not give any information about the angles of the pentagon.

167. **(B)**

The area of a circle is πr^2, where r is the radius of the circle. Since O is a point on the line AB, AB is a diameter of the circle. Therefore, since a radius is one half of a diameter, the radius of the circle is 3.5 inches. Thus, STATEMENT (2) alone is sufficient.

STATEMENT (1) alone is insufficient since there is no relation between DE and the radius.

168. **(C)**

Using STATEMENT (2) alone we have $\$10,000 + x + y = \$34,000$, where x is the taxable income for 1972 and y is the taxable income for 1973. So STATEMENT (2) alone is not sufficient.

STATEMENT (1) alone is not sufficient since no relation is given between taxable income in 1972 and 1973.

STATEMENTS (1) and (2) together give the equation $\$10,000 + \$12,000 + y = \$34,000$, which means $y = \$12,000$, where y is the taxable income for 1973.

169. **(B)**

STATEMENT (2) alone is sufficient. 3 feet, 2 inches is more than half of 6 feet so the piece of string 3 feet 2 inches long must be longer than the other 2 pieces put together.

STATEMENT (1) alone is insufficient. There is not enough information to find the length of *any* of the three pieces of string.

170. **(D)** Let r be the fraction of the job the 4 apprentices finish in 1 hour. Then $\frac{1}{r}$ is the amount of time in hours that it will take the 4 apprentices to finish the job. So it is sufficient to find r. The group of 5 craftsmen finishes $\frac{1}{3}$ of the job per hour, so each craftsman does $\frac{1}{15}$ of the job per hour.

STATEMENT (1) alone is sufficient. An apprentice will do $\frac{2}{3}$ of $\frac{1}{15} = \frac{2}{45}$ of the job per hour, so $r = \frac{8}{45}$.

STATEMENT (2) alone is sufficient. The craftsmen and the apprentices together will finish $\frac{1}{3} + r$ of the job per hour. Since it takes them $1\frac{22}{23}$ hours to finish the job, $(\frac{1}{3} + r)(\frac{45}{23}) = 1$ which can be solved for r.

171. **(C)**

STATEMENT (2) alone is not sufficient. −1 is less than 2 and $\frac{1}{-1}$ is less than $\frac{1}{2}$ but 1 is less than 2 and $\frac{1}{1}$ is greater than $\frac{1}{2}$.

STATEMENT (1) alone is insufficient since there is no information about y.

STATEMENTS (1) and (2) together imply that x and y are both greater than 1 and for two positive numbers x and y, if x is less than y then $1/x$ is greater than $1/y$.

172. **(A)**

STATEMENT (1) alone is sufficient. Since angle CAD is bisected by AO, the triangles AOD and AOC are congruent by side-angle-side ($AO = AO$). Therefore, angle AOD = angle AOC. Since the sum of the angles is 180° (CD is a straight line) the two angles are right angles and AB is $\perp CD$.

STATEMENT (2) alone is insufficient. We can choose B so that $BC = AD$ whether or not $AB \perp CD$.

173. **(E)**

Since C is closer to A, if plane X is flying faster than plane Y it will certainly fly over C before plane Y. However, if plane X flys slower than plane Y, and C is very close to A, plane X would still fly over C before plane Y does. Thus, STATEMENTS (1) and (2) together are not sufficient.

174. **(C)**

STATEMENT (1) gives $x + y = 4 - x$ and since there is no further information about x, STATEMENT (1) alone is insufficient.

STATEMENT (2) alone is also insufficient because STATEMENT (2) only implies $x + y = 5 - y$. However, if you multiply STATEMENT (2) by −2 and add it to STATEMENT (1), the result is $-3y = -6$ or $y = 2$. So $x + y = 5 - 2 = 3$.

Therefore, STATEMENTS (1) and (2) together are sufficient and (C) is the answer.

175. **(E)**

Since the area of a circle is πr^2, the area of the circular section AOB is the fraction $x/360$ times πr^2, where angle $AOB = x°$. (There are 360° in the entire circle.) Using STATEMENT (1), we know $x = 36$ so $(x/360)\pi r^2 = 1/10\,\pi r^2$. However, STATEMENT (1) gives no information about the value of r, so STATEMENT (1) alone is insufficient.

STATEMENT (2) gives no information about the value of r, so STATEMENTS (1) and (2) together are insufficient.

176. **(B)**

An integer k is divisible by another integer m if $k = mr$, where r is an integer. So STATEMENT (1) implies $k = 4r$ for some integer r. STATEMENT (1) alone is insufficient because 12 is divisible by 4 ($4 \cdot 3 = 12$) but 12 is not divisible by 8.

STATEMENT (2) alone is sufficient. STATEMENT (2) implies that $k = 16r$ for some integer r, but since $16 = 8 \cdot 2$ that means $k = 8 \cdot 2r$ and $2r$ is an integer, so k is divisible by 8.

177. **(D)**

STATEMENT (1) is sufficient. Since the foreman's salary is \$12,000, the total of the assembly workers' salaries is \$300,000. Therefore, the average salary is \$300,000 ÷ 30 = \$10,000.

STATEMENT (2) is sufficient. If A is the average salary of the assembly workers, then 120% of A is \$12,000. Therefore, A = \$12,000 ÷ $6/5$ = \$10,000.

178. **(C)**

STATEMENT (2) alone is insufficient since you need to know what direction town B is from town C.

STATEMENT (1) alone is insufficient, since you need to know how far it is from town B to town C.

Using both STATEMENTS (1) and (2), A, B and C form a right triangle with legs of 9 miles and 12 miles. The distance from town A to town B is the hypotenuse of the triangle, so the distance from town A to town B is $\sqrt{9^2 + 12^2} = 15$ miles.

179. **(C)**

STATEMENTS (1) and (2) by themselves are insufficient since you need to know the area of the floor, and STATEMENT (1) only gives the length and STATEMENT (2) only gives the width. Using STATEMENTS (1) and (2) together, the area of the floor is $5 \times 10 = 50$ square feet. Since the area of each square is $5^2 = 25$ square inches, each square has area $^{25}/_{144}$ square feet. Therefore, the number of squares is $50 \div {}^{25}/_{144} = 288$.

180. **(E)**

STATEMENTS (1) and (2) only give relations between Mary's wages and Jim's wages and tell you the cost of the set of luggage in terms of hours of wages. Since there is no information about the value of the hourly wages in dollars, STATEMENTS (1) and (2) together are not sufficient.

181. **(C)**

STATEMENT (1) alone implies $x = 3y$. Since there is no more information about y, STATEMENT (1) alone is insufficient.

STATEMENT (2) alone gives $x = 9 + y$ but there is no information about y, so STATEMENT (2) alone is not sufficient.

STATEMENTS (1) and (2) together are sufficient. If $x = 9 + y$ and $x = 3y$, then $3y = 9 + y$ which gives $y = {}^{9}/_{2}$, so $x = (3)({}^{9}/_{2}) = {}^{27}/_{2}$.

182. **(A)**

Since in similar triangles corresponding angles are equal, angle CED = angle CBA. Therefore, DE is parallel to AB and STATEMENT (1) alone is sufficient.

STATEMENT (2) alone is insufficient since D could be *any* point on the line CA and there is at most one point on CA which will make DE parallel to AB.

183. **(B)**

If $x + y = 24$ then at least one of the numbers x or y is positive. If x is positive then $y = 24 - x$ and since x is less than 20, $24 - x = y$ is positive. The same argument shows that if y is positive so is x. Therefore, STATEMENT (2) alone is sufficient to show that both numbers are positive.

STATEMENT (1) alone is insufficient, since the fact that x is less than 5 does not tell whether x is positive and no information is given about y.

184. **(C)**

STATEMENT (2) alone implies $x = y$ since equal sides have equal angles in a triangle. Since there is no information about y, STATEMENT (2) alone is insufficient.

STATEMENT (1) alone is insufficient since there is no relation between x and y without STATEMENT (2).

STATEMENTS (1) and (2) together imply $x = y = 30$, so STATEMENTS (1) and (2) together are sufficient.

185. **(E)**

Denote by w_1 the weight of the first volume, by w_2 the weight of the second volume, by w_3 the weight of the third volume and by w_4 the weight of the fourth volume. STATEMENT (1) gives $w_1 + w_2 + w_3 = 4$ and STATEMENT (2) gives $w_2 + w_3 + w_4 = 3\frac{1}{2}$. Using STATEMENTS (1) and (2) you can obtain $w_1 - w_4 = \frac{1}{2}$ so $w_1 = w_4 + \frac{1}{2}$ but no other information is given about w_4. Therefore, STATEMENTS (1) and (2) together are insufficient.

Evaluating Your Score

Tabulate your score for each section of Sample Test 5 according to the directions on pages 3–4 and record the results in the Self-scoring Table below. Then find your rank for each score on the Self-scoring Scale and record it in the appropriate blank.

Self-scoring Table

PART	SCORE	RANK
1		
2		
3		
4		
5		
6		

Self-scoring Scale

	ACHIEVEMENT			
PART	POOR	FAIR	GOOD	EXCELLENT
1	0–15	16–21	22–25	26–30
2	0–29	30–40	41–47	48–55
3	0–20	21–28	29–34	35–40
4	0–7	8–10	11–12	13–15
5	0–10	11–14	15–16	17–20
6	0–12	13–17	18–21	22–25

Study again the Review sections covering material in Sample Test 5 for which you had a rank of FAIR or POOR.

SEVEN

A LIST OF SCHOOLS REQUIRING THE GMAT

The following list represents graduate schools of business which require GMAT scores as part of their admissions procedure. All the schools included are members of the American Assembly of Collegiate Schools of Business.

Adelphi University
School of Business Administration
Garden City, NY 11530

The American University
School of Business Administration
Washington, DC 20016

Angelo State University
Business Administration Department
San Angelo, TX 76901

Arizona State University
College of Business Administration
Tempe, AZ 85281

Armstrong College
Berkeley, CA 94704

Auburn University
School of Business
Auburn, AL 36830

Augusta College
Department of Business Administration
Augusta, GA 30904

Babson College
Babson Park, MA 02157

Ball State University
College of Business
Muncie, IN 47306

Baylor University
Hankamer School of Business
Waco, TX 76706

Bentley College
Waltham, MA 02154

Boise State College
School of Business
1910 Campus Drive
Boise, ID 83725

Boston College
School of Management
Chestnut Hill, MA 02167

Boston University
College of Business Administration
685 Commonwealth Avenue
Boston, MA 02215

Bowling Green State University
College of Business Administration
Bowling Green, OH 43403

Bradley University
College of Business Administration
Peoria, IL 61606

Brigham Young University
College of Business
Provo, Utah 84601

Bryant College
Smithfield, RI 02917

Butler University
College of Business Administration
Indianapolis, IN 46208

California State College, Bakersfield
School of Business and Public Administration
9001 Stockdale Highway
Bakersfield, CA 93309

California State College, Dominguez Hills
Business Administration
Carson, CA 90747

California State College, San Bernardino
Department of Administration
550 State College Parkway
San Bernardino, CA 92407

California State College, Stanislaus
Division of Business Administration
Turlock, CA 95380

California Polytechnic State University
School of Business and Social Sciences
San Luis Obispo, CA 93401

California State Polytechnic University, Pomona
School of Business Administration
Pomona, CA 91768

California State University, Chico
School of Business
Chico, CA 95926

California State University, Fresno
School of Business
Fresno, CA 93710

California State University, Fullerton
School of Business Administration and Economics
Fullerton, CA 92634

California State University, Hayward
School of Business and Economics
Hayward, CA 94542

California State University, Humboldt
School of Business and Economics
Arcata, CA 95521

California State University, Long Beach
School of Business Administration
Long Beach, CA 90840

California State University, Los Angeles
School of Business and Economics
Los Angeles, CA 90032

California State University, Northridge
School of Business Administration and Economics
Northridge, CA 91324

California State University, Sacramento
School of Business Administration
6000 Jay Street
Sacramento, CA 95819

California State University, San Diego
School of Business Administration
San Diego, CA 92115

California State University, San Francisco
School of Business
1600 Holloway Avenue
San Francisco, CA 94132

California State University, San Jose
School of Business
San Jose, CA 95192

Canisius College
School of Business Administration
Buffalo, NY 14208

Capital University
Department of Business Administration and Economics
Columbus, OH 43209

Carnegie-Mellon University
Graduate School of Industrial Administration
Pittsburgh, PA 15213

Case Western Reserve University
School of Management
Cleveland, OH 41106

Central Michigan University
School of Business Administration
Mt. Pleasant, MI 48858

Central Missouri State University
School of Business and Economics
Warrensburg, MO 64093

Central State University
School of Business
Edmond, OK 73034

City University of New York
The Bernard M. Baruch College
School of Business and Public Administration
17 Lexington Avenue
New York, NY 10010

Clarion State College
Division of Business Administration
Clarion, PA 16214

Clark University
Division of Business Administration
Worcester, MA 01610

Clemson University
College of Industrial Management and Textile Science
Clemson, SC 29631

Cleveland State University
The James J. Nance College of Business Administration
Cleveland, OH 44115

College of William and Mary
School of Business Administration
Williamsburg, VA 23185

Colorado State University
College of Business
Fort Collins, CO 80521

Columbia University
Graduate School of Business
New York, NY 10027

Cornell University
Graduate School of Business and Public Administration
Ithaca, NY 14850

Creighton University
College of Business Administration
Omaha, NE 68178

Dartmouth College
The Amos Tuck School of Business Administration
Hanover, NH 03755

DePaul University
College of Commerce
Chicago, IL 60604

Drake University
College of Business Administration
25th and University
Des Moines, IA 50311

Drexel University
College of Business and Administration
Philadelphia, PA 19104

Drury College
Breech School of Business Administration
Springfield, MO 65802

Duquesne University
Graduate School of Business and Administration
Pittsburgh, PA 15219

East Carolina University
School of Business
Greenville, NC 27834

East Tennessee State University
College of Business Administration and Economics
Johnson City, TN 37601

East Texas State University
College of Business Administration
Commerce, TX 75428

East Illinois University
School of Business
Charleston, IL 61920

Eastern Kentucky University
College of Business
Richmond, KY 40475

Eastern Michigan University
College of Business
Ypsilanti, MI 48197

Eastern Washington State College
School of Business and Administration
Cheney, WA 99004

Emory University
Graduate School of Business Administration
Atlanta, GA 30322

Fairleigh Dickinson University
College of Business Administration
Teaneck, NJ 07666

Florida State University
School of Business
Tallahassee, FL 32306

Florida Technological University
College of Business Administration
Orlando, FL 32916

Furman University
Department of Economics and Business Administration
Greenville, SC 29613

Gannon College
Division of Business Administration
Erie, PA 16501

George Washington University
School of Government and Business Administration
Washington, DC 20006

Georgia Institute of Technology
College of Industrial Management
225 North Avenue, NW
Atlanta, GA 30332

Georgia Southern College
School of Business
Statesboro, GA 30458

Georgia State University
School of Business Administration
33 Gilmer Street, SE
Atlanta, GA 30303

Gonzaga University
School of Business Administration
Spokane, WA 99202

Governors State University
College of Business and Public Service
Park Forest South, IL 60466

Grand Valley State College
School of Business and Economics
Allendale, MI 49401

Harvard University
Graduate School of Business Administration
Soldiers Field
Boston, MA 02163

Hofstra University
School of Business
1000 Fulton Avenue
Hempstead, NY 11550

Howard University
School of Business and Public Administration
Washington, DC 20001

Idaho State University
College of Business
Pocatello, ID 83201

Illinois Institute of Technology
Stuart School of Management and Finance
Chicago, IL 60616

Illinois State University
School of Business
Normal, IL 61761

Indiana State University
School of Business
Terre Haute, IN 47809

Indiana University
The Graduate School of Business
Bloomington, IN 47401

Iona College
School of Business Administration
New Rochelle, NY 10801

John Carroll University
School of Business
Cleveland, OH 44118

Kansas State Teachers College
Division of Business and Business Education
Emporia, KS 66801

Kansas State University
College of Business Administration
Manhattan, KS 66506

Kent State University
College of Business Administration
Kent, OH 44242

Lake Forest College
Advanced Management Institute
Lake Forest, IL 60045

Lehigh University
College of Business and Economics
Bethlehem, PA 18015

Long Island University
Brooklyn Center
School of Business Administration
New York, NY 11201

Long Island University
C.W. Post Center
School of Business Administration
Greenvale, NY 11548

Louisiana State University
College of Business Administration
Baton Rouge, LA 70803

Louisiana Tech University
College of Administration and Business
Box 5796, Tech Station
Ruston, LA 71270

Lowell Technological Institute
College of Management Science
Lowell, MA 01854

Loyola College
Department of Accounting and Business Administration
Baltimore, MD 21210

Loyola University
School of Business Administration
Lewis Towers
820 North Michigan Avenue
Chicago, IL 60611

Loyola University
College of Business Administration
New Orleans, LA 70118

Mankato State College
School of Business
Mankato, MN 56001

Marquette University
The Robert A. Johnston College of Business Administration
Milwaukee, WI 53233

Marshall University
School of Business
Huntington, WV 25701

Massachusetts Institute of Technology
Alfred P. Sloan School of Management
Cambridge, MA 02139

McNeese State University
School of Business
Lake Charles, LA 70601

Memphis State University
College of Business Administration
Memphis, TN 38152

Miami University
School of Business Administration
Oxford, OH 45056

Michigan State University
The Graduate School of Business Administration
East Lansing, MI 48823

Michigan Technological University
School of Business and Engineering Administration
Houghton, MI 49931

Middle Tennessee State University
School of Business and Economics
Murfreesboro, TN 37130

Mississippi College
Division of Business and Economics
Clinton, MS 39058

Mississippi State University
College of Business and Industry
Mississippi State, MS 39762

Monmouth College
Department of Business Administration
West Long Branch, NJ 07764

Moorhead State College
Division of Business
Moorhead, MN 56560

Morgan State College
Department of Economics and Business
Baltimore, MD 21239

Murray State University
School of Business
Murray, KY 42071

New Mexico State University
College of Business Administration and Economics
Las Cruces, NM 88003

New York Institute of Technology
Division of Business and Management
888 Seventh Avenue
New York, NY 10019

New York University
College of Business and Public Administration
Washington Square
New York, NY 10003

Nicholls State University
College of Business Administration
Thibodaux, LA 70301

North Texas State University
College of Business Administration
Denton, TX 76203

Northeast Louisiana University
College of Business Administration
Monroe, LA 71201

Northeastern University
College of Business Administration
Boston, MA 02115

Northern Arizona University
College of Business Administration
Flagstaff, AZ 86001

Northern Illinois University
College of Business
DeKalb, IL 60115

Northwest Missouri State University
Department of Business and Economics
Maryville, MO 64468

Northwestern State University of Louisiana
College of Business
Natchitoches, LA 71457

Northwestern University
Graduate School of Management
Leverone Hall
2001 Sheridan Rd.
Evanston, IL 60201

Oakland University
School of Economics and Management
Rochester, MI 48063

Ohio State University
College of Administrative Science
Columbus, OH 43210

Ohio University
College of Business Administration
Athens, OH 45701

Oklahoma State University
College of Business Administration
Stillwater, OK 74074

Old Dominion University
School of Business Administration
Norfolk, VA 23508

Oregon State University
School of Business and Technology
Corvallis, OR 97331

Pace University
Lubin School of Business Administration
New York, NY 10038

Pacific Lutheran University
School of Business Administration
Tacoma, WA 98447

The Pennsylvania State University
College of Business Administration
120 Boucke Building
University Park, PA 16802

Pennsylvania State University, Capitol Campus
Administration and Business Graduate and Undergraduate Programs
Middletown, PA 17057

Pepperdine University
School of Business and Management
Los Angeles, CA 90044

Portland State University
School of Business Administration
P.O. Box 751
Portland, OR 97207

Providence College
Department of Business Administration
Providence, RI 02918

Purdue University
Krannert Graduate School of Industrial Administration
West Lafayette, IN 47907

Rensselaer Polytechnic Institute
School of Management
Troy, NY 12181

Rider College
School of Business Administration
Trenton, NJ 08602

Rochester Institute of Technology
College of Business
Rochester, NY 14623

Rollins College
Roy E. Crummer School of Finance and Business Administration
Winter Park, FL 32789

Roosevelt University
Walter E. Heller College of Business Administration
430 South Michigan Avenue
Chicago, IL 60605

Rutgers University
Graduate School of Business Administration
Newark, NJ 07102

Rutgers University, Camden
Department of Business and Economics
Camden, NJ 08102

Saint Cloud State College
School of Business
Saint Cloud, MN 56301

St. John's University
College of Business Administration
Utopia and Grand Central Parkways
Jamaica, NY 11432

Saint Louis University
School of Business and Administration
St. Louis, MO 63108

St. Mary's University
School of Business Administration
2700 Cincinnati Avenue
San Antonio, TX 78284

Samford University
School of Business
Birmingham, AL 35209

Seattle University
School of Business
Seattle, WA 98122

Seton Hall University
School of Business Administration
South Orange, NJ 07079

Shippensburg State College
Department of Business Administration
Shippensburg, PA 17257

Southern Illinois University at Carbondale
School of Business
Carbondale, IL 62901

Southern Illinois University at Edwardsville
Division of Business
Edwardsville, IL 62025

Southern Methodist University
School of Business Administration
Dallas, TX 75222

Stanford University
Graduate School of Business
Stanford, CA 94305

State University of New York at Albany
School of Business
Albany, NY 12222

State University of New York at Binghamton
School of Management
Binghamton, NY 13901

State University of New York at Buffalo
School of Management
Crosby Hall, Library Circle
Buffalo, NY 14214

Stephen F. Austin State University
School of Business
Nacogdoches, TX 75961

Suffolk University
College of Business Administration
Boston, MA 02114

Syracuse University
School of Management
116 College Place
Syracuse, NY 13210

Temple University
School of Business Administration
Philadelphia, PA 19122

Texas Christian University
M. J. Neeley School of Business
Fort Worth, TX 76129

Trinity University
School of Business Administration
San Antonio, TX 78284

Troy State University
School of Business
Troy, AL 36081

Tulane University
Graduate School of Business
Administration
New Orleans, LA 70118

United States International University
School of Business Administration
San Diego, CA 92131

University of Akron
College of Business Administration
Akron, OH 44304

University of Alabama
College of Commerce and Business
Administration
Graduate School of Business
University, AL 35486

University of Alabama in Birmingham
School of Business
Birmingham, AL 34294

University of Arizona
College of Business and Public
Administration
Tucson, AZ 85721

University of Arkansas at Little Rock
Division of Business Administration
Little Rock, AR 72204

University of Arkansas at Monticello
Department of Business Administration
Monticello, AR 71655

University of Baltimore
School of Business
Baltimore, MD 21201

University of Bridgeport
College of Business Administration
Bridgeport, CT 06602

University of California
Graduate School of Business
Administration
Berkeley, CA 94720

University of California, Los Angeles
Graduate School of Management
Los Angeles, CA 90024

University of Chicago
The Graduate School of Business
Chicago, IL 60637

University of Cincinnati
College of Business Administration
Cincinnati, OH 45221

University of Colorado
Graduate School of Business
Administration
Boulder, CO 80302

University of Connecticut
School of Business Administration
Storrs, CT 06268

University of Dayton
School of Business Administration
Dayton, OH 45409

University of Delaware
College of Business and Economics
Newark, DE 19711

University of Denver
College of Business Administration
University Park
Denver, CO 80210

University of Detroit
College of Business and Administration
Graduate School
McNichols Road at Livernois
Detroit, MI 48221

University of Evansville
School of Business Administration
Evansville, IN 47701

University of Georgia
College of Business Administration
Athens, GA 30602

University of Hawaii
College of Business Administration
2404 Maile Way
Honolulu, HI 96822

University of Houston
College of Business Administration
3801 Cullen Boulevard
Houston, TX 77004

University of Idaho
College of Business and Economics
Moscow, ID 83843

University of Illinois
College of Commerce and Business Administration
Urbana, IL 61801

University of Illinois at Chicago Circle
College of Business Administration
Box 4348
Chicago, IL 60680

University of Iowa
College of Business Administration
Iowa City, IA 52242

University of Kansas
School of Business
Lawrence, KS 66044

University of Kentucky
College of Business and Economics
Lexington, KY 40506

University of Louisville
School of Business
Louisville, KY 40208

University of Maine
College of Business Administration
Orono, ME 04473

University of Maryland
College of Business and Management
College Park, MD 20742

University of Massachusetts
School of Business Administration
Amherst, MA 01002

University of Miami
School of Business Administration
Coral Gables, FL 33124

The University of Michigan
Graduate School of Business Administration
Ann Arbor, MI 48104

University of Minnesota
Graduate School of Business Administration
Minneapolis, MN 55455

University of Mississippi
School of Business Administration
University, MS 38677

University of Missouri, Columbia
College of Administration and Public Affairs
Columbia, MO 65201

University of Missouri, Kansas City
School of Administration
5100 Rockhill Road
Kansas City, MO 64110

University of Missouri, St. Louis
School of Business Administration
8001 Natural Bridge Road
St. Louis, MO 63121

University of Montana
School of Business Administration
Missoula, MT 59801

University of Nebraska, Lincoln
College of Business Administration
Lincoln, NE 68508

University of Nebraska, Omaha
College of Business Administration
Omaha, NE 68101

University of Nevada, Las Vegas
College of Business and Economics
Las Vegas, NV 89154

University of Nevada, Reno
College of Business Administration
Reno, NV 89507

University of New Hampshire
Whittemore School of Business and Economics
Durham, NH 03824

The University of New Mexico
School of Business and Administrative Sciences
Albuquerque, NM 87131

University of New Orleans
College of Business Administration
New Orleans, LA 70122

University of North Carolina, Chapel Hill
Graduate School of Business Administration
Chapel Hill, NC 27514

The University of North Carolina, Charlotte
College of Business Administration
Charlotte, NC 28213

University of North Carolina, Greensboro
School of Business and Economics
Greensboro, NC 27412

University of North Dakota
College of Business and Public Administration
Grand Forks, ND 58201

University of Northern Iowa
Department of Business
Cedar Falls, IA 50613

University of Notre Dame
College of Business Administration
Notre Dame, IN 46556

University of Oklahoma
College of Business Administration
Norman, OK 73069

University of Oregon
Graduate School of Management and Business
Eugene, OR 97403

University of Pennsylvania
The Wharton School
3620 Locust Walk
Philadelphia, PA 19174

University of Pittsburgh
Graduate School of Business
Pittsburgh, PA 15213

University of Portland
School of Business Administration
Portland, OR 97203

University of Puget Sound
School of Business and Public Administration
Tacoma, WA 98416

University of Rhode Island
College of Business Administration
302 Ballentine Hall
Kingston, RI 02881

University of Rochester
The Graduate School of Management
Rochester, NY 14627

University of San Francisco
College of Business Administration
San Francisco, CA 94117

University of Santa Clara
Graduate School of Business and Administration
Santa Clara, CA 95053

University of South Carolina
Graduate School of Business
Columbia, SC 29208

University of South Dakota
School of Business
Vermillion, SD 57069

University of Southern California
Graduate School of Business
Administration
University Park
Los Angeles, CA 90007

University of Southern Mississippi
School of Business Administration
Hattiesburg, MS 39401

University of Tennessee
College of Business Administration
Knoxville, TN 37916

University of Tennessee, Chattanooga
Department of Economics and Business
Administration
Chattanooga, TN 37401

The University of Tennessee, Martin
School of Business Administration
Martin, TN 38237

The University of Texas, Arlington
College of Business Administration
Arlington, TX 76010

University of Texas, San Antonio
College of Business
San Antonio, TX 78284

University of Toledo
College of Business Administration
Toledo, OH 43606

University of Tulsa
College of Business Administration
Tulsa, OK 74104

University of Utah
College of Business
Salt Lake City, UT 84112

University of Virginia
McIntire School of Commerce
Charlottesville, VA 22903

University of Washington
Graduate School of Business
Administration
Seattle, WA 98195

University of Wisconsin, LaCrosse
School of Business Administration
La Crosse, WI 54601

University of Wisconsin, Madison
Graduate School of Business
Madison, WI 53706

University of Wisconsin, Milwaukee
School of Business Administration
Milwaukee, WI 53201

University of Wisconsin, Oshkosh
School of Business Administration
Oshkosh, WI 54901

University of Wisconsin, Whitewater
College of Business and Economics
Whitewater, WI 53190

University of Wyoming
College of Commerce and Industry
Laramie, WY 82070

Utah State University
College of Business
Logan, UT 84321

Vanderbilt University
Graduate School of Management
Nashville, TN 37203

Virginia Commonwealth University
School of Business
Richmond, VA 23220

Virginia Polytechnic Institute
College of Business
Blacksburg, VA 24061

Wake Forest University
Charles H. Babcock School of Business
Administration
Winston-Salem, NC 27109

Washington State University
College of Economics and Business
Pullman, WA 99163

Washington University
The Graduate School of Business
Administration
St. Louis, MO 63130

Wayne State University
School of Business Administration
Detroit, MI 48202

West Georgia College
School of Business
Carrollton, GA 30117

West Texas State University
School of Business
Canyon, TX 79016

West Virginia University
College of Business and Economics
Morgantown, WV 26506

Western Carolina University
School of Business
Cullowhee, NC 28723

Western Kentucky University
College of Business and Public Affairs
Bowling Green, KY 42101

Western Michigan University
College of Business
Kalamazoo, MI 49001

Wichita State University
College of Business Administration
Wichita, KS 67208

Woodbury College
Los Angeles, CA 90017

Wright State University
College of Business and Administration
Dayton, OH 45431

Xavier University
College of Business Administration
Cincinnati, OH 45207

Youngstown State University
School of Business Administration
Youngstown, OH 44503